Libel and Lampoon

LAW AND LITERATURE

The Law and Literature series publishes work that connects legal ideas to literary and cultural history, texts, and artefacts. The series encompasses a wide range of historical periods, literary genres, legal fields and theories, and transnational subjects, focusing on interdisciplinary books that engage with legal and literary forms, methods, concepts, dispositions, and media. It seeks innovative studies of every kind, including but not limited to work that examines race, ethnicity, gender, national identity, criminal and civil law, legal institutions and actors, digital media, intellectual property, economic markets, and corporate power, while also foregrounding current interpretive methods in the humanities, using these methods as dynamic tools that are themselves subject to scrutiny.

Series Editors
Robert Spoo, University of Tulsa
Simon Stern, University of Toronto

Libel and Lampoon

Satire in the Courts, 1670–1792

ANDREW BENJAMIN BRICKER

OXFORD
UNIVERSITY PRESS

OXFORD
UNIVERSITY PRESS

Great Clarendon Street, Oxford, OX2 6DP,
United Kingdom

Oxford University Press is a department of the University of Oxford.
It furthers the University's objective of excellence in research, scholarship,
and education by publishing worldwide. Oxford is a registered trade mark of
Oxford University Press in the UK and in certain other countries

First Edition published in 2022

Impression: 1

Published in the United States of America by Oxford University Press
198 Madison Avenue, New York, NY 10016, United States of America

British Library Cataloguing in Publication Data
Data available

Library of Congress Control Number: 2021953109

ISBN 978-0-19-284615-0

DOI: 10.1093/oso/9780192846150.001.0001

Printed and bound by
CPI Group (UK) Ltd, Croydon, CR0 4YY

Acknowledgements

In *Libel and Lampoon*, I explain how emerging laws, courtroom procedures, and legislation influenced English satire between the seventeenth and eighteenth centuries, and how those same laws were shaped by the evasions of satirists, their printers, and their booksellers. This book has also been shaped by the many wonderful friends, readers, colleagues, and interlocutors I have had over the past decade. I would like to thank some of them here.

A few deserve special attention. John Bender, Blair Hoxby, Nick Hudson, Bob Spoo, Simon Stern, and Blakey Vermeule all read multiple drafts of this book as it evolved and offered insight and feedback that always shaped my arguments and analysis for the better. Over the years I have also been lucky enough to work alongside so many magnificent colleagues, including Simon Macdonald, Derek Nystrom, Fiona Ritchie, Peter Sabor, Darren Wagner, and Katie Zien at McGill University; and Alex Dick, Sandra Tomc, Siân Echard, and Scott MacKenzie at the University of British Columbia. A huge debt of gratitude goes to my former colleagues at Stanford University, and especially the informal group for eighteenth-century studies. Claude Willan, James Wood, Hannah Doherty, Steve Osadetz, Jenna Sutton, and Erik Johnson all read and improved chapters of this book. Over the last few years, I have worked on *Libel and Lampoon* alongside *mijn fantastische collega's* at Ghent University, including Elizabeth Amann, Lars Bernaerts, Chris Chan, Gert Buelens, Marco Caracciolo, Stef Craps, Marysa Demoor, Teodoro Katinis, Georges Martyn, Mara Santi, Fauve Vandenberghe, Kornee van der Haven, and Marianne Van Remoortel. *Iedereen bedankt!*

Numerous colleagues and friends have also offered me insightful feedback, help, and companionship. They include David Alvarez, John Baird, Charity Bengert, David Brewer, Esther Chadwick, Dennis Choquette, Michael Cobb, Rosemary Coombe, Darryl Domingo, Stephanie DeGooyer, Helen Deutsch, Simon Dickie, Gary Dyer, Melissa Ganz, Katie Gemmill, Alberto Godioli, Philip Hamburger, Eckhart Hellmuth, Hilda Hoy, Michelle Karnes, Sarah Kareem, Tom Keymer, Rachael Scarborough King, Emily Kopley, Jonathan Kramnick, Fiona MacMillan, Ashley Marshall, Andrew McKendry, Michael McKeon, Melina Moe, Jesse Molesworth, Marissa Nicosia, Daniel O'Quinn, Stephen Orgel, Natalie Phillips, Claude Rawson, Paul Saint-Amour, Hillary Schroeder, Carrie Shanafelt, Patricia Meyer Spacks, Dustin Stewart, Michael Suarez, Kathryn Temple, David Vander Meulen, Bill Warner, Seth Williams, Kyle Wyatt, Martin Zeilinger, and Eugenia Zuroski—and, of course, my many fellow fellows at the Andrew W. Mellon Society of Fellows in Critical Bibliography at Rare Book School at the University of Virginia.

I have also been assisted by too many people to name while researching and writing this book, but a few have been instrumental. They include Margaret Powell, Kristen MacDonald, Cynthia Roman, and Susan Walker of the Lewis Walpole Library at Yale University; Molly Gipson, Jaeda Snow, and Steve Hindle of the Huntington Library; Aaron Pratt at the Ransom Center at the University of Texas at Austin; Karla Nielsen of the Rare Book & Manuscript Collection at the Butler Library at Columbia University; John Bidwell at the Morgan Library & Museum; John Pollack in Special Collections at the Van Pelt Library at the University of Pennsylvania; Thomas Lannon of the Manuscripts and Archives Division and Madeleine Viljoen of the Print Collection, both at the New York Public Library; Anne-Marie Diffley, Paul Ferguson, and Shane Mawe of the Department of Early Printed Books and Special Collections at Trinity College Library at the University of Dublin; John Chalmers, formerly of Special Collections at the Chicago Public Library; and the staffs of the William Andrews Clark Memorial Library at UCLA, the Newberry Library, the Patricia D. Klingenstein Library at the New-York Historical Society, the Folger Shakespeare Library, the Beinecke Rare Book & Manuscript Library at Yale University, the Houghton Library at Harvard University, the British Library, the National Archives (UK), and the Prints and Drawings Division of the Library of Congress.

Finally, the research for this book was supported by the tremendous generosity of several organizations and institutions. I would like to thank the Social Sciences and Humanities Research Council of Canada, the Department of English and School of Humanities and Sciences at Stanford University, and the American Council of Learned Societies for their support. Additional research funds have come from a Mellon Foundation Fellowship at the Huntington Library, a Modern British History and Culture Research grant from Stanford, a visiting research fellowship at the Lewis Walpole Library at Yale University, an ASECS fellowship from the William Andrews Clark Memorial Library at UCLA, an ASECS Bibliographical Studies Fellowship from the Bibliographical Society of America, a Swann Foundation Fellowship from the Library of Congress, and an Andrew W. Mellon Fellowship in Critical Bibliography from Rare Book School.

Two chapters of *Libel and Lampoon*, previously published, appear here in expanded form. Chapter four was published by Johns Hopkins University Press as 'Libel and Satire: The Problem with Naming', *English Literary History* 81, no. 3 (Fall 2014): pp. 889–921. Chapter six, also published by Johns Hopkins University Press, appeared as 'After the Golden Age: Caricature, Libel, and the Deverbalization of Satire', *Eighteenth-Century Studies* 51, no. 3 (Spring 2018): pp. 305–36 (© American Society for Eighteenth-Century Studies). My thanks to the editorial staffs of *ELH* and *ECS* and to Johns Hopkins University Press for permission to republish those materials here.

This book is dedicated to my parents, Drew and Allison, who have always supported me, despite not always knowing what, exactly, I was doing.

Contents

Abbreviations   ix
List of Illustrations   xi
Epigraph   xiii

Introduction: The Perils of Satire   1
  I.1 The Perils of Satire   1
  I.2 Libel and Lampoon, 1670–1792   6
  I.3 Verbal and Bibliographical Evasions   9
  I.4 Libel and Satire, Law and Literature   16

1. Keeping Out of Court I: Libel and Lampoon after Hale and Dryden   26
  1.1 'Common Intendment' and the Regulation of the Press   29
  1.2 Libel and Lampoon: Manuscript Satire during the Later
     Seventeenth Century   36
  1.3 Lampoon without Libel: *Mac Flecknoe*, Verbal Evasion, and
     the Language of Satire   43
  1.4 The Legitimation of Lampoon: *Mac Flecknoe* and the Satiric
     Shadow Canon   47

2. Keeping Out of Court II: Swift and the Illicit Book Trade   58
  2.1 The Book Trade and the Law   60
  2.2 The Act of Anne: Authorship, Ownership, and the Authorities   66
  2.3 Deception and Detection: Projecting Readers, Evading
     the Authorities   74
  2.4 Editing Authors: Language, Libel, and Liability   84

3. Irony in the Courts: Defoe and the Law of Seditious Libel   93
  3.1 *The Shortest Way* and Extrinsic Irony   94
  3.2 Malice, Intention, and Irony in the Law of Seditious Libel   107
  3.3 'Be Wise as *Somerset*': Intention and Irony in *R. v.
     Dr. Browne* (1706)   111
  3.4 Defending Defoe: 'Plain *English without Design*'   121

4. Naming in the Courts: Pope and the *Dunciad*   127
  4.1 Gutted Names in Court: Before and After *R. v. Hurt* (1713)   129
  4.2 Perceptions of Law: Slippage and the Problem of Legal Meaning 134
  4.3 Gutted Names in Eighteenth-Century Satire   138
  4.4 More Precious than Life: Reputation in Early Modern England   149
  4.5 Naming Victims: Pope and the *Dunciad Variorum* (1729)   152

5. Allegory in the Courts: Satire and the Problem of 'Libellous
   Parallels'   160
   5.1 Delarivier Manley, *The New Atalantis*, and the Limits of
       R. v. Tutchin (1704)   162
   5.2 The '*Insolence* of Drawing Parallels': *The Craftsman* and the
       Uses of Allegory   173
   5.3 'The Generality of Readers': *R. v. Clerk* (1728/9), the 'Persian
       Letter', and *Mist's Weekly Journal*   182

6. Keeping Out of Court III: Caricature, Mimicry, and the
   Deverbalization of Satire   195
   6.1 Satire in the Courts, 1695–1792: Legal Strategies for Regulating
       the Press   199
   6.2 The Deverbalization of Satire: Caricature and the Limits of
       Libel Law   209
   6.3 The Deverbalization of Drama: Samuel Foote, Mimicry, and
       Impersonation after the Stage Licensing Act (1737)   233

Epilogue: A Shandean History of the Press   248

Bibliography   271
Index   319

Abbreviations

Baker, *ELH*	John H. Baker. *An Introduction to English Legal History*, 4th ed. (Oxford: Oxford University Press, 1995).
Beattie, *Crime*	J. M. Beattie. *Crime and the Courts, 1660–1800* (Princeton: Princeton University Press, 1986).
Bein.L	Beinecke Library, Yale University, New Haven, CT, USA
BL	The British Library, London, UK
Black, *Press*	Jeremy Black. *The English Press in the Eighteenth Century* (London: Croom Helm, 1987).
Bogel, *Satire*	Fredric V. Bogel. *The Difference Satire Makes: Rhetoric and Reading from Jonson to Byron* (Ithaca: Cornell University Press, 2001).
LOC	Library of Congress, Washington, DC, USA
Clark L	William Andrews Clark Memorial Library, University of California, Los Angeles, CA, USA
CSR	John Harold Wilson (ed.). *Court Satires of the Restoration* (Columbus: Ohio State University Press, 1976).
CUL	Cambridge University Library, Cambridge, UK
Eng. Rep.	*The English Reports, Full Reprint.* 176 vol. (Edinburgh: W. Green and Sons, Limited, 1900–1930).
Green, *Verdict*	Thomas A. Green. *Verdict According to Conscience: Perspectives on the English Criminal Trial Jury, 1200–1800* (Chicago: University of Chicago Press, 1985).
Griffin, *Satire*	Dustin Griffin. *Satire: A Critical Reintroduction* (Lexington: University Press of Kentucky, 1994).
Hamburger, 'Seditious Libel'	Philip Hamburger. 'The Development of the Law of Seditious Libel and the Control of the Press', *Stanford Law Review* 37, no. 3 (February 1985): pp. 661–765.
Hanson, *Government*	Laurence Hanson. *Government and the Press, 1695–1763* (Oxford: Clarendon Press, 1967).
Holdsworth, *History*	Sir William Holdsworth. *A History of English Law.* 2nd ed. 10 vol. (London: Methuen, 1937).
Hought.L	Houghton Library, Harvard University, Cambridge, MA, USA
Hunt.L	The Huntington Library, San Marino, CA, USA
Keymer, *Poetics*	Thomas Keymer. *Poetics of the Pillory: English Literature and Seditious Libel, 1660–1820* (Oxford: Oxford University Press, 2019).
Mansfield MSS	James C. Oldham. *The Mansfield Manuscripts and the Growth of English Law in the Eighteenth Century.* 2 vol. (Chapel Hill: University of North Carolina Press, 1992).
Marshall, *Satire*	Ashley Marshall. *The Practice of Satire in England, 1658–1770* (Baltimore: Johns Hopkins University Press, 2013).

Mezey, 'Law'	Naomi Mezey. 'Law as Culture', in *Cultural Analysis, Cultural Studies, and the Law: Moving Beyond Legal Realism*, edited by Austin Sarat and Jonathan Simon (Durham: Duke University Press, 2003), pp. 37–72.
NYHS	New-York Historical Society Library, New York, NY, USA
OED	*Oxford English Dictionary* (Oxford: Oxford University Press, 2020): http://www.oed.com/.
ODNB	*The Oxford Dictionary of National Biography*. Edited by H. C. G. Matthew and Brian Harrison (Oxford: Oxford University Press, 2004): http://www.oxforddnb.com.
OHECS	Paddy Bullard (ed.). *The Oxford Handbook of Eighteenth-Century Satire* (Oxford: Oxford University Press, 2019).
POAS	George deF. Lord (ed.). *Poems on Affairs of State: Augustan Satirical Verse, 1660–1714*. 7 vol. (New Haven: Yale University Press, 1963).
Plucknett, *CHCL*	Theodore F. T. Plucknett. *A Concise History of the Common Law*. 5th ed. (Boston: Little, Brown and Co., 1956).
RA	Royal Archives, Windsor Castle, UK
SCSU	Special Collections, Stanford University, Stanford, CA, USA
Siebert, *Freedom*	Fredrick Seaton Siebert. *Freedom of the Press in England, 1476–1776: The Rise and Decline of Government Control* (Urbana: University of Illinois Press, 1965).
SMA	Soane Museum Archives, London, UK
Sources	J. H. Baker and S. F. C. Milsom (ed.). *Sources of English Legal History: Private Law to 1750* (London: Butterworths, 1986).
State Law	*State Law: Or, the Doctrine of Libels, Discussed and Examined*. 2nd ed. ([London], [1730]).
State Trials	William Cobbett, et al. *Complete Collection of State Trials*. 21 vol. (London, 1809–1826).
TNA	The National Archives, Kew, UK

List of Illustrations

2.1 [Thomas Stretzer], Titlepage, *A New Description of Merryland*, 2nd ed. (Bath [i.e., London], 1741, for W. Jones [pseud. Edmund Curll]). The Huntington Library (309238)   76

2.2 [Thomas Stretzer], 'Editor to the Reader', in *A New Description of Merryland*, 2nd ed. (Bath [i.e., London], 1741, for W. Jones [pseud. Edmund Curll]), p. i. The Huntington Library (309238)   77

2.3 [Hildebrand Jacob], *The Silent Flute, A Poem: Being the Members Speech to their Sovereign* (London, 1729). Harry Ransom Center, The University of Texas at Austin (Ak J150 +A729s)   85

2.4 [Hildebrand Jacob], 'The Curious Maid', in *A New Collection of Poems on Several Occasions* (London, 1725), p. 93. Courtesy of the Department of Special Collections, Stanford University Libraries (PR3640 .A12 1725)   86

4.1 *The Lawyers Answer to the Country Parson's good Advice to My Lord Keeper*. (C) British Library Board (General Reference Collection 1493.a.6)   144

4.2 'Dund [ass]' (i.e., Dundas). Detail from [John Kay], *A [Letter] [toe] Sir L___e Dund[ass]* (1762). Courtesy of the Lewis Walpole Library, Yale University (762.00.00.04)   145

4.3 [J. Hill?], The Retort [:] an Hieroglyphic Epistle from the Revd. Dr. [Whitefield] to Saml. [foot] Esqr. (C) Trustees of the British Museum (AN356907001)   147

4.4 *I am Kick[']d Out of Doors/No Screen*. (C) Trustees of the British Museum (AN471477001)   148

6.1 *John of Gant in Love, or Mars on his Knees* (1749). Courtesy of the Lewis Walpole Library, Yale University (749.07.15.01+ Impression 1)   214

6.2 Henry Fuseli, *The Nightmare* (1781). Detroit Institute of Arts (55.5.A). Founders Society Purchase with funds from Mr. and Mrs. Bert L. Smokler and Mr. and Mrs. Lawrence A. Fleischmanf. Bridgeman Images   217

6.3 [Thomas Rowlandson], *The Covent Garden Night Mare* (1782). Courtesy of the Lewis Walpole Library, Yale University (784.04.20.01+)   218

6.4 Benjamin West, *The Death of General Wolfe* (1770). © National Trust Images/J. Whitaker (NT 851783)   220

6.5 [John Boyne], *General Blackbeard wounded at the Battle of Leadenhall* (5 January 1784). General Collection, Beinecke Rare Book & Manuscript Library, Yale University (11810304)   221

6.6 Friedrich Rehberg, *Drawings Faithfully Copied from Nature at Naples*
(1794) (London, 1797). Courtesy of the Lewis Walpole Library, Yale
University (Quarto 75 R266 797)   222

6.7 [James Gillray?], *A New Edition Considerably Enlarged, of Attitudes
Faithfully Copied from Nature and Humbly Dedicated to all Admirers
of the Grand and Sublime* (1807). Courtesy of The Lewis Walpole
Library, Yale University (Quarto 75 G41 807)   223

6.8 [Frederick George Byron], *Don Dismallo, after an Absence of Sixteen
Years, Embracing his Beautiful Vision* (18 November 1790).
© The Trustees of the British Museum (1868,0808.5973)   224

6.9 R. Lyford (pseud.), *A Certain Dutchess Kissing Old Swelter-in-Grease the
Butcher for his Vote* (1784), for H. Macphail (pseud.). © The Trustees
of the British Museum (1868,0808.5215)   226

6.10 [James Gillray], *A Democrat, or Reason & Philosophy* (1 March 1793).
Courtesy of the Lewis Walpole Library, Yale University (793.03.01.01)   228

6.11 [Robert Cruikshank], *Royalty in a Rage or Family Quarrels* (1820).
Prints and Photographs Division, Library of Congress (PC 3-1820 [A size])   230

E.1 Laurence Sterne, *The Life and Opinions of Tristram Shandy, Gentleman*,
vol. 6 (York and London, 1759–67), p. 152. (C) British Library Board
(General Reference Collection Ashley1770)   264

For let me ask the most zealous *Reformer* what regimen he would prescribe for these crafty Incendiaries. Would you regularly bring them into *Westminster-Hall*, as the Authors of *Libels*, Movers of *Sedition*, and Disturbers of the *Peace*? ... And can it be imagined that old Foxes will be taken in a Snare they are so well apprised of, or that they will venture their Necks within the Reach of a Rope, the Length of which is their daily Contemplation? These cunning Proteus's are deeply read and experienced in the Arts of Jugling and Metamorphosis. They are always prepar'd to evade the Blow, to shelter their Heads, and to make their escape, under the false *Colours* of *Irony*, *Anagram*, or *Double Entendre*; so that instead of a decent Satisfaction, what a Jest would he made of an *English Magistrate*, or *Counsellor of State*, if he should take it into his Head gravely to complain, and formally to apply to his own Person a Scandal or Invective very harmlessly dated in the Empire of *Lilliput*, or the Land of *Eutopia*?

You will find the greatest Difficulty in the World, with *Honour* and *Justice*, to lay your Hand on these *Sophists in Calumny*; so perfect are they in all the Tricks and Wiles of Ambiguity, and Equivocation; in the Mysterious Art of raising Ideas by the Use of Words of a *contrary* Signification, of abusing and vilifying by affected *Encomiums*, of sneering Truth by Writing in *Italicks*, of *assassinating* with a *Smile*, or *betraying* with a *Kiss*.

—[Francis Squire], *A Faithful Report of a Genuine Debate Concerning the Liberty of the Press* (London, 1740), pp. 17–18.

Introduction

The Perils of Satire

1 The Perils of Satire

After the Restoration in 1660, few writers needed reminding about the dangers of composing, printing, and distributing controversial, oppositional, and satiric works. Reminders, in fact, were everywhere. Think only of the many satirists roughed up for pointing an incautious finger in the wrong direction.[1] As one poet quipped,

> Believe me, 'tis an evil trade to rail;
> The angry poet's hopes do often fail,
> Instead of bays a cudgel oft does find.

He had a specific example in mind: John Dryden, who was set upon in December of 1679 in Covent Garden by three men 'who beat him very severely'.[2] As the wit continued, 'Some lines, for being praised when they were read, / Were once a cause of Dryden's broken head'.[3] Rumour had it that the Duchess of Portsmouth, one of the king's mistresses, had sent the toughs after Dryden for *An Essay upon Satire*, in which she is depicted as 'False, foolish, old, ill-natur'd and illbred'.[4] (Little consolation that the poem was actually by John Sheffield, Earl of Mulgrave.) This was all the worse for Dryden, who had claimed, years earlier, that he had given up 'Lampoon' and 'forsworn that dangerous part of wit, not so much out of good nature, But least from the inkhorn vanity of poets, I should show it to others, and betray my self to a worse mischief than what I designed my Enemy'.[5]

---

[1] J. Paul Hunter, 'Political, satirical, didactic and lyric poetry (I)', in *The Cambridge History of English Literature, 1660–1800*, edited by John Richetti (Cambridge: Cambridge University Press, 2005), p. 174n13. Even if, importantly, retributive violence for words waned over the course of the eighteenth century, especially after 1750. See Robert Shoemaker, 'Male Honour and the Decline of Public Violence in Eighteenth-Century London', *Social History* 26, no. 2 (May 2001): pp. 190–208, esp. 203–4.

[2] Narcissus Lutrell, *A Brief Historical Relation of State Affairs, from September 1678 to April 1714*, vol. 1 (Oxford: Oxford University Press, 1857), p. 50.

[3] 'Utile Dulce' (1681), rpt. *CSR*, p. 49, ll. 3–7.

[4] 'An Essay upon Satire' (1679), rpt. *POAS*, vol. 1, p. 405, l. 3.

[5] Dryden to Rochester, *The Letters of John Wilmot, Earl of Rochester*, edited by Jeremy Treglown (Oxford: Basil Blackwell, 1980), p. 89.

Libel and Lampoon: Satire in the Courts, 1670–1792. Andrew Benjamin Bricker, Oxford University Press.
© Andrew Benjamin Bricker 2022. DOI: 10.1093/oso/9780192846150.003.0001

Physical peril was one threat to the practising satirist. But reminders of the grisly legal punishments writers faced were also everywhere.[6] Few could forget William Prynne, twice tried and convicted of sedition for his writings during the 1630s. As part of his punishment, his ears were amputated, his nose was slit, and his cheeks were branded with S.L., for 'seditious libeller'.[7] Prynne lived until 1669, and anyone passing through London's increasingly fashionable West End might have seen his ghoulish, mutilated figure as he walked the streets to and from his preacher's appointment at Lincoln's Inn. To any writer, he was a living warning.

Other reminders of risk came fast and quick. One could make a long list of printers and booksellers who were harassed, interrogated, tried, and convicted during the first decades of the Restoration for publishing the incendiary and seditious, the oppositional and polemical.[8] The printer John Twyn, for instance, was executed for treason in 1664 after the Surveyor of the Press (or Imprimery), Roger L'Estrange, caught him printing *A Treatise of the Execution of Justice* in 1663, a work that called for King Charles II to be deposed and executed.[9]

Writers had to be on constant guard. According to Samuel Butler, one of the many wits who also studied the law, 'our modern Satyr has enough to do, to secure himselfe against the Penaltys of Scandalum Magnatum, and Libells'.[10] A hot-headed satirist could even find himself hanged for his verses. Take Stephen College—'The Protestant Joiner', as he was known to his contemporaries—who was twice tried for treason in 1681.[11] At the centre of both trials was his satirical ballad, *The Ra-Ree Show* (1681). There Charles shows up as a political puppet master, skilled in 'sleight of hand'. The poem closes with a jaunty call for the king's execution, 'Like father, like son'.[12] College's first trial foundered in Westminster, where a Whig opposition managed to have a sympathetic jury of nonconformists and tradesmen impanelled. The Crown countered, however, that College's treason had taken place in both London and Oxford and set up a second prosecution. Tried on 17 and 18 August 1681, the hapless poet was convicted and then executed in Oxford Castle yard two weeks later. To his contemporaries and successors, 'good Stephen College' was a hero and a 'martyr for the people's

---

[6] For an overview of Restoration 'censorship', see Geoff Kemp, 'Introduction', in *Censorship and the Press, vol. 3: 1660–1695*, edited by Geoff Kemp (London: Pickering & Chatto, 2009), pp. xi–xxvii.

[7] William Lamont, *Marginal Prynne, 1600–1669* (Toronto: University of Toronto Press, 1963), p. 39. See also Annabel Patterson, *Censorship and Interpretation: The Conditions of Writing and Reading in Early Modern England* (Madison: University of Wisconsin Press, 1984), pp. 44–8, 105–7.

[8] Andrew McRae, *Literature, Satire and the Early Stuart State* (Cambridge: Cambridge University Press, 2004), p. 7.

[9] Stephen Bardle, *The Literary Underground in the 1660s: Andrew Marvell, George Wither, Ralph Wallis, and the World of Restoration Satire and Pamphleteering* (Oxford: Oxford University Press, 2013), p. 3.

[10] Samuel Butler, *Characters and Passages from Note-Books*, edited by A. R. Waller (Cambridge: Cambridge University Press, 1908), p. 469; and *ODNB*.

[11] *Burnet's History of My Own Time*, edited by Osmund Airy, vol. 2 (Oxford: Clarendon Press, 1900), p. 296.

[12] 'The Raree Show' (1681), rpt. *POAS*, vol. 2, pp. 425–31, ll. 72, 87.

privileges'.[13] But he was also a reminder to every satirist to mind one's meaning in the perilous world of political lampooning. As College himself warned in his final letter to his son (not without, perhaps, an ironist's final twist of litotes), 'Pray do not endeavour after that folly of Riming, for on my word it will do you hurt'.[14]

College was hardly alone. We could just as easily point to a long list of writers, both before and after the Restoration, who were imprisoned, interrogated, fined, and pilloried.[15] Physical retribution and prosecution were, however, only two forms of peril. Part of the risk that satirists faced was the peril of writing satire at all, of dealing in the shadowy world of sarcastic invective and mocking irony, of veiled meanings and obscure intentions. Such evasive rhetorical procedures were expanded during the eighteenth century in an extension of the 'functional ambiguity' first studied by Annabel Patterson, through which early modern writers and readers 'knowingly exploited...the indeterminacy inveterate to language'.[16] As I document throughout *Libel and Lampoon*, satirists came increasingly to rely on verbal evasions to counter developments in libel law during the late seventeenth and early eighteenth centuries. These same evasions led to further legal developments, including the emergence of innovative courtroom procedures for delimiting verbal ambiguity. In effect, the courts devised specific legal protocols of reading and interpretation: doctrines and procedures that began to make sense of the evasive verbal models so common in satiric works written and circulated between roughly 1680 and 1740.

This new hermeneutics also entailed a new peril: accidental or even active misunderstanding by the authorities. Satires, so many authors worried, could be wilfully misinterpreted by ingenious prosecutors, hard-headed justices, and dim-witted and recalcitrant jurors alike. In his second trial for *The Ra-Ree Show*, for instance, College was convicted of treason in part because the Crown purposefully misread his anti-papal satire as pro-Catholic propaganda, a rotten turn of events for a Presbyterian and occasional conformist who had hoped for a rapprochement between dissenters like him and Charles II's bullying Church of England.[17]

---

[13] 20 August 1683, in *Calendar of State Papers Domestic: Charles II, 1683: July–September*, edited by F. H. Blackburne Daniell and Francis Bickley (London: His Majesty's Stationery Office, 1934), p. 309.

[14] *The Life and Times of Anthony Wood, Antiquary, of Oxford, 1632–1695, described by Himself*, edited by Andrew Clark, vol. 2 (Oxford: Clarendon Press, 1894), p. 553n. For more on College's prosecution, see Jane Wessel, 'Performing "A Ra-ree Show": Political Spectacle and the Treason Trial of Stephen College', *Restoration* 38, no. 1 (Spring 2014): pp. 3–17; Harold Weber, *Paper Bullets: Print and Kingship under Charles II* (Lexington: University Press of Kentucky, 1996), ch. 5; and B. J. Rahn, 'A Ra-ree Show—A Rare Cartoon: Revolutionary Propaganda in the Treason Trial of Stephen College', in *Studies in Change and Revolution: Aspects of English Intellectual History 1640–1800*, edited by Paul J. Korshin (Menston, Yorkshire: The Scolar Press, 1972), pp. 77–98.

[15] Siebert, *Freedom*, pp. 107–304, *passim*; and Ian Higgins, *Swift's Politics: A Study in Disaffection* (Cambridge: Cambridge University Press, 1994), pp. 160–5.

[16] Patterson, *Censorship and Interpretation*, p. 18. See also Randy Robertson, *Censorship and Conflict in Seventeenth-Century England: The Subtle Art of Division* (University Park: Pennsylvania State University Press, 2010), pp. 13–15.

[17] Gary S. De Krey, 'College [Colledge], Stephen (c. 1635–1681)', *ODNB*.

The determined misinterpretation of potentially seditious works proved a significant worry in the early eighteenth century. Even seemingly innocent writers found themselves in court when this new legal hermeneutics, devised to suss out latently defamatory and seditious meaning, detected incendiary undertones where none was intended. In 1722, for instance, John Trenchard argued that the Crown—in 'a stretch of discretionary power [that] must subvert all the principles of free government, and overturn every species of liberty'—was actively misreading works, even wholly innocent works, by 'strain[ing] their genuine signification' to secure convictions.[18] A writer for *The Craftsman*, a journal in almost unending legal trouble during the 1720s and 1730s, wholly agreed. Whether it was the interpretation of libel laws or the meaning of slippery satire, he wrote in 1726, 'No man is safe against the Subtilties and Finesses of *Lawyers* and *State-Chymists*; who can extract Poison out of the most innocent Things'.[19]

Such fishy forms of courtroom interpretation were perhaps to be expected, though, in an era when writers relied so heavily on verbal evasion. The Crown and the courts had no choice but to work concertedly to devise new measures that might fill the yawning regulatory chasm that had opened up between the permanent lapse of prepublication licensing in 1695 and the emergence of postpublication prosecution under hastily repurposed libel laws. Looking back in 1740 on the radical encroachments of the courts against works of satire, one writer reasoned that '*Judges* and *Juries*' had been forced 'to stretch the Laws' to convict 'these *Sophists in Calumny*'. Writers were 'so perfect . . . in all the Tricks and Wiles of Ambiguity, and Equivocation; in the Mysterious Art of raising Ideas by the Use of Words of a *contrary* Signification, of abusing and vilifying by affected Encomiums', that the authorities had no other choice.[20] For some, satire's verbal evasiveness actually promoted greater latitude in the courts' interpretation of both purposefully ambiguous works and the repurposed laws used increasingly to police them.

This multi-sided perilousness is the focus of *Libel and Lampoon*. One of those perils was in circulating satiric works at all, in making them 'public', as the courts put it, and thus subject to official scrutiny.[21] But the seeds of an even larger peril were built into satire itself. The verbal evasiveness that came to characterize satire during this era entailed the dual problem of interpretation. In the first place, readers routinely misunderstood ironic and allegorical works and often found implied insults where none was intended. In the irritable words of Daniel Defoe, a

---

[18] *Cato's Letters: Or, Essays on Liberty, Civil and Religious, and Other Important Subjects*, edited by Ronald Hamowy, vol. 2 (Indianapolis: Liberty Fund, 1995), p. 720.

[19] *The Craftsman* no. 2 (9 December 1726).

[20] [Francis Squire], *A Faithful Report of a Genuine Debate Concerning the Liberty of the Press* (London, 1740), pp. 17–18.

[21] *John Lamb's Case* (1610), 9 Coke 59 (S.C.), 77 Eng. Rep. 822; and *Trial of Dover, Brewster and Brooks* (1663), 6 *State Trials* 563.

writer who repeatedly found himself at odds with the authorities for his satire, readers 'fancy themselves Lampoon'd, and Expos'd, in some Characters which were never design'd for them: And so take a Coat which never was cut out for that use'.[22] These same misunderstandings imperilled satirists in the courts. In the hazy mechanics of interpreting verbal ambiguity—whether ironic compliments, dense allegorical worlds, or euphemisms dressed in comic circumlocutions and winkingly tedious pleonasms—judges, prosecutors, plaintiffs, and jurors at times proved precisely the kinds of readers that satirists most feared. They were those 'Naughty People', one poet scoffed, who 'make Naughty Applications; as Vicious Stomachs turn the best Food to Flegme'.[23] Libel laws were also subject to analysis, expansion, refinement, and instrumentalization, and such laws, once reinterpreted, could be used in new and sometimes shocking ways, as many satirists soon discovered. It is a routine complaint among writers during this period that both the Crown and the courts had stretched libel laws during the first decades of the eighteenth century in an attempt to regulate the press more generally.[24] Regulation was fine and needed, *The Craftsman* admitted, but 'the Nature and several Species of *Libels* are not ascertain'd by any of [our] Laws'. Instead, they 'are left to the Judgment and Discretion of the *Courts of Justice*; from whence it comes to pass, that in bad Reigns, many *real Patriots* have been severely punished under the Character of *infamous Libellers*'.[25] How a reader, whether lay or legal, was to understand a satiric work *or* libel laws, and the relationship that existed between them, was simply a point of frequent and anxious debate during this period.

The story this book tells is about how satire and the law mutually shaped one another: how satire triggered legal responses, how legal pressures changed the physical production of satire—the material forms in which satiric works circulated, whether in manuscript or print—and how an awareness of the difficulties of legal interpretation promoted the often deeply ambiguous language that came to typify much of the satire written during this period. This relationship often played out in unpredictable ways. Precisely because libel laws changed so quickly and so radically between the late seventeenth and early eighteenth centuries, satirists, printers, and booksellers routinely misunderstood the current status of the law— whether it was the growing legal liability of publishers, the changing qualifications for establishing malice, or the legal status of satiric naming itself. I take up these and other issues in the chapters that follow, showing how a focus on the legal concerns of both satirists and those in the book trade draws important attention to the question of legal reception. Even the *mis*interpretation of extant laws and evolving courtroom procedures among satirists and members of the book trade

---

[22] Daniel Defoe, 'An Explanatory Preface', in *A True Collection of the Writings of the Author of The True Born English-man*, 2nd ed. (London, 1705), p. iv.

[23] *The Law Corrupted; A Satire* (London, 1706), p. iii.

[24] Hamburger, 'Seditious Libel', pp. 725–58.   [25] *The Craftsman*, no. 2 (9 December 1726).

had important effects on both the physical forms and the language of satire during this era. Such a reading of satire's evolution, of how satirists proactively responded to the law, also helps to explain why English satire changes so radically during this era. One of my major goals is thus to reshape how we think about the rhetorical qualities of satire, and especially verbal irony and allegory, during this period.

In addition, emerging satirical practises also helped to shape legal developments, whether courtroom procedures or doctrinal innovations. My focus, as a result, is not only on how satire changes rhetorically and bibliographically. I also track the evolution of the law during the eighteenth century, including debates over juror competence and the century-long struggle between jurors and judges over issues of fact and law in jury deliberations; the incremental adoption of an abstract, generalized, or 'objective' conception of the typical English reader for the interpretation of verbal ambiguity in satiric works; and press freedom and the pervasive belief shared, perhaps surprisingly, by both the authorities *and* writers that the press ought to be regulated (even if they disagreed about precisely how). In all of this, I attempt to trace a strange and sometimes unpredictable reciprocity between legal and literary developments—between the practise of satire, the authorities that sought to regulate it, and the courts that were tasked with interpreting it.

2 Libel and Lampoon, 1670–1792

This legal and literary back and forth, between legal restrictions and satiric evasion, begins especially to play out in the decades following 1660. In my opening chapter, on Dryden's *Mac Flecknoe,* I focus on the development of libel law in the 1670s and how the authorities and the courts drew newfound attention to the rhetorical qualities of satire. By focusing on the interpretation of potentially defamatory language, the courts accidentally and unwittingly encouraged satirists in the latter part of the seventeenth century to write in more verbally ambiguous ways. Dryden, of course, did not 'invent irony', as Steven N. Zwicker has observed. But he explored 'the uses of irony' and, in the process, 'turned a mere figure of speech into an arresting mode of literary self-consciousness'.[26] *Mac Flecknoe* was at the forefront of an important rhetorical shift in satiric practise. His poem helped to devise a model of deeply ironic attack that allowed one to lampoon a satiric victim both directly and yet obliquely, while implicitly thwarting the emerging interpretive procedures of libel laws. To borrow a term from Caroline Levine, irony was an old rhetorical form, but within the legal ecology of the later

---

[26] Steven N. Zwicker, 'Dryden and the Invention of Irony', in *Swift's Travels: Eighteenth-Century Satire and its Legacy,* edited by Nicholas Hudson and Aaron Santesso (Cambridge: Cambridge University Press, 2008), p. 75.

seventeenth century, Dryden found a new or at least heightened 'affordance' for irony within satire.[27] That satiric model, a combination of heavy irony and verbal ambiguity, in turn became a rough rhetorical template for writers engaged in the production of political and personal satire in the final decades of the seventeenth century and the first decades of the eighteenth century.

At the heart of *Libel and Lampoon* is the question of how the courts responded to the verbal and bibliographical evasions that came to typify much of the satire that succeeded Dryden's poem. In trials for libel, beyond showing that a work had been intentionally made public, whether in manuscript or print, the prosecutor or plaintiff was required to prove two things.[28] First, that the words in question referred to someone in particular. This was a slight but not insurmountable problem during the final decades of the seventeenth century, especially when satiric victims appeared under gutted names (such as J—D—for John Dennis).[29] The identities of satiric victims became increasingly easy to prove, especially after 1713, when Chief Justice Thomas Parker ruled that gutted names were no defence in trials for defamation.[30]

Second, prosecutors and plaintiffs had to demonstrate that the imputation was defamatory, either in itself or given the context. This required showing that the words relating to the victim carried the meaning that the prosecution or plaintiff claimed them to mean, and that those words were legally defamatory rather than merely insulting. But delimiting defamatory meaning in heavily ironic works proved, at least in the last few decades of the seventeenth century, deeply difficult, a lesson quickly learned by Dryden's many successors. Satiric works like *Mac Flecknoe* provided a model for mocking one's victims without openly libelling them; such poems lack the bluntly defamatory language so common in manuscript satires from the mid- to late seventeenth century. In the process, Dryden and his successors established a form of slippery ironic locution steeped in mock-praise.

Early on, irony was a specific problem for the Crown and satiric victims. How could one prove that an ostensibly innocent utterance was actually a defamatory accusation? This is the major question addressed in my third chapter, but one that always had to be taken up in trials based on satiric writings. And both writers and judges knew it. In 1714, for instance, Justice Thomas Powys observed that vague

---

[27] Caroline Levine, *Forms: Whole, Rhythm, Hierarchy, Network* (Princeton: Princeton University Press, 2015), pp. 6–14.

[28] For an overview of defamation law, see Holdsworth, *History*, vol. 8, pp. 333–78, esp. 343–351; and Baker, *ELH*, pp. 336–47.

[29] In all of the known manuscript copies of *Mac Flecknoe* (excepting one from 1684), Shadwell's name is written out in full, a common practise in clandestine satires throughout the latter part of the seventeenth century. But his name was gutted, often appearing as 'S—', in both the 1682 unauthorized and 1684 authorized editions of the poem, a naming practise that came to typify printed satire throughout the eighteenth century. See *Mac Flecknoe*, in *The Poems of John Dryden*, vol. 1: 1649–1681, edited by Paul Hammond (New York: Longman, 1995), p. l. 15n.

[30] *R. v. Hurt* (1713), in William Hawkins, *Pleas of the Crown*, 2nd ed., vol. 1 (London, 1724), p. 194.

accusations were such a routine problem for the courts 'that people had taken advice of counsel upon a sheet of paper full of scandalous words in order to know which they might out with safety'.[31] What qualified as a legally defamatory imputation was often perfectly clear; yet dubious phrasing and mocking circumlocutions sometimes made it impossible to secure favourable rulings in court. In 1730, one legal commentator even suggested that his 'Hints for private Use' might address a question that every satirist faced: 'Whether a witty Man may not write or publish Things of a scandalous Import, yet so glossed over and disguised, so wrapp'd up in Implications and Allegories, as not to come within Reach of the Law, nor be construed a Breach of them'.[32] Evasion, circumlocution, allegory, irony—all of these became handy legal contrivances in the satirist's rhetorical toolbox. In turn, the courts, plaintiffs, and prosecutors were burdened with proving the opposite. When presented with verbally evasive forms of defamation—whether an allegorical portrait or an ironic compliment—they were forced to address another question: How was one to go from a text's seemingly innocent surface meaning to an author's supposedly libellous intention?

Delimiting ironic meaning was one hurdle. But an even larger procedural problem that was linked to the courtroom exegesis of vaguely defamatory language was jury competence. Two large interpretive questions loomed over each trial. The first was a question of fact: whether a given statement meant what the prosecutor or plaintiff claimed it to mean. Juries, rather than the bench, exclusively addressed such questions of fact. To the profound frustration of not only satiric victims but also presiding justices, however, jurors frequently rejected a prosecutor or plaintiff's defamatory interpretation of an offending document's language, especially in trials for seditious libel.[33] In 1756, for example, Lord Chancellor Hardwicke complained to the prime minister, the Duke of Newcastle, of 'the impossibility of getting Juries to convict' for 'libellous papers', even when they were 'most provoking and infamous'.[34] Such recalcitrance was one way in which jurors across the eighteenth century stifled actions and prosecutions for libel, especially in trials focusing on works critical of the government or featuring unsympathetic victims.

This question of fact—what a given statement meant—was only one interpretive hurdle prosecutors and complainants faced. The second was a question of law: whether a given statement was legally defamatory. Such questions of law, the courts contended (and prosecutors agreed), were subject to judicial interpretation. If the jury accepted the prosecutor or plaintiff's interpretation of a given statement, then the bench was tasked with determining whether that same statement

---

[31] *Harrison v. Thornborough* (1714), rpt. *Sources*, p. 646.   [32] *State Law*, p. [ii], 6.
[33] Green, *Verdict*, pp. 249, 329.
[34] Hardwicke to Newcastle (29 August 1756), BL Add. MS 32867, f. 146, qtd. Black, *Press*, p. 168.

qualified as legally defamatory. For instance, jurors might agree that to be 'Pox'd by her love', as Alexander Pope put it of Lady Mary Wortley Montagu, meant to be infected with a venereal disease; but it was the jurisdiction of the bench to decide whether that same imputation of communicable disease qualified as legally defamatory.[35]

Here, too, jurors pushed back. Whether juries could speak to questions of both fact *and* law—'to the whole matter', as it was then known—was one of the major legal debates of the seventeenth and eighteenth centuries.[36] In trials for libel, juries routinely took on legal issues (whether, for instance, a given statement was defamatory or seditious), despite directions from the bench to confine themselves solely to questions of fact (whether, for instance, a work had been published). Such debates could result in 'jury nullification'—that is, when jurors opted to 'nullify' a law by refusing to convict a defendant, often because they believed that the application of libel laws to certain kinds of writing or speech was unjust, or because they as jurors had been denied adequate purview to assess the 'libellous-ness' of the language being tried.[37] This larger debate over jury competence was not settled until Fox's Libel Act in 1792 (32 Geo. 3, *c.*60), the terminal date for *Libel and Lampoon* and the statute by which juries were finally and definitively given the scope to decide questions of both fact and law.[38] Until then, however, prosecutors, plaintiffs, and justices alike frequently battled jurors over the inter-pretation of defamatory and seditious language, a problem only exacerbated when the words in question, especially in works of satire, proved ambiguous.

3 Verbal and Bibliographical Evasions

Throughout *Libel and Lampoon*, I return to these debates over jury competence and nullification, situating them within a larger legal drama over the courtroom interpretation of satire. One of the most valuable early opinions, I argue in my first chapter, was the ruling in *King v. Lake* (1671) under Justice (later Lord Chief

---

[35] Alexander Pope, *The First Satire of the Second Book of Horace Imitated*, in *The Poems of Alexander Pope*, edited by John Butt (New Haven: Yale University Press, 1963), l. 84.

[36] Richard H. Helmholz, 'Civil Trials and the Limits of Responsible Speech', in *Juries, Libel, & Justice: The Role of the English Juries in Seventeenth- and Eighteenth-Century Trials for Libel and Slander* (Los Angeles: William Andrews Clark Memorial Library, University of California, Los Angeles, 1984), pp. 24–5.

[37] On the evolving relationship between nullification and the fact-law distinction in jury deliber-ations, see Simon Stern, 'Between Local Knowledge and National Politics: Debating Rationales for Jury Nullification after *Bushell's Case*', *The Yale Law Journal* 111, no. 7 (May 2002): 1815–59; and Green, *Verdict*, pp. xxxi, xviii–xx, chs. 7 and 8.

[38] Siebert, *Freedom*, p. 391. On the 'historically unprecedented number of prosecutions for seditious libel' following the passage of the act, when 'juries frequently sided with the administration' (p. 4), see Trevor Ross, *Writing in Public: Literature and the Liberty of the Press in Eighteenth-Century Britain* (Baltimore: Johns Hopkins University Press, 2018), esp. ch. 5.

Justice) Sir Matthew Hale.[39] This case was important in part because it belongs to a series of developments in libel law in the later seventeenth century that helped to lay the groundwork for the government's post-licensing regulatory strategy for the press. As Philip Hamburger has shown, this critical intervention was perhaps unintentional: only following the lapse of licensing in 1695 did the authorities entirely turn to post-publication press prosecutions using newly repurposed libel laws.[40]

The opinion in *King v. Lake* was important in particular, though, because it helped to model the bench's directions to juries across the seventeenth and eighteenth centuries for the interpretation of defamatory language, precisely at a moment in the 1670s when older, more permissive doctrines of courtroom interpretation were under intense judicial scrutiny.[41] *King v. Lake* simply afforded Hale and his colleagues on the bench the opportunity to repurpose an alternative interpretative principle—known as 'common intendment'—that was already being employed to elucidate imprecise language in other branches of law. In short, Hale and his fellow justices insisted that jurors interpret words in their most natural sense given the context of their utterance.[42] This theory of 'common intendment' set the groundwork for a supposedly reasonable standard of interpretation that was employed in trials for libel throughout the eighteenth century. The result was a theoretically objective means of assessment based on the assumption that there is an average or typical reader or listener, one who ought to be able to deduce a speaker or satirist's intended meaning from a shared or 'common' set of beliefs about the primary denotations and connotations of a word, locution, or idiom.

Over time, the courts expanded the use of these 'reasonable' standards.[43] In 1694, for instance, Chief Justice Sir John Holt ruled that all words, no matter how ambiguous, should be understood in sociocentric terms. They should be taken, that is, 'in a common sense according to the vulgar intendment of the bystanders'.[44] He extended this notion of commonality in 1706 to even ironic statements, again by focusing on how such statements were understood by listeners—in this case, jurors—rather than on the precise linguistic mechanism that made them ironic.[45] Finally, in 1728/9, Chief Justice Sir Robert Raymond ruled that the interpretation

---

[39] *King v. Lake* (1671), 2 Vent. 28 (K.B.), 89 Eng. Rep. 12; *King v. Lake* (1671), 2 Vent. 28 (K.B.), 86 Eng. Rep. 289; and *King v. Lake* (1671), 1 Freeman 14–15 (K.B.), 89 Eng. Rep. 12–13.

[40] Hamburger, 'Seditious Libel', pp. 725–6.

[41] Baker, *ELH*, p. 443; and *Hamond and Kingsmill* (1647), Style 22–3, 82 Eng. Rep. 500. For the ecclesiastical origins and common-law development of defamation, see Richard H. Helmholz, preface to *Select Cases on Defamation to 1600* (London: Selden Society, 1985) and *The Oxford History of the Laws of England*, vol. 1: The Canon Law and Ecclesiastical Jurisdiction from 597 to the 1640s (Oxford: Oxford University Press, 2003), pp. 577–93.

[42] *King v. Lake* (1671), 2 Vent. 28 (C.P.), 89 Eng. Rep. 12.

[43] For the codification of sociocentric doctrines of interpretation, see *State Law*, pp. 59–62, 74–6.

[44] *Somers v. House* (1694), Holt 39 (K.B.), 90 Eng. Rep. 919.

[45] *R. v. Dr. Brown* [sic] (1706), 11 Mod. 86 (Q.B.), 88 Eng. Rep. 912.

of allegorical libels should rely on an abstract 'generality of readers': how a juror believed *most* people would have understood a work, rather than the manner in which a potentially idiosyncratic juror actually did.[46]

Reasonable standards were valuable not only because they created objective rules for elucidating verbal ambiguity, but also because they slowly eroded the interpretive latitude of jurors by limiting their deliberations. They allowed the Crown to defer to the jury in the abstract while effectively displacing the capricious interpretations of actual jurors in court. 'Common intendment', 'vulgar intendment', and 'the generality of readers' all suggested that jurors should reject their personal interpretations in favour of a rational projection: a community of predictable readers around whom semantic consensus could be built.[47] The Crown could not simply do away with jurors, but it could attempt to control the heuristic of their interpretation. As a result, these rulings together in part helped to neutralize recalcitrant and unpredictable jurors, even if those same jurors continued to resist the directions of the bench across the century.[48] Just as importantly, these same doctrines permitted the Crown to skirt the linguistic-evidentiary issues posed by evasive language. By deferring to a broader, more sociocentric understanding of satiric meaning, the Crown was no longer required to demonstrate the precise textual qualities that furnished satiric intent, whether a series of ironic clues or internal semantic evidence that linked an allegorical world to its real-world counterpart. In short, the Crown was able to claim that a satire could be understood by an abstract generality of readers in a certain manner; but the Crown was not obliged to decipher the precise linguistic mechanism that made a statement ironic or allegorical.

In response to the increasing refinement of libel law and especially the development of legal methods for the interpretation of ambiguous language, satirists, their printers, and their booksellers developed new ways to evade both the authorities and the courts. Those evasions came in two forms, bibliographic and verbal, and it is one of my primary goals to show how these emerging satiric practises shaped the law and how, in turn, legal responses further spurred on the development of satire. As I argue in my first chapter, Dryden's *Mac Flecknoe* offered an important rhetorical break from the Restoration's most virulent and bald-faced political and personal manuscript satires. He and his successors also offered a new model for satire itself—one steeped in irony and verbal evasion, one whose criticisms were couched in circumlocution and ambiguity, and one that proved immensely difficult, in the coming decades, to prosecute in the courts.

---

[46] *R. v. Clerk* [*sic*] (1728/9), 1 Barn. 305 (K.B.), 94 Eng. Rep. 207.

[47] See also Michael McKeon, who has argued that the 'political and legal policy' around the courtroom interpretation of libels 'fostered the coalescence of a virtual "reading public"' (*The Secret History of Domesticity: Public, Private, and the Division of Knowledge* [Baltimore: Johns Hopkins University Press, 2005], pp. 94–5).

[48] Beattie, *Crime*, pp. 400–49; Baker, *ELH*, pp. 143–4, 151; and Green, *Verdict*, chs. 7 and 8.

Often working together, the Crown and the courts continued to develop new ways of redressing these satiric evasions. I take up these legal responses in the following chapters, offering a series of case studies on the back and forth between the law and satire. In each instance, I offer a combination of macro- and micro-level analyses of the broad relationship between law and satire—such as the means of publication and circulation, the interpretation of verbal irony and allegory, the function of satiric naming practises, and whether visual satires were defamatory—while also offering insights into the practises of particular authors, including John Dryden, Jonathan Swift, Daniel Defoe, Alexander Pope, Delarivier Manley, and the pseudonymous Junius; major periodicals from this period, including *Mist's Weekly Journal* and *The Craftsman*; and later visual and dramatic satirists, such as James Gillray, Thomas Rowlandson, the Cruikshanks, and Samuel Foote. As a result, each chapter moves both in and out, offering general observations on the relationship between law and literature alongside specific readings of this period's most important satiric works and practitioners.

In my second chapter, for instance, I study Swift and the illicit book trade, exploring how the semi-underground publishing industry worked in eighteenth-century London. After the Press Licensing Act lapsed in 1695, writers and their booksellers were ostensibly free to publish anything they wished. But the authorities quickly responded to this largely unwanted expansion of press freedom with a series of prosecutions that increased the liabilities of printers and booksellers while also clamping down on the book trade's most routine evasions.

Swift was both an exemplary and exceptional figure within this world of everyday subterfuge. His printers and booksellers employed all the same methods with his works that they did with others—they revised his publications with an eye towards the legally actionable, doctored the publication information present on his title pages, and employed shadowy figures to distribute and circulate his most virulent texts. But Swift also craftily used the provisions of the Act of Anne (1709/10), the first formal copyright law, to insulate himself against the authorities. Swift in effect created a form of reverse indemnification by trading the economic benefits of copyright for a higher degree of legal safety. In exchange for ownership over his copyrights, Swift's publishers took on legal liability for a given work, obscuring his involvement and withholding his name in those frequent instances in which they were called to account for his writings. Swift's canny use of copyright was seemingly typical of the illicit book trade more generally. As a result, I seek to reorient discussions of copyright law away from the nuts-and-bolts historical model—what intellectual property was—towards the law's instrumentality: how those in the book trade and authors exploited the provisions of intellectual property to create covert legal protections.

My third chapter moves my discussion of this reciprocal relationship between law and satire from the booksellers' stalls and shops and the material forms in which these works were distributed to the courtrooms in which such satires were interpreted. There I focus on ironic works in trials for libel and the prosecution of Defoe for his widely misunderstood and, as I argue, deeply ironic pamphlet *The Shortest Way with the Dissenters* (1702). I begin by offering an overview of the law of seditious libel and the courts' methods for interpreting semantics, intentionality, and malice in verbally ironic satires. This debate came to a head in Dr Joseph Browne's 1706 trial for seditious libel for his satiric poem, *The Country Parson's Honest Advice* (1705). In his opinion on the case, Chief Justice Holt contentiously ruled, without precedent, that verbal irony was no defence for libel.

This discussion of satire and intention in seditious works also opens up larger questions about the interpretation of irony and how jurors (and, by proxy, lay readers) made sense of satiric works. This is a story, in short, about how readers learned to read, and especially how they learned to interpret the massive body of ironic works that had suddenly emerged after 1695. Modern theorists have abstracted a general type of verbal irony in eighteenth-century satiric works—what we might call internally signalled irony—from a small body of satiric texts, and especially from Swift's *A Modest Proposal*. Other works, however, some even by Swift, follow a different model built around what I call extrinsic irony. This form of irony relies less on internal clues than on the reader's knowledge of information that lies definitively outside of the text. *The Country Parson's Honest Advice* is a prime example. In it, the speaker openly praises eighteen noble lords for precisely the virtues they were widely thought to lack, and yet the poem offers no *internal* linguistic clues that it is anything other than overt encomium. Take the speaker's compliment for William Cavendish, fourth earl and first duke of Devonshire, who is praised for his 'Chastity',[49] despite his well-earned reputation 'for Debauchery, Lewdness, &c'.[50] (One can only imagine what that pregnant et cetera contains.) Browne's poem, moreover, was not alone in its use of extrinsic irony, and it is only through tremendous blinkering that we have been able to ignore its critical role in the complex operations of this period's satires. Browne's trial for the poem is likewise deeply suggestive about how irony was understood during this period. This was the precise question addressed in the run-up to and then during his trial: how readers were supposed to make sense of satiric and specifically ironic works, when such coded insults at a purely semantic level looked simply like compliments.

In my conclusion to this chapter, I apply my findings about irony and the law of seditious libel to Defoe's case. I argue that *The Shortest Way* is in fact ironic (a point of routine disagreement among Defoe scholars), and show that his prosecution, as his contemporaries well understood, was the result of Chief Justice

---

[49] [Joseph Browne?], *The Country Parson's Honest Advice to The Judicious Lawyer, and Worthy Minister of State, My Lord Keeper* (London, 1706), rpt. *POAS*, vol. 7, p. 158, l. 13.

[50] Thomas Hearne, *Remarks and Collections*, edited by C. E. Doble, et al., vol. 2 (Oxford: Clarendon Press, 1885–1921), p. 40.

Holt's surprising revisions to the law of seditious libel. Especially important, and shocking, was Holt's decision to dispose of malice (that is, intent) as an element of the crime of seditious libel, which in turn made it easier to prosecute politically subversive works of satire. Irony was and should have been a defence for seditious libel—all of which suggests that Defoe did have a defence for *The Shortest Way*, but one that was only of value before Holt's judicial tenure, and one missed by scholars who have presumed that Holt's reading of the law was unexceptional.

In my fourth chapter, I turn to satiric naming practises, especially the use of gutted names, such as 'J— S—' for John Smith, and Pope's *Dunciad Variorum* (1729). The courts ruled in 1713 that gutted names were no defence for libel and that missing letters could simply be plugged in. Yet gutted names continued to be used in satiric works. Why? In part, many satirists simply misunderstood the law—an important reminder that even misinterpretation in legal reception should be a part of our understanding of how the law shapes literary behaviour. Above all, however, gutted names served important commercial, aesthetic, and pseudo-ethical functions. In closing, I return to Pope and show how he handled the contentious issue of outright naming in his *Dunciad Variorum*. Having decided to name his dunces in full, Pope was forced to grapple with what was, at its core, a socio-literary rather than legal issue. In a clever turn, however, he did so by adopting the language of the courts.

In my fifth chapter, I turn to allegory, which writers, journalists, and satirists in a variety of media found a flexible tool for political criticism. Like verbal irony, allegory posed a particular problem for the courts. How were prosecutors and plaintiffs to demonstrate legally that a fantastical allegorical world actually referred to real victims in quotidian England? I begin by studying the failed prosecution of Manley's *The New Atalantis* (1709), a work widely perceived to be an allegory (or so-called secret history) of the Whigs and the Junto that wielded control over Queen Anne. Her prosecution should have been enabled by a crucial decision from 1704, in which Chief Justice Holt ruled that criticism of not only specific officials but also the government as a whole was criminal.[51] Though this ruling broadened the definition of libel, it nonetheless failed to provide a mechanism by which prosecutors could prove that allegorical depictions referred to real-world individuals or government institutions.

Given these procedural hurdles, allegorical satire flourished during this period, especially in the growing opposition periodical press of the 1710s and 1720s. The remainder of this chapter focuses on two of the most important journals from this era: *The Craftsman*, which devised a sophisticated and flexible model for political commentary and satire built largely around allegorical news from abroad and the implicit application of history to the present; and *Mist's Weekly Journal*, perhaps

---

[51] Hamburger, 'Seditious Libel', p. 735.

the most widely read periodical of the 1710s and 1720s. The government repeatedly failed throughout the later 1720s to prosecute either periodical successfully, thanks in large measure to the limits of libel law when it came up against allegory. However, all of that changed in early 1729, when the government successfully prosecuted John Clarke, a printer for *Mist's*. The case against Clarke revolved around the 'Persian Letter', a Jacobite allegory of the royal family that intimated that Walpole was secretly manipulating the illegitimate king, George II. The decision in the case—in which Chief Justice Raymond argued that jurors should rely on an abstract 'generality of readers' when confronted with allegorical materials—proved pivotal, the final piece in the decades-long puzzle of how best to delimit the courtroom interpretation of verbally ambiguous satires.[52]

My final chapter brings together the rulings and satiric practises examined throughout *Libel and Lampoon* to answer a question that has long vexed literary historians. Why does satire seemingly disappear in the middle of the eighteenth century? Rather than dying, as literary scholars routinely claim, satire begins a period of migration at mid-century, especially to visual satire and, to some degree, dramatic mimicry and impersonation. Over the course of the later seventeenth century and the first half of the eighteenth century, the courts closed the verbal and bibliographical loopholes that satirists and their booksellers had opened up. The perils of satire, rather than diminishing, actually increased during this period. By 1741, as David Hume remarked, 'The general laws against sedition and libelling [were] as strong as they possibly can be made'.[53] Satire, though, does not vanish—and it certainly does not die, as earlier scholars asserted, because of changing tastes, the rise of sentimentality, or the entrenchment of politeness.

Instead, by mid-century the courts had devised largely effective procedures for handling the most routine verbal evasions. This increased legal pressure in turn led to the migration of satire to visual media like caricature, which relied less on verbal evasion and was not subject to the courtroom procedures and laws that had enabled the prosecution of printed satire. Legal rulings unintentionally promoted the 'deverbalization' of satire. Over the latter half of the century, caricaturists increasingly used words sparingly and punningly. In lieu of language, visual satirists developed a range of non-verbal representational strategies, such as repetition, intimation, and juxtaposition. The most broadly libellous aspects of such satires were visual and often irreducible to actionable language. Deverbalization thus describes a purely legalistic understanding of language. In visual satires, words typically serve a secondary function, while images often contain the satire's central defamatory imputation. The result was a form of visual defamation that was almost impossible to pin down, let alone prosecute.

---

[52] *R. v. Clerk* [*sic*] (1728/9), 1 Barn. 305 (K.B.), 94 Eng. Rep. 207.
[53] David Hume, 'Essay of the Liberty of the Press', in *Essays, Moral and Political*, edited by Eugene F. Miller, rev. ed. (Indianapolis: Liberty Fund, 1987), p. 605.

In closing, I argue that the Stage Licensing Act of 1737, which required the pre-performance censorship of plays performed at the two patent theatres in London, also promoted forms of deverbalization. Like libel laws from this same period, the Licensing Act was especially preoccupied with the verbal regulation of perform-ance through the censorship of play texts. However, this emphasis on textual regulation also created a loophole in licensing. Dramatic satires from the last half of the eighteenth century, and especially the plays of Samuel Foote, the most prominent satiric mimic of this period, are teeming with non-verbal satire and pointed impersonations. Such forms of physical and acoustic mimicry never showed up in the playscripts submitted to the Lord Chamberlain's office for licensing and could only retroactively be subjected to censorship.

4 Libel and Satire, Law and Literature

In stressing the role that legal pressures played in shaping literary production, my goal is not to downplay other factors in the development of satire, but to draw greater attention to the law. The rise of neoclassicism, the spread of generic theory, the entrenchment of politeness, the growth of literacy, the rise of the novel, the changing role of women in society—all of these, too, shaped the satire written and published during this period and have been closely and ably studied over the past half century by such scholars as Ian Jack, James Sutherland, Alvin B. Kernan, Ronald Paulson, Pat Rogers, Felicity Nussbaum, Leon Guilhamet, Howard D. Weinbrot, Claude Rawson, Dustin Griffin, Helen Deutsch, and Ashley Marshall, among many others.[54]

However, the lack, until recently, of sustained studies of the relationship between satire and the law is in part surprising, because scholars for decades have routinely gestured to the importance of libel laws in shaping literary and

---

[54] Ian Jack, *Augustan Satire: Intention and Idiom in English Poetry, 1660–1750* (Oxford: Clarendon Press, 1952); James Sutherland, *English Satire* (Cambridge: Cambridge University Press, 1958); Alvin Kernan, *The Plot of Satire* (New Haven: Yale University Press, 1965); Ronald Paulson, *Fictions of Satire* (Baltimore: Johns Hopkins University Press, 1967) and *Satire and the Novel in Eighteenth-Century England* (New Haven: Yale University Press, 1967); Pat Rogers, *The Augustan Vision* (London: Weidenfeld and Nicolson, 1974); Felicity Nussbaum, *The Brink of All We Hate: English Satires on Women, 1660–1750* (Lexington: University Press of Kentucky, 1984); Leon Guilhamet, *Satire and the Transformation of Genre* (Philadelphia: University of Pennsylvania Press, 1987); Howard Weinbrot, *The Formal Strain: Studies in Augustan Imitation and Satire* (Chicago: University of Chicago Press, 1969), *Augustus Caesar in 'Augustan' England: The Decline of a Classical Norm* (Princeton: Princeton University Press, 1977), *Alexander Pope and the Traditions of Formal Verse Satire* (Princeton: Princeton University Press, 1982), *Eighteenth-Century Satire: Essays on Text and Context from Dryden to Peter Pindar* (Cambridge: Cambridge University Press, 1988), and *Menippean Satire Reconsidered: From Antiquity to the Eighteenth Century* (Baltimore: Johns Hopkins University Press, 2005); Claude Rawson, *Satire and Sentiment 1660–1830* (Cambridge: Cambridge University Press, 1994); Griffin, *Satire*; and Helen Deutsch, *Resemblance and Disgrace: Alexander Pope and the Deformation of Culture* (Cambridge: Harvard University Press, 1996).

especially satiric production. Those gestures have often led back to a single article by C. R. Kropf from the 1970s.[55] Kropf brought to light the profound role legal considerations played in the production of satire, but in the process accidentally closed down discussion of that relationship. In the intervening decades, most scholars have simply accepted his conclusions, dutifully citing him in passing while repeating some of his errors, which have become commonplaces of eighteenth-century scholarship.[56] All of this has rapidly changed, just in the last five years, as such literary scholars as Roger Lund, Joseph Hone, and Thomas Keymer have sought to re-evaluate Kropf's conclusions while offering compelling new studies of the relationship between eighteenth-century satire and libel laws.[57] My own research has also contributed to this burgeoning trend, and the primary goal of *Libel and Lampoon* is not simply to correct our assumptions about libel law from this period but to make the law central to our understanding of how and why satire developed during the eighteenth century.[58] Just as Joss Marsh did with nineteenth-century literature and Sean Latham did with modernism, I want to put laws relating to language regulation at the centre of eighteenth-century literature more generally—to show how legal pressures shaped satiric production, to trace the complicated ways in which satirists and their booksellers both interpreted and responded to legal pressures, and to demonstrate how legal developments encour-aged the eventual migration of satire to increasingly non-verbal media during the last half of the century.[59]

In putting the law at the centre of literary history, I am especially interested in the sometimes unpredictable ways in which this relationship played out—how satirists, printers, and booksellers understood the law and their legal responsibil-ities and liabilities. To some extent, earlier literary scholars, and especially those working in the field of law and literature, were too willing to read the law in simplistic terms, as Julie Stone Peters cuttingly observed in a widely cited article

---

[55] C. R. Kropf, 'Libel and Satire in the Eighteenth Century', *Eighteenth-Century Studies* 8, no. 2 (Winter 1974–1975): pp. 153–68.

[56] See Edward P. Nathan, 'The Bench and the Pulpit: Conflicting Elements in the Augustan Apology for Satire', *English Literary History* 52, no. 2 (Summer 1985): p. 394n1; Vincent Carretta, *The Snarling Muse: Verbal and Visual Political Satire from Pope to Churchill* (Philadelphia: University of Pennsylvania Press, 1983), p. 265n10; Gregory Colomb, *Designs on Truth: The Poetics of the Augustan Mock-Epic* (University Park: Pennsylvania State University Press, 1992), p. 65n15; Black, *Press*, p. 313; Higgins, *Swift's Politics*, p. 160; and Howard D. Weinbrot, 'Masked Men and Satire and Pope: Toward a Historical Basis for the Eighteenth-Century Persona', *Eighteenth-Century Studies* 16, no. 3 (Spring 1983): p. 283n31.

[57] Roger Lund, '"An Alembick of Innuendos": Satire, Libel, and *The Craftsman*', *Philological Quarterly* 95, no. 2 (Spring 2016): pp. 243–68; Joseph Hone, 'Legal Constraints, Libellous Evasions', in *OHECS*, pp. 525–41; and Keymer, *Poetics*. See also McKeon, *Secret History of Domesticity*, pp. 95–9.

[58] Andrew Benjamin Bricker, 'Libel and Satire: The Problem with Naming', *English Literary History* 81, no. 3 (Autumn 2014): pp. 889–921 and 'After the Golden Age: Caricature, Libel, and the Deverbalization of Satire', *Eighteenth-Century Studies* 51, no. 3 (Spring 2018): pp. 305–36.

[59] Joss Marsh, *Word Crimes: Blasphemy, Culture, and Literature in Nineteenth-Century England* (Chicago: University of Chicago Press, 1998); and Sean Latham, *The Art of Scandal: Modernism, Libel Law, and the Roman à Clef* (Oxford: Oxford University Press, 2009).

from 2005.[60] Much has changed in the intervening decade and a half, and scholars of law and literature have increasingly come to the important conclusion that the law must always be interpreted by lay actors.

In attempting to make sense of these intersections between law and satire, I have drawn especially on the work of the legal theorist Naomi Mezey, who has foregrounded the complicated ways in which law and culture function reciprocally. Mezey has drawn particular attention to what she calls 'slippage': those 'inconsistencies between the production of legal meaning and its cultural reception'.[61] During this period, a kind of interpretive interference existed between libel law, as it gradually evolved and slowly appeared in legal opinions and statutes, and the law as it was popularly understood by non-legal actors. Two versions of libel law existed side by side: one was professional, shared by judges and lawyers at Westminster and the Inns of Court; the other was looser and more socio-literary, common among satirists and their booksellers—and even their victims—all of whom believed, sometimes mistakenly, that certain verbal and bibliographic evasions could stymie legal proceedings. In the case of the lampooned, their misapprehension of the law often directly benefited satirists.

In this regard, libel laws from this period were not 'crystalline', to use Carol M. Rose's terminology, but 'muddy'. Rather than signalling the precise liabilities of satirists and booksellers, the courts, in their haste to refurbish libel laws and develop interpretive doctrines, often produced confusion over individual 'rights and obligations' and sometimes even substituted 'fuzzy, ambiguous rules' for 'perfectly clear...demarcations and entitlements'.[62] Throughout *Libel and Lampoon*, I identify these moments of doctrinal muddiness in eighteenth-century libel law and track instances of slippage in lay legal interpretation, this disconnect between legal theory and literary practise. In doing so, I am interested in recovering what Simon Stern has called the 'enabling conditions' that bridge the spheres of law and literature.[63]

In foregrounding the law's role in the history of satire, I also seek to revise, especially in my epilogue, our standard accounts of press freedom during this period. In particular, I push back against the somewhat Whiggish tendency among scholars to assume that press freedom ineluctably grew over the course of the eighteenth century. Since Herbert Butterfield's attack on 'Whig history', literary historians and historians of the press have slowly if not fully backed away from

[60] Julie Stone Peters, 'Law, Literature, and the Vanishing Real: On the Future of an Interdisciplinary Illusion', *PMLA* 120, no. 2 (March 2005): pp. 442–53.

[61] Mezey, 'Law', p. 54.

[62] Carol M. Rose, 'Crystals and Mud in Property Law', *Stanford Law Review* 40, no. 3 (February 1988): pp. 577–610.

[63] Simon Stern, 'Literary Analysis of Law: Reorienting the Connections Between Law and Literature', *Critical Analysis of Law* 5, no. 2 (2018): p. 3.

such teleological thinking.[64] At the same time, we have failed to fill this vacuum with a narrative that ever fully accounts for the wild and routine vacillations in press freedom that run across the century.[65] In arguing for a history that accounts for the simultaneous expansion and contraction of press freedom, I build on the work of scholars studying earlier periods, including Laura Gowing, Cyndia Susan Clegg, M. Lindsay Kaplan, and Debora Shuger, who have emphasized the authorities' often piecemeal responses to unruly writers and booksellers.[66] Despite fluctuations in enforcement, the authorities and the courts developed a flexible set of regulatory tools that could be used systematically when required.[67] Following the fates of satirists and members of the book trade over the course of the eighteenth century provides a salutary reminder that the Crown continued to believe that the press should be closely monitored, and at times strictly regulated, even after licensing lapsed in 1695.

This is all to say that satire is also a stand-in for a larger, less intuitive, and much more complicated history of the press. For all of our progressive stories about press freedom during this period—that it inevitably grows and grows, part and parcel with our progression towards ever greater liberty—there can be little doubt that there were also sudden and stunning moments of intense legal pressure across the eighteenth century. Press freedom does grow, but it does so only between moments of contraction, especially in the routine government crackdowns during moments of domestic unrest, and despite the growth of ever more restrictive court rulings and procedures. The government eagerly prosecuted those it could and routinely harassed those it could not. Satirists, printers, and booksellers responded as best they knew how, devising new bibliographical and verbal sleights until the most virulent satire began to migrate to increasingly non-verbal media.

[64] Hanson, *Government*; Siebert, *Freedom*; Robert R. Rea, *The English Press in Politics: 1769–1774* (Lincoln: University of Nebraska Press, 1963); and Arthur M. Schlesinger, *Prelude to Independence: The Newspaper War on Britain, 1764–1776* (New York: Knopf, 1958). For an assessment of this 'evolutionary model', see Stephen Botein, Jack Censer, and Harriet Ritvo, 'The Periodical Press in Eighteenth-Century English and French Society: A Cross-Cultural Approach', *Comparative Studies in Society and History* 23, no. 3 (July 1981): pp. 466–7.
[65] Herbert Butterfield, *The Whig Interpretation of History* (1932; New York: Norton, 1965), p. v.
[66] Laura Gowing, *Domestic Dangers: Words, Women and Sex in Early Modern London* (Oxford: Clarendon Press, 1996); Cyndia Susan Clegg, *Press Censorship in Jacobean England* (Cambridge: Cambridge University Press, 1991), *Press Censorship in Elizabethan England* (Cambridge: Cambridge University Press, 1997), and *Press Censorship in Caroline England* (Cambridge: Cambridge University Press, 2008); M. Lindsay Kaplan, *The Culture of Slander in Early Modern England* (Cambridge: Cambridge University Press, 1997); and Debora Shuger, *Censorship and Cultural Sensibility: The Regulation of Language in Tudor-Stuart England* (Philadelphia: University of Pennsylvania Press, 2006).
[67] In so claiming, I also follow Joad Raymond and others in their recent re-evaluation of 'revisionist' accounts of early modern press regulation. Revisionists have tended to emphasize the ad hoc nature of regulation, downplaying its effectiveness, whereas Raymond and others have argued for the 'utility of the blurred relationship between legislation and legal practice', which 'could be more effective than overwhelming systematization' (p. 514). See Joad Raymond, 'Censorship in Law and Practice in Seventeenth-Century England: Milton's *Areopagitica*', in *The Oxford Handbook of English Law and Literature, 1500–1700*, edited by Lorna Hutson (Oxford: Oxford University Press, 2017), pp. 507–28.

Finally, by reading the development of satire through the lens of legal history, I examine a wide range of works and, in so doing, complicate tidy descriptions of what satire was and is. Critical and abstract models often fail to describe the diverse and even anarchic literary practises of this period. Our current theories for irony, for instance, so carefully worked out by scholars like Wayne Booth and D. C. Muecke, are simply too limited to account for a period steeped in ironic writings that followed a range of literary procedures, many of which are too inconsistent or too unlike our own twentieth- and twenty-first-century models to fall neatly into our carefully arranged theoretical bins.[68]

In a similar way, some scholars have favoured limited definitions of what satire was or is. Whether addressing satire as a genre or a mode, one of our longest-standing and yet least resolved debates, such critics have fallen back on often extremely broad or painfully crabbed definitions. Like Ashley Marshall, Robert Phiddian, and others, I have my reservations about generic criticism.[69] The failures of generic definitions are legion and the debate around how we define satire in particular has often proven unproductive, especially in light of a growing interest in 'historical poetics', in which all parties more or less agree on one thing: generic, transhistorical, and transcultural definitions of satire are bound to fail.[70] As a result, I have adopted a broad definition of satire, for at least two reasons. The first is that a specific sub-categorical definition of satire—something like formal verse satire—fails to account for so many types of works, such as ranting pamphlets, allegorically satiric novels, or gently mocking comedies, that seem to fall in the hinterlands of our descriptive terminology, and would exclude their consideration from a study like this one.

I also have a second and, for this project, more important reason for resisting a limiting definition of satire. My goal is not to define satire into existence but to understand it within a 'process theory of genre', as Ralph Cohen and Jonathan Culler have called it, in which genres are 'open systems' that 'are named and placed within hierarchies or systems of genres'.[71] The evolution and generic reformulation of satire over time permits one to see the reciprocal relationship between satire and the law, and in particular how satire was viewed and interpreted by legal actors, potential plaintiffs, and the authorities at different points during this period. My view of satire is, one might say, ground up. I want not

---

[68] Wayne Booth, *A Rhetoric of Irony* (Chicago: University of Chicago Press, 1975); and D. C. Muecke, *The Compass of Irony* (London: Methuen, 1969).

[69] Marshall, *Satire*, pp. 2–8; Robert Phiddian, 'Satire and the Limits of Literary Theories', *Critical Quarterly* 55, no. 3 (October 2013): pp. 48–51; and Paul Simpson, *On the Discourse of Satire: Towards a Stylistic Model of Satirical Humour* (Amsterdam: John Benjamins, 2003), pp. 47–67.

[70] Yopie Prins, 'What is Historical Poetics?', *Modern Language Quarterly* 77, no. 1 (2016): pp. 13–40; Marshall, *Satire*, pp. xiii–xiv; and William R. Jones, *Satire in the Elizabethan Age: An Activistic Art* (New York: Routledge, 2018), pp. 1–6.

[71] Ralph Cohen, 'History and Genre', *New Literary History* 17, no. 2 (Winter 1986): pp. 203–18; and Jonathan Culler, 'Lyric, History, and Genre', *New Literary History* 40, no. 4 (Autumn 2009): pp. 879–99.

simply to track those who wrote, read, and wrote about satire, but also to understand how those who had little interest in generic definitions and yet much at stake in the effect of certain types of writing read such works: the victims of satire, the authorities, the courts. Satire, like the law, was a moving target during this period; it often reacted to the law, reformulating itself in newly evasive ways.

As a result, I have adopted a broad formulation of satire that takes into account all of the works that make up the primary materials in *Libel and Lampoon*. First, satire is not only a literary art but also a mode that can inhabit a range of genres, as Alastair Fowler has written, and an assortment of media—from written to visual works, from private and street performances to material objects, such as decorative ceramics and novelty coins—that typically fall outside of literary studies.[72] Second, satire offers some form of commentary on its object, whether we call that an 'attack' on a 'target', as Northrop Frye, Edward W. Rosenheim, and other scholars have concluded, or a milder form of 'critique' that might lack 'hostility', as Marshall has argued.[73] Finally, satire requires some form of comic leavening agent, something to push it beyond mere invective.

Such a definition might seem too generous, even too broad, but it does bring into view, if not crisp focus, the objects that make up my primary body of materials. My interest lies not in defining and delimiting those objects; this is not a project concerned with forwarding a specific generic theory of satire. Instead, it lies in the ways satiric works entered the world; how they were understood and often misunderstood; how they were interpreted and misinterpreted; and how the authorities, through a host of legal instruments, and satirists and those in the book trade, in response, shaped the works written and circulated during this period.

A looser approach to the definition of satire during this period—one in which genres operate, in Peter Seitel's words, as 'frameworks of expectation' or as 'social contracts between a writer and a specific public', as Fredric Jameson has written— has a few added benefits.[74] In the first place, the courts and the authorities proved remarkably bad generic critics. As we will see throughout this book, the courts often refused to specify the precise verbal mechanisms by which things like verbal irony or allegory might work. In addition, the government was not so much concerned with *how* satires worked as with controlling the undesirable social and political *effects* of its most pernicious kinds. The very word 'satire' was a kind of flare for the authorities—so much so that Roger Lund has argued that the

---

[72] Alastair Fowler, *Kinds of Literature: An Introduction to the Theory of Genres and Modes* (Cambridge: Harvard University Press, 1982), p. 110.

[73] Northrop Frye, *Anatomy of Criticism* (Princeton: Princeton University Press, 1957), p. 224; Edward W. Rosenheim, *Swift and the Satirist's Art* (Chicago: University of Chicago Press, 1963), p. 31; and Marshall, *Satire*, p. 3.

[74] Peter Seitel, 'Theorizing Genres: Interpreting Works', *New Literary History* 34, no. 2 (Spring 2003): p. 277; and Fredric Jameson, *The Political Unconscious: Narrative as a Socially Symbolic Act* (Ithaca: Cornell University Press, 1981), p. 106.

authorities sought 'to criminalize satiric indeterminacy' itself during the eighteenth century.[75]

Another benefit of a formally loose definition is that it tends, by necessity, to bring more writers under the broad umbrella of satire. We have been told time and again, for instance, that women did not write satire in this era. Even Marshall, in her exhaustive study of over 3,000 works of satire, has managed to unearth only eleven female satirists.[76] One question we should ask, however, is whether our definitions of satire for this period have tended categorically to exclude feminocentric forms of literary expression. Such theories—often derived from male practitioners, who self-servingly defined satire as high-minded, corrective, and didactic—have led literary critics to think about satire in highly phallogocentric terms. But if we were to step back for a moment and ask what a poetics of female satire might look like, we might also come to see a range of female-authored works from this period in a very new and perhaps even satiric light.[77] Melinda Alliker Rabb, for instance, has asked what happens when 'we consider the power dynamic of secret history' in relation to not equality and the novel but to aggression and satire. For Rabb, both secret history and amatory fiction, in their commitment to the exposure of secrets, are formally related to 'the ironic aggression of satire'.[78] This formal intimacy is especially clear in my fifth chapter, in which I have tried actively to think about satire in less dogged terms and in which I insist on referring to Manley's allegorical secret history—like many but not all secret histories—as satiric. One useful aspect of a loosely formal rather than strictly generic definition of satire is the extent to which it permits us not simply to identify satires but also to locate the satiric in its most fleeting moments—to link writings by women to satire more generally, and not only through the role of women as satiric booksellers and publishers during this era, following Paula McDowell.[79]

A more deeply formalist approach, like Fredric V. Bogel's, whom I refer to throughout, is one way out of this generic morass.[80] Another, which I am proposing here, is to focus on verbal ambiguity itself. Verbal ambiguity is not satire and need not be satiric; but it is one way to think about an often fundamental or at least common aspect of the satiric enterprise. This is not to dismiss or flatten out the tonal variability or diverse agendas and politics of satire from this period. But it is to see the forest for the trees a bit more: to see that the forest is largely green is not to claim that the plants that are not green are not, therefore, part of the forest.

[75] Lund, '"An Alembick of Innuendos"', pp. 245, 258.   [76] Marshall, *Satire*, pp. 28, 314n43.

[77] Fauve Vandenberghe, 'Caustic Burns and Moving Hearts: Satire and Affect in Eliza Haywood's *The Masqueraders*', *Restoration: Studies in English Literary Culture, 1660–1700* 44, no. 1 (Spring 2020): pp. 39–66.

[78] Melinda Alliker Rabb, *Satire and Secrecy in English Literature, 1650–1750* (New York: Palgrave Macmillan, 2007), pp. 82, 31.

[79] Paula McDowell, *The Women of Grub Street: Press, Politics, and Gender in the London Literary Marketplace, 1678–1730* (Oxford: Clarendon Press, 1998).

[80] Bogel, *Satire*, pp. 41–83.

This book, then, is not about every work of satire or even every form it took. Satire from the long eighteenth century appeared in a variety of forms and served motley ends. Here, however, I am concerned primarily with political and personal works of satire, and lampoon remains a key and recurring term, a capacious literary category that encompasses attacks on both persons and institutions.[81] Moreover, that term, like 'satire' itself, underwent an important connotative if not denotative shift during this period. In the 1640s, when 'lampoon' was introduced to English from the French, it was intimately tied to satire itself. Lampoon was merely a 'virulent or scurrilous satire upon an individual'.[82] As Michael Seidel has observed, 'satire, libel, lampoon, and slander were inextricably mixed' during this era and the term 'satire...was often used synonymously with lampoon'.[83] My retention of the term lampoon in the title of this book thus belongs to a larger literary archaeology: an attempt to see, historically, how two nearly interchangeable terms took on increasingly specialized meanings during the eighteenth century—how satire and lampoon grew further apart, if not in function and content, then perhaps in style and above all socio-literary meaning. That process began in the late seventeenth century, when Dryden rewrote those very terms in an attempt to distinguish between and thus hold aloft legitimate satires from libellous lampoons. As a result, more than a half century later, Samuel Johnson was able to claim that a satire is 'A poem in which wickedness or folly is censured' and which 'is distinguished, by the generality of its reflections, from a *lampoon* which is aimed against a particular person', even if he was also forced to concede that such crisp generic distinctions were all 'too frequently confounded' in practise.[84]

Despite my qualms about how we define satire, I do want to emphasize one larger transhistorical point. Namely, that if satire does have a defining characteristic—especially the satire produced during its so-called Golden Age between the 1670s and 1740s, but also thereafter—it is its verbal or even non-verbal forms of ambiguity. This is not to deny the existence of other forms of satire, but to locate a major qualitative aspect of satire from this period, which was produced by legal pressures, and that trickled down to the practise of satire more generally.

The law simply pushed satire into verbally ambiguous and then increasingly non-verbal forms, and those forms came in large measure to define what satire was during the eighteenth century. This is the massive rhetorical break I track

---

[81] Metin Özdemir, 'Lampoon', in *Encyclopedia of Humor Studies*, edited by Salvatore I. Attardo (Thousand Oaks: Sage, 2014), p. 435.

[82] *OED*.

[83] Michael Seidel, 'Satire, lampoon, libel, slander', in *The Cambridge Companion to English Literature, 1650-1740*, edited by Steven Zwicker (Cambridge: Cambridge University Press, 1998), p. 33.

[84] *Samuel Johnson's Dictionary: A Modern Selection*, edited by E. L. McAdam, Jr. and George Milne (New York: Dover, 1964), p. 357.

between pre-Restoration English satires, including many of the verse satires circulated in manuscript in the first few decades after 1660, and the satires that succeeded and rhetorically imitated works like *Mac Flecknoe* during the first few decades of the eighteenth century and beyond. That rhetorical break is between a literary culture of open attack and one of verbal evasion, one defined by irony and sarcasm, by parody and allegory, by periphrasis and circumlocution, by litotes and apophasis—by an entire vocabulary and satiric rhetoric that purposefully veiled its jokes and its attacks, whether on people or institutions.

This, I would argue, is the defining characteristic not only of works from this so-called Golden Age but also of satire thereafter: of the generation of satirists who succeeded Pope and Swift, including Samuel Johnson, Peter Pindar, and Charles Churchill; of the Romantic-era satirists and of *Punch* in the nineteenth century; of the satiric experiments of the modernist novel studied most closely by Jonathan Greenberg; of playful postmodernism; even of the late twentieth and twenty-first centuries, in the pungent satire of *The Daily Show* and *The Colbert Report* and in the at times trenchant sketch comedy of *Saturday Night Live*, *Kids in the Hall*, *In Living Color*, *That Mitchell and Webb Look*, *Chappelle's Show*, and *Key & Peele*. Across this massive swathe of time, this 350-year period, I would argue that the most common denominator of satire has been its reliance on ambiguity and indirection, in one form or another; this 'modern' form of satire, as a complicated linguistic or visual act demanding a reader or viewer's interpretive engagement, which is so familiar to us today, was worked out during the final decades of the seventeenth century and refined during the first half of the eighteenth. Think only of that classic twentieth-century euphemism of the British press, a circumlocution that would not have been out of place in 1720, of referring to a publicly drunk politician as 'tired and emotional'.[85]

Perhaps most interestingly, this quality of ambiguity and indirectness was an accident at the intersections of legal and literary history. The reliance of eighteenth-century satirists, printers, and booksellers on verbal and bibliographical sleights, and later of caricaturists, print sellers, and dramatic mimics on non-verbal evasions, was largely the product of legal pressures. And though these legal pressures gradually diminished as ever broader definitions of press freedom emerged, and though satirists could have spoken more directly, the legal evasion of verbal ambiguity had become so entrenched, such a fundamental texture and quality of satire itself, that practitioners of satire continued to write in much the same way that their forebears had. As Caroline Levine has written, 'aesthetic and social forms outlive the specific conditions that gave birth to them'.[86] In this instance, even though verbal evasions like irony and mock-encomium no longer

[85] Jessica Hodgson, '*Private Eye* hails libel victory', *The Guardian* (7 November 2001): https://www.theguardian.com/media/2001/nov/07/pressandpublishing1.
[86] Levine, *Forms*, p. 12.

served an effective legal function—they had become in large measure legally useless thanks to court ruling after court ruling—they had by the last half of the eighteenth century become so absorbed into the architecture of satire that to practise satire at all meant to utilize the language of evasion. That verbal ambiguity came to be the most central qualitative characteristic of later seventeenth-century satire, and up to today, is perhaps the broadest claim in this book. My more central claim is about the practical and fundamental ways in which the law and satire shaped one another over the course of the eighteenth century. That shaping often played out in unpredictable and surprising ways. This was the peril of satire.

1

Keeping Out of Court I

Libel and Lampoon after Hale and Dryden

One of the defining features of the political and personal satires published after the lapse of licensing in 1695 is their verbal ambiguity: their often deeply ironic or at least evasive language, their tendency to couch their most inflammatory accusations in roundabout expressions and vague circumlocutions. Satire's verbal evasiveness had not always been a fundamental part of its rhetorical armature. English satire had existed for centuries, yet medieval and early modern lampoons, in comparison especially with early eighteenth-century works, were for the most part more openly defamatory: they tended to accuse their subjects by name and in the most bald-faced language of wrongdoing, attacking everything from piddling acts of everyday malfeasance to the grossest breaches of moral and ethical life.[1] It was precisely these lashingly Juvenalian works that the authorities were most interested in suppressing following the Bishops' Ban (1599), which ordered that 'noe Satyres or Epigramms be printed hereafter'.[2]

It was also this libellous culture of satire that the English in large measure inherited at the Restoration in 1660.[3] Prepublication licensing laws were again reinstituted in 1662, and during this period political and personal satires were circulated almost exclusively in manuscript, safe theoretically from the inquisitorial quill of the licenser. Manuscript circulation and underground printing soon

---

[1] Tiffany Stern, 'Nashe and Satire', in *The Oxford History of the Novel in English*, vol. 1: Prose Fiction in English from the Origins of Print to 1750, edited by Thomas Keymer (Oxford: Oxford University Press, 2017), pp. 180–95; John N. King, 'Traditions of Complaint and Satire', in *A New Companion to English Renaissance Literature and Culture*, 2 vol., edited by Michael Hattaway (Malden: Blackwell, 2010), pp. 326–40; Laura Kendrick, 'Medieval Satire', in *A Companion to Satire*, edited by Ruben Quintero (Malden: Blackwell, 2007), pp. 52–69; Alvin Kernan, *The Cankered Muse: Satire of the English Renaissance* (New Haven: Yale University Press, 1959); A. R. Heiserman, *Skelton and Satire* (Chicago: University of Chicago Press, 1961); and John Peter, *Complaint and Satire in Early English Literature* (Oxford: Clarendon Press, 1956).

[2] For the text of the Bishops' Ban, and its specific application to satire, see Richard A. McCabe, 'Elizabethan Satire and the Bishops' Ban of 1599', *Yearbook of English Studies* 11, no. 2 (1981): pp. 188–93. See also William R. Jones, 'The Bishops' Ban of 1599 and the Ideology of English Satire', *Literature Compass* 7, no. 5 (2010): pp. 332–46; Debora Shuger, *Censorship and Cultural Sensibility: The Regulation of Language in Tudor-Stuart England* (Philadelphia: University of Pennsylvania Press, 2006), p. 85; and Cyndia Susan Clegg, *Press Censorship in Elizabethan England* (Cambridge: Cambridge University Press, 1997), ch. 9.

[3] For a counter-tradition of 'indirect satire', see Rachel E. Hile, *Spenserian Satire: A Tradition of Indirection* (Manchester: Manchester University Press, 2017).

Libel and Lampoon: Satire in the Courts, 1670–1792. Andrew Benjamin Bricker, Oxford University Press.
© Andrew Benjamin Bricker 2022. DOI: 10.1093/oso/9780192846150.003.0002

became the two greatest problems the authorities faced in the regulation of the press. Licensing nonetheless persisted as the government's central regulatory tool, though it was limited to certain *forms* of publication. Prepublication censorship thus offered an easy mechanism for vetting works, but only those intended for print; works anonymously circulated in manuscript, including literally thousands of satiric poems during these decades, proved more difficult to police for they bypassed the central means of licensing itself.

Eventually, with the permanent lapse of licensing in 1695, the Crown turned to the courts to regulate the press. During this later period, judges routinely expanded the common law's capacity to redress the verbal ambiguity that had come increasingly to typify printed satires. This opening chapter documents this emerging legal hermeneutics, an issue I return to throughout *Libel and Lampoon*. Here I focus on legal developments from the early 1670s, and especially *King v. Lake* (1671), which helped to develop the use of 'common intendment' in cases of defamation. The doctrine itself was already being employed to elucidate imprecise language in other branches of the law, including in trials for defamation. But *King v. Lake* opened up an opportunity for the justices to contemplate how they might procedurally delimit the interpretation of imprecise or ambiguously defamatory language in particular, during an era when older interpretive doctrines were under intense judicial scrutiny. Ultimately, the justices held that jurors should understand such language using a supposedly objective or reasonable standard. In the process, the bench unintentionally laid the groundwork for a model that would come to dominate directions given to jurors throughout the eighteenth century in trials and prosecutions for libel. In those later decisions, judges expanded the logic of common intendment in an attempt to displace and mitigate jurors' subjective deliberations. The end result was something like an ideal reader in trials for satire: a juror who might, at least theoretically, understand verbal ambiguity in objective and thus more predictable ways.

My overarching goal in this opening chapter is to document two parallel tracks in literature and the law that developed during the last decades of the seventeenth century and that came directly into contact in the early eighteenth century. On the one hand, the courts had begun to refurbish interpretive doctrines in an attempt to delimit how jurors assessed verbal ambiguity in trials for defamation. At the same time, the language of satire was changing: satirists increasingly came to rely on forms of verbal indirection that would later complicate trials for libel. Again, these two tracks, between satire and the courts, did not come fully to a head until the early eighteenth century. But the terms of that later confrontation were accidentally and almost simultaneously devised in the 1670s, as verbal evasion became an increasingly regular feature of satire's rhetorical structure and at the very moment when the courts were also revising procedures for delimiting verbal ambiguity itself. Eventually, when the authorities turned to the courts as the primary means of regulating the press in the eighteenth century, they uncovered the procedural tools they needed to facilitate trials and prosecutions for defamatory and seditious materials.

As a result, I track not only the early emergence of reasonable or objective standards in jury deliberations over defamatory language, but also a significant rhetorical break between the unequivocally libellous verse satires circulated in manuscript during the later seventeenth century and the much more verbally evasive satires that succeeded them in print, especially in the early eighteenth century. Such verbal evasion was a new or at least an uncommon feature of later seventeenth-century manuscript satire, part of a rhetorical trend that starts, in its most sustained form, with John Dryden's *Mac Flecknoe*, but that is continued by satirists in the decades after his death. *Mac Flecknoe*'s enduring importance, I argue, was a product of both its literary and its legal virtues. In devising a deeply ironic and evasive language, one structured around mock-encomium and saturated with epic and classical allusions, Dryden was helping to legitimate satire through its promotion as a verbal art. He did not, of course, invent irony. But, as Steven N. Zwicker observes, 'none before Dryden . . . had so widely explored the uses of irony', and his own experiments in this peculiar figure of speech helped to model the 'double-tongued utterance, or quality of double-mindedness' that Margaret Anne Doody has defined as an 'essential technique . . . of Augustan poetry'.[4] In this regard, Dryden's enduring contribution to the verbal texture of satire cannot be overstated. During the early modern period, throughout the later seventeenth century, and well into the eighteenth century, personal and political satire, often referred to as 'lampoon' by contemporaries, was thought to be an irredeemably low genre, one intimately associated with demotic language and vulgar personal abuse. *Mac Flecknoe*, conversely, created an alliance between mock-encomium and the classical and epic traditions, establishing the rhetorical and generic foundations of a satiric shadow canon, which writers like Alexander Pope would later inherit, while also distancing his 'true Satires' from the supposed 'lampoons' alongside which his poems circulated.

In tracking this rhetorical break, I am also documenting the challenge that satire's verbal evasiveness would eventually pose to courtroom procedures during the first decades of the eighteenth century. In *Mac Flecknoe* in particular, with its richly coy and ironic personal attack on Thomas Shadwell, Dryden taught writers how to satirize without libelling, how to attack obliquely without openly defaming one's target. In doing so, he also implicitly established the question that the courts in one form or another would come to struggle with in the succeeding decades: How was one to prove, to the satisfaction of sometimes finicky and literal-minded

---

[4] Steven N. Zwicker, 'Dryden and the Invention of Irony', in *Swift's Travels: Eighteenth-Century Satire and its Legacy*, edited by Nicholas Hudson and Aaron Santesso (Cambridge: Cambridge University Press, 2008), p. 75; and Margaret Anne Doody, *The Daring Muse: Augustan Poetry Reconsidered* (Cambridge: Cambridge University Press, 1985), p. 211.

jurors, that an ambiguously worded attack, even an ironic compliment, could be just as defamatory as an open accusation?

1.1 'Common Intendment' and the Regulation of the Press

The government and private complainants had a host of statutes, regulations and laws at their disposal for enacting legal retribution on wayward satirists and their printers and booksellers during the last half of the seventeenth century. The Crown could turn to the medieval law of treason, heresy laws for the prosecution of blasphemous works, and a series of Tudor statutes that defined certain types of dissent as felony and even treason. Private individuals could use *scandalum magnatum*, an action based upon a series of thirteenth- and fourteenth-century statutes that protected eminent individuals and especially peers from damage to their reputations,[5] or could turn to the ecclesiastical courts, if the injury had not resulted in either monetary loss or public unrest.[6] However, as Philip Hamburger has shown, each of these solutions also had certain limitations.[7]

It was more effective, the authorities realized, to nip a satire in the bud before it even saw the light of day, by preventing works from becoming public instead of hounding down offenders after they had already appeared. That was part of the goal of the Press Licensing Act (1662; 14 Car. II, c. 33), which mandated government censorship of manuscripts intended for print publication.[8] The act was renewed by successive parliaments, lapsing first for a period between 1679 and 1685 and then permanently in 1695. The authorities never gave up on their attempts to regulate the press, however, even during the Act's temporary lapse, when they relied on royal prerogative, the regulation of hawkers, judicial warrants, and the enforcement of the Stationers' Company bylaws. Most importantly, even before licensing's final lapse, the government had begun to turn to the common law courts, and especially to the law of seditious libel, to regulate the press.[9]

Licensing had the useful effect, at least theoretically, of keeping the most incendiary works out of print and thus out of the hands of the widest possible readership. In response to the restrictions of the Press Licensing Act, which

---

[5] 1275, 3 Edw. 1, c. 34; 1378, 2 Rich. 2, c. 5; 1388, 12 Rich. 2, c. 11; 1554 1 & 2 Phil. & M., c. 3; and 1559, 1 Eliz., c. 6. See John C. Lassiter, 'Defamation of Peers: The Rise and Decline of the Action for *Scandalum Magnatum*, 1497–1773', *American Journal of Legal History* 22, no. 3 (July 1978): pp. 216–36.

[6] Baker, *ELH*, 438; and Richard H. Helmholz, Introduction, in *Select Cases on Defamation to 1600* (London: Selden Society, 1985), pp. xli–lvii.

[7] Hamburger, 'Seditious Libel', pp. 666–71.   [8] Siebert, *Freedom*, pp. 237ff.

[9] Hamburger, 'Seditious Libel', pp. 697–700; Timothy Crist, 'Government Control of the Press After the Expiration of the Printing Act in 1679', *Publishing History* 5 (1979): pp. 49–77; Paul Mitchell, *The Making of the Modern Law of Defamation* (Oxford: Hart, 2005), p. 6; and Raymond Astbury, 'The Renewal of the Licensing Act in 1693 and its Lapse in 1695', *The Library*, 5th series 33, no. 4 (1978): pp. 296–322.

limited London to a mere twenty master printers, an underground book trade emerged for illicit works. A staggering number of pieces were published without an official license at all during this period, perhaps as many as half of all printed works.[10] Many writers simply bypassed print publication altogether, though, choosing to circulate their most inflammatory wares in manuscript. As the Surveyor of the Press (or Imprimery), Roger L'Estrange, complained, 'Libells... in Manuscript' were 'comonly ye more seditious, & scandalous' than those printed.[11] This was particularly the case with satiric verse during the seventeenth century. A stunning number of verse lampoons circulated solely in manuscript, only occasionally finding their way into print, often in unauthorized and unlicensed editions after their topicality and contentiousness had worn out. Today, 1,200 verse satires from this period survive exclusively in manuscript; an additional 3,000 pieces were eventually printed, of which 1,200 appeared only later, between 1689 and 1716, in the various collections of poems on affairs of state.[12]

Despite the existence of so many rulings and statutes to control or at least punish those involved in the production of incendiary works, the law remained riddled with loopholes. Licensing only worked for those pieces submitted to the censors; treason laws could only be used against publications touching on the king's life; *scandalum magnatum* was limited to peers; the ecclesiastical courts were unable to award damages, and so on. The broad common law canopy of libel laws offered a different and more effective route, as prosecutors and complainants came to discover following the lapse of licensing in 1695. During the later seventeenth century and across the eighteenth century, the courts, the Crown, and plaintiffs revealed the remarkable versatility of libel laws to punish wayward writers and stationers. According to Hamburger, libel laws proved a flexible stopgap measure for the failures of prepublication censorship between 1662 and 1695 and, after licensing permanently lapsed, became the government's primary means of regulating the press.[13]

Part of the usefulness of libel law lay in the bench's willingness to accept the Crown's broad interpretations of supposedly libellous and seditious works. Despite our sometimes Whiggish accounts of judicial freedom in the wake of the Glorious Revolution, prosecutorial misprision and juridical complicity remained major problems during the later Stuart Monarchy and a considerable

---

[10] Siebert, *Freedom*, p. 243; D. F. McKenzie, *Making Meaning: 'Printers of the Mind' and Other Essays*, edited by Peter D. McDonald and Michael F. Suarez (Amherst: University of Massachusetts Press, 2002), p. 131. For a re-evaluation of those statistics, see Joad Raymond, 'Censorship in Law and Practice in Seventeenth-Century England: Milton's *Areopagitica*', in *The Oxford Handbook of English Law and Literature, 1500–1700*, edited by Lorna Hutson (Oxford: Oxford University Press, 2017), pp. 509–10.

[11] SP 29/51/10, TNA.   [12] *POAS* vol. 1, p. xxvi.

[13] Hamburger, 'Seditious Libel', pp. 725–53.

point of concern about the Hanoverian justices.[14] I address judicial freedom more extensively in my third chapter on seditious libel prosecutions under Queen Anne through her sometimes servile chief justice, Sir John Holt, but it is worth observing at this point that a willing bench made prosecutions easier for the Crown and continued to exist in new, less overt ways even after 1688.[15] Above all, the profound malleability of libel laws made them an effective candidate for press regulation. As a common law offence, libel was subject to the latitudes of judicial interpretation, and a common theme of the period between 1670 and 1792 is the routine willingness of the bench to expand the scope of the law while compressing the number of legitimate defences a satirist or stationer might offer.[16]

The increased focus on the language of defamation happened, almost accidentally, over a series of lawsuits in the early 1670s between Edward King and Sir Edward Lake.[17] King had first sued Lake in ecclesiastical court in 1664, in a recondite matter involving excommunication and oath taking.[18] The two then spent years squabbling both in and out of court. Of particular interest are two separate cases from 1670 and 1671—both confusingly named *King v. Lake*—in which Justice Sir Matthew Hale played a critical role, first as Lord Chief Baron of the Exchequer (1660–71) and then as Lord Chief Justice (1671–76). First, in 1670, in an appellate case in the Court of Exchequer Chamber, Hale and his fellow justices parsed slander (spoken defamation) from libel (written defamation), a distinction not always observed in the common law courts, and made libel the more serious offence.[19] In addition, the justices laid out three forms of defamation: calling into question an individual's professional competence, accusing him or her of a criminal act, and/or claiming that he or she had a communicable disease—all

---

[14] Alfred F. Havighurst, 'James II and the Twelve Men in Scarlet', *Law Quarterly Review* 69 (October 1953): pp. 522–46, 'The Judiciary and Politics in the Reign of Charles II (Part I, 1660–1676)' and 'The Judiciary and Politics in the Reign of Charles II (Part II, 1676–1685)', *Law Quarterly Review* 66 (January and April 1950): pp. 62–78 and 229–52; D. A. Rubini, 'The Precarious Independence of the Judiciary, 1688–1701', *The Law Quarterly Review* 83 (July 1967): pp. 343–5; W. J. Jones, *Politics and the Bench: The Judges and the Origins of the English Civil War* (New York: Barnes & Noble, 1971), p. 17; and Keymer, *Poetics*, p. 18.

[15] Wilfrid Prest, 'Judicial Corruption in Early Modern England', *Past & Present* 133 (November 1991): pp. 67–95; David Lemmings, 'The Independence of the Judiciary in Eighteenth-Century England', *The Life of the Law*, edited by Peter Birks (London: The Hambledon Press, 1993), pp. 125–49; and Stewart Jay, 'Servants of Monarchs and Lords: The Advisory Role of Early English Judges', *American Journal of Legal History* 38, no. 3 (April 1994): pp. 117–96.

[16] Harold J. Berman, 'The Origins of Historical Jurisprudence: Coke, Selden, Hale', *Yale Law Journal* 103, no. 7 (May 1993): pp. 1651–738; Harold J. Berman and Charles J. Reid, Jr, 'The Transformation of English Legal Science: From Hale to Blackstone', *Emory Law Journal* 45, no. 2 (Spring 1996): pp. 444–67; and Gerald J. Postema, 'Classical Common Law Jurisprudence (Part I)' and 'Classical Common Law Jurisprudence (Part II)', *Oxford University Commonwealth Law Journal* 2, no. 2. and 3, no. 1 (Winter 2002 and Summer 2003): pp. 155–80 and 1–28.

[17] See *King v. Lake* (1667), rpt. *Sources*, pp. 652–4; and *King v. Lake* (1668), rpt. *A Source Book of English Law*, edited by A. K. R. Kiralfy (London: Sweet & Maxwell Ltd, 1957), pp. 154–63.

[18] *King v. Lake* (1664), Hard. 364 and 388, 145 Eng. Rep. 499 and 511.

[19] *King v. Lake* (1670), Hard. 470–1 (Ex. Ch.), 145 Eng. Rep. 552–3. J. M. Kaye, 'Libel and Slander— Two Torts or One?', *Law Quarterly Review* 91, no. 4 (October 1975): p. 526; and Baker, *ELH*, p. 506.

of which might jeopardize an individual's public standing and thus capacity to carry on one's trade.[20] Finally, the justices ruled that complainants were not obliged to prove damages in such instances.[21]

The ruling in the case had a number of practical but unintended consequences for satire. Most immediately, with libel the more serious offence than slander, writers and stationers would implicitly face greater scrutiny under the law. In addition, the claim that a manuscript had been circulated discreetly, thereby causing a victim no harm, ceased to be an accepted defence. Most importantly, the ruling drew attention to the language of libel by both formulating and clarifying rules around what qualified as defamation per se. Even a cursory review of the manuscript satires produced between the 1660s and 1680s makes it clear that the 'directly pejorative' language of lampoon in no way troubled extant courtroom procedures.[22] As we will see in the next section, individuals are cavalierly named and defamed often using the very imputations enumerated in *King v. Lake* (1670): professional incompetence, communicable disease, and criminality.

The second *King v. Lake* case, from 1671, proved even more important. This is in part surprising because the case itself focused not on an ambiguously libellous satire but on an overtly defamatory private letter that Lake had written and sent to Anne, Countess of Lincoln, calling King, a counsellor at law, 'a griping lawyer' who would 'milk [her] purse' in a 'vexatious suit'.[23] On its surface, *King v. Lake* (1671) had nothing to say directly about satire, and yet the justices' contemplation of the procedural and interpretive issues that defamatory language might pose, whether those imputations were ambiguously idiomatic or purposefully evasive, opened up a larger discussion of how to delimit procedurally the deliberations of jurors.

The justices' ruling in *King v. Lake* (1671) was in part important because it further eroded and displaced *mitior sensus*, a doctrine traditionally used to guide the jury's interpretation of defamatory language.[24] According to the rule, jurors were encouraged to understand ambiguously defamatory language in its lesser, more innocuous sense, theoretically providing quick-witted defendants and their

---

[20] Certain words, given the right context, could also be defamatory, if not in and of themselves (Baker, *ELH*, 444). See *Smale v. Hammon* (1610), 1 Bulst. 40 (K.B.), 80 Eng. Rep. 743; and Anon. (1580), Misc. MS 488/76, Lincoln's Inn (Q.B.), rpt. *Sources*, pp. 638–9.

[21] Holdsworth, *History*, vol. 8, pp. 364–5; Plucknett, *CHCL*, p. 497; Peter F. Carter-Ruck, *Libel and Slander* (Hamden: Archon, 1973), p. 42; and Mitchell, *Making of the Modern Law of Defamation*, pp. 4–8.

[22] Harold Love, 'Rochester and the Traditions of Satire', in *Restoration Literature: Critical Approaches*, edited by Harold Love (London: Methuen, 1972), p. 161.

[23] *King v. Lake* (1671), 2 Vent. 28 (C.P.), 89 Eng. Rep. 12; *King v. Lake* (1671), 2 Vent. 28 (C.P.), 86 Eng. Rep. 289; and *King v. Lake* (1671), 1 Freeman 14–15 (C.P.), 89 Eng. Rep. 12–13.

[24] Richard H. Helmholz, *The Oxford History of the Laws of England*, vol. 1: The Canon Law and Ecclesiastical Jurisdiction from 597 to the 1640s (Oxford: Oxford University Press, 2003), p. 577.

slippery legal counsel with an opening to claim that even the most sadistic insults were nothing more than harmless wind.[25] As one of Hale's colleagues on the bench observed, to claim a man was a 'murderer' might be defamatory, though this might only mean, *in mitiori sensu*, that he was a murderer of 'hares'.[26] The doctrine was not officially abolished until 1714, but by the 1670s *mitior sensus* was already under intense judicial scrutiny, and *King v. Lake* (1671) simply opened up an opportunity for Hale and his colleagues to revisit the absurdities that such a doctrine might permit by demonstrating the dire need for less impressionistic and more objective standards for the interpretation of defamatory language.[27]

That discussion also led to a second revision to trial procedure in actions for defamation. With *mitior sensus* and its generous accommodation of far-fetched defences set aside, the justices were able to install in its stead a theory of 'common intendment'.[28] By the 1670s, common intendment already had a long history at law, especially in discussions of contracts and wills.[29] The doctrine had even occasionally been invoked in early seventeenth-century trials for defamation.[30] But it was only after mid-century, when judicial opposition to the older doctrine of *mitior sensus* was at its height, that common intendment became a feasible candidate for guiding the interpretation of defamatory language.[31] In effect, rather than always deferring to the lesser, non-defamatory meaning of words, jurors were instructed to interpret those words in their most natural sense given the context of their utterance. Importantly, this theory of common intendment would eventually help to create a standard of interpretation in trials for defamation: a theoretically objective means of assessment based on the a priori assumption that a supposedly average or typical reader exists who ought to be able to deduce a speaker's (or, later, satirist's) intended meaning from a shared or 'common' set of beliefs about the primary denotations and connotations of a word, locution, or idiom.

---

[25] *Select Cases on Defamation*, pp. xcii–xcv; Knightley D'Anvers, *A General Abridgment of the Common Law*, vol. 1 (London, 1722–1725), p. 140; and William Sheppard, *Action Upon the Case for Slander*, 2nd ed. (London, 1674), p. 20.

[26] *King v. Lake* (1671), 2 Vent. 28 (C.P.), 89 Eng. Rep. 12.

[27] *Harrison v. Thornborough* (1714), Gilb. Cas. 114, 10 Mod. 196 (Q.B.), 93 Eng. Rep. 277; *Morrison v. Cade* (1607), Cro. Jac. 162, in John March, *Actions for Slander*, 2nd ed. (London, 1674), p. 31; *Foster v. Browning* (1624), Cro. Jac. 688 (C.P.), 79 Eng. Rep. 596; and *Kilvert v. Roe* (1625), Bendl. 155 (K.B.), 73 Eng. Rep. 1022.

[28] *King v. Lake* (1671), 2 Vent. 28 (C.P.), 89 Eng. Rep. 12.

[29] See, for instance, Sir Thomas Littleton (or de Littleton), *Littleton's Tenures in English*, trans. Eugene Wambaugh (Littleton, CO: Rothman, 1985), §646; and John Cowell, *The Interpreter: Or Booke, Containing the Signification of Words* (London, 1637), p. [I³]. See also Roger T. Simonds, *Rational Individualism: The Perennial Philosophy of Legal Interpretation* (Amsterdam: Rodopi, 1995).

[30] *Stamp v. White* (1621), Cro. Jac. 600 (K.B.), 79 Eng. Rep. 513; and *Peard v. Jones* (1635), Cro. Car. 382 (K.B.), 79 Eng. Rep. 934.

[31] See Henry Rolle, *Un Abridgment des Plusieurs Cases et Resolutions del Common Ley* (London, 1668), quoted in Baker, *ELH*, p. 443.

As Hale's colleagues on the bench readily conceded, however, even this interpretive procedure nonetheless failed to isolate language in a heuristic vacuum. Words that seemed explicitly defamatory, for instance, could be deemed innocent given the context in which they were spoken. As the justices observed, even an apparently absurd defence in the abstract might prove entirely reasonable, justifiable, and obvious if 'the circumstances do evince it'.[32] Again, to call a man a 'murderer', a seemingly straightforward accusation of criminality, might be defamatory, but within the context of its utterance—perhaps a discussion of hunting—one might only be understood as a murderer of 'hares'. In this instance, the innocent interpretation relies not on the lesser sense of the word 'murderer' but on the circumstances of its use. Nonetheless, in the coming decades, even when allowing for the complicated interplay of abstraction and context that attends any locution, judge after judge cited the doctrine of common intendment, foregrounding and reasserting the objective intelligibility of defamatory language.[33]

That appeal to objectivity is itself interesting, given the dubious socio-linguistic assumptions already built into the doctrine. In the courts, common intendment was partly understood as simply 'common meaning', as John Rastell, an early sixteenth-century barrister, put it.[34] 'Common' also carried a specific legal designation: a form of meaning or intention at common law; or a customary or reasonable interpretation, as determined by the law.[35] What exactly was 'common' about those forms of intentionality or meaning, however, was harder to pin down. For instance, when applied to the interpretation of language, 'common' by extension also pointed to a broader sociological application: what was commonly, or generally, held to be the most obvious meaning of a given phrase among a group of listeners or readers. In this latter sense of commonality, the doctrine performed an important legal-hermeneutic function. The most obvious interpretation of a given phrase, such as 'murderer', ought to mean a killer or someone who has murdered a person. But that meaning was common only insofar as it was coextensive with a linguistically typical English listener or reader. In effect, the justices were attempting to establish an objective standard of assessment in understanding and interpreting words.

As a result, the doctrine of common intendment later provided an important model for jury directions in at least two ways. First, in its implicit appeal to an objective means or standard of assessment, the doctrine might be understood as an important precursor, forerunner, or analogue to the 'reasonable man' standard,

---

[32] *King v. Lake* (1671), 2 Vent. 28 (C.P.), 89 Eng. Rep. 12.

[33] Case 114 (Anon.), 1 Comyns 263, 92 Eng. Rep. 106.

[34] John Rastell, *Les Termes de la Ley: Or, Certain Difficult and Obscure Words and Terms of the Common and Statute Laws of this Realm*, rpt. *An Exposition of Certaine Difficult and Obscure Words* (1579) (London, 1721), p. 147. In this sense, see the entry for '*Domus instructa*', in William Fulbecke, *A Direction or Preparatiue to the study of the Lawe* (London, 1600), [n.p.].

[35] *OED*, vide: 'Intendment', 4.

first fully promulgated in 1837.[36] Both means of assessment implicitly posit some theoretically objective entity: in the former, an abstract or hypothetical community of readers or listeners who understand a given word, phrase, or locution within its context of utterance in uniform and predictable ways; in the latter, a personified abstraction that offers an objective means of assessment, especially when determining the grounds of liability.[37] The doctrine of common intendment did not directly influence the emergence of the reasonable person standard. But it did critically develop an emerging line of legal logic, like the reasonable man, in its implicit recourse to an objective personification.[38] Already in *King v. Lake* (1671) we can glimpse the beginnings of a supposedly objective means of assessment in trials for defamation in the courts' appeal to an abstract standard, one that continues today to influence jury directions in Anglo-American law.[39]

Second, this theorization of a hypothetically ideal reader or interpreter is important because the courts would later devise similar doctrines to guide jurors in their handling of the common rhetorical features of eighteenth-century satire. For instance, in interpreting verbal irony and allegory, jurors were instructed to read like an abstract 'generality of readers', an imagined hermeneutic community for whom authorial intentions were always coherent and self-evident.[40] In each of these later rulings, the courts sought to isolate the impressionable subjectivity of jurors, and thus readers, that accompanied verbal ambiguity itself. More importantly, judges were creating a practical tool for deliberations by effectively displacing *actual* jurors, and their capricious interpretations, with an abstract juror or even theoretical reader, who interpreted defamatory and seditious language in supposedly more coherent, more reasonable, and therefore more predictable ways. However, the precise problem that common intendment and its doctrinal successors attempted to solve—of how best to interpret idiomatic and ambiguous forms of defamation—only grew more unwieldy as satire itself changed: as it became more verbally evasive and as it distanced itself from the overtly libellous manuscript lampoons that were seemingly everywhere during the final decades of the seventeenth century.

---

[36] *Vaughan v. Menlove* (1837), 3 Bing (N.C.) 468, 173 Eng. Rep. 232. See also Baker, *ELH*, p. 414; [Francis Buller], *An Introduction to the Law relative to Trials at Nisi Prius* (London, 1767), p. 25; William Jones, *Treatise on the Law of Bailments* (London, 1781), p. 6; and *Jones v. Bird* (1822), 5 B. & Ald. 845–6.

[37] Simon Stern, 'R v Jones (1703)', in *Landmark Cases in Criminal Law*, edited by Phil Handler, Henry Mares, and Ian Williams (Oxford: Hart, 2017), pp. 59–79.

[38] Alan D. Miller and Ronen Perry, 'The Reasonable Person', *New York University Law Review* 87, no. 2 (May 2012): pp. 323–92.

[39] Mayo Moran, *Rethinking the Reasonable Person: An Egalitarian Reconstruction of the Objective Standard* (Oxford: Oxford University Press, 2003), p. 1.

[40] *R. v. Clerk* [sic] (1728/9), 1 Barn. 305 (K.B.), 94 Eng. Rep. 207. See also *Somers v. House* (1694), Holt 39 (K.B.), 90 Eng. Rep. 919, in which Chief Justice Holt argued that words should be taken 'in a common sense according to the vulgar intendment of the bystanders'.

1.2 Libel and Lampoon: Manuscript Satire during the Later Seventeenth Century

To appreciate the degree to which *Mac Flecknoe* developed mock-encomium as a vehicle for verbally evasive satire, it is worth reviewing the overtly defamatory manuscript lampoons of the last decades of the seventeenth century.[41] Take 'A New Ballad to an Old Tune Call'd Sage Leafe', a manuscript satire in circulation in the 1680s that explicitly attacks George Villiers, the second duke of Buckingham, a common whipping boy throughout the period for his double-dealing during the Civil Wars and his perceived political incompetence. The poem, sometimes attributed to Dryden, openly identifies its object—'all true English curse Buckingham'—and imputes to him a range of criminal offences, including 'Treason and Bugg'ry'.[42] Other poems were just as blatant, such as this widely copied parody of the Anglican litany, also attacking Buckingham, in which each stanza ends '*Libera nos*' ('deliver us [from evil]'):

> From sensual, proud, atheistical life,
> From arming our lackeys with pistol and knife,
> From murd'ring the husband and whoring the wife,—
>   *Libera nos.*[43]

Many of these poems are brutal—nasty, misogynistic, xenophobic, and hateful lampoons that name names and chastise without reservation. Frequently they follow a shotgun model, providing capsule attacks on a host of notorious and semi-public figures in rapid succession, such as this almost giddily defamatory poem from 1663, which picks up on a rumour that Eleanor, Lady Byron, purportedly infected Richard Lane, a Groom of the Bedchamber to Charles II:

> Byron fain would conquer still,
> But now she only hath the will;
> Her killing power is over;
> And yet 'tis plain
> She hurt Dick Lane,
> But he's like to recover.[44]

Perhaps predictably, such manuscript satires tend to be obsessed with the sex life of the court—profoundly churlish works that make even something like John

---

[41] Harold Love, *English Clandestine Satire, 1660–1702* (Oxford: Oxford University Press, 2004), p. 146.
[42] OSB MS b105, 369–371, Bein.L.
[43] 'The Litany of the Duke of Buckingham' (1680), rpt. *POAS* vol. 2, p. 192–3.
[44] '[On the Ladies of the Court]' (1663), rpt. *CSR*, p. 6, ll. 95–101.

Wilkes's *Essay on Woman*, privately printed a century later, look relatively tame.[45] As one poet put it:

> This way of writing I observed by some
> Is introduced by an exordium,
> But I will leave to make all that ado,
> And in plain English tell you who fucks who.[46]

Poetic accounts of bed swapping typically accused almost every last named victim of spreading venereal disease, one of the primary defamatory imputations laid out in *King v. Lake* (1670). Consider this jauntily libellous ballad on the widow Susannah Williams:

> Williams, with her chatted foam,
> Has chancred half the pit,
> And is the only she of whom
> No scandal can be writ.
> Of Lumley and of twenty more
> Whom she has soundly poxed,
> I'll nothing say because I hear
> She has of late been fluxed.[47]

Her 'chatted foam' is just as revolting as one might suspect, a kind of venereal rabies—Williams is half woman, half animal, lusty and out of control—and the source of the syphilitic sores or ulcers that she has given to the rakish bucks of the theatre (to be 'chancred'). Other than that, she has done nothing wrong, the poet offers tongue in cheek. In the final lines, owing to her mercury treatment (to be 'fluxed'), the poet resists saying anything more, a pregnant moment of defamatory apophasis after eight lines that have given her entire sexual and medical history. Really, nothing worse can be said of her—but, then again, what's left to report?

So many poems gleefully catalogue every last pox, fingering bed-hopping court-goers and their lubricious ladies. These were the manuscript libels (eagerly reprinted, without apology, in later decades) that appeared alongside the printed satires that tended to condemn women not only individually but also as an entire sex.[48] Such works list with almost breathless delight the mistresses, courtesans,

---

[45] Wilke's *Essay* is perhaps an early example of what Rachel Potter has called 'luxury obscenity' (*Obscene Modernism: Literary Censorship and Experiment, 1900-1940* [Oxford: Oxford University Press, 2013], pp. 62–3).

[46] 'Satire' (1682), rpt. *CSR*, p. 81, ll. 1–4.

[47] 'A Ballad to the Tune of Cheviot Chace, or Whenas King Henry Ruled this Land' (1682), rpt. *CSR*, p. 106, ll. 105–12.

[48] Felicity A. Nussbaum, *The Brink of All We Hate: English Satires on Women, 1660-1750* (Lexington: University Press of Kentucky, 1984), introduction, *passim*.

and bawds who were seemingly the only members of Charles II's court. In the shotgun satire 'The Ladies' March' from 1681, for instance, Mary Sackville, the estranged wife of Roger Boyle, second earl of Orrery, shows up to assure the Envoy Extraordinary from Denmark to England, M. de Lindenau, that it was not her syphilis that killed him but the mercury treatment provided by the king's surgeon, Florente Fourcade:

> Then came pensive Orrery,
> "Oh, Lindano, why should'st thou die?
> 'Twas Fourcard killed thee and not I,
> Oh, destructive mercury!"[49]

From there it is more of the same. 'Betty Felton', one of the king's mistresses, is 'lewd and pocky' (l. 45), but so is the oversexed Catherine Crofts, guardian to Mary Tudor, Charles' illegitimate daughter by Moll Davis, who's 'Still itching though [Henry Jermyn, earl of] St. Albans fucks her' (l. 70). So syphilitic is Susan Armine, the widow of Sir Henry Belasyse, that she 'can pox you with a kiss' (l. 76). Every last disease was part of a larger inheritance of depravity. Think of Katherine Sedley—maid of honour to Mary of Modena, duchess of York, and mistress to the Duke—whose illegitimate daughter is 'Soaked in pox and Popery' (l. 82). It was more of the same in another shotgun satire circulated just a few years later. Some men get the better of the women, like Sir Henry Hobart, who gives Dorothy Mason the court's most routine gift: 'His damned pocky seed in her womb is just knit' (l. 43). Other men prove less adept, such as 'Poor bedchamber [Richard Leveson], how hard is thy hap / To purchase another man's bastard and clap' (ll. 49–50). Other women make out little better. Take the 'sage lady mother' (l. 52), Anne Margaretta, widow of Sir Richard Mason, whose teeth have been reduced to jagged nubs from her mercury treatment:

> Of her teeth she could save but the black rotten stocks,
> From the flux she endured in France for the pox. (ll. 59–60)[50]

At a rhetorical level, such openly libellous poems show a total lack of legal caution. Where care is taken in the words chosen, it is a contest of baleful wit—who can say the worst, in the most minute detail.

Attacks on the lurid sexual life of the court were one element of these satires, and such muckraking might seem like an undue attack on private life. But the creeping suspicion underlying so many of these lampoons is that private vices are intimately tied to public wrongs. One poem goes so far as to suggest that Elizabeth,

---

[49] 'The Ladies' March' (1681), rpt. *CSR*, p. 56, ll. 11–14.
[50] 'Julian's Farewell to the Coquets' (1687), rpt. *CSR*, pp. 199–203.

Lady Ogle had traded sexual favours for the murder of her second husband, Thomas Thynne, in 1682:

> Ogle's returned and will consider further
> Who next she'll show her arse to for a murder.[51]

As part of their exposure of shameless criminality, such poems also eagerly documented quotidian malfeasance and traitorous double-crossing. Sometimes these were broad though equally libellous denouncements—Lord Thomas Howard, for instance, is 'A forward, testy thief' in one poem—but other pieces were gossipy accounts of treasonable coteries.[52] The author behind one poem, written following the Rye House Plot hatched by a group of anti-Catholic Whigs to kill Charles and his brother the Duke of York (later James II), attacks everyone equally. After naming and skewering more than a dozen Whigs, the poet decides to cut his catalogue short, lest the final product end up looking like a perverse inversion of John Foxe's book of martyrs, *The Acts and Monuments* (1563):

> To name 'em all, with all their villainies,
> Their follies, shames, their treasons, blasphemies,
> Their fine amours, debauches, claps, and pox,
> Would fill a volume like our history Fox.[53]

Such lampoons did not evolve out of a vacuum, and yet we might be surprised by the extent to which manuscript libels from the latter half of the seventeenth century belonged squarely to a tradition largely devised in the first decades of the Restoration and then only marginally and often tangentially influenced by earlier English, classical, or Continental models. Interestingly, at least during the latter part of the seventeenth century, there was little in the way of a readily available canon of English satire upon which to draw.[54] English satirists certainly predated 1660—figures like William Langland, Geoffrey Chaucer, Thomas Nashe, John Skelton, John Marston, and John Donne—but, besides Donne, few of these authors were reprinted during the latter part of the seventeenth century, making access to their works (even if understood) extremely difficult.[55] As J. Paul Hunter has written,

> Chaucer seemed remote and inaccessible, and the Elizabethans and Jacobeans seemed, despite vast accomplishments, still rough and crude.... Even though

---

[51] 'Satire' (1682), rpt. *CSR*, p. 83, ll. 51–2.   [52] 'Satire to Julian' (1682), rpt. *CSR*, p. 87, l. 37.

[53] 'Satire on Both Whigs and Tories' (1683), rpt. *CSR*, p. 123, ll. 71–5.

[54] Robert D. Hume, '"Satire" in the Reign of Charles II', *Modern Philology* 102, no. 3 (February 2005): p. 338.

[55] Hume, '"Satire" in the Reign of Charles II', pp. 335–6.

they admired the poetry of their immediate predecessors enormously, Restoration critics had larger doubts about its power as a distinct and continuing body of work, and there was a strong tendency to think of it as providing a kind of workshop or pre-tradition on which to build: certainly early poetry needed to be polished, 'refined' and 'improved' ... What the 'previous age' had done was too little, too tentative, too unself-conscious, too rugged and perhaps still too European to fully create, in a modern spirit, a literature fully appropriate to the English language, British temperament and modern 'refinement'.[56]

This is not to say that English satire lacked extant models.[57] Much of the manuscript satire from this period seems to draw, for instance, on the carnival-esque rough-and-tumble energy of the English skimmington with its public shaming or flytings with their open poetical abuse.[58] As Harold Love has written, 'the Restoration lampoon has a characteristic tone, even a characteristic kind of viciousness, that was foreign to its [poetic] precursors'.[59] So many verse libels are closer to contemporary sung forms and especially ballads from this period.[60]

With their rapid, disconnected successions of piquant thumbnail portraits, these poems sometimes read like collections of topical epigrams, works themselves generically associated with 'libellous satire' during this period.[61] Many writers, including Abraham Cowley, Sir John Denham, John Wilmot, the second earl of Rochester, Dryden, and John Oldham, translated or loosely adapted Martial's epigrams. It is in their witty syntactic reversals that we hear the clearest classical echoes in the libellous poems of this period, rather than Juvenal, Horace, or Persius, classical satirists who only later came to influence satiric practise and

[56]   J. Paul Hunter, 'Political, satirical, didactic and lyric poetry (I)', *The Cambridge History of English Literature, 1660–1800*, edited by John Richetti (Cambridge: Cambridge University Press, 2005), p. 178. See also Howard Weinbrot, *Britannia's Issue: The Rise of British Literature from Dryden to Ossian* (Cambridge: Cambridge University Press, 1995).

[57]   Love, *English Clandestine Satire*, p. 19.

[58]   Douglas Gray, 'Rough Music: Some Early Invectives and Flytings', *Yearbook of English Studies* 14 (1984): pp. 21–43; and Martin Ingram, 'Ridings, Rough Music and Mocking Rhymes in Early Modern England', in *Popular Culture in Seventeenth-Century England* (London: Routledge, 1985), pp. 166–97. Market-square satires, often satirical ballads nailed up at the centre of some English town or impromptu oral ballads, also have their classical forebears in the public verse satires inscribed on Pompeii's and Herculaneum's walls. See Adam Fox, *Oral and Literate Culture in England, 1500–1700* (Oxford: Oxford University Press, 2000), pp. 229–334; and Laura Gowing, *Domestic Dangers: Women, Words, and Sex in Early Modern London* (Oxford: Oxford University Press, 1996), p. 84. For an English example, see 'A friendly caution to all Malsters, Millers, & other dealers in Corn', a market-square satire on a certain John Wing for using false weights (Add. MS 33230, BL).

[59]   Love, *English Clandestine Satire*, p. 23.

[60]   Harold Love, *Scribal Publication in Seventeenth-Century England* (Oxford: Clarendon Press, 1993), pp. 232–4; Love, *English Clandestine Satire*, pp. 249–59; and Fox, *Oral and Literate Culture*, ch. 6.

[61]   Kate Loveman, 'Epigram and Spontaneous Wit', in *OHECS*, p. 492. See also Roger D. Lund, 'The Ghosts of Epigram, False Wit, and the Augustan Mode', *Eighteenth-Century Life* 27, no. 2 (Spring 2003): pp. 67–95.

especially critical discussion of individual satires.[62] Take these lines on John Grobham Howe, a one-time rakish hanger-on of Charles II's court who in 1678 openly bragged about a non-existent affair with Frances, Duchess of Richmond. Later banished from court, he soon found himself a double-dealing writer of minor satiric verse, before entering politics in the late 1680s. An oft-copied manuscript satire on 'Jack Howe' claims that 'His whole design is to be thought a wit' (l. 33), and through 'downright lies' (l. 28) he 'Writes what he sees, feigns and makes out the rest' (l. 40). The best shot at him was not for his scandalmongering libels but for his foppish vanity and psychosomatic ugliness. 'His person too he much admires' (l. 41), the poet writes, but:

> A face he has much like a skeleton,
> Two inches broad and fifteen inches long.
> His cheeks sunk, a visage pale as death,
> Adorned with pimples and a stinking breath.
> His scragged carcass moves with antic grace,
> And every limb as awkward as his face.
> His poisoned corpse wrapped in a wicker skin,
> Dismal without and ten times worse within.[63]

In such lines we can easily detect echoes of Martial: so much of the tone of the ad hominem attack is caught up with its (largely) metrical feet, punchy couplets, and an easy, almost demotic register. It offers a vivid picture of a hideously pocky and elongated face, attached to a body that lumbers like a half-resurrected corpse. Howe is not simply a whited sepulchre but a sepulchre through and through—a putrid mass encased by a cross-hatching of desiccated skin. Paradoxically, the heroic couplet both mitigates and intensifies the attack. It gives the speaker a restrained condescension, but through a kind of Martialian inversion drives home the insult with a force that direct invective never could.

Such libels were seemingly everywhere between the 1660s and the 1680s. As Thomas Cogswell has put it, the outpouring of topical satire was 'as close to a mass media as early Stuart England ever achieved'.[64] Predictably, the authorities became more and more deeply concerned about the spread of satires, the vast majority of which were opposition works—Whig, exclusionist, and sometimes even anti-royalist assaults on everything the court and the two Houses of Parliament

---

[62] J. P. Sullivan and A. J. Boyle (eds.), *Martial in English* (New York: Penguin, 1996), pp. 87–158; and Howard D. Weinbrot, *Augustus Caesar in 'Augustan' England: The Decline of a Classical Norm* (Princeton: Princeton University Press, 1978), pp. 150–3.

[63] 'An Answer to the Satire on the Court Ladies' (1680), rpt. *CSR*, pp. 42–3, ll. 47–54.

[64] Thomas Cogswell, 'Underground Verse and the Transformation of Early Stuart Political Culture', in *Political Culture and Cultural Politics in Early Modern England: Essays Presented to David Underdown*, edited by Susan D. Amussen and Mark A. Kishlansky (Manchester: Manchester University Press, 1995), pp. 277–300.

touched.[65] In hopes of halting their dissemination, Charles issued a proclamation in late 1675 calling for the closure of the coffeehouses. It was perhaps almost impossible to stop such satires from coming into being, the Crown reasoned, but in the absence of a gathering place for their recitation and dissemination the market for them would at the very least be severely hampered. Coffeehouses, the authorities worried, were utter hotbeds of rash talking and sedition. In L'Estrange's view, 'every *Coffee-house* [is] *furnished* with *News-Papers* and *Pamphlets* (both *written* and *Printed*) of *Personal Scandal, Schism* and *Treason*'.[66] Charles's first proclamation attacked 'the great resort of Idle and disaffected persons', where 'by the occasion of the meetings of such persons therein, divers False, Malitious and Scandalous Reports are devised and spread abroad, to the Defamation of His Majesties Government, and the Disturbance of the Peace and Quiet of the Realm'.[67] The proclamation was soon withdrawn—the coffeehouses were given a reprieve—and replaced with another forcing each coffeehouse proprietor to take the oaths of allegiance and enter £500 into recognizance 'to prevent and hinder all Scandalous Papers, Books or Libels'.[68] Prevention gave way to policing.

This first proclamation was followed by a second, just over a week later. It attacked the lampoonists more directly, targeting those 'Writing, [and] Printing, sundry false, infamous, and scandalous Libells' that 'stir up and dispose the minds of His Majesties Subjects to Sedition and Rebellion'. The proclamation even offered a reward of £20 to anyone who might snitch on the underground network of go-betweens, including 'the person or persons to whom any such Libell...be brought, and by him or them received, or order to Print or transcribe the same; Or the Place where such Libell shall be printing or transcribing [...or] any private Printing-Press'. The king more than doubled the reward, to £50, for anyone who might discover 'the Author of any such Libell', so that 'said Libells may be suppressed, and the parties offending may be effectually prosecuted'.[69] The government needed only to flush out such 'hireling scribblers', Chief Justice William Scroggs observed, 'for they are only safe whilst they can be secret; but so are vermin, so long as they can hide themselves...[T]hey shall know that the law wants not power to punish a libellous and licentious press'.[70]

The authorities' emphasis on modes of transmission made sense. With their out-and-out accusations of criminality and disease, manuscript lampoons did little at a rhetorical level to hamper prosecutions and actions. Their authors relied almost exclusively on their modes of circulation for protection—in manuscripts passed from hand to hand, transcribed in professional scriptoria, or printed on

[65] Love, *Scribal Publication*, p. 240.
[66] Roger L'Estrange, *A Word Concerning Libels and Libellers* (London, 1681), p. 12.
[67] *A Proclamation for the Suppression of the Coffee-Houses* (London, 1675), p. 1.
[68] *An Additional Proclamation Concerning Coffee-Houses* (London, 1676), p. 2.
[69] *A Proclamation for the better Discovery of Seditious Libellers* (London, 1676), p. 1.
[70] 7 *State Trials* 703.

underground presses.[71] Such works did little to upset even the literary-legal nomenclature of the period in which they were known almost uniformly as 'libels'.[72] Manuscript verse satirists, even when mocking the tradition within which they wrote, openly identified their own works among the 'loose-writ libels of the age'.[73] Throughout the decades that followed the Restoration, two trends were simply at odds and on a collision course: the growth of verse libels as a wellspring of personal satire and political opposition, and the refinement of the law, and especially of libel laws, to police written works.

1.3 Lampoon without Libel: *Mac Flecknoe*, Verbal Evasion, and the Language of Satire

During the first decades of the Restoration, satirists had to rely almost exclusively on those who circulated, copied, and sometimes printed and sold their most outrageous wares for protection. The defamatory overtness of such libels provided no defence, and it became clear that something about the way in which satire was not only circulated but also written needed to change. It was in John Dryden's *Mac Flecknoe* that later satirists found an implicit model. This is perhaps to claim too much for a single poem. The literary and legal virtues of *Mac Flecknoe* can be found scattered across dozens of pieces and employed by a range of satirists during the final decades of the seventeenth century. It is nonetheless worth emphasizing the ways in which Dryden brought these techniques together by establishing a model for the legitimation of satire and by devising an evasive language built around mock-encomium that would later complicate the bench's interpretive directions given to jurors in defamation cases. *Mac Flecknoe* was not a direct response to developments in defamation law in the 1670s (even if Dryden knew of Hale, whom he referred to as 'doubtless an Uncorrupt and Upright Man').[74] Nor did every satirist after Dryden write so-called 'neoclassical' satire or even look directly to him as an exemplar. Instead, later satirists found in Dryden's poetry, and in his imitators and successors, the rhetorical tools that would most trouble the courts in the coming decades. *Mac Flecknoe* demonstrated the legal value of verbal evasion and sustained irony in particular and, in so doing, later forced the courts to address the problem of ambiguity in defamatory and seditious works.

Dryden first composed *Mac Flecknoe* in the summer of 1676, and shortly thereafter the poem began to circulate in manuscript. It attacks Thomas

---

[71] Love, *Scribal Publication*, chs. 2 and 3.   [72] Love, *English Clandestine Satire*, p. 7.
[73] John Sheffield, Earl of Mulgrave, 'An Essay Upon Satire' (1679), rpt. *POAS*, vol. 1, p. 403, l. 37.
[74] *Discourse concerning the Original and Progress of Satire*, in *The Works of John Dryden*, vol. 4: Poems 1693–1696, edited by A. B. Chambers, William Frost, and Vinton A. Dearing (Berkeley and Los Angeles: University of California Press, 1956–90), p. 50. Hereafter cited parenthetically by page number(s).

Shadwell, a prominent playwright and poet, and extends from a literary quarrel the two writers had been carrying on since 1668. At its core, the debate was over the nature of drama and how it should be practised. Dryden preferred Shakespeare and the comedy of repartee; Shadwell, Ben Jonson and the comedy of humours.[75] As Dryden put it in his prologue to *The Tempest* in 1667:

> *Shakespear* who (taught by none) did first impart
> To *Fletcher* Wit, to laboring *Johnson* Art.
> He, Monarch-like, gave those his subjects Law,
> And is that Nature which they print and draw.
> *Fletcher* reach'd that which on his heights did grow,
> Whilst *Johnson* crept and gather'd all below.[76]

After his pointed remarks about the two Renaissance dramatists, Dryden and Shadwell went back and forth in barbed epilogues and prefaces, hashing out their squabble in half-veiled allusions to each other's works. Some attacks were more personal than others. In Shadwell's play *The Humourists* (1670), for instance, Dryden appears as Drybob, a name that most obviously echoes his own, but also intimated that he was a feckless, sexually impotent poet in need of a good slapping: a dry bob could mean both a glancing blow and 'coition without emission'.[77]

Their dustup finally reached its apex in June 1676, when Shadwell attacked comedies that rely on 'downright silly folly' in his dedication to *The Virtuoso* (1676). Better is Jonson, he wrote, 'who was incomparably the best Drammatick Poet that ever was, or, I believe, will ever be; and I would rather be Author of one Scene of his best Comedies, than of any Play this Age has produced'.[78] Dryden picked up the prompt and ran with it in *Mac Flecknoe*: Shadwell implicitly claims to be the dramatic inheritor to Jonsonian comedy of humours. Rather than accept Shadwell's dramatic genealogy, however, Dryden turned Shadwell into the progeny of the poet-playwright Richard Flecknoe, who had earlier identified himself with Jonson and whose copious outpouring of bad and hastily written works had already turned him into his age's archetypal hack. In Dryden's poem, Flecknoe has 'governed long' his literary 'empire' (l. 4):

> In prose and verse was owned without dispute
> Through all the realms of nonsense absolute.
>
> (ll. 5–6)[79]

---

[75] R. Jack Smith, 'Shadwell's Impact Upon John Dryden', *Review of English Studies* 20, no. 77 (January 1944): pp. 29–44.

[76] Dryden, Prologue, in *The Tempest* (London, 1667), p. [i], ll. 6–10.

[77] *OED*, n3.1; *POAS* vol. 1, p. 362, l. 75n. See Howard Weinbrot, *Eighteenth-Century Satire: Essays on Text and Context from Dryden to Peter Pindar* (Cambridge: Cambridge University Press, 1988), p. 75n26.

[78] Thomas Shadwell, Dedication, in *The Virtuoso* (London, 1676), pp. [ii–iii].

[79] *Mac Flecknoe*, in *The Poems of John Dryden*, vol. 1: 1649–1681, edited by Paul Hammond (New York: Longman, 1995), pp. 306–36. Hereafter cited parenthetically by line number(s).

Flecknoe attempts 'To settle the succession of the state' (l. 10) and decides that

> "Shadwell alone my perfect image bears,
> Mature in dullness from his tender years;
> Shadwell alone, of all my sons, is he
> Who stands confirmed in full stupidity".
>
> (ll. 15–18)

After a few less than gracious words about Shadwell—all dressed up in dry mock-praise—Shadwell is crowned and 'Empress Fame' (as in 'rumour') (l. 94) spreads word of his coronation. Soon a world of hack authors from the City and Bunhill Fields, the epicentre of bad poetry in London, join to welcome the new Prince of Dullness. However,

> No Persian carpets spread th' imperial way,
> But scattered limbs of mangled poets lay:
> From dusty shops neglected authors come,
> Martyrs of pies, and relics of the bum.
>
> (ll. 98–101)

His coronation train is all remaindered poems—'Much Heywood, Shirley, Ogilby there lay, / But loads of Shadwell almost choked the way' (ll. 102–3)—that have been converted into pie liners and bog paper, the most fitting end for the Kingdom of Dullness's subjects. The scene plays out with mock-dignity and inverted regality, and echoes with allusions to Milton's *Paradise Lost* and Virgil's *Aeneid*. Like Satan, Shadwell sits 'High on a throne of his own labours reared' (l. 107) ('High on a throne of royal state', as Milton puts it).[80] But instead of the life-giving light that envelops the head of Ascanius, Aeneas's son—'A lambent Flame arose, which gently spread / Around his brows, and on his Temples fed'[81]—Shadwell is predictably engulfed by stultifying fogs:

> His brows thick fogs, instead of glories, grace,
> And lambent dullness played around his face.
>
> (ll. 110–12)

Finally crowned, Flecknoe offers a concluding prophecy, predicting that Shadwell will follow in this line of 'filial dullness' (l. 136):

---

[80] Milton, *Paradise Lost*, edited by John Leonard (New York: Penguin, 2000), II.1.
[81] *The Works of Virgil containing his Pastorals, Georgics and Aeneis*, trans. John Dryden (London, 1697), II. pp. 930–2.

"My son, advance
Still in new impudence, new ignorance".

(ll. 145–6)

Then, with a puff of flatulence—his 'drugget robe' is 'Born upwards by a subter-
ranean wind' (ll. 214–5)—Flecknoe falls through a trapdoor, leaving only his heir
behind. Thomas Shadwell, son of Richard Flecknoe: a new poetic hero for a fallen
literary age.

Like Flecknoe, Shadwell is not only the false inheritor to poetic greatness, but
also a clown ill-suited to heroic fame. One of the subtle syntactic jokes running
throughout *Mac Flecknoe* is the inappropriateness not only of Shadwell to the epic
but also of Shadwell's very name. Routinely in the poem his trochaic surname falls
awkwardly into the iambic pentameter of the Dryden's heroic couplets.[82] In
several instances, a line begins with the bumbling hero: 'Shadwell alone my perfect
image bears' (l. 15). Such moments force readers into unsatisfactory sonic decisions: either to distort his name into an iamb (shad-*WELL*), thus maintaining the
symmetry of the iambic pentameter; or to retain the natural trochee of his name
(*SHAD*-well), but disrupt the line's metre. Such metrical violations are not
unknown in heroic poetry, but the cumulative effect of such syntactic awkward-
ness exposes at a metrical level what should be painfully obvious at a thematic one:
Shadwell, right down to the trochee of his name, is at best a clumsy fit and at worst
a totally inappropriate subject for either heroic poetry or heroic meter.

The pungency of this syntactic juxtaposition, its comic strength and satiric cut,
belongs to the poem's implicit high burlesque: the fool as the subject of heroic
verse. This was the very feature, too, for which Dryden later praised Nicolas
Boileau, whose *Le Lutrin* had foregrounded the comic virtues of the mock-heroic:[83]

His Subject is Trivial, but his Verse is Noble...This, I think,...to be the most
Beautiful, and most Noble kind of Satire. Here is the Majesty of the Heroique,
finely mix'd with the Venom of the other; and raising the Delight which
otherwise wou'd be flat and vulgar by the Sublimity of the Expression.   (83–4)

In a similar manner, *Mac Flecknoe* balances and exposes two disparities. At a local
level, the poem juxtaposes Shadwell's own perverse view of himself as Jonson's
inheritor and Dryden's humiliating insight that he is actually Flecknoe redux.
'Thou art my blood', Flecknoe announces—one can almost see Dryden's finger-
wagging glee—'where Jonson has no part' (l. 175). At a grander level, the poem

---

[82] In later printed satires, Shadwell's name is gutted. It appears, for instance, as either 'Shad—' or
'Sh—' in the authorized 1684 printed version of *Mac Flecknoe*. In almost all of the 17 known
manuscript copies of the poem, his name is written out in full. See *Mac Flecknoe*, l. 15n.
[83] James Fowler, 'Moralizing Satire: Cross-Channel Perspectives', in *OHECS*, pp. 601–4.

articulates a juxtaposition that is the thematic basis of the mock-epic itself: the gross mortification of a bumbling fool on a heroic stage. Within these juxtapositions, Shadwell implicitly becomes an example of the poem's deflating precept: the eternal threat to good poetry is bad poets.

1.4 The Legitimation of Lampoon: *Mac Flecknoe* and the Satiric Shadow Canon

By the standards of contemporary ad hominem poetry, *Mac Flecknoe* was a masterpiece of attack.[84] As Lord Mulgrave wrote years later, satire is most effective not when it brutally lambasts its object, but when it expresses itself in disinterested mock-praise: "Rage you must hide, and prejudice lay down: / A Satyr's Smile is sharper than his Frown."[85] Decades later, in 1693, Dryden would come to a similar conclusion in his *Discourse concerning the Original and Progress of Satire*, arguing that style or tone was the central formal feature of satire, one that made it "well-manner'd" and a kind of "fine Raillery" (70). As he put it in the *Discourse*'s most quoted passage:

> How easie is it to call [a man] Rogue and Villain, and that wittily! But how hard to make a Man appear a Fool, a Blockhead, or a Knave, without using any of those opprobrious terms! To spare the grossness of the Names, and to do the thing yet more severely, is to draw a full Face, and to make the Nose and Cheeks stand out, and yet not to employ any depth of Shadowing...there is still a vast difference betwixt the slovenly Butchering of a Man, and the fineness of a stroke that separates the Head from the Body, and leaves it standing in its place.   (70–71)

For Dryden, a satire's ethics and verbal method were intimately linked. Moreover, that verbal indirectness—the obliqueness of the attack, the ability to show a man's foolishness and depravity, without the name-calling and imputation mongering that typified manuscript satires from this period—was also the source of its decapitating power.

Dryden had done more, however, than simply adopt an arch tone of pseudo-disinterestedness. With *Mac Flecknoe*, he had also devised a model for personal attack by gathering and refashioning a range of literary forms. In part, Dryden draws on the tradition of 'sessions' poems in which a range of figures, often poets, are summoned for lashing judgement. (Such poems share something in common with shotgun satires, which served much the same function—attacking as many figures as possible—without the scaffolding of a parodic sub-tradition.) Sessions

---

[84] Pat Rogers, *The Augustan Vision* (London: Methuen, 1974), p. 174.
[85] John Sheffield, Earl of Mulgrave, *An Essay Upon Poetry* (London, 1682), p. 10.

satires were common throughout the last half of the seventeenth century and drew broadly on Sir John Suckling's 'A Session of the Poets' (1637?).[86] In Suckling's poem, 'the wits of the Town' appear before Apollo to decide who should be crowned with a laurel wreath.[87] Each poet is paraded out and lashed for his failures, but ultimately Apollo realizes that that no poet will do. He

> Openly declared that 'twas the best signe
> Of good store of wit to have good store of coyn,
> And without a Syllable more or lesse said,
> He put the Laurel on the Aldermans head.
>
> (ll. 107–10)

Later sessions satires loosely followed Suckling's model, trotting out living poets and playwrights for a heap of abuse before laying the laurel, in the most damning of all reversals, on some non-writer. In a sessions satire from 1668, for instance, Apollo eventually crowns two actors, John Lacy and Henry Harris, 'Because they alone made the plays go off'.[88]

In *Mac Flecknoe*, Dryden clearly draws on this sub-tradition of lambasting poets. But by focusing on one supposed hack rather than a blunderbuss of bad writers, he is able to create movement and action—something approaching a narrative. *Mac Flecknoe*, in fact, is more structured than any of the verse satires that preceded it. Almost all of the satiric poems from this period, especially the closely related shotgun pieces, tend to be random catalogues of hacks listed in no particular order. In most instances, one could pick up almost any portrait or stanza and move it wholesale, or even read it in isolation, without jeopardizing the poem's organizing precept. Sessions satires tend to move in much the same way. The only parts that we might think of as conscientiously placed—the exordium, which introduces the contest, and the crowning of not a poet but some tertiary figure to the action—are concretely bookended in each poem; they come first and last, and it hardly matters what goes between, beyond a litany of boisterously self-important scribblers.[89] Conversely, *Mac Flecknoe* possesses a series of dramatic units in a structure: it opens with a soliloquy by Flecknoe, is followed by Shadwell's coronation, and is closed by Flecknoe's prophecy.

---

[86]   For examples of 'sessions' poems, see 'The Session of the Poets' (1668) and 'A Session of the Poets' (1676), rpt. *POAS* vol. 1, pp. 327–37 and 352–6; and 'Colin' (1679) and 'The Lovers' Session' (1687), rpt. *CSR*, pp. 23–31 and 175–98.

[87]   Sir John Suckling, '[The Wits] (A Session of the Poets)', in *The Works of Sir John Suckling: The Non-Dramatic Works*, edited by Thomas Clayton (Oxford: Clarendon Press, 1971), pp. 71–6, l. 5. The poem circulated in manuscript in the late 1630s, and was published posthumously in Sir John Suckling, *Fragmenta Aurea* (London, 1646), pp. 7–9.

[88]   'The Session of the Poets' (1668), rpt. *POAS* vol. 1, p. 337, l. 172.

[89]   Love, 'Rochester', p. 148.

Perhaps most importantly, Dryden built his narrative around a single person-age rather than a host of poets. In doing so, *Mac Flecknoe* paradoxically helps to transmute a particular satire, one might argue, into a general one. Between 1676 and 1682, *Mac Flecknoe* circulated only in manuscript, and then seemingly only among a limited audience of readers.[90] As a result, the poem's enduring import-ance is to some degree thanks to the unauthorized edition published in 1682, which prompted Dryden to print his own version in 1684 (that the poem saw wide circulation in print at all is also in large part thanks to the temporary lapse in the Press Licensing Act between 1679 and 1685). Printing the poem accommodated a shift in the print market itself and the rapid expansion of literacy. Circulating lampoons in manuscript worked well enough when they were intended for a limited and knowing audience.[91] They created a closed circle of information sharing in which cumulative gossip filled in the gaps in a backstory. As one poet quipped of Mary Lewis, wife of Robert Leke, earl of Scarsdale, 'To speak of Scarsdale is but loss of paper; / She's called a stinking whore in every satire'.[92]

But beyond a limited circle—and, to a considerable extent, as Michael McKeon has argued, even within the coterie circles of the ostensibly informed—such poems were profoundly difficult to make sense of.[93] Wider distribution failed to change at first what readers outside of certain charmed circles knew. As more and more works were printed, however, a critical mass of knowledge began to fill this informational vacuum. Print had the advantage of broadening Dryden's audience, with *Mac Flecknoe* demonstrating how a fully fleshed-out depiction of a single figure could supply many of the details needed for less-informed readers to read a particular work in a general way. That is, through the internal accumulation of details in the poem itself, the individual and deeply personalized shots at Shadwell made internal sense. But also through that same accumulation, readers were able to understand the most personal elements of an attack as a generalized satiric fiction. It hardly mattered whether Flecknoe or Shadwell were real people or fictional characters; there is enough in the poem, even if read wholly in isolation, to interpret it as a satire on a general type—the archetypal poetaster—rather than a single, identifiable individual.

In addition, by putting one figure at the heart of the poem, Dryden was also able to draw on a second, much larger literary tradition through parodic inversion: the epic. Genre theory held epic as the highest accomplishment in poetry, and those like Dryden and later Pope who adopted the Virgilian progression model would

[90] 17 contemporary manuscript copies are known. Headnote to *Mac Flecknoe*, in *The Poems of John Dryden*, vol. 1: 1649–1681, edited by Paul Hammond (New York: Longman, 1995), p. 312.

[91] Love, *English Clandestine Satire*, p. 248, ch. 8, *passim*. For manuscript circulation more generally, see Love, *Scribal Publication*, esp. chs. 2 and 3.

[92] 'Satire' (1682), rpt. *CSR*, 83, ll. 43–4.

[93] Michael McKeon, 'What Were Poems on Affairs of State?', *1650–1850: Ideas, Aesthetics, and Inquiries in the Early Modern Era* 4 (1997): pp. 363–82.

only move on to writing epics, or at least long-form narrative poems, having successfully executed pastorals and didactic works.[94] By aligning *Mac Flecknoe* with the most regarded of all genres, and drawing on the heroic manner of especially Virgil, Milton, and Cowley, Dryden was able not only to plunder a host of epic works for pointed allusions but also to secure the poem's place in a satiric shadow canon.

This alignment with the epic gave *Mac Flecknoe* a prominence and a permanence that few parodies, which often repurposed a single work within a minor sub-tradition, could ever hope to achieve. All of the 'Advice to a Painter' poems that started to appear in the later 1660s and 1670s, for instance, drew implicitly on Edmund Waller's bloated and sycophantic panegyric, *Instructions to a Painter* (1665), which celebrated the Duke of York, Lord High Admiral, for his naval victory off Lowestoft on 3 June 1665 during the Second Anglo-Dutch War. Waller's poem, which was based on Giovanni Francesco Busenello's *Prospettiva del nauale ripotato dall Republica Serenissima contra il Turco* (1656; translated by Thomas Higgons as *A Prospective of the Naval Triumph of the Venetians* in 1658), introduced the Horatian *ut pictura poesis* ('as is painting, so is poetry') analogy to English poetry, in which the speaker of the poem directs a painter.[95] The first parody, 'The Second Advice To a Painter' (likely written by Andrew Marvell), appeared in manuscript perhaps less than a month after Waller's poem was licensed in March 1666, and worked to supply the many defects missing from Waller's glowing depiction of the duke.[96]

Advice poems, though, were a literary experiment at the intersections of satire and ekphrasis that eventually fizzled out. Marvell's poem and the many that followed it (some also authored by Marvell) belonged to a scathing parodic subtype, one too limited in scope to serve as the basis for a long-standing satiric model. For all of their intertextual allusions to preceding parodies, such works were based almost solely on one embarrassingly commendatory poem rather than a massive transhistorical canon. Conversely, the mock-epic could never knock the epic off of its pedestal (though it did, perhaps, tarnish its solemnity).[97] The entire

---

[94] James Sambrook, 'Poetry, 1660–1740', in *The Cambridge History of Literary Criticism*, edited by H. B. Nisbet and Claude Rawson (Cambridge: Cambridge University Press, 1997), p. 115.

[95] Henryk Markiewicz and Uliana Gabara, 'Ut Pictura Poesis... A History of the Topos and the Problem', *New Literary History* 18, no. 3 (Spring 1987): pp. 535–58.

[96] See Andrew Marvell, 'The Advice-to-a-Painter and Associated Poems', in *The Poems of Andrew Marvell*, edited by Nigel Smith (New York: Pearson Longman, 2003), pp. 321–71. On the intersections between print and manuscript during this period, see Martin Dzelzainis, 'L'Estrange, Marvell and the *Directions to a Painter*: The Evidence of Bodleian Library, MS Gough London 14', in *Roger L'Estrange and the Making of Restoration Culture*, edited by Anne Dunan-Page and Beth Lynch (Aldershot: Ashgate, 2008), pp. 53–66.

[97] Ulrich Broich, *The Eighteenth-Century Mock-Heroic Poem* (1968), trans. David Henry Wilson (Cambridge: Cambridge University Press, 1990), pp. 58–9; and Brean Hammond, *Professional Imaginative Writing in England, 1670–1740: 'Hackney for Bread'* (Oxford: Clarendon Press, 1997), ch. 4.

classical epic tradition remained openly celebrated and widely read, if only rarely attempted as the following century wore on.[98] Waller's poem could be and was superseded, as his royalist praise became more and more embarrassing in the final years of the 1660s and as the poem itself fell into disregard. By the 1680s, writing additional advice poems was little better than beating a dead horse.

This is not to say that the advice poems, and especially Marvell's, had little enduring effect on satire after the 1670s. Dryden knew Marvell's mock-encomiastic depiction of the Duke of York's mock-heroic exploits, perhaps just as well as he knew the language of panegyric.[99] His own poems, including *Astraea Redux* (1660), *To His Sacred Majesty: A Panegyric on his Coronation* (1661), and *To My Lord Chancellor* (1662), had come in for their fair share of derision as the obsequious outpourings of a mercenary place-seeker. But he also knew, as Marvell taught in his 'Last Instructions to a Painter' (1667), that panegyric's most effective opposite was not invective but mock-praise.

In a similar way, Dryden drew on and gave cohesion to a half-formed mock-heroic tradition. For Love, *Mac Flecknoe* is a 'brilliant marriage of vulgar content to Virgilian stylistic pastiche'.[100] Indeed, the poem was, strictly speaking, the first mock-heroic poem in English—Dryden later claimed to have authored 'the first piece of ridicule written with heroics'—but it was not the first of its kind.[101] There were the classic progenitors like the mock-Homeric *Battle of the Frogs and Mice* and the mock-Virgilian *Culex* (*The Gnat*). One could likewise point to Alessandro Tassoni's *Secchia Rapita* (*The Stolen Bucket*) (1622), which Dryden knew; or Boileau's *Le Lutrin* (1674), a mocking account of a religious squabble over the placement of a lectern (though Dryden seemingly only read this poem after he had composed *Mac Flecknoe*). *Mac Flecknoe*'s punch is likewise tied up intimately with Dryden's epigrammatic turns of phrase—so much so that two scholars have gone as far as to say that Martial 'informed his whole compositional style' and that his longer satires could be read as 'constructs of epigrams'.[102] We can see this Martialian inheritance in Dryden's portraits of both Flecknoe and Shadwell, for instance, but especially later in his pungent mock-encomiastic reversals in *Absalom and Achitophel*.

Again, all of these works were in some capacity forerunners. As Steven N. Zwicker has observed, 'Dryden did not invent irony' and he knew well the

[98] Claude Rawson, 'Mock-heroic and English Poetry', in *The Cambridge Companion to Epic*, edited by Catherine Bates (Cambridge: Cambridge University Press, 2010), p. 167.
[99] Keymer, *Poetics*, p. 58.   [100] Love, *English Clandestine Satire*, p. 245.
[101] Joseph Spence, *Observations, Anecdotes, and Characters of Books and Men*, edited by James M. Osborn, vol. 1 (Oxford: Clarendon Press, 1966), pp. 274–5.
[102] *Martial in English*, edited by J. P. Sullivan and A. J. Boyle (New York: Penguin, 1996), p. 114. See also Love, 'Rochester', pp. 147–9. On the influence of Martial in earlier periods, see Peter, *Complaint and Satire*, pp. 160–7.

ironies of Lucian, Horace, Juvenal, Persius, and Tacitus. Yet his employment of irony was also unusual. As Zwicker continues:

> none before Dryden . . . had so widely explored the uses of irony, who had turned a mere figure of speech into an arresting mode of literary self-consciousness, and who used irony not only to humiliate antagonists but as well to refuse simplifications and singularity. From early in his career, Dryden was engaged with a progressive unfolding of the ways irony might furnish a shield against commitments and enable a writer to walk away from the most overt demonstration of damaging truths while at the same time insinuate them into his writing.[103]

In this regard, Dryden helped to instantiate what Margaret Anne Doody has called the 'essential technique or habit of Augustan poetry': 'its double-tongued utterance, or quality of double-mindedness'.[104] Moreover, Dryden's 'growing mastery of ventriloquism' is important, because it permitted him to couple 'proximity and distance': the ability to convincingly espouse positions he intuitively abhorred.[105]

In this regard, Dryden also helped to shape what Fredric V. Bogel has called the 'formal structure' that undergirds satire more generally. For Bogel, satire is 'a literary mechanism for the production of differences', a means of producing a gulf between a satirist (and reader) and victim:

> satirists identify in the world something or someone that is both attractive and curiously or dangerously like them, or like the culture or subculture that they identify with or speak for, or sympathetic even as repellent—something, then, that is *not alien enough* . . . The 'first' satiric gesture . . . is not to expose the satiric object in all its alien difference but to *define* it as different, as other . . . Satire, then, is a rhetorical means to the production of difference in the face of a potentially compromising similarity, not the articulation of differences already securely in place.[106]

In its attempt to establish this satiric distance, *Mac Flecknoe* offers a case study in 'self-irony'.[107] Even its Ovidian opening—'All human things are subject to decay' (l. 1)—intimates that Dryden is subject to the same historical forces as any other fallen poet, an implicit concession that further undermines the confident anaphoric claim that 'Shadwell *alone*' (ll. 15, 17) is Flecknoe's true inheritor. What starts as emphatic identification of an alien other becomes a desperate repetition and a hopeful denial of Dryden's own futurity. He might become the very thing he loathes as much as fears: one of those 'mangled poets' or 'neglected authors'. It is

---

[103] Zwicker, 'Dryden and the Invention of Irony', p. 75.   [104] Doody, *Daring Muse*, p. 211.
[105] Zwicker, 'Dryden and the Invention of Irony', pp. 76–7.   [106] Bogel, *Satire*, pp. vii, 21, 41–2.
[107] Matthew C. Augustine, 'The Invention of Dryden as Satirist', in *OHECS*, p. 163.

worth keeping in mind that 'Heywood, Shirley, [and] Ogilby' were all once Drydens just a few decades earlier, before their remaindered paper selves were converted into Shadwellian pie liner and bog paper. Dryden's rhetorical gesture, to put it in Bogel's terms, is the hopeful articulation of a *future* difference not yet known, a similarity glimpsed and yet denied, despite the troubling realization that 'All human things'—Dryden's poems and reputation included—'are subject to decay'.

The semantic doubleness of *Mac Flecknoe* points to how the poem repurposed a canon of literary works while introducing a sustained tone of ironic, Parnassian judgement without the kinds of openly defamatory shots so typical of contemporary manuscript satires. The poem accomplishes this through collocations of ironic reversals, tempering dignified acclaim with condescending modification. In the same way that the speaker praises Flecknoe—he has 'governed long… Through all the realms of nonsense absolute' (ll. 4–6)—Dryden builds up a series of mock-commendatory inversions. 'Absolute' suggests a monarchical (or in hindsight, as the poem progresses, Satanic) dominion, but it is only a kingdom of nonsense he governs. Shadwell comes in for the same sort of abuse. We are told by Flecknoe that Shadwell 'never deviates'—suggesting a kind of commendatory steadfastness—and yet we find in quick reversal that he never deviates 'into sense' (l. 20). He is the 'last great prophet', Flecknoe commends Shadwell with formal solemnity, but only 'of tautology' (l. 30). He possesses 'true dullness' (l. 90), Flecknoe explains to Shadwell, as if this were a quality others dutifully struggled to attain, so 'Trust nature, do not labour to be dull' (l. 166). We might even think of this as a satiric instantiation of the 'moderate style', the ideal of neoclassical rhetoric.[108] It was the success of such rhetoric, Love has argued, that 'eroded the prestige and effectiveness of the lampoon by making it seem crude and unmodish'. As he continues, lampooners

> spoke their truth or spite as plainly and forcefully as possible. In an age that increasingly prided itself on its polish and savoir faire, this very directness came to be seen as self-defeatingly crude: persuasion in this new world was more likely to be secured by more refined kinds of ridicule uttered in the measured tones of the metropolitan man and woman of sense.[109]

This tone of arch condescension, deeply ironic and bounded by a kind of mock-dignity, created a cohesive model of cool detachment for the satires that succeeded *Mac Flecknoe*.

This is not, however, to recast the poem as the disinterested work of some public-minded satirist. Simply put, *Mac Flecknoe* was a nasty smear campaign

---

[108] David Malouf, 'Made in England', *Quarterly Essay* 12 (2003): pp. 46–7.
[109] Love, *English Clandestine Satire*, pp. 146–7.

against a rival with whom Dryden had tetchily bickered for years.[110] John Dennis saw Dryden's poems, including *Mac Flecknoe* and *Absalom and Achitophel*, exactly for what they were: 'libels which have pass'd for Satires ... They are indeed, if you please, beautiful Libels, but they are every where full of Flattery and Slander, and a just Satire admits of neither'.[111] Dryden was able to mitigate the nastiness of this attack, to disguise the personal animus that charged his lampoon, by dressing his 'beautiful Libels' in the mock-solemn rhetoric of an inverted epic. The entire vocabulary and stance of disaffected spite that typifies verse libels from this period Dryden sublimated into a grand poetic gesture: the ability to deflate an opponent while also assuming the ostensibly disinterested man-on-the-hill condescension of implicit superiority.

Some took more from Dryden's model than others and most obviously Pope later on. Love has rightfully called *Mac Flecknoe* Dryden's 'most important contribution to clandestine satire'.[112] We can already see part of Dryden's enduring legacy in the 'classicizing lampoons' that start to appear in the late 1670s—works 'distinguished by learned allusions, antithetical wit of the Popean kind, and self-conscious use of rhetorical figures'.[113] We can likewise detect faint Drydenian echoes in works circulated between 1676 and 1682, while *Mac Flecknoe* was still only available in manuscript.[114] Other works adopted what we might call an Augustan tone of knowing condescension peppered with insults delivered in well-turned couplets, even if such poems failed to accomplish Dryden's seeming disinterestedness.[115]

The history of *Mac Flecknoe*, as both as an important transitional poem in the history of English satire but also more locally within the manuscript culture of verse 'libels' during the later seventeenth century, eventually became for Dryden part of his larger socio-literary agenda. Satire, so irredeemably low during the early modern period, begins to undergo with *Mac Flecknoe* a profound shift, one both rhetorical and cultural. As Michael Seidel has written, during the 'Restoration and eighteenth century, satire, libel, lampoon, and slander were inextricably mixed'

---

[110] Hume, '"Satire" in the Reign of Charles II', p. 344; and Marshall, *Satire*, p. 76.

[111] John Dennis, *The Characters and Conduct of Sir John Edgar* (London, 1720), p. 3.

[112] Love, *English Clandestine Satire*, p. 178.

[113] Love, *English Clandestine Satire*, p. 84. See, for instance, Sir Carr Scroope, 'In Defence of Satyr' (1677), rpt. *POAS* vol. 1, p. 364–70; 'Rochester's Farewell' (1680), rpt. *POAS* vol. 2, pp. 217–27; 'Barabara Piramidum Sileat Miracula Memphis' (1680?), Harleian MS 6913, f. 5, BL; and 'An Heroic Poem' (1681), rpt. *CSR*, pp. 68–75.

[114] See, for instance, 'A Session of the Poets' (1676), rpt. *POAS* vol. 1, p. 353, ll. 26–36; John Oldham, *Satyrs upon the Jesuits* (1679), in *The Poems of John Oldham*, edited by Harold F. Brooks (Oxford: Clarendon Press, 1987), pp. 5–54; and 'Advice to Apollo' (1677), rpt. *POAS* vol. 1, p. 392–4.

[115] Throughout the first half of the eighteenth century, Dryden remained an important model for those writing within the neoclassical satiric tradition. But other models also emerged and there is remarkable discontinuity between satiric models across the eighteenth century (Marshall, *Satire*, pp. xii–xiv, 14–20).

and satire 'was often used synonymously with lampoon'.[116] In opening up this cleft between proper satire and libellous lampoon—a historical generic intimacy clearest in the so-called 'verse libels' of Renaissance England and Scotland and in the generic satiric theory of the early modern period, when satirists were expected to model their practises after Juvenal as aggressive attacks in rude and derisive language—Dryden was attempting to create in practise a normative literary distance.[117] Part of Dryden's legacy as a practitioner and theorist of satire is the extent to which he helped to rewrite its mid-seventeenth-century history. Nigel Smith has argued that the 'meanings of the word "satire"', and its radical ties to the Civil War and Interregnum, 'have been largely obscured by the Restoration itself' and especially by Dryden, whose 'prefaces to his major satires and his essay on satire extract the genre from the uncertain state in which it had existed between 1640 and 1660, and ultimately claim it for High Tory neo-Catholicism'.[118] This era is the beginning of what came to be known as the Great Age of Satire, when satire was—shockingly, given its historical status in English literature—proudly practised and openly published by this period's most famous and most respected writers. We can do little to overstate just how radical a revision of fortunes this was, both in how satire was written and how it came to be evaluated and even valued, both commercially and culturally, in the succeeding decades. Dryden could plausibly claim to have legitimated satire, an argument both he and his successors relied on heavily when attempting to vindicate their works. They did so through a double gesture: not only by linking their satires to a celebrated classical inheritance, but also by distinguishing and distancing themselves from contemporary libellers and their lampoons.

Years later, in his *Discourse concerning the Original and Progress of Satire*, Dryden would look back on the satiric culture he had lived inside and had attempted to dissociate himself from. Part of that distancing entailed a prescriptive generic redefinition of satiric subtypes. Most of his scribbling contemporaries were nothing more than 'dull Makers of Lampoons' (9), he remarked, who had trafficked in 'Rubbish' (61). His goal in the *Discourse* was to 'give the Definition and Character of true Satires' (9), to rewrite the past and future of satire, and through that qualitative rethinking redefine satire in relation to its possible social

---

[116] Michael Seidel, 'Satire, lampoon, libel, slander', in *The Cambridge Companion to English Literature, 1650–1740*, edited by Steven Zwicker (Cambridge: Cambridge University Press, 1998), p. 33. On the 'synonymity of libel and satire in the print culture' of the eighteenth century, see Ian Higgins, 'Censorship, Libel and Self-censorship', in *Jonathan Swift and the Eighteenth-Century Book*, edited by Paddy Bullard and James McLaverty (Cambridge: Cambridge University Press, 2013), pp. 192–3.

[117] Steven M. May and Alan Bryson, *Verse Libel in Renaissance England and Scotland* (Oxford: Oxford University Press, 2016), p. v; Kernan, *Cankered Muse*, pp. 64–8, 79–80; and Griffin, *Satire*, pp. 10–14.

[118] Nigel Smith, *Literature and Revolution in England, 1640–1660* (New Haven: Yale University Press, 1994), ch. 9, esp. pp. 295–6, 317–19. See also Harold F. Brooks, 'English Verse Satire, 1640–1660: Prolegomena', *The Seventeenth Century* 3, no. 1 (Spring 1988): pp. 17–46.

and epistemological functions. 'In our Modern Languages', he complained, we apply the name of satire only 'to invective Poems' (48). Such deeply personal satires had an ugly ethical dimension. Lampoon, he argued, was 'a dangerous sort of Weapon, and for the most part Unlawful. We have no Moral right on the Reputation of other Men' (even if he was willing to justify lampoon for the purposes of revenge or to dispose of a 'Publick Nuisance' [59–60]). Instead, satire should serve a valuable and legitimate intellectual end, 'as being instructive' (55). This, as I have already noted, was all a bit too heavy-handed and noble-minded for John Dennis. But like *Mac Flecknoe* itself, Dryden's *Discourse* belongs to a decades-long project to reimagine the function and history of satire. As Dustin Griffin has argued, 'Dryden's theory [of satire] represents not so much what satire was and had been as what Dryden and his followers wanted it to be'.[119] That later theorizing also had an important effect, one that established the terms of debate and offered satirists the language, genealogy, and arguments needed to justify their most cutting lampoons.[120] That reconceptualization of satiric subtypes has had important generic consequences for how we think about satire today, producing an at times paper-thin distinction between lampoons and 'true Satires'. And yet the topical (if not formal) proximity of manuscript satires to works like *Mac Flecknoe* and its successors is worth articulating: both kinds of satire belong properly to the category of lampoon—both involve political and personal attacks—even if *Mac Flecknoe* radically revised the tone, language, and genealogy of lampooning itself.

I have gone to lengths in this chapter to place *Mac Flecknoe* in direct contact and contrast with so many of the hastily scribbled lampoons that it circulated alongside to demonstrate Dryden's unique or at the very least inventively synthetic take on personal satire. From the vantage point of literary history, few early works could claim as much importance to the satiric canon (except, perhaps, *Absalom and Achitophel*, which in many ways was to religious allegory what *Mac Flecknoe* was to the panegyric and epic traditions). That the poem offered a model for non-defamatory personal satire is not to say that every writer after Dryden was able to imitate it to the same stunning effect. But neither is this to downplay the poem's importance.

In all of this, my goal has been to emphasize the later legal value of rhetorically evasive satire. *Mac Flecknoe* was not a direct response to revisions in courtroom procedures, and yet we might trace, as Thomas Keymer has recently suggested, 'a correlation between the richness and complexity of Dryden's verse and the context of expressive constraint from which it emerged'.[121] It was this rhetorical

[119] Griffin, *Satire*, p. 21.
[120] P. K. Elkin, *The Augustan Defense of Satire* (Oxford: Clarendon Press, 1973), pp. 71–89; and Marshall, *Satire*, pp. 48–53, 62.
[121] Keymer, *Poetics*, p. 38.

density—of effectively saying one thing and yet meaning another—to which later satirists turned, finding in his poetry the verbally ironic and mock-encomiastic models that would trouble courtroom procedures. One might even suggest that the long-term aesthetic consequences of Dryden's satiric experiment were an accident, the product of a rupture in legal practise that no one could have anticipated, when licensing finally ended and the Crown turned fully to libel laws to regulate the press. It was only then that the courts were forced to decide how one was to demonstrate that a seemingly commendatory ironic locution could also be a libellous attack on an individual or the government. The bench's earlier recourse to common intendment in turn provided eighteenth-century judges with a model for redressing this newfound rhetorical problem while also conceptualizing interpretive directions for jurors.

Before any of that could happen, however, the authorities and complainants needed to haul those same satirists into court. In 1695, when licensing finally and permanently came to an end in England, writers and stationers were suddenly and supposedly free to print, publish, and sell whatever they wanted. Very quickly it became clear, however, that the lapse of licensing hardly signalled the end of regulation, as the Crown swiftly moved from a regime of prepublication licensing to a system of post-publication prosecutions. In response, stationers began to expand on the bibliographical tricks of the illegal printing operations of the seventeenth century to obscure their involvement and to protect their authors. This also led to a practical problem for the authorities—how to squirrel out those responsible for a given work, whether the author or his or her stationers. This, and the Crown's response, is the focus of the next chapter: with a new and verbally evasive language at their disposal, how satirists and their stationers responded to the authorities and the courts, by devising new bibliographical subterfuges that further exacerbated the difficulties that the authorities and complainants already faced in prosecuting those responsible for the eighteenth century's most virulent satires.

2

Keeping Out of Court II

Swift and the Illicit Book Trade

In 1755, the Treasury Solicitor, Jonathan Sharpe, complained about the printer Richard Nutt, whose 'artfull means' had again vexed the government in its attempt to prove that he was behind a seditious edition of the *London Evening Post*.[1] Nutt was hardly alone in the tricks he used to evade the authorities and even, occasionally, stymie prosecution. Take the bookseller William Moore, who in 1770 employed a twelve-year-old boy to run his shop (the ruse worked).[2] Sharpe's complaint about 'artfull means' was also hardly new. After the lapse of the Press Licensing Act in 1695, those charged with monitoring the press routinely worried about the ploys so common among the printers and booksellers who produced and sold the salacious, incendiary, blasphemous, and seditious. Somehow, authorities like Sharpe grumbled, those in the book trade were always devising new stratagems to sidestep evolving regulations.

As I argue throughout *Libel and Lampoon*, verbal ambiguity was the main tool authors had at their disposal. Such verbal evasions operated at a textual level; they were concerned with a satire's rhetoric—what it said, how it said it, and about whom. This, though, was only one aspect of a dual approach to publication. The other element concerned what we might call bibliographical evasions: the tricks used to print, market, distribute, and circulate those same works. This chapter studies how members of the book trade responded to the vagaries of the legal system—how they anticipated potential legal crackdowns, how they circulated illicit works, and how they shielded themselves and their authors through a host of evasive publishing and distribution practises. Such evasions were not always successful, but they did throw a wrench in the regulatory works by forcing the authorities to sort out the most basic bibliographical aspects of a publication before they could even begin to locate, depose, arrest, and potentially prosecute those responsible. More importantly, though these tactics were used to distribute a range of illicit materials, they became fundamental bibliographic features of printed satire in the eighteenth century. As a result, one of my goals in this chapter is to show how legal pressures on the book trade both encouraged and shaped not

---

[1] SP 36/131, f. 87 (11 July 1755), TNA.   [2] TS 11/1078/5360, TNA.

Libel and Lampoon: Satire in the Courts, 1670–1792. Andrew Benjamin Bricker, Oxford University Press.
© Andrew Benjamin Bricker 2022. DOI: 10.1093/oso/9780192846150.003.0003

only the language of satire but also the evasive physical forms in which such works were circulated.

I begin with an account of the legal tools the authorities had at their disposal, including a series of rulings from the first half of the eighteenth century that increased the liability of members in the book trade—those often known as 'stationers', a term I use throughout this chapter and a category that includes both the printers who manufactured such libels and booksellers, who served not only as wholesalers and retailers during this period, but also as publishers. Successful prosecutions were one branch of the Crown's strategy for regulating the press. Such trials frequently targeted prominent troublemakers and agitators, in hopes of shutting down or at least dissuading the most incendiary publishing outfits. But even unsuccessful prosecutions could serve an important hortatory role. Failed prosecutions were financially burdensome, even for successful defendants, and had an important chilling effect that promoted a cautious self-censorship across the book trade.

In addition, in 1709 parliament passed the first copyright law, the Act for the Encouragement of Learning (often known today as the Act or Statute of Anne or the Copyright Act), which helped formally to tie writers and booksellers to potentially libellous works. Despite debate about its drafters' original intentions, the Act of Anne contained the important provision that authors were required to register their publications with the Stationers' Company to protect their intellectual property. But even this provision, I argue, could benefit authors, who were afforded a new legal mechanism by which they could sell their rights over a work to a publisher in exchange for protection from the authorities. One of my goals in this chapter is to reorient discussions of copyright law away from the nuts-and-bolts historical model—what intellectual property was—toward a question of the law's instrumentality: how those in the book trade, and especially authors, exploited the provisions of intellectual property to create legal protections.

In response to such legal pressures, stationers devised a series of subterfuges to throw the authorities off their scent. One of the most routine evasions was the doctoring of title pages and imprints, which disguised inflammatory works as the plain and innocuous and sometimes had the effect of sending the authorities off on the wrong path. But such title pages were also bibliographic codes that hailed astute readers. Beyond disguising title pages and imprints, those in the book trade employed a range of other methods to shield their authors, to get their hands on sensitive materials for publication, and to distribute their more dubious wares. In closing, I show how this dual strategy of bibliographical and verbal evasion came together in the illicit publishing outfits of the eighteenth century: beyond disguising the libellous as the everyday, booksellers also carefully edited potentially defamatory and seditious works for publication.

Throughout this chapter, I focus on Jonathan Swift's dealings with the London book trade. Swift is in many ways an ideal case study, a writer whose publications were subject to inquiries and investigations and criminal prosecutions and civil actions for more than four decades.[3] Yet Swift himself was never once prosecuted. Moreover, there is little evidence that those who had hoped to bring an action or prosecution against him or his writings even knew of his authorship—and in those rare instances when they had squirreled him out, there remained no way to prove it. What emerges in a study of Swift's career and his strategies for avoiding prosecution is a profoundly resourceful author. Swift felt it was safest to distance himself from those who brought his works to print. As a result, when hoping to publish a work, he had to find willing accomplices to absorb the legal repercussions of his outspokenness, which he exchanged for considerable editorial freedom with his texts and the profits extending from copyright holdings. Such an analysis of the eighteenth-century illicit book trade offers one critical half of *Libel and Lampoon*'s central claim: that the production of satire was shaped by the development of the law and the legal procedures used to police satire, and that satirists and their stationers responded by devising new evasions. The most effective responses were verbal, as I argue throughout, but the law also shaped the physical media in which satire circulated, producing the bibliographically dubious forms that came to characterize printed satire across the century.

2.1 The Book Trade and the Law

Naughty books sold well: it was an incontrovertible fact of the trade. As one poet remarked in 1733:

Can Statutes keep the *British* Press in awe,
When that sells best, that's most against the law.[4]

Simply put, 'The Vulgar are eager after Scandal', Henry Fielding scoffed, 'from the same Curiosity that makes them flock to Executions'.[5] Selling scandal produced its own legal problems, though, and the authorities remained eager to make an example of not simply stationers but authors. As Chief Justice William Scroggs put it in 1680, 'one author found is better than twenty printers'.[6] Already by the later seventeenth century, Harold Weber has argued, the government was attempting 'to stabilize the dynamic and fluid field of print by defining the author

---

[3] Ian Higgins, 'Censorship, Libel and Self-censorship', in *Jonathan Swift and the Eighteenth-Century Book*, edited by Paddy Bullard and James McLaverty (Cambridge: Cambridge University Press, 2013), ch. 9.

[4] James Bramston, *Man of Taste* (London, 1733), p. 8.

[5] Henry Fielding, *Jacobite's Journal*, no. 15 (12 Mar. 1748), in *The Jacobite's Journal and Related Writings*, edited by W. B. Coley (Oxford: Clarendon Press, 1974), p. 200.

[6] *R. v. Carr* [or *Care*] (1680), 7 *State Trials* 1118.

as a fundamental object of punishment and agent of transgression'.[7] Hence the Walpole government's approach decades later. In 1730, for instance, agents raided the shop of Richard Francklin, the printer-publisher behind *The Craftsman*, in a failed attempt to discover the periodical's most incendiary authors.[8] Francklin, though, had the good sense to dispose of (or perhaps deposit elsewhere) manuscripts that would have linked any piece back to his anonymous authors—including such opposition politicians as Henry St John, Viscount Bolingbroke, and William Pulteney, earl of Bath.[9]

The authorities also had other means. Raids were one strategy, along with open warrants (which were later deemed illegal). The government also relied on intelligence gathered by official and unofficial informants. The secret service had its tentacles everywhere, its oily underlings slithering around every bookshop in London and Westminster looking for seditious wares or eavesdropping on conversations in coffeehouses.[10] The messengers of the press often snooped around, and unofficial government informants filled a void in insider knowledge.[11] The MP George Townshend, for instance, instructed the messenger of the press, Samuel Gray, to begin a general crackdown in 1729. '[B]uy up one of every sort of pamphlet or News Paper that shall be published', he wrote to Gray, 'in case such Pamphlet or News Paper shall contain anything liable to a prosecution'.[12]

Authors not forthcoming, the government often settled for stationers. For Charles Delafaye, who seemingly managed press policy between 1717 and 1734 as an undersecretary to the Secretary of State, this was the preferred method. As he put it, 'fall[ing] upon printers and publishers', who often simply hired 'scoundrels' to pump out lampoons, was the 'more effectual way to put a stop to Libelling'.[13] Already by the last half of the seventeenth century, the government had devised a broad understanding of 'authoring' a work—an 'authoriality of the press', in Joseph F. Lowenstein's words—in order to hold members of the book trade

[7] Harold Weber, Paper Bullets: *Print and Kingship under Charles II* (Lexington: University Press of Kentucky, 1996), p. 134. See also Jane Wessel, 'Performing "A Ra-ree Show": Political Spectacle and the Treason Trial of Stephen College', *Restoration* 38, no. 1 (2014): pp. 3–17.

[8] James J. Caudle, 'Richard Francklin: A Controversial Publisher, Bookseller and Printer, 1718–1765', in *The Cambridge History of the Book in Britain*, Vol. 5: 1695–1830, edited by Michael F. Suarez, S. J., and Michael L. Turner (Cambridge: Cambridge University Press, 2009), p. 384.

[9] Cholmondeley (Houghton) Papers, MS, CUL. See Michael Harris, 'Figures Relating to the Printing and Distribution of the *Craftsman*, 1726 to 1730', *Historical Research* 43, no. 108 (1970): pp. 233–42.

[10] Ian Higgins, *Swift's Politics: A Study in Disaffection* (Cambridge: Cambridge University Press, 1994), p. 160.

[11] Hanson, *Government*, pp. 36–9.   [12] KB 33/5/6, TNA.

[13] SP 43/66, TNA. On Delafaye, see J. C. Sainty, 'Delafaye, Charles (1677–1762)', *ODNB*; Michael Harris, 'Newspaper Distribution during Queen Anne's Reign: Charles Delafaye and the Secretary of State's Office', in *Studies in the Book Trade: In Honour of Graham Pollard*, edited by R. W. Hunt, I. G. Philip, and R. J. Roberts (Oxford: Oxford Bibliographical Society, 1975), pp. 139–51; and Black, *Press*, pp. 108, 115–16.

liable.[14] This had at least one advantage for the authorities: cases against printers and booksellers were often airtight. Legally speaking, to publish was simply to make public, a charge any bookseller had difficulty ducking if the offending pamphlet was found for sale in one's shop. Though some tried. Think of how many booksellers claimed that they hadn't read everything they sold—how were they to know that this title advocated Jacobitism, another called for the prime minister's impeachment, another pushed for every last Huguenot, dissenter, and Jew to be booted out of England?

The law was clear, though. In 1712 the courts ruled that it was 'not material whether he who disperses a Libel knew any Thing of the Contents'.[15] Five years later, during the trial of the bookseller George Strahan (or Strachan, father of William and grandfather to George and Andrew), the courts found that printers were presumed guilty of printing any libels found in their shops unless their innocence could be proven.[16] These rulings were shored up and expanded repeatedly over the succeeding decades.[17] In 1724, for instance, the courts ruled that printers were responsible for anything printed by their servants, even without their knowledge, a ruling confirmed in 1729 and then again in 1770.[18] Stationers could also be found guilty of printing if not publishing a libel, even if they had only served as compositor for a part.[19] No pleas of ignorance, no matter how genuine, were admissible.

As a result, those in the book trade had good reason to worry. Gone, supposedly, were the bad old days of Charles II and James II—the prepublication censorship, the toadying judges, the inquisitorial mad men like Roger L'Estrange—but the press remained a major point of concern, and any stationer worth his or her ink was sure to hear the rumblings of government crackdowns, deposed apprentices, and packages opened at the Post Office.[20] Almost every notable bookseller from this period faced some form of criminal investigation. One thinks of John Dunton—'A broken Bookseller and abusive scribler', as Pope

[14] Joseph F. Lowenstein, 'Legal Proofs and Corrected Readings: Press-Agency and the New Bibliography', in *The Production of English Renaissance Culture*, edited by David Lee Miller, Sharon O'Dair, and Harold Weber (Ithaca: Cornell University Press, 1994), p. 93.

[15] *R. v. Hurt* (1712), rpt. Williams Hawkins, *A Treatise of the Pleas of the Crown*, vol. 1 (London, 1716–1721), p. 194.

[16] Hanson, *Government*, p. 18.

[17] Tamara L. Hunt, 'Servants, Masters and Seditious Libel in Eighteenth-Century England', *Book History* 20 (2017): pp. 83–110.

[18] *R. v. Nutt* (1729), 1 Barn. 306 (K.B.), 94 Eng. Rep. 208; John Almon, *Memoirs of a Late Eminent Bookseller* (London, 1790), pp. 182, 185; and Hamburger, 'Seditious Libel', pp. 749, 752.

[19] *R. v. Knell* (1729), 1 Barn. 305–306 (K.B.), 94 Eng. Rep. 207–8.

[20] Darrick N. Taylor, 'L'Estrange His Life: Public and Persona in the Life and Career of Sir Roger L'Estrange' (PhD diss., University of Kansas, 2011); Hanson, *Government*, 41; Joad Raymond, 'The Newspaper, Public Opinion, and the Public Sphere in the Seventeenth Century', *Prose Studies* 21, no. 2 (1998): p. 109; Peter Fraser, *The Intelligence of the Secretaries of State and Their Monopoly of Licensed News, 1660–1688* (Cambridge: Cambridge University Press, 1956), pp. 20–5; and Alan Marshall, *Intelligence and Espionage in the Reign of Charles II, 1660–1685* (Cambridge: Cambridge University Press, 1994), ch. 2.

put it in his notes to the *Dunciad*—who is best remembered today as the founder, editor, and printer of the *Athenian Mercury*, a periodical premised on the existence of the fictional Athenian Society, which gathered to answer readers' questions. Or, inevitably, of Edmund Curll, whose frequent run-ins with the law, from at least 1709 on, have been expertly documented by Paul Baines and Pat Rogers.[21] Other members of the book trade were in constant, almost unending trouble.[22]

After the lapse of licensing in 1695, Philip Hamburger has shown, the authorities moved from an era of prepublication censorship to post-publication prosecution to regulate the press.[23] Moreover, such prosecutions seemingly worked—both on those who faced a trial and on onlookers in the trade who carefully considered just what could be printed and sold. Even failed prosecutions promoted self-censorship and had an important chilling effect.[24] This, we might say, was the larger objective of the authorities: not simply to secure convictions among guilty booksellers, but to devastate repeat offenders through costly legal procedures while also scaring off those in the trade without the stomach or means to withstand official scrutiny. *The Craftsman* argued that this was the precise function of '*seizing Persons and Papers*', '*strict Examinations, Commitments* and *Confinement*', demanding '*Bail*', issuing multi-year '*diverse Recognizances*', and forcing 'the Expence of *several Trials*, and of *preparing* for several others'. All had one goal: '*intimidating Booksellers, Printers* and *Publishers*'.[25]

As the most controversial anti-Walpole journal of the late 1720s and early 1730s, *The Craftsman* had good reason to worry. Its printer-publisher, Francklin, was repeatedly arrested between 1727 and 1731 alone.[26] After a few false starts, the government finally convicted him in 1731.[27] This was a major blow to Francklin, who was at his height in the early 1730s. The Francklin imprint appeared on more than thirty works in 1731—an astonishing number in an era when even the most enterprising publisher barely cracked twenty titles a year. After his conviction, Francklin went more or less underground, publishing almost exclusively apolitical

---

[21] Stephen Parks, *John Dunton and the English Book Trade: A Study of his Career with a Checklist of his Publications* (New York: Garland, 1976); and Paul Baines and Pat Rogers, *Edmund Curll, Bookseller* (Oxford: Oxford University Press, 2007), p. 34.

[22] See the depositions routinely given by stationers in KB10, TNA; Hanson, *Government*, pp. 36–83; and H. R. Plomer et al., *A Dictionary of the Printers and Booksellers who were at Work in England, Scotland and Ireland from 1668 to 1725* (Oxford: The Bibliographical Society, 1922) and *A Dictionary of the Printers and Booksellers who were at Work in England, Scotland and Ireland from 1726 to 1775* (Oxford: The Bibliographical Society, 1968), *passim*.

[23] Hamburger, 'Seditious Libel', 662.

[24] For more on this 'most arbitrary Punishment' and 'very oppressive...manner of Proceeding', see [Hugh Hume, Earl of Marchmont], *A Serious Exhortation to the Electors of Great Britain* (London, 1740), p. 16.

[25] *The Craftsman*, no. 179 (6 December 1729).

[26] Eckhart Hellmuth, 'Towards Hume—The Discourse on the Liberty of the Press in the Age of Walpole', *History of European Ideas* 44, no. 2 (2018): p. 161; and Roger Lund, '"An Alembick of Innuendos": Satire, Libel, and The Craftsman', *Philological Quarterly* 95, no. 2 (Spring 2016): p. 258.

[27] Increasingly, after 1730, the Crown employed 'special' juries (see ch. 6), a tactic it seemingly used to re-prosecute and finally convict Francklin, whom I in part focus on in ch. 5.

works between 1732 and 1739. Few of his titles from this period feature his name alone on the imprint. Instead, he distributed ownership and thus responsibility for his publications across a range of figures in the book trade or, more commonly, used a false imprint.[28] Anything even slightly touchy fell under a 'Haines' imprint—first Henry Haines and then his wife, M. Haines, after Henry was imprisoned in 1736.[29] In the decade following his conviction, the once brazen Francklin simply became more cautious. As he observed, the laws are 'like a Bogg, fair to the Eye and dangerous to the Tread'.[30] He trod carefully.

Across the century, the authorities systematically targeted prominent stationers to send a warning throughout the trade. The Jacobite printer and publisher Nathaniel Mist, proprietor of *Mist's Weekly Journal*, the most important and popular political periodical of the later 1710s and '20s (and the partial focus, along with *The Craftsman*, of my fifth chapter), had as many as fourteen run-ins with the law in a mere twelve years. To protect himself, Mist walked 'very carefully the fine line between what could be proved to be treasonable and what could not' and 'deliberately held back from political controversy... [at] difficult times'.[31] Others were equally cautious. Up until the late 1760s, the printer-bookseller John Almon had done a swift business in political muckraking as the opposition's go-to printer-bookseller. Increasingly, though, he had run into difficulties with the Crown.[32] He was one of six printers taken in for Junius's infamous 1769 Letter to the King.[33] Worst of all, he was the only one tried in government-friendly Westminster (the other cases took place in London) and the only one convicted and sentenced. Almon was fined and ordered to pay £800 as sureties for good behaviour for two years—and thus forced to keep his nose clean for the duration of his sentence.[34] Almon clearly saw the effect. 'This sentence, though calculated to appear light and moderate, is, in fact, most heavy, cruel and oppressive; as it amounts to a total prohibition of [Almon's] following his trade or business as a bookseller... without running the risque of forfeiture of the sum of eight hundred pounds; which would tend to [his] ruin'. Silencing him, he reasoned, 'was the sole object; for if [Almon] will print no more political pamphlets, he suffers nothing

---

[28] Caudle, 'Richard Francklin', table 18.1.

[29] Caudle, 'Richard Francklin', pp. 390–1. For Haines's version, see Henry Haines, *Treachery, Baseness, and Cruelty Display'd to the Full; in the Hardships and Sufferings of Mr. Henry Haines, Late Printer of the Country Journal, or, Craftsman* (London, 1740).

[30] SP 36/23/215–216, TNA.

[31] Paul Chapman, 'Mist, Nathaniel (d. 1737)', *ODNB*. For more on Mist, see Paul Kléber Monod, *Jacobitism and the English People, 1688–1788* (Cambridge: Cambridge University Press, 1989), pp. 29–37.

[32] Almon, *Memoirs*, p. 31.

[33] John Cannon (ed.), Introduction, *The Letters of Junius* (Oxford: Clarendon Press, 1978), pp. xv–xvi.

[34] Deborah D. Rogers, *Bookseller as Rogue: John Almon and the Politics of Eighteenth-Century Publishing* (New York: Peter Lang, 1986), p. 43.

from the sentence'.[35] And it worked. After his conviction, Almon shied away from political publications for two years, the exact period of his mandated 'good behaviour', opting instead to publish on literary issues or to reissue safe reprints of poems from earlier miscellanies.[36]

Moreover, the government believed that such prosecutions, even when unsuccessful, served an important cautionary role, one that promoted self-policing among writers, printers, and booksellers.[37] In 1731, for instance, a grand jury recommended 'Exemplary Punishment' of 'All the Authors, Actors Printers and Publishers' to serve as 'a Terror to All Offenders of the like kind for the future'.[38] The government simply knew that it could not go after every callous scribbler. Douglas Hay has shown that the administration of the criminal law was a balancing act between 'delicacy and circumspection' in the eighteenth century.[39] It needed to be administered tactically and selectively to be an effective tool for social regulation. Convictions were thus desirable but unnecessary, for the goal in most instances was financially to sabotage printers and booksellers while also warning others. Already in 1723 as much was clear. The *True Briton* noted that stationers were subject to 'daily arrests', and even if 'they should be discharg'd [,] ... such proceedings against them, will as certainly reduce them at length to want and a gaol'.[40] Decades later, Henry Sampson Woodfall, the lead publisher of the Junius letters, endured a similar campaign of harassment: he had been '*fined* by the House of Lords; confined by the court of the king's bench, and indicted at the Old Bailey'.[41] The lone function of prosecuting a prominent stationer like Woodfall, Junius argued, was 'stopping the press' more generally.[42]

Publishing the smutty, sensational, and scandalous was simply risky business. The authorities and their underlings were everywhere, and libel laws were vague— vague to the point of being seemingly ad hoc, as many stationers complained. From 1695 on, those in the book trade routinely found themselves interrogated and deposed, summoned to the House of Lords, reprimanded in the Commons,

---

[35] Almon, *Memoirs*, pp. 71, 74–5.   [36] Rogers, *Bookseller as Rogue*, pp. 49, 54n18.

[37] Siebert, *Freedom*, p. 380.   [38] KB 33/5/6, TNA.

[39] Douglas Hay, 'Property, Authority and the Criminal Law', in *Albion's Fatal Tree: Crime and Society in Eighteenth-Century England*, rev. ed., edited by Douglas Hay, et al. (New York: Verso, 2011), pp. 49–65, *passim*. On the selectiveness of government censorship, in response to particular events and publications, see Blair Worden, 'Literature and Political Censorship in Early Modern England', in *Too Mighty to Be Free: Censorship and the Press in Britain and the Netherlands*, edited by A. C. Duke and C. A. Tamse (Zutphen: De Walburg Press, 1987), ch. 3; Cyndia Susan Clegg, *Press Censorship in Caroline England* (Cambridge: Cambridge University Press, 2008), *Press Censorship in Elizabethan England* (Cambridge: Cambridge University Press, 1997), and *Press Censorship in Jacobean England* (Cambridge: Cambridge University Press, 1991); and Debora Shuger, *Censorship and Cultural Sensibility: The Regulation of Language in Tudor–Stuart England* (Philadelphia: University of Pennsylvania Press, 2006).

[40] *True Briton* 18 (2 August 1723).

[41] Donald W. Nichols, *Literary Anecdotes of the Eighteenth Century*, 6 vol., vol. 1 (London, 1812–1814), p. 301.

[42] Junius to Woodfall (November 1771), *The Letters of Junius*, edited by John Cannon (Oxford: Clarendon Press, 1978), p. 378.

dragged into the courts, and pilloried, fined, and imprisoned. This was no secret among those in the trade and was routinely commented on in the London papers. For all of the risk, however, there remained the economic rewards, and not every bookseller found him- or herself in court. Scandal, granted, was the surest commodity. But the question wasn't what sells; it was how one was to sell it. Some got away. How?

2.2 The Act of Anne: Authorship, Ownership, and the Authorities

Those in the book trade were the first port of call for the authorities, and authors often expected their publishers to take the fall for their writings. In emphasizing this aspect of the relationship between authors and booksellers, my goal in this section is to focus attention on a lesser-studied aspect of eighteenth-century intellectual property law. Research on the advent of intellectual property has largely focused on contemporary debates about the privileges provided by and the limitations of the Act of Anne (1709/10): who owned the property, whether ownership preceded the act, and how long that ownership remained in place after composition, publication, and revision.[43]

This emphasis on the technical dimensions of the law has produced important work, but it has also occluded how authors and booksellers simultaneously used copyright law to shield themselves.[44] This same act raised vexing questions about how a written work could be a property; who retained the ownership of and thus responsibility for a work; and how one could exploit the ambiguities and weaknesses of cultural policing through the thimblerig of ownership. As Jody Greene has shown, the Act of Anne could be a double-edged sword for authors: it not only provided them with formal copyright protections but also increased the degree of

---

[43] For an important recent exception, see Trevor Ross, *Writing in Public: Literature and the Liberty of the Press in Eighteenth-Century Britain* (Baltimore: Johns Hopkins University Press, 2018), chs. 1 and 2.

[44] See, for instance, Simon Stern, 'From Author's Right to Property Right', *University of Toronto Law Journal* 62 (2012): pp. 29–91, 'Copyright, Originality, and the Public Domain in Eighteenth-Century England', in *Originality and Intellectual Property in the French and English Enlightenment*, edited by Reginald McGinnis (New York: Routledge, 2009), pp. 69–101, and '*Tom Jones* and the Economies of Copyright', *Eighteenth-Century Fiction* 9, no. 4 (1997): pp. 429–44; Jody Greene, *The Trouble with Ownership: Literary Property and Authorial Liability in England, 1660–1730* (Philadelphia: University of Pennsylvania Press, 2005); Ronan Deazley, *On the Origin of the Right to Copy: Charting the Movement of Copyright Law in Eighteenth-Century Britain (1695–1775)* (Oxford: Hart, 2004); John Feather, *Publishing, Piracy and Politics: An Historical Study of Copyright in Britain* (New York: Mansell, 1994); Martha Woodmansee, *The Author, Art and the Market: Rereading the History of Aesthetics* (New York: Columbia University Press, 1994); and Mark Rose, *Authors and Owners: The Invention of Copyright* (Cambridge: Harvard University Press, 1993).

their legal liability.[45] At the same time, I would argue, copyright in many ways could be used to mitigate an author's responsibility for a work, a kind of reverse indemnification through an informal verbal agreement. For the very reason that ownership could be formally attributed, authors were able to exchange the economic benefits of copyright for a higher degree of legal safety. In the eighteenth-century book trade, it was 'established practice' for authors to assign outright their rights over a new work to the bookseller who would publish it.[46] In exchange for those rights, the bookseller-publisher took on responsibility for a work, obscuring the author's involvement and withholding his or her name in those frequent instances in which they were called to account.

On the whole, such a strategy worked well. Take Swift. During his forty-year career as an author, his works were subject to criminal prosecutions and civil actions in both Ireland and England a remarkable number of times.[47] Yet Swift himself was never once prosecuted or even, seemingly, officially examined. Moreover, there is little evidence that those who had hoped to bring an action against his writings knew of his authorship—and, in those rare instances when they had found him out, there remained no way to prove it. How did such a pugnacious and polemical author, and especially one of such considerable renown from at least 1708 on, manage to avoid litigation over so many decades?[48]

To avoid prosecution, the holders of Swift's copyrights often edited his texts considerably (a strategy I discuss in the final section of this chapter) and withheld his name when called to account. Those in the book trade simply took on legal responsibility for Swift's publications in exchange for copyrights. If they kept up their end of the bargain, the same figures put themselves in a position to secure further copyrights for future Swift works. In 1732, for instance, when the grandfathered protections for his pre-April 1710 works were set to expire, Swift assigned all of his copyrights to the bookseller William Bowyer, through Matthew Pilkington.[49] As he wrote, with his usual guardedness, 'I do here without specifying the sd Papers, give all manner of Right I may be thought to have in the sd Papers, to Mr Mathew [*sic*] Pilkington aforesd, who informs me that he intends to

[45] Greene, *Trouble with Ownership*, Introduction, *passim*, and ch. 4. On the conflation of legal and aesthetic authorship, and the frequent conflation of authorship and liability, see Robert J. Griffin, 'Anonymity and Authorship', *New Literary History* 30, no. 4 (Autumn 1999): pp. 877–95, esp. 889–91.

[46] Betty A. Schellenberg, 'The Eighteenth Century: Print, Professionalization, and Defining the Author', in *The Cambridge Handbook of Literary Authorship*, edited by Ingo Berensmeyer, Gert Buelens, and Marysa Demoor (Cambridge: Cambridge University Press, 2019), p. 140.

[47] Sabine Baltes, '"The Grandson of that Ass Quin": Swift and Chief Justice Whitshed', *Swift Studies* 23 (2008): pp. 126–46.

[48] Stephen Karian, *Jonathan Swift in Print and Manuscript* (Cambridge: Cambridge University Press, 2010), p. 45.

[49] Ian Gadd, 'Leaving the Printer to His Liberty: Swift and the London Book Trade, 1701–1714', in *Jonathan Swift and the Eighteenth-Century Book*, edited by Paddy Bullard and James McLaverty (Cambridge: Cambridge University Press, 2013), p. 57.

give up the sd right to Mr Bowyer aforesd'.[50] Swift predictably worked with the same cluster of individuals in the London book trade—figures like the bookseller Benjamin Tooke, Jr, and the printer John Barber, who were responsible for almost all of Swift's London publications between 1701 and 1714—who had proven their allegiance and those who, unknowingly, had been appending their names to the imprints that had accompanied Swift's anonymous publications all along.[51]

Members of the book trade were simply expected to take the fall for their authors. This was a biblio-ethical covenant of sorts, an often unspoken and implicitly understood agreement between booksellers hungry for works and authors hoping to maintain an arm's length distance from them. (The exception was the exceptional Edmund Curll, who regularly squealed on authors and printers to protect himself.)[52] For the most part, those in the book trade held fast under interrogation, in interviews, and during depositions, often performed by the Secretary of State for the Southern Department, his undersecretaries, or those at the Attorney General's office. Stationers who ratted out their authors and co-conspirators were ostracized from the trade. Think only of poor Michael Curry, the printer for John Wilkes's private press—an idiotic affair, no doubt, as Richard Grenville, Lord Temple pointed out to the improvident Wilkes, urging him to get rid of the thing.[53] Curry was blacklisted by his fellow stationers for giving information against Wilkes. 'His treachery was deemed so ignominious', the Gentleman's Magazine reported, 'that no person in the metropolis would ever afterwards give him employment, considering the offence of the greatest magnitude to a profession in which secrecy is essentially requisite'.[54] Curry, though, was in an odd situation. Many stationers, especially those being secretly funded by an opposition figure, had only a faint or circumstantial sense of who their authors were. And yet Curry was hardly alone, as Laurence Hanson has shown in his catalogue of those squeezed from the trade for snitching. Think only of John Matthews' apprentice, who turned government patsy: at his funeral a pack of journeyman printers showed up simply to insult his corpse.[55]

[50] Swift (22 July 1732), MS Eng. 827, Hought.L.

[51] The Act of Anne did not apply to Ireland until the Importation Act of 1739, though Dublin booksellers had their own arrangements (M. Pollard, Dublin's Trade in Books, 1550–1800 [Oxford: Clarendon Press, 1989], p. 71). Swift maintained similarly close relationships with his Dublin stationers, including John Harding and then his widow, Sarah, and then, from the 1730s on, George Faulkner. See Adam Rounce, 'Swift's Texts between Dublin and London', in Jonathan Swift and the Eighteenth-Century Book, edited by Paddy Bullard and James McLaverty (Cambridge: Cambridge University Press, 2013), ch. 10. For more, see M. Pollard, 'Who's for Prison? Publishing Swift in Dublin', Swift Studies 14 (1999): pp. 37–49 and A Dictionary of Members of the Dublin Book Trade 1550–1800 (London: Bibliographical Society, 2000), passim; Michael Treadwell, 'Swift's Relations with the London Book Trade to 1714', in Author/Publisher Relations During the Eighteenth and Nineteenth Centuries, edited by Robin Myers and Michael Harris (Oxford: Oxford Polytechnic Press, 1983), ch. 1; and Gadd, 'Leaving the printer to his liberty', ch. 2.

[52] Baines and Rogers, Edmund Curll, p. 7.   [53] Rogers, Bookseller as Rogue, p. 22.

[54] Gentleman's Magazine 58 (July–December 1788), p. 752.   [55] Hanson, Government, p. 52.

Protecting authors was one element of a relationship that was, at its core, primarily economic. Those in the book trade needed authors with juicy goods, and authors expected a level of protection from those who profited by their risk. Some were more steadfast than others. Horace Walpole was certain that Almon, the bookseller behind Wilkes's *North Briton*, was not to be trusted (even if Walpole had secretly employed Almon in 1764 to distribute his own political pamphlets).[56] As he cautioned William Mason, who had anonymously published his satiric *An Heroic Epistle to Sir William Chambers* in 1773 through that 'rogue' Almon, 'remember if he guesses the author, that you must manage him. Money will be offered him to tell, and he will take it and tell'.[57] Walpole's paranoia proved misguided. In 1805, Almon wholeheartedly denied that Mason was the author of anything he had ever published; he even claimed not to know who the author was.[58] And Mason, it seems, had grown to trust Almon.[59] As he later wrote of his anonymous satires,

Bind in poetic sheaves the plenteous crop,
And stack my full-ear'd load in ALMON's shop.[60]

Others trusted him too. 'I think I may say without vanity', Almon wrote decades later, 'that no man now alive was more in Temple's confidence from the year 1762 till his death'.[61] Others also suspected it. Almon was known publicly as 'Temple's man', and their entire bibliographical affair was recounted in a satirical 'Dialogue between Vamp and his Patron'.[62] Almon, in fact, spent years covertly publishing works by not only Temple, Mason, Walpole, and Wilkes, but also Charles Townshend, Christopher Smart, William Knox, John Hall Stevenson, and Charles Lloyd.[63] Years later, in 1784, he was hired by members of the 'Whig

---

[56] Robert R. Rea, 'Mason, Walpole, and That Rogue Almon', *Huntington Library Quarterly* 23, no. 2 (February 1960): p. 188.

[57] Walpole to Mason (14 January 1774), *Yale Edition of the Correspondence of Horace Walpole*, 48 vol., edited by W. S. Lewis, et al., vol. 8 (New Haven: Yale University Press, 1937–1983), p. 402.

[58] Rea, 'Mason, Walpole, and That Rogue Almon', pp. 192–3.

[59] Mason to Walpole (7 May 1773), *Correspondence of Horace Walpole*, vol. 28, p. 82.

[60] Mason, 'Heroic Postscript', in *Poetical Works* (London, 1805), p. 29.

[61] Almon to [?] (6 September 1804), Correspondence and Papers, [c.1760–1808], MS f. 84, NYHS.

[62] Almon, *Memoirs*, p. 32; and 'A Dialogue between Vamp and his Patron', in *A Letter to the Right Honourable The E— T—* (London, 1766), pp. v–xvi.

[63] Rogers, *Bookseller as Rogue*, 12. See Almon, Correspondence and Papers, [c.1760–1808], 1, f. 1.15, NYHS. For the relationship of the press to government propaganda, see J. A. Downie, *Robert Harley and the Press: Propaganda and Public Option in the Age of Swift and Defoe* (Cambridge: Cambridge University Press, 1979); Bertrand A. Goldgar, *Walpole and the Wits: The Relation of Politics to Literature, 1722–1742* (Lincoln: University of Nebraska Press, 1976); Tone Sundt Urstad, *Sir Robert Walpole's Poets: The Use of Literature as Pro-Government Propaganda, 1721-1742* (Newark: University of Delaware Press, 1999); John Brewer, *Party Ideology and Popular Politics at the Accession of George III* (Cambridge: Cambridge University Press, 1976), esp. chs. 8 and 11; and Paul Korshin, 'Types of Eighteenth-Century Literary Patronage', *Eighteenth-Century Studies* 7, no. 4 (Summer 1974): pp. 453–73.

Club', which included the Duke of Portland, Earl Fitzwilliam, Sheridan, and Lord Robert Spencer, to print propaganda in the *General Advertiser* in exchange for a tidy £300 a year. Party publishing paid handsomely, and Almon seems to have had no qualms about taking dirty money. As Horace Walpole acidly remarked, he retired with 'a fortune of £10,000 by publishing and selling libels'.[64]

The same held true for Woodfall, who was the most reliable choice according to many part-time satirist-politicians. Woodfall regularly printed anonymous pieces by John Montagu, the fourth earl of Sandwich, Lord George Gordon, John Horne Tooke, and Wilkes. Many authors simply treasured their anonymity, even for the most innocuous publications.[65] Think only of Woodfall's most infamous correspondent, the pseudonymous Junius (perhaps Sir Philip Francis, the leading if by no means certain author of the letters, among some sixty others who have been trotted out over the centuries).[66] Between 21 January 1769 and 21 January 1772, Woodfall published nearly seventy letters by Junius in the *Public Advertiser*. These were deeply ironic, lashingly satiric works of High Whig philosophy, which lashed George III and the Tory administrations of the Duke of Grafton and Lord North. They were, as one biographer has put it, 'one of the most effective uses of slanderous polemic ever employed in English political controversy'.[67] During those three years, Junius was also at his height, the scathing critic against whom no one was safe. As Edmund Burke complained in November 1770 in the Commons, 'How comes the Junius to have broke through the cobwebs of the law, and to range uncontrolled, unpunished, through the land? ... No sooner has he wounded one than he lays down another dead at his feet'.[68] (Burke would finally find some satisfaction years later, in 1784, in an action against Woodfall for libel. Burke won the case, though perhaps not as decidedly as he had hoped. He had claimed damages of £5,000; the jury felt £100 was more appropriate.)[69] Yet for all of the hardship Woodfall faced, he kept mum about Junius's identity—he seemingly had no idea who his most infamous author was.

In the world of libels and lampoons, the cooperation of intermediaries remained critical. Swift, for instance, often employed an endless chain of hands merely to bring a work to press. Take *An Epistle to a Lady* (1733), a cutting satiric apologia laced with a few well-placed jibes at parliament, George II ('the strutting chatt'ring Vermin...the brisk Baboon'), and Walpole (by whom 'the Helm is

---

[64] Horace Walpole, *Memoirs of the Reign of King George III*, 4 vol., edited by G. F. Russell Barkey, et al., vol. 3 (London: Lawrence and Bullen, 1894), p. 83, 4.106.

[65] Thomas Eagles to R. D. Woodforde (23 June 1787), 'Letters on Literature', Osborn c252, Bein.L.

[66] See *Letters of Junius*, pp. 540–72. As early as 1783, Almon pointed to Hugh Macaulay Boyd as the author of the Junius letters. See John Almon, Correspondence and Papers, [c.1760–1808], 1, f. 1.7 and Almon to George Chalmers (25 August 1800), 2, f. 6.1, NYHS.

[67] Francesco Cordasco, 'Junius (fl. 1768–1773)', *ODNB*.

[68] *Parliamentary History* (27 November 1770), 16. p. 1154.

[69] Hannah Barker, 'Woodfall, Henry Sampson (1739–1805)', *ODNB*.

rul'd').[70] In this instance, Mary Barber, one of Swift's protégés, transported a packet of poems—copied in someone else's hand—from Dublin to London and gave them to Matthew Pilkington, another protégé. Pilkington passed the manuscripts on to Benjamin Motte, Jr, who had a part in a publishing firm owned by Benjamin Tooke, Jr, with whom Swift had worked before.[71] Through Motte's connection to *The Grub-Street Journal*, he persuaded Lawton Gilliver to bring the manuscript to print, promising to pay half of his legal expenses if the poem led to a prosecution. Gilliver then convinced Samuel Aris to print the piece and paid John Wilford, who also had a share in *The Grub-Street Journal*, to act as its trade publisher, appending his name to the imprint, though knowing nothing of the poem's authorship.[72]

With the *Epistle*, Swift got off the hook—though just barely. Over a twenty-day period, between 11 and 30 January 1733/4, almost everyone involved in the publication snitched. Predictably, Wilford was the first to be arrested. He fingered Aris, the printer. Aris then pointed to Gilliver, who implicated Pilkington and Motte. Pilkington then squealed on Mary Barber.[73] But Barber held strong, refusing to name Swift. Unable to get to the author, the Crown decided to charge Barber with 'making' a libel that upset the peace and causing it to be published.[74] In the Crown's information against Barber, three sets of lines were identified as libellous. The first set (ll. 155–72) compares the king and Commons to slaves, ruled by Walpole, before the speaker's most violent shot—'I would hang them if I cou'd' (l. 170). The second set (ll. 221–30) is little better. Swift attacks parliament and the king, who are loaded with 'Vices odious' (l. 226). The final set (ll. 239–44) is more ambiguous, comparing the 'Lady' gently chastised in the poem to the king while calling the House of Commons, indirectly, 'Hirelings' (l. 244). Despite the testimony of so many witnesses, Barber's trial never got off the ground. Again and again, it was delayed until the Attorney General, John Willes, in May 1735 caused a *nolle prosequi*, putting an end to the prosecution.[75] The failed prosecution of Barber is neither here nor there. She eventually got off (though perhaps with the help of John Barber, no relation, who might have meddled in the case, as he had

---

[70] *An Epistle to a Lady* (London, 1734 [1733]), pp. 152–70.

[71] Treadwell, 'Swift's Relations', pp. 9–11.

[72] As Pope had earlier, Gilliver seems to have fudged the imprint, which states Dublin as the site of publication. It wasn't, as Lord Harrington, Secretary of State for the Northern Department, was later to find out. See his letter to the Attorney General, John Willes, SP 63/396, f. 124, TNA.

[73] SP 44/83, 123–124, TNA. See McLaverty, 'Lawton Gilliver: Pope's Bookseller', *Studies in Bibliography* 32 (1979): p. 119; and John Irwin Fischer, 'The Legal Response to Swift's *The Public Spirit of the Whigs*', in *Swift and his Contexts*, edited by John Irwin Fischer, et al. (New York: AMS Press, 1989), p. 43.

[74] To assist or even encourage the publication of a libel was criminal; moreover, to write down a libel for the first time was to 'make' it and such making was an offence (though not second and third 'makings'), even if never published. *Rex v. Paine* (1696), 5 Modern 163 (KB), 87 Eng. Rep. 584. See Hamburger, 'Seditious Libel', pp. 726–8.

[75] John Irwin Fischer, 'The Government's Response to Swift's "An Epistle to a Lady"', *Philological Quarterly* 65, no. 1 (Winter 1986): pp. 39–59.

on behalf of Francklin during an earlier *Craftsman* trial).[76] The point is that Swift's roundabout efforts to preserve his anonymity and to shield himself from later legal entanglements, typical of the satiric book trade, ultimately worked. With the *Epistle*, Swift came closest in his career to being fingered. Luckily, Barber stepped in and took the blow, perhaps in appreciation of and in implicit exchange for the four letters Swift had written on her behalf to drum up subscriptions for her forthcoming collection of poems.[77]

Swift was hardly alone in his comically circuitous means. Junius also faced the problem of getting his letters to Woodfall. Public meetings would vanquish his disguise, and the Post Office, run by the government, could not be trusted. Instead, mail between the two of them, addressed sometimes to either William Middleton or John Fretley, was left at one of three coffeehouses roughly a mile from Woodfall's shop.[78] Wilkes struck upon a similar ruse with Almon.[79] After being exiled to France, Wilkes had his letters delivered by hand, using his friend, Humphrey Coates.[80] Years later, in 1767, when he was back in London, he directed Almon to send correspondence through three successive contact points: to a Mary Jackson, either through Mr Tukes, a distiller in Fleet St, or through another address in Westminster; or to Abraham Long through Samuel Bladon, a bookseller in Paternoster Row.[81] 'I shall know whether there has been any trick or mistake in the delivery of any of them', Wilkes explained. If a letter materialized at Bladon's before another found its way to him through Jackson, then someone had found them out.[82]

Getting information from printer to author could be even more complicated. Whenever Woodfall had a package for Junius, for instance, he printed a signal in the *Public Advertiser*. Cloak and dagger, perhaps, but early on Woodfall proved a clumsy encrypter. Junius wrote privately to Woodfall, telling him to 'direct a letter to Mr. William Middleton, to be left at the bar of the new Exchange Coffee house'.[83] Admittedly, there were plenty of coffeehouses in the Strand, but Woodfall's first signal, from 18 July 1769, almost let the cat out of the bag. 'Reasons why the Hint was not printed are sent to the last-mentioned Coffeehouse in the Strand, from whence our *old* Correspondent will be pleased to send for them'.[84] He did little better on his second attempt, two days later, letting anyone smart enough to notice that Woodfall had supplied Junius's pseudonym: 'Mr. *William Middleton*'s Letter is sent as desired'.[85] At this point Junius stepped

[76] Hanson, *Government*, p. 23; Fischer, '*Epistle*', pp. 51–2.

[77] See Swift to Mrs. Caesar (30 July 1733), to Sir Andrew Fountaine (30 July 1733), to the Earl of Orrery (2 Aug. 1733), and to the Earl of Oxford (2 Aug. 1733), *Correspondence of Swift*, vol. 3, pp. 677–84.

[78] Cannon, *Letters of Junius*, p. 533.   [79] Almon, *Memoirs*, pp. 30, 38, 40.

[80] Add. MS 30868, f. 136, BL.   [81] Plomer, et al., *Dictionary, 1726–1775*, p. 27.

[82] Add. MS 30869, ff. 110, 119, 123, BL.

[83] Junius to Woodfall (15 July 1769), *Letters of Junius*, p. 349.

[84] *Public Advertiser* 10832 (16 July 1769).   [85] *Public Advertiser* 10834 (20 July 1769).

in. 'Whenever you have any thing to communicate to me', he explained to Woodfall, perhaps with some early hints of frustration, 'let the hint be thus *C at the usual place* & so direct to Mr. John Fretley at the same Coffee house'.[86] Over the next three months, into the fall of 1769, Woodfall did as he was told.[87] Likely worrying that the disguise had grown thin, Junius suggested a new code word: 'say only *a Letter*, when you have occasion to write to me again.—I shall understand you'.[88]

Over the next year, Woodfall alternated between code words, including 'A Letter', 'This Day', and 'C'.[89] But, again, Junius sought to change the signals. 'When you send to me, instead of the usual signal, say, *Vindex shall be considered*'.[90] Woodfall, again, did what he was told, though rather to the letter than the spirit. A few days later, an exasperated Junius was back at him. 'Don't always use the same signal.—any absurd Latin verse will answer the purpose'.[91] Woodfall understood and over the next two years inserted Latin tags largely from Horace, Virgil, Cicero, and Persius. For the most part, they seemingly had no bearing on the letters themselves, but occasionally Woodfall was clever enough to use his code words to other ends. Sometimes these were harmless enough, if ultimately rather silly, like a bad Latin pun, thanks to the drop spot at Munday's Coffee-House: 'Sic *transit Gloria* Mundy'.[92] But they also occasionally served a real purpose. In the 18 January 1772 issue of the *Public Advertiser*, Woodfall used the code word to signal a change in location. 'Mutare *necessarium est*' (it is necessary to change).[93] At another point, Woodfall signalled to Junius that 'the *usual Method* of Conveyancing is shut up', owing to a frosty January, before adding 'Sat verbum Sapienti' (a word to the wise).[94]

Such bizarrely elaborate evasions and workarounds were in fact essential, if authors were to conceal their identities and if booksellers were to protect those behind their most valuable commodities. The larger point worth observing is that copyright, rather than merely being a tool through which the government could tie authors and publishers by their own admission to potentially illicit works, could afford authors a degree of protection. Some booksellers felt the economic benefits of copyright holdings easily exceeded their legal risks. Protecting authors was only one part of a larger equation, however. Not getting caught altogether had its obvious advantages. It was foolish to leave an overtly scandalous work lying about in one's shop. It made more sense to hold some wares below the counter or distribute them by subterfuge. Apparently, booksellers looking to tip off

[86] Junius to Woodfall (21 July 1769), *Letters of Junius*, p. 351.

[87] See the signal to Junius, 'C. in the usual Place', in *The Public Advertiser* 10883 (16 September 1769).

[88] Junius to Woodfall (12 November 1769), *Letters of Junius*, p. 357.

[89] See, for instance, *The Public Advertiser* 10934 (16 November 1769).

[90] *Letters of Junius* letter 42.   [91] *Letters of Junius*, letter 44.

[92] *Public Advertiser* 11779 (23 December 1772).

[93] *Public Advertiser* 11615 (18 January 1772).   [94] *Public Advertiser* 11616 (20 January 1772).

smut-hunting customers needed only to have a 'naked male figure' in the shop, as *The Times* reported, to let them know 'what *kinds of books* the proprietor had to dispose of'.[95] Such evasions abounded in the London book trade. Customers on the hunt for scandal simply needed to know where to look and how to read the coded bibliographical signals so cautiously laid out for them.

2.3 Deception and Detection: Projecting Readers, Evading the Authorities

Given the perils of publishing the seditious and the obscene, the blasphemous and the defamatory, those in the book trade employed a host of evasions to duck the authorities. Printers and booksellers knew that they were under routine if haphazard surveillance and that it was foolish to parade their most incendiary wares without a layer of subterfuge. This, though, was part of a delicate balancing act. How could booksellers both evade the authorities while also effectively advertising their most contentious and thus perhaps most saleable wares to customers? The answer in large measure was the title page, the main point of entry for any reader and a code that often furnished a potential buyer with clues about its contents.[96] In what follows, I lay out the semiotics of such illicit satires: how the title, its purported author, and its imprint served both to confuse authorities and to signal discerning readers.

Title pages during this period were rife with meaning. As Jerome McGann has written, 'Every literary work that descends to us operates through the deployment of a double helix of perceptual codes: the linguistic codes, on one hand, and the bibliographical codes on the other'.[97] This was perhaps at no point truer than in the eighteenth century, when readers were expected to interpret not only titles but title *pages*. Titles were only one piece of information; moreover, they could be just as misleading as imprints, which contained the supposed (and yet often doctored) city of publication, stationers' names, and their places of business. We might even say that misleading is the wrong word. Title pages created misdirection, but they also furnished readers with crucial information which, when read suspiciously, intuitively, critically, and closely, told one more about a work than the most accurate title page could. As Catherine Gallagher has observed, this was an era

---

[95] *The Times* (20 August 1788).

[96] James Raven, *The Business of Books: Booksellers and the English Book Trade, 1450–1850* (New Haven: Yale University Press, 2007), pp. 55, 112, 170–1, 177; and Nicolas Barker, 'Typography and the Meaning of Words: The Revolution in the Layout of Books in the Eighteenth Century', in *Buch und Buchhandel in Europa im achtzehnten Jahrhundert*, edited by Giles Barber and Bernhard Fabian (Hamburg: Hauswedell, 1981), pp. 127–65, esp. 129, 131.

[97] Jerome J. McGann, *The Textual Condition* (Princeton: Princeton University Press, 1991), p. 77.

when one had the 'desire to open every book to some extra-textual reality, to read everything double'.[98]

Think only of how often titles were both a disguise and a code. Curll, a 'Manufacturer of Sodomy', as Daniel Defoe put it in his most puritanical language, hid some of his bawdiest publications behind titles that were ostensibly only works of medicine.[99] Curll capitalized on a tradition that held throughout the century, as other enterprising pornographers dished out the mildly salacious and outright obscene as supposed works of medicine and natural philosophy. Thus the *Natural History of the Frutex Vulvaria, Or Flowering Shrub* (1732), an earthy botanical guide featuring the research of Leonard Fucksius, or *The Electrical Eel, or Gymnotus Electricus* (1777), a lewd poem that punningly capitalized on (and satirized) a spate of published experiments in the mid-1770s. The squeamish bookseller John Murray knew exactly how obscenity was camouflaged. He was cautious about publishing even actual medical texts or home cures for venereal disease, lest they be taken the wrong way.[100] Other titles were just as pregnant with half-veiled signals. The writer-bookseller John Dunton, for instance, dressed up his mildly salacious guide to London prostitutes, *The Night Walker; Or, Evening Rambles in Search after Lewd Women, with the Conferences held with Them* (1694?), as the missionary work of a concerned Christian looking to convert so many souls given over to contamination.[101]

But most pornography was disguised, sometimes shabbily, behind double entendres. An author's name, at first glimpse barely meaningful, could quickly morph into something as smutty as a well-thumbed *L'école des filles*. Take *A New Description of Merryland* (Figure 2.1), a work of what we might call 'erotic topography' (all 'Rivers, Canals, &c.' described with schoolboy subtlety: 'At the End of the Great Canal toward the *Terra Firma*, are two Forts called LBA ... There are two other pleasant little Mountains, called BBY').[102] The piece was ostensibly authored by the pseudonymous Roger Pheuquewell, a four-letter word perhaps only clear when spoken aloud. Even then, the name was cautiously broken up by a calculated hyphen and lodged safely in the volume's sexually suggestive preface (Figure 2.2).[103] Other pseudonyms announced themselves more brazenly: Captain

---

[98] Catherine Gallagher, *Nobody's Story: The Vanishing Acts of Women Writers in the Marketplace, 1670–1820* (Berkeley: University of California Press, 1994), p. 124.

[99] *Daniel Defoe: His Life and Recently Discovered Writings*, edited by William Lee, vol. 2 (London, 1869), p. 32; Baines and Rogers, *Edmund Curll*, pp. 109–10, 114–17.

[100] William Zachs, *The First John Murray and the Late Eighteenth-Century Book Trade: With a Checklist of his Publications* (New York: The British Academy, Oxford University Press, 1998), p. 176.

[101] Parks, *John Dunton*, p. 72.

[102] [Thomas Stretzer], *A New Description of Merryland*, 2nd ed. (Bath [London], 1741, for W. Jones [Edmund Curll]), pp. 15, 28. In 1745 the printer-bookseller Thomas Read was deposed for the never-published 'A Compleat Set of Charts of the Coasts of Merryland', an illustrated version; in one of the great losses to the genre, the plates were seemingly destroyed. See SP 36/70/67 and SP 36/65, TNA.

[103] [Stretzer], *A New Description of Merryland*, pp. i. The strategic hyphen, despite different type-settings, is present in all of the editions I have been able to view.

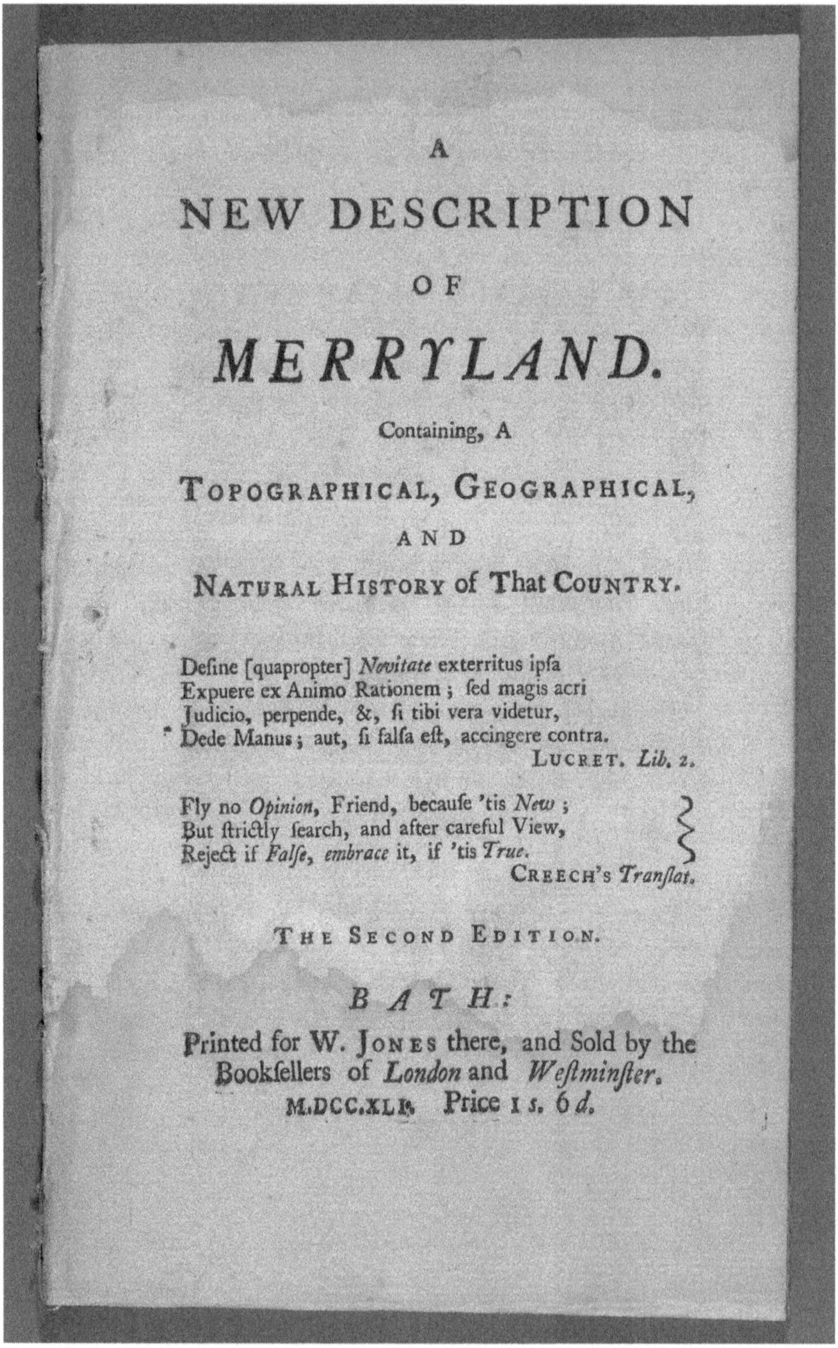

A

NEW DESCRIPTION

O F

MERRYLAND.

Containing, A

TOPOGRAPHICAL, GEOGRAPHICAL,

AND

NATURAL HISTORY of That COUNTRY.

Define [quapropter] *Novitate* exterritus ipfa
Expuere ex Animo Rationem ; fed magis acri
Judicio, perpende, &, fi tibi vera videtur,
Dede Manus ; aut, fi falfa eft, accingere contra.
                                    LUCRET. *Lib. 2.*

Fly no *Opinion*, Friend, becaufe 'tis *New* ;
But ftrictly fearch, and after careful View,
Reject if *Falfe*, *embrace* it, if 'tis *True*.
                                    CREECH's *Tranflat.*

THE SECOND EDITION.

B A T H :

Printed for W. JONES there, and Sold by the
Bookfellers of *London* and *Weftminfter.*
M.DCC.XLI. Price 1 *s.* 6 *d.*

Figure 2.1 [Thomas Stretzer], Titlepage, *A New Description of Merryland*, 2nd ed. (Bath [i.e., London], 1741, for W. Jones [pseud. Edmund Curll]). The Huntington Library (309238)

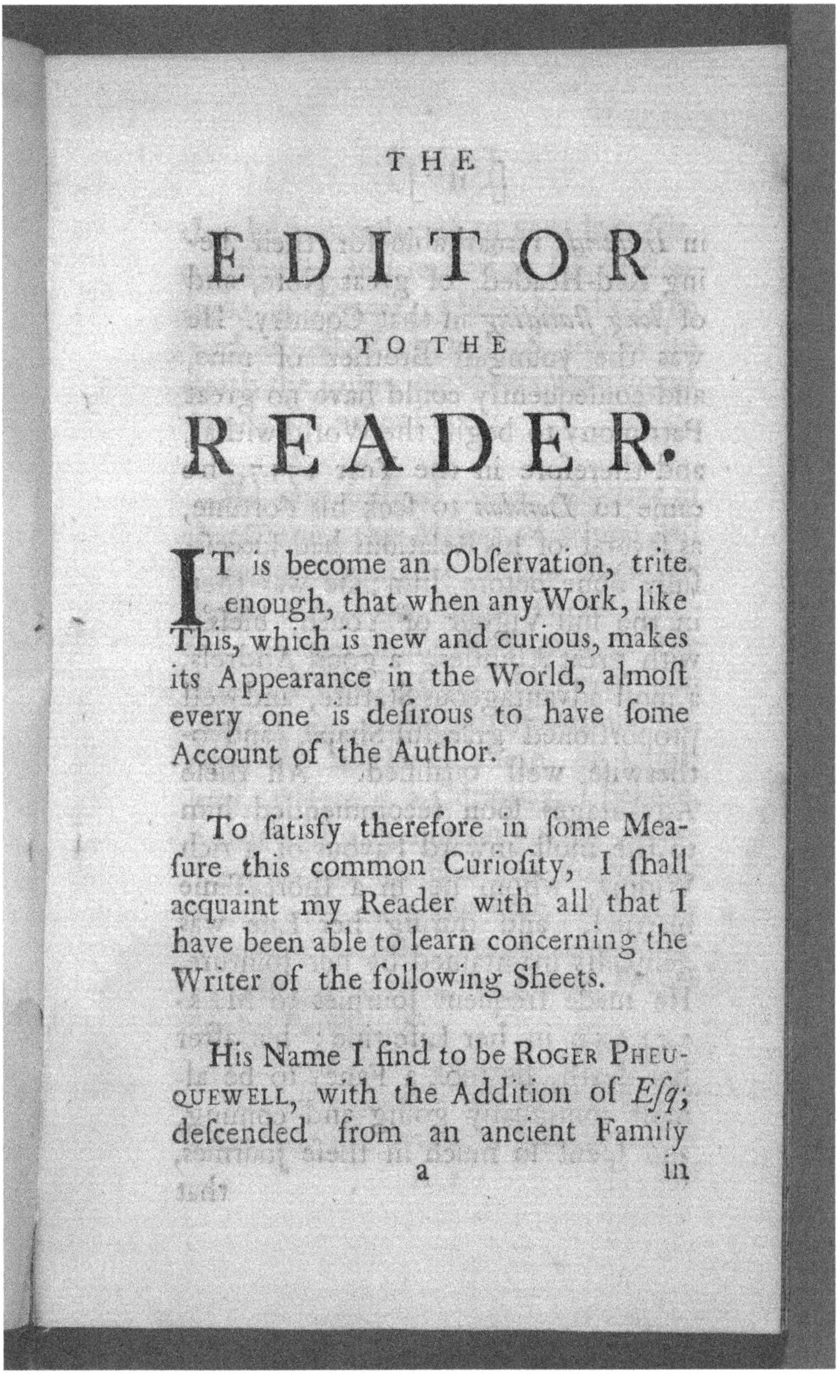

THE

EDITOR

TO THE

READER.

IT is become an Obſervation, trite enough, that when any Work, like This, which is new and curious, makes its Appearance in the World, almoſt every one is deſirous to have ſome Account of the Author.

To ſatisfy therefore in ſome Meaſure this common Curioſity, I ſhall acquaint my Reader with all that I have been able to learn concerning the Writer of the following Sheets.

His Name I find to be ROGER PHEUQUEWELL, with the Addition of *Eſq;* deſcended from an ancient Family

a in

Figure 2.2 [Thomas Stretzer], 'Editor to the Reader', in *A New Description of Merryland*, 2nd ed. (Bath [i.e., London], 1741, for W. Jones [pseud. Edmund Curll]), p. i. The Huntington Library (309238)

Samuel Cock, Philogynes Clitorides, Thomas Longtool, or Timothy Touchit.[104] The point is that title pages and authors, rather than being purely descriptive or deceptive, were also allusive. Like the verbally ambiguous language that saturated the satires they mediated, title pages needed to be interpreted by readers.

Imprints were both the clearest and yet most confusing port of entry for the authorities and readers alike. At its most superficial level, the imprint provided straightforward bibliographic information guided by a series of conventions: the place of publication (usually London), the printer ('printed by'), the publisher ('printed for'), the bookseller ('sold by'), and the date of publication. But rarely was this information complete or wholly accurate. Printers, for instance, were rarely identified. Further, throughout the century, joint publication—in which a group of publishers shared the copyright for a title and the costs of production— remained common, meaning that not all of the publishers were always identified in the imprint. Booksellers also proved a problem. All too often, the imprint simply read 'sold by the booksellers in London and Westminster'—a not terribly useful way to pinpoint a place of sale. Finally, the date of publication was often fudged to make a publication look fresher. A work printed near year's end often carried the succeeding year as the date of publication. Most troublingly, this information could be doctored again and again. For works that sold poorly, or perhaps needed to be recast to capitalize on a newly simmering controversy, printers could cancel the title page and sew in a new one, which reoriented the contents to the topical or revised the date of publication. Like titles, imprints too demanded close reading.

This is nowhere clearer than in the routine use of false or misleading imprints, which could themselves become a form of advertisement.[105] Over time, some publishers became associated with certain wares, a kind of corporate identity for the salacious and seditious, the lewd and libellous. As a result, names of particular value could be and frequently were appropriated by lesser-known printers and booksellers looking to tap a fast-selling imprint. Francklin, the printer-publisher behind the quick-selling Craftsman, soon discovered that some stationers, without permission, were using his name in the late 1720s and early '30s. In the hands of others, the Francklin imprint itself became part marketing tool, part protection for controversial wares.[106]

[104] Captain Samuel Cock, A Voyage to Lethe (London, 1741); Philogynes Clitorides, Natural History of the Frutex Vulvaria, Or Flowering Shrub (London, 1732); Thomas Longtool, The New Epicurean (London, 1740); and Timothy Touchit, La Sourciè, Or The Mouse-trap (London, 1794). For more on the 'erotic' book trade, see Julie Peakman, Mighty Lewd Books: The Development of Pornography in Eighteenth-Century Britain (New York: Palgrave Macmillan, 2003), ch. 2, especially pp. 39–44, on 'censorship'.
[105] Michael Treadwell, 'On False and Misleading Imprints in the London Book Trade, 1660–1750', in Fakes and Frauds: Varieties of Deception in Print & Manuscript, edited by Robin Meyers and Michael Harris (Detroit: St Paul's Bibliographies, 1989), pp. 29–46.
[106] Simon Varey, 'The Craftsman', Prose Studies 16, no. 1 (1993): p. 57.

Most frequently, though, publishers simply used fictional names in their imprints to distance themselves from potentially seditious or defamatory works. These were often plausible-sounding but generic pseudonyms like B. Dickinson, T. Atkin, or A. Price. The most routinely used name during the first half of the eighteenth century is 'Moore' (often 'A. Moore' or 'Moor'), which appears on some five hundred works in fifty years.[107] Had he existed, Moore would have been one of the most prolific booksellers of the early eighteenth century. However, it was also clear to those in the book trade—and among consumers—that the A. Moore imprint was both an inside joke among booksellers and a half-veiled signal to readers.[108] 'The Study of Bookseller is as difficult as the Law; and there are as many Tricks in the one as the other', the bookseller in Henry Fielding's *The Author's Farce* laughingly reveals. 'Sometimes we give a Foreign Name to our own Labours, . . . so we have Messieurs Moore near St. Paul's, and Smith near the Royal Exchange'.[109] Others also noticed. One contemporary conjectured that it 'It must be premised that the name of the printer is on these occasions omitted & A Moor near St. Pauls generally put where the law directs the printers name to be'.[110] The A. Moore imprint was used for a range of wares. Much of the period's 'erotica', for instance, features an A. Moore imprint, a pun ('*amour*') that perhaps signalled to readers some form of salacious content, as Janine Barchas has argued.[111] So routine was the A. Moore imprint during the first half of the eighteenth century that numerous printers and publishers were actually using it simultaneously.[112]

Not all imprints carried wholly dubious information, however. Some carried the names of real people, though not always those associated with the production and distribution of a particular work. Take the *London Evening Post*. The government had twice managed to halt the paper's sale by prohibiting its distribution through the Post Office — once in 1733 during the excise crisis and a second time during the general election of 1754. The Walpole administration likewise initiated a series of unsuccessful prosecutions against the paper. But Nutt remained (just barely) a step ahead of the government. First he changed the imprint, by using the name of his journeyman, Samuel Neville, and then, starting in 1737, John Meres, a printer related to him apparently by marriage.

[107] Evan R. Davis, 'Pope's Phantom Moore: Plagiarism and the Pseudonymous Imprint', in *Producing the Eighteenth-Century Book: Writers and Publishers in England, 1650–1800*, edited by Laura L. Runge and Pat Rogers (Newark: University Delaware Press, 2009), p. 193, fig. 3.

[108] Treadwell, 'On False and Misleading Imprints', pp. 41–3.

[109] *The Author's Farce* (1734), in *Henry Fielding: Plays*, Vol. 1: 1728–1731, edited by Thomas Lockwood (Oxford: Clarendon Press, 2004), p. 328.

[110] Cholmondeley (Houghton) MS 74 (34), CUL, qtd. in David Foxon, 'The Phantom Moore', *Bibliography Newsletter* 1, no. 12 (1973): p. 6.

[111] Janine Barchas, Introduction, *Eighteenth-Century British Erotica*, Vol. 1: 1700–1735 (London: Pickering & Chatto), pp. xxiv–xxv.

[112] Andrew Benjamin Bricker, 'Who was "A. Moore"?: The Attribution of Eighteenth-Century Publications with False and Misleading Imprints', *Papers of the Bibliographical Society of America* 110, no. 2 (June 2016): pp. 194–201.

Having some low-level stationer take the fall was useful, but beyond the social contract of the book trade there was no way to be certain that a printer could resist turning on his bookseller. Better was some form of economic security. Starting in the later seventeenth century, this position in the trade—the person hired to protect the actual printer, publisher, and author—was being filled by enterprising intermediaries. Today, following D. F. McKenzie's coinage and the pioneering research of Michael Treadwell, we call them 'trade publishers' (they were less helpfully known as 'publishers' in the seventeenth and eighteenth centuries).[113] In effect, trade publishers were employed by booksellers, whom we would today call publishers (those who funded publication and retained copyrights), and were paid small fees to append their names to the imprints of different works.[114] Trade publishers emerged in the last quarter of the seventeenth century to fill a void in the book trade created by the period's licensing laws.[115] Their primary function, Treadwell argues, was 'concealment': a controversial pamphlet might be danger-ous, though not dangerous enough to justify a fully fictional imprint, but none-theless 'worth the slight added expense of paying a [trade] publisher to stand between the authorities and the person really responsible'.[116] As Treadwell observes, 'It was simply one of the trade publisher's functions (and not the least important) to stand mute between the real proprietors and the authorities'.[117] Some trade publishers had stunning careers. John Morphew's name, for instance, appeared on more than two hundred imprints between 1714 and 1717 alone.

For scandal-mongering authors and stationers, doctoring imprints was routine. Take Swift's *The Publick Spirit of the Whigs* (1713/4). In this instance he bypassed Tooke, the bookseller he had consistently used since 1701, and dealt directly with Barber, his printer, a practise he continued to employ with politically sensitive materials, such as *The Conduct of the Allies* (1711) and *The Importance of the Guardian Considered* (1713).[118] For all three of these works, neither Tooke's nor Barber's name appears on the imprint. Instead, they employed Morphew, who was then also serving as a trade publisher to Dunton and Curll, among others. For Swift, Morphew served as a wall to authorial access; for Barber, though, he was an inlet to sales, a problem every printer faced in a market in which printers were largely excluded from copyright ownership thanks to a concerted effort on the part of booksellers.[119] Morphew was also the right choice—at least according to

---

[113] D. F. McKenzie, 'The London Book Trade in the Later Seventeenth Century' (Sandars Lectures, Cambridge, 1976), pp. 24–28, MISC 217, SCSU; and Michael Treadwell, 'London Trade Publishers, 1675–1750', *The Library*, sixth series, 4, no. 2 (June 1982): p. 99.

[114] Treadwell, 'London Trade Publishers', pp. 100, 101.

[115] Treadwell, 'London Trade Publishers', p. 103.

[116] Treadwell, 'London Trade Publishers', pp. 113, 121.

[117] Treadwell, 'London Trade Publishers', p. 125. John Morphew claimed that such papers were free gifts. SP 35/1/100 (20 August 1714), TNA.

[118] Michael Treadwell, 'London Book Trade', pp. 9–11.

[119] Treadwell, 'London Trade Publishers', p. 120; Terry Belanger, 'Booksellers' Sale of Copyright: Aspects of the London Book Trade, 1718–1768' (PhD diss., Columbia University, 1970), pp. 146–7.

Tooke, who employed him again and again on behalf of Swift—though even he was not enough in this case. Summoned to the House of Lords, Morphew was forced to finger Barber as the pamphlet's printer. The government in turn brought an information against Barber in Queen's Bench. Barber held fast, though, and refused to name Swift (it might have helped that Robert Harley, who had hired Swift to write Tory propaganda in *The Examiner*, had given Swift a bill for £100 to offset the men's 'exigencys').[120] Parliament offered a £300 reward to anyone who would name its author. No one came forward.[121]

As we have already seen, dizzying authorial arrangements were not uncommon for Swift. Consider, for example, his 'most vicious satire', the *Short character of his Ex. T.E. of W., LL of I__*, an essay on Thomas, the earl of Wharton, who had served as Lord Lieutenant of Ireland. The *Short character* bore the imprint 'London for William Coryton, Book-seller, at the Black Swan on Ludgate-hill. 1711'. Whoever the text was printed for did a plausible job of creating the impression of a factual imprint, employing a place name, a bookseller, an address, and a sign (all features typically falsified in or omitted from false imprints). For all that, Coryton never existed and no black swan was to be found on Ludgate-hill.[122]

Later, with *Gulliver's Travels* (1726), the only work for which Swift was paid, it was more of the same. As Pope wrote to Swift in November 1726, 'Motte [the bookseller] receiv'd the copy (he tells me) he knew not from whence, nor from whom, dropp'd at his house in the dark, from a Hackney-coach: by computing the time, I found it was after you left England'.[123] This was apparently stock in trade, especially for political works that might run afoul of the government.[124] As Morphew explained to the Secretary of State in 1714, it was 'a very usual thing to leave books & papers at [Morphew's] house and at the houses of other publishers'. Only 'a long time after' publication, when authors knew they were safe, would they 'call for the value' of the publication 'without making themselves known to the said publishers'. But, 'if the Government makes enquiry concerning the authors', then 'it often happens that nobody comes to make any demand for the value of the said books'.[125] Swift knew the dangers he ran. 'I have writ some things that would make people angry', he later reflected in a letter to Motte.

[120] Harley to Swift (3 March 1713/4), *Correspondence of Swift*, vol. 1. p. 589; and Downie, *Robert Harley and the Press*, pp. 126–7.

[121] J. A. Downie, 'Swift and the Oxford Ministry: New Evidence', *Swift Studies* 1 (1986): pp. 2–8; Charles A. Rivington, '*Tyrant': The Story of John Barber, 1675–1741: Jacobite Lord Mayor of London and Printer and Friend to Dr. Swift* (York: William Sessions, 1989), pp. 31–7, 42–68, 126–30, 138–42, 148–60, 201–21; Maurice J. Quinlan, 'The Prosecution of Swift's *Public Spirit of the Whigs*', *Texas Studies in Literature and Language* 9, no. 2 (1967): pp. 173–4; and John Irwin Fischer, 'The Legal Response to Swift's *The Public Spirit of the Whigs*', in *Swift and his Contexts*, edited by John Irwin Fischer et al. (New York: AMS Press, 1989), pp. 21–38.

[122] Treadwell, 'On False and Misleading Imprints', pp. 29–69, esp. 43–4.

[123] Pope to Swift (16 November 1726), *The Correspondence of Alexander Pope*, edited by George Sherburn, vol. 2 (Oxford: Clarendon Press, 1956), p. 412.

[124] Higgins, *Swift's Politics*, p. 153.   [125] SP 35/1/100, TNA.

'I always sent them by unknown hands, [so] the Printer might guess [who the author was], but he could not accuse me'.[126] Even with *Gulliver's Travels* the ruse worked. Shortly after the book's publication in London, John Gay wrote to Swift: 'About ten days ago a Book was publish'd here of the Travels of one Gulliver, which hath been the conversation of the whole town ever since:... 'Tis generally said that you are the Author, but I am told, the Bookseller declares he knows not from what hand it came'.[127]

Swift, moreover, was hardly alone in the precautions he took and in the manner he manipulated copyright ownership. When Pope moved to publish the *Dunciad Variorum* in 1729, he carefully obscured not only his involvement but also the responsibility of his intermediaries by creating new and seemingly untouchable routes of distribution.[128] First, on 12 March 1729, he somehow managed to have Sir Robert Walpole present a handsome quarto edition of the *Variorum* to George II.[129] Then, having implicitly gained something like royal and ministerial approval for the poem, Pope used his high-ranking friends to distribute the work.[130] 'You are now at full liberty to publish all my faults & Enormities', he wrote the following day to the Earl of Oxford, who along with the Earl of Burlington and Lord Bathurst began to distribute copies to the *beau monde*.[131] Part of this ruse also meant keeping the poem out of the booksellers'—and thus the general public's—hands. As he begged Oxford, the poem was 'by no means to be given to any Bookseller, but dispos'd of as by your own Order at 6s. by any honest Gentleman or Head of a House'.[132] He kept this wile going for roughly a month, which served both to protect Pope legally while drumming up demand for the poem. On 8 April he wrote to John Caryll, his friend and long-time correspondent, sheepishly claiming that the poem should have 'reached your hands a week ago'. But 'the publishers had not then permitted any to be sold, but only dispersed by some lords of theirs and my acquaintance, of whom I procured yours. But I understand that now the booksellers have got 'em by the consent of Lord Bathurst'.[133] The publishers here seem a mere fiction of Pope's; the lords were the publishers even if they did not retain copyright. On 10 April, Lawton Gilliver,

---

[126] Swift to Motte (4 November 1732), *The Correspondence of Jonathan Swift, D.D.*, 5 vol., edited by David Woolley, vol. 3 (Frankfurt am Main: Peter Lang, 1999–2014), p. 556.

[127] Gay to Swift (28 November 1726), *The Letters of John Gay,* edited by C. F. Burges (Oxford: Oxford University Press, 1966), pp. 60–2.

[128] James Sutherland (ed.), Alexander Pope, *The Dunciad*, 2nd ed., rev. ed., (1953), in *The Twickenham Edition of the Poems of Alexander Pope*, 11 vol., vol. 5 (London: Methuen, 1939–1967), p. 460ff.

[129] *The Dunciad, Twickenham Edition* V, p. xxvii. Jody Greene claims that Pope 'sent Walpole a copy of the work and asked him to present it to George II' (*Trouble with Ownership*, p. 175), but does not cite any source for this information.

[130] Vander Meulen, Preface, *Pope's* Dunciad *of 1728*, p. ix, n1.

[131] Pope to the Earl of Oxford (13 March 1728/9), *Correspondence of Pope*, vol. 3, pp. 25–6.

[132] Pope to the Earl of Oxford (29 March [1729]), *Correspondence of Pope*, vol. 3, p. 26.

[133] Pope to Caryll (8 April 1729), *Correspondence of Pope*, vol. 3, p. 31.

the work's new bookseller, advertised the poem.[134] On 12 April, he entered its title in the Stationers' Register, though he did not, at this point, own the copyright.[135]

Through such ruses, and given his public statute, Pope was in a fairly safe position.[136] To begin with, he refused to own the poem publicly (though he was also equally unwilling to disown the poem, as his critics routinely observed). That wouldn't happen until 1735.[137] The real question was the liability of his printer and bookseller, as he noted in a letter to Burlington. This proved a concern well founded. On 18 April, ten days after Gilliver had advertised the poem, Pope wrote anxiously to the Earl of Oxford: 'the Gentlemen of the Dunciad intend to be vexatious to the Bookseller & threaten to bring an action of I can't tell how many thousands against him'.[138] Gilliver, young and inexperienced, was easy to fright.[139] He did not own the copyright, despite registering the work, though it appears that Pope had promised Gilliver that he could buy it as soon as it was safe to do so.[140] Despite such tenuous ties to the poem's copy, Gilliver was irritated by the supposedly unauthorized editions of the *Variorum*, and bluffed his ownership, filing a suit at Chancery on 6 May against James Watson, a printer, and the booksellers Thomas Astley, John Clarke, and John Stagg, before asking for and receiving an injunction on 8 or 19 May to put a stop to the supposed piracies.[141] On 6 June, though, Gilliver's suit failed and the injunction was dissolved, when it turned out that he, like Stagg, another bookseller, had bought copies of the poem for 5 shillings. Gilliver merely cancelled the title page in his octavo versions and inserted a new one, so that his copies appeared to have been printed for him.[142] At some point between April and November of 1729, Pope seemingly assigned the *Dunciad* to Burlington, Oxford, and Bathurst. On 16 October, a reassignment was drawn up, transferring copyright.[143] On 21 November 1729, Gilliver made an entry in the Stationers' Register, noting that the author had assigned the copyright to the three lords, who had in turn assigned it to him.[144]

[134] *The Daily Post* (10 April 1729).
[135] Pope, *The Works of Pope*, edited by Whitwell Elwin and William John Courthope, vol. 8 (London, 1871–1886), p. 309.
[136] Keymer, *Poetics*, p. 106.
[137] Pope to Caryll (8 April 1729), *Correspondence of Pope*, vol. 3. p. 31.
[138] Pope to Oxford (18 April 1729), *Correspondence of Pope*, vol. 3, p. 31.
[139] Gilliver had been set up as a bookseller for just over a year by the time the *Variorum* went to press. See James McLaverty, 'Lawton Gilliver: Pope's Bookseller', *Studies in Bibliography* 32 (1979): p. 103.
[140] This according to the bookseller Thomas Wooton in a sworn affidavit from 2 June 1729. Wooton asked Gilliver, on 26 April, or there around, 'why he made such a rout about ye publishing of ye [pirated editions]'. Gilliver responded that 'he had then no assignment of ye said Copy but should have it in a little time' (C 41/43 n. 566, TNA, qtd. Sutherland, 'The Dunciad of 1729', p. 349).
[141] For confusion over the date, see Sutherland, who writes 19 May ('The Dunciad of 1729', p. 349); Greene notes that the entry in the Chancery reads 'Jovis May 8' (*Trouble with Ownership*, p. 246n66). C 33/351, f. 284, TNA.
[142] C 11/2581/36 (2), TNA.   [143] Egerton MS. 1951 f. 7, BL.
[144] All of this is helpfully outlined in Sutherland, 'The Dunciad of 1729', pp. 347–53 and supplemented and corrected in *The Dunciad, Twickenham Edition* vol. 5, p. 462. See also Greene, *Trouble with Ownership*, p. 175ff.

Given the vagaries of such circuitous arrangements, title pages were simply not to be trusted by readers. But they were not to be wholly disregarded, either, as I have tried to make clear: they were both a disguise and a signal to knowledgeable readers. Take the title page of *The Silent Flute, A Poem: Being the Members Speech to their Sovereign* (1729) (Figure 2.3). By the standards of early eighteenth-century printing, *The Silent Flute* could not be more run-of-the-mill, though its elegant folio format, during an era when even serious poetry was typically printed in quarto, might have raised an inquisitive eyebrow.[145] To an eye trained to scandal, the poem's title page was packed with half-veiled signals. As I noted above, by the 1720s, the 'A. Moore' imprint was itself a clue, even a key to the salacious, but at the very least it always appeared in imprints to works that warranted closer inspection. The imprint to *The Silent Flute*, then, might have sent the reader up to the poem's allusive authorial attribution: 'By the Author of the Curious Maid'. A smutty bestselling parody of Matthew Prior from the mid-1720s, *The Curious Maid* recounts a young woman's attempt to glimpse her own genitalia, in hopes of figuring out why men are so obsessed with women's nether regions (the poem culminates with the maid squatting over a mirror, a comically anticlimactic scene later depicted in woodcut [Figure 2.4]).[146] This would have linked *The Silent Flute* to the illicit world of mildly pornographic satire and to the poem's author, Hildebrand Jacob, a lesser satiric light of the period. In turn, the would-be consumer might have re-evaluated the title. The members' speech to their sovereign was not a conversation between MP and king, as one might have at first suspected, but between a man and his penis: the silent flute.

Title pages and their imprints, rife with meaning and the learned language of covert consumerism, simply demanded deciphering. When brought together, these various evasions amounted to a carefully managed bibliographical map, an allusive guide to would-be readers in the know. In short, the law shaped not only the way books were written, but also the physical forms they took and how readers came to understand them.

2.4 Editing Authors: Language, Libel, and Liability

Even still, given the authorities' constant scrutiny of the press and the court rulings that had increased the liability of stationers, such bibliographical evasions had their limits. Verbal self-policing remained the primary means of mitigating legal responsibility, and booksellers often extensively edited their most

---

[145] Bertrand H. Bronson, *Printing as an Index of Taste in Eighteenth-Century England* (New York: New York Public Library, 1963), pp. 11–12 and, more generally, 5–30, *passim*.

[146] [Hildebrand Jacob], 'The Curious Maid', in *A New Collection of Poems on Several Occasions* (London, 1725), 93. PR3640 .A12 1725, SCSL.

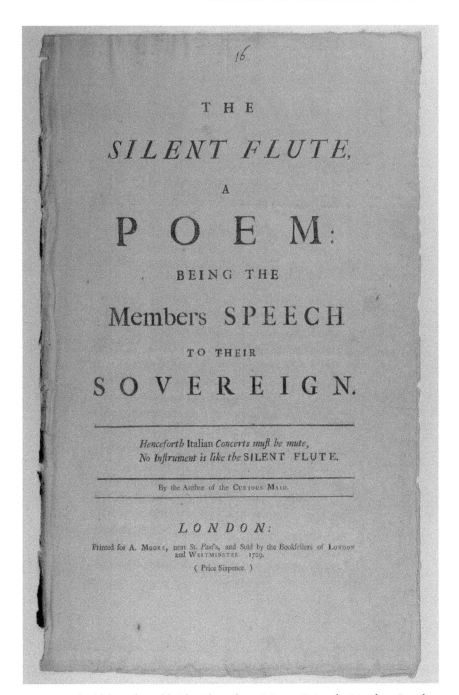

Figure 2.3 [Hildebrand Jacob], *The Silent Flute, A Poem: Being the Members Speech to their Sovereign* (London, 1729). Harry Ransom Center, The University of Texas at Austin (Ak J150 +A729s)

Figure 2.4 [Hildebrand Jacob], 'The Curious Maid', in *A New Collection of Poems on Several Occasions* (London, 1725), p. 93. Courtesy of the Department of Special Collections, Stanford University Libraries (PR3640 .A12 1725)

provocative publications.[147] A knowledge of the relevant laws was learned on the spot, handed down from printer to apprentice, and passed on from family member to family member, especially within the dynastic publishing outfits of the eighteenth century. Moreover, legal training, especially among fledgling authors, was stunningly routine. One could make a long list of stationers who were lawyers, had studied law, or had spent some time in the Inns of Court.[148]

For those without either formal or on-the-job training, there were always the lay legal works, printed and reprinted throughout the century, which laid out the basics of defamation law, sometimes even openly signalling those readers who were also writers. One legal commentator went so far as to suggest that his digest of libel law might be used to answer a knotty if obvious question: 'Whether a witty Man may not write or publish Things of a scandalous Import, yet so glossed over and disguised, so wrapp'd up in Implications and Allegories, as not to come within Reach of the Law, nor be construed a Breach of them'.[149] In addition, both authors and stationers legally vetted their works. Pope relied on the lawyer Nicholas Fazakerley to assess the legal repercussions of the *Dunciad Variorum*; Samuel Johnson's *London* (1738) was carefully edited for libel before publication, possibly by the bookseller Robert Dodsley or the printer Edward Cave; Wilkes used the bookseller William Johnston and the lawyer Charles Sayer to assess the legality of the *North Briton*; and Murray and the Longmans relied on Sharon Turner, an attorney and solicitor, for advice on copyright matters and potential libel proceedings.[150]

Editing potentially libellous works was routine for those in the book trade. John How, the printer for *The Observator*, admitted during his 1704 examination in court that he 'altered [the copy] oftentimes to make it safe'.[151] The goal, Paula McDowell has shown, was the erasure of 'seditious intentions', the careful editing of a text, perhaps even an overtly libellous oral ballad, in light of the broad canopy of libel laws.[152] Again, take Swift. Some of his printed works attracted no legal attention, and for good reason: many of those who shepherded his works into print often excised or revised pricklier passages. Importantly, Swift permitted and even expected his intermediaries to delete legally dubious passages from his works. He bristled, however, at the wrong kinds of edits—not omissions, but emendations and additions. With *Gulliver's Travels*, for instance, Benjamin Motte, Jr

[147] John Feather, 'The English Book Trade and the Law, 1695–1799', *Publishing History* 12 (1982): p. 51.

[148] Plomer et al., *Dictionary, 1726 to 1775, passim.*   [149] *State Law*, pp. [ii], 6.

[150] For more on Pope, see chapter 4, below; for Johnson, see Keymer, *Poetics*, pp. 210–13; for Wilkes, see Arthur Cash, *John Wilkes: The Scandalous Father of Civil Liberty* (New Haven: Yale University Press, 2006), pp. 70, 89; and, for Murray, Longman, and Turner, see Gary Dyer, 'Publishers and Lawyers', *The Wordsworth Circle* 44, no. 2–3 (Spring–Summer 2013): pp. 121–6.

[151] *The Trial of John Tutchin*, in 16 *State Trials* 1106.

[152] Paula McDowell, *The Women of Grub Street: Press, Politics, and Gender in the London Literary Marketplace, 1678–1730* (Oxford: Clarendon Press, 1998), ch. 2.

employed his brother, Andrew, to edit the work. He did a crummy job, and Swift was predictably galled. 'Had there been onely omissions, I should not care one farthing', he tetchily wrote to Charles Ford. 'But change of Style, new things foysted in, that are false facts, and I know not what, is very provoking'.[153] In any case, Swift took it for granted that those who printed his works, and thus faced the first round of legal inquiries, would edit as they saw fit. As he had earlier written to Motte, the printer 'ran the whole risk, and well deserved the property'.[154]

It was more of the same for Junius. For all of his prized author's reassurances, Woodfall knew some materials could never be printed as is. One of Junius's Letters in the *Public Advertiser* (from 22 February 1771 and published under the pseudonym Vindex) addressed the recent skirmish between Britain and Spain over the possession of Jamaica, Gibraltar, and Minorca.[155] In short, Vindex asserts that the ministry had been too spineless to rebuff the Spanish. These were all criticisms above board, at least in Woodfall's view. But the latter part of the letter—in which Vindex calls George III 'degraded' and 'dishonoured' and asserts that he had displayed 'Cowardice' and an 'Excess of Infamy', before signing off 'I am, Sir, (With all possible Contempt for a *stigmatised* Coward)'—was too contemptuous to print, and Woodfall omitted it with Junius's explicit approval. Woodfall had gone to trial half a year earlier, in the summer of 1770, for Junius's letters, and already that month he had been threatened with a separate prosecution for Junius's letter from 30 January 1771, also on the government's weak-kneed dealings with Spain. 'I hope you will not be offended at my declining to publish your Letter', Woodfall replied to Junius. 'I am convinced the Subject of it must, if I was to publish it, render me liable to very severe reprehension'. It was Woodfall's hope that 'some little regard to Prudence will not by you be deemed Squeamishness'.[156] Junius begrudgingly allowed that the 'Satyrical part' could be omitted, ceding editorial control to Woodfall's more cautious judgement. 'The risque is yours', he reasoned, '& you must determine for yourself'.[157]

Even with Junius's private letters, Woodfall found himself editor in chief. By late 1771, Junius was under the mistaken impression that David Garrick—yes, that Garrick, actor-manager of Drury Lane—was running reconnaissance for the Crown. As Junius wrote in a private letter to Woodfall, 'secret [:] beware of David Garrick. he was sent to pump you, & went directly to Richmond to tell the king I shd. write no more'.[158] Junius decided to confront Garrick himself, and accordingly used Woodfall, telling him to have his letter to Garrick 'copied in any

---

[153] Swift or Ford (20 November 1733), *Correspondence of Swift*, vol. 3, p. 708.

[154] Swift to Motte (4 November 1732), *Correspondence of Swift*, vol. 3, p. 556.

[155] *Letters of Junius*, pp. 487–8. For a complete version of this letter in Junius's hand, see Add. MS. 27777, f. 13, BL.

[156] Woodfall to Junius (19 February 1771), *Letters of Junius*, p. 370.

[157] Junius to Woodfall (21 February 1771), *Letters of Junius*, pp. 370–1.

[158] Junius to Woodfall (1 November 1771), *Letters of Junius*, p. 374.

hand, & sent by the penny post'.[159] 'I am very exactly informed of your impertinent inquiries', Junius wrote to the actor-manager. 'Now mark me, vagabond.—keep to your pantomimes, or be assured you shall hear of it. Meddle no more, thou busy informer!'[160] This was all a bit too much for Woodfall—too rude, to be sure, but also a touch too histrionic. It was bad enough calling Garrick impertinent, a particularly venomous term for a busybody, but the business about vagrancy only fingered the sore spot of thespian pride.[161] Vagrancy laws remained on the books, and actors like Garrick who harboured some pretence to gentility were certain to take such affronts badly. Woodfall softened the language, changing 'impertinent inquiries' to 'practices', and sent the letter on to an admittedly shocked Garrick, who found the affair 'rather too Inquisitorial for the great Champion of our Liberties!'[162] The whole thing had been a gross misunderstanding, Garrick explained in his response to Woodfall. He was on some personal business at Richmond, and happened only to mention to the king, who was upset that Garrick had not acted for him, what Woodfall himself (!) had earlier told Garrick, perhaps in a star-struck moment.[163]

With Swift, this process of careful editing is clearest in On Poetry: A Rapsody (December 1733).[164] The version of the poem readers bought in 1733 was nothing like the manuscript that eventually found its way into the hands of John Huggonson, who published it in London. The work in full was only printed in 1758 (though it is a bewildering question as to what the complete poem should be).[165] In addition, it seems many of the cuts were made not by Swift but by Huggonson. These edits include forty-eight lines and, possibly, a series of couplets written by Swift that were either not included in the manuscript sent to Huggonson, excised by the bookseller before the poem was published, or produced after the poem had gone to print. (Here, just as he had time and again before, Swift used a series of intermediaries and gave the copyright to Matthew Pilkington.)[166]

After the poem was printed, it seems Swift, either to supplement the work or to return it to its original form, supplied a group of close friends with the additional lines, including John Boyle, fifth earl of Orrery, a man whom both Swift and

[159] Junius to Woodfall (10 November 1771), Letters of Junius, p. 376.
[160] Junius to Woodfall (10 November 1771), Letters of Junius, p. 376.   [161] OED, def. 2.
[162] Junius to Garrick (18 November 1771) and Garrick to Woodfall (20 November 1771), Private Correspondence of David Garrick, 2 vol., edited by H. Colburn and R. Bentley, vol. 1 (London, 1831), pp. 443–4.
[163] Garrick to Woodfall (20 November 1771), Private Correspondence, vol. 1, pp. 444–5.
[164] A. C. Elias, et al., 'The Full Text of Swift's On Poetry: A Rapsody (1733)', Swift Studies 9 (1994): pp. 17–32; and Karian, Jonathan Swift, ch. 4.
[165] Karian, Jonathan Swift, p. 103.
[166] Laetitia Pilkington, Memoirs of Laetitia Pilkington, 2 vol., edited by A. C. Elias, vol. 1 (Athens: University of Georgia Press, 1997), p. 64.

Pope trusted.[167] At present, there are seven printed editions of the poem that possess the additional lines, transcribed in contemporary hands. Among these is Boyle's copy, which contains several legally objectionable passages: an eight-line section attacking the bishops for heterodoxy and atheism; a seditious couplet on the House of Lords and George II; a couplet on the king's parsimony; and a thirty-six-line passage attacking monarchs as beasts.[168] Whether Huggonson chose to excise the passages or whether Swift chose not to send them along at all, crucial editing was done to make the poem fit for print.

The authorities, however, took little interest in the printed version of the poem.[169] Why? In its published form, the Crown might have found a few things objectionable enough, though it is doubtful whether any passage alone would have been legally actionable. Too much of the work is sustained by a combination of heavy verbal irony and mock-encomiastic criticism. Had the Crown knowledge of the excised lines, however, they most likely would have taken more interest in the poem. In an obvious sense, any addition to the text of the poem would have changed the way its readers interpreted and understood it. But what is so interesting about the excised lines is the way in which they severely qualify—and undermine—the preceding and succeeding lines that *were* published with the poem. Take just one example. How much harder would it have been to read the section beginning 'Fair *Britain* in thy Monarch blest', in which Swift displays George II's 'Magnanimity', with a straight face, if the following excised couplet, part of a series of overt comparisons and a distastefully anti-Semitic shot at George's notorious stinginess with patronage, were included: 'A House of Peers, or Gaming Crew, / A griping Monarch, or a Jew'? Two things should be clear. First, the poem existed in two radically different versions in 1733 and became, with its addenda, overtly instead of covertly seditious. Second, the poem needed to be edited—perhaps by Swift but most likely by Huggonson—if it was going to make it into print and evade the authorities.

Despite all the precautions taken with *On Poetry*, it is also clear that some works, even if assiduously redacted, could not be printed at all. Swift knew this, and so did his publishers. Some writings he thus simply held back from the press—so often, in fact, that Stephen Karian has advocated for thinking of Swift as primarily a manuscript poet.[170] 'On the Words "Brother Protestants and Fellow Christians"' (1733), a scornful take on the attempt to repeal the Test Clause in the Irish House of Commons and the Irish MP Richard Bettesworth, is a particularly

---

[167] Swift had earlier entrusted Orrery with a copy of Pope's epitaph for John Gay (1 May 1733), *Correspondence of Swift*, vol. 3, p. 637. On Pope's trust of Orrery, see a series of letters exchanged between them: 8 October 1735 and 17 May 1737, *Correspondence of Pope*, vol. 3, pp. 502–6, 4.69.

[168] Lindsay SwJ 203, CUL.   [169] Fischer, 'Epistle', p. 46.

[170] Stephen Karian, 'Swift as a manuscript poet', in *Jonathan Swift and the Eighteenth-Century Book*, edited by Paddy Bullard and James McLaverty (Cambridge: Cambridge University Press, 2013), pp. 31–2.

good example. Swift had already attacked the repeal attempt three times in print.[171] After the repeal had failed, Swift circulated a manuscript of his poem, attacking Bettesworth's Whig slogan 'Brother Protestants and Fellow Christians', comparing it to the conversation between a piece of horse dung and an apple during a flood in Aesop's fable: 'See, Brother, how we Apples swim'.[172] Eventually, Bettesworth got his hands on a copy, before confronting and threatening the poet—a quarrel Swift later recounted with some malicious glee.[173] The story doesn't stop there, however. In the poem, Swift clumsily rhymes Bettesworth with 'Sweat's Worth', an awkward solecism that set off a game of poetic one-upmanship. Other anonymous works soon succeeded Swift's in both print and manuscript, all trying to find better rhymes for the MP's name.[174] So vexed was Bettesworth by the whole affair that he was soon pronouncing his surname with three syllables instead of two, in hopes of distancing himself from the poem's many mocking successors.[175]

In general, Swift was extremely cautious with such manuscripts. Between 1722 and 1733, for instance, he privately circulated two other highly polemical poems, both in response to topical political events: 'The Storm; or Minerva's Petition' (1722–23) and 'On the Irish Bishops' (1732).[176] With these, he was careful that they moved in limited circles. On occasion, though, some things were simply too dangerous to pass around, such as his poem 'A Wicked Treasonable Libel' (1718), a nasty attack on George I and the royal family's succession and sexual problems between 1717 and 1718.[177] The poem today exists in a lone holograph in the Lockwood Collection at SUNY Buffalo, a more or less sure sign that Swift did not circulate the poem, though he might have shown it to an inner circle of friends in Dublin.[178]

What we need to keep in mind, above all, is that the mediation of printers and booksellers was essential to the protection of satirists during this period. This was part of a largely unspoken arrangement, one that had long been in place before 1710 but that had, paradoxically, been given greater force through the provisions of copyright. More to the point, the mediation of stationers fundamentally shaped how satiric works were printed, the language they ultimately contained, how they

---

[171] The Advantages Propos'd by Repealing the Sacramental Test, Impartially Considered (1732), Queries Wrote by Dr. J. Swift (1732), and The Presbyterians Plea of Merit (1733).

[172] The Poems of Jonathan Swift, edited by Harold Williams, vol. 3 (Oxford: Clarendon Press, 1958), p. 811.

[173] Swift to the Duke of Dorset (Jan. 1734), Correspondence of Swift, vol. 3, p. 719.

[174] Karian, Jonathan Swift, p. 88.

[175] Deane Swift (ed.), Letters Written by the Late Jonathan Swift, 6 vol., vol. 5 (London, 1768), p. 391n.

[176] Karian, Jonathan Swift, p. 82ff.

[177] James Woolley, 'Writing Libels on Germans: Swift's "Wicked Treasonable Libel"', Swift: The Enigmatic Dean, Festschrift for Hermann Josef Real, edited by Rudolf Freiburg, et al. (Tübingen: Stauffenburg Verlag, 1998), pp. 303–16.

[178] Woolley, 'Writing Libels', p. 311n28.

were distributed and sold, and the physical forms in which they circulated. Legal concerns encouraged such bibliographical evasions, and those bibliographical evasions shaped the perceptions of readers and consumers. As I argue over the next three chapters, however, the law affected not only how stationers acquired and published such satires, but also the verbally evasive language those satires contained and how readers made sense of them. Verbal irony, satirists soon realized, was the greatest literary and legal tool at their disposal. So too did the Crown and members of the pro-ministry bench. Ask only poor Daniel Defoe, the subject of my next chapter.

3

Irony in the Courts

Defoe and the Law of Seditious Libel

Among the rhetorical evasions that came to typify eighteenth-century satire, none was quite as effective as verbal irony: to say one thing and yet simultaneously mean something else. However, though it remained one of the most useful tools for complicating courtroom interpretive procedures for both the authorities and the courts, verbal irony was also one of the great perils of satire: the ambiguous rhetorical figure that routinely confused both readers and jurors alike. No better example exists than Daniel Defoe's *The Shortest Way with the Dissenters* (1702), a mocking impersonation of the orthodox Anglican attack on Protestant dissent that sought to expose the ghastly consequences of High-Church rhetoric. Defoe's satire not only led to his prosecution, conviction, and pillorying, but also contributed to a massive revision in the handling of irony in trials for libel in the first years of the eighteenth century.

This chapter tells the story of how the courts came to understand irony and especially the rules devised for making sense of ambiguous language in trials for libel. That story is important for understanding the reciprocal relationship between law and literature—between courtroom procedure, in this instance, and one of the defining rhetorical features of eighteenth-century satire. This chapter is also, therefore, about irony itself during this period. By the time Defoe's mocking pamphlet was published, irony was becoming an increasingly prominent feature of satire's verbal armature. And yet readers, early on, were deeply confused by *The Shortest Way*, just as critics today have puzzled over its precise rhetorical structure.

To make sense of Defoe's vexing satire and the readerly difficulties such works presented, I begin with a discussion of irony during the first half of the eighteenth century. My goal is to describe *The Shortest Way*'s rhetorical method and especially Defoe's use of what I call extrinsic irony. Extrinsic irony differs from more modern theories of internally signalled irony, I argue, in its presumption of and implicit reliance on the shared prejudices of readers. In short, rather than leaving verbal and argumentative *internal* clues for a reader to decode—what we might think of as the breadcrumb method—extrinsic irony offers seemingly plausible statements that nonetheless jar with the common extra-textual perceptions of

Libel and Lampoon: Satire in the Courts, 1670–1792. Andrew Benjamin Bricker, Oxford University Press.
© Andrew Benjamin Bricker 2022. DOI: 10.1093/oso/9780192846150.003.0004

readers. A straight-faced poem praising Sir Robert Walpole for honesty might be easy enough to imagine early in his premiership, but readers would have seen how that same commendatory poem in 1742, after he was forced to resign for widely rumoured backdoor dealing, butted violently up against popular perceptions, pointing through implicit juxtaposition to the very virtue the prime minister seemed most visibly to lack. Extrinsic irony is a delicate balancing act, however, and Defoe, I would argue, misjudged his readers' prejudices. Where he saw a horrifying persecutorial regime of High-Church Anglicanism, many of his readers saw a plausible and even reasonable response to the problem of dissent.

These same interpretive difficulties around irony troubled prosecutions, especially in trials for seditious libel. I spool out those challenges in two stages. I begin by outlining how the courts revised the law of seditious libel, before showing how verbal irony complicated the most radical revisions to the law. I do so by turning to another example of extrinsic irony: *The Country Parson's Honest Advice* (1706), a mock-encomiastic poem on the parliamentary establishment that eventually led to Dr Joseph Browne's prosecution, conviction, and pillorying. The poem's irony, however, raised the spectre of authorial intent that had all along haunted Chief Justice Sir John Holt's boldest revisions to the law, which sought to remove intent as an element of seditious libel. In the end, Holt ruled that ironic works, even those subject to innocent interpretations, could be libellous. He did so by establishing a sociocentric procedure for establishing ironic intent, an interpretive doctrine that relied not on demonstrable internal textual clues that furnished an author's libellous intended meaning, but on an appeal to the jurors' collective impression that a given text was ironic.

In closing, I bring together these revisions to the law and the ruling in Browne's case to re-evaluate Defoe's hasty trial just a few years earlier. Doing so helps us to see that Defoe did have a defence, but one of value only in the years prior to or following Holt's tenure on the bench. Such a re-evaluation might be nothing more than an exercise in counterfactual history. But in uncovering the long-term doctrinal effects of Holt's sociocentric understanding of irony, we might also recognize the extent to which Defoe was merely one victim during a troubling era of conservative judicial activism, when a new regulatory regime for policing an increasingly unruly—and verbally evasive—press was coming into being.

3.1 *The Shortest Way* and Extrinsic Irony

By December of 1702, when *The Shortest Way with the Dissenters: Or Proposals for the Establishment of the Church* was anonymously published, all of England was seemingly debating occasional conformity, 'the most bitterly contested of all the battlegrounds of the political parties in the years between 1702 and 1705'.[1] According to the Corporation Act of 1661, only those who had taken the Anglican Sacrament within a twelve-month period were eligible to hold municipal offices. Starting in the 1690s, civic-minded dissenters began to take communion in the Church of England before standing for local office in an effort to obviate the act. Hardline and orthodox Anglicans were horrified.[2] Even Defoe, a Presbyterian (and thus a dissenter himself), was disgusted by such religious cynicism. Occasional conformity was a rotten ruse, he wrote, little better than '*playing Bo-peep* with God Almighty'.[3] High-Church Tories agreed. In three failed bills and over three sessions between 1702 and 1704, the Commons attempted to stamp out the practise through heavy fines.[4] For Defoe, though, this was a step too far. Though he abhorred occasional conformity, he was also troubled by the proposed legislation, which he viewed as a vile attempt to persecute religious dissent.

By 1702, Defoe had already spent years hammering away at the issue. His first swipe was *An Enquiry into the Occasional Conformity of Dissenters* (1697), written after the Presbyterian Sir Humphrey Edwin was elected mayor of London. Defoe archly asks how someone like Edwin, who infamously took communion at St Paul's before attending a dissenting service at Pinners' Hall on the same day, could be '*a* Conformist *in the Morning, and a* Nonconformist *before Night*'.[5] Such debates only intensified after Anne's accession. In May of 1702, the ornery High-Church fanatic Henry Sacheverell urged his fellow Anglicans to 'Hang out the *Bloody Flag*' and eradicate 'These Crafty, Faithless, and Insidious Persons'.[6] Defoe responded by attacking the High Churchmen.[7] Shortly thereafter, as the first bill was moving through parliament, Defoe published his *Enquiry into Occasional Conformity. Shewing that the Dissenters are no way Concern'd in it*, rehashing his

[1] Geoffrey Holmes, *British Politics in the Age of Anne* (1967), rev. ed. (London: Hambledon Press, 1987), p. 99. See also John Flaningam, 'The Occasional Conformity Controversy: Ideology and Party Politics, 1697–1711', *Journal of British Studies* 17 (1977): pp. 38–62.

[2] Geoffrey Holmes, *The Making of a Great Power: Late Stuart and Early Georgian Britain, 1660–1722* (New York: Longman, 1993), pp. 350–66.

[3] Daniel Defoe, *An Enquiry into the Occasional Conformity of Dissenters, in Cases of Preferment* (1697), in *Political and Economic Writings of Daniel Defoe*, vol. 3: Dissent, edited by W. R. Owens (London: Pickering & Chatto, 2000), p. 46.

[4] Clyve Jones, ' "Too Wild to Succeed": The Occasional Conformity Bills and the Attempts by the House of Lords to Outlaw the Tack in the Reign of Anne', *Parliamentary History* 30, no. 2 (2011): pp. 414–27.

[5] Defoe, *An Enquiry into the Occasional Conformity of Dissenters, in Cases of Preferment* (1697), pp. 45, 55.

[6] Henry Sacheverell, *The Political Union: A Discourse Shewing the Dependance of Government on Religion in General: And of the English Monarchy on the Church of England in Particular* (Oxford, 1702), pp. 50, 59. For more, see Brian Cowan, *The State Trial of Doctor Henry Sacheverell* (Malden: Wiley-Blackwell, 2012).

[7] Defoe, *A New Test of the Church of England's Loyalty* (1702), in *Political and Economic Writings of Daniel Defoe*, p. 65.

arguments to show that every single party of interest to the bill was wholly mistaken—dissenters, Anglicans, High Churchmen, and politicians alike.[8]

His next attempt, *The Shortest Way with the Dissenters*, appeared as the first occasional conformity bill was being read in the Lords. Defoe took a different tack. On its face, the pamphlet reads like a straight-faced if rabid High-Church assault on dissent. Scholars have debated its tone, but many have concluded that it is a pitch-perfect act of ventriloquism, echoing and to some degree inflating the language of earlier critics of occasional conformity, including notorious ideo-logues like Charles Leslie and Sacheverell.[9] Defoe's speaker, for instance, merci-lessly attacks the dissenters, that 'viperous Brood', who for too long now had 'huff'd and bully'd' good Anglicans.[10] After laying out a brief history of dissent, from James I's 'fatal Lenity' to William III, the enraged speaker clarifies the grievous threat that dissenters pose to Anglicanism and parliament. For the most part, these early sections read like the worst kind of High-Church jeremiad, a relentlessly one-sided declaration that dissent will tear England and its beloved institutions to pieces.

At the same time, the positions advocated by the speaker could seem like little more than common sense, at least to High-Church Anglicans. Two arguments stand out in particular. First, the speaker notes, dissenters have misunderstood the queen's obligations to Protestant minorities. Here Defoe was rehashing Anne's declaration from 25 May 1702 (and printed the next day). The queen assured parliament that she would be 'very careful to preserve and maintain the Act of Toleration', before clarifying that 'My own Principles must always keep me entirely firm to the Interests and Religion of the Church of England'.[11] The dissenters, however, had misconstrued the queen, Defoe's speaker argues. Yes, she was willing to safeguard religious nonconformity, but the Anglican Church was her primary concern. 'Her Majesty has promised to Protect and Defend the Church of *England*', he explained, 'and if she cannot effectually do that without the Destruction of the Dissenters, she must of course dispence with one Promise to comply with the other'. In effect, he was asking, if the Church and dissent came

[8] Defoe, *Enquiry into Occasional Conformity. Shewing that the Dissenters are no way Concern'd in it* (London, 1702), pp. 5–6. See also Henry L. Snyder, 'The Defeat of the Occasional Conformity Bill and the Tack: A Study in the Techniques of Parliamentary Management in the Reign of Queen Anne', *Bulletin of the Institute of Historical Research* 41 (1968): p. 79.

[9] Maximillian E. Novak, 'Defoe's *Shortest Way with the Dissenters*: Hoax, Parody, Paradox, Fiction, Irony, and Satire', *Modern Language Quarterly* 27 (1966): pp. 402–17; J. A. Downie, 'Defoe's *Shortest Way with the Dissenters*: Irony, Intention and Reader-Response', *Prose Studies* 9, no. 2 (September 1986): pp. 120–39; and L. S. Horsley, 'Contemporary Reactions to Defoe's *Shortest Way with the Dissenters*', *Studies in English Literature, 1500–1900* 16, no. 3 (Summer 1976): pp. 407–20.

[10] Defoe, *The Shortest Way with the Dissenters: Or Proposals for the Establishment of the Church* (1702), in *Political and Economic Writings of Daniel Defoe*, pp. 98, 99. Hereafter cited parenthetically.

[11] *History and Proceedings of the House of Commons*, vol. 3 (London, 1741–42), pp. 203; and *Her Majesties Most Gracious Speech to Both Houses of Parliament, on Monday the Twenty Fifth Day of May 1702* (London, 1702). See Edward Gregg, *Queen Anne* (New Haven: Yale University Press, 2001), p. 159.

to a head, guess which one would lose? Put most bluntly, 'Her Majesty did never promise to maintain the Tolleration, to the Destruction of the Church' (103). This was a rhetorical fudge on Defoe's part. At the time, Anne was not speaking to the threat of dissent, but only reassuring a wary English people that the monarch was solidly Anglican. And though a logical shell game, it was also the kind of creeping verbal chicanery that was all too easy to miss. What anxious dissenter would have quibbled over a High Churchman's account of a staunchly Anglican queen's promise to the Church?

In a second and equally interesting argument, Defoe's speaker advocates for the end of dissent, but sensibly opposes the wholesale lynching of dissenters. Instead, he calls for exemplary punishment—the kind of punishment routinely handed out in criminal trials throughout the early modern period.[12] In one of the pamphlet's least heated passages, his speaker clarifies: 'I am not supposing that all the Dissenters in *England* shou'd be Hang'd or Banish'd, but as in cases of Rebellions and Insurrections, if a few of the Ring-leaders suffer, the Multitude are dismist, so a few obstinate People being made Examples there's no doubt but the Severity of the Law would find a stop to the Compliance of the Multitude' (106). In short, string up a few figureheads, and the rest will sheepishly follow the flock back to the Church. The reason was simple. For the most part, moderate dissenters saw nonconformity as a matter of '*Modes and Accidents*'. Even dissenters believed that the Church of England was legitimate, quibbling only over aspects of its government and liturgical practises, such as kneeling for Holy Communion. One thinks of Presbyterians and dissenters like Defoe, who based on their reading of the New Testament only objected to the rule of bishops.[13] 'Why shou'd we expect that they will suffer Gallows and Gallies, corporeal Punishment and Banishment for these Trifles?' (107).

No one, however, immediately caught Defoe's irony, not even those embroiled in such partisan skirmishes, which encouraged the very kinds of close reading needed to decipher and expose ambiguously propagandistic agendas.[14] At least early on, Defoe's irony was not obvious; many of his readers simply took the pamphlet at face value.[15] As Kate Loveman has remarked, 'one has to wonder how

---

[12] Frank McLynn, *Crime and Punishment in Eighteenth-Century England* (London: Routledge, 1989), p. xiii; David Lemmings, *Law and Government in England during the Long Eighteenth Century: From Consent to Command* (New York: Palgrave Macmillan, 2011), pp. 96ff.; and Simon Devereaux, 'In Place of Death: Transportation, Penal Practices, and the English State, 1770–1830', in *Qualities of Mercy: Justice, Punishment, and Discretion*, edited by Carolyn Strange (Vancouver: University of British Columbia Press, 1996), p. 62.

[13] W. R. Owen, Introduction, *Political and Economic Writings of Daniel Defoe*, p. 8.

[14] Mark Knights, *Representation and Misrepresentation in Later Stuart Britain: Partisanship and Political Culture* (Oxford: Oxford University Press, 2005), pp. 356–8.

[15] *The Observator* 71 (23–6 December 1702); and Charles Leslie, *The New Association, Part II* (London, 1703), p. 6. Howard Weinbrot has argued, however, that 'A heavily annotated copy of the *Shortest Way* in the British Library makes plain that at least one reader, surely among many others, promptly or at least reasonably soon saw through the speaker's presumed persona' (*Literature, Religion,*

even a careful reader could detect Defoe's irony'.[16] This is perhaps predictable. Linda Hutcheon has written that the vagueness of irony is what makes it such 'risky business'. Readers operate in different 'discursive context[s]' or 'participation framework[s]', which mediate their understanding of a given work. Such interpretive difficulties are only exacerbated by the 'transideological nature' of irony itself: its ability to be both 'conservative or authoritarian' or 'oppositional and subversive'.[17] Nonetheless, Defoe's contemporaries had few doubts about his irony—but only *after* his authorship became known. Overwhelmingly, his critics agreed: he was 'a very *Ironical* Gentleman all over', as one exasperated reader tartly put it.[18] The problem, they argued, was that *The Shortest Way*'s vexing irony was either too obscure or too poorly executed to have led its readers to Defoe's intended conclusions.[19] It was Defoe's own fault, one critic argued, for relying too heavily on irony, that slippery and obscure '*Clavis Rhetorica*'.[20]

The Shortest Way has come in for similar debate in recent decades. Many scholars have agreed: *The Shortest Way* is ironic, but its internal signals, which should have alighted Defoe's readers to his intended meaning, were simply too subtle.[21] Others have disagreed, arguing that the pamphlet's ironic signals are 'conspicuous'.[22] One such signal is the speaker's bungling of the number of Israelites Moses killed: not 'Three and thirty thousand', as Defoe's speaker writes, but three thousand. This would have been a glaring error—and, the numbers being written out, one not easily chalked up to a boozy typesetter's mere clumsiness. We might also conjecture that Defoe, who had seemingly memorized much of the Bible as a child, intended it.[23]

And yet doubts creep in. Was this so certainly an *ironic* signal, or was this merely a key to the speaker's own sloppiness, a synecdochic jab at High-Church scriptural illiteracy? Even the number of Israelites massacred raises questions. In the King James Version (1611), Defoe's preferred translation, Exodus pegs the number at 'about three thousand men' (32:28), but Numbers octuples the sum, putting it at 'twentie and foure thousand' (25:9). Has the speaker perhaps

---

and the Evolution of Culture, 1660–1780 [Baltimore: Johns Hopkins University Press, 2013], p. 79). Yet it is unclear *when* annotations were added, or whether the annotator thought the speaker was being ironic or was simply a fool.

[16] Kate Loveman, *Reading Fictions, 1660–1740: Deception in English Literary and Political Culture* (Burlington: Ashgate, 2008), p. 134, and ch. 6, *passim*.

[17] Linda Hutcheon, *Irony's Edge: The Theory and Politics of Irony* (London: Routledge, 1994), pp. 9, 15, 95.

[18] *The Fox with his Fire-brand Unkennell'd and Insnared* (London, 1703), pp. 3–4.

[19] John Dunton, *The Shortest Way with Whores and Rogues* (1703); and *The Protestant Jesuite Unmask'd* (London, 1704), p. 50.

[20] *The Shortest Way... With its Author's Brief Explanation Consider'd* (London, 1703), pp. 6, 7, 9, 15.

[21] Horsley, 'Contemporary Reactions', p. 409.

[22] Downie, 'Defoe's *Shortest Way*', pp. 133–4; Howard D. Weinbrot, *Literature, Religion, and the Evolution of Culture*, p. 79; and Keymer, *Poetics*, pp. 128–30.

[23] Maximillian E. Novak, *Daniel Defoe, Master of Fictions: His Life and Ideas* (Oxford: Oxford University Press, 2001), p. 32.

confused or conflated the two numbers? Is the speaker deliberately exaggerating?[24] Perhaps the speaker, even Defoe, was confusing one of the Bible's interminable streams of figures, such as the lists of tribes who came to David's support in his war with Saul (1 Chronicles 12:23–37), or the 33,000 mercenaries organized by the Ammonites to fight David (2 Samuel 10:6). Even granting the obviousness of the error, and presuming Defoe intended it, we need to ask whether this numeric bungling was an *ironic* signal. Would Defoe's readers have so easily assumed that the speaker was a mere mask? That the pamphlet was an elaborate hoax? That the call for the dissenters to be strung up en masse, like so many idolatrous and lusty Israelites, was nothing more than a cheeky biblical joke on those boorish High-Church fanatics?

The botched sum does seem like a signal, yet I doubt whether it was either unambiguously ironic or functionally clear.[25] For readers of one cast of mind, the numbers business was indirect proof that the speaker was an ass, an exemplary fool among so many doltish fanatics; readers of another stripe might have understood it sympathetically, believing it the kind of mistake anyone might make when confronted with the Bible's glaring inconsistencies. John Tutchin simply chalked up the speaker's errors to the haphazard reading of some lesser cleric.[26] In any case, the claim that this is an overt, easily discernible ironic signal seems hasty. J. A. Downie allows that such passages function ambiguously: 'Does [the inflation of the number of Israelites killed] draw deliberate attention to the unreliability of the narrator? Is it Defoe's muddle, or his speaker's?'[27] To be sure, someone made a mistake—whether it was Defoe or his speaker—but nothing suggests that that mistake was a simple, unmissable ironic clue. Like Joseph Hone, I do not want to deny the *potential* 'ironic edge' of these 'rhetorical flourishes'. Instead, such moments only become 'visible and ironic when one knows what one is looking for, which readers in 1702 did not'.[28]

In almost all instances, such clue-hunting readings of *The Shortest Way* have relied on a surprisingly recent and tidily theoretical view of irony. Perhaps we should ask, in the first place, whether internal signalling was what Defoe had in mind.[29] Instead of working from normative notions about what irony is and how it ought to function—the presupposition that all ironic works always contain

---

[24] W. R. Owens, *Political and Economic Writings of Daniel Defoe*, vol. 3, p. 363n22.
[25] For a similar scepticism, see Joseph Hone, *Literature and Party Politics at the Accession of Queen Anne* (Oxford: Oxford University Press, 2017), pp. 162–3.
[26] *The Observator* (23–6 December 1702).
[27] 'Defoe's *Shortest Way with the Dissenters*', pp. 133, 134.   [28] Hone, *Party Politics*, p. 163.
[29] In this regard, I partly agree with Ian Watt, who called *The Shortest Way* 'a masterpiece not of irony but of impersonation' (*The Rise of the Novel* [Berkeley: University of California Press, 1957], p. 126); Ashley Marshall, who reads it as not 'insufficiently ironic but as a counterfeit, an intentional fake not meant to be decoded' ('The Generic Context of Defoe's *The Shortest-Way with the Dissenters* and the Problem of Irony', *Review of English Studies* 61, no. 249 [2010]: pp. 235–6); and Keymer, who interprets the pamphlet both ways: 'when casually read, it functioned first as a hoax...It could then function as irony when more carefully read' (*Poetics*, p. 130).

internal signals that attentive readers should be able to decipher—we should step back and ask a few more rudimentary questions. What was irony at the beginning of the eighteenth century, and how did readers and critics think it worked? To literary scholars today, the answers to those questions might be surprising.

One of the major faults of our current theoretical models is the extent to which they simplify the messy mechanics of irony itself. Satires from this period are often rhetorically clumsy affairs. Norman Knox has observed that 'the worst aspect of run-of-the-mill controversial irony in the Restoration and first years of the eighteenth century [was] its half-heartedness. Even when a combatant found an effective ironic premise or mask he was likely after a few pages to drop it for downright abuse'.[30] Part of the reason *The Shortest Way* was misunderstood extends from the fact that Defoe kept up the High-Church front so relentlessly.[31] As I have already tried to make clear, the pamphlet's errors, rather than being straightforward ironic clues, were simply the kinds of errors that any foolish, one-sided ideologue might have made. *The Shortest Way* lacks, that is, the kinds of manifest internal clues—psychological discontinuities, drops in tone, a hastily discarded mask—that would have allowed Defoe's readers to decode his pamphlet definitively as a work of satire, or at least to identify some disparity between writer and speaker, without recourse to the author function of a proper name. Defoe's rhetorical consistency was exceptional—and, as a result, confusing.

Perhaps this is to be expected. In 1702, irony was a poorly understood and even obscure term. Sixteenth- and seventeenth-century rhetoricians (and some in the eighteenth century) had profound difficulty pinning irony down. For some, it was a synonym for sarcasm, antiphrasis, inversio, or simulatio; for others, a substitute for more obscure rhetorical figures, such as asteimus, epiceriomesis, micterismus, or charientismus.[32] This imprecision only grew as more colloquial language cluttered the lexical landscape. One man's irony was another man's ridicule, banter, humour, drolling, or burlesque.[33] Lay writers and readers, rather than technical rhetoricians, were also more inclined to use a term like raillery—forms

---

[30] Norman Knox, *The Word Irony and Its Context, 1500–1755* (Durham: Duke University Press, 1961), p. 173.

[31] As Weinbrot has noted, eighteenth-century 'commentators assumed that authorial role-playing was common to many literary forms, and frequently used terms like *masks, person, personate, character, part* and *figurative* speaker' (*Eighteenth-Century Satire: Essays on Text and Context from Dryden to Peter Pindar* [Cambridge: Cambridge University Press, 1988], p. 47).

[32] Richard Sherry, *A Treatise of the Figures of Grammer and Rhetorike* (London, 1555), f. xxvi; Abraham Fraunce, *The Arcadian Rhetorike*, vol. 1 (London, 1588), ch. 6; George Puttenham, *Arte of English Poesie* (London, 1589), pp. 128, 157–60; Henry Peacham, *The Garden of Eloquence* (London, 1593), pp. 37–8; Thomas Hall, *Vindiciae literarum; The Schools Guarded* (London, 1655), pp. 163ff; John Smith, *The Mysterie of Rhetorique Unvail'd* (London, 1657), pp. 79–80; John Prideaux, *Sacred Eloquence, Or the Act of Rhetorick* (London, 1659), pp. 12–14; Anthony Blackwall, *Introduction to the Classics* (London, 1718), pp. 195–8; and Ephraim Chambers, *Cyclopaedia: Or, An Universal Dictionary of Arts and Science*, vol. 1 (London, 1728), p. 111.

[33] Knox, *Irony*, p. 181.

of contemptuous ridicule, light-hearted or cruel jesting, or epideixis (praise-by-blame and blame-by-praise)—for what later critics would identify as irony.[34]

Not until the 1720s and '30s did irony start to feature more prominently in general and critical literature.[35] Even then, though, critics often fell back on a stock formulation, one that did little to explain how readers were expected to jump from a surface meaning to an intended one: irony was saying the contrary, or opposite, of what one means.[36] The perception that irony was a slippery, unstable device endured throughout the first half of the eighteenth century. As Henry Fielding remarked in 1748, 'no kind of Humour [is] so liable to be mistaken[:] it is, of all others, the most dangerous to the Writer'.[37] As a result, irony was often greeted with an air of scepticism or even outright distrust. Ephraim Chambers listed it among the four primary rhetorical tropes but cautioned that ironies 'should always be clear; they are vicious, if they be obscure, or too far fetched'.[38]

How, then, were readers supposed to locate, decode, and interpret irony? Thomas Gordon felt that the '*Ironical Stile*' could only be detected by putting 'fantastical Expressions into the pompous Eulogium', or by 'print[ing] some ambiguous Words in significant *Italick* Characters'.[39] This might be the most intriguing observation, one common throughout the last half of the seventeenth century and the first half of the eighteenth: irony, if it was to be detected at all, required not internal linguistic signalling but overt typographical cues.[40] To quote the childish pitter-patter of Swiftian instruction: 'To Statesmen wou'd you give a Wipe, / You print it in *Italick Type*'.[41]

Easier said—or printed—than done. Italics were hardly the preserve of satirists, nor was their presence a guarantee of verbal irony. Some uses (for proper names, place names, and quotations) were printing conventions rather than typographical cues to signification. Then, as today, italics could also be used to add verbal stress.[42] In the 1680s, for instance, the printer Joseph Moxon noted that '*Words of great Emphasis*' should be 'set in *Italick*'.[43] Italics could even serve a more precise communicative purpose. In his 1755 *Printer's Grammar*, for instance, John

---

[34] Knox, *Irony*, ch. 5, especially pp. 192–208.   [35] Knox, *Irony*, p. 141.

[36] Knox, *Irony*, p. 30. In his *Dictionary*, for instance, Samuel Johnson calls it 'A mode of speech in which the meaning is contrary to the words'.

[37] Henry Fielding, *Jacobite's Journal*, no. 17 (26 March 1748), in *The Jacobite's Journal and Related Writings*, edited by W. B. Coley (Oxford: Clarendon Press, 1974), p. 211.

[38] Ephraim Chambers, *Cyclopaedia*, vol. 2, p. 256.

[39] Thomas Gordon, *Humourist*, vol. 2 (London, 1725), pp. 99–102.

[40] [Thomas Gordon], *The Art of Railing at Great Men* (London, 1723), p. 16. See also *The Craftsman* 580 (12 September 1730); and [Francis Squire], *A Faithful Report of a Genuine Debate Concerning the Liberty of the Press* (London, 1740), p. 18.

[41] Swift, *On Poetry: A Rapsody* (1733), ll. 95–6.

[42] M. B. Parkes, *Pause and Effect: An Introduction to the History of Punctuation in the West* (Aldershot: Scolar Press, 1992), p. 70.

[43] Joseph Moxon, *Mechanick Exercises on the Whole Art of Printing (1683–4)*, edited by Herbert Davis and Harry Carter, 2nd ed. (Oxford: Oxford University Press, 1962), p. 216. My thanks to James McLaverty for bringing the conventions of italicization to my attention.

Smith asserted that italics should be used 'for words, terms, or expressions which some authors would have regarded as more nervous; and by which they intend to convey to the reader either instructing, satyrizing, admiring, or other hints and remarks'.[44] Particularly interesting here is Smith's use of the word 'nervous', whose more common meaning today (as in an anxious temperament) was only coming into currency in the mid-eighteenth century.[45] Instead, Smith's usage points to its now obsolete rhetorical meaning. To be 'nervous', in this sense, is to have a particular concern to be 'vigorous, powerful, [or] forcible', with the goal of precise semantic transfer between writer and reader. In such instances, italics become a visible, typographical means of signalling, by which authors 'intend to convey to the reader' some 'hints and remarks'.[46] As James McLaverty has written, 'Italics, at least in their most interesting appearances, have to do with these little pushes that draw our attention to the author's intention and cause us to identify it'.[47] With 'nervous' italics, the outright typographical signalling of irony would appear to be a textbook case of how 'linguistic codes' can merge with 'biblio-graphical codes'.[48] In short, during this period, irony was discernible not only through verbal signals but also, and perhaps even primarily, through typograph-ical cues that would have drawn attention to those complicated verbal gestures.

With *The Shortest Way*, all of the conventional uses of italics are in place, and yet it would be difficult to argue that Defoe, even if he were fully aware of those conventions, took an active part in directing the compositor. Today, we possess only one major manuscript in his hand, the autograph copy of *The Compleat English Gentleman*, and Defoe's successive editors have repeatedly remarked on the messiness, irregularity, randomness, and general perplexity of his orthography and punctuation.[49] As a result, most scholars have followed G. A. Starr in concluding that 'no valid stylistic comments can be based on

---

[44] John Smith, *The Printer's Grammar* (London, 1755), p. 14.

[45] Nervous 9.a.: *OED*: 'Of a person or temperament: excitable, highly strung, easily agitated, anxious, timid; hypersensitive; worried, anxious (about); afraid, apprehensive (of)'.

[46] *Nervous*: 4.a.: *OED*: 'Of argument, prose, poetry, literary style, etc.: vigorous, powerful, forcible; free from insipidity and diffuseness'.

[47] James McLaverty, 'Italics in Swift's Poems', *Swift Studies* 28 (2011): p. 27. On the manner in which 'typographic features offer alternative solutions to . . . semantic and pragmatic problems', see David Crystal, *Making a Point: The Pernickety Story of English Punctuation* (London: Profile Books, 2015), p. 318. See also James McLaverty, 'Swift and the Art of Political Publication: Hints and Title Pages, 1711–1714', in *Politics and Literature in the Age of Swift*, edited by Claude Rawson (Cambridge: Cambridge University Press, 2010), pp. 116–39; and Simon Dickie, *Cruelty and Laughter: Forgotten Comic Literature and the Unsentimental Eighteenth Century* (Chicago: University of Chicago Press, 2011), pp. xii, 191, 238.

[48] Jerome J. McGann, *The Textual Condition* (Princeton: Princeton University Press, 1991), p. 77.

[49] Autograph copy of Defoe's 'The Compleat Gentleman', Add. MS 32555, BL. See Karl D. Bülbring (ed.), Introduction to *The Compleat English Gentleman by Daniel Defoe* (London: D. Nutt, 1890), pp. xvii–xix; and G. H. Healey (ed.), Preface to *The Letters of Daniel Defoe* (Oxford: Clarendon Press, 1969), pp. vii–viii.

nuances of punctuation, capitalization, italicization, or spelling in [Defoe's] texts'.[50] *The Shortest Way* simply lacks the kinds of overt typographical signalling that would have theoretically helped even the most perceptive reader to arrive at more subtle internal linguistic clues. And again, we have good reason to doubt that those specifically *verbal* cues would have been so self-evident in 1702.

Only by the late 1720s was irony finally coming into sharper focus, with a greater concern for its verbal rather than typographical nature. Theoretically, at least, it was beginning to be thought of in ways a lot like our own: irony should be understood by easy-to-identify internal signals. In 1702, though, hardly was that the case. If *The Shortest Way* is in fact ironic, and yet lacks *internal* signals, how then were readers supposed to identify the disparity between Defoe's position and his High-Church speaker's? One clue comes from Quintilian's *Orations*, a text central to early modern thinking about rhetoric. Quintilian writes that irony 'is made evident to the understanding either by the delivery, the character of the speaker or *the nature of the subject*'.[51] The first two of these we would call internal signals: they would include variations in the speaker's tone (which suggest the speaker holds a view different from the author's) or the character of the speaker (including the speaker's perceived reliability or sanity).

Quintilian's third way—the nature of the subject—offers a hint to Defoe's method. This third way might be either an internal signal or a competing external reality or perception. If internal, the nature of the subject would be at odds with either the tone of the piece or the speaker's mask. This would include the presentation of impossible or largely implausible views that no wholly sane or non-ironic individual would likely hold (think only of the projector's solution of eating Irish babies in *A Modest Proposal*). If external—or what I call an 'extrinsic' irony—then the writer would make his intended meaning known by seemingly offering an earnest defence of or by advocating for a position that he presumes his intended reader would not hold or would object to. The position per se would be both possible and plausible, but it would nonetheless be at odds with the presumably shared prejudices of the work's intended readers.

How then were readers supposed to jump from a surface meaning to an intended one with extrinsic irony? The answer, I would argue, is *shared prejudices*. The writer presumes that the reader holds a view of a given subject that is at odds with the surface meaning of the ironic piece. Imagine a poem praising Walpole in 1742, shortly after his resignation. By then, both the poet and the vast majority of his readers would have shared the belief (or been aware of the popular perception) that Walpole was the very portrait of backdoor dealing, cronyism, and political

[50] G. A. Starr, 'Defoe's Prose Style: 1. The Language of Interpretation', *Modern Philology* 71, no. 3 (February 1974): pp. 278–9.

[51] *The Orator's Education*, edited by and trans. Donald A. Russell, vol. 3 (Cambridge: Harvard University Press, 2002), bk. 8, ch. 6, sect. 54 (emphasis mine).

corruption. A poem that overtly praised Walpole for his honesty would therefore have awkwardly butted up against a commonly held, yet textually external, perception of his dishonesty. As a result, readers would have been forced to square the disparity between the poem's praise and a widely held view of Walpole, causing them (one hopes) to see the praise as ironic.

Hardly, though, should we call this disparity between the speaker's position and the presumably shared prejudices of his readers an *internal* signal. It is worth noting that to praise a man for honesty is something we do every day, but this does not make it necessarily ironic. Instead, in the abstract, such praise—person X is honest—is both possible and plausible. The praise or proposition of an *internally* signalled irony is often neither of these things. In an internally signalled poem, for instance, Walpole would be praised for something impossible—say, the angel's wings growing out of his back—or something implausible: Walpole has miraculously cured all political corruption. In either case, the reader would need little to understand the praise as ironic beyond a few basic facts or platitudes and the help of a simple syllogism: angels don't exist, say, or corruption is an endemic feature of politics. With extrinsic irony, however, the reader would have to hold certain views or at least be aware of potentially shifting public perceptions or values. The reader's ability to locate the irony would therefore rely on his or her ability to identify the disparity between the praise or proposition (e.g., Walpole is honest) and an external reality (e.g., the popular view that Walpole is dishonest).

This kind of extrinsic irony, I would argue, also typifies Defoe's pamphlet, though classical, early modern, and modern theorists have only made passing mention of it.[52] *The Shortest Way* also relies on shared prejudices, though Defoe presumed, wrongly I would argue, that his readers would be just as horrified as he was by the High-Church position, if he simply laid out the precise conclusions that he felt Orthodox Anglicans were implicitly advocating for. This, a decade later, was also how Defoe attempted to rationalize the 'True and Onely Design' behind a series of mock-Jacobite pamphlets, for which he was again arrested in 1713. In an ill-advised manuscript petition to the queen, he clarified his method: 'by Ironicall Discourse of Recomending The Pretender, in the strongest and Most Forcible Manner to Expose his designs, and The ruinous Consequences of his Succeeding

---

[52] Northrop Frye, for instance, calls this mode *sophisticated irony*, 'which lets the reader add the ironic tone himself' (*Anatomy of Criticism* [Princeton: Princeton University Press, 1957], p. 41). D. C. Muecke likewise offers a separate category, 'covert irony', and he briefly mentions 'external contradiction': 'when the ironist thinks he can rely upon his audience having the requisite prior knowledge' (*The Compass of Irony* [London: Methuen, 1969], p. 59). Like Frye, Wayne Booth parses out irony into two general categories: stable irony, in which the reader can deduce the implied author's covert intention; and unstable irony, in which the implied author's beliefs, propositions, or intentions are unknowable or inconsistent. Like other critics, Booth claims that irony becomes known by signals. He disposes, however, with the distinction between internal and external signals, which he calls 'strangely irrelevant' (*A Rhetoric of Irony* [Chicago: University of Chicago Press, 1975], pp. 3–7, 240–5, 11).

Therein'.[53] In this instance, as Defoe himself acknowledged, the irony was derived not from explicit verbal cues, but from the deductive reasoning of readers, who would arrive at the text's ironic intentions when they were presented with the full repercussions of the Jacobite agenda.

In *The Shortest Way*, however, the disparity between the speaker's proposition (exemplary punishment) and the external reality (the threat of dissent hardly warranted corporal punishment) was simply too weak to prod his readers on: his speaker's conclusions almost felt too reasonable. Defoe wrongly believed that his readers would have perceived the stringing up of a few dissenters for quibbles over church governance and the liturgy as a grossly overblown response to religious nonconformity (it is worth keeping in mind that even Tory-led bills at this point were comparatively moderate, proposing only a tax on occasional conformity). Rather than identifying the pamphlet's overt aims as an untenable form of persecution, however, some High-Church readers thought this was a perfectly reasonable plan. Defoe's speaker did not call for the culling of dissenters, only for the selective and exemplary punishment of church leaders to incentivize the return of dissenting congregants to the Anglican church. And dissenters, while no doubt objecting, also thought the application of exemplary punishment the sort of plan that a staunchly Anglican government might plausibly have pursued. If Defoe had called for the killing of *all* dissenters—the kind of argument that the vast majority of his readers, from High Churchmen to dissenters, would have found so obscenely outlandish that no sane or non-ironic speaker would plausibly advocate for it—he might, perhaps, have been better understood.

The problem Defoe encountered—in this case, a disparity between the preju-dice a writer presumes his readers to hold and the actual prejudices of his readers—is the very problem of extrinsic irony. It is often misunderstood when external information remains unknown or, in Defoe's case, when a presumably shared prejudice turns out to be a narrow or idiosyncratic one. In Defoe's view, he was doing exactly what Allan Ramsay had thought the best method of ironic attack more than half a century later: by 'representing the obvious consequences of such a proceeding [from false principles], convincing the reader of the falshood and absurdity of such principles and opinions'.[54] Defoe, however, overestimated the extent to which his readers would find the High-Church position grossly overblown. A few decades later, Gordon urged satirists, when writing '*Ironical* or *Mock Panegyrick*', 'always [to] make…the Subject of your Panegyrick [that] which other People complain of'.[55] In effect, Gordon was articulating the notion

---

[53] 'To The Queens Most Excellent Majesty [:] The Humble Peti[ti]on of Daniel De Foe' (November 1713 [?]), SP 34/37/11, TNA.

[54] Allan Ramsay, *An Essay on Ridicule* (London, 1753), p. 54.

[55] Gordon, *Humourist*, vol. 2, pp. 96, 105. See also Antoine Arnauld and Pierre Nicole, *The Art of Speaking*, trans. Bernard Lamy (London, 1676), p. 146.

that, in readers' eyes, it is the impossibility of praising that which is uniformly repellent—taxes *are* great!—that makes an author's true position known.

Still, even the clearest example of extrinsic irony was tricky to identify. One critic implored ironists to be certain that there be 'sufficient prejudice' against the position being sent up.[56] 'Where would be the *Irony*, or the *Satire*', the pseud-onymous Caleb D'Anvers asked, 'in calling *Lucretia* chaste, *Caesar* valiant, or *Cato* just?'[57] Such mock-praise would always be missed by readers. It would simply confirm what everybody, more or less, thought to be true. Lucretia *was* chaste, Caesar *was* valiant, Cato *was* just. A writer might have thought otherwise, but there was no good way to express such condemnation through unmitigated encomium, because such an inverse understanding so readily contradicted the most prevalent view. According to Wayne Booth, prejudice itself inhibits a reader from understanding an ironic statement. He has called these prejudices, after I. A. Richards, 'doctrinal adhesions', which can 'prevent my inferring ironies when the implied author's norms seem to me less plausible than the surface statement that violates them'.[58] Defoe, for instance, thought everyone would be aghast when he laid out the High-Church position clearly, by making it obvious that it led to punishments so needlessly gruesome that no one should take the pamphlet as a plausible solution to the question of dissent. He was wrong. Defoe's readers didn't misread *The Shortest Way*; Defoe, instead, misread his readers.

The problem of Defoe's readers—their inability to access what, exactly, he rather than his speaker was aiming at—was only exacerbated by the pamphlet's parody of High-Church rhetoric. Fredric V. Bogel has argued that parody 'is inescapably imitative and therefore identificatory...the imitative impulse can produce hostile parody as well as positive criticism or even tribute...A tribute may devolve into a hostile parody; a satiric mimicry may emerge as unwitting tribute'.[59] In an effort to expose the grievousness of the High-Church position, Defoe was forced to perform an act of parodic ventriloquism: he had to think and speak like those whom he most detested. In the transitional process of identifica-tion, however, he seemingly failed to re-emerge. For Linda Hutcheon, parody, especially in the twentieth century, is 'extended repetition with critical distance'.[60] In the end, a discernible distance is what Defoe failed to produce. Rather than exposing the consequences of the attack on dissent, he offered an accidental tribute to the pragmatics of religious persecution.

I have gone to some lengths to emphasize this sociocentric aspect of Defoe's extrinsic irony because such readerly perceptions came to serve a crucial

[56] Obadiah Walker, *Art of Oratory* (1659), p. 93.   [57] *Craftsman*, vol. 1 (1731), pp. 102ff.
[58] I. A. Richards, *Practical Criticism: A Study of Literary Judgment* (London: K. Paul, Trench, Trubner & Co., ltd., 1929), pp. 13–18; and Booth, *A Rhetoric of Irony*, p. 224.
[59] Bogel, *Satire*, pp. 73–4.
[60] Linda Hutcheon, *A Theory of Parody: The Teachings of Twentieth-Century Art Forms* (London: Methuen, 1985), p. 7.

hermeneutic function in trials for defamation. As we will see over the next two sections, authorial intentions were at the heart of the changes made to libel law as the Crown moved from an era of prepublication licensing to a regime of post-publication prosecutions: first in the revisions Chief Justice Sir John Holt made to the law; and, second, in Dr Joseph Browne's trial, which brought to a head the question of irony in court.

3.2 Malice, Intention, and Irony in the Law of Seditious Libel

When licensing lapsed in 1695, the Crown knew it had a problem on its hands. Presses were suddenly abundant, print was remarkably cheap, coffeehouses had sprung up in stunning numbers, and tensions routinely flared up into full-fledged paper wars.[61] Many in parliament hoped, even expected, that prepublication censorship would be re-enacted, and yet more than a dozen new licensing bills failed between 1695 and 1714.[62] In its efforts to fill this regulatory chasm, the government had a few options—including *scandalum magnatum*, Tudor felony statutes, and prosecutions for heresy and treason—but none of these proved a useful enough tool for policing the press more generally.[63]

As Philip Hamburger has shown, the Crown eventually struck upon a new solution: the law of seditious libel, an early seventeenth-century offshoot of the law of the libel of magistrates, a subcategory of written defamation, and an early remedy to protect officials from manuscript defamation.[64] The Crown's turn to the courts was nonetheless unexpected. Trials for seditious libel were almost wholly for unprinted materials in the seventeenth century—that is, manuscripts that were not subject to licensing laws—and for writings that were not necessarily even seditious or defamatory.[65] Moreover, such trials were rare. The lapse of licensing changed everything. Between 1695 and 1707, Crown prosecutions for 'print, writing, and speech', and primarily for seditious libel, grew exponentially, and those numbers continued to rise across the century.[66] Between 1702 and 1760,

---

[61] Knights, *Representation and Misrepresentation*, pp. 220–59; and Paul Halliday, *Dismembering the Body Politic: Partisan Politics in England's Towns, 1650–1730* (Cambridge: Cambridge University Press, 2003), pp. 276ff.

[62] Hanson, *Government*, pp. 260–3; John Feather, 'The Book Trade in Politics: The Making of the Copyright Act of 1710', *Publishing History* 8 (1980): table 1, pp. 19–44, *passim*; and Raymond Astbury, 'The Renewal of the Licensing Act in 1693 and its Lapse in 1695', *The Library*, fifth series, 33, no. 4 (1978): pp. 296–322.

[63] Hamburger, 'Seditious Libel', p. 671.

[64] *Case de Libellis Famosis*, 5 Coke 125 (1605), 77 Eng. Rep. 250; Hamburger, 'Seditious Libel', p. 691. See also Irving Brant, 'Seditious Libel: Myth and Reality', *New York University Law Review* 39, no. 1 (January 1964): pp. 8–11.

[65] Hamburger, 'Seditious Libel', p. 674.

[66] Wendell Bird, *Press and Speech Under Assault: The Early Supreme Court Justices, the Sedition Act of 1798, and the Campaign against Dissent* (Oxford: Oxford University Press, 2016), p. 38–9; Michael Lobban, 'From Seditious Libel to Unlawful Conspiracy: Peterloo and the Changing Face of Political

for instance, some 115 informations and indictments for seditious libel were filed in King's Bench, with additional trials taking place at the Old Bailey.[67] By the mid-eighteenth century, what was once an obscure law for dealing with occasional manuscript offences had become the Crown's chief means of controlling the press.[68]

It was under John Holt, appointed Chief Justice of King's Bench by King William on 17 April 1689, that this transformation from an obscure manuscript law to the Crown's chief weapon against the press was performed. By 1660, indictments and informations for seditious libel contained three essential allega-tions. First, the writing had to be defamatory. This meant that *someone* had been defamed—a government official, for instance, and not simply a government body—and that he or she was clearly identifiable.[69] In practise, the courts them-selves determined whether a writing was defamatory, not the jury.[70] Second, the libel had to be published, meaning distributed to some third party, which the courts broadly understood as any aspect of the physical or textual production of an offending libel, such as printing, stitching, and binding, which were aspects of 'making'. But printing alone was not enough, as Chief Justice Sir Robert Hyde observed, 'for if a man print a book to make a fire on, that's no offence'.[71]

Third, and most important, was the defendant's state of mind.[72] By 1660, there were largely clear rules, borrowed from the law of murder, for establishing this.[73] The courts ruled that the act of killing created a rebuttable presumption of malice—an *implied* intention.[74] In the same way, a supposedly seditious libel created a rebuttable presumption of malice. Thus the words, 'by construction of law', as jurists put it, supplied the defendant's state of mind.[75] Despite the

---

Crime, c.1770–1820', *Oxford Journal of Legal Studies* 10, no. 3 (1990): pp. 307–9 and 'Treason, Sedition and the Radical Movements in the Age of the French Revolution', *Liverpool Law Review* 22 (2000): pp. 205–34; Clive Emsley, 'Repression, "Terror" and the Rule of Law in England During the Decade of the French Revolution', *The English Historical Review* 100, no. 397 (October 1985): pp. 801, 824; and Philip Harling, 'The Law of Libel and the Limits of Repression, 1790–1832', *Historical Journal* 44, no. 1 (March 2001): p. 108.

[67] *An Account of the Persons Held to Bail to Answer in the Court of King's Bench for Libels, From 1 Anne to 57 Geo. 3*, ed. E. H. Lushington (1818), p. 4. KB 33/24/2, TNA.

[68] James C. Oldham, *English Common Law in the Age of Mansfield* (Chapel Hill: University of North Carolina Press, 2004), pp. 209ff.

[69] *Proceedings against Mr. Baxter* (1685), 11 *State Trials* 502.

[70] Hamburger, 'Seditious Libel', p. 702.

[71] *Trial of Dover, Brewster and Brooks* (1663), 6 *State Trials* 563.

[72] For conflicting opinions on whether a defendant's knowledge of the contents of a given libel was a necessary aspect of the offence, or only whether publication or the intent to publish were necessary, see *Want's Case* (1600), More 628 (S.C.), 72 Eng. Rep. 802; *Trial of Dover, Brewster and Brooks* (1663), 6 *State Trials* 564; and *Lamb's Case* (1610), 9 Coke 59 (S.C.), 77 Eng. Rep. 822.

[73] For example, see *Trial of Dover, Brewster and Brooks* (1663), 6 *State Trials* 547; *Trial of Sir Samuel Barnardiston* (1684), 9 *State Trials* 1349; and *Seven Bishops' Trial* (1688), 12 *State Trials* 401.

[74] Edward Coke, *Institutes of the Laws of England*, vol. 3 (London, 1641), p. 52; William Hawkins, *A Treatise of the Pleas of the Crown*, vol. 2 (London, 1716–21), ch. 13; and Matthew Hale, *History of the Pleas of the Crown* (London, 1736), pp. 229, 455, 508.

[75] *Trial of Dover, Brewster and Brooks* (1663), 6 *State Trials* 547.

simplicity of the rule, establishing a rebuttable presumption of malice was difficult, because malice, legally speaking, was only a product of the publication's defamatory content. That is, if the contents of a given libel were ambiguously defamatory, then the malicious intentions of the defendant required additional proof. Lord Chief Justice George Jeffreys clarified that 'there must be some accusations, or words of the person accused, that in their own nature will bear the interpretation of such crimes'.[76] As a result, defendants often argued that they had acted without knowledge or with good intentions. The question of whether the defendant had acted knowingly (i.e., with malice) in publishing the defamation only went to the jury if either the judge or the defence, offering proof of good intentions, raised the issue. By the 1680s, however, judges were treating questions of knowledge and malice as mere formalities in an attempt to remove such ticklish issues from the jury's purview.

Holt further modified the law in two stages. First, between 1696 and 1702, when trials for seditious libel were still only being used against manuscript offences, he began to relax the publication requirement.[77] Traditionally, the mere making or composing of a libel was not criminal without additional proof that the defendant had knowingly published the libel (made it public, that is, to some other individual) or had at least intended to do so.[78] Holt went so far as to argue that the mere transcribing of a libel was a 'making'. This argument was a crucial first step in reducing the publication requirement in trials for seditious libel. Holt in effect argued that simply writing a libel—rather than publishing it—was criminal. This argument he returned to years later, claiming that neither the publication of the libel nor the intent to publish was an essential element of the crime.[79] Holt further argued that the mere writing had *always* constituted the crime.[80] The publication requirement, as Hamburger has shown, he 'simply evaded ... There were, in fact, no plausible precedents for Holt's ruling'.[81] Instead, Holt pointed to Roman law and general political exigencies: 'this Opinion we give is no Novelty in the World, It is founded upon the preservation of All Government, and Safety of all Civil Society: And if it Should be no Crime to Write Libels, the Government & the Magistrates, must be Exposed to the Malice & Discontents of Disaffected

---

[76] *Trial of Sir Samuel Barnardiston* (1684), 9 *State Trials* 1350.

[77] *R. v. Paine* (1696), 5 Modern 163 (K.B.), 87 Eng. Rep. 584.

[78] *John Lamb's Case* (1610), 9 Coke 59 (S.C.), 77 Eng. Rep. 822; and *Trial of Dover, Brewster and Brooks* (1663), 6 *State Trials* 563.

[79] *R. v. Bear* [sic] (1698), Holt 442 (K.B.), 90 Eng. Rep. 1132; 2 Salkeld 417, 91 Eng. Rep. 363; Lord Raymond 414, 91 Eng. Rep. 1175. Also, see Holt's verbatim opinion: *R. v. Bear* [sic] (1699), Hardwicke Papers, Add. MS 35981, BL.

[80] Holt cited *Dr. Edwards v. Dr. Wooton* (1607), 12 Coke 35 (S.C.), 77 Eng. Rep. 1316; *Sir Baptist Hicke's Case* (1618), Popham 139, Hobart 215 (S.C.), 79 Eng. Rep. 1240; *Barrow v. Lewellin* (1615), Hobart 62 (S.C.), 80 Eng. Rep. 211; *Goodrick's Case* (1612), Moore 821 (S.C.), 71 Eng. Rep. 927—none of which was relevant. See *R. v. Bear* (1699), Hardwicke Papers, Add. MS 35981, 8–16, BL.

[81] Hamburger, 'Seditious Libel', pp. 730–1.

persons'.[82] His language is telling. Holt knew that his opinion lacked sturdy precedents but found that the preservation of the Revolution settlement simply outweighed such niggling jurisprudential concerns.[83]

Not only was Holt's opinion a substantial revision of the law of seditious libel; it also reduced the Crown's evidentiary burden. Now the government needed only to prove that the words had been committed to writing, not that they had been published. Moreover, with publication no longer an element of the crime, the defendant's state of mind was no longer at issue, because it no longer mattered whether the defendant had acted knowingly (i.e., maliciously). And, if it were immaterial whether the defendant had acted with malice, then the defendant could in no way attempt to rebut the presumption of malice that was supplied, by construction of law, by the nature of words used in the libel. With publication no longer an element of the offence, the defendant's intentions were irrelevant. Under Holt, all that mattered was whether the writing was seditious or not.

Simply put, Holt was taking profound liberties. But he was also creating a springboard upon which the Crown could bounce from prosecuting manuscript materials to prosecuting supposedly seditious printed materials. This is exactly what happened. It was during this second stage, between 1702 and 1710, that Holt continued to refine the law of seditious libel. First, in John Tutchin's 1704 trial for the *Observator*, he ruled that not only government representatives but also government institutions could be defamed.[84] Then, in 1706, in James Drake's trial, he argued that the sense or substance of the supposedly libellous words had to appear in the indictment or information, thus allowing judges rather than juries to decide whether the contents of the offending document were defamatory—a question of fact, rather than law, that juries had traditionally taken within their purview.[85]

These were all important and major changes executed in a stunningly short period of time. What matters here, though, is how irony should have been considered in the court's interpretation of the defendant's intentions. Later in this chapter, I return to Defoe and his trial for seditious libel in 1703. At this point, though, it is worth keeping in mind the relationship between Holt's redefinition of the offence and Defoe's pamphlet. In disposing of malice as an element of the crime, Holt was arguing that an offender's intentions were irrelevant. To some extent, this revision made sense. Both Holt and the Crown were preoccupied with the repercussions of anti-government criticism; it simply did not matter whether those criticisms were intentional. As Holt remarked at Tutchin's trial, the law is

[82]   *R. v. Bear* (K.B. 1699), Hardwicke Papers, Add. MS 35981, 16, BL.

[83]   This view of seditious libel did not survive Holt, though. See Hawkins, *Pleas of the Crown*, ch. 73; Hamburger, 'Seditious Libel', pp. 753–4; and *Mansfield MSS*, vol. 2, pp. 781, 783–805, *passim*.

[84]   *Trial of John Tutchin* (Q.B. 1704), 14 *State Trials* 1195. See also 87 Eng. Rep. 922, 1014; 90 Eng. Rep. 929; and 91 Eng. Rep. 50, 165.

[85]   *R. v. Drake* (Q.B. 1706), Hardwicke Papers, Add. MS 35980, BL.

primarily concerned with 'the nature and the consequences of such Libelous and Scandalous Papers, and what evil Effects such Libels might produce'.[86] The difficulty, however, is that ironic materials necessitate an interpretation of the writer's or, in this case, the defendant's intentions. The interpretation of ironic writings, that is, always turns on the disparity between an intended and a surface meaning. This exact tension between Holt's revisions to the law and the role of irony soon came to a head. It did so in Joseph Browne's trial for seditious libel in 1706—a case that finally raised the spectre of irony and intended meaning that had haunted Holt's revisions all along.

3.3 'Be Wise as *Somerset*': Intention and Irony in *R. v. Dr. Browne* (1706)

On 30 January 1706, Dr Joseph Browne had printed *The Country Parson's Honest Advice to The Judicious Lawyer, and Worthy Minister of State, My Lord Keeper*. Directed at William Cowper, the Whig MP nominated to Lord Keeper of the Great Seal, the poem praises a host of Whigs in a series of choppy heroic couplets. Of the eighteen noble lords the poem openly names in full, all had supported Cowper's nomination to Lord Keeper; sixteen had also voted against the failed second and third bills to penalize occasional conformity.[87] The speaker of the poem is a plain-talking country parson. Each lord is praised for a certain virtue, ostensibly to lay out the best possible example for Cowper:

> Be Wise as *Somerset*, as *Somers* Brave,
> As *Pembroke* Airy, and as *Richmond* Grave;
> Humble as *Orford* be; and *Wharton*'s Zeal;
> For Church and Loyalty wou'd fit thee well;
> Like *Sarum*, I wou'd have thee love the Church;
> He scorns to leave his Mother in the Lurch.
> For well governing your Family,
> Let pious *Haversham* thy Pattern be:
> And if it be thy Fate again to Marry,
> And *Seymour*'s Daughter will thy Year out tarry,
> May'st thou use her as *Mohun* his tender Wife,
> And may she lead his virtuous Lady's Life.
> To sum up all; *Devonshire*'s Chastity,
> *Bolton*'s Merit, *Goldolphin*'s Probity,
> *Halifax* his Modesty, *Essex*'s Sense,

---

[86] *Tryal and Examination of Mr John Tutchin* (London, 1704), p. [2].
[87] Holmes, *British Politics*, pp. 425–35.

Montague's Managment, *Culpepper*'s Pence,
Tenison's Learning, and *Southampton*'s Wit,
Will make thee for an able States-man fit.[88]

At a remove of more than three hundred years, the parson's advice to Cowper seems clear enough: be an amalgam of these many great men's finest virtues. In 1706, though, hardly were these lines so easy to read with a straight face. To Browne's contemporaries, the poem was a tongue-in-cheek shot at the parliamentary establishment, an elaborate work of glaring mock-praise. As Thomas Hearne observed, the poem 'severely reflects (but Ironically) on divers Great Men'.[89] Each virtue Browne associates with each lord points precisely to the quality each man painfully lacked. Who would have contended, especially among High-Church Tories, that the known occasional conformist and adulterer John Thompson, Lord Haversham was 'pious' or even a husband after whom one ought to find a 'Pattern' for 'well governing your Family'? What of William Cavendish, fourth earl and first duke of Devonshire, who is praised for his 'Chastity'? This about a man 'famous for Debauchery, Lewdness, &c'. and said to have ravished 'more Women than any Five Keepers of Quality besides'.[90] Or Sidney Godolphin, 'a cunning, sagacious Ambidexter', a man not exactly known for his 'Probity'.[91]

Even the parson's recommendation to the Lord Keeper, 'if it be thy Fate again to Marry', dredged up a notorious piece of libertine gossip. The story ran that a rakish young Cowper had seduced Elizabeth Culling, orchestrated a sham marriage ceremony, and had impregnated her not once but twice. A few years later, in 1688, Cowper married Judith Booth in a ceremony some thought bigamous. In any case, the allusion to marrying again was a nasty piece of business. Browne almost certainly knew that Judith had died only eight months before the poem was published. (For Cowper it hardly mattered. In September 1706, he was secretly married again, this time to Mary Calvering.) According to the poem, Cowper's hypothetical wife was in for some less-than-gallant treatment. The Lord Keeper is urged to 'use her as [Charles] Mohun his tender Wife', a man known as 'one of the arrantest Rakes in Town'.[92]

Given the density and prominence of names, even a modestly informed reader would have seen through the parson's naïve advice. For Browne's readers, the poem was manifestly ironic, despite lacking the kinds of internal signals that so

[88] [Joseph Browne?], *The Country Parson's Honest Advice to the Judicious Lawyer, and Worthy Minister of State, My Lord Keeper* (London, 1706), rpt. *POAS*, vol. 7, pp. 156–9.

[89] Thomas Hearne, *Remarks and Collections*, 11 vol., ed. C. E. Doble, et al., vol. 1 (Oxford: Clarendon Press, 1885–1921), p. 176.

[90] John Dunton, *The Hazard of a Death-Bed Repentance* (London, 1708), p. 38; and Hearne, *Remarks and Collections*, vol. 2, pp. 39–40.

[91] *The English Theophrastus: Or, The Manners of the Age*, 2nd ed. (London, 1706), p. 369.

[92] John Macky, *Memoirs of the Secret Services of John Macky* (London, 1733), p. 93.

routinely typify discussions of irony today.[93] Thomas Keymer has likewise argued that *The Country Parson's Honest Advice*'s 'patently untenable surface meaning' depends entirely on the reader's awareness of extra-textual information about each man's reputation that implicitly contradicted Browne's faux praise.[94] But it is also worth emphasizing two further implications of this. First, *The Shortest Way* operates under a similar structural principle: readers, that is, should have arrived at Defoe's irony through recourse to extra-textual or *extrinsic* information rather than internally signalled textual clues. Second, despite Browne's irony being obvious, the poem's epideixis was unambiguously positive at a purely semantic or linguistic level. That surface quality hardly hindered lay interpretation—it was, as Keymer puts it, a 'blatant sarcasm' for its first readers—but it did trouble courtroom procedures that early on remained focused on surface rather than intended meanings.[95]

Browne's manner, in fact, is entirely straight-faced—no hedging phrases, no dips in tone, no slips of the mask. Instead, the poem relies on its readers to see the disparity between what it praises and what readers commonly thought of each man. As we saw above, this is the very '*Ironical* or *Mock Panegyrick*' mode that Gordon later encouraged '*Ironical Defamers*' to use. Such satirists should draw attention to a victim's failings by praising those precise virtues: 'take a particular Care that you do not in any of your Mock-Applauses, praise any one for good Qualities which he is thought to *Possess*, but dwell entirely upon those which he is known to *want*'.[96] Alexander Pope agreed: 'A vile Encomium double ridicules', for 'Praise undeserv'd is scandal in disguise'.[97] Browne relied on his readers to piece together the irony by identifying the disparity between his praise of the Whigs who had voted against the occasional conformity bills and the widespread public perception that those men lacked the very moral attributes for which they were being commended.

On 30 January 1706, just two days after the poem was published, the authorities questioned Browne, the poem's suspected author.[98] The next day he was committed to Newgate to await trial, before being indicted on a charge of seditious libel on

---

[93] Browne's poem seems to be a prime example of the New Critical precept that all language has 'ironic potential', for any '"statement" made in [a] poem bears the pressure of the context and has its meaning modified by the context'. See Cleanth Brooks, *The Well Wrought Urn: Studies in the Structure of Poetry* (New York: Harcourt Brace, 1947), p. 191. Of course, Brooks's definition of irony is so broad as to encompass almost every kind of utterance. See Booth, *A Rhetoric of Irony*, p. 17n11.

[94] Keymer, *Poetics*, p. 124.   [95] Keymer, *Poetics*, p. 99.

[96] [Gordon,] *The Art of Railing*, pp. 13–15.

[97] Alexander Pope, *The First Epistle of the Second Book of Horace Imitated*, in *The Poems of Alexander Pope*, edited by John Butt (New Haven: Yale University Press, 1963), ll. 410–13.

[98] Historical Manuscripts Commission, *Manuscripts of the Duke of Portland*, 10 vol., vol. 4 (London, 1899), p. 282. Browne all along denied his authorship. See [Joseph Browne], *A Letter To the Right Honourable Mr. Secretary Harley, by Dr. Browne* (London, 1706), pp. 3–4.

12 February.[99] When Browne finally went to trial in November 1706, he faced Holt and a version of the law that had hardly existed a mere ten years earlier.

It is worth focusing on Browne's poem because it exposed the glaring paradox at the heart of Holt's revisions. It did so by dragging the problem of irony into court, which in turn forced the bench and the jury to consider questions of intentionality in determining the meaning of words that, on their face, seemed to mean something other than what they overtly said. It is also worth exploring the mechanics of Browne's irony for the ways in which they trouble more modern conceptions of satire. Through an eagerness to define satire in largely formalist terms during the mid-twentieth century, most scholars rejected the supposed fallacy of authorial intention. This, though, has had the troubling consequence of making satire 'close to untheorisable', as Robert Phiddian has written, because so much satire entails a thoughtful 'shaping intention': 'a deliberate intent to persuade an audience'.[100]

This sense of both present and yet inaccessible intentionality was not only at the centre of Browne's poem with its suggestive wink-and-nudge ironic reversals, which required readers to contemplate the intentional and not merely accidental disparity between the virtues attributed to each man and the incompatible public perception of them. But it was also Browne's defence of the poem. Turn the words which way you will, he publicly argued both before and during the trial, but one cannot turn a bland compliment, such as 'Be Wise as *Somerset*', into an insult. Holt disagreed. In his view, irony was established not through internal verbal signals—no set of necessary and sufficient verbal conditions guaranteed irony—but by a community of readers, in this case the jurors, who understood the work not as a series of compliments but as a volley of veiled insults. Irony was not an abstractable, self-evident verbal mechanism, but a product of actual interpretation. Whether an author intended a work to be ironic or not hardly mattered, in Holt's view. What mattered were the intuitions of on-the-ground readers.

Nonetheless, Browne's case has received at most limited attention from legal and literary historians. However, when we consider Holt's revisions to the law of seditious libel—and especially his claim that publication was not an element of the crime and that, as a result, the intention of the work's maker or author was immaterial—we get into some rather sticky and recursive ground. The only way to establish that an ironic piece of writing means something other than what it seems to mean on its face is to get into the muddle of asking what the author had intended the piece to mean and how readers were to understand such murky

---

[99]   *Portland MSS*, vol. 4, p. 283.

[100]   Robert Phiddian, 'Satire and the Limits of Literary Theories', *Critical Quarterly* 55, no. 3 (October 2013): pp. 48–9, 51. On the difference between motive and intention, see Mark Vareschi, *Everywhere and Nowhere: Anonymity and Mediation in Eighteenth-Century England* (Minneapolis: University of Minnesota Press, 2018), pp. 145–9.

language. Jurors, charged with determining a locution's meaning, were thus forced to consider intentionality—an element of the crime of seditious libel with which Holt had attempted to dispense. Moreover, Browne's trial raises important legal and literary issues around *The Shortest Way*, showing clearly the relevance of intention, malice, and interpretation in trials for irony.

Browne raised the issue of irony before he even went to court. His primary tool was his public *Letter* to the Secretary of State, Robert Harley. Despite its fumbling and seemingly earnest meekness, the *Letter* undergoes massive dips in tone— bizarre shifts in reverence; catty, sarcastic, know-it-all asides; and huffy and peevish half-spoken and outright accusations against Harley. It was an ill-judged method for gaining the Secretary's ear. (The *Letter* also proved a seditious libel, for which Browne faced a second prosecution in the fall.[101]) The *Letter* nonetheless is an interesting defence and a clear (if comically tetchy) exploration of the problem of intended meaning. As Browne argued, 'I think it the greatest Folly imaginable, to suppose any Body shou'd make any other Construction of the Word, than what it naturally intends'. The real problem were the verbal quibblers, those wont to read every word as a subtle piece of irony and who 'can understand Words in a harsher Meaning than the natural and genuine Sense of them will bear'.[102]

Again and again, Browne resorts to this kind of wilful obtuseness, an almost bumpkinish thickheadedness about what words mean and when. To help dispel the troubling accusation of insult and irony, he clumsily works through every epithet in the poem. Take 'Be Wise as *Somerset*', he writes. 'I never had the Honour to partake of the abundance of his Grace's Wisdom, nor have I ever had the Opportunity to judge, that he wanted either that or Discretion; if there is any other Meaning in the Words, they are out of my Knowledge, and conse-quently beyond my Interpretation'.[103] Browne's semantic sluggishness—the dolt-ish writer, baffled to find himself in an almost Kafkaesque situation, awaiting trial for a crime he hardly understands and certainly did not commit—also squared the problem any prosecutor, any judge, and any juror would have to face. How is one to prove that overt praise was actually veiled mockery? Be wise as Somerset: how was this an insult?

Despite Browne's protestations, his trial for seditious libel went forward. On 3 May, he returned to Queen's Bench, where he faced Holt.[104] The prosecution, it seemed, had a tidy case to argue. Browne had made a few surprising concessions, first in his deposition to Erasmus Lewis, the undersecretary to Harley, and then in his *Letter*. After his printer, Hugh Mear, had identified him, Browne admitted to Lewis that he had handed the poem over to Mear to be printed and sold (i.e.,

---

[101]   Harley to the Attorney General, Sir Edward Northey (22 February 1706), Portland Loan 29/263, ff. 172–173, BL.
[102]   Browne, *A Letter*, p. 5.   [103]   Browne, *A Letter*, p. 11.
[104]   Luttrell, *A Brief Historical Relation of State Affairs*, vol. 6, p. 43.

published).[105] This quickly established a few facts for the prosecution. According to Holt, by simply copying the libel down, Browne had satisfied an element of the crime. This would not have been enough before 1696, when publication or the intent to publish was an essential element of the offence, but by 1706 it was.[106]

That Browne was guilty of copying the poem (or even publishing it) was clear enough. But was the poem really a seditious libel? Almost immediately, the Crown got into the rigmarole of fixing the poem's language. In order for it to be interpreted as criminal, the Crown needed to demonstrate to the jurors, who were charged with determining the meaning of a given libel, that the poem was ironic, rather than the mere praise it appeared.[107] With an ironic locution, though, the meaning of the words hardly inheres. 'Be Wise as *Somerset*', if strictly interpreted *in mitiori sensu*—that is, in their lesser sense, as all words in trials for defamation were expected to be understood up until 1714, when the rule was abolished—means only what it seems, on its surface, to mean.[108] Simply put, Somerset was wise. How ever then to get from wise to dim-witted? This was a question for the jury. Moreover, by putting this issue of fact to the jury the Crown was also inevitably muddying the waters, dragging in questions that Holt had earlier deemed immaterial to the crime. Malice, for instance, was out, but it was impossible to establish that Browne's poem was a seditious libel without dipping into the ticklish issue of intent. To do so, the jury would first have to establish the actual meaning of the poem's encomiastic language; and in order to establish the meaning of that language, the jury would have to ask both what the poem was intended to say and how its readers were supposed to understand it.

This in part is why the *Letter* is so interesting. Browne had a seemingly sturdy sense of libel law—at least libel law before Holt got his hands on it. The poem's language, he protested again and again, is too slippery to pin down. To do so is only to get into the morass of intentionality: 'I cannot pretend to understand the Intentions of [the poem] . . . because it is impossible for me to know another Man's

---

[105] *Portland MSS*, vol. 4, p. 282.

[106] Harley Papers, Portland Deposit, Loan 29/193, f. 172–173, BL. A large number of manuscript versions of the poem have survived, suggesting that it had circulated widely, even though only three printed broadsheets exist today. See J. A. Downie, *Robert Harley and the Press: Propaganda and Public Option in the Age of Swift and Defoe* (Cambridge: Cambridge University Press, 1979), p. 95; and *POAS*, vol. 7, pp. 642–3.

[107] Richard H. Helmholz, 'Civil Trials and the Limits of Responsible Speech', in *Juries, Libel, & Justice: The Role of the English Juries in Seventeenth- and Eighteenth-Century Trials for Libel and Slander* (Los Angeles: William Andrews Clark Memorial Library, University of California, Los Angeles, 1984), pp. 3–36.

[108] *Harrison v. Thornborough* (1714), Gilb. Cas. 114, 10 Mod. 196 (Q.B.), 93 Eng. Rep. 277. See Richard H. Helmholz, *Select Cases on Defamation to 1600* (London: Selden Society, 1985), pp. xcii–xcv; Knightley D'Anvers, *A General Abridgment of the Common Law*, vol. 1 (London, 1722–25), p. 140; and William Sheppard, *Action Upon the Case for Slander*, 2nd ed. (London, 1674), p. 20. For resistance to the rule in the later seventeenth century, see my discussion in ch. 1; Baker, *ELH*, pp. 440–2; Plucknett, *CHCL*, pp. 495–8; and Holdsworth, *History*, vol. 8, pp. 355–6.

thoughts'.[109] This was the problem echoed time and again in the courts.[110] As we saw earlier, the malicious nature of a libel was established 'by construction of law'. In effect this meant that the very nature of the words created a rebuttable presumption of malice. To say 'Thou art a pocky whore and the pox hath eaten out the bottom of thy belly that thy guts are ready to fall out' seems, by the violence of its language and self-evident cruelty, to suggest a malicious intent.[111] In Browne's view, because the intentions of the poet were obscure, so too was the charge upon which the prosecution was grounded. Moreover, the poem in no way evinced a malicious intent—a necessary element of the offence (at least according to Browne and Holt's predecessors). The 'Law only censure[s] according to [a publication's] Intention, tho' it may appear to be evil in its Effect', Browne concluded. The only reason he was being tried was Harley, who had glommed a meaning onto the poem that no man in his right mind would have seen.[112]

For all of his objections, and despite his sturdy understanding of the law in the 1690s, Browne's defence proved a shambles. In the first place, his sense of the law was obsolete. As satirists and their stationers would time and again discover while on trial during the first half of the eighteenth century, their view of the law had suddenly become outdated—a perfect example of what Naomi Mezey has called 'slippage', those 'inconsistencies between the production of legal meaning and its cultural reception'.[113] Moreover, having established the lone necessary question of fact—that Browne had copied the libel down—the case was open and shut. The verdict came back: Browne was guilty of seditious libel.

Browne's counsel, however, submitted a motion in arrest of judgment. In the defence's view, Holt had denied the jury the opportunity to speak to a further question of fact: whether the poem meant what the prosecution claimed it to mean in the information. The words of the poem, they argued, 'did not import a scandal, but, in their natural signification, carry a credit, as "to be wise as Somerset, &c" .... So here [in the information] the manner of speaking ought to be set out'. The Attorney General shot back that the jury had already spoken to that particular fact, and that it was incumbent on the defence to demonstrate that the poem was innocuous praise. The Crown argued that the poem 'gives every lord a character ironically; and so 'tis set forth in an information, and the jury find him guilty'. 'It was laid to be wrote *ironicè*', the Attorney General continued, 'and [Browne]

---

[109] Browne, *A Letter*, p. 11.

[110] *Trial of Dover, Brewster and Brooks* (1663), 6 *State Trials* 537; and *Trial of Sir Samuel Barnardiston* (1684), 9 *State Trials* 1334.

[111] *Prekington's Case* (1610), 1 Rolle Abr. 66, l. 53. However, defendants could claim the words were merely impetuously spoken in heat, offered in mere jest, or simply too trifling to import a purely malicious intent. See *Carpenter's Case* (1558); Anon. (1565), Maynard MS 87, f. 34; and Anon. (1580), MS Misc. 488/76, all rpt. *Sources*, pp. 637–8. Or the defendant, through the use of a special traverse, in which he or she admitted to having said or written some words about the plaintiff, but not the exact words alleged in the plaintiff's declaration, could have an additional issue submitted to the jury: the manner and form of the words. See Helmholz, 'Civil Trials', pp. 3–36, esp. 6–19.

[112] Browne, *A Letter*, pp. 19–20.   [113] Mezey, 'Law', p. 54.

ought to have shewed at the trial that he did not *intend* to scandalize them; and the jury are judges *quo animo* how this was done, and they have found the *ill intent*.[114] In effect, the Attorney General was combining two aspects and two eras of libel law: by 1706, Browne's intent should have been beside the point.

Moreover, in claiming that the work was written ironically, the Crown was shifting the burden of proof from the prosecution to the defence. Suddenly, after months of arguing that words only mean what they seem to mean, Browne was charged with proving that this proposition was necessarily true. This meant showing, like some thickheaded linguist, that words only denote; connotations and ironic reversals, surprisingly, were not the satirist's but the prosecutor's best friend. The Crown needed only to claim that something was ironic, thereby shifting the exegetical burden to the defence, which was then required to show otherwise to the satisfaction of the jury. Holt likewise agreed: defendants were responsible for demonstrating that an ostensibly ironic phrase was a wholly innocent construction. But he also took this argument a step further. In this instance, he summarized,

> 'twas shewn for cause to arrest judgment, that there was no cause to charge the defendant, because he said no ill thing of any person, and all he said was good of them; to which it was answered and resolved by the Court, that this was laid to be ironical, and whether 'twas so or not, the jury were judges; they found it so.[115]

A statement was not ironic simply because the prosecution said so. Instead, the prosecution's claim raised the possibility of irony, and the jurors confirmed it.

From the outside, this might seem odd: the courts in effect refused to clarify the messy mechanics of an important procedural rule. But Holt's decision to defer to the jury was undergirded by a clear sense that ironic meaning was produced by a community of readers, rather than a mechanistic set of verbal signals. In this way, Holt might be thought to hold a 'sociocentric' view of ironic interpretation: a belief that readers are ultimately responsible for ironic meaning, and that the means of interpretation is a learned set of conventions produced by the institutions that have authorized them.[116] Put slightly differently, we understand locutions as ironic not because they contain simple ironic signals that all (or at least most)

---

[114] *R. v. Dr. Brown* [sic] (1706), 11 Mod. 86 (Q.B.), 88 Eng. Rep. 911–12 (italics mine).

[115] *R. v. Dr. Brown* [sic] (1706), 11 Mod. 86 (Q.B.), 88 Eng. Rep. 912.

[116] Wayne C. Booth, 'A New Strategy for Establishing a Truly Democratic Criticism', *Daedalus* 112, no. 1 (Winter 1983): p. 197. For Booth there is a way, in most instances, to decode irony: either a set of signals, which are not always present, or a series of mechanisms of interpretation, which do not always produce the same results. Conversely, for Fish we have different ironic and non-ironic readings because we hold different 'assumptions'; that is, 'what is ironic will be for the reader to decide', he writes, but 'only in relation to the decision procedures that have been authorized by the institution' ('Short People Got No Reason to Live: Reading Irony', *Daedalus* 112, no. 1 [Winter 1983]: p. 188). Yet both agree that a group will cluster around a particular interpretation, even if Fish is unwilling to admit that majorities of readers emerge in practise in many instances. See Booth, 'A New Strategy', pp. 200–1.

readers should be able to identify and decode, but because our entire practise of reading and interpretation is an unrecognized product of habits authorized by the institutions within which we read. As Stanley Fish has written,

> when a community of readers agrees that a work, or a part of a work, is ironic, that agreement will have come about because the community has been persuaded to a set of assumptions, to a *way* of reading, that produces the ironic meanings that all of its members 'see' . . . Irony, then, is neither the property of works, nor the creation of an unfettered imagination, but a way of reading, an interpretive strategy that produces the object of its attention, an object that will be perspicuous to those who share or have been persuaded to share the same strategy.[117]

We might disagree with Fish that all ironic statements are merely the product of 'an interpretive strategy that produces the object of its attention', while still pointing to the broadest similarities between Fish's theory—that readers arrive at ironic meanings through certain interpretive practises—and Holt's. Holt was simply willing to defer to readers, both those who smelled something rotten when Browne's poem was first published and the jurors who found that the seemingly laudatory poem harboured an 'ill intent'. For Holt (unlike Fish), it hardly mattered how readers stumbled on that interpretation: the jury deemed the work ironic, and it was on Browne to show otherwise. In addition, Holt saw the perversity of allowing irony as a defence. It was a patent absurdity, he argued, that irony in some way circumvented the law. 'If this were not a crime', he reasoned, then any writer 'might by contraries libel any person'. Simply put, he concluded, 'An information will lie for speaking *ironically*'.[118]

Holt's sociocentric take on irony is important because it belongs to a series of rulings that sought to isolate the fuzzy subjectivity of jurors, who had tremendous discretion in trials for libel and often happily bucked against the directions of the bench.[119] As we saw in my first chapter, the doctrine of 'common intendment' held that jurors were expected to interpret words in their most natural sense given the context of their utterance.[120] This 'reasonable' standard was important because it created an objective interpretive rule that was theoretically isolated from jurors' subjective deliberations. In a similar way, Holt extended this form of legal thinking to trials for ironic materials. Under Holt, the prosecution was not required to demonstrate the linguistic mechanism by which a superficially innocent locution could denote or connote a defamatory intended meaning. As a result, this procedure also mitigated the impressionability of individual jurors. As Holt had

---

[117] Fish, 'Reading Irony', p. 189.
[118] *R. v. Dr. Browne* (1706), 11 Mod. 86 (Q.B.), 90 Eng. Rep. 1134.
[119] Beattie, *Crime*, pp. 400–49; and Baker, *ELH*, pp. 143–4, 151.
[120] *King v. Lake* (1671), 2 Vent. 28 (C.P.), 89 Eng. Rep. 12.

earlier argued, words should be taken 'in a common sense according to the vulgar intendment of the bystanders'.[121] That is, interpretation should rely on an abstract 'generality of readers', as the courts would later claim—on how a juror believed *most* people would have understood a phrase, rather than merely the way that an individual juror did.[122] Such a rule in practise meant that the courts could defer to the jury in the abstract while effectively displacing the capricious interpretations of actual jurors by creating a theoretical juror who read in more coherent, more reasonable, and more predictable ways.

This proved an important shift in trials for satiric and ironic materials, as Holt's view of irony came to dominate the courts' understanding of authorial intent.[123] Libel could be legally established by focusing not on what the writing said, even if wholly laudatory. Instead, the courts could defer to a sociocentric understanding of the text's meaning through implicit juxtaposition and inference. As one legal commentator noted, just a decade later, such libels worked by

> pretending to recommend to one the Characters of several great Men for his Imitation, instead of taking Notice of what they are generally esteemed famous for, pitches on such Qualitie only which their Enemies charge them with the Want of, as by proposing such a one to be imitated for his Courage, which is known to be a great Statesman, but no Soldier, and another to be imitated for his Learning, who is known to be a great General, but no Scholar, &c. Which kind of Writing is as well understood to mean only to upbraid the Parties with the Want of these Qualities.[124]

Satirists, once seemingly liberated by irony—its curious reversals in meaning, its susceptibility to both innocuous and lacerating interpretations—were now its clearest victims. Prosecutors needed only to assert its mere existence, forcing the defendant to prove that a dubious locution was perfectly innocent.

Browne's poem is no masterpiece of early modern satire, but his prosecution is deeply suggestive. Most importantly, his trial should remind us that, despite Holt's radical revisions to the law, the courts and jurors clearly needed to take into account not merely the surface meaning of a given text in trials for libel but also its intended meanings and by extension the author's intentions. This is precisely what the courts did. Browne was convicted not for what the poem said on its face, but for its veiled ironic meaning. Holt, the government, and the jury read the poem the same way Browne's readers did, by looking past its straight-faced catalogue of

---

[121] *Somers v. House* (1694), Holt 39 (K.B.), 90 Eng. Rep. 919.

[122] *R. v. Clerk* [sic] (1728/9), 1 Barn. 305 (K.B.), 94 Eng. Rep. 207. Michael McKeon, *The Secret History of Domesticity: Public, Private, and the Division of Knowledge* (Baltimore: Johns Hopkins University Press, 2005), pp. 94–5, on the 'coalescence of a virtual "reading public"' (p. 95).

[123] Treasury Solicitor's Papers, TS 11/10766, no. 5338, TNA.

[124] Hawkins, *Pleas of the Crown*, vol. 1, p. 194.

bland compliments. In addition, this poem and Browne's trial offer important insights into Defoe's trial just a few years earlier. Perhaps Defoe did have a defence for *The Shortest Way*—even if he, like Browne, eventually found himself pilloried for a satiric work too clever by half.

3.4 Defending Defoe: 'Plain *English without Design*'

By late December 1702, the skirmish around *The Shortest Way* had exploded into a full-fledged paper war. On 3 January, a warrant was issued for Defoe's arrest. Like Browne, Defoe quickly produced a second piece, *A Brief Explanation of a Late Pamphlet*, that sought to sort out the entire affair. In his view, *The Shortest Way*'s purpose was as clear as day: 'If any man take the pains seriously to reflect upon the Contents, the Nature of the Thing and the Manner of the Stile, it seems Impossible to imagine it should pass for any thing but a Banter upon the High-flying Church-Men'.[125] According to him, the pamphlet was 'plain *English without design*'. Further, he felt that the pamphlet served an obvious end. 'When the Persecution and Destruction of the *Dissenters, the very thing they* [the High Churchmen] *drive at*, is put into plain *English*, the whole Nation will start at the Notion, and Condemn the Author to be Hang'd for his Impudence' (114). Moreover, the pamphlet had nothing to do with the 'Publick Bills in Parliament' that sought to outlaw occasional conformity or 'of either House, or of the Government'. Instead, it was 'a fair answer to several Books published *in this Liberty of the Press*', a response to the 'Virulent Spirits of some Men, who have thought fit to express them selves to the same Effect in their printed Books, *tho' not in words so plain and at length*, and by an *Irony not Unusual*' (114).

Defoe's defence should be taken with a grain of salt, and yet in this second pamphlet he was also offering a coherent explanation for *The Shortest Way*. Its job was to put all that High-Church nonsense down in the clearest possible language, showing the odious inferences one was forced to draw if such arguments were followed all the way down to their logical—and abhorrent—conclusions. His '*Irony not Unusual*', in 'plain *English without design*', as far as Defoe was concerned, was clear: to state explicitly what the High Churchmen were actually driving at before leaving it to readers to see how this led to 'the Persecution and Destruction of the *Dissenters*'.

---

[125] Defoe, *A Brief Explanation of a Late Pamphlet, Entituled, The Shortest Way with the Dissenters* (1703), in *Political and Economic Writings of Daniel Defoe*, vol. 3: Dissent, edited by W. R. Owens (London: Pickering & Chatto, 2000), p. 113.

The story of Defoe's time on the run and eventual capture, trial, and pillorying are well known and have been ably told.[126] Nonetheless, a few points are worth returning to. First, when Defoe was indicted in absentia at the Old Bailey, the Crown quoted at length from the pamphlet, focussing in particular on *The Shortest Way*'s most divisive claim: that 'Her Majesty did never promise to maintain the Tolleration to the Destruction of the Church'. According to the indictment, Defoe attempted to provoke 'discord between the Queen and her Subjects, and to Disunite and set at variance the Protestant Subjects of...the Queen'. The queen, apparently, was especially furious over Defoe's mincing depiction of her. In addition, the indictment continued, Defoe's pamphlet sought 'to alarm All her Protestant Subjects Dissenting from the church of England with the Fear of being deprived of the Exemption...and to persuade All the English people Conforming to the Church of England to procure the destruction of the same Protestant Subjects'.[127] As I noted earlier, this was the pamphlet's most glaring—and, indeed, most potent—argument against the government's claim to preserving dissent, one intended 'to set the Nation in a Flame', as one reader argued, 'and to engage us in an intestine War'.[128] It was also the thing mostly likely to drive a wedge between both the queen and her subjects and Anglicans and dissenters.

When finally caught, Defoe had seemingly little choice but to plead guilty. In the first place, he knew he had run aground of the Tory administration. His pamphlet proved a bizarre cause célèbre, igniting a paper war and bringing decidedly unwanted attention to the Commons' legislative attempts to ban occasional conformity. There was also the problem of the Secretary of State, Daniel Finch, earl of Nottingham, whom Defoe had spent months ducking and dodging, and to whom he had even sent a presumptuous letter, just days after his *Brief Explanation* appeared, begging for some sort of deal.[129] During this period Defoe's finances had also grown perilous after months on the run and then in gaol. He also believed that he could use a plea for better treatment. Nottingham had promised to use him 'tenderly' in exchange for a guilty plea.[130] Defoe kept his end of the bargain, but the Crown did not. Nonetheless, Defoe suspected that a guilty plea was part of a larger, more secretive deal, in which leniency would be exchanged for his services as a government propagandist. Even before writing *The Shortest Way*,

[126] Paula R. Backscheider, 'No Defense: Defoe in 1703', *PMLA* 103, no. 3 (May 1988): pp. 274–84 and *Daniel Defoe: His Life* (Baltimore: Johns Hopkins University Press, 1989), pp. 84–135; and Novak, *Daniel Defoe*, pp. 173–90.

[127] SF 472, City of London Record Office. Qtd. in Backscheider, 'Defoe in 1703', p. 277, trans. Pauline Sidell.

[128] *Reflections Upon a Late Scandalous and Malicious Pamphlet Entitul'd, The Shortest Way with the Dissenters* (London, 1703), p. 22. See Hone, *Party Politics*, p. 131.

[129] Defoe to Daniel Finch, Earl of Nottingham (9 January 1702), *The Letters of Daniel Defoe*, ed. George Harris Healey (Oxford: Clarendon Press, 1955), pp. 1–4.

[130] Qtd. Backscheider, *Daniel Defoe*, p. 108.

Defoe had seemingly been in contact with Harley about working as a pro-ministry writer, as J. A. Downie has shown.[131]

As a result, most scholars, including Paula Backscheider and Maximillian Novak, with a few caveats, have concluded that Defoe's conviction was a fait accompli.[132] More recently, Thomas Keymer has argued that the 'finer points of literary interpretation have limited relevance to a case' in which the seditious was defined 'in the simple sense of rocking the boat', whether *The Shortest Way* was a 'non-ironic work attacking Dissenters' or 'an ironic work attacking High-Church Tories'.[133] I fully agree, and yet the question I would like to raise is not whether Defoe had a feasible defence in 1703, but whether he had a defence that would have been of value in the years either before or after Holt ascended to the bench. This might seem like quibbling. Whether Defoe had a defence in 1690 or one in 1715, at least in one sense, hardly matters. After 1699, Holt's interpretation of the law was straightforward: Defoe had a hand in 'making' the pamphlet, which was deemed a seditious libel, and he was therefore guilty.[134] In addition, the Attorney General Sir Simon Harcourt was working under a reduced evidentiary burden. He only needed to prove that the words had been committed to writing, thereby rendering the pamphlet's publication irrelevant. As a result, the defendant's state of mind was no longer at issue. It simply did not matter whether the defendant had acted knowingly (i.e., maliciously). And, if it were immaterial whether the defendant had acted with malice, then the defence could in no way attempt to rebut the presumption of malice that was supplied, by construction of law, by the nature of the words used in the libel. Defoe was guilty: case closed.

Such an account, though, ignores both how radically Holt had modified the law and how ironic works, as we saw in Browne's trial, severely troubled precisely those revisions. Holt's view that the mere writing had always constituted the offence was not only historically without foundation; it also failed to survive the chief justice's tenure.[135] In this sense, Holt's modifications to the law were, in part, only temporary. Further, a closer consideration of *The Shortest Way* points to the oddity of Holt's decision to shift the burden of proof from the prosecution to the defence. In effect, Defoe would have been in the strange position of proving to the jury that his act of ventriloquism meant *other* than what it seemed to on its face; rather than demonstrating his pamphlet's surface meaning, à la Browne, he would have been required to demonstrate its non-textual intended meaning. This was an odd double reversal of both trial procedure and the usual obligation of defendants

---

[131] Downie, *Harley and the Press*, p. 60. See also Owens and Furbank, Introduction, in *Political and Economic Writings of Daniel Defoe*, p. 18; and Backscheider, *Daniel Defoe*, p. 119.

[132] Backscheider, 'Defoe in 1703', pp. 279–80; and Novak, *Daniel Defoe*, p. 188.

[133] Keymer, *Poetics*, pp. 130–1.

[134] *R. v. Bear* (K.B. 1699), Hardwicke Papers, Add. MS 35981, 16, BL.

[135] Hawkins, *Pleas of the Crown*, ch. 73; Hamburger, 'Seditious Libel', pp. 753–4; and *Mansfield MSS*, vol. 2, pp. 781, 783–805, *passim*.

for ironic writings. In the past, prosecutors were required to prove to jurors that works of mock-praise were damning pieces of seditious criticism. Now, under Holt, defendants had taken on the exculpatory burden of proof. Defendants, not prosecutors, had to prove to juries that works of mock-praise meant exactly what they seemed to mean—that they were catalogues of bland compliments rather than pregnant lists of virtues some public figures were thought to lack. Browne, for instance, was obliged to show that the poem was not mock-praise at all. Instead, *The Country Parson's Honest Advice* was simply honest advice—no irony intended.

At Defoe's trial, this shift entailed a further complication. Unlike Browne, Defoe was not obliged to prove that his pamphlet meant exactly what it seemed to mean. Instead, he was under the burden to prove that his pamphlet was ironic, that it was intended to mean something other than what it seemed to mean, and something that few if any of his readers actually understood upon first reading. Rather than being a rabid High-Church screed against occasional conformity and the dissenters—which, indeed, the *Shortest Way* very much looks and sounds like—Defoe had to show that the pamphlet was something else entirely.

This again raises the issue of malice. As I have already noted, under Holt, Crown prosecutors were no longer required to demonstrate that the defendant had acted intentionally. Granted, Defoe had wilfully brought the pamphlet to publication. But he also viewed the piece differently from either the Crown or his earliest readers. By construction of law, *The Shortest Way* was both defamatory and malicious, even if, for Defoe, such a reading was only surface deep. Like Browne, Defoe was hoping to attach a very specific meaning to his words. For Browne, that was the poem's superficial meaning—a mere catalogue of praise. For Defoe, that meant unearthing the pamphlet's ironic meaning: not that we should selectively cull dissenting ministers, but that the logic of the High Churchmen inexorably led to ghastly forms of systematic persecution. Defoe was not advocating for a breach of the peace; he was trying to prevent one. According to him, there was no intent to do harm.

Further, Defoe's pamphlet seemingly failed to defame any one individual in particular—the lone element that strung together the various branches of defamation law. Perhaps his pamphlet had attacked the queen, or at least wilfully misread her words to parliament, as the government claimed. On closer inspection, though, even this seems a stretch. Defoe's speaker had in effect misread the queen's guarantee to preserve dissent, casting it as a half-hearted promise that could be easily discarded should dissent come head-to-head with the Church of England. This obviously was not Defoe's argument, but his speaker's. In effect, then, in the most curious paradox in his case, Defoe was prosecuted and convicted based on a misreading of his own words, which, the Crown argued, had constituted a misreading of the queen's promise to preserve her many Protestant subjects.

Perhaps at first blush, questions of irony should have little to do with the law of seditious libel, maybe even less to do with Defoe's trial and his precarious defence. But by understanding the changes the law of seditious libel underwent in the years leading up to Defoe's trial, we can see just how crucial a nuanced sense of authorial intention and thus irony should have been in trials for seditious libel. By the time Defoe went to trial in 1703, irony hung in a form of legal limbo. In the preceding years, Holt had modified the law, and in the process disposed of the element of malice. In doing so, he had gutted a defence upon which any ironist might have relied: that he had intended no harm by his pamphlet—that he had not produced it maliciously—because the work's ostensible surface meaning, upon which the prosecution was grounded, was at odds with the author's intentions. In short, before Holt ascended the bench in 1689, irony was a satirist's best friend; after Browne's trial, irony was no longer a defence. More to the point, irony was an actual problem for those writers who found themselves on trial with the exegetical burden of having to demonstrate the intended meaning of a given work.

My hope is that this interpretation of *The Shortest Way* might reshape our perceptions of Defoe's most misunderstood piece of writing. Such a reading also has broader implications for the study of satire, and especially political satire, in the early decades of the eighteenth century. In the first place, we need to keep in mind that irony was not a simple and stable rhetorical device during this period. *The Shortest Way* was ironic, but its rhetorical method—its use of extrinsic irony—heightened the role readers played in piecing together the disparity between the text's surface and intended meaning. Moreover, by focusing on Defoe's and Browne's trials, we can see how satiric prosecutions under Holt were part of a larger attempt to regulate the press following the lapse of licensing. By 1706, the courts had gained a reputation for coming down hard on Grub Street's most incendiary scribblers. As Harley wrote to John Churchill, the Duke of Marlborough on 7 May, just three days after Browne's conviction, the judges, and especially Holt, had begun 'to make examples of the libellers and printers'. The hope was that 'Some few examples . . . will cure, in great measure, the abominable vice'—the same logic of exemplary punishment that Defoe's speaker had advocated for against dissenters.[136] But even these examples were a surprise. Defoe, Browne, Robert Ferguson, John Tutchin, James Drake, William Stephens, and Ned Ward, among many others—all were prosecuted for a crime that simply did not exist in 1696 in the way it had to come to function under Holt during the final years of the Stuart monarchy.[137]

This attention to the ways Holt revised the law should also direct us to two important observations. The first is the instability of the law during the early modern period. It is worth keeping in mind that precedent at this point was a

---

[136] Portland MSS, v, f. 49, Longleat House Library, qtd. Downie, *Harley and the Press*, p. 92n60.
[137] *An Account of the Persons Held to Bail*, 4, KB 33/24/2, TNA.

foggy science.[138] We should not be surprised that Holt took a lax view of the common law in revising the elements of seditious libel, but we should note that his revisions were radical, idiosyncratic, and in part only temporary. Doing so should remind us that the judiciary of the eighteenth century, despite the promises of independence contained in the Act of Settlement (1701), was never a wholly independent branch of government. The early modern legal system was not a systematized code of sturdy precedents administered by a disinterested judiciary, but an ever-shifting body of laws subject to the interpretation of fallible human actors with their own implicit political, religious, and social allegiances and biases.[139]

A second observation extends from the first. The instability of the law during the early modern period helps to explain why practising satirists and their stationers so often found themselves confused by the current state of libel law throughout the eighteenth century. In 1729, one legal commentator spoke directly to this very problem: 'What is a Libel?' This 'has of late Years been a Question frequently debated, and by some so loosely handled, that it almost became a Question if any thing was a Libel'.[140] As the law had changed and grown more complicated, its actual state had only become more opaque or 'muddy'.[141] As we saw in Defoe's and Browne's trials, that confusion was at the heart of how irony itself was to be handled in trials for libel. And irony was only one issue. Many also wondered whether naming a satiric victim was itself defamatory. This, at least, was a question that Alexander Pope raised—and then tested—in his *Dunciad*, the subject of my next chapter.

---

[138] Michael Lobban, *The Common Law and English Jurisprudence* (Oxford: Oxford University Press, 1991), pp. 83, 87; Harold J. Berman and Charles J. Reid, Jr, 'The Transformation of English Legal Science: From Hale to Blackstone', *Emory Law Journal* 45, no. 2 (Spring 1996): pp. 437–522; and Andrew Benjamin Bricker, 'Is Narrative Essential to the Law?: Precedent, Case Law and Judicial Emplotment', *Law, Culture and the Humanities* 15, no. 2 (June 2019): pp. 319–31 and 'The Functions of Legal Literature and Case Reporting before and after *Stare Decisis*', in *The Oxford Handbook of Law and Humanities*, edited by Simon Stern, Bernadette Meyler, and Maksymilian Del Mar (Oxford: Oxford University Press, 2020), pp. 617–36.

[139] Wilfrid Prest, 'Judicial Corruption in Early Modern England', *Past & Present* 133 (November 1991): pp. 67–95; David Lemmings, 'The Independence of the Judiciary in Eighteenth-Century England', *The Life of the Law*, edited by Peter Birks (London: The Hambledon Press, 1993), pp. 125–49; and Stewart Jay, 'Servants of Monarchs and Lords: The Advisory Role of Early English Judges', *American Journal of Legal History* 38, no. 3 (April 1994): pp. 117–96.

[140] *State Law*, p. [i].

[141] Carol M. Rose, 'Crystals and Mud in Property Law', *Stanford Law Review* 40, no. 3 (February 1988): pp. 577–610.

4

Naming in the Courts

Pope and the *Dunciad*

At the intersection of the verbal and bibliographical evasions that came to typify eighteenth-century satire, authors and their stationers devised a new typographical sleight. During this period, the names of satiric victims were regularly gutted—or 'emvowelled', as it was then known—and plugged full of asterisks, dashes, and ellipses.[1] Following C. R. Kropf, literary historians have routinely argued that such typographical tricks stymied actions and prosecutions for defamation.[2] Gutted names were legally safe, the reasoning went, because the courts could never quite wrap their heads around such omissions.[3] In theory, the idea works well enough. If you want to block some form of legal comeuppance, don't name your target, even if you and every one of your readers knows that J—S— is John Smith.

The legal record, however, tells a very different and a much more complicated story, one that shuttles between the worlds of legal history, lay legal theory, and rhetorical provocation. Early on, such naming practises usually provided satirists with little or no legal protection. Any lingering ambiguity was stamped out in 1713, when Lord Chief Justice Thomas Parker ruled that gutted names in no way hindered potential prosecutions. One could simply read through the bundles of asterisks and the interminable dashes, filling in blanks as if the names had been wholly written out. In addition, it was perfectly legal to name a person in full. The

---

[1] 'Emvowel' does not appear in the *Oxford English Dictionary*, but the term was seemingly common in the eighteenth century. See, for instance, Henry Fielding, *The Jacobite's Journal and Related Writings*, edited by W. B. Coley (Middleton: Wesleyan University Press, 1975), p. 96.

[2] C. R. Kropf, 'Libel and Satire in the Eighteenth Century', *Eighteenth-Century Studies* 8, no. 2 (Winter 1974–75): p. 159. See, for instance, Noelle Gallagher, *Historical Literatures: Writing about the Past in England, 1660–1740* (Manchester: Manchester University Press, 2018), pp. 214–15n33; Anne Toner, *Ellipsis in English Literature: Signs of Omission* (Cambridge: Cambridge University Press, 2015), p. 59; Melinda Alliker Rabb, *Satire and Secrecy in English Literature from 1650 to 1750* (New York: Palgrave Macmillan, 2007), p. 65; Ian Higgins, *Swift's Politics: A Study in Disaffection* (Cambridge: Cambridge University Press, 1994), p. 160; Black, *Press*, p. 313; Vincent Carretta, *The Snarling Muse: Verbal and Visual Political Satire from Pope to Churchill* (Philadelphia: University of Pennsylvania Press, 1983), p. 40; and Howard D. Weinbrot, 'Masked Men and Satire and Pope: Toward a Historical Basis for the Eighteenth-Century Persona', *Eighteenth-Century Studies* 16, no. 3 (Spring 1983): p. 283n31.

[3] Edward P. Nathan, 'The Bench and the Pulpit: Conflicting Elements in the Augustan Apology for Satire', *English Literary History* 52, no. 2 (Summer 1985): p. 387; and Gregory Colomb, *Designs on Truth: The Poetics of the Augustan Mock-Epic* (University Park: Pennsylvania State University Press, 1992), p. 63.

Libel and Lampoon: Satire in the Courts, 1670–1792. Andrew Benjamin Bricker, Oxford University Press.
© Andrew Benjamin Bricker 2022. DOI: 10.1093/oso/9780192846150.003.0005

real question was not whether someone had been named, or even whether they could be identified through the oblique allusion of a gutted name, but whether what was imputed to a satiric victim qualified as legally defamatory.

In short, after 1713, such naming strategies offered no *formal* legal defence, and yet the emvowelment of victims' names remained a routine feature of eighteenth-century satire. Why? In part, many writers and victims simply misunderstood the law, a predictable outcome, as we saw in the last chapter, during a period when libel laws were rapidly evolving and courtroom interpretive procedures were radically revised. As a result, and despite widespread confusion among satirists and stationers about the legal permissibility of naming, emerging legal protocols continued to affect the production of satire, though in this instance in unpredictable ways. Rather than dismissing such misunderstandings, though, I would argue that widespread legal misperceptions should be central to our understanding of early modern law and literature: misinterpretations effectively shaped the practise of satire and readers' responses to it.

Nonetheless, some writers and satiric victims understood that gutted names served no formal legal purpose, and yet we see relatively few cases for libel during the first half of the eighteenth century. Slow-moving, confusing, and costly legal procedures were in part to blame. Above all, though, victims believed that they had little to gain by airing their private squabbles in a public courtroom. Most importantly for this chapter, gutted names came to serve a host of commercial, aesthetic, and pseudo-ethical functions. What started as legal ruse, and one that became increasingly transparent as the century wore on, eventually evolved into a central aspect of eighteenth-century printed satire's typographical visuality. The pregnant title pages of such works promised readers the sordid details of some potentially scandalous affair. Gutted names were part of the larger role that readers played in the construction of satiric meaning, in which the decoding of names was one act of participation among many. Above all, satirists employed strategic naming practises to fulfil a pro forma ethical obligation. During this period, legal and literary commentators asserted again and again the truism that no one has the right to damage the reputation of another. Gutted names were a way to skirt this ethical rule. They offered a form of mock-candidness, a kind of transparent circumspection.

Some writers, however, did directly name their satiric targets. One thinks of Alexander Pope's wildly provocative decision to name all of his dunces in the revised Variorum edition of the *Dunciad*. This was an exceptional act in the history of eighteenth-century satire and serves, in this chapter, as an intriguing case study: an opportunity to examine how one author mitigated his liability after disposing of a typographic precaution that served no legal function but nonetheless tended to inhibit legal action. As I show in closing, the *Variorum* was a poem at the intersection of the rules that governed satiric exposure and defamation: the poem served both as a litmus test for the socio-ethical limits of satire and as a pre-emptive defence of Pope's decision to name his victims in full.

Part of my goal in this chapter is to help clear away what we might call the legal-defence fallacy—the belief that gutted names *did* provide satirists with formally recognized legal protection—which has tended to reduce emvowelment to a one-dimensional typographical idiosyncrasy of this period's satire. As a result, I am more interested in demonstrating how this pseudo-legal evasion impacted the production and reception of satire and in documenting the aesthetic, commercial, and pseudo-ethical functions that gutted names served. This was a typographical sleight that bridged the worlds of verbal and bibliographical evasion and that played a precise if at times ambiguous role in the satires and courts of this period. Such a case study thus demonstrates how the bizarre and occasionally confusing world of early modern legal precedent and procedure influenced the choices of not only satirists and their stationers but also their victims.

4.1 Gutted Names in Court: Before and After *R. v. Hurt* (1713)

In the decades following the Restoration, gutted names might have served a legal function. During this period, we lack a crisp formulation of their legal status. Still, we can piece together a pre-1713 working theory of naming from the existing records and the legal commentary of the period. That theory tends to fly in the face of much received literary-historical wisdom. Satirists who indirectly named their victims were provided at best with slight protection before 1713 and none thereafter.

In trials for defamation, the plaintiff or prosecutor was required to establish two things. First, one had to prove that the words themselves were defamatory—that the words spoken or written of the victim meant what the prosecution or plaintiff claimed them to mean (a question of fact) and that those words were defamatory rather than merely insulting (a question of law).[4] Words could be defamatory either in themselves or within the context of their utterance. Defamatory words per se fell under three kinds of imputation. One would have to impugn an individual's professional competence, accuse him or her of a criminal act, or claim that he or she had a communicable disease.[5] But certain words, given their context, could also be defamatory.[6] For instance, to call a man an

---

[4] Holdsworth, *History*, vol. 8, pp. 367–8.
[5] *King v. Lake* (1670), Hard. 470–1 (Ex. Ch.), 145 Eng. Rep. 552–3.
[6] Baker, *ELH*, p. 444. See *Smale v. Hammon* (1610), 1 Bulst. 40 (K.B.), 80 Eng. Rep. 743. Justices in the eighteenth century sought to limit defamatory imputations to words that exposed a plaintiff to 'publick Hatred, Contempt or Ridicule' (William Hawkins, *A Treatise of the Pleas of the Crown*, vol. 1 [London, 1716], p. 193) or tended to cause a plaintiff to be 'shunned or avoided' (Villers v. Monsley [1769], 2 Wils. 403 [K.B.]).

'ambidexter'—a double-dealer, one who takes bribes from both sides—was legally permissible. But the same insult made against a lawyer might damage his business and was therefore defamatory.[7]

The plaintiff or prosecutor was also required to prove that the words referred to the plaintiff or victim.[8] To establish both of these points—that the words were defamatory and that they had been spoken of the victim or plaintiff—the prosecutor or plaintiff used an information or a colloquium, respectively. These fussy documents delimited any ambiguities about the defendant's defamatory language through the use of 'innuendoes', a legal term for any word whose referent was not immediately obvious when taken out of context (the term came from Latin: *innuere*, to hint or indicate).[9] In a civil action, for instance, the colloquium might read 'J— S— (*innuendo*, John Smith)'. But innuendoes were also subject to interpretation and could not be used, the courts asserted, to infer meanings, only to clarify what had already been said or written. An innuendo, one legal commentator observed in 1733, can only 'mark out a Thing or Person more certainly than it was before described'. It 'cannot make that certain which had no certainty before; nor can it alter the Matter by enlarging or restraining the Sense of the Words'.[10] Despite lawyers' best efforts to twist their function, innuendoes often performed a very specific and even banal role: either to clarify the meaning of an obscure insult or to designate an individual already named who then later, in speech or writing, appeared under a metonym like 'preacher' or a pronoun like 'he' or 'she'. If the plaintiff or victim had not been openly named by the defendant, then no innuendo was going to prove that he had.[11]

This is not to say that satiric victims who appeared under gutted names were simply denied legal relief. For the most part, prosecutors and plaintiffs spent most of their efforts establishing whether the defendant had defamed the victim or plaintiff—not whether the ostensibly defamatory language referred to him or her. What we might call onomastic innuendoes—those that established the victim or plaintiff's identity—were open and shut. Either it was clear to the courts that the victim had been named (or substantively alluded to) or not.

The legal status of strategic naming before 1713, however, is to some degree unclear. Our own uncertainty in part extends from the doctrine of *mitior sensus*, a

---

[7] Anon. (1580), Misc. MS 488/76, Lincoln's Inn (Q.B.), rpt. *Sources*, pp. 638–9.

[8] Holdsworth, *History*, vol. 8, pp. 370–1. In addition to these elements—that the words were defamatory and that they had been written or spoken of the plaintiff or victim—the prosecution or plaintiff was required to show that the words were spoken or written in the manner alleged; that they had been published to some third party, which was easy enough to prove with printed materials that were distributed or sold; and that this had been done maliciously, meaning they had been published without just cause, excuse (like the truth, in case of the tort of slander, or the plea of justification), or privilege. See Holdsworth, *History*, vol. 8, pp. 367–77.

[9] Baker, *ELH*, p. 444n53.

[10] William Bohun, *Declarations and Pleadings in the Most Usual Actions* (London, 1733), p. 2.

[11] *Jeames v. Rutlech* (1599), 4 Co. Rep. 17 (Q.B.), rpt. *Sources*, pp. 642–3.

procedural rule used to clarify the interpretation of defamatory language.[12] The
doctrine held that jurors were to interpret supposedly defamatory language in its
lesser, more innocuous sense, but only in instances in which both senses—the
worse and the better—seemed equally tenable.[13] Perhaps predictably, this rule
often led to outlandish defences. The plaintiff in one 1608 case argued that
the defendant had accused him of murder upon the words he 'struck his cook
on the head with a cleaver, and cleaved his head; the one part lay on the one
shoulder and the other on the other'. The defence countered that 'it is not averred
that the cook was killed'. Surprisingly, the court ruled in favour of the defendant.
'Notwithstanding such wounding', Chief Justice Sir Thomas Fleming reasoned,
'the party may yet be living, and it is then but a trespass'.[14] That is, the defendant
had merely accused the plaintiff of a misdemeanour, not a felony, and therefore
the imputation was not slanderous. Under a strict interpretation of the rule, a
quibbling counsellor and a hard-headed judge could twist almost any statement
into innocuous wind.[15]

As a result, some legal historians have viewed the doctrine with bemusement,
though others have severely questioned the extent to which the rule prevented
rulings that favoured plaintiffs.[16] Even in the ecclesiastical courts, where *mitior
sensus* was first formulated, it was argued that 'words should be interpreted in
their most natural sense, as they would have been understood among hearers'.[17] In
the common law courts, judges for the most part followed suit. One legal commentator noted that words should always be understood in their 'vulgar and
common sense'.[18] Again and again, legal historians have concluded the rule itself
had 'very little ultimate effect on the law'.[19] By the mid-seventeenth century,

[12]   Richard H. Helmholz, *The Oxford History of the Laws of England*, vol. 1: The Canon Law and
Ecclesiastical Jurisdiction from 597 to the 1640s (Oxford: Oxford University Press, 2003), p. 577.
[13]   Richard H. Helmholz, preface to *Select Cases on Defamation to 1600* (London: Selden Society,
1985), pp. xcii–xcv; Knightley D'Anvers, *A General Abridgment of the Common Law*, vol. 1 (London,
1722–1725), 140; and William Sheppard, *Action Upon the Case for Slander*, 2nd ed. (London, 1674),
p. 20.
[14]   *Holt v. Astrigg* (1608), Cro. Jac. 184, pl. 4 (K.B.), rpt. *Sources*, pp. 643–4.
[15]   For example, see *Poe v. Mondford* (1598), Cro. Eliz. 620 (Q.B.), 78 Eng. Rep. 861; *Morrison v. Cade*
(1607), Cro. Jac. 162, in John March, *Actions for Slander*, 2nd ed. (London, 1674), p. 31; *Foster v.
Browning* (1624), Cro. Jac. 688 (C.P.), 79 Eng. Rep. 596; and *Kilvert v. Roe* (1625), Bendl. 155 (K.B.), 73
Eng. Rep. 1022.
[16]   Baker, *ELH*, p. 443; and Richard H. Helmholz, 'The Mitior Sensus Doctrine', *Green Bag* 7 (Winter
2004): p. 133.
[17]   Helmholz, *Laws of England*, vol 1, p. 577. For the ecclesiastical origins and common law
development of defamation, see Helmholz, *Select Cases on Defamation*; and Helmholz, *Laws of
England*, vol. 1, pp. 590–3.
[18]   Sheppard, *Action Upon the Case*, p. 30. See also *Watson v. Vanderlash* (1628), Hetley 71 (C.P.),
124 Eng. Rep. 351.
[19]   Baker, *ELH*, pp. 442–3; Holdsworth, *History*, vol. 8, p. 356; and Helmholz, 'The Mitior Sensus
Doctrine', 135, 136. See, for example, *Hamond v. Kingsmill* (1647), 22 Style 23 (K.B.); and *King v. Lake*
(1671), 2 Vent. 28, 1 Freem. 14 (C.P.), rpt. *Sources*, p. 654.

judicial opposition to the doctrine was at its height.[20] In case after case, the rule was rejected along with counsellors' preposterous interpretations of their clients' words.[21] Finally, in 1714, Chief Justice Thomas Parker formally abolished the doctrine. As he put it, 'the rule now was that words shall be taken in the sense that the hearers understood them, and not *in mitiori sensu* as formerly'.[22] Once again, and as with irony earlier, the courts continued to formulate sociocentric doctrines for the interpretation of ambiguous language in order to mitigate the subjective deliberations of individual jurors.

In addition, *mitior sensus* had little effect on establishing a victim's identity. When debate arose in the courtroom, the issue at hand tended not to be whether the victim or plaintiff was the person named, even if somewhat obliquely. Instead, such questions of fact centred on the nature of the imputation. When a name proved vague, an innuendo often did the work of fixing an attribution, unless the allusion was hopelessly opaque. As we will see in the next chapter, until 1728, allegory was a particular problem for the courts, where innuendoes were useless in establishing the real-world identities of allegorical victims.[23]

Any lingering uncertainty about the legal status of gutted names was stamped out in 1713, when the printer William Hurt was tried, pilloried, fined, and imprisoned for publishing a version of *The British Embassadress's Speech to the French King*. First printed in March, the poem tells the apocryphal story of the British ambassador Charles Talbot, duke of Shrewsbury on his trip to Paris to negotiate the terms of peace for the War of Spanish Succession. His wife, Adellinda Paleotti, tells Louis XIV that Queen Anne is racked with guilt having taken the throne from her half-brother. As a consolation, the queen has instructed the duke to give his middle-aged duchess over to the seventy-four-year-old French king. The poem closes with 'The Duke o'erjoy'd, that his *Italian* Dame / Could in so Old an Hero raise a flame'.[24] Jonathan Swift called the poem 'the cursedest Libel in Verse [to] come out, that ever was seen'.[25] Hurt was arrested in April and tried in June.[26]

[20] Henry Rolle, *Un Abridgment des Plusieurs Cases et Resolutions del Common Ley* (London, 1668), qtd. in Baker, *ELH*, p. 443.

[21] See *Somers v. House* (1694), Holt 39 (K.B.), 90 Eng. Rep. 919; and *Baker v. Pierce* (1704), 6 Mod. 24 (Q.B.), 87 Eng. Rep. 788.

[22] *Harrison v. Thornborough* (1714), Gilb. Cas. 114, 10 Mod. 196 (Q.B.), 93 Eng. Rep. 277.

[23] *R. v. Clerk* (1728/9), 1 Barn. 305 (K.B.), 94 Eng. Rep. 207.

[24] 'The British Embassadress's Speech to the French King', *POAS*, vol. 7, pp. 590–6 (where, however, the blanks are filled in). The original version (Williams.410, no. 12, CUL) can be found under *The Br— sh Embassadress's Speech. To the French King* ([London], [1713]) in *Eighteenth Century Collections Online* (Gale Document no. CB3327149562). For the copy sent to Harley on 25 March 1713, see Dartmouth MSS, 1/315, BL.

[25] Jonathan Swift, *Journal to Stella: Letters to Esther Johnson and Rebecca Dingley, 1710–1713*, edited by Abigail Williams (Cambridge: Cambridge University Press, 2013), p. 517.

[26] Bolingbroke to Northey (7 April 1713), SP 44/114, TNA. For more on Hurt, see P. B. J. Hyland, 'Liberty and Libel: Government and the Press during the Succession Crisis in Britain, 1712–1716', *English Historical Review* 101 (October 1986): pp. 866–72.

For the most part, Hurt blots out the names that appear in the poem. Robert Harley, by then the earl of Oxford, shows up as '*Ox—d*'; the two Secretaries of State, William Legge, earl of Dartmouth, and Henry St John, viscount Bolingbroke appear as '*D——th*' and '*B——ke*'; while Queen Anne is either '*A—*' or '*Q—*'. Nonetheless, this sleight proved useless. Parker ruled that

> a Defamatory Writing expressing only one or two Letters of a Name, in such a Manner, that from what goes before and follows after, it must needs be understood to signify such a particular Person, in the plain, obvious, and natural Construction of the Whole, and would be perfect Nonsence if strained to any other Meaning, is as properly a Libel, as if it had expressed the whole Name at large.

In short, there was no difference between a gutted name and one written out in full. Moreover, Parker continued, 'it brings the utmost Contempt upon the Law, to suffer its Justice to be eluded by such trifling Evasions: And it is a ridiculous Absurdity to say, That a Writing which is understood by every the meanest Capacity, cannot possibly be understood by a Judge and Jury'.[27] By 1713, the legal status of gutted names was clear—they served no legal function.

The ruling proved pivotal. A few years later William Hawkins quoted Parker in his influential *Pleas of the Crown*.[28] Thereafter, Parker's ruling was routinely cited by legal commentators and invoked time and again in the courts.[29] In one of the most widely printed legal compendia of the period, Matthew Bacon shored up this newer, more common-sense understanding of words:

> [if] the Whole [of the words] taken together, or from the Circumstances which attended the speaking of them, it do appear that a certain Charge and a certain Person were intended by the Speaker, an Action does lie.... The Want of Certainty in the words themselves may be supplied by Averment.[30]

Missing letters could simply be plugged in. As William Blackstone commented on a case in 1769, a certain John Wing had been 'plainly indicated' in a libellous poem

---

[27] *Hurt's Case* (1713), in Hawkins, *Pleas of the Crown*, vol. 1, p. 194.

[28] Hawkins, *Pleas of the Crown*, vol. 1, p. 194.

[29] Sir John Gonson, *A Charge to the Grand Jury* (London, [1729]), p. 38; *State Law*, p. 63; Matthew Bacon, *A New Abridgment of the Law*, vol 3 (London, 1740), p. 493; Richard Burn, *The Justice of the Peace and Parish Officer*, 8th ed., vol. 2 (London, 1764), p. 88; and John Rayner, *A Digest of the Law Concerning Libels* (London, 1765), p. 6. See *R. v. Cooper* (1734), KB 1/4/2, TNA; *R. v. Meres* (1740), KB 10/25/1, TNA; *Roach v. Garvan* (1742), 2 Atk. 469 (Ch.), 26 Eng. Rep. 683; *R. v. Barnes* (1749), KB 10/29, TNA; *R. v. Harrop* (1754), KB 1/11/6, TNA; *R. v. Tiffen* (1768), D/DO/B24/5, Essex Record Office; *R. v. Woodfall* (1774), KB 33/5/8, TNA; *R. v. Miller* (1781), KB 33/5/9, TNA; *Bourke v. Warren* (1826), 2 Carr. & P. 307 (N.P.), 172 Eng. Rep. 138; and *Cook v. Ward* (1830), 6 Bing 409 (C.P.), 130 Eng. Rep. 1388.

[30] Matthew Bacon, *A New Abridgment of the Law*, vol. 4 (London, 1759), pp. 503–4.

nailed up in a market square, despite 'the cautious Intervention of a Blank' in 'W-NG'd'.[31] According to another legal commentator, the 'Mystery of [a] Satir'— its ambiguous language, its pseudonyms, its onomastic gaps—was no defence.[32]

In short, gutted names served no legal function in most instances prior to Parker's ruling and none thereafter. In addition, overt naming was itself neither a crime nor a tort. What mattered, above all, was whether what had been written or said about an individual amounted to defamation. As a result, innuendoes were almost exclusively used to establish that a given imputation was defamatory, not whether such imputations had been directed at the victim or plaintiff. Nonetheless, literary historians have continued to insist that gutted names provided satirists with some form of legal refuge. This was simply untrue, but it also raises important questions. If such onomastic omissions provided no defence, and if naming itself was legally permissible, why then did satirists continue to gut names? Why did they continue to cloud attribution? What did such practises and strategies actually do?

4.2 Perceptions of Law: Slippage and the Problem of Legal Meaning

Part of the confusion over the legal status of naming extends from a broad misunderstanding of defamation procedure among satirists and their victims. Writers wrongly assumed that gutted names offered legal protection, just as victims often mistakenly believed that the courts offered no redress for such evasions. Such varying perceptions demonstrate a central thesis of *Libel and Lampoon*: that competing interpretations of the law during this period, whether accurate or not, shaped not only the practise of satire during this period—the language it used and the physical forms it circulated in—but also its reception among readers. Such an account also suggests the extent to which strictly black-letter legal history, in which the law is depicted as both obvious and accessible, fails to account for the natural interpretive interference that we witness between the production of legal meaning and its reception by non-legal actors. These grey zones between socio-literary and legal history—this muddled working through of the law as lived—reveal the intersections between perceptions of law, no matter their accuracy, and the aesthetic and social arenas in which such views played out. The question we should be asking is not whether writers and readers understood the law; instead, we should be asking how their understanding of the law ultimately affected their actions and how, in this particular instance, those perceptions shaped this period's satire.

---

[31] Add. MS 33230, fos. 34, 36, BL.   [32] *The Doctrine of Libels*, p. 136.

In this instance, many writers wrongly believed that such practises were some sure-fire defence. One wag, mocking the nuisance of modern lawyers, wrote that gutted names stopped satiric victims short. 'Let them therefore stay till that one Defect of the Law here complain'd of is remedied, and then ——. What then? Here are no Names. No particular Persons; unless they can form 'em out of the Consonant Kind, the *P*s. and *B*s. and so forth'.[33] Joseph Addison, writing of the abuse the better sorts so routinely underwent, likewise claimed that not even they could have recourse to the courts under *scandalum magnatum*, an action based upon a series of thirteenth- and fourteenth-century statutes that protected emi-nent individuals and especially peers from damage to their reputations.[34] 'Some of our Authors indeed, when they would be more Satyrical than ordinary', he noted,

> omit the Vowels of a great Man's Name, and fall most unmercifully upon all the Consonants. This way of writing was first of all introduced by *T—m Br—wn*, of facetious Memory, who, after having gutted a Proper Name of all its intermediate Vowels, used to plant it in his Work, and make as free with it as he pleased, without any danger of the Statute.[35]

Addison, however, was confusing two issues: whether *scandalum magnatum* would have offered legal redress, and whether anyone was willing to go to court over so much wind. By 1714, when he was writing, the action was all but officially dead, thanks in part to a 1687 ruling that barred even successful plaintiffs from recovering court costs.[36] In addition, the courts had grown increasingly unwilling to award vast sums for damages in such actions. As a result, there was only 'a thin stream of cases' for *scandalum magnatum* in the eighteenth century, before the last in 1773.[37]

Writer after writer simply assumed that gutted names afforded legal protection. Such a misperception has influenced later literary historians, who have turned to such writers—and especially Jonathan Swift—to elaborate the legal safety that typographical mechanisms ostensibly provided. In the preface to *A Tale of a Tub*, for instance, Swift advocates for the use of gutted names, for 'whoever, I say, should venture to be thus particular, must expect to be imprisoned for *Scandalum Magnatum*: to have *Challenges* sent him; to be sued for *Defamation*; and to be

---

[33] *The Law Corrupted; A Satire* (London, 1706), p. iii.

[34] 3 Edw. 1, c. 34 (1275); 2 Rich. 2, c. 5 (1378); and 12 Rich. 2, c. 11 (1388). The scope and jurisdiction of the offence was expanded twice: 1 & 2 Phil. & M., c. 3 (1554) and 1 Eliz., c. 6 (1559).

[35] Joseph Addison, *The Spectator*, no. 567 (14 July 1714), edited by Donald F. Bond, vol. 4 (Oxford: Clarendon Press, 1965), p. 537.

[36] *Earl of Peterborough v. Williams* (1687), 2 Show. 505 (K.B.), 89 Eng. Rep. 1068.

[37] John C. Lassiter, 'Defamation of Peers: The Rise and Decline of the Action for Scandalum Magnatum, 1497–1773', *American Journal of Legal History* 22 (July 1978): p. 233.

brought before the Bar of the House'.[38] In *The Importance of the Guardian Considered* he also laughed, in a sideswipe at Richard Steele, that 'we are careful never to print a Man's Name out at length; but as I do that of Mr. *St—le*: So that although every Body alive knows whom I mean, the Plaintiff can have no Redress in any Court of Justice'.[39] Scholars have generally taken such claims of legal safety at face value. But it is difficult to read either *A Tale* or *The Importance of the Guardian Considered* as simple, earnest, or unambiguous observations on the law. Perhaps Swift was cheekily parodying a common piece of Grub Street logic; he might even have thought gutted names were some sort of legal impediment. Whatever the case, Swift's satiric writings seem an odd if not unreliable source for information about the rules of legal evidence.

Moreover, at other times Swift seems to have understood (or at least been indifferent to) the legal repercussions of naming. As he pleaded to Pope, after the *Dunciad* with almost every name gutted first appeared:

> I would have the names of those scriblers printed indexically at the beginning or end of the Poem, with an account of their works, for the reader to refer to.... How it passes in Dublin I know not yet; but I am sure it will be a great disadvantage to the poem, that the persons and facts will not be understood, till an explanation comes out, and a very full one.... Again I insist, you must have your Asterisks fill'd up with some real names of real Dunces.[40]

This might be Swift's clearest statement on the practise of naming—you might as well name, he writes, or no one will know who you are talking about—and yet even here it is difficult to assert confidently whether he felt gutted names served some legal end. In any case, it hardly matters. Swift was no legal expert and, from the safety of Dublin, he seems to have either cared little for the legal repercussions of naming or thought correctly that gutted names served no officially recognized function. In the end, whether Swift or other writers fully understood the legal dimensions of naming, satirist after satirist continued to gut names in pro forma ways, often assuming that such sleights provided some measure of defence.

Misunderstandings about libel law were also prevalent among satiric victims. They too assumed that there was no legal redress for satires in which they had been obliquely named.[41] This is not to say, however, that such views, though unjustified, were also irrelevant. Our perception of the law is just as likely to

---

[38] Swift, preface, in *A Tale of a Tub and Other Works*, edited by Marcus Walsh (Cambridge: Cambridge University Press, 2010), p. 32.

[39] Swift, *The Importance of the Guardian Considered*, in *English Political Writings, 1711–1714: The Conduct of the Allies and Other Works*, edited by Bertrand A. Goldgar and Ian Gadd (Cambridge: Cambridge University Press, 2008), p. 229.

[40] Swift to Alexander Pope (16 July 1728), *The Correspondence of Jonathan Swift, D.D.*, edited by David Woolley, vol. 3 (Frankfurt am Main: Peter Lang, 1999–2014), p. 89.

[41] *Doctrine of Libels*, pp. 135–6.

influence our actions as its actual existence in seemingly abstract and remote legal rulings and statutes. Naomi Mezey has called such gaps between our perception of the law and its black-letter status 'slippage'—those 'inconsistencies between the production of legal meaning and its cultural reception'.[42] In effect there is a feedback loop between the law, as it appears in legal rulings and statutes, and the law as it is popularly understood by non-legal actors. In this instance, many satirists thought they were skirting the law (other writers likely gave little thought to why names were routinely gutted, perhaps deducing a legal rule from a satiric commonplace). In the same way, potential plaintiffs followed suit, unaware they could actually bring such libellers to court. In the eighteenth century, two under-standings of defamation law existed side by side: the one that prevailed in the Inns of Court and at Westminster, where such omissions were at best a far-fetched defence, and a more socio-literary understanding, common among satirists, sta-tioners, and their victims, in which such evasions were wrongly thought to protect against legal proceedings. As a result, for those lampooned, ignorance of the law could be a powerful if accidental prohibition against dragging a satirist or book-seller into court.

Such misperceptions have also blurred our view of the relationship between defamation and satire during this period. Yet such moments of 'slippage' might tell us much about the social experience of the law among non-legal actors and especially among eighteenth-century writers and their stationers, whose percep-tions of the law, despite their wrongheadedness, influenced the language of their satires and the bibliographical forms in which they were published. The law is not a homogeneous, monolithic, and immovable force, as some earlier scholars of law and literature have characterized it.[43] Early modern legal actors, and especially judges, prosecutors, and jurors, had tremendous discretionary powers to decide which cases would go forward, which summarily decided or dismissed, and which punished in the most harsh and exemplary manner or slight and sympathetic way.[44] Misperceptions about the legal safety of naming are simply one more aspect of this instability, of the lived experience of the law. Handling such views with more caution and with a deeper sense of the legal system's ambiguities and inconsistencies allows us to understand the important and yet uncertain role the law played in the lives of early modern individuals, be they satirists or readers, while illustrating the limits to and confusions created by treating legal meaning as coherent, self-evident, and readily accessible.

---

[42] Mezey, 'Law', p. 54. Mezey's example comes from the U.S. Supreme Court's finding in *Dickerson v. US* (2000). There the court dizzyingly ruled that Miranda rights were constitutionally protected not because they were constitutionally required but because of a broad popular understanding (and misperception) that they were in fact constitutionally protected (see pp. 51–3).

[43] Julie Stone Peters, 'Law, Literature, and the Vanishing Real: On the Future of an Interdisciplinary Illusion', *PMLA* 120, no. 2 (March 2005): p. 443.

[44] Beattie, *Crime*, pp. 400–49; and Baker, *ELH*, pp. 143–4, 151.

4.3 Gutted Names in Eighteenth-Century Satire

Others, though, did know better, especially the considerable minority of writers who were lawyers or had legal training. A mere misunderstanding of the law fails to explain by itself why we see so few criminal and civil trials for libel in the first half of the eighteenth century when personal satire is everywhere. In part, procedural issues inhibited complainants and litigants. Moreover, by the beginning of the eighteenth century, a sense had developed that a public courtroom was no place to air one's private grievances. Gutted names, though, were not merely prohibitive. They also served commercial and aesthetic functions: they advertised intrigues and invited readers to be part of the construction of a scandal. Onomastic gaps always needed to be filled—and readers seem happily to have played their role.

To some extent, legal procedures discouraged potential plaintiffs and victims. It was simply a nuisance either to initiate a prosecution or originate an action.[45] Actions and prosecutions, for both of which the victim was required to pay the expenses, could also be costly. Then there was the tedious business of bringing the offence to the attention of the authorities, assembling witnesses, gathering evidence, and presenting it all in court.[46] In any case, what was the point? There were no set rules for determining damages, meaning that even fairly confident plaintiffs could find the courts ruling in their favour only to have the jury fine the defendant a piddling 1d.[47]

Moreover, in libel law's most glaring paradox, plaintiffs and complainants were denied the opportunity to rebut a libel's accusations. Truth was immaterial in actions and prosecutions for libel (though not for the tort of slander), which meant that victims and plaintiffs were prevented from refuting a satire's imputations. This gave the impression, at least superficially, that even a successful plaintiff had conceded the truth of the supposed libel, if only to collect damages or to see the defamer punished. As Adam Smith observed, 'taking notice of a libell makes the [victim] appear more probably to be guilty than if he had despised them'.[48] Even worse, if one were to lose a case, the implicit impression was given, though not legally justified, that the accusations were true. More troublingly, a suit always garnered unwanted attention on the pamphlet or poem, drumming up interest and spurring on sales. Animosity and publicity were as likely to be quashed by such actions, one legal commentator observed, as 'fire can be extinguished by adding fewell into it'.[49] When all had been tallied up, most victims

---

[45] Beattie, *Crime*, pp. 35–50; and John Langbein, *The Origins of Adversary Criminal Trial* (Oxford: Oxford University Press, 2003), ch. 5.

[46] Beattie, *Crime*, pp. 35–6, 41.

[47] *Knowlys v. Castleton* (1754), Harrowby MSS 12/14, Lincoln's Inn.

[48] Adam Smith, *Lectures on Jurisprudence*, edited by R. L. Meek, D. D. Raphael, and P. G. Stein (Oxford: Clarendon Press, 1978), p. 125.

[49] March, *Actions for Slander*, p. 9.

concluded that the drawbacks of an action or a prosecution simply outweighed the benefits.

This only added to the intuitive sense that hauling some no-name scribbler into court was profoundly embarrassing. By the close of the seventeenth century, there was something *déclassé* about hashing out such pettish squabbles in a public courtroom filled with gawking rows of tittering onlookers. Martin Ingram has shown that 'changed legal and social conditions gradually made it less necessary or less appropriate to defend aspects of reputation in the courts, less desirable and perhaps less respectable to bring interpersonal quarrels into the legal arena in the guise of slander suits'.[50] This in part helps to explain why so few suits actually made it to the courts. Legal fees along with sometimes glacial and confusing courtroom procedures are certainly part of the equation, but above all the fashion for civil suits over words had simply passed by the beginning of the eighteenth century.[51] It all had the unpleasant stench of so much dirty laundry being put out to air.

Perhaps most importantly, plaintiffs and prosecutors were required to prove that a publication's imputations were themselves defamatory. Unfortunately for such complainants, the overwhelming majority of satires, if interpreted strictly, failed to constitute defamation: no crimes, no disease, no professional incompetence had been alleged. Satirists and their booksellers simply took caution when sending someone up. Those efforts were aided by the many lay guides to defamation published and republished throughout the period.[52] Satirists for the most part played it safe, opting for merely nasty insults over legally defamatory accusations, while stationers, as we saw in my second chapter, often carefully edited their most provocative wares before publication.[53]

Pope, for instance, in his attempt to mitigate his legal liability for the Variorum edition of the *Dunciad*, consulted the lawyer Nicholas Fazakerley (a few years later, Fazakerley also defended Richard Francklin, the printer-publisher of the *Craftsman*, in his trial for seditious libel brought by the

---

[50] Martin Ingram, 'Law, Litigants and the Construction of "Honour": Slander Suits in Early Modern England', in *The Moral World of the Law*, edited by Peter Cross (Cambridge: Cambridge University Press, 2000), p. 160.

[51] On the decline in civil litigation during the final quarter of the seventeenth century and throughout the eighteenth, see Christopher Brooks, 'Interpersonal Conflict and Social Tension: Civil Litigation in England, 1640–1830', in *The First Modern Society: Essays in English History in Honour of Lawrence Stone*, edited by A. L. Beier, David Cannadine, and James M. Rosenheim (Cambridge: Cambridge University Press, 1989), ch. 10; W. A. Champion, 'Recourse to Law and the Meaning of the Great Litigation Decline', in *Communities and Courts in Britain, 1150–1900*, edited by Christopher Brooks and Michael Lobban (London: Hambledon Press, 1997), p. 180; and David Lemmings, *Law and Government in England During the Long Eighteenth Century: From Consent to Command* (New York: Palgrave Macmillan, 2011), ch. 4 and *Professors of the Law: Barristers and English Legal Culture in the Eighteenth Century* (Oxford: Oxford University Press, 2000), pp. 78–84.

[52] *Doctrine of Libels*, pp. ii, 6.

[53] John Feather, 'The English Book Trade and the Law, 1695–1799', *Publishing History* 12 (1982): p. 51.

Walpole administration).[54] Pope had good reason to exercise caution, having been questioned, in an obscure incident from 1723, over 'a seditious and scandalous Libel'.[55] 'I am grown more Prudent than ever, the less I think others so', Pope wrote to the Earl of Burlington shortly before the Variorum edition was published. 'The whole Question is only this', he continued:

> If there be any thing in these sheets (for the other two can have nothing of that sort) which an Action may be grounded upon? and if there be, which those things are? that Mr F[azakerley] would mark or alter them in this Copy. The time of publication pressing, I could wish he read them as soon as possible. Your Lordship needs not even name *me* as any way concern'd in that publication, which Mr F. will observe is guarded against by the manner in which it is publish'd, but the apprehension is only, lest if the Printer & Publisher be found, any such Action could be brought; for we would be safe even against this.[56]

That Pope exercised such caution is remarkable. As Thomas Keymer has observed, 'It speaks volumes about the uncertainties faced by poets in the post-licensing era that the most accomplished ironist of the day felt compelled... to take professional advice'.[57] Interestingly, despite Fazakerley's cautious intervention, Pope still libelled the bookseller Edmund Curll, who was, in a certain sense, a safe target. During the poem's mock-epic battle, Curll and another bookseller, William Rufus Chetwood, engage in a literal pissing contest—'the glorious strife' (l. 159)—filled with burlesque Homeric similes, to publish the works of Eliza Haywood. Chetwood goes first, accidentally urinating on himself: 'A second effort brought but new disgrace, / For straining more, it flies in his own face' (ll. 169–70). The gonorrhoeal Curll then tries his luck:

> Not so from shameless Curl: Impetuous spread
> The stream, and smoking, flourish'd o'er his head.
> So, (fam'd like thee for turbulence and horns,)
> Eridanus his humble fountain scorns,
> Thro' half the heav'ns he pours th' exalted urn;
> His rapid waters in their passage burn.
>
> (ll. 171–6)

Legally speaking, Curll easily could have brought a successful suit for libel against Pope for the imputation of communicable disease. Pope knew, however, that Curll

[54] Roger Turner, 'Fazakerley, Nicholas (bap. 1682, d. 1767)', *ODNB*. See also Pope to Earl of Burlington (23 December 1728) and Pope to Earl of Burlington (1728/9), *Correspondence of Alexander Pope*, edited by George Sherburn, vol. 3 (Oxford: Clarendon Press, 1956), pp. 532, 4.

[55] Keymer, *Poetics*, pp. 106–7; and Maynard Mack, *Alexander Pope: A Life* (New York: W. W. Norton & Company in association with Yale University Press, 1985), p. 397.

[56] Pope to Earl of Burlington (1728/9), *Correspondence of Pope*, vol. 3, p. 4.

[57] Keymer, *Poetics*, p. 110.

wasn't about to spend his hard-filched pounds dragging the little poet to court. Above all, Curll was a bookseller, and for all the infamy he had suffered at the pen of Pope, he had also benefited from it. Every charge Pope had laid at Curll's door the bookseller had batted back in one-off squibs, all scribbled and sold almost as quickly as they could be printed. In libelling Curll, Pope's tactic was not merely rhetorical but economic. He counted on the one thing he knew about booksellers and about Curll in particular: little would he pass up the chance to print something in response with an almost guaranteed audience. And that is exactly what he did.[58] For Curll, business, books: these came first; reputation, second, if at all.

Caution over one's imputations was thus essential, but the obliqueness of gutted names also helped to shelter satirists and their booksellers. If a victim could not be confidently identified, then it was uncertain whether he or she could find redress in the courts. However, this trade-off between overt identification and oblique allusion meant that third-party readers were sometimes left in the dark about who exactly was being sent up. As I noted above, Swift felt readers twenty miles outside of London had no idea to whom all those obscure initials referred in the first edition of the *Dunciad*.[59] Such obscurity also occasionally backfired, though not always in the worst way. A vague allusion could also produce some profitable humour, especially when a reader or critic mistakenly fingered the wrong fool. Pope had played up this ambiguity in the first edition of the *Dunciad*. In a disingenuous letter to the much-besmirched Aaron Hill, he claimed that the poem's initials 'were set at random to occasion what they did occasion [:] the suspicion of bad and jealous writers'.[60] (Even still, who but the densest dunce would have mistaken J. D. and J. O. for anyone other than John Dennis and John Oldmixon?) He and Swift had done the same in the sixth chapter of *The Art of Sinking in Poetry*, with its seemingly endless catalogue of obscure initials—thirty in all, five of which were duplicates. 'Such was the number of poets eminent in *that* art [of sinking]', Richard Savage laughed, 'that some one or other took every letter to himself'.[61] Critic after critic attempted to clear up the mess, often with little success.[62] Obscure allusions often proved too ticklish to pin down. Unsurprisingly, misidentifications were stock-in-trade in the world of personal satire. Pope hardly thought it a problem, but others were less pleased.[63] Daniel Defoe, for one,

---

[58] Paul Baines and Pat Rogers, *Edmund Curll, Bookseller* (Oxford: Oxford University Press, 2007), ch. 10; and J. V. Guerinot, *Pamphlet Attacks on Alexander Pope, 1711–1744: A Descriptive Bibliography* (London: Methuen, 1969).

[59] Swift to Pope (16 July 1728), *Correspondence of Swift*, vol. 3, p. 189.

[60] Pope to Aaron Hill (26 January 1730/1), *Correspondence of Pope*, vol. 3, p. 165.

[61] Qtd. Samuel Johnson, *The Yale Edition of the Works of Samuel Johnson*, vol. 23: *The Lives of the Poets*, edited by John H. Middendorf (New Haven: Yale University Press, 1958–2019), p. 1111.

[62] For the confusion over whom Pope had intended for the initials, see Edna Lake Steeves' commentary *The Art of Sinking in Poetry* (New York: King's Crown Press, 1952), pp. 109–36.

[63] Maynard Mack, *The Last and Greatest Art: Some Unpublished Poetical Manuscripts of Alexander Pope* (Newark: University of Delaware Press, 1984), p. 99; and Shef Rogers, 'Pope, Publishing, and Popular Interpretations of the *Dunciad Variorum*', *Philological Quarterly* 74 (Summer 1995): pp. 279–95, esp. 285–6.

bemoaned the imbecility of readers. 'The Case is this', he explained. 'They fancy themselves Lampoon'd, and Expos'd, in some Characters which were never design'd for them: And so take a Coat which never was cut out for that use'.[64] Another poet agreed, settling the blame on those 'Naughty People [who] make Naughty Applications; as Vicious Stomachs turn the best Food to Flegme'.[65]

These same satiric misidentifications could also have disastrous consequences. One thinks of Pope's mocking depiction of Timon's villa in his *Epistle to Burlington*. Soon after the poem's publication, rumour began to circulate that the villa was Cannons, the lavish Berkshire estate of James Brydges, duke of Chandos.[66] The playwright James Miller encountered a similar situation in 1737. According to him, his play *The Coffee-House* had been damned for 'Personal Reflexions' on both the family that ran the coffeehouse in Temple Bar at which the play was thought to take place and 'several Persons who frequent it'. The real problem, he claimed, was his audience—those rabble rousers too ready to find a personal reference in a general send-up. In his words: "tis impossible to write anything but may, in some Particular or other, be apply'd'.[67] (Then again, Miller's purported innocence was hard to swallow. Charles Macklin, who acted the part of the coffeehouse's resident poet, Bays, was dressed as Richard Savage.) Such mistakes were in part obviated, sometimes corrected, or even exacerbated by the satiric 'keys' published during this period.[68] Curll was notorious for them, some of which he simply scrawled out and posted in the windows of his shop for the benefit of confused readers and curious passers-by.[69] Some writers, with spleen to vent, happily joined in, outing their fellow scribblers in vengefully printed catalogues of satiric wrongdoing.[70]

At the same time, the obliqueness of an attack could also benefit the victim of a satire, offering him a degree of half-wished-for deniability. If the allusion were obscure and readers uncertain, then a victim had little to gain by dragging some scribbler to court only to prove that he was the satire's prize boob. Even if the victim's name was less than totally cryptic, perhaps even obvious given a host of circumstantial details—a semi-notable work, a well-known quotation, or a physical or professional description—then one could simply choose to keep mum. If I can't clearly identify myself in the piece, the logic went, then how likely are others to? In any case, who ever wanted openly to identify himself as the fool sent

[64] Daniel Defoe, preface, in *A True Collection of the Writings of the Author of The True Born Englishman*, 2nd ed. (London, 1705), p. [iv].

[65] *The Law Corrupted*, p. iii.   [66] Mack, *Alexander Pope*, pp. 498–501.

[67] James Miller, *The Coffee-House* (London, 1737), pp. i, iii.

[68] Nicola Parsons, *Reading Gossip in Early Eighteenth-Century England* (New York: Palgrave, 2009), p. 47.

[69] Baines and Rogers, *Edmund Curll*, pp. 178, 189.

[70] *A Compleat Collection Of all the Verses, Essays, Letters and Advertisements* (London, 1728), p. 51; and *Characters of the Times; Or, An Impartial Account of...the several Noblemen and Gentlemen, libell'd in a Preface to a late Miscellany* (London, 1728), p. v.

up in a poem? What pleasure was there in showing up some workaday hack in court for at best a few pounds damages? Who wanted to look not just a dolt but the tetchy bully who couldn't take a joke? Edward P. Nathan comes closest to identifying how this half-veiled prohibition worked. 'These satiric techniques of indirection, or obliquity', he writes, 'almost achieve the status of *de facto* legality'.[71] This is not to say they were *de jure* legal—quite the opposite, as Nathan notes. But there was little to gain by openly identifying oneself as a satire's victim, and such indirection functioned in effect as a prohibition, if not a formal legal check, that drained one's desire to pursue an action or a complaint.

Such naming practises were, however, more than just impediments. They also served a host of aesthetic and commercial functions and were something like a marketing tool.[72] As Catherine Gallagher has argued, a half-hidden name does more to hint at scandal than to hide it.[73] Similarly, these teasing, rebus-like absences produced moments of textual indeterminacy that encouraged readers to participate: they were literal 'gaps' that solicited intervention.[74] Readers were thus invited to fill in such blanks—and often, in fact, did (Figure 4.1).[75] There was simply a delectable pleasure in piecing together a satire. As Thomas Gordon put it, 'the Ambiguity or *double Entendre* of a Fable raises the Curiosity of every Reader, to discover the secret Sting which it contains, and gratifies his Chagrin with more than ordinary Satisfaction when discovered'.[76] Readers eagerly attempted to crack the onomastic codes upon which both the amusement the satire provided and its personal element were based.

Gutted names could also serve a host of aesthetic ends. They were part of a riddle-like game that forced readers to identify a satiric victim while decoding the half-veiled scandal itself. Think of the printed versions of *Mac Flecknoe*, with their punning visual-verbal confusion over whether a line should read Shadwell or shit:

> From dusty shops neglected Authors come,
> Martyrs of Pies, and Reliques of the Bum.
> Much Heywood, Shirly, Ogleby [all dead by 1684] there lay,
> But loads of Sh— almost choakt the way.[77]

---

[71] Nathan, 'Bench and the Pulpit', p. 387.

[72] P. K. Elkin, *The Augustan Defense of Satire* (Oxford: Clarendon Press, 1973), p. 122.

[73] Catherine Gallagher, *Nobody's Story: The Vanishing Acts of Women Writers in the Marketplace, 1670–1820* (Berkeley: University of California Press, 1995), p. 100.

[74] Wolfgang Iser, 'Indeterminacy and the Reader's Response in Prose Fiction', in *Prospecting: From Reader Response to Literary Anthropology* (Baltimore: Johns Hopkins University Press, 1993), pp. 9–10.

[75] See, for instance, a facsimile of Jonathan Richardson, Jr's heavily annotated copy of the first *Dunciad* (David L. Vander Meulen [ed.], *Pope's Dunciad of 1728: A History and Facsimile* [Charlottesville: University Press of Virginia, 1991], pp. 73–140).

[76] Thomas Gordon, *The Humourist*, vol. 2 (London, 1735), p. 98.

[77] John Dryden, *Mac Flecknoe*, in *The Poems of John Dryden*, vol. 1: 1649–1681, edited by Paul Hammond (New York: Longman, 1995), p. 323, ll. 100–3.

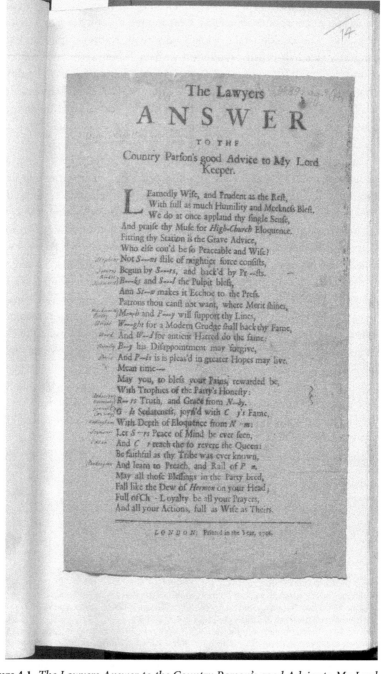

Figure 4.1 *The Lawyers Answer to the Country Parson's good Advice to My Lord Keeper.* (C) British Library Board (General Reference Collection 1493.a.6)

Or think of the fad for hieroglyphic letters in the latter half of the eighteenth century. These pieces signalled their recipients or ostensible senders through either a portrait or some sort of phonetic rebus—say, a boot for John Stuart, third earl of Bute.[78] At other times, the rebuses could be comically insulting. In one, produced by the engraver and caricaturist John Kay, the Scottish MP Sir Lawrence Dundas is identified using the letters 'Dund' and an image of an ass (Figure 4.2). Such games

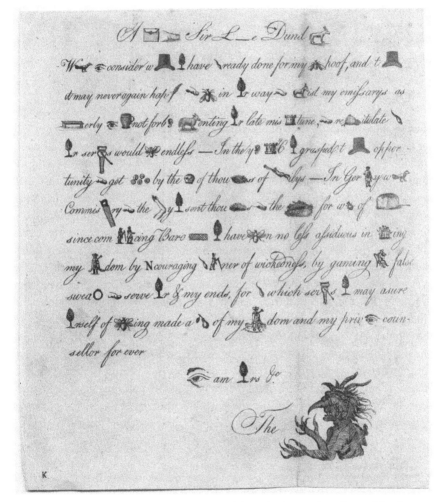

Figure 4.2 'Dund [ass]' (i.e., Dundas). Detail from [John Kay], *A [Letter] [toe] Sir L___e Dund[ass]* (1762). Courtesy of the Lewis Walpole Library, Yale University (762.00.00.04)

[78] *The [boot] Interest in the [city] or a [bridge] in the [hole]* (1760), BM Satires 3741, the British Museum.

also forced readers to do some contextual or phonetic guesswork when decoding a letter's larger message and the sordid details of the squabble itself. Take, for example, *The Retort [:] an Hieroglyphic Epistle from the Revd. Dr. [Whitefield] to Saml. [foot] Esqr.*, a piece occasioned by Foote's play *The Minor*, a send-up of Methodism and George Whitefield, whom Foote mocked in the play's epilogue as Mr. Squintum (an allusion to the preacher's deformed eye) (Figure 4.3).[79] Such visual-verbal games had the ability to offer complicated and pungent statements. For instance, on one side of a pewter medal from 1742, after Robert Walpole had been forced to resign his premiership, the fallen minister reclines on a bag of money—a sure sign of his backdoor dealing—while bemoaning his fate (Figure 4.4). On the other side is a wall with a pole (wall-pole). But atop the pole is a head—visual shorthand for a traitor. No wonder readers not only tittered at a satire's pointed jabs but also relished decoding its shabby backstory.

A published satire was often nothing more than the last and most prominent blow in some evolving, semi-public scandal. The various editions of the *Dunciad*, for instance, served as ever-changing satiric gallows for Pope's enemies, both new and old.[80] Take his attack on William Broome, whom Pope had employed for his translations of the *Iliad* (1715–20) and the *Odyssey* (1725–26).[81] For his own reasons, Pope attempted to obscure the extent to which both Broome and another poet, Elijah Fenton, had assisted him. Predictably irritated, Broome planned to publish a full account of the affair, though Fenton, perhaps hoping to avoid publicizing the fact that the worst part of the *Odyssey* was his, successfully cautioned him against it.[82] Later that year, the eccentric John Henley, a spy for Walpole and a hack for Curll, circulated a couplet, punningly bringing the matter to light: 'Pope came off clean with Homer, but they say / Broome went before, and kindly swept the way'.[83] In Pope's mind, Broome's failure to respond publicly to the couplet was tantamount to a tacit declaration of paper war. Shortly thereafter, he sent Broome up in *The Art of Sinking*, where he listed him among the class of authors known as '*Parrots*'—'they that repeat *another's* Words, in such a *hoarse, odd* Voice, that it makes them seem *their own*'—before poaching and misquoting several couplets from two of Broome's poems.[84] Apparently the parrot's feathers were ruffled, but Fenton again brokered a peace, and Broome bit his tongue.

---

[79] Thanks to the brouhaha that surrounded the play's premiere, the phrase 'new birth'—a favourite Methodist idiom—was axed from a third version of the play by Edward Capell, the Examiner of Plays, when submitted to the Lord Chamberlain. See mssLA 177, in the Papers of John Larpent, 1737–1824, Hunt.L.

[80] Paul Baines, 'Crime and Punishment', in *The Cambridge Companion to Alexander Pope*, edited by Pat Rogers (Cambridge: Cambridge University Press, 2007), pp. 152–4.

[81] Many of the biographical details that follow have been taken from Anna Chahoud, 'Broome, William (bap. 1689, d. 1745)', *ODNB*.

[82] Arthur Sherbo, 'Fenton, Elijah (1683–1730)', *ODNB*.

[83] Qtd. Johnson, *The Lives of the Poets*, vol. 23, p. 1031. For more on Henley, see Graham Midgley, 'Henley, John (1692–1756)', *ODNB*.

[84] Pope, *The Art of Sinking in Poetry*, pp. 27, 31–2; 139–40n, 176–7n.

Figure 4.3 [J. Hill?], The Retort [:] an Hieroglyphic Epistle from the Revd. Dr. [Whitefield] to Saml. [foot] Esqr. (C) Trustees of the British Museum (AN356907001)

Figure 4.4 *I am Kick[']d Out of Doors/No Screen*. (C) Trustees of the British Museum (AN471477001)

Pope, though, refused to let the matter pass. He again dredged up the affair, complaining in the *Dunciad Variorum* of 'translating three whole years with Broome'.[85] He eventually retracted the jab in 1735, when the men were reconciled. Even then, Pope could hardly resist boasting of his retroactive magnanimity, telling Broome 'I have prevailed with much ado to *cancel an impression of a thousand leaves to* insert that alteration'.[86] The translator's name appeared again in the poem in 1742, when the four-book *Dunciad* was published (though Pope was quick to note that the 'Broome' there was actually the long-dead Richard Brome, 'a serving-man' to Ben Jonson).[87] According to Curll, notwithstanding the careful omission, even this was the upshot of too much spleen. As he tartly observed in his key to the *Dunciad*, pointing out another such emendation, 'this Poem is to mimic a *Weather-Glass* and vary every Impression as the Author's Malice *Increases* to one, or *abates* to *Another*'.[88] To some, the *Dunciad* looked like a capricious Grub Street blacklist—malicious, petty, even seemingly random. But behind every gutted name, as others knew and readers quickly gathered, lay an entire antisocial history in need of decryption.

Gutted names were thus not simply prohibitive, despite serving no formal legal function, but were part of a satire's larger aesthetic and commercial functions. They invited readers in, signalling to them the promise of a scandal. They also created multilayered messages, some comic, some trenchant, while at the same time coaxing readers to construct the meaning of a particular piece by filling in the blanks and making sense of a satire's ticklish ambiguities. Readers were thus guiltily complicit, playing a central role not simply in the demand for and consumption of particular satire, but also in the very act of personalizing the piece, plugging in the names satirists did not, ostensibly, have a right to supply.

---

[85] Pope, *The Dunciad Variorum*, in *The Poems of Alexander Pope*, vol. 3: *The Dunciad (1728) & The Dunciad Variorum (1729)*, edited by Valerie Rumbold (New York: Longman, 2007), p. 305, bk. 3, l. 328.

[86] Pope to Broome (12 January 1735/6), *Correspondence of Pope*, vol. 4, p. 3.

[87] Pope, *The Dunciad in Four Books*, edited by Valerie Rumbold (New York: Longman, 1999), p. 120, bk. 1, l. 146n.

[88] Edmund Curll, *A Compleat Key to the Dunciad* (London, 1728), p. 22.

4.4 More Precious than Life: Reputation in Early Modern England

The role of readers also suggests the extent to which gutted names served more than aesthetic and commercial ends. Above all, satirists employed such practises to satisfy a dubious literary-ethical standard. Contemporary critics and writers understood that particular rather than general satire was a nasty business, even a violent breach of an abstract ethical standard. Gutted names were thus a form of apophasis: a way to name but not name; a questionable way to skirt an ethical commonplace—particular satire was callous, and naming even worse—while also implicitly violating it. Such practises allowed satirists to feign a margin of ethical safety. What looked like circumspection was simply mock-discretion.

That satirists relied so heavily upon gutted names for fishy ethical reasons is perhaps unsurprising. Again and again during this period, we hear the same refrain. We have absolutely no right, as critics routinely argued and satirists begrudgingly admitted, to attack another.[89] Dryden was clear: 'Lampoon ... is a dangerous sort of Weapon, and for the most part Unlawful. We have no Moral right to the Reputation of other Men. 'Tis taking from them, what we cannot restore to them'.[90] Even those willing to concede the utility of particular satire were revolted by the idea that satirists should overtly name their victims.[91] Joseph Trapp, for instance, felt personal satire could be justified, but that naming itself was reprehensible: 'To characterize by Name ... [is] a Property which I should much rather leave to the Libeller, than the Poet'.[92] Personal satire could be accomplished simply through description and allusion or, at its limits, the shoddy guise of a gutted name. Naming in full, though, was a stunning violation of what seemed to many a commonplace even in the lowliest back stalls of Grub Street. To name was 'a potentially shameful revelatory endeavor', Helen Deutsch has argued, whether one legally defamed one's victim or not.[93] Ethically, there was no way to justify it. There may be no surer sign that overt identification was a gross violation

---

[89] John Dennis, *An Essay upon Publick Spirit* (London, 1711), pp. 26–9; and *The London Journal*, no. 479 (5 Oct. 1728), which observed that, 'tho' 'tis true, that to come at general Knowledge, we must be left at full liberty to reason and to publish our Reasons upon all *Subjects*; yet, it does not follow, that, to come at Knowledge or Happiness, we must write and publish our Opinions freely about *all Persons*, or *any Persons*'.

[90] John Dryden, *Discourse concerning the Original and Progress of Satire*, in *The Works of John Dryden*, edited by A. B. Chambers, William Frost, and Vinton A. Dearing, vol. 4 (Berkeley and Los Angeles: University of California Press, 1956–90), pp. 59–60.

[91] *The Art of Poetry* (London, 1741), p. 7; and Richard Steele, no. 61 (30 August 1709), in *The Tatler*, edited by Donald F. Bond, vol. 3 (Oxford: Clarendon Press, 1987), p. 221.

[92] Joseph Trapp, *Prælectiones Poeticæ* (Oxford, 1711–19), trans. William Bowyer and William Clarke as *Lectures on Poetry* (London, 1742), p. 231.

[93] Helen Deutsch, *Resemblance & Disgrace: Alexander Pope and the Deformation of Culture* (Cambridge: Harvard University Press, 1996), p. 192.

of a largely accepted socio-literary covenant than the stunningly tedious, circuit-ous, and belaboured explanations satirists offered for naming their victims.[94]

Men were simply tender of their reputations, and part of the reason satirists omitted names extended from a somewhat more social understanding of defam-ation as a perverse form of theft.[95] As Sir Edward Coke argued, defamation 'robs a Man of his good Name, which ought to be more precious to him than his Life'.[96] Quite literally, to defame a man was not simply to remove his good fame, but also, in church law, to replace it with an 'evil reputation'.[97] No matter how far back we go into late medieval and early modern culture, we hear the same statements again and again.[98] Like so many others, John Dennis found that reputation was 'dearer to every good Man, even than Life it self'.[99] So precious was a man's reputation that Adam Smith listed 'an unspoiled character' (*jus sincerae aestimationis*) among man's natural rights (*iura hominum naturalia*). In his view, at the hands of a defamer a man 'receives one of the most affecting and atrocious injuries that possibly can be inflicted on him'. Perhaps inevitably, many satiric victims took it into their own hands to correct this 'deficientia juris'.[100] Think only of all the poets and booksellers roughed up for pointing an incautious finger in the wrong direction.[101] Hence too, the vengeful paper wars that flared up constantly in London—all the hot-headed pamphlets and catty poems teeming with sadistically retributive fantasies.[102]

As a result, defamation proceedings in their earliest forms in England's medi-eval ecclesiastical courts primarily sought 'the restoration of a person's reputation, a task that came to be regarded in England as a normal goal of the [common] law'.[103] Chief Justice Sir John Holt rejected the doctrine of *mitior sensus* precisely because he felt that the law should be flexible enough to 'give satisfaction to those whose reputation is hurt'.[104] The courts asserted that the law needed to function

---

[94] 'A Letter to the Publisher', in the *Dunciad Variorum*, pp. 127–34.

[95] Helmholz, *Select Cases on Defamation*, p. 135.

[96] Sir Edward Coke, *De Libellis Famosis* (1606), 5 Coke 125 (S.C.), 77 Eng. Rep. 251. See also March, *Actions for Slander*, p. 4.

[97] Plucknett, *CHCL*, p. 484.

[98] William Shakespeare, *Othello*, in *The Arden Edition of the Works of William Shakespeare*, edited by M. R. Ridley (Cambridge: Harvard University Press, 1958), 3.3.161–5. For more on the 'cult of reputation', see Lawrence Stone, *The Crisis of the Aristocracy* (Oxford: Oxford University Press, 1967), pp. 25ff; Keith Thomas, *The Ends of Life: Roads to Fulfilment in Early Modern England* (Oxford: Oxford University Press, 2009), ch. 5; and J. A. Sharpe, *Defamation and Sexual Slander in Early Modern England*, Borthwick Paper 58 (York: Borthwick Institute, University of York, 1980).

[99] Dennis, *An Essay upon Publick Spirit*, p. 30.

[100] Smith, *Lectures on Jurisprudence*, pp. 8, 399, 13, 124.

[101] J. Paul Hunter, 'Political, satirical, didactic and lyric poetry (I)', *The Cambridge History of English Literature, 1660–1800*, edited by John Richetti (Cambridge: Cambridge University Press, 2005), p. 174n13.

[102] *A Popp upon Pope*, in *The Popiad* (London, 1728), pp. 5–7.

[103] Helmholz, *Laws of England*, pp. 571–2.

[104] *Somers v. House* (1694), Holt 39 (K.B.), 90 Eng. Rep. 919.

pragmatically, both to help victims and plaintiffs and to prevent retributive violence.[105] Smith agreed. 'When the laws do not give satisfaction somewhat adequate to the injury', he pointed out, 'men will think themselves intitled to take it at their own hand'.[106]

This is not to say, though, that satirists particularly cared about the reputations of those they so relentlessly ridiculed. As later theorists have noted, satire seemingly requires an object of attack.[107] We can only sustain the fiction that the reputations of others truly mattered to satirists by fabricating exactly the same kinds of over-rationalizations for satire that such writers themselves repeatedly fell back on. Much of the period's most energetic satire is simply prodded along by a relentless and almost giddy contempt for the suffering of others.

Nonetheless, readers seemingly required satirists to make such pro forma claims. Considered in the abstract, direct satiric naming was a gross violation of an ethical standard to which all readily assented. Disingenuous declarations about the propriety of gutted names thus offered a wink-and-nudge gesture—no ethical codes violated here, so to speak. And yet moralizing readers were also the same people who less than squeamishly purchased pamphlet after pamphlet and poem after poem of materials purporting to reveal the amours of the D— of Ch— and the scandals of Sir H—. As Dennis lamented, 'we find that the Generality of Mankind' was simply too apt to take a perverse 'Pleasure...in particular Satyr'. The result was not only a general decline in human decency, he argued, but also the spread of a rancorous misanthropy. By buying satires, readers 'have a kind of Ostracism of Reputations establish'd by implicit Consent among us'.[108] Readers found themselves in a bizarre conundrum, insisting upon some form of half-cocked ethical undergirding for the scandal-mongering satires that they nonetheless gleefully and insatiably consumed.[109] As the notorious pamphlet-seller Ann Dodd sheepishly admitted after once again being questioned by the authorities, 'the business sometimes compels me to sell Papers that give Offense'.[110] Scandal simply sold well.

Such a paradox—this almost unthinking demand for high-mindedness to prop up such lowly squibs—also suggests the extent to which readers were and are complicit in the production of satire. Robert C. Elliott was certainly right when he brought to light a half-century ago the withering, almost magical power that the

---

[105] *Harrison v. Thornborough* (1714), Gilb. Cas. 114, 10 Mod. 196 (Q.B.), 93 Eng. Rep. 278.

[106] Smith, *Lectures on Jurisprudence*, p. 124.

[107] Edward W. Rosenheim, *Swift and the Satirist's Art* (Chicago: University of Chicago Press, 1963), p. 31.

[108] Dennis, *An Essay upon Publick Spirit*, pp. 27, 29.

[109] On the tension between eighteenth-century satire as an ethical practise and its mobilization of the CAD triad of negative emotions (contempt, anger, and disgust), see Robert Phiddian, *Satire and the Public Emotions* (Cambridge: Cambridge University Press, 2019), pp. 4–32.

[110] May 1731, SP 36/23/134, TNA.

satirist wielded.[111] But with a move to predominantly printed satire, we should emphasize that satirists did not and could not work alone: they needed printers and booksellers, who in turn needed readers. In the first place, the economics of eighteenth-century printing and bookselling prohibited willy-nilly runs of venomous and unsellable squibs.[112] Booksellers almost solely brought books to press for which they believed a market existed, even if small or marginal. Often, they were right.

None of this should be a surprise, but it should enlighten us to the sense that readers were callously casual about buying works that obdurately exposed the embarrassing and damaging escapades of some satiric victim. The rambling title pages of such pieces advertised as much, hailing readers and signalling the promise of intrigue. For all of the scorn heaped upon the satirists of the day, it is perhaps surprising that few critics pointed an accusing finger at scandal-hungry readers and their Hobbesian laughter at the suffering of others, as if they were nothing more than helpless and passive recipients.[113] Granted, one could argue that moral responsibility starts with the satirist: if only he had turned his cheek, the logic goes, then these scabrous things would never have been printed in the first place. This in any case was Curll's high-handed position. 'Satires *should not be Printed*', Pope had told him. No, Curll tartly responded, '*they should not be wrote*'.[114]

But should we not also ask whether such works would have found a home in booksellers' shops and stalls if readers were not so ready to turn a blind eye to the ethical paradox staring them squarely in the face? The market for personal satire implicated every actor—satirist, bookseller, and buyer alike. We should keep in mind that readers both prodded along the printing of satires and participated in the very production of meaning that the decoding of such works entailed. Satirists may have committed the crime, but readers proved rather willing accomplices.

4.5 Naming Victims: Pope and the *Dunciad Variorum* (1729)

Some satirists did expose their victims, and yet Pope's decision to name all of his dunces in the *Dunciad Variorum* was shocking. It was also, in its extensiveness

---

[111] Robert C. Elliott, *The Power of Satire: Magic, Ritual, Art* (Princeton: Princeton University Press, 1960).

[112] James Raven, 'The book as a commodity', in *The Cambridge History of the Book in Britain*, vol. 5: 1695–1830, edited by Michael F. Suarez, S. J., and Michael L. Turner (Cambridge: Cambridge University Press, 2009), pp. 102–4.

[113] Andrew Benjamin Bricker, '"Laughing a Folly out of Countenance": Laughter and the Limits of Reform in Eighteenth-Century Satire', in *The Power of Laughter and Satire in Early Modern Britain: Political and Religious Culture, 1500–1820*, edited by Mark Knights and Adam Morton (Woodbridge: Boydell Press, 2017), pp. 165–6.

[114] Edmund Curll, *The Curliad* (London, 1729), p. 21.

and by the standards of eighteenth-century satire, almost entirely unprecedented. In naming his victims, Pope was abandoning a precaution with no legal function, but one that still had the tendency to inhibit legal action. For this very reason, the *Variorum* also offers an intriguing case study. In openly identifying its victims, the poem isolated the potential legal repercussions of naming. With such legal confusions set aside, we can examine how Pope exercised caution for a work that so many of his contemporaries found defamatory in a socio-literary if not strictly legal sense. He did so by usurping the legal function of the courts themselves and by turning the poem's new apparatuses into a venue for a mock literary trial. In this sense, the *Variorum* takes part in a long tradition of satire as court or legal brief and evinces a broader tendency of Pope's: the desire to make his satire a '*Supplement . . . to the public Laws*'.[115] The sustained juridical rhetoric of the *Variorum* also makes it clear that this was, to some degree, *the* function of the revised poem. We can see it not only in the poem's mock-sentencing, but also in the legalese that saturates the *Variorum*'s additions: offender, correction, crime, malice, motive, accusation, judgment, plea, slander, libel, defamation, and calumny. The sheer frequency of such language only reinforces the poem's greatest rhetorical feat: the way it turns what should be a defence into a prosecution, with the poet going from defendant to plaintiff, before judging and sentencing those who had been foolhardy enough to attack Pope.

Pope's court of opinion is most blatant in the poem's 'Letter to the Publisher', ostensibly authored by his friend, William Cleland.[116] The letter reads like a grandiloquent jurist's mock-pompous brief, chock-full of arch turns of phrase and cunning asides, unflagging inventories of half-conflated offences and puffed-up charges, and winking deferrals to jurors and justices—all rounded off in comically pleonastic locutions. Pope's critics, for instance, were the 'first Aggressors', the 'offenders' who had written 'slanders' against their 'lawful superiors'. The real question, Cleland argues, are the laws governing naming in the republic of letters. His preliminary answer is clear. One is fit to judge another's writings—and his writings alone—when they appear in public: 'whoever publishes, puts himself on his tryal by his country'. The rationale for such a rule is supplied by a simple if misleading juxtaposition. The 'Letter' is closed out by a few

---

[115] Owen Ruffhead, *The Life of Alexander Pope, Esq.* (London, 1769), p. 342. See also Oliver Goldsmith, *An Enquiry into the Present State of Polite Learning in Europe*, in *Collected Works of Oliver Goldsmith*, edited by Arthur Friedman, vol. 1 (Oxford: Oxford University Press, 1966), pp. 314–35; Griffin, *Satire*, pp. 39, 43; Nathan, 'The Bench and the Pulpit', pp. 375–96; Elkin, *The Augustan Defense of Satire*, pp. 75–7; James Sutherland, *English Satire* (Cambridge: Cambridge University Press, 1958), pp. 2–4; and Maynard Mack, 'The Muse of Satire', *Yale Review* 40 (1951): p. 85.

[116] 'A Letter to the Publisher', in *The Poems of Alexander Pope: The Dunciad (1728) & The Dunciad Variorum (1729)*, pp. 127–34. Cleland seemingly appended his name to the Pope's words, a view echoed by Pope's critics. See *The Curliad*, p. 1; John Dennis, *Remarks Upon Mr. Pope's Dunciad* (London, 1729), p. 38; and *Pope Alexander's Supremacy* (London, 1729), p. 4. See also James McLaverty, *Pope, Print, and Meaning* (Oxford: Oxford University Press, 2001), p. 106.

free-floating quotations, including a strategic paraphrase from the preface to Charles Gildon's *A New Rehearsal, or Bays the Younger* (1714) (a dramatic dialogue that in part satirizes Pope as Sawney Dapper, 'a small Dabbler in *Helicon*', and a refurbishing of *The Rehearsal* [1671], likely co-written by George Villiers, the second Duke of Buckingham, which had earlier sent up Pope's modern progenitor, Dryden[117]):

> The Judges and Magistrates may with full as good reason be reproach'd with *Ill-nature*, for putting the Laws in execution against a Thief or Impostor—The same will hold in the Republick of Letters, if the Criticks and Judges will let every *Ignorant Pretender* to Scribling, pass on the World.[118]

The analogy holds at face value. Judges are not to be scolded for simply enforcing the laws; the same goes for critics, who need to keep the standards of composition up. Further, both judges and critics make use of an analogous science. Judges have case law; critics, 'the *Antecedent* Labours and Pains of Criticism'.[119] Like Pope, Gildon is concerned with policing letters by identifying bad works and judging them accordingly. Unlike Pope, though, Gildon retains what Swift and Pope had earlier called the 'Rule': 'The wisest Way is not once to name' those one criticizes, a maxim openly violated in the *Variorum*.[120]

Cleland, however, pushes Gildon's analogy even further. The quotation implies that the dunces need to be not only identified but also disciplined: 'there is no publick punishment left, but what a good writer inflicts'. This, he reasons, is the role of the poet, the poem, and its extensive new apparatus. But this was also a shell game, a rationalization parading as an inevitable form of jurisprudence, as Pope goes from defendant to prosecutor, and then from prosecutor to judge, in punishing those who judged him first. Granted, the law can only pronounce on open facts. But having opened up those facts—who the offenders are—the poet-judge's jurisdiction should come to an end and the law should enter to offer the punishment. Pope, moreover, was hardly a judge in the case, disinterestedly applying case law; he was, instead, one of the litigants.

The poem's function is thus both to name and punish, as the Advertisement makes clear, before offering '*a word or two*' upon '*the chief Offenders*'. The commentary then '*'tis only as a paper pinn'd upon the breast, to mark the*

---

[117] Charles Gildon, *A New Rehearsal, or Bays the Younger* (London, 1714), p. 39.

[118] 'A Letter', p. 135. Gildon's actual words are more extensive, but are similar in spirit: '*The Judges and Magistrates may, with full as strong Reason, be reproach'd with ill Nature in putting the Laws in Execution against a successful Thief, Cheat or Impostor; ... The same will hold in the Republic of Letters, if Critics and Judges let every ignorant Pretender to Scribling pass on the World*' (Preface, *A New Rehearsal*, pp. [i–ii]).

[119] Preface, *New Rehearsal*, p. ii.   [120] Swift-Pope *Miscellanies* (London, 1728), p. viii.

Enormities for which they suffer'd; lest the Correction only should be remember'd, and the Crime forgotten'.[121] The *Variorum* becomes an instrument of law: the paper appended to pilloried criminals, announcing their crimes. This not only expands the function of naming—it is necessary in certain situations and serves a punitive function—but also marks a radical shift in Pope's view of naming, as James McLaverty has argued.[122] For years, he had avoided identifying his victims. With the *Variorum*, naming became compulsory. As he explained to John Arbuthnot a few years later:

> General Satire in Times of General Vice has no force, & is no Punishment: People have ceas'd to be ashamed of it when so many are joind with them; and tis only by hunting One or two from the Herd that any Examples can be made. If a man writ all his Life against the Collective Body of the Banditti, or against Lawyers, would it do the least Good, or lessen the Body? But if some are hung up, or pilloryed, it may prevent others. And in my low Station, with no other Power than this, I hope to deter, if not to reform.[123]

He offered a similar logic in his *Epilogue to the Satires* (1738), but then high-handedly claimed that naming was both a corrective and a deterrent. His unnamed interlocutor asks whether satire should be general or particular: Should one 'Spare then the Person, and expose the Vice'? Of course not, Pope retorts. 'How Sir! not damn the Sharper, but the Dice?' Vice is produced only by the vicious. To send up the one without touching upon the other would be to chastise an effect while ignoring its cause. Moreover, satire corrects where others fail—those 'Safe from the Bar, the Pulpit, and the Throne, / Yet touch'd and sham'd by *Ridicule* alone'—and is the 'sacred Weapon' that promotes virtuous behaviour:

> To rowze the Watchmen of the Publick Weal,
> To Virtue's Work provoke the tardy Hall,
> And goad the Prelate slumb'ring in his Stall.[124]

Naming is thus both a corrective that targets not simply the vice but also the vicious, prompting them to better behaviour, and a deterrent that keeps the potentially guilty on their toes.

---

[121] '*Advertisement*', in *The Dunciad Variorum*, in *The Poems of Alexander Pope: The Dunciad (1728) & The Dunciad Variorum (1729)*, p. 123.

[122] James McLaverty, 'Naming and shaming in the poetry of Pope and Swift, 1726–1745', in *Swift's Travels: Eighteenth-Century Satire and its Legacy*, edited by Nicholas Hudson and Aaron Santesso (Cambridge: Cambridge University Press, 2008), ch. 10.

[123] Pope to Arbuthnot (23 August [1734]), *Correspondence of Pope*, vol. 3, p. 423.

[124] Pope, *Epilogue to the Satires* (1738), in *Imitations of Horace: With An Epistle to Dr. Arbuthnot and The Epilogue to the Satires*, 2nd ed., edited by John Butt (New Haven: Yale University Press, 1953), Dialogue II, ll. 12–13, 210–12, 217–19.

The Scriblerians' nom de plume, Martin Scriblerus, takes a different tack in the *Variorum*'s collection of 'Testimonies', offering a kind of cross examination of 'the various Judgments of the Learned concerning our Poet'.[125] The result is a series of irreconcilable opinions. According to his critics, Pope was either 'a great hypocrite, or a very honest man; a terrible imposer upon both parties, or a very moderate to either' (154). This is the purposeful destruction of the middle ground, an example of the rhetorical blacks and whites with which jurists paint and a feature of the law's either/or rigidity—what the legal theorist Leo Katz has called the law's 'perversity'.[126] Scriblerus returns to these same binaries throughout, closing off the 'Testimonies' in a breathless *enumeratio* of opposed ills:

> If he *singly* enterpris'd one great work, he was tax'd of Boldness and Madness to a prodigy: If he took *assistants* in another, it was complain'd of, and represented as a great injury to the public. The loftiest Heroicks, the lowest ballads, treatises against the state and church, satyrs on lords and ladies, raillery on wits and authors, squabbles with booksellers, or even full and true accounts of monsters, poysons, and murders: of any hereof was there nothing so good, nothing so bad, which hath not at one or other season been to him ascribed. If it bore no author's name, then lay he concealed; if it did, he father'd it upon that author to be yet better concealed. If it resembled any of his styles then was it evident; if it did not, then disguis'd he it on set purpose. Yea, even direct oppositions in religion, principles, and politics, have equally been supposed in him inherent. Surely a most rare and singular character! of which let the reader make what he can. (pp. 160–1)

He thus could not write on his own or with others; no form was below him; no genre resistant to the ends of his scurrility. Then there was the paradox of authorship. If anonymous, he therefore wrote it; if owned, then pseudonymous. Even worse, his stylistic fingerprints are everywhere. If even faintly his writing, then his; if different, then his in disguise. On its surface, the whole catalogue is incomprehensible. As Paul Baines has observed, 'the Dunces provided more evidence merely by contesting it'.[127] Throughout, Scriblerus is a prosecutor masquerading as a docent. In his deferrals and his unwillingness to do anything more than juxtapose contradictions, he traps his readers, pressuring them to draw conclusions based on a limited view of the evidence. In Pat Rogers' view, 'Pope forces the Dunce to convict himself out of his own mouth, whilst the author

---

[125] 'Testimonies of Authors, Concerning our Poet and his Works', in *The Poems of Alexander Pope: The Dunciad (1728) & The Dunciad Variorum (1729)*, 138. Hereafter cited parenthetically. These were likely gathered by Pope, who collected dozens of printed works attacking him and his publications (Elkin, *Augustan Defense of Satire*, p. 90n2). See ['Libels on Pope'], General Reference Collection C.116. b.1–4, BL.

[126] Leo Katz, *Why the Law Is So Perverse* (Chicago: University of Chicago Press, 2011), pp. 142–5.

[127] Baines, 'Crime and Punishment', p. 153.

himself remains seemingly detached'.[128] At the same time, this argumentative claustrophobia is mitigated by the laughing, incredulous persona, a kind of soft rhetorical power: it persuades, but does so gently; it interprets the evidence, but appears only to present it; it makes conclusions inevitable, but never states them outright.

One might argue that the rhetorical efficacy of the *Variorum* is most clearly on display in the way Pope's critics adopted his juridical language. Theirs is not the woolly language of justice and equity—the bland claims about being treated unfairly and unjustly that are so common in the pamphlets of the day—but the legalese of eighteenth-century defamation law, used purposefully if somewhat imprecisely: imputation, scandal, libel, calumny.[129] One critic calls the *Dunciad* a '*virulent Libel*'.[130] Another dubs Pope a 'Libeller', calling the poem 'a leud and infamous Libel'.[131] For John Dennis the work is all 'Scandal or Calumny', full of 'malicious and infamous Libels'.[132] Moreover, many of the 'Gentleman libell'd in the *Dunciad*' not only claimed that the poem was defamatory, but also worked out, like barristers trained in the Inns of Court, detailed cases against Pope.[133] The *Curliad*, for instance, offers a systematic rebuttal of the claims made in the *Variorum*'s 'Letter'.[134] The same charges were taken up in the collection *Pope Alexander's Supremacy and Infallibility examin'd*: 'every one knows he is liable to the Laws of the Land to be punish'd when he shall be discovered'.[135] John Dennis also adopted Pope's legalese, invoking the legal principle justifying self-defence ('*laesit prior*') and explaining 'I only retort in the Language he gave'.[136] Like *The Curliad* before, Dennis outlines how the *Variorum* sought to turn the tables, '*accusing innocent Persons of the Accuser's Crimes*'.[137]

The decision to reframe this literary debate not merely in the vituperative language of a Grub Street squabble or through the weighty metaphors of war but in the fussy legalese of the courtroom was seemingly intentional. One language always had to be matched and outdone by its natural counterpart. Such a shift in

---

[128] Pat Rogers, *Grub Street: Studies in a Subculture* (London: Methuen & Co Ltd, 1972), p. 198.

[129] *The Martiniad*, in *Pope Alexander's Supremacy and Infallibility examin'd* (London, 1729); the Advertisement to John Dennis's *Remarks Upon Mr. Pope's Dunciad* (London, 1729); the 'After-Thought' to the second edition of *Claudian's Rufinus* (London, 1729); and *The Dulcinead Variorum* (London, 1729).

[130] *The Curliad*, pp. 6, 7. This was a charge he knew well enough, having twice been prosecuted and pilloried years earlier. See Pat Rogers and Paul Baines, 'The Prosecutions of Edmund Curll, 1725–28', *Library* 5, no. 2 (2004): pp. 176–94. For Curll's account, see *The Curliad*, p. 18.

[131] *Pope Alexander's Supremacy and Infallibility examin'd* (London, 1729), pp. 3, 5.

[132] *Remarks Upon Mr. Pope's Dunciad* (London, 1729), pp. 9, [iv], 53. For similar accusations, see [Edward Ward], *Apollo's Maggot in his Cups* (London, 1729), pp. 26, 34; and [Leonard Welsted and James Moore Smythe], *One Epistle to Mr. A. Pope*, 2nd ed. (London, 1729), p. vi.

[133] *Daily Journal*, no. 2926 (23 May 1730).   [134] *The Curliad*, pp. 5–8.

[135] *Pope Alexander's Supremacy*, p. 3.

[136] Nathan, 'The Bench and the Pulpit', p. 385; and *Remarks Upon Mr. Pope's Dunciad*, p. 11.

[137] *Remarks Upon Several Passages In The Preliminaries to the Dunciad*, advertisement.

jurisdiction, away from the common law and toward socially constructed views of defamation, also helps to explain the accusations of libel so routinely issued against Pope. Many of these allegations were founded on the belief that Pope had violated socio-literary rules, not legal ones. The overlap in language is pronounced: defamation, libel, scandal, calumny—like the socio-legal terminology around libels and lampoons that we saw in the first chapter—all of these words carried both legal *and* literary connotations.[138] Sometimes these charges reflected the belief that Pope had legally defamed his dunces. Just as often, though, such claims mirror the belief that Pope had breached the ethical limits of personal satire. For the punningly named Will. Flogg, the poet had become 'a *Libeller* instead of a *Satyrist*', having failed to observe the border between 'scandal and satire'.[139] Eliza Haywood offered a similar view, noting 'there is a Distinction between *Scandal* and *Sauciness, Scurrility* and *Satire*'.[140]

Both the *Dunciad* and the *Variorum* tested the legal limits of defamation and the ethical limits of satire. Legally speaking, Pope had shown that open naming only required a bit of restraint: one could say some profoundly nasty and insulting things about another, but provided such language was not defamatory, plaintiffs had little they could do, and courts were perfectly happy to leave the matter to the London literary world. Despite the success of Pope's legal litmus test, he fared less well when it came to the rules governing the republic of letters. In choosing to name his dunces, Pope had violated an ethical code held sacrosanct in the literary marketplace, a self-regulating community with its own rules, its own tools of policing, and its own ways of punishing its members.

For too long, the legal-defence fallacy—that satiric naming practises provided writers with some sort of legal refuge—has prevented literary historians from asking what other functions emvowelment might have served in eighteenth-century satire. I have tried to show that the widespread belief, common among satirists and their victims alike, that gutted names stymied prosecutions and actions for defamation nonetheless influenced the production and reception of satire, even though such practises served no formal legal purpose. Such pseudo-legal concerns shaped the uses of gutted names, especially as vehicles for aesthetic and commercial functions. Above all, satirists employed gutted names for vaguely ethical reasons. Eighteenth-century critics of satire firmly held it best to omit names and, for the most part, practitioners adhered to this decree. Such naming practises thus offered a nominally decent way to signal a victim while also ostensibly preserving that same victim's anonymity. To depict a vicious man was one thing, perhaps offering his initials and describing his loathsome behaviour and person in such a way that any informed reader might guess his identity. But never—*never*—should writers name their objects in full. Satirists responded to

---

[138] Elkin, *The Augustan Defense of Satire*, pp. 20–4.
[139] *Pope Alexander's Supremacy*, pp. 17, 12.   [140] *The Parrot*, no. 2 (2 October 1728).

this pressure with a typographical sleight. We might have no right to another man's reputation, they reasoned with a mocking shrug of the shoulders, but were a few coy asterisks and one or two pregnant dashes really the same thing?

Throughout this chapter, I have also pointed to the role readers played. They were by no means impotent partners. They proved time and again hungry consumers and willing participants in the construction of a scandal. They plugged in names just as readily as satirists half-omitted them; they decoded intrigues with obdurate relish. I have argued throughout *Libel and Lampoon* that readers, as both lay consumers and impanelled jurors, played a critical role in the construction of satiric meaning. Communities of readers, whether they gathered in the streets around St Paul's Cathedral or were assembled in juries at Westminster, coalesced around the meaning of given works, especially the period's ironic and deeply ambiguous satires. Those sociocentric habits and practises of reading were redeployed in the courts when plaintiffs, prosecutors, and judges were presented with verbally ambiguous texts. The importance of those interpretive communities was nowhere more evident than in the prosecution of allegory, one of the final hurdles that the government faced in the prosecution of satirists, and the focus of the next chapter.

5

Allegory in the Courts

Satire and the Problem of 'Libellous Parallels'

Over the final years of the seventeenth century and the first decades of the eighteenth century, the Crown worked concertedly to target satire's most routine evasions. Many of those efforts focused on legal procedures for delimiting verbal ambiguity. In 1706, for instance, Chief Justice Sir John Holt devised a new interpretative doctrine for handling verbal irony.[1] The ruling built on the court's earlier conceptions of 'common' or 'vulgar intendment': the notion, that is, that jurors should interpret words in their most natural sense given the context of their utterance.[2]

Although these new courtroom procedures had facilitated the prosecution of ironic materials, they had nonetheless failed early on to make sense of allegorical works. This is perhaps surprising. Both verbal irony and allegory operate under a similar structural principle of semantic doubling, presenting locutions that possess both surface and intended meanings, as we would say in verbal irony, or a vehicle and a tenor, as in allegory. But irony and allegory also differ in one critical regard. Typically for literary theorists today, the intended meaning of a 'stable' irony is accessed by readers through recourse to internal verbal clues.[3] One thinks of Jonathan Swift's Projector, who grants, in perhaps the most obvious internal clue that *A Modest Proposal* was less than a wholly serious project for alleviating the sufferings of the Irish poor, that 'this food [i.e., Irish babies] will be somewhat dear, and therefore *very proper for Landlords*, who, as they have already devoured most of the Parents, seem to have the best Title to the Children'.[4]

Unlike verbal irony, however, an allegory might contain few direct clues to its application. Access to the tenor is instead frequently left in the hands of readers; they must deduce the analogue to a surface fiction, often without recourse to internal verbal evidence. Despite the court's earlier creation of a non-textual,

---

[1] *R. v. Dr. Brown* [*sic*] (1706), 11 Mod. 86 (Q.B.), 88 Eng. Rep. 912.
[2] *King v. Lake* (1670), 2 Vent. 28 (C.P.), 89 Eng. Rep. 12; and *Somers v. House* (1694), Holt 39 (K.B.), 90 Eng. Rep. 919.
[3] Wayne C. Booth, *A Rhetoric of Irony* (Chicago: University of Chicago Press, 1974), pp. 47–86.
[4] [Jonathan Swift], *A Modest Proposal for Preventing the Children of Poor People from Being a Burthen to their Parents, or Country; and for Making Them Beneficial to the Publick*, in *The Cambridge Edition of the Works of Jonathan Swift*, Irish Political Writings after 1725: *A Modest Proposal* and Other Works, edited by D. W. Hayton and Adam Rounce (Cambridge: Cambridge University Press, 2018), p. 151.

Libel and Lampoon: Satire in the Courts, 1670–1792. Andrew Benjamin Bricker, Oxford University Press.
© Andrew Benjamin Bricker 2022. DOI: 10.1093/oso/9780192846150.003.0006

sociocentric rule to overcome the interpretive problem of intended meaning in verbal irony, this same doctrine was not immediately employed in trials for allegory. It was as if Holt, even in devising such a non-textual rule—one built around hypothetical communities of readers—was implicitly conceding that internal verbal signalling, which was nonetheless, according to the bench, inessential to demonstrate, still created in the courts an unbridgeable cleft between irony and allegory.

The focus of this chapter is how writers in a variety of media during the first few decades of the eighteenth century used allegory as a flexible tool for political satire and how the authorities responded. As I show in the first section of this chapter, the Crown early on believed that it had solved this most ticklish of literary devices. In 1704, Holt ruled that criticism of the government as a whole was criminal and not only specific officials, meaning that the indeterminability of allegorical names was theoretically no longer a bar to prosecution.[5] The procedural and practical limits of Holt's ruling became clear in 1709, however, when the government moved to prosecute Delarivier Manley for *The New Atalantis*, a scandal-mongering political allegory, or 'secret history', of the sordid inner workings of the Whigs and Queen Anne's court. As the Secretary of State soon discovered, it was still profoundly difficult in 1709 to create positive identifications between allegorical pseudonyms and the real-world politicians and monarchs they supposedly stood in for, even if, according to Holt's 1704 ruling, the prosecution needed only to demonstrate that government institutions, rather than specific individuals, had been libelled.

Given these procedural hurdles, allegorical satire flourished during this period, especially in the growing periodical press of the 1710s and 1720s. In the final two sections of this chapter, I focus on two of the most important, popular, and widely circulated journals of this era. I begin with *The Craftsman*, which devised a sophisticated and yet flexible model for political commentary and satire built largely around allegorical fake news from abroad and the implicit application of history to the present. *The Craftsman* and its provoking attacks on the government were the bane of Sir Robert Walpole's administration. Nonetheless, the government repeatedly failed throughout the later 1720s to prosecute the periodical successfully, thanks in large measure to the limits of libel law to redress allegorical ambiguity.

As I show in my final section, that all changed in 1728/9 when the government successfully prosecuted John Clarke, a printer for *Mist's Weekly Journal*, perhaps the most important political periodical of the 1710s and '20s. The case against Clarke revolved around the so-called 'Persian Letter', a Jacobite allegory of the royal family which intimated that Walpole was secretly manipulating George

---

[5] *R. v. Tutchin* (1704), Holt 424 (Q.B.), 90 Eng. Rep. 1133.

II. The decision in the case proved pivotal. In it, Chief Justice Sir Robert Raymond found that the interpretation of allegorical materials should rely on an abstract 'generality of readers'—that is, on how a juror believed *most* people would have understood a text rather than the manner in which an actual juror did.[6] The result was, as in Holt's 1706 ruling against verbal irony, a sociocentric rule for interpreting allegorical satires that obviated the prosecution's need to demonstrate the precise verbal mechanism by which the fictional worlds of allegory were necessarily tied to the government actor or institution being libelled.

My larger goal in this chapter is to document how the government, through dozens of interrogations and in numerous court cases across several decades following the lapse of licensing in 1695, developed a legal doctrine for the courtroom interpretation of allegories—those '*libellous Parallels*' that so provoked and befuddled the authorities and the courts alike.[7] Moreover, through a mock-deference to the 'generality of readers' in trials for allegory, the courts devised and thus enabled a means not only to prosecute works of political allegory but also to discipline satirists and their stationers more generally. Such rulings almost always did so by creating 'reasonable' procedures for delimiting verbal ambiguity that foregrounded hypothetical rather than literal jurors. This permitted the courts to defer to jurors in the abstract, by forcing them to interpret dubious materials in more predictable ways, while also effectively displacing the capriciousness and idiosyncrasy of actual jurors in practise. The result, as satirists and their stationers soon saw, was that libel law—once a minor feature of the common law for arbitrating interpersonal squabbles during the era of licensing—had become a flexible post-publication tool for managing an increasingly unruly press.

5.1 Delarivier Manley, *The New Atalantis*, and the Limits of *R. v. Tutchin* (1704)

Delarivier Manley's *The New Atalantis* was the *cause célèbre* of 1709. With its veiled disclosure of the embarrassing sexual scandals of the court's hangers-on and the sleazy self-interest of every underhanded Whig, *Atalantis* was perhaps 'the most infamous text published in early eighteenth-century England'.[8] Moreover, everyone presumed the work to be a so-called 'secret history' of the Whigs and, in particular, the Junto that wielded frightful control over Queen Anne. Bradford

[6] *R. v. Clerk* [*sic*] (1728/9), 1 Barn. 305 (K.B.), 94 Eng. Rep. 207.
[7] *The Craftsman*, no. 140 (8 March 1728/9). *The Craftsman* changed its title to *The Country Journal: Or, The Craftsman* in no. 45 (13 May 1727). For clarity's sake, I refer to the periodical as *The Craftsman* throughout.
[8] Nicola Parsons, 'Secrecy and Enlightenment: Delarivier Manley's *New Atalantis*', in *Libertine Enlightenment: Sex, Liberty and Licence in the Eighteenth Century*, edited by Peter Cryle and Lisa O'Connell (London: Palgrave MacMillan, 2003), p. 145.

K. Mudge has gone so far as to argue that Manley's scandalous allegory of Anne's court and its interminable political intrigues was an 'intervening event in the cultural life of early eighteenth-century Britain'.[9]

Why, then, was it so difficult to prosecute and convict Manley for *Atalantis*, a thinly camouflaged or even transparent libel, as some claimed, on almost every person of power tied to the monarch? In this section, I focus on the Crown's prosecutorial challenges, showing how Manley's run-in with the law revealed the procedural limitations that the government faced in prosecuting works of allegory. I focus especially on the failure of Chief Justice Sir John Holt's ruling in *R. v. Tutchin* (1704). Holt had attempted to correct the problem of individual identification by arguing that government institutions and not only government actors could be defamed. However, in order to substantiate the claim that parliament and in particular the monarchy and the House of Commons had been libelled, Crown prosecutors were required to demonstrate the essential verbal link between those allegorized individuals, such as the queen or individual MPs, and the allegorized institutions for which they served as representatives. What Holt's ruling had promised to correct had simply displaced the interpretive burden, as the Secretary of State soon discovered during his fumbling interrogation of Manley.

For theorists today, allegory always entails two levels of signification, between a surface meaning (the vehicle) and an intended meaning (the tenor).[10] How one got from vehicle to tenor was less than clear to early eighteenth-century readers, writers, and jurists alike, who often had profound difficulty explaining the practical mechanics of allegory.[11] Take Manley's *Atalantis*. Astrea, the Goddess of Justice, returns to Earth, where her bedraggled mother, Virtue, disgusted with the behaviour of the mortals, conducts a tour of the New Atalantis (England) and eventually Angela (London), where they encounter Lady Intelligence (as in secrecy), who serves as Groom of the Stole to Princess Fame (as in rumour). Their arrival in London coincides with the crowning of the new Princess Olympia (Queen Anne). The resulting narrative is a disjointed jumble of scenes recounting the political and sexual corruption of Atalantis's slimy politicians and the court's devious lackeys.

It was an open question, though, how one was to link the fictional world of Atalantis to England. By its very nature, allegory always forces readers into provisional or even sceptical interpretations, often subject to re-evaluation. We

---

[9] Bradford K. Mudge, *The Whore's Story: Women, Pornography, and the British Novel, 1684–1830* (Oxford: Oxford University Press, 2000), p. 137.

[10] That the vehicle was thought a means to the end of the tenor is clear in the term's etymological roots: allegory was always 'other-speaking' (from the Greek *allos* [other, different] and *agoreuein* [to speak in public]). See Rita Copeland and Peter T. Struck, Introduction, *The Cambridge Companion to Allegory*, edited by Rita Copeland and Peter T. Struck (Cambridge: Cambridge University Press, 2010), p. 2; and Jeremy Tambling, *Allegory* (New York: Routledge, 2010), p. 3.

[11] Eve Tavor Bannet, *Eighteenth-Century Manners of Reading: Print and Popular Instruction in the Anglophone Atlantic World* (Cambridge: Cambridge University Press, 2017), pp, 237–41.

might even suggest, after Michael Riffaterre, that allegory entails a heightened process of 'hermeneutic reading': a tentative or 'heuristic' reading of a text, followed by a deeper 'retroactive' reading.[12] This process of reading, interpretation, and retrospection was only complicated in this era by disparities in insider information and by the idiosyncrasies of individual readers. As Wolfgang Iser has reminded us, the 'meanings in literary texts are generated in the act of reading; they are the product of a complex interaction between text and reader, and not qualities that are hidden in the text'. This quality of textual 'indeterminacy' is central to the readerly interpretive act.[13]

It was precisely this indeterminacy that was foregrounded, both literarily and legally, by satirists during this period. Allegory simply prevented straightforward decoding and stable interpretation. Think only of A Tale of a Tub or Gulliver's Travels—suggestively allegorical works with complicated underlying tenors.[14] In Ashley Marshall's words, the Tale would have left Swift's contemporary readers, like critics today, 'thoroughly befuddled'.[15] Moreover, we should resist the broad twentieth-century critical tendency to read politically allusive satires like Gulliver's Travels in strictly allegorical terms. J. A. Downie has argued for a less rigorous formulation, what he calls the 'Scriblerian technique of commenting on topical politics': 'implying criticism by drawing parallels between the existing situation and what might otherwise obtain'. Such a method is closer, he concludes, to 'parallel history' than 'allegory'.[16] However, we should be equally cautious about simplifying allegory itself during the first half of the eighteenth century. As I try to make clear throughout this chapter, rigid parallelism, generally speaking, was not a feature of allegory during this period and allegory, by virtue of its inexplicit nature, always functions in suggestive and potentially misunderstandable ways.

One way to bridge allegory's two levels of signification was through its long-standing association with personification or *prosopopoeia*, especially in satiric works in which a fictional character stands in for a real one.[17] As Rita Copeland and Peter T. Struck have written, 'Neoclassical criticism isolated personification as the principal mark of allegory'. For those writing in the seventeenth and

---

[12] Michael Riffaterre, *Semiotics of Poetry* (London: Methuen, 1980), pp. 4–6.

[13] Wolfgang Iser, 'Indeterminacy and the Reader's Response in Prose Fiction', in *Prospecting: From Reader Response to Literary Anthropology* (Baltimore: Johns Hopkins University Press, 1993), pp. 5, 6.

[14] Gordon Teskey, *Allegory and Violence* (Ithaca: Cornell University Press, 1996), p. 5; Phillip Harth, 'The Problem of Political Allegory in *Gulliver's Travels*', *Modern Philology* 73, no. 4.2 (May 1976): pp. S40–S47; and Lennard Davis, *Factual Fictions: The Origins of the English Novel* (Philadelphia: University of Pennsylvania Press, 1996), pp. 149–53.

[15] Marshall, *Satire*, pp. 186–7.

[16] J. A. Downie, 'The Political Significance of *Gulliver's Travels*', in *Swift and His Contexts*, edited by John Irwin Fischer, Hermann J. Real, and James Woolley (New York: AMS Press, 1989), pp. 1–19. For the reception of *Gulliver's Travels* as personal satire, see Bertrand A. Goldgar, *Walpole and the Wits: The Relation of Politics to Literature* (Lincoln: University of Nebraska Press, 1976), pp. 49–63.

[17] James J. Paxson, *Poetics of Personification* (Cambridge: Cambridge University Press, 1994), pp. 6, 12–13.

eighteenth centuries, allegory had come to entail a 'stricter formal limitation': 'a clear, symmetrical, and fixed correspondence between a figure and the abstraction it represents'.[18] This reliance on personification meant that allegories, despite their inherent indirectness, tended to focus not simply on an institution (such as the House of Commons) but on one figure or group of figures in particular.

In *Atalantis*, Manley's use of personification facilitated the reader's identification of the latent central actors who populated the inner and outer rings of Anne's court. This happens in two ways. First, Manley created connections between her pseudonymous characters and the real-world individuals they were thought to stand in for through positive, laudatory descriptions, which openly linked certain individuals to the characters depicted in *Atalantis*. For example, in her dedication to the first volume, published in late May of 1709, Manley praises Henry Somerset, second duke of Beaufort, suggesting that Atalantis's Duke de Beaumond (i.e., good- or beautiful-world) shares '*so near a resemblance of Yours*'.[19] Everything Manley has to say about both Somerset and Beaumond is extremely flattering, the type of praise to which Somerset was unlikely to object. At the same time, through overt comparison, Beaumond-Somerset becomes one piece in the social puzzle that is both Atalantis and by extension England. If readers are told, effectively, that Somerset is Beaumond, then they also know that Beaumond's 'Grand-father' is Henry Somerset, first duke of Beaufort, a committed loyalist during the Civil War, who later defended Bristol against the Duke of Monmouth's forces in 1685 (in John Dryden's *Absalom and Achitophel* he appears as Bezaliel).[20] From there, the interlocking familial and social relationships spool outward. At the same time, the decision to dedicate the work to Somerset was a clever ruse, if a seemingly odd one. Hardly did Manley sympathize with Somerset's Jacobite tendencies, but it would have been too risky to dedicate the work to, for instance, Robert Harley, earl of Oxford, Manley's later secret supporter and a man whom Sarah Churchill, duchess of Cambridge and the queen's closest confidante, already held in firm distrust.[21] With Somerset, Manley had found one pawn in an interpretive game— a linking figure in the world of Westminster politics and a cover for her own political allegiances and allies.

Second, Manley helped her readers by creating constellations of clearly defamed figures, often presented in close succession, which created layers of circumstantial evidence that enabled individual identifications. Take her dense description of the Churchill family. John Churchill, the earl of Marlborough, is Count Fortunatus, a punning allusion to the Churchill family motto *Fidelis sed infortunatus* (in this case, though, Marlborough was thought to be more fortunate

[18] Copeland and Struck, Introduction, *Cambridge Companion to Allegory*, pp. 8–9.
[19] *The New Atalantis (1709)*, in *The Selected Works of Delarivier Manley*, edited by Rachel Carnell and Ruth Herman, with W. R. Owens, vol. 3 (London: Routledge, 2005), pp. 7, 111.
[20] Manley, *Atalantis*, vol. 2, p. 111.   [21] Downie, *Robert Harley and the Press*, pp. 115–16.

than faithful, especially to James II); he was 'rais'd by concurrent Favour of two
Monarchs [James II, who made him baron, and William III, who made him earl],
his own [charms: his military victories, but also his affair with Barbara Palmer,
duchess of Cleveland, mistress to Charles II, depicted as Duchess de L'Inconstant],
and his Sisters Charms [Arabella Godfrey, mistress to James II], from a meer
Gentleman'.[22] Then there is his wife, the 'She-favourite' of the 'new Empress',
Sarah Churchill, who had been Anne's closest advisor since the 1680s (at least
until their later falling-out).[23] Once again, through association, readers were able
to spool out identifications, starting with a single figure.

This, at least in theory, is how allegorical personifications were supposed to
work. Yet this emphasis on rigid symmetrical personification also entailed its own
problems both for lay readers and for prosecutors hoping to decode an uncertain
vehicle as an undeniable tenor—what Fredric V. Bogel has called 'allegory's failure
to master and localize by means of the figure of personification'.[24] In his study of
allegorical identifications and misidentifications, David Brewer has likewise
argued that misattributions were par for the course:

> the discrepancies and competing marginal identifications that we have pushed
> aside as outliers and exceptions are, in fact, completely typical... [They] allow us
> to see how even the most seemingly straightforward equations between an
> allegorical figure and its putative referent are shot through with discrepancies,
> departures from the supposed parallel, details that do not correspond, and so
> on.[25]

In practical terms this meant that readers, at the moment of publication, were
often uncertain who, precisely, lay behind a text's supposedly symmetrical personifications. This was by no means a new problem in 1709. Alan Roper, for
instance, has examined 149 copies of *Absalom and Achitophel*, demonstrating that
readers often had tremendous difficulty decoding Dryden's densely allegorical
biblical satire.[26] Routine misidentification simply troubled the entire satiric landscape. The omission of a victim's name, whether by allegorical personification,
pseudonym, or 'emvowelment', only exacerbated such interpretive difficulties as
the reader moved farther outside the charmed circles of metropolitan literary and

---

[22] Manley, *Atalantis*, vol. 2, pp. 20, 312n66, 314n83.
[23] For Sarah Churchill's (admittedly biased) version of events, see her *An Account of the Conduct of the Dowager Duchess of Marlborough, from Her First Coming to Court to the Year 1710* (London, 1742).
[24] Bogel, *Satire*, p. 129.
[25] David A. Brewer, 'Secret History and Allegory', in *The Secret History in Literature, 1660–1820*, edited by Rebecca Bullard and Rachel Carnell (Cambridge: Cambridge University Press, 2017), p. 61.
[26] Alan Roper, 'Who's Who in *Absalom and Achitophel?*', *Huntington Library Quarterly* 63, no. 1–2 (2000): pp. 93–138.

political life.[27] The 'instability' of allegorical acts of 'translation and interpretation' could even be leveraged as a satiric tool. Ros Ballaster, for instance, has pointed to the ways that Eliza Haywood 'destabilizes the allegorical enterprise, the search for a direct correspondence between text and referential world', in *The Adventures of Eovaai*, through the 'pluralizing interpretive tendencies of the text's machinery': 'readers are encouraged to snigger not only at her satiric targets, but at the allegorical seriousness of satire itself'.[28]

Such interpretive problems had always plagued allegory, but they were compounded by the particular nature of political allegory in the late seventeenth and early eighteenth centuries. Allegory was both a familiar and ancient literary device that remained central to political debate throughout the seventeenth century.[29] But earlier moral allegories tended to be more readily decipherable than political allegories of the late seventeenth and early eighteenth centuries, which often required minute insider knowledge about specific political actors during short-lived and sometimes obscure controversies.[30] Earlier moral allegories, such as *The Pilgrim's Progress* or *The Faerie Queene*, were instead 'naïve', as Northrop Frye has put it (even if such works, Edmund Spenser admitted in a letter to Sir Walter Ralegh, contain a 'darke conceit . . . clowdily enwrapped in Allegoricall devises').[31] Already by the beginning of the eighteenth century, an almost de Manian or Benjaminian sense of allegory obtained among readers and critics alike—the double imperative of allegory as a 'sign of deferred or absent meaning, both calling for and resisting interpretation'.[32]

Despite the recalcitrance of allegory, readers felt a strange and yet familiar compulsion to furnish textual lacunae at moments of authorial reticence. Sceptical readers often actively sought out real-world analogues for characters and events, even and perhaps especially when cautioned by a work's paratexts not to.[33] As Catherine Gallagher has observed, this was an era when one had the 'desire to open every book to some extra-textual reality, to read everything double'.[34] The

---

[27] Jonathan Swift to Alexander Pope (16 July 1728), *The Correspondence of Jonathan Swift, D. D.*, edited by David Woolley, vol. 3 (Frankfurt am Main: Peter Lang, 1999–2014), p. 189.

[28] Ros Ballaster, 'A Gender of Opposition: Eliza Haywood's Scandal Fiction', in *The Passionate Fictions of Eliza Haywood: Essays on Her Life and Work*, edited by Kirsten T. Saxton and Rebecca P. Bocchicchio (Lexington: University Press of Kentucky, 2000), pp. 158, 164.

[29] Mark Kishlansky, 'Turning Frogs into Princes: Aesop's *Fables* and the Political Culture of Early Modern England', in *Political Culture and Cultural Politics in Early Modern England: Essays Presented to David Underdown*, edited by Susan Dwyer Amussen and Mark A. Kishlansky (Manchester: Manchester University Press, 1995), pp. 338–60.

[30] Northrop Frye, *Anatomy of Criticism: Four Essays* (1957; Princeton: Princeton University Press, 1990), p. 90.

[31] Edmund Spenser, 'The Letter to Ralegh', in *The Faerie Queene*, edited by Carol V. Kaske, vol. 1 (Indianapolis: Hackett, 2006–7), p. 179.

[32] Copeland and Struck, Introduction, *Cambridge Companion to Allegory*, p. 10.

[33] Kate Loveman, *Reading Fictions, 1660–1740: Deception in English Literary and Political Culture* (Burlington: Ashgate Publishing, 2008), pp. 3–8.

[34] Catherine Gallagher, *Nobody's Story: The Vanishing Acts of Women Writers in the Marketplace, 1670–1820* (Berkeley: University of California Press, 1994), p. 124.

shocking preponderance of satires from this period that feature careful marginal annotations in contemporary hands suggests just how eagerly readers sought to solve the puzzle of deferred onomastic meaning. Moreover, it is worth keeping in mind that such moments of readerly participation entailed not merely a straight-forward game of fill-in-the-blank. Instead, they are a critical intervention in the text itself, an implicit signal that a reader believes that he or she has access to authorial intentions.[35] Satiric naming, moreover, was a game played both ways. Readers who chose to intervene in a text were often *invited* to do so by the author and printer alike. In Kathryn Temple's words: 'Neither Manley nor her characters were meant to be disguised by anonymity; instead it worked as a tease'.[36]

Such readerly interventions were also enabled by so-called satiric 'keys', stun-ningly routine extra-textual publications that promised to disclose the names of every figure obliquely represented in a text.[37] Even these posed problems, though, especially when competing keys advanced incompatible readings of the same text or offered far-fetched attributions. Nicola Parsons has argued that the 'actual relationship between the key and the text is one of supplementation, not super-session'.[38] Manley might even have had a hand in producing keys for *Atalantis*. Almost immediately following the publication of the second volume in mid-October 1709, a two-part broadside turned up, listing the names of over two hundred figures, all helpfully linked to page numbers.[39] Later editions went so far as to print the key with the book itself. But even these keys present inconsistencies and readers continued to make mistakes. Parsons has shown that two of Manley's successive readers even quibbled over the decoding of specific figures.[40] But what was one to do? Thomas Hearne admitted that *Atalantis* 'was not easily under-stood' without the 'key that was handed about'.[41]

Lay interpretation was one thing, however, and legal interpretation something else. Manley's encounter with the law intriguingly drew attention to the interpret-ive obstacle every lawyer faced in the prosecution of allegorical satires: how to demonstrate, to the satisfaction of finicky jurors, that an allegorical personification amounted to a defamatory imputation against a real-world individual. This issue raises two ticklish problems. First, in the past each minister would have been

---

[35] H. J. Jackson, *Marginalia: Readers Writing in Books* (New Haven: Yale University Press, 2001), p. 90.

[36] Kathryn Temple, 'Manley's "Feigned Scene": The Fictions of Law at Westminster Hall', *Eighteenth-Century Fiction* 22, no. 4 (Summer 2010): p. 585.

[37] For example, see Paul Baines and Pat Rogers, *Edmund Curll, Bookseller* (Oxford: Oxford University Press, 2007), pp. 178, 189.

[38] Nicola Parsons, *Reading Gossip in Early Eighteenth-Century England* (New York: Palgrave, 2009), p. 47.

[39] *The Key to Atalantis. Part I* [London?: 1709?]; and *The Key to Atalantis. Part II* [London?: 1709?].

[40] Parsons, *Reading Gossip*, pp. 52–3. For the copy in question, See Manley, *The New Atalantis* (London, 1709), EC7.MC3148.709s vol. 2, Hought.L.

[41] Thomas Hearne, *Remarks and Collections*, 11 vol., edited by C. E. Doble, et al., vol. 2 (Oxford: Clarendon Press, 1885–1921), p. 292.

required to identify himself as one of the overtly vicious figures obscurely depicted in the work. In so doing, however, each minister would then have been required to admit tacitly that he *was* that vicious figure. Unfortunately, having done so, no minister could contest the factual basis of the personification, because the truth of a libel was immaterial to its prosecution.[42]

Luckily for the Crown, a recent development in libel law theoretically meant that individual ministers could avoid the embarrassing task of self-identification. In November 1704, John Tutchin was prosecuted for seditious libel for a series of articles in *The Observator*.[43] In his decision on the case, Chief Justice Holt ruled that criticism of the government as a whole was criminal, and not only specific officials, countering the arguments of the defence who, rightfully citing English precedents, claimed that only individuals could be defamed.[44] In Holt's account, the mere assertion that 'corrupt officers are appointed to administer affairs' constituted 'a reflection on the Government', and because 'no Government can subsist' unless 'the people have a good opinion of it', Tutchin's efforts 'to procure animosities as to [its] management' required that he 'be called to account'.[45] Although the decision in the case was later nullified on a procedural error, the original ruling proved at least the theoretical capacity of the Crown to prosecute individuals for libel against institutions rather than the individual representatives of those institutions.[46]

Nonetheless, in prosecuting Manley, the Crown also faced a second difficulty: how to demonstrate that the world of Atalantis was England, a problem that made Holt's 1704 ruling less useful than it at first appeared. To link Atalantis to England, one had to follow the allegory from the bottom to the top: first the individual victims had to be identified, then the institutions to which they belonged. At this point, however, it was legally impossible to create definitive identifications between allegorical figures and the people they stood in for. The Crown, for instance, might easily have claimed that the 'Country Chevalier' was the Whig MP Sir Thomas Colepeper, but it remained legally improbable that any juror would have accepted such an interpretation in the absence of *internal* textual evidence. As a result, Holt's 1704 ruling meant little in practise when it came to allegory. Jurors, rather than judges, continued to interpret innuendoes, a legal term for any word whose referent was not immediately obvious when taken out of

---

[42] *Case de Libellis Famosis* (1605), 5 Coke 125, 77 Eng. Rep. 250.

[43] Lee Sonsteg Horsley, 'The Trial of John Tutchin, Author of the *Observator*', *Yearbook of English Studies* 3 (1973): pp. 124–40.

[44] Hamburger, 'Seditious Libel', p. 735.

[45] *R. v. Tutchin* (1704), Holt 424 (Q.B.), 90 Eng. Rep. 1133–4; and Hamburger, 'Seditious Libel', p. 735.

[46] *R. v. Tutchin* (1704), Holt 56 (Q.B.), Mod. Cas. 268, 274, 285, 1 Salk. 51, 90 Eng. Rep. 929–30.

context.[47] Moreover, as we saw in the last chapter, innuendoes could not be used to infer meanings. They could be used only to clarify what had already been said or written, such as the meaning of an obscure insult or the designation of individuals *already* named in the offending text who later, in the same text, appeared under a metonym like 'minister' or a pronoun like 'she'.[48] In this regard, allegory posed a unique interpretive challenge. Gutted or 'emvowelled' names required jurors merely to fill in the blanks literally left open for attribution; allegory, conversely, entailed the wholesale substitution of real-world names for proper nouns that never appeared anywhere in a text.[49]

The legal-hermeneutic issues posed by allegory became clear when the authorities finally moved to interrogate Manley. On 28 October 1709, roughly two weeks after the second volume of *Atalantis* appeared, the Secretary of State, Charles Spencer, third earl of Sunderland, issued a joint warrant for the work's two trade publishers, John Morphew and James Woodward, both of whom are named in the imprint.[50] Likely later that day, as information arose around the identity of *Atalantis*'s author, Sunderland issued a second joint warrant for Manley and the work's printer, John Barber (with whom she carried on a decades-long common law relationship).[51] Almost immediately Woodward and Morphew were arrested. A day later, on 29 October 1709, Manley was reportedly in custody.[52] There Manley was examined by Sunderland in an exchange she later recounted in *The Adventures of Rivella* (1714), a provoking fictionalization that nonetheless is corroborated by both extant and recently discovered legal documents.[53] In *Rivella*, Manley freely admits to Sunderland that she authored the piece—thereby cavalierly setting aside one of the most common alibis of writers—but archly argues that *Atalantis* was a mere work of fiction. Any real-world similitudes one

[47] Richard H. Helmholz, 'Civil Trials and the Limits of Responsible Speech', *Juries, Libel, & Justice: The Role of the English Juries in Seventeenth- and Eighteenth-Century Trials for Libel and Slander* (Los Angeles: William Andrews Clark Memorial Library, University of California, Los Angeles, 1984), pp. 3–25; and Green, *Verdict*, ch. 8.

[48] See *Jeames v. Rutlech* (1599), 4 Co. Rep. 17 (Q.B.), rpt. *Sources*, 642–3; and William Bohun, *Declarations and Pleadings in the Most Usual Actions* (London, 1733), p. 2.

[49] *Hurt's Case* (1713), in Hawkins, *Pleas of the Crown*, vol. 1, p. 194; and *Harrison v. Thornborough* (1714), Gilb. Cas. 114 (Q.B.), 10 Mod. 196.

[50] SP 44/78/64 and SP 34/11/69, TNA. On Morphew's and Woodward's activities as trade publishers, see Michael Treadwell, 'London Trade Publishers, 1675–1750', *The Library*, sixth series-IV, 2 (June 1982): pp. 106–7, table 3. For the chronology of arrests, see John McTague, 'The New Atalantis Arrests: A Reassessment', *The Library* 15, no. 4 (December 2014): pp. 439–46, which corrects some inconsistencies in both Rachel Carnell, *A Political Biography of Delarivier Manley* (London: Pickering & Chatto, 2008) and Ruth Herman, *The Business of a Woman: The Political Writings of Delarivier Manley* (Newark: University of Delaware Press, 2003).

[51] Ros Ballaster, 'Manley, Delarivier (c.1670–1724)', *ODNB*.

[52] SP 44/78/65, TNA; and *The Post Boy*, no. 2256 (27–9 October 1709).

[53] McTague, 'The New Atalantis Arrests', p. 446. On the 'gendered interdependence of literary and legal representations' (p. 64) in *Rivella*, see Susan Sage Heinzelman, *Riding the Black Ram: Law, Literature, and Gender* (Stanford: Stanford University Press, 2010), pp. 61–6.

might find in the text were nothing more than an unhappy accident. Manley's examination is recounted in *Rivella* by the character Sir Charles Lovemore:

> They us'd several Arguments to make her discover who were the Persons concern'd with her in writing her Books; or at least from whom she had receiv'd Information of some special Facts, which they thought were above her own Intelligence: Her Defence was with much Humility and Sorrow, for having offended, at the same Time denying that any Persons were concern'd with her, or that she had a farther Design than writing for her own Amusement and Diversion in the Country; without intending particular Reflections or Characters: When this was not believ'd, and the contrary urg'd very home to her by several Circumstances and Likenesses; she said then it must be *Inspiration*, because knowing her own Innocence she could account for it no other Way: The Secretary reply'd upon her, that *Inspiration* us'd to be upon a good Account, and her Writings were stark naught; she told him, with an Air full of Penitence, that might be true, but it was as true, that there were evil Angels as well as good; so that nevertheless what she had wrote might still be by *Inspiration*.[54]

Sure, she wrote it, but the whole thing was made up. Even if it were an allegory, Manley was innocent, having been inspired to write it. A few days later, on 3 November 1709, Manley sued for *habeas corpus*. On 5 November 1709, she was officially charged and released on bail until her trial, which was scheduled for the first day of the following Hilary term in mid-January 1709/10 at Queen's Bench.

Manley's tale of interrogation, obfuscation, and fictionalization has been ably told time and again by such scholars as Catherine Gallagher, Kathryn Temple, and Rachel Carnell, among others.[55] All have, to some degree, marvelled at Manley's use of 'Inspiration' and her claim of naïveté as a defence for the supposedly accidental correspondence between the fictional world of Atalantis and the sleazy horse-trading of Queen Anne's court. But scholars have also underestimated the degree to which allegory remained a surprisingly effective satiric device in preventing prosecutions for libel. Gallagher, for instance, has claimed that allegory was *not* a useful legal defence in 1709.[56] But her conclusion is based on a reading of *State Law; Or, the Doctrine of Libels* ([1730]), a text first published in 1728 as *The Doctrine of Libels Discussed and Examined*, almost two decades after *Atalantis* had been published and after fundamental changes to libel law had facilitated the

---

[54] Manley, *The Adventures of Rivella* (1714), edited by Rachel Carnell, in *The Selected Works of Delarivier Manley*, vol. 4 (London: Pickering & Chatto, 2005), p. 55.

[55] Gallagher, *Nobody's Story*, pp. 88–144; Temple, 'Manley's "Feigned Scene"', pp. 573–98; Carnell, *A Political Biography of Delarivier Manley*, pp. 180ff; Herman, *The Business of a Woman*, ch. 3; and Fidelis Morgan, *A Woman of No Character: An Autobiography of Mrs Manley* (Boston: Faber and Faber, 1986), pp. 146–51.

[56] Gallagher, *Nobody's Story*, pp. 98–104.

prosecution of satirical works.[57] As we will see in the final section of this chapter, allegory remained a useful satiric tool in fending off prosecutions for libel until 1728/9, when the Crown devised a new doctrine for the courtroom interpretation of allegory.

With nothing more to go on than the widely held assumption that *Atalantis* was a political allegory, Sunderland was in a bind. Faced with the impossible evidentiary burden—at least in 1709—of proving that Atalantis was England, Sunderland put off Manley's prosecution term after term for more than a year. It appears, moreover, that Sunderland had very little to go on. He and other prominent Whigs simply suspected that Manley had high-ranking informants who had provided her with intelligence about insider affairs. (Even still, as Parsons has shown, few found her allegorized tales of backdoor dealing revelatory.[58] For the Whig MP Arthur Maynwaring, it was nothing more than 'a nauseous book' full of 'very old, false, and incredible scandal'.[59]) Some pointed to the earl of Peterborough, others to Harley, whom Manley obsequiously depicted in *Atalantis* as Don Geronimo de Haro: 'He was *Honest*! he was *Brave*! understood the Interest of the Nation, and fearlesly proclaim'd and pursu'd it'.[60] Some disagreed. As Maynwaring sardonically wrote to Sarah Churchill, 'Could any one but an idiot call him honest, in a good sense?'[61]

With a change in the ministry in 1710, the charges against Manley were quietly dropped.[62] On 13 February 1710/11, Scandalosissima Scoundrelia, as she came to be known, was set free.[63] Sunderland's efforts had failed miserably either to secure a conviction or to suppress the work. As Sarah Churchill complained to the queen, 'notwithstanding the prosecution', *Atalantis* was still being 'sold at every shop'.[64] The entire affair proved an unintended boon for Manley, paving the way for a

---

[57] *Hurt's Case* (1713), in Hawkins, *Pleas of the Crown*, vol. 1, p. 194; *Harrison v. Thornborough* (1714), Gilb. Cas. 114, 10 Mod. 196 (Q.B.), 93 Eng. Rep. 277; and *R. v. Clerk* [*sic*] (1728/9), 1 Barn. 305 (K.B.), 94 Eng. Rep. 207. Gallagher rightly opposes C. R. Kropf's reading of satire's relationship to libel law ('Libel and Satire in the Eighteenth Century', *Eighteenth-Century Studies* 8 [Winter 1974–75]: pp. 153–68), but her misreading of allegory at law is largely the product of Donald Thomas's own promulgation of a specific error: that the critical ruling against allegory, in 1728/9, was *already* the 'interpretation [of the law] accepted' at the time of Manley's examination in 1709. This is not true, as the failed prosecutions of numerous allegories in periodicals in the intervening years make clear. See Gallagher, *Nobody's Story*, pp. 99–100, 100n25; and Thomas, *A Long Time Burning: The History of Literary Censorship in England* (London: Routledge and Kegan Paul, 1969), pp. 57–9.

[58] Parsons, *Reading Gossip*, pp. 60–1.

[59] Maynwaring to Sarah Churchill (October 1709 [?]), *Private Correspondence of Sarah, Duchess of Marlborough*, vol. 1 (London, 1838), p. 237. See Blenheim Papers, Add. MS 61460, f. 85v, BL.

[60] Manley, *Atalantis*, vol. 2, p. 235.

[61] Maynwaring to Sarah Churchill (October 1709 [?]), *Private Correspondence of Sarah, Duchess of Marlborough*, vol. 1, p. 238.

[62] Narcissus Luttrell, *A Brief Historical Relation of State Affairs*, vol. 6 (London, 1857), p. 546.

[63] *General Postscript* (27 September 1709), qtd. John Wilson Bowyer, *The Celebrated Mrs. Centlivre* (Durham: Duke University Press, 1952), p. 125.

[64] *Correspondence*, vol. 1, p. 237.

sequel, *The Memoirs of Europe* (1710), and her veiled biographical account of the entire affair in *Rivella* a few years later.

That Sunderland's pursuit of Manley had gone awry is intriguing. Foolishly, it seems, he had simply assumed that Manley would fess up, naming names and owning the allegory. Manley had turned the tables back around, stymieing what Holt's 1704 ruling was supposed to have taken care of. An institution, like a representative of that institution, could be defamed. But how was one to prove that the institution being defamed was the same one to which the allegory supposedly referred? Was Atalantis really England? Was Angela undoubtedly London? More to the point, was Princess Olympia so surely Anne? Were her controlling lackeys indisputably the Whig Junto? Manley had brought the entire legal-interpretive issue back to square one. The question, time and again, was not who or what could or could not be defamed. The question was how to prove to the satisfaction of jurors that an allegorical representation meant what everybody so surely knew it to mean.

Manley's run-in with the authorities is important because it was one piece in a decades-long legal puzzle, as the Crown and the courts worked to devise court-room mechanisms for the interpretation of allegory. *Atalantis* unintentionally served as a satiric test run—an abandoned prosecution that illustrated the limits of earlier legal developments and signalled the need for a new interpretive doctrine. That procedure was finally devised in 1728/9, in *R. v. Clerk*, the subject of the final section of this chapter, and drew on the framework of sociocentric interpretation that the courts had been developing since the late seventeenth century. But between Manley's interrogation and the court's conceptualization of this new doctrine in 1728/9, writers continued to employ and refine allegory, especially in the burgeoning periodical press of the 1710s and '20s, where it became an allusive—and elusive—tool for both opposition and Jacobite satire.

5.2 The '*Insolence* of Drawing Parallels': *The Craftsman* and the Uses of Allegory

Central to the difficulty of prosecuting such satires was allegory's 'protean' quality, as Angus Fletcher has put it—its perceived slipperiness and instability.[65] For writers, critics, and lay readers alike at the beginning of the eighteenth century, allegory's mechanics and signifying procedures were anything but self-evident. In the fleeting commensurability of vehicle and tenor, an incongruity always seemed to haunt allegory. Even an 'initially straightforward' text, Claude Rawson has

---

[65] Angus Fletcher, *Allegory: The Theory of a Symbolic Mode* (Ithaca: Cornell University Press, 1964), p. 1.

argued, could move easily 'outside the clean lines of allegory'.[66] Yet it was precisely this semantic indeterminacy and the problems it posed for courtroom interpretation that the opposition press increasingly instrumentalized in its attacks on the government. My goal in this section is to account for the growth of allegorical political satire during the 1710s and '20s. I focus especially on the periodical press and in particular on *The Craftsman*, the most prominent and virulently anti-Walpole journal of the later 1720s.[67] By studying the instrumental ambiguity of allegory, and its recalcitrance to definitive interpretation, we can see why political satirists routinely resorted to allegory and why the Crown still had tremendous difficulty in prosecuting allegorical libels.

For Sir Robert Walpole, the press was a particular worry during the first years of his administration. The periodical market had quickly expanded following the lapse of licensing in 1695, when the government-funded *London Gazette* was the lone source of state-sponsored news. By the time Walpole was in power, about 20 daily, tri-weekly, and weekly newspapers and periodicals had come into existence.[68] Serial publications played a critical role not only in the distribution of information, but also in the interpretation of contemporary politics:

> The impact of the Revolution [of 1688] on the structure of politics also had considerable importance for the development of the news and news-related serial. The emergence of a formally constituted two-party system, whereby distinct sets of ideology were identified within an acknowledged framework of authority, created an environment in which public debate became an integral part of the political process. The post-1695 London papers were engulfed by the publications generated by party conflict which, during Queen Anne's reign, centred on a series of dedicated essay sheets linked in various ways to the leading Whig and Tory politicians.[69]

With the periodical press as the main venue for publicly hashing out politics, Walpole remained eager both to silence and undermine his critics while also publicizing and promoting his policies. His dual-pronged approach to the press was evident not only in his administration's funding and embedding of counter-propagandistic journalists (the costs of which rose to as much as £20,000 per

---

[66] Claude Rawson, *Gulliver and the Gentle Reader: Studies in Swift and Our Time* (London: Routledge & Kegan Paul, 1973), p. 56.

[67] James J. Caudle, 'Richard Francklin: A Controversial Publisher, Bookseller and Printer, 1718–1765', in *The Cambridge History of the Book in Britain*, vol. 5: 1695–1830, edited by Michael F. Suarez, S. J., and Michael L. Turner (Cambridge: Cambridge University Press, 2009), p. 385.

[68] Michael Harris, 'London newspapers', in *The Cambridge History of the Book in Britain*, vol. 5: 1695–1830, p. 422.

[69] Harris, 'London newspapers', p. 417. For an overview of periodical regulation across the century, see Black, *Press*, ch. 6.

annum), but also in its active efforts to hamper Tory critics, both legally in the courts and extra-legally through counter-intelligence subterfuges.[70]

No periodical of the last half of the 1720s quite provoked his administration like *The Craftsman*, an explicitly anti-Walpole vehicle edited by the satirist Nicholas Amhurst and founded, funded, and furnished by a group of well-connected Tories, including William Pulteney (the later earl of Bath); his brother, Daniel Pulteney; and Henry St John, Viscount Bolingbroke. Walpole routinely appeared in the pages of *The Craftsman* under a breathtaking range of 'feigned names', literary stand-ins, and contemptuous historical and present-day parallels: he was Volpone, the 'sly fox' of Ben Jonson's satiric embodiment of lust and greed; Lucius Sergius Catilina, the conspiratorial Roman senator; Lucius Aelius Sejanus, the power-hungry confidant of the Roman emperor Tiberius; Cardinal Thomas Wolsey, the *alter rex* (or 'other king') controlling Henry VIII; Captain Macheath, John Gay's double-dealing thief catcher; Aleksander Danilovich Menshikov (or 'Menzikoff'), the corrupt advisor to Peter the Great turned de facto ruler of Russia under Empress Catherine in the 1720s; and the highwaymen Joseph 'Blueskin' Blake and Jonathan Wild.[71] With Walpole appearing in almost every issue of the journal, *The Craftsman* was subject to routine government inquiries, examinations, and prosecutions throughout this period.[72] Its printer-publisher, Richard Francklin, was arrested a remarkable eight times between 1727 and 1731 alone.[73]

Despite the legal pressures brought to bear by the Walpole administration on the press, the government was hamstrung by allegorical criticism. Periodical writers in turn often employed 'parallel history' to offer a veiled critique of the present. As Brian Cowan has written, a 'deep sensitivity to the past, along with the dangers posed by censorship or prosecution for sedition, provided a powerful incentive for people to think about politics allegorically'.[74] That recourse to allegory had deeper roots in the rise of so-called 'secret history'. Literary scholars have often traced the emergence of secret history in English to seventeenth-century

---

[70] Michael Harris, 'Print and Politics in the Age of Walpole', in *Britain in the Age of Walpole*, edited by Jeremy Black (New York: St. Martin's Press, 1984), pp. 189–210; and Simon Varey, 'Growth of Capitalism and the Rise of the Press in the Age of Walpole', in *Politics, Politeness and Patriotism: Papers Presented at the Folger Institute Seminar 'Politics and Politeness: British Political Thought in the Age of Walpole'*, edited by Gordon J. Schochet (Washington: Folger Institute, 1993), pp. 250–1. See also Tone Sundt Urstad, *Sir Robert Walpole's Poets: The Use of Literature as Pro-Government Propaganda, 1721–1742* (Newark: University of Delaware Press, 1999), pp. 32–7, 56–97; and Simon Targett, '"The premier scribbler himself": Sir Robert Walpole and the Management of Political Opinion', *Studies in Newspaper and Periodical History* 2, no. 1–2 (1994): pp. 19–33.

[71] Varey, 'The Growth of Capitalism', pp. 67–8.

[72] Eckhart Hellmuth, 'Towards Hume—The Discourse on the Liberty of the Press in the Age of Walpole', *History of European Ideas* 44, no. 2 (2018): p. 161.

[73] Roger Lund, '"An Alembick of Innuendos": Satire, Libel, and *The Craftsman*', *Philological Quarterly* 95, no. 2 (Spring 2016): p. 258.

[74] Brian Cowan, 'The History of Secret Histories', *Huntington Library Quarterly* 81, no. 1 (Spring 2018): p. 136.

translations of Procopius of Caesarea's previously unpublished *Anekdota*, a salacious account of the Roman Emperor Justinian and his wife.[75] The term 'secret history' itself was a product of the text's translations from the Greek *Anekdota* (literally 'unpublished-things') to the Latin *Historia Arcana* in 1623, before being re-translated into French as *Histoire Secrète* (1669) and into English as *The Secret History of the Court of the Emperor Justinian* (1674). Annabel Patterson and Rebecca Bullard have shown that Procopius's subversive retelling of Justinian's rule offered an intriguing analogue to official history for readers worried about abuses of power in the courts of Charles II and Louis XIV.[76] Hundreds of 'secret histories' were published in the succeeding decades; an even greater number appeared as 'anecdotes', a virtual synonym at the time, though most writers were less brazen, allowing their texts quietly to enter the world while leaving it to readers to decode the scandals within.[77] In the process, secret history was given a quasi-classical precedent in its association with Procopius's *Anekdota*—one not unlike Dryden's larger project of satiric legitimation that we saw in the first chapter.[78]

Such temporal-generic definitions have offered one approach to allegory, allowing literary historians in recent years to link secret history to the increasingly politicized literary culture of the late Stuart era and to connect a historically neglected and even denigrated form to an evergreen interest in the supposed 'rise of the novel' during the eighteenth century.[79] However, the practise of secret history extends even further back into the early modern period, and historians have tended to study secret history in less formally discrete terms than literary critics. They have simply been less concerned with 'notions of canon and genre'

[75] Peter Burke, 'Publicizing the Private: The Rise of "Secret History"', in *Changing Perceptions of the Public Sphere*, edited by Christian J. Emden and David Midgley (Oxford: Berghahn Books, 2012), pp. 67–9.

[76] Annabel Patterson, *Early Modern Liberalism* (Cambridge: Cambridge University Press, 1997), pp. 183–98; and Rebecca Bullard, *The Politics of Disclosure, 1674–1725: Secret History Narratives* (London: Pickering & Chatto, 2009), pp. 29–43.

[77] April London, 'Secret History and Anecdote', in *The Secret History in Literature, 1660–1820*, edited by Rebecca Bullard and Rachel Carnell (Cambridge University Press, 2017), p. 176; and Eve Tavor Bannet, 'Secret History and Censorship', in *The Secret History in Literature, 1660–1820*, edited by Rebecca Bullard and Rachel Carnell (Cambridge: Cambridge University Press, 2017), p. 166.

[78] Rebecca Bullard, 'Introduction: Reconsidering Secret History', in *The Secret History in Literature, 1660–1820*, edited by Rebecca Bullard and Rachel Carnell (Cambridge: Cambridge University Press, 2017), p. 4.

[79] See, for instance, Rachel Carnell, 'Slipping from Secret History to Novel', *Eighteenth-Century Fiction* 28, no. 1 (Fall 2015): pp. 1–24; Michael McKeon, *The Secret History of Domesticity: Public, Private, and the Division of Knowledge* (Baltimore: Johns Hopkins University Press, 2005), pp. 621–59; Eve Tavor Bannet, '"Secret History": Or, Talebearing Inside and Outside the Secretoire', *Huntington Library Quarterly* 68, no. 1–2 (March 2005): pp. 375–96; Karen O'Brien, 'History and the Novel in Eighteenth-Century Britain', *Huntington Library Quarterly* 68, no. 1–2 (March 2005): pp. 397–413; Aaron Santesso, '*The New Atalantis* and Varronian Satire', *Philological Quarterly* 79, no. 2 (Spring 2000): pp. 177–204; Ros Ballaster, *Seductive Forms: Women's Amatory Fiction from 1684 to 1740* (Oxford: Oxford University Press, 1992); and Davis, *Factual Fictions*, pp. 110–22.

than the 'legitimation crises of early modern monarchy'.[80] The larger point is that early modern writers and readers understood 'secret history' in capacious generic terms: a secret history might be a factual history assembled from unpublished documents; it might equally be a political allegory, full of fabricated events stitched together by rumour and falsehood and dressed in the guise of an amatory novel. The flexibility of the category has led cautious critics into the many twists and turns of generic definition.

I have no interest in litigating the formal limits of secret history, but I am interested for the sake of this chapter in the allegorical link between secret histories, like Manley's *Atalantis*, and the 'parallel histories' that regularly appeared in periodicals like *The Craftsman* and *Mist's Weekly Journal*.[81] 'Not all secret histories are allegories', David Brewer has reminded us.[82] But a deep vein of allegorical thinking seemingly marked all discourses in the last half of the seventeenth century, whether political, literary, or religious.[83] It was, moreover, this allegorical overlap that linked secret history and parallel history for the authorities—the semantic doublings that undergirded such texts both marked them out and unified them as a form of verbal evasion that the government eagerly sought to suppress during the first decades of the eighteenth century.

During the 1710s and '20s, writers for *The Craftsman* and *Mist's* were especially canny in their reapplication of history to the present. Perhaps most infamous were Bolingbroke's contributions to *The Craftsman*.[84] He seemingly knew the limits of libel law better than most, having served as Secretary of State for the Northern Department between 1710 and 1714 (he also knew a thing or two about satire, having enlisted Swift to write for *The Examiner*).[85] Bolingbroke wrote dozens if not hundreds of pieces for *The Craftsman*, including a series of infamous allegorical articles known as 'Remarks on the History of England' between 1730 and 1731 under the pseudonym Humphrey Oldcastle.[86] James Pitt, the editor of the pro-Walpole

---

[80] Cowan, 'The History of Secret Histories', p. 138. See, for instance, Peter Lake, *Bad Queen Bess?: Libels, Secret Histories, and the Politics of Publicity in the Reign of Queen Elizabeth I* (Oxford: Oxford University Press, 2016); Noah Millstone, 'Evil Counsel: *The Propositions to Bridle the Impertinency of Parliament* and the Critique of Caroline Government in the Late 1620s', *Journal of British Studies* 50, no. 4 (October 2011): pp. 813–39; and Alastair Bellany and Thomas Cogswell, *The Murder of King James I* (New Haven: Yale University Press, 2015), pp. xxv, xxx–xxxi.

[81] For a similarly broad conceptualization of 'secret history', see McKeon, *Secret History of Domesticity*, pp. 470–2.

[82] Brewer, 'Secret History and Allegory', p. 62. On the contentiousness of defining 'secret history', see Rebecca Bullard, 'Secret History, Politics, and the Early Novel', in *The Oxford Handbook of the Eighteenth-Century Novel*, edited by J. A. Downie (Oxford: Oxford University Press, 2016), p. 137.

[83] Steven N. Zwicker, *Lines of Authority: Politics and English Literary Culture, 1649–1689* (Ithaca: Cornell University Press, 1993), pp. 3–5.

[84] Alexander Pettit, *Illusory Consensus: Bolingbroke and the Polemical Response to Walpole, 1730-1737* (Newark: University of Delaware Press, 1997), pp. 58–87.

[85] Leo Damrosch, *Jonathan Swift: His Life and His World* (New Haven: Yale University Press, 2013), p. 195.

[86] Simon Varey, Introduction to Henry St John, Lord Bolingbroke, *Contributions to the* Craftsman (Oxford: Oxford University Press, 1982), pp. xxiii–xxvii.

London Journal, had objected years earlier to this 'Manner of Writing' and pointed to *The Craftsman* and *Mist's* as 'notorious Instances'. As Pitt's pseudonym Publicola argued, Caleb D'Anvers, Amhurst's fictional author-editor of *The Craftsman*, had been 'Weekly libelling the Government and Ministry ... for Two Years together'. But little could be done, he concluded, as D'Anvers had 'wisely wrapp'd himself in Fable and Allegory': 'He has applied Scraps of Plays, Farces, Beggars Operas and Songs; ransacked ancient and modern History for Parallels, and then produced 'em without any other Resemblance than that they were Ministers'.[87]

Despite its obscurity, allegory could be good for business. In 1723, one author argued that the '*allegorical* Mode', whether in the '*Historical*' mode of '*drawing Parallels*' or the '*Foreign* Mode' of false news abroad, was the best way to prick up a reader's ears: 'the Ambiguity or *double Entendre* of a Fable raises the Curiosity of every Reader, to discover the secret Sting which it contains, and gratifies his Chagrin with more than ordinary Satisfaction when it is discover'd'.[88] This, moreover, was the goal. For Maureen Quilligan, 'allegory appeals to readers as readers of a system of signs ... [;] its purpose is always to make its reader correspondingly self-conscious'.[89]

In addition, by passing interpretive agency off on readers, authors were also pawning off responsibility. Readers, not writers, *The Craftsman* argued, were the ones apt to make unflattering—and perhaps even false—applications. All this talk of 'calumniating men in high stations under *feigned characters*, and by other indirect methods, such as ironies, allegories, parallels, and remote *innuendoes*'. Hardly could an author be blamed: 'if two Cases happen to be so much alike, that the generality of the world will compare what I relate of *former* Times to the *present*; or any *Great Men* will apply bad Characters to themselves, I do not think my self answerable for such *applications*'.[90] This, simply, was why allegory was so effective: it provoked readers into defining into existence a libel nowhere literally present in the text. As a result, Lennard Davis has argued, surface narratives were used to encode real-world applications as 'a mere tactic or ploy for the concealed message'. In turn, the vehicle becomes 'the alibi for the genuine material it conceals'.[91]

Faux-naïveté was not simply a provoking and yet legally insoluble authorial strategy; it was also a rhetorical device that registered the paradoxical perversity of allegory for its victims. It was difficult, if not impossible, for the purported subject of an unflattering allegory both to identify him- or herself as the intended tenor of a satiric allegory while also simultaneously denying the accuracy of the

---

[87] *London Journal*, no. 477 (21 September 1728).

[88] [Thomas Gordon], *The Art of Railing at Great Men* (London, 1723), pp. 12, 16, 18.

[89] Maureen Quilligan, *The Language of Allegory: Defining the Genre* (Ithaca: Cornell University Press, 1979), p. 24.

[90] *The Craftsman*, no. 31 (24 March 1728).   [91] Davis, *Factual Fictions*, p. 150.

imputations. For satiric victims, allegory always entailed a double gesture of identification and rejection that was tantamount to saying, 'he is supposed to be me, but I am not like him'. For a man to 'construe every Reflection...as a Satyr upon himself', one commentator provokingly remarked, might make one 'imagine that he is conscious of...some secret Guilt'.[92]

This is in part why, despite the supposed transparency of historical parallels, the government found its hands tied. According to one legal commentator,

> The Remarks are laid down in such a plain and ingenuous Manner, that one would imagine they could give no Offence to any one; and as they are Matters of Fact extracted from the best Historians, of Things transacted some Ages ago, how invidious is it in any Man to wrest an Author's meaning, and draw Parallels where none were design'd?[93]

Periodical writers likewise understood that allegory always troubled both lay and legal interpretation (little surprise that the legal-minded D'Anvers was resident in 'Gray's-Inn', as the banner of The Craftsman proudly declared). But journalists also suspected that the authorities were actively manipulating the law in order to enable the courtroom interpretation of allegory.[94] One of the great worries of satirists during this period was that legal innuendoes that established the nature of a libellous imputation or the identity of a victim were undergoing a troubling form of judicial creep—that, through them, the authorities could glom almost any libellous meaning onto any guiltless text. 'These *Innuendoes*', D'Anvers argued, 'have often been made use of, in *Crown Prosecutions*, to fix a *criminal* Meaning upon Words and Expressions, which are either *dubious* or naturally import an *innocent Meaning*'.[95] Others also noticed. As the Tory MP Archibald Hutcheson argued in 1722, 'all the *Senses* clapt upon the *Heathen* Authors by their *Scholiasts*...were not so *wild*, *absurd*, and *arbitrary*, as what the single force of an *Innuendo* can fix upon any *Passage*, when play'd, *secundum artem*, in the Hand of a nice *State-Empirick*'.[96]

The dubiousness of innuendoes was, moreover, an extension of the plasticity of defamation law itself during this period. Philip Hamburger has shown that libel laws had come to serve a radically new purpose as the government's primary means of regulating the press over the first three decades of the eighteenth century.[97] The Craftsman made the entire problem clear in 1726: 'the Misfortune is, that the Nature and several Species of *Libels* are not ascertain'd by any of these

---

[92] *The Doctrine of Innuendo's Discuss'd, Or the Liberty of the Press Maintain'd* (London, 1731), pp. 7–8.
[93] *Doctrine of Innuendo's Discuss'd*, p. 6.   [94] Lund, '"An Alembick of Innuendos"', pp. 252–5.
[95] *The Craftsman*, no. 179 (6 December 1729).
[96] *The Freeholder's Journal*, no. 39 (26 September 1722).
[97] Hamburger, 'Seditious Libel', pp. 725–6.

Laws; but are left to the Judgment and Discretion of the *Courts of Justice*'. Whether it was the interpretation of libel laws or the meaning of a slippery satire, 'No man is safe against the Subtilties and Finesses of *Lawyers* and *State-Chymists*; who can extract Poison out of the most innocent Things, and, by tortured Constructions, apply the Penalties of Statutes, where the Legislators never design'd them'.[98] Even supporters of the administration occasionally worried that the government had grown too liberal in its unscrupulous manipulation of innuendoes. The pro-Walpole *London Journal*, for instance, questioned whether there was any legal basis for reading '*Historical* Parallels' in an allegorical manner at all. Francis Osborne, another of Pitt's letter-writing pseudonyms for the journal, found it all incomprehensible: 'What a Libel is *in* Law, I don't know, nor desire to know'.[99]

In response, periodical writers again and again advocated for courtroom rules that presumed the innocence of journalists. Some even called for the reinstitution of *mitior sensus* more than a decade after its abolishment.[100] That doctrine had held that jurors were to interpret supposedly defamatory language in its lesser sense, but only in instances in which both the worse and the better sense seemed equally tenable.[101] *The British Journal*, for instance, complained in 1722 that government prosecutors were always 'strain[ing] their genuine signification to make [words or texts] intend Sedition'.[102] D'Anvers made the question explicit: 'if his Words, in their first and most obvious Signification, bear an *inoffensive Meaning*, how can any conscientious Man take upon Him to say that he had any *other Meaning*; or resort to a *less natural Construction*, in order to find Him *guilty*?' Simply put, 'if the Words will *equally* bear an *innocent* and a *criminal* Meaning, the most *favourable* is always the most *just*; especially in a Court of Judicature'. To rummage around after unstated meanings was, 'in Effect, to set up a Court of Inquisition over a Man's *Thoughts*, and to punish Him for *criminal Intentions*, which perhaps never enter'd into his Heart'.[103]

The prosecution and persecution of writers for innocuous or, at the very least, prohibitively ambiguous language offered a vivid demonstration of an already

---

[98] *The Craftsman*, no. 2 (9 December 1726), rpt. in Caleb D'Anvers, *The Craftsman* (London, 1731), pp. 11–12.

[99] *London Journal*, no. 582 (26 September 1730); Headnote, *London Journal* (1720), 17th and 18th Century Burney Collection Newspapers.

[100] *Harrison v. Thornborough* (1714), Gilb. Cas. 114, 10 Mod. 196 (Q.B.), 93 Eng. Rep. 277.

[101] See Richard H. Helmholz, *The Oxford History of the Laws of England*, vol. 1: The Canon Law and Ecclesiastical Jurisdiction from 597 to the 1640s (Oxford: Oxford University Press, 2003), p. 577; Knightley D'Anvers, *A General Abridgment of the Common Law*, vol. 1 (London, 1722–1725), p. 140; and William Sheppard, *Action Upon the Case for Slander*, 2nd ed. (London, 1674), p. 20.

[102] *The British Journal*, no. 6 (27 October 1722).

[103] *The Craftsman*, no. 179 (6 December 1729). For more, see Steven N. Zwicker, *The Arts of Disguise: Politics and Language in Dryden's Poetry* (Princeton: Princeton University Press, 1984), pp. 3–34, esp. 6–9.

decades-old scepticism about verbal reference.[104] In the seventeenth century, John Locke had argued that relative signification was endemic to language itself. As he put it, words '*signify* only Men's peculiar *Ideas*, and that *by a perfectly arbitrary Imposition*, is evident, in that they often fail to excite in others (even that use the same Language) the same *Ideas*, we take them to be the Signs of'.[105] *The Craftsman* agreed, later protesting that one must rely on the most 'literal and common Acceptation' of words and phrases as they 'must import to every unprejudiced Understanding'. If not, 'no writer can be safe in Writings of any kind; since the Wit of man has not yet been able to invent Words, that can possibly carry but *One Interpretation*'.[106] According to Roger Lund, the authorities' repeated attacks on the periodical press through the strategic use of innuendoes were seemingly part of a larger effort 'to criminalize satiric indeterminacy' itself.[107]

The Craftsman's hand-wringing over the slipperiness of signification was also, of course, a tacit defence. Parallel history and allegory were the periodical press's preferred vehicles of political criticism precisely for their semantic indeterminacy—the lurking sense that implied analogies, no matter how carefully constructed and scaffolded, always entailed small ruptures of time, place, character, and motive that flummoxed the deliberations of judge and jury alike. In Samuel Johnson's view: 'allegories drawn to great length will always break'.[108] Indeterminacy was thus not an accidental feature of allegorical double-speak, but seemingly intrinsic to and inseparable from its very structure. In their semantic doublings, allegories always seemed to produce the conditions of a deconstructionist aporia: they always conditioned, as Paul de Man has argued and as sceptical early modern readers already knew, sets of seemingly contradictory and incompatible codes and messages—identifications undermined by incommensurate local details, analogies stymied by sequential incompatibilities.[109] How, journalists marvelled, could one ever know for certain that Jonathan Wild was Walpole or that the Lilliputian King was so undoubtedly George I? And how, the authorities wondered, might the courts overcome the legal-interpretive problem that allegories always posed? That was the question, and a solution, almost by accident, was finally found in early 1729.

---

[104] See, for instance, Ronald Paulson, *Breaking and Remaking: Aesthetic Practice in England, 1700-1820* (New Brunswick: Rutgers University Press, 1989), pp. 20-2; and Andrew Benjamin Bricker, 'Fielding after Mandeville: Virtue, Self-Interest, and the Foundation of "Good Nature"', *Eighteenth-Century Fiction* 30, no. 1 (Fall 2017): pp. 79-85.

[105] John Locke, *An Essay concerning Human Understanding*, edited by Peter H. Nidditch (Oxford: Clarendon Press, 1975), p. 408.

[106] *The Craftsman*, no. 228 (14 November 1730).

[107] Lund, '"An Alembick of Innuendos"', pp. 245, 258.

[108] Samuel Johnson, *The Yale Edition of the Works of Samuel Johnson*, vol. 21: *Life of John Dryden*, edited by J. A. V. Chapple (New Haven: Yale University Press, 1958-2019), p. 463.

[109] Paul De Man, *Allegories of Reading: Figural Language in Rousseau, Nietzsche, Rilke, and Proust* (New Haven: Yale University Press, 1979), p. 245.

5.3 'The Generality of Readers': *R. v. Clerk* (1728/9), the 'Persian Letter', and *Mist's Weekly Journal*

Given the procedural problems the Crown faced, it perhaps comes as little surprise that the first decades of the eighteenth century witnessed a boom in political allegory. As one writer remarked in 1723, '*drawing Parallels*' was a '*Mode of Political Scandal* . . . at present very much in vogue'.[110] The abandoned prosecution of Manley for *Atalantis* had already hinted at the legal hurdles that the authorities faced, and opposition periodicals like *The Craftsman* increasingly understood that allegory could be a strategic tool for covert criticism, one whose elusive significations resisted strict courtroom procedures for the identification of satiric victims.

This all came to a head in 1728/9, when the government successfully prosecuted the printer John Clarke for the 'Persian Letter', a Jacobite allegory first published in *Mist's Weekly Journal*. Clarke's trial has received little attention, but the case was pivotal to the government's larger project of turning libel law into an effective mechanism of press regulation. In his ruling on the case, Chief Justice Sir Robert Raymond argued that the interpretation of allegorical libels should rely on an abstract 'generality of readers'.[111] The new rule was valuable, because it obviated the Crown's need to demonstrate the precise verbal mechanism by which the fictional worlds of allegory were necessarily tied to the government actor or institution being defamed—a semantic rather than purely legal problem, as we saw in the first section, that *R. v. Tutchin* had failed to resolve decades earlier. Suddenly, and as a result, allegory—a stunningly common satiric device for issuing coded attacks on the government that had stymied the courts for decades—was useless as a formal legal defence.

Mist's Weekly Journal was perhaps the most important and popular political periodical of the late 1710s and '20s, selling upwards of 8–10,000 copies per issue at its height. Its publisher-editor, Nathaniel Mist, was a fervent Tory and rabid Jacobite who had taken over the periodical from Robert Mawson in December of 1716, when it was still known as the *Weekly Journal, or, Saturday's Post*. As with *The Craftsman*, Mist's writers often relied on allegory and parallel history in their criticisms of the government.[112] Soon it was one of the most outspoken and sought-after journals in London, and Mist, seeking to capitalize on his growing infamy, relaunched the paper as *Mist's Weekly Journal* in May of 1725. Today it is best known for one of its major contributors, Daniel Defoe, who wrote often for Mist between 1717 and 1724, and who was secretly paid by the government to

---

[110] [Gordon], *Art of Railing*, p. 16.

[111] *R. v. Clerk* [sic] (1728/9), 1 Barn. 305 (K.B.), 94 Eng. Rep. 207.

[112] James Sutherland, *The Restoration Newspaper and Its Development* (Cambridge: Cambridge University Press, 1986), pp. 38–40; and Harris, *London Newspapers*, p. 115.

moderate the journal's anti-Whig and anti-Hanoverian tendencies.[113] Despite Defoe's careful (if often unsuccessful) interventions, the journal under Mist continued to rile the authorities. Already, by August of 1718, the government was complaining about the 'numbers of these papers [being] distributed' and believed that the publication did 'more mischief than any other Libel being wrote'.[114] But what was one to do? Arrests always had the troubling repercussion of re-advertising the wares they sought to suppress. As one government agent noted in a memorandum in 1722, 'There never was a Mist or any other Person taken up or tryed but double the number of papers were sold upon it'.[115]

Nonetheless, throughout his run as the journal's editor and lead proprietor, Mist found himself repeatedly arrested, interrogated, fined, pilloried, and imprisoned—at least fourteen times, in fact, during his mere dozen years in London publishing.[116] Those run-ins with the law finally came to a head when *Mist's* published the Persian Letter, a Jacobite allegory of a Persian usurpation. According to the letter writer, Persia had long been governed by the 'old Usurper *Meryweis*' (George I), before being handed over to the bumbling misgovernance of '*Esreff*, the present Usurper' (George II). Apparently, though, Esreff was illegitimate, a fact disclosed by two secret 'Writings' held in the possession of a 'High Priest' and Meryweis's 'Favorite Concubine' (the Duchess of Kendall, George I's former mistress). The 'Chief Scribe' (Walpole), however, had gained access to the writings, and was using the secret to 'purchase [Esreff's/George I's] Friendship'; the Chief Scribe was also being '*screened* by *Esreff's* Authority, from the Cries of the People, who were groaning under the Load of his Depredations' (a further allusion to Walpole, who had been dubbed 'Screenmaster-General' for protecting his allies during the fallout from the South Sea Bubble).[117] The High Priest has kept quiet to save his hide, and the Concubine to save the fortune she had amassed under Meryweis. Esreff, who is all 'Avarice', 'Ambition', and 'Vanity', is a 'Tyrant' who has displaced 'the lawful Sophi' (James Francis Edward Stuart), whose 'Sufferings have added Experience and Patience to those endearing Qualities, in order to compleat the greatest Character that ever Eastern Monarch bore'. Sophi, nonetheless, retains his 'Patience', knowing providence will set the kingdom right.[118]

The details of the allegory were all later laid out in breathtakingly tedious detail in the criminal information and then reiterated in court.[119] And yet this ostensible

---

[113] Paula R. Backscheider, *Daniel Defoe: His Life* (Baltimore: Johns Hopkins University Press, 1989), pp. 430–4.
[114] SP 35/3/31 (1 August 1718), TNA.   [115] SP 35/30/52, TNA.
[116] Pat Rogers, 'Nathaniel Mist, Daniel Defoe, and the Perils of Publishing', *The Library* 10, no. 3 (September 2009): pp. 298–313; and Matthew Thomas Symonds, 'Grub Street Culture: The Newspapers of Nathaniel Mist, 1716–1737' (PhD diss., University College London, 2007), ch. 7.
[117] Christine Gerrard, 'Poems on Politics', in *The Oxford Handbook of British Poetry, 1660–1800*, edited by Jack Lynch (Oxford: Oxford University Press, 2016), p. 297.
[118] *Mist's Weekly Journal*, no. 175 (24 August 1728).   [119] *R. v. Nutt*, TS 11/157, TNA.

letter from abroad also proved a dense and elusive rewriting of present-day politics, clear in its broadest strokes, but still requiring a degree of insider knowledge and some sense of monarchical history. Certain minor characters, for instance, are less than entirely self-evident. The High Priest might have been Edmund Gibson, the Bishop of London, a man colloquially known as Walpole's 'pope', but he might also have been William Wake, the Archbishop of Canterbury, who had found himself politically on the outs since the mid-1710s.[120] Who was Aga, the 'Buffoon' who had been sent abroad by Esreff? What about the Grand Seignior, or his 'Favourite Mufti', whose 'chief View is to prevent a War'? Then there was the rewriting of Jacobite history itself, which muddied any strict correspondence between Persia and England. The 'warming-pan' myth held that James Francis Edward Stuart—the son of James II and his wife, Mary of Modena—was a 'changeling' smuggled into the queen's bedchamber in a warming pan to replace her stillborn child and thus settle on England a Catholic male heir.[121] The Persian Letter, though, wholly reverses the myth: suddenly George II, rather than the Stuart heir, was an illegitimate bastard foisted on George I. Whether or not each and every reader identified every actor and deduced every single parallel is hard to say. But the Crown knew that this remained the precise interpretive problem it would have to face when presenting the allegory to jurors.

In short order, the Persian Letter proved a hot commodity, an outcome Mist had anticipated. As was later revealed in court, almost 11,000 copies of the journal's 24 August 1728 edition had been printed.[122] A month later, the paper was still selling well, with manuscript copies being sold for half a guinea each.[123] Published under the pseudonym Amos Dudge, the Persian Letter was likely the work of Philip, duke of Wharton, a wishy-washy Jacobite and a figure notorious in English politics between the late 1710s and 1720s.[124] Wharton's reputation in part extended from his God-given gift for oratory, which he often exercised to devastating effect in the House of Lords (his speech against the government on 4 February 1721, following his personal loss of £120,000 in the South Sea Bubble, had supposedly caused the death of James, Earl Stanhope). Admittedly, Wharton's infamy was in large measure a product of his sometimes very public private life.

---

[120] Stephen Taylor, '"Dr. Codex" and the Whig "Pope": Edmund Gibson, Bishop of Lincoln and London, 1716–1748', in *Lords of Parliament: Studies, 1714–1914*, edited by R. W. Davis (Stanford: Stanford University Press, 1995), pp. 9–28.

[121] Symonds, 'Grub Street Culture', p. 252; Rachel J. Weil, 'The Politics of Legitimacy: Women and the Warming-Pan Scandal', in *The Revolution of 1688–89: Changing Perspectives*, edited by Lois G. Schwoerer (Cambridge: Cambridge University Press, 1992), ch. 4; and McKeon, *Secret History of Domesticity*, pp. 549–57.

[122] *Monthly Chronicle* (26 February 1729), rpt. *Monthly Chronicle*, vol. 2 ([London,] [1728–1732]), p. 29.

[123] Wharton to Stuart (18 September 1728), Stuart Papers, 120/85, Royal Archives, Windsor Castle.

[124] Many of the succeeding biographical details are drawn from Lawrence B. Smith, 'Wharton, Philip James, duke of Wharton and Jacobite duke of Northumberland (1698–1731)', *ODNB*.

He was perhaps best known as the founder and chairman on the Hellfire Club, a mixed-sex secret society that supposedly delighted in satanic rituals, parodies of established religion, and general licentiousness. So famous was he for rakish villainy that Samuel Richardson, who had earlier printed Wharton's anti-Walpole journal the *True Briton* (1723–24), ostensibly modelled *Clarissa*'s aristocratic rapist Lovelace after him.[125]

Nonetheless, by the time of the Persian Letter, Wharton had firmly established his bona fides as a provoking if sometimes half-hearted Jacobite.[126] In 1723 he had defended the Jacobite conspirator Francis Atterbury, the Bishop of Rochester, who had hastily colluded with the Pretender's agents in the fall of 1721 for an armed landing in England, and even accompanied Atterbury on the ship that carried him into exile.[127] He likewise closely aligned himself throughout the mid-1720s with Charles Boyle, fourth earl of Orrery, the face of English Jacobitism after Atterbury's banishment. Having finally accepted the role of Stuart plenipotentiary to the imperial court at Vienna, Wharton foolishly drank the Pretender's health before departing—an exemplary blunder, perhaps, by a man whom Alexander Pope deemed 'Too quick for Thought'.[128] It hardly helped that Wharton had suspiciously converted to Roman Catholicism to marry the Spanish maid of honour Maria Theresa O'Neill O'Beirne, before joining other Jacobite exiles in the Spanish army against the British in a siege of Gibraltar in 1727.

The Persian Letter was not Wharton's first missive for Mist. In 1728, Walpole even offered Wharton a complete pardon, the preservation of all of his estates, and the retention of all of his titles if he would simply stop attacking his administration publicly.[129] Looking at the Persian Letter, it is easy to understand Walpole's apprehension. The letter not only exploited the interpretive weaknesses of libel law; it also cleverly balanced the literal and literary. On one level, the letter seems merely to allude to the actual situation in Persia, part of a bewildering era of dynastic turnover in the Middle East during the 1720s that fascinated segments of the London press and which *Mist's* had been suggestively reporting on since 1722.[130]

---

[125] Tom Keymer, *Richardson's* Clarissa *and the Eighteenth-Century Reader* (Cambridge: Cambridge University Press, 1992), pp. 160–2.

[126] Eveline Cruickshanks, 'Lord Cowper, Lord Orrery, the Duke of Wharton, and Jacobitism', *Albion* 26, no. 1 (Spring 1994): pp. 27–40.

[127] D. W. Hayton, 'Atterbury, Francis (1663–1732)', *ODNB*.

[128] Pope, *Moral Essays: Epistle I. To Sir Richard Temple, Viscount Cobham* (1734), in *The Poems of Alexander Pope*, edited by John Butt (New Haven: Yale University Press, 1963), l. 201.

[129] Smith, 'Wharton', *ODNB*.

[130] See, for instance, Sir John Chardin, *A New and Accurate Description of Persia*, 2 vol. (London, 1724); Thomas Salmon, *Modern History: Or, The Present State of All Nations* (London, 1726), pp. 375–84; and Judas Thaddeus Krusinski, *The History of the Late Revolutions of Persia*, 2 vol. (London 1728). For more, see Ros Ballaster, *Fabulous Orients: Fictions of the East in England, 1662–1785* (Oxford: Oxford University Press, 2005), ch. 3, esp. p. 79; and Parvin Loloi, 'The Image of the Safavids in English and French Literature (1500–1800)', in *Iran and the World in the Safavid Age*, edited by Willem Floor and Edmund Herzig (London: I. B. Taurus, 2012), pp. 347–55. For Mist's semi-allegorical reporting on Persia, see Symonds, 'Grub Street Culture', pp. 262–73, and entries for *The*

The Safavid Dynasty, which had controlled Persia since the early sixteenth century, had finally been ousted in 1722, when Pashtun rebels besieged the city of Isfahan (in present-day Iran) and defeated Sultan Husayn, before the Safavids were temporarily restored in late 1729 by Nader Shah Afshar. Persian politics only added a troubling layer of contemporary reality to the letter's allegorical rewriting of a half-century of British monarchical and parliamentary history. Persia in the 1720s—part of a moment that one historian has called 'the blackest period in the whole history of Islamic Iran'—simply had too many queasily familiar parallels to an England now ruled by a recently ascendant German king.[131]

At the same time, beyond this literal layer of deposed Persian dynasties lay the letter's most direct allegorical-satirical forebear. Just years earlier, Charles de Secondat, Baron de Montesquieu's *Persian Letters* (1721) had proven a bestseller in both England and France.[132] On its surface, Montesquieu's *Persian Letters* was nothing more than the correspondence of Usbek and Rica, two Persian noblemen travelling through France. But at moments, this rambling tale, for all of its topical and tonal disjointedness, offered an outsider's cutting glimpse into the regency of Philippe d'Orléans between 1715 and 1723 following the death of Louis XIV. In writing ostensibly about Persia, Wharton had found a ready-made analogue for the politics of contemporary England: a literal history of the present that not only alluded to a range of domestic monarchical and parliamentary intrigues, but also carried with it the suggestion of a pointed satirical intertext.

Despite its literal source and literary allusions, however, few baulked at reading the Persian Letter as a coded Jacobite attack on Walpole and George II. As one writer for the pro-ministry *London Journal* scoffed, the letter was nothing more than 'High Treason among the People against their King and Country...under the Notion of a *Persian Story*'.[133] The authorities responded swiftly. According to the government, the letter had both undermined the administration and tacitly questioned the legitimacy of the newly ascended George II by raising doubts about the parentage of the king himself, the last of the German-born monarchs of Great Britain.[134] Correspondence between the Secretary of State and Solicitor General also reveals that the government was seeking not merely a conviction for seditious libel, but also perhaps a charge of treason and capital punishment, one that would build upon the earlier prosecution and execution of the printer John Matthews for

Weekly Journal, or, Saturday's Post (before its renaming as *Mist's*), no. 168 (17 February 1722), no. 186 (23 June 1722), no. 188 (7 July 1722), no. 191 (28 July 1722), no. 212 (17 November 1722), and no. 270 (28 December 1723).
[131] Qtd. John Foran, 'The Long Fall of the Safavid Dynasty: Moving beyond the Standard Views', *International Journal of Middle East Studies* 24, no. 2 (May 1992): p. 281.
[132] Charles de Secondat, baron de Montesquieu, *Persian Letters* (1721), 2 vol., trans. John Ozell (London, 1722).
[133] *London Journal*, no. 477 (21 September 1728).
[134] Varey, 'Growth of Capitalism', pp. 250–1.

Vox Dei, Vox Populi in 1719.[135] The king too was pushing for those responsible to be 'punisht with the utmost Severity of Law'.[136]

Nonetheless, the authorities had very little they could directly do to either the letter's author or the journal's editor-proprietor. Wharton was already exiled abroad and, shortly after the letter's publication, Mist went into hiding. With its hands largely tied, the government decided to hamper the journal's operations, a strategy that ultimately proved disastrous for Mist. Following the letter's appearance on 24 August, some twenty pressmen, printers, hawkers, and booksellers tied to *Mist's* were arrested. Nonetheless, a few weeks later, Mist managed to have published a joint issue of the journal, for 7 and 14 September, which led to further arrests and Grand Jury Indictments in Middlesex, Westminster, and Bristol.[137] Throughout, the authorities continued to dismantle Mist's operation. They quite literally destroyed his press during another round of arrests in September.[138] In harassing every last stationer with any tie to him, the government hoped to send a message. As the Attorney General, Sir Philip Yorke (later first earl of Hardwicke), argued in a letter to Thomas Pelham-Holles, the duke of Newcastle, even in the absence of a prosecution, the Grand Jury indictment of Edward Farley, *Mist's* Bristol printer, for treason should have been enough to instil a 'fear' of similar consequences for other stationers.[139] (That his prosecution came to nothing was little consolation to Farley, who died in prison while awaiting trial.)[140] One more issue of *Mist's* appeared on 21 September, but soon thereafter Mist fled to France and the short-lived protection of Wharton. Starting on 28 September, *Mist's Weekly Journal*—perhaps the most popular periodical in all of Great Britain— ceased to exist and was renamed *Fog's Weekly Journal*. Though Mist continued to run the journal from France with the assistance of his friends, he had difficulty steering its content towards anti-Hanoverian outrage from abroad. In the decade that followed, Mist remained exiled in France, from where he continued to advocate for Jacobite causes.[141] In May of 1737, he severed his final ties with *Fog's*, and died a few months later, on 20 September 1737, in Boulogne.

With Mist on the run in 1728, however, the government had little choice but to go ahead with a series of prosecutions against the stationers tied to the journal. At least eight had criminal informations presented against them, four of whom were eventually prosecuted for and found guilty of seditious libel.[142] None of these

---

[135] SP 36/151/56–58, TNA. Paul Kléber Monod, *Jacobitism and the English People, 1688–1788* (Cambridge: Cambridge University Press, 1989), pp. 39–40.

[136] SP 36/8/75, TNA.

[137] *The Trial of Mr. Richard Francklin* (1731), rpt. 17 *State Trials* 666–7n.

[138] Paul Chapman, 'Mist, Nathaniel (d. 1737)', *ODNB*.   [139] SP 36/13/69, TNA.

[140] Hannah Barker, *Newspapers and English Society, 1695–1855* (2000) (London: Routledge, 2014), p. 72.

[141] Stuart Papers, 119/42, Royal Archives, Windsor Castle.

[142] *Monthly Chronicle* (28 November 1728), rpt. *Monthly Chronicle*, vol. 1, p. 247; and *Monthly Chronicle* (25 February 1729), rpt. *Monthly Chronicle*, vol. 2, p. 33.

trials, however, proved quite as useful to the Crown in the long term as the ruling in the prosecution against John Clarke, a minor printer for Mist, about whom we know very little today beyond the fact that his name was Clarke, not Clerk, as he came to be known in the decision on the case.[143] In Clarke's case, the Crown knew that it was facing the old procedural conundrum always posed by allegory. How was one to demonstrate legally that this supposedly innocent letter from abroad was actually teeming with 'odious Parallels'?[144] It is worth keeping in mind that the letter had been naïvely printed in *Mist's* as nothing more than 'a perfect Relation of the Present State of Affairs in *Persia*' (an example, perhaps, of the manner in which 'significant *Italick* Characters' could be used, even with proper nouns, to signal satiric or pregnant content).[145] In their correspondence on the Persian Letter, Attorney General Yorke and Solicitor General Charles Talbot clearly recognized that 'the whole paper is Allegorical' and understood that their central task was to convince 'a Jury that the name *Sophi*', for example, 'was intended by the persons concern'd in printing to signify the Pretender [,]...a term never used for him before'.[146] The central issue, then, was how to demonstrate to *whom* the libel actually referred. Nonetheless, the Crown remained confident that at trial it would be able to prove that 'several of the Royal Family' had been 'scandalously traduced under borrowed names'.[147]

Clarke's trial took place on 25 February 1728/9 at King's Bench. He was defended by William Hawkins, a serjeant-at-law who knew well the procedural limits of the law. As he wrote in 1716, 'I have heard it agreed in the Court of King's Bench' that 'no Writing whatsoever is to be esteemed a Libel, unless it reflect upon some particular Person'.[148] In court, Hawkins raised this exact issue, arguing that the Persian Letter could not be construed as a reflection on either Walpole or George II. His reasoning for this conclusion, however, gave the Crown precisely the means by which the Attorney General was able to demonstrate the tenor of the allegory. As Hawkins argued, there was simply a disparity between those supposedly depicted in the letter and their reputations in real life. For instance, the letter's representations, even if allegorical—and he was not yet willing to grant that point—were wholly negative: 'the characters that are here drawn, are by no means agreeable to the persons supposed to be represented' and that 'anything related to

---

[143] See, for instance, *An Account of Persons Held to Bail to Answer in the Court of King's Bench for Libels, From 1 Anne to 57 Geo. 3 both inclusive*, edited by E. H. Lushington (3 March 1818), p. 10, entry 74, KB 33/24/2, TNA.

[144] *Monthly Chronicle* (25 February 1729), rpt. *Monthly Chronicle*, vol. 2, p. 32.

[145] [Gordon], *Art of Railing*, p. 16. On the tonal function of italics, see my discussion in ch. 3; see also Joseph Moxon, *Mechanick Exercises on the Whole Art of Printing (1683–4)*, edited by Herbert Davis and Harry Carter, 2nd ed. (Oxford: Oxford University Press, 1962), p. 216; John Smith, *The Printer's Grammar* (London, 1755), p. 14; James McLaverty, 'Italics in Swift's Poems', *Swift Studies* 28 (2011): pp. 22–37; and Simon Dickie, *Cruelty & Laughter: Forgotten Comic Literature and the Unsentimental Eighteenth Century* (Chicago: University of Chicago Press, 2011), pp. xii, 191, 238.

[146] SP 36/151/56–57, TNA.   [147] *R. v. Clerk* [sic] (1728/9), 1 Barn. 304 (K.B.), 94 Eng. Rep. 207.

[148] Hawkins, *A Treatise of the Pleas of the Crown*, vol. 2 (London, 1716–1721), p. 195.

them [is] entirely opposite to what each are known to deserve'.[149] In short, he was asking, how could honest, upstanding Walpole ever be equated with the crafty High Scribe, who was shielding an illegitimate monarch, whom the Crown, incredibly, claimed to be the wholly lawful King George II?

On its surface, this was a familiar argument. Hawkins was pushing the Crown not simply to decode the allegory—to state that George II was Esreff—but also to demonstrate *how* the text corresponded with a public perception of George II as an illegitimate tyrant. But in so doing, Hawkins was also returning to a defence that had failed more than twenty years earlier, claiming, in effect, that irony itself prohibited jurors from reading ostensibly innocent constructions in a defamatory manner. This was all the more surprising because Hawkins knew the ruling in *R. v. Browne* and had argued years earlier that something composed in an 'ironical Manner' was 'properly a Libel'. Moreover, as he himself had written, the intended meaning of a verbally ironic satire could be accessed through ironic reversals, such as praising a man for his 'Learning, who is known to be a great General, but no Scholar'. This, the courts had earlier held, was as clearly defamatory 'as if [the writer] had directly and expresly' written out the libel.[150]

By suggesting the possibility of ironic inversion in the Persian Letter, however, Hawkins had also seemingly provided the Crown with a way to explain the mechanism by which a reader could access even the most fleeting of tenors. Chief Justice Raymond picked up immediately on Hawkins' claim about the uninterpretability of ironic reversals and rejected it, citing the earlier ruling in *R. v. Browne*. This is why we might think of Hawkins' foray as an argumentative misstep. While denying the justness of representing George II, for instance, as a hapless Persian tyrant, he was also pointing directly to the form of ironic inversion that had permitted the conviction of Browne—a kind of distorted satiric mirroring, in which one's virtues were one's vices. Hawkins was revealing, that is, how one could arrive at a libellous reading of the allegory: there was not a *direct* allegorical correspondence between the satiric representation and the real-world victim; there was, instead, an *inverse* correspondence between the two. We know the tyrannical Esreff is George II not because George II is tyrannical, but precisely because he is *not*.

Hawkins' own explanation thus opened the door for the Attorney General to pursue a new argument, at least as it pertained to allegory, but one that likewise drew on the sociocentric interpretation of verbal irony expounded earlier in *R. v. Browne*. As Attorney General Yorke argued,

it lies upon the counsel for the King only to shew, that this construction, which they've put upon the paper, is such, as the generality of readers must take it in

---

[149] *R. v. Clerk* [sic] (1728/9), 1 Barn. 305 (K.B.), 94 Eng. Rep. 207.
[150] Hawkins, *A Treatise of the Pleas of the Crown*, vol. 1, p. 194.

according to the obvious and natural sense of it; and if upon the hearing of the paper read the jury are of that opinion, they are bound in their consciences to find the defendant guilty.[151]

The Crown, that is, was only obliged to assert the allegorical meaning of the text, based on a theoretical community of idealized readers. The jury, in turn, only had to agree that the hypothetical 'generality of readers' would, indeed, read this allegory in this manner. Chief Justice Raymond also 'agreed the law should be so', and again explicitly pointed to *R. v. Browne*.[152] Moreover, not only was allegory equally libellous, Raymond argued, but 'the Crime was even greater for making the Parallel'.[153] Clarke was convicted and, on 19 May 1729, ordered to stand in the pillory in three locations across London—the Royal Exchange, Temple Bar, and Charing Cross—before performing six months of hard labour at Bridewell.[154] After his sentence, Clarke returned to printing and his bookshop at the Bible in the Royal Exchange, just a stone's throw from where he had been pilloried years earlier; there he perhaps predictably sold 'all Sorts of Statutes and Common Law Books'.[155]

Of the many arrests, interrogations, and trials stemming from the Persian Letter, none proved as useful to the Crown as *R. v. Clerk*, which built on Chief Justice Holt's 'reasonable' standards for interpreting ambiguous language from decades earlier. In that case, the prosecution was not required to demonstrate the precise linguistic mechanism by which a superficially innocent locution also carried a defamatory intended meaning. Instead, the Crown only had to claim that the average group of readers or 'bystanders' would understand a given locution according to its most common meaning or its 'vulgar intendment'.[156] The decision in *R. v. Clerk* likewise built on Holt's reasonable standard, by suggesting that the interpretation of allegory should rely on an abstract 'generality of readers'—on how a juror believed *most* people would have understood a phrase, rather than merely the way in which an individual juror did.[157] In so doing, the ruling permitted the Crown to skirt the technical linguistic issue: how one was to demonstrate the intended meaning of a supposedly allegorical statement in the absence of internal textual evidence. Such a rule in practise meant that the Crown could defer to the jury in the abstract while effectively displacing the capricious interpretations of actual jurors in court. In this sense, the decision in *R. v. Clerk* also belongs to an important series of eighteenth-century rulings that sought to

[151] *R. v. Clerk* [sic] (1728/9), 1 Barn. 304–305 (K.B.), 94 Eng. Rep. 207.
[152] *R. v. Clerk* [sic] (1728/9), 1 Barn. 304–305 (K.B.), 94 Eng. Rep. 207.
[153] *Monthly Chronicle* (25 February 1729), rpt. *Monthly Chronicle*, vol. 2, p. 33.
[154] *Monthly Chronicle* (19 May 1729), rpt. *Monthly Chronicle*, vol. 2, p. 106.
[155] *Books printed for, and sold by John Clarke at the Bible under the Royal-Exchange Cornhill, London* ([London?], [1734?]), p. 3.
[156] *Somers v. House* (1694), Holt 39 (K.B.), 90 Eng. Rep. 919.
[157] *R. v. Clerk* [sic] (1728/9), 1 Barn. 305 (K.B.), 94 Eng. Rep. 207.

neutralize jurors, who often had tremendous discretion in trials for libel and who often happily fought the directions of the bench, especially in trials for seditious libel.[158] The Crown could not simply stop jurors, but it could control the heuristic of their interpretation.

The ruling in *R. v. Clerk* has, nonetheless, received scant attention. Of the many trials that resulted from the Persian Letter, most scholars have pointed to Raymond's decision in *R. v. Knell* (1729) that one can be found guilty of printing a libel, even if evidence of publication cannot be proven.[159] But the decision in Clarke's case was a major advancement in the government's ongoing efforts to develop courtroom procedures for fixing verbal ambiguity in politically sensitive publications. Eventually, this notion of the 'generality of readers' became the commonly accepted doctrine.[160] As one legal commentator noted just two years later, allegory and verbal ambiguity more generally no longer offered any camouflage: 'whether it be done directly or obliquely, whether by Hint or Surmize, Allegory or Riddle, open Invective or ironical Reproach, the Person so doing, assisting, or publishing, is guilty of a Libel, and punishable as a Libeller'.[161] Finally, the government had solved the problem of '*libellous Parallels*'.[162]

With Mist out of the way, or at least pacified in France, his journal effectively under new editorship, and the hurdle of prosecuting works of allegory cleared, the Walpole administration turned its efforts back to *The Craftsman* and its printer-publisher, Richard Francklin.[163] The Crown was especially interested in a series of allegorical essays in *The Craftsman* entitled 'Remarks on the History of England', authored by Bolingbroke under the pseudonym of Humphrey Oldcastle.[164] Though the Crown's 1728 prosecution of Francklin for seditious libel had failed thanks in large measure to a recalcitrant Tory jury, new juror legislation passed in 1730 permitted a special jury of Whigs to be impanelled in 1731 to prosecute Francklin again—this time successfully for a fictitious 'private Letter from the Hague' concerning the Treaty of Seville.[165] In his final statement to the jury in Francklin's case, Attorney General Yorke pointed to the decision in Clarke's case, noting that 'fictitious names' should be 'plainly . . . understood as if their names were particularly mentioned'. The law, Yorke argued, was clear: for judges and jurors alike, allegorical names should be 'understood . . . as every common reader would'.[166] Francklin's conviction, moreover, had the intended effect: after his

---

[158] Beattie, *Crime*, 400–49; and Baker, *ELH*, pp. 143–4, 151; and Green, *Verdict*, chs. 7 and 8, esp. pp. 249, 329.

[159] *R. v. Knell* (1729), 1 Barn. 305–6 (K.B.), 94 Eng. Rep. 207–8. For later citations, see *Baldwin v. Elphinston* (1775), 2 Black. W. 1038 (Ex.Ch.), 96 Eng. Rep. 610; and *R. v. Burdett* (1820), 3 B & Ald. 727–9, 750–2 (K.B.), 106 Eng. Rep. 827, 835.

[160] Hanson, *Government*, p. 24.   [161] *State Law*, p. 57.

[162] *The Craftsman*, no. 140 (8 March 1728/9).

[163] Lund, '"An Alembick of Innuendos"', p. 258.   [164] Pettit, *Illusory Consensus*, p. 60.

[165] *The Craftsman*, no. 235 (2 January 1730); *An Act for the better Regulation of Juries*, 3 Geo. 2, ch. 25 (1730); and Hamburger, 'Seditious Libel', p. 760n312.

[166] *The Trial of Mr. Richard Francklin* (1731), rpt. 17 *State Trials* 666–8.

sentencing, the once-audacious stationer went more or less underground, publishing almost exclusively apolitical works between 1732 and 1739.[167] With Mist exiled in France and Francklin subdued, the Walpole administration had managed to silence two of its most vocal critics of the 1710s and '20s.

Nonetheless, the Crown was strategic in how it wielded its power. Alexander Pettit has marvelled at the Walpole administration's reluctance during the later 1730s to prosecute those who spoke out against the government.[168] This reluctance, however, was central to the Walpole administration's revised approach to the press.[169] In short, the government had become increasingly aware of the counterproductiveness of pursuing every last anti-ministerial squib.[170] For instance, Charles Delafaye, who helped manage press policy between 1717 and 1734 as an undersecretary to the Secretary of State, found himself increasingly uncertain about the efficacy of directly prosecuting stationers. He somewhat sheepishly conceded in 1732 that 'We can not govern authors and printers'.[171] For Jeremy Black, Delafaye's retirement in 1734 'symbolised a shift in the ministerial attitude to the regulation of the press'.[172] Then there was the issue of promotion. Legal attention, simply put, always led to increased sales.[173]

Moreover, prosecutions were only one branch of a regulatory regime that found ad hoc and selective attacks on the press, including arrests and strategic indictments, more effective than wholesale persecution in promoting a greater degree of self-censorship.[174] As one grand jury put it in 1731, such forms of 'Exemplary Punishment [of] All the Authors, Actors Printers and Publishers' served as 'a Terror to All Offenders of the like kind for the future'.[175] Such restraint was also part of a larger public relations campaign. As Walpole proudly remarked, 'No Government, I will venture to say, ever punished so few Libels, and no Government ever had Provocation to punish so many'.[176]

---

[167] Caudle, 'Richard Francklin', pp. 390–1, table 18.1.   [168] Pettit, *Illusory Consensus*, p. 62.

[169] Ian Higgins, *Swift's Politics: A Study in Disaffection* (Cambridge: Cambridge University Press, 1994), pp. 160–5.

[170] Michael Harris, *London Newspapers in the Age of Walpole: A Study of the Origins of the Modern English Press* (Rutherford: Fairleigh Dickinson University Press, 1987), p. 147.

[171] Charles Delafaye to James, first Earl Waldegrave (31 March 1732), Papers of James, first Earl Waldegrave, Chewton House, Chewton Mendip, UK, qtd. Black, *Press*, p. 115.

[172] Black, *Press*, p. 116. On Delafaye, see J. C. Sainty, 'Delafaye, Charles (1677–1762)', *ODNB*; and Michael Harris, 'Newspaper Distribution during Queen Anne's Reign: Charles Delafaye and the Secretary of State's Office', in *Studies in the Book Trade: In Honour of Graham Pollard*, edited by R. W. Hunt, I. G. Philip, and R. J. Roberts (Oxford: Oxford Bibliographical Society, 1975), pp. 139–51.

[173] On the shifting dynamics of prosecution, authorial celebrity, and sales, see Keymer, *Poetics*, pp. 159–65.

[174] Siebert, *Freedom*, p. 380; Hellmuth, 'Liberty of the Press', p. 160; Douglas Hay, 'Property, Authority and the Criminal Law', in *Albion's Fatal Tree: Crime and Society in Eighteenth-Century England*, rev. ed., edited by Douglas Hay et al. (New York: Verso, 2011), p. 49; and Philip Harling 'The Law of Libel and the Limits of Repression, 1790–1832', *Historical Journal* 44, no. 1 (March 2001): p. 120.

[175] KB 33/5/6, TNA.

[176] *The History and Proceedings of the House of Commons from the Restoration to the Present Times*, vol. 10 (London, 1742), p. 287.

Sometimes, even, venomous libels could be turned to profitable use, as we will see in the next chapter. Walpole was eager to institute pre-performance theatrical censorship against the raucous dramatic satires of the 1720s and '30s and seemingly bribed Henry Giffard, the theatre manager and co-owner of the Theatre in Goodman's Fields, to stage a now-lost dramatic version of 'The Vision of the Golden Rump', a two-part allegorical satire of George II that had appeared in the journal *Common Sense* in March of 1737.[177] Walpole then circulated extracts of the play to other MPs, read portions to the king, and recited lines during parliamentary debate in May. His crafty manipulation of the entire event led to the almost wholly unopposed passage of the Theatrical Licensing Bill, and then Act (10 Geo. 2, c. 28), in late May and June of 1737. The act itself would remain in effect for more than two hundred years.[178] No doubt the authorities could have initiated a successful prosecution for seditious libel against *Common Sense*, but Walpole had the cunning foresight to see that this same allegory could be leveraged in service of even greater regulatory control. In any case, the Walpole administration hardly gave up on prosecutions for seditious libel. It brought another against *The Craftsman* in 1737—this time, in a tart paradox, for its satirization of the Stage Licensing Act—and again in 1739.[179]

What needs to be kept in mind is that the authorities, through the courts, had slowly but surely devised new courtroom procedures for the prosecution of verbally ambiguous satires. Following the lapse of licensing, the courts had repeatedly ruled in favour of the Crown and complainants against rabble-rousing writers and their recalcitrant stationers, often targeting the verbal and bibliographical evasions that had come to typify the writing and circulation of satiric texts. Through this series of rulings, the courts had developed new doctrines of interpretation that mitigated the unpredictability of juror deliberations. These doctrines proved immensely effective in redressing the evasive language of eighteenth-century satire. As David Hume first remarked in 1741, 'The general laws against sedition and libelling are at present as strong as they possibly can be made'.[180]

This emphasis on the verbal qualities of satire, however, also had an unintended effect. Since the early seventeenth century, the courts had claimed that not only words but also images could be defamatory.[181] But the extensive use of verbal evasions among satirists meant that the courts had consequently focused the

---

[177] Vincent J. Liesenfeld, *The Licensing Act of 1737* (Madison: University of Wisconsin Press, 1984), pp. 92, 129–37. See *Common Sense: Or, The Englishman's Journal* nos. 7 and 8 (19 and 26 March 1737).

[178] David Thomas (ed.), *Theatre in Europe: A Documentary History: Restoration and Georgian England, 1660–1788* (Cambridge: Cambridge University Press, 1989), pp. 211–14.

[179] Simon Varey, 'Printers as Rivals: The Craftsman, 1739–40', *The Library*, sixth series, 2, no. 2 (June 1980): pp. 220–2.

[180] David Hume, 'Essay of the Liberty of the Press', in *Essays, Moral and Political*, edited by Eugene F. Miller, rev. ed. (Indianapolis: Liberty Fund, 1987), p. 605.

[181] *Case de Libellis Famosis* (1605), 5 Coke 125 (K.B.), 77 Eng. Rep. 250.

majority of their efforts on devising mechanisms for delimiting the linguistic components of defamatory imputations; in comparison, procedures for interpreting the meaning of images remained woefully underdeveloped. This was a problem that neither the authorities nor the courts could have anticipated in the media ecology of the early eighteenth century. As I go on to argue in my next and final chapter, however, the rise of satirical caricature in the mid-eighteenth century changed all of that. Caricature simply threw into disarray all the careful ordering that the courts had incrementally and conscientiously put into place.

6

Keeping Out of Court III

Caricature, Mimicry, and the Deverbalization of Satire

Throughout *Libel and Lampoon* I have focused on a back and forth between literature and the law. Between the late seventeenth and early eighteenth centuries, satirists and their stationers developed and expanded a host of verbal and bibliographical evasions that early on created procedural problems for plaintiffs and the authorities, who had increasingly turned to the courts to regulate the press. Such legal efforts led to a range of innovations, including the development of novel prosecutorial strategies and the employment of extrajudicial forms of harassment. During this same period, the bench repeatedly expanded courtroom procedures for the interpretation of verbal ambiguity while also increasing the liability of stationers.

In this final chapter, I bring together these legal and satiric developments to address a paradox that has long vexed literary historians. For more than two centuries, scholars have claimed that satire entered terminal decline in the mid-eighteenth century. Literary historians of the eighteenth and nineteenth centuries tended to explain this fall from grace biographically. The story went that the literary field had simply dried up following the deaths of such major satirists as Alexander Pope and Jonathan Swift.[1] Over the last half of the twentieth century, such theories were largely displaced by more socio-historical explanations. Following Stuart M. Tave, scholars began to argue that satire became gentler over the course of the century, contending that the rise of sentimentality had rendered the at times aggressive and venomous energies of earlier eighteenth-century satire passé.[2] Others expanded on this thesis, suggesting that satire was

---

[1] See Horace Walpole to Horace Mann (21 March 1746), *Yale Edition of the Correspondence of Horace Walpole*, edited by W. S. Lewis, et al., vol. 19 (New Haven: Yale University Press, 1937–83), p. 229; and William Cowper, 'Table Talk', in *The Poems by William Cowper*, edited by John D. Baird and Charles Ryskamp, vol. 1: 1748–1782 (Oxford: Clarendon Press, 1980–95), p. 260, l. 728.

[2] Stuart M. Tave, *The Amiable Humorist: A Study in the Comic and Theory and Criticism of the Eighteenth and Early Nineteenth Centuries* (Chicago: University of Chicago Press, 1960), p. viii.; Eric Rothstein, *Restoration and Eighteenth-Century Poetry, 1660–1780* (Boston: Routledge & Kegan Paul, 1981), p. 125; P. K. Elkin, *The Augustan Defense of Satire* (Oxford: Clarendon Press, 1973), p. 64; William Dowling, *The Epistolary Moment: The Poetics of the Eighteenth-Century Verse Epistle* (Princeton: Princeton University Press, 1991), pp. 105–6; Jennifer Keith, '"Pre-Romanticism" and

Libel and Lampoon: Satire in the Courts, 1670–1792. Andrew Benjamin Bricker, Oxford University Press.
© Andrew Benjamin Bricker 2022. DOI: 10.1093/oso/9780192846150.003.0007

domesticated by and absorbed into the novel.[3] In recent years, however, even these accounts have come under pressure, as social and literary historians have begun to question the influence of the cult of sensibility.[4] At the same time, scholars studying the last half of the eighteenth century and the Romantic era have amply demonstrated that the supposed death of satire has for more than two hundred years been grossly overstated.[5]

Nonetheless, integral elements of this story of literary decline have remained intact: satire does not die after mid-century—it continues to be written and published—but it is massively diminished in social, political, and literary importance during the last half of the century and is most frequently practised by lesser writers and only occasionally by the period's most important figures.[6] In addition, as the novel grows over the last half of the century, in the overall number of both titles and pages published, satire comes to constitute a smaller and smaller portion of the print marketplace.[7] The old story, with some important modifications,

---

the Ends of Eighteenth-Century Poetry', in *The Cambridge Companion to Eighteenth-Century Poetry*, edited by John Sitter (Cambridge: Cambridge University Press, 2001), p. 286; Brean Hammond, 'Verse Satire', in *A Companion to Eighteenth-Century Poetry*, edited by Christine Gerrard (Malden: Blackwell, 2006), ch. 27; and Marshall, *Satire*, p. 239. For an early account of sentiment's effect on satire, see Andrew M. Wilkinson, 'The Decline of English Verse Satire in the Middle Years of the Eighteenth Century', *Review of English Studies* 3, no. 11 (1952): pp. 222–3.

[3] Ronald Paulson, *Satire and the Novel in Eighteenth-Century England* (New Haven: Yale University Press, 1967), pp. 237–45; Joseph F. Bartolomeo, 'Restoration and Eighteenth-century Satiric Fiction', in *A Companion to Satire: Ancient and Modern*, edited by Ruben Quintero (Malden: Blackwell, 2007), ch. 14; and Frank Palmeri, *Satire, History, Novel: Narrative Forms, 1665–1815* (Newark: University of Delaware Press, 2003), pp. 14–15.

[4] Simon Dickie, *Cruelty and Laughter: Forgotten Comic Literature and the Unsentimental Eighteenth Century* (Chicago: University of Chicago Press, 2011) and 'Deformity Poems and Other Nasties', *Eighteenth-Century Life* 41, no. 1 (2017): pp. 197–230; Vic Gatrell, *City of Laughter: Sex and Satire in Eighteenth-Century London* (New York: Walker & Co., 2007), pp. 172–6; and David Fairer, *English Poetry of the Eighteenth Century* (London: Longman, 2003), pp. 2–3.

[5] Thomas Lockwood, *Post-Augustan Satire: Charles Churchill and Satirical Poetry, 1750–1800* (Seattle: University of Washington Press, 1979); Marcus Wood, *Radical Satire and Print Culture, 1790–1822* (Oxford: Clarendon Press, 1994); Gary Dyer, *British Satire and the Politics of Style, 1789–1832* (Cambridge: Cambridge University Press, 1997); Steven Jones, *Shelley's Satire: Violence, Exhortation, and Authority* (DeKalb: Northern Illinois University Press, 1994) and *Satire and Romanticism* (London: Macmillan Press, 2000); and John Strachan, *Advertising and Satirical Culture in the Romantic Period* (Cambridge: Cambridge University Press, 2007).

[6] Lockwood, *Post-Augustan Satire*, p. 4; Lance Bertelsen, *The Nonsense Club: Literature and Popular Culture, 1749–1764* (Oxford: Clarendon Press, 1986), p. 5; Claude Rawson, *Satire and Sentiment, 1660–1830: Stress Points in the English Augustan Tradition*, rev. ed. (New Haven: Yale University Press, 2000), p. x; James Engell, 'Satiric Spirits of the Later Eighteenth Century: Johnson to Crabbe', in *A Companion to Satire: Ancient and Modern*, edited by Ruben Quintero (Malden: Blackwell, 2007), p. 235; John Sitter, *The Cambridge Introduction to Eighteenth-Century Poetry* (Cambridge: Cambridge University Press, 2011), p. 109; and Marshall, *Satire*, pp. 286–8.

[7] See Michael F. Suarez, S. J., 'Towards a Bibliometric Analysis of the Surviving Record, 1701–1800', in *The Cambridge History of the Book in Britain*, vol. 5: 1695–1830, edited by Michael F. Suarez, S. J., and Michael L. Turner (Cambridge: Cambridge University Press, 2009), pp. 39–65. Suarez's analysis is both cautious and at times necessarily conjectural. We might nonetheless also deduce a per capita decline in satire across the latter half of the eighteenth century, when novels come to constitute more and more of the literary marketplace in terms of not only imprints but also the total number of pages printed.

seems still to hold true: satire does not die after mid-century, but it was certainly in decline, qualitatively and quantitatively, following its Golden Age.

Other factors also complicate the stories we tell about satire during this period. How, for instance, might we explain the massive expansion of the marketplace for visual satire during the latter half of the century? Between 1770 and 1830 alone, some 20,000 individual prints totalling millions of individual copies were produced.[8] During this era, the market for satire seems simultaneously both to have expanded and contracted. My goal in this final chapter is to account for this paradox in satiric production: the shrinking of the marketplace for printed satire and the staggering growth of visual satire during the last half of the eighteenth century. I argue in particular that satire, rather than vanishing, as earlier scholars have contended, began to migrate to non-verbal and especially visual media in the middle of the eighteenth century. To explain this migration, I bring together the findings from my first five chapters, including the Crown's emerging tactics for regulating print and the courts' refinement of libel laws and courtroom interpretive procedures, which enabled the prosecution of writers for verbally ambiguous works and increased the liability of stationers during the first half of the eighteenth century.

Despite the restrictiveness of this legal regime, however, visual satirists and printsellers were largely given a free pass. Why? In short, earlier eighteenth-century court rulings focused almost exclusively on satire's verbal elements, ignoring the then comparatively minor field of visual satire. As a result, these same legal developments had little bearing on later visual satires, which contained fewer and fewer words and tended to operate through forms of visual repetition, juxtaposition, and intimation. As part of its migration, I claim, satire underwent a process of *deverbalization*: as the century progressed, caricaturists made increasingly sparing use of words. Such visual satires were not, of course, wordless. Eirwen Nicholson has shown that 'word/image relationships' are 'a defining and broadly common characteristic' of late eighteenth- and early nineteenth-century visual satire.[9] However, the most libellous aspects of such satires were visual and often irreducible to unambiguously prosecutable language. Deverbalization thus describes not only the growth of visual satire but also a purely legalistic understanding of language in caricature. From a prosecutorial perspective, the verbal aspects of visual satire served largely *secondary* functions; it was the image itself that often contained the satire's central defamatory message, and it was these forms of visual defamation that most troubled prosecutors and the courts. In short, the legal protocols of the first half of the century, which had focused

---

[8] Gatrell, *City of Laughter*, p. 9.
[9] Eirwen Nicholson, 'Soggy Prose and Verbiage: English Graphic Political Satire as a Visual/Verbal Construct', *Word & Image: A Journal of Verbal/Visual Enquiry* 20, no. 1 (2004): p. 33.

intensely on mitigating the verbal ambiguity that had come to typify written satire, later proved useless at policing increasingly non-verbal visual works.

Throughout this chapter, I describe this paradox of diminishment and growth in terms of 'migration'. But this story is more complicated than a simple shift from one medium to another. When placed under pressure, satire did not need to emerge elsewhere. Instead, we might understand this transition as an accident in media history: at the moment that printed satire faced its greatest pressure from the law, the new visual medium of caricature emerged. This aesthetic development led to the expansion of the visual marketplace and the eventual and accidental realization among artists and printsellers that libel laws were ineffectual when applied to largely visual forms of defamation. This is all to say that the law was only *one* factor in the diminishment of written satire. But it is a factor worth emphasizing, not only because libel laws played such a critical role in the shaping of satire both rhetorically and bibliographically during this period, but also because an attention to emergent legal procedures helps to explain the imperviousness of visual satire to prosecution.

I begin this chapter by examining the legal regimes governing the press during the last half of the eighteenth century. I draw special attention to two legal tactics that the authorities developed and relied on extensively, especially during the last half of the century and into the Romantic era: special juries and ex officio informations. The Crown employed both strategies to harass satirists and members of the book trade while obviating the nuisance of recalcitrant jurors—a problem itself finally redressed with Fox's Libel Act in 1792.

In the remainder of the chapter, I study two forms of satiric deverbalization. I argue, first, that increased legal pressure led to the migration of satire to visual media, such as caricature, which was less reliant on verbal evasion and therefore resistant to courtroom protocols for the interpretation of verbally ambiguous forms of defamation. The most libellous aspects of such satires were instead visual, a form of imagistic defamation built around cryptic imputations and enigmatic accusations, which was seemingly impossible to prosecute.

In the final section of this chapter, I turn to a second kind of deverbalization: the use of non-verbal theatrical forms, such as mimicry and impersonation, in dramatic satires from the last half of the eighteenth century, especially in the plays of Samuel Foote, the most prominent satiric mimic of this period. This move towards non-verbal forms of theatrical satire, I argue, is in part the product of the 1737 Stage Licensing Act, which required the pre-performance censorship of plays staged at the two patent theatres in London. Like the procedures and doctrines of libel law developed in the preceding decades, the Licensing Act was especially preoccupied with the *verbal* regulation of performance through the play texts submitted for censorship. However, this emphasis on textual regulation also created a gap in licensing: non-verbal forms of satire, such as suggestive costuming and pointed impersonations, often through physical imitation and acoustic mimicry, never showed up in the playscripts submitted to the Lord Chamberlain's office for licensing. My focus in these final two sections is thus on two types of deverbalization as a form of evasion during the last half of the eighteenth century, when both stage and visual satirists came to understand not only the limits of libel law, but also the utility of the non-verbal.

6.1 Satire in the Courts, 1695–1792: Legal Strategies for Regulating the Press

Following the lapse of licensing in 1695, the Crown turned increasingly to the courts to regulate the press through post-publication prosecution.[10] The authorities were particularly eager to close the loopholes in the law that had been exposed by satirists and their stationers. In what follows, I offer an overview of these legal developments, before turning to special juries and ex officio informations—two legal procedures that the Crown used to obviate the problem of recalcitrant jurors. My goal in this section is to lay out the legal regime writers and stationers had come to live under by the mid-eighteenth century to explain in part the migration of satire to visual media while also tempering more optimistic accounts of expanding press freedom during this period.

Rulings against satiric practises came fast and quick after the lapse of licensing. In *R. v. Bear* (1698), for instance, Chief Justice Sir John Holt ruled that neither the publication of a libel nor the intent to publish were essential elements of the crime, but that merely copying a libel down for the first time was 'making' it and thus criminal.[11] Most rulings from this period targeted satire's verbal ambiguity. Holt expanded the ambit of libel law, ruling in *R. v. Tutchin* (1704) that not only individuals but also institutions, such as the House of Commons, could be defamed.[12] In *R. v. Drake* (1706) he ruled that the substance of a defamatory statement was to be determined not by sometimes sympathetic jurors but by the bench.[13]

Perhaps most critically, Holt held in *R. v. Browne* (1706) that verbal irony was no defence for libel.[14] This ruling was important in part because it targeted irony, an increasingly central verbal mechanism in satire from this period. But it was also important because it critically expanded the logic of the rulings in both *King v. Lake* from 1671 and *Somers v. House* in 1694 that all words should be understood

---

[10] Hamburger, 'Seditious Libel', pp. 661–765. See also Roger Lund, '"An Alembick of Innuendos": Satire, Libel and *The Craftsman*', *Philological Quarterly* 95, no. 2 (Spring 2017): pp. 243–68.

[11] *R. v. Bear* [sic] (K.B. 1698), Holt 442, 90 Eng. Rep. 1132 and 2 Salkeld 417, 91 Eng. Rep. 363; and Lord Raymond 414, 91 Eng. Rep. 1175. For Holt's opinion, see *R. v. Bear* [sic] (K.B. 1699), Hardwicke Papers, Add. MS 35981, BL.

[12] *R. v. Tutchin* (1704), Holt 424 (Q.B.), 90 Eng. Rep. 1133.

[13] *R. v. Drake* (Q.B. 1706), Hardwicke Papers, Add. MS 35980, BL.

[14] *R. v. Dr. Brown* [sic] (1706), 11 Mod. 86 (Q.B.), 88 Eng. Rep. 912.

in sociocentric terms—an interpretive logic that would come to dominate direc-tions to obstinate jurors especially in trials for satire and allegory.[15] In all of these rulings, the bench sought to instil an objective rule for interpreting ambiguous language theoretically isolated from jurors' unpredictable and subjective deliber-ations. Holt expanded on this protocol, ruling that prosecutors were not required to demonstrate how an ironic locution might actually mean something other than what it superficially said. Instead, the meaning of the statement should be under-stood 'in a common sense according to the vulgar intendment of the bystanders'—that is, how a juror believed *most* people would have understood a phrase, rather than merely the way in which an individual juror did.[16]

Following Holt's tenure, the courts continued to target satire, expanding these doctrines of reasonable interpretation. In *R. v. Hurt* (1713), Chief Justice Sir Thomas Parker deemed gutted names (like J—S— for John Smith) useless at preventing prosecutions.[17] He likewise formally abolished the doctrine of *mitior sensus*, a procedural rule for interpreting ambiguously defamatory language in its lesser, more innocuous sense.[18] Finally, in 1728, allegory was targeted.[19] With the help of the Crown, the courts concocted a supposed 'generality of readers' to interpret allegorical works. This fictional group of readers constituted an abstract rather than literal community whom prosecutors and plaintiffs could have recourse to in the absence of verifiable internal textual evidence. Rather than delimiting the linguistic mechanism by which readers came to understand alle-gories, the courts conceptualized an imagined and theoretically objective commu-nity of readers. As a result, defendants were obliged to demonstrate that this same hypothetical 'generality of readers' either did not exist or that those literal readers of the allegory—the jurors themselves—were mistaken in deducing real worlds and real figures from innocent fictional ones. Taken together, these rulings allowed the courts to defer to jurors in the abstract without raising the issue of jury purview, a debate that raged across the eighteenth century over whether jurors could speak to issues of both fact *and* law.[20] At the same time, these rulings sought to displace the capricious interpretations of actual jurors by installing a theoretical juror who read in more coherent, more reasonable, and more predictable ways.

During this same period, parliament also passed law after law that tightened regulations on the press. The Act of Anne (1709/10), for instance, required that

[15] *King v. Lake* (1671), 2 Vent. 28 (C.P.), 89 Eng. Rep. 12; and *Somers v. House* (1694), Holt 39 (K.B.), 90 Eng. Rep. 919.

[16] *R. v. Clerk* [sic] (1728/9), 1 Barn. 305 (K.B.), 94 Eng. Rep. 207; and *Somers v. House* (1694), Holt 39 (K.B.), 90 Eng. Rep. 919.

[17] *R. v. Hurt* (Q.B. 1713), in William Hawkins, *Pleas of the Crown*, 2nd ed., vol. 1 (London, 1724), p. 194.

[18] *Harrison v. Thornborough* (1714), rpt. *Sources*, p. 646.

[19] *R. v. Clerk* [sic] (1728/9), 1 Barn. 305 (K.B.), 94 Eng. Rep. 207. *State Law*, p. 57.

[20] Green, *Verdict*, chs. 7 and 8.

imprints appear on publications and that works be registered with the Stationers' Company in exchange for copyright protection, thereby pinning works to specific publishers, and sometimes authors, by their own admission.[21] Even for those willing to forego copyright protection and thus registration for especially incendiary works, imprints were eventually required by the Stamp Act (1712; 10 Anne c. 19, c. 13), which stipulated that 'no person whatsoever shall sell, or expose to sale, any [such] pamphlet, without the true respective names, and place or places of abode, of some known person or persons, by or for whom the same was really printed or published, written or printed thereupon'.[22] Throughout the century parliament renewed the act while also increasing its levies.[23] The popular press fared particularly poorly. A 1743 act allowed for heavy fines and the imprisonment of those caught selling unstamped newspapers; a 1789 act banned the hiring of newspapers from hawkers; a 1798 act made the publication of the names and addresses of printers and publishers mandatory; and, in 1799, a register of printing presses was finally introduced.[24] Such legislation only added to a series of rulings that markedly increased the liability of stationers, attacking the sometimes genuinely and sometimes coyly naïve defences that printers and booksellers so routinely offered up when deposed—I didn't know this was in my shop, I wasn't there when it was printed, I didn't understand its contents.[25]

For all of our stories about the growth of press freedom over this period, there can be little doubt that there were also sudden and stunning moments of contraction after mid-century, a point I take up most fully in my epilogue on how we might begin to narrativize press regulation more generally during the eighteenth century. During the last half of the century we could easily point to the most obvious moments of pressure on the press—during the brouhaha over John Wilkes, the *North Briton*, and the perverse ministerial mismanagement of Lord Bute in the 1760s; during the Junius trials and the severe mishandling of the American Revolution in the 1770s; during the domestic terror of the French

---

[21] Jody Greene, *The Trouble with Ownership: Literary Property and Authorial Liability in England, 1660–1730* (Philadelphia: University of Pennsylvania Press, 2005), pp. 1–22; and Ronan Deazley, *On the Origin of the Right to Copy: Charting to the Movement of Copyright Law in Eighteenth-Century Britain (1695–1775)* (Oxford: Hart, 2004).

[22] J. A. Downie, *Robert Harley and the Press: Propaganda and Public Opinion in the Age of Swift and Defoe* (Cambridge: Cambridge University Press, 1979), ch. 7.

[23] Bob Harris, 'Print Culture', in *A Companion to Eighteenth-Century Britain*, edited by H. T. Dickinson (Malden: Blackwell, 2002), p. 285.

[24] Hannah Barker, *Newspapers, Politics and English Society, 1695–1855* (New York: Longman, 2000), pp. 67–9.

[25] Hamburger, 'Seditious Libel', p. 752; Tamara L. Hunt, 'Servants, Masters and Seditious Libel in Eighteenth-Century England', *Book History* 20 (2017): pp. 83–110; and Ian Higgins, *Swift's Politics: A Study in Disaffection* (Cambridge: Cambridge University Press, 1994), pp. 160–5. For example, see *R. v. Hurt* (1712), rpt. Williams Hawkins, *A Treatise of the Pleas of the Crown*, vol. 1 (London, 1716–1721), p. 194; *R. v. Knell* (K.B. 1729), 1 Barn. 305–6, 94 Eng. Rep. 207–8; and *R. v. Nutt* (1729), 1 Barn. 306 (K.B.), 94 Eng. Rep. 208; and the extensive collection of stationers' depositions held in KB 1, TNA.

Revolution in the 1790s; or between 1817 and 1822, during the post-war period, the Peterloo Massacre, the reform agitation, the Queen Caroline affair, and the accession of George IV. The current of judicial rulings and legislation both before and after mid-century is simply clear.

On closer inspection, the legal landscape during the last half of the century looks uncannily like the first few decades after the lapse of licensing in 1695, when parliament unsuccessfully attempted to reinstitute licensing again and again.[26] Parliament's efforts were also supported by an often-willing judiciary. Thanks to the Act of Settlement (1701), judges were certainly more independent during the first half of the eighteenth century than they had been at any time during the seventeenth century, when they served at the king's pleasure.[27] However, a facile faith in judicial independence occludes a much more complicated historical reality. Then, as today, judges continued to be vetted for political allegiances; they served the monarch under whom they were appointed and sat; they mingled with members of both parliamentary houses and routinely consulted with the monarch; and they continued to be part of a larger state structure that lacked a crisp separation of powers. Moreover, before ascending the bench, most justices served a spell in the Commons, where their political beliefs were made publicly available to the monarch under whom they would eventually be appointed.[28] After mid-century, parliament found a willing justice in William Murray, first earl of Mansfield, Chief Justice of the King's Bench between 1756 and 1788. Like Holt before him, Mansfield found trials for seditious libel a useful tool for patrolling print. He took, in James C. Oldham's words, a 'conservative, royalist approach', and 'was accused in the popular press of having created a restrictive seditious libel apparatus that imprisoned freedom of the press'.[29]

This is in part why satirists and their booksellers became only more cautious during the second half of the century. One had constantly to be on guard, measuring not only the heat of one's rhetoric but also the temperature of the times. This was especially true during and after the 1790s and into the 1820s, when the publication of radical satire was particularly dangerous. Evan Lloyd, Thomas

---

[26] Hanson, *Government*, pp. 260–3; and John Feather, 'The Book Trade in Politics: The Making of the Copyright Act of 1710', *Publishing History* 8 (1980): table 1, pp. 19–44.

[27] Alfred F. Havighurst, 'James II and the Twelve Men in Scarlet', *Law Quarterly Review* 69 (October 1953): pp. 522–46, 'The Judiciary and Politics in the Reign of Charles II (Part I, 1660–1676)' and 'The Judiciary and Politics in the Reign of Charles II (Part II, 1676–1685)', *Law Quarterly Review* 66 (January and April 1950): pp. 62–78 and 229–52.

[28] For a reevaluation of judicial independence during the eighteenth century, see Wilfrid Prest, 'Judicial Corruption in Early Modern England', *Past & Present* 133 (November 1991): pp. 67–95; David Lemmings, 'The Independence of the Judiciary in Eighteenth-Century England', in *The Life of the Law*, edited by Peter Birks (London: Hambledon Press, 1993), pp. 125–49; and Stewart Jay, 'Servants of Monarchs and Lords: The Advisory Role of Early English Judges', *American Journal of Legal History* 38, no. 3 (April 1994): pp. 117–96.

[29] James C. Oldham, *English Common Law in the Age of Mansfield* (Chapel Hill: University of North Carolina Press, 2004), pp. 209, 221.

Spence, Leigh Hunt, William Cobbett, William Hone, Thomas Wooler, Richard Carlile, John Hunt—all were brought up on libel charges, often more than once.[30] As Marcus Wood has observed, 'Virtually every ultra-radical author of any importance was prosecuted for either sedition, libel, or seditious blasphemy' between 1790 and 1832.[31] Not all satirists were 'ultra radicals', as Gary Dyer has amply demonstrated, nor were all 'ultra radicalists' satirists, as Wood has argued, even if such writers and publishers found their 'wellsprings in the popular political and social satire of the eighteenth century'.[32] The larger point, though, simply holds: satire remained legally perilous during this later period, as scholar after scholar has shown.[33]

This threat to the practise of satire was nowhere more evident than in the rash of Crown prosecutions for seditious libel initiated between the 1750s and 1770s, especially during tense moments of domestic and political unrest.[34] Such trials did not always bring convictions, but they did serve an important hortatory function.[35] Take the Junius letters, first published in Henry Sampson Woodfall's *Public Advertiser* and then reprinted in other London papers, which led to a series of printers and booksellers being prosecuted in 1770. Woodfall was tried twice, but got off on a technicality; John Miller, the printer of the *London Evening Post*, and Henry Baldwin, the printer for the *St James's Chronicle*, were also acquitted; the charges against Charles Say, printer for the *Gazetteer*, and George Robinson, printer of the *Independent Chronicle*, were dropped; only the bookseller John Almon was found guilty.[36] From the outside, the government's prosecutions looked like a disaster. But they were also an uncomfortable reminder that a writer, and one so suddenly prominent and respected—Robert Southey called Junius one of the most important satirists of the age—could lead his printers down the road to prosecution, persecution, and financial ruin.[37]

Moreover, the government believed that such prosecutions, even when unsuccessful, served an important cautionary role, one that would promote self-policing

---

[30] 'Libels on the House of Common prosecuted (*inter alia*) by the government', KB 33/24/2, TNA.

[31] Marcus Wood, 'Radical Publishing', in *The Cambridge History of the Book in Britain*, vol. 5: 1695–1830, edited by Michael F. Suarez, S. J., and Michael L. Turner (Cambridge: Cambridge University Press, 2009), p. 835.

[32] Dyer, *British Satire and the Politics of Style*, pp. 3–5; and Wood, *Radical Satire and Print Culture*, p. 3.

[33] Gary Dyer, 'The Circulation of Satirical Poetry in the Regency', *Keats-Shelley Journal* 61 (2012): pp. 66–74; and Andrew McKendry, 'Will the Public Please Step Forward?: Libel Law and Public Opinion in Byron's *The Vision of Judgment*', *Studies in Romanticism* 54, no. 4 (2015): pp. 525–49.

[34] Bob Harris, *Politics and the Nation: Britain in the Mid-Eighteenth Century* (Oxford: Oxford University Press, 2002), p. 7.

[35] Eckhart Hellmuth, 'Towards Hume—The Discourse on the Liberty of the Press in the Age of Walpole', *History of European Ideas* 44, no. 2 (2018): p. 160.

[36] John Cannon, *The Letters of Junius* (Oxford: Clarendon Press, 1978), p. xvi. See *The Trial of John Almon, Bookseller* (London, 1770); *R. v. Almon* (1770), rpt. *Mansfield MSS*, vol. 2, pp. 833ff; and *R. v. Baldwin* (1770), rpt. *Mansfield MSS*, vol. 2, pp. 842ff.

[37] Robert Southey, 'On the Rise and Fall of Popular Disaffection', in *Essays, Moral and Political*, vol. 2 (London, 1832), p. 82.

among writers, printers, and booksellers.[38] The Crown knew it could never go after every callous scribbler, even if some in government believed that they could be more systematic in documenting the production and dissemination of potentially prosecutable works.[39] Douglas Hay has argued that the administration of the criminal law in the eighteenth century was a balancing act between 'delicacy and circumspection'. It needed to be administered tactically and selectively to be an effective tool for social regulation: 'the discretion embodied allowed the authorities to use terror with great flexibility'.[40] Convictions were thus desirable but unnecessary, for the goal in many instances was to financially devastate printers and booksellers while warning others. Almon, for instance, was fined and ordered to pay £800 as sureties for good behaviour for two years. 'This sentence', he recalled, is 'most heavy, cruel and oppressive; as it amounts to a total prohibition of [Almon's] following his trade or business as a bookseller . . . without running the risque of forfeiture of the sum of eight hundred pounds; which would tend to [his] ruin'.[41] Silencing him was the entire point, he reasoned: 'for if [Almon] will print no more political pamphlets, he suffers nothing from the sentence'.[42] Following his conviction, in fact, Almon avoided publishing anything political for two years, the exact period of his mandated good behaviour.[43] The 'machinery of prosecution harassed [those in the book trade] at every turn', Philip Harling has observed, and it was through such strategic prosecution, arrest, and indictment that the authorities were able to ensure a degree of self-censorship.[44]

The authorities were also strategic about whom they went after. Prosecutions could hurt the government's cause, drumming up interest in and support for the very thing it sought to tamp down. The Essex magistrate Thomas Kynaston, for instance, questioned the prosecution of a group of 'incendiary Publications', worrying that 'our mistaken and intemperate Zeal should injure the Cause we

---

[38] Siebert, *Freedom*, p. 380.

[39] See, for instance, a letter from Charles Townshend, Secretary of State for the Northern Department, to the messenger of the press, Samuel Gray (1 March 1728/9), calling for his agents to buy up a copy of every pamphlet and newspaper to create an evidentiary record for later prosecutions (KB 33/5/6, TNA). Walpole also made Robert Paxton, a Treasury Solicitor, a 'specialist', who was instructed to coordinate measures against the opposition press. See Hellmuth, 'The Discourse on the Liberty of the Press in the Age of Walpole', p. 160.

[40] Douglas Hay, 'Property, Authority and the Criminal Law', in *Albion's Fatal Tree: Crime and Society in Eighteenth-Century England*, rev. ed., edited by Douglas Hay et al. (New York: Verso, 2011), pp. 49–65.

[41] John Almon, *Memoirs of a Late Eminent Bookseller* (London, 1790), p. 71.

[42] Almon, *Memoirs*, pp. 74–5.

[43] Deborah D. Rogers, *Bookseller as Rogue: John Almon and the Politics of Eighteenth-Century Publishing* (New York: Peter Lang, 1986), pp. 49, 54n18.

[44] Philip Harling, 'The Law of Libel and the Limits of Repression, 1790–1832', *Historical Journal* 44, no. 1 (March 2001): p. 120; Michael Treadwell, 'London Trade Publishers, 1675–1750', *The Library*, 6th ser., 4 (1982): pp. 99–134; Andrew Benjamin Bricker, 'Who Was "A. Moore"?: The Attribution of Eighteenth-Century Publications with False and Misleading Imprints', *Papers of the Bibliographical Society of America* 110, no. 2 (June 2016): pp. 202–10; and Keymer, *Poetics*, pp. 178–9.

meant to serve'.[45] 'Whenever a libel is prosecuted', one critic observed in 1794, 'it draws it into a second course of agitation, and ... the very observations made upon the libel in a Court of Justice, become, as it were, a promulgation of the libel itself'.[46] Accordingly, enforcement and prosecution, as in earlier periods, was selective and piecemeal, responding to tense moments.[47]

Trials also tended to inflame the press, sprouting a fresh crop of articles and pamphlets calling for greater press freedom. Especially after mid-century, critics focused on the issue of jury competence, a tempest that had been brewing since at least the days of Holt.[48] The jury's purview should be enlarged, such critics argued, allowing jurors to comment not only on issues of fact—what a given statement meant and whether it had been published—but also questions of law: whether a given statement constituted libel.[49] Some jurors simply ignored the directions of the bench, offering a verdict of not guilty even when the facts of the case had been amply proven, especially in prosecutions for seditious libel.[50] Juries finally got their way with Fox's Libel Act in 1792 (32 Geo. III, c. 60)—the terminal date for *Libel and Lampoon* and the act that once and for all determined the jury's purview in trials for defamation. The act reversed the view of judges, from Sir Edward Coke, almost two centuries earlier, to Holt and Mansfield, and established that a jury could offer either a general verdict on the 'whole issue', including questions of fact *and* law, or a special verdict.[51] We should be careful in overestimating just how liberatory this act ultimately was, as Trevor Ross has recently argued, and yet from the government's perspective things only got worse after Fox's Libel Act.[52] In 1794, for instance, when the Crown was contemplating the prosecution of Solomon Lyons, Treasury Solicitor Joseph White voiced his qualms: 'The words are extremely offensive yet it is very doubtful whether a Jury could, under the circumstances stated, be induced to find him guilty and acquittal would be very

[45] Qtd. in Clive Emsley, 'An Aspect of Pitt's "Terror": Prosecutions for Sedition during the 1790s', *Social History* 6, no. 2 (May 1981): p. 174.

[46] Daniel Isaac Eaton, *The Trial of Daniel Isaac Eaton, for Publishing a Supposed Libel* (London, 1794), p. 21.

[47] Hellmuth, 'Liberty of the Press', p. 160; for earlier periods, see Blair Worden, 'Literature and Political Censorship in Early Modern England', in *Too Mighty to be Free: Censorship and the Press in Britain and the Netherlands*, edited by A. C. Duke and C. A. Tamse (Zutphen: De Walburg Press, 1987), ch. 3; Cyndia Susan Clegg, *Press Censorship in Elizabethan England* (Cambridge: Cambridge University Press, 1997), *Press Censorship in Jacobean England* (Cambridge: Cambridge University Press, 1991), and *Press Censorship in Caroline England* (Cambridge: Cambridge University Press, 2008); and Debora Shuger, *Censorship and Cultural Sensibility: The Regulation of Language in Tudor-Stuart England* (Philadelphia: University of Pennsylvania Press, 2006).

[48] Green, *Verdict*, ch. 6–8.   [49] Holdsworth, *History*, vol. 8, pp. 367–8.

[50] Green, *Verdict*, p. 329; and Beattie, *Crime*, pp. 406–9, 420–1, 423–30.

[51] Siebert, *Freedom*, p. 391. On jury nullification and the fact–law distinction, see Simon Stern, 'Between Local Knowledge and National Politics: Debating Rationales for Jury Nullification after *Bushell's Case*', *The Yale Law Journal* 111, no. 7 (May 2002): pp. 1815–59; and Green, *Verdict*, pp. xxxi, xviii–xx, chs. 7 and 8.

[52] Trevor Ross, *Writing in Public: Literature and the Liberty of the Press in Eighteenth-Century Britain* (Baltimore: Johns Hopkins University Press, 2018), pp. 4, 213–17.

mischievous'.[53] As Sylvester Douglas, later Lord Glenbervie, bluntly put it in 1798, there was 'always something of a Lottery in juries'.[54] Then, as now, jurors could be capricious.

To overcome the unruliness of jurors, the courts instantiated and then expanded a theory of interpretation in trials for libel that limited the unpredictable subjectivity of jury deliberations. In addition, the Crown developed an innovative two-pronged strategy to redress obstinate jurors, especially after 1760. The first tactic was the use of 'special juries', based on legislation first passed in 1730 (3 Geo. II, c. 25). This act allowed the Crown a heavy hand in limiting who could be selected for jury service, and often to great effect—at least for Samuel Johnson, who listed special juries alongside government spies as plagues on not only the press but also justice itself.[55] Harling has shown that 'there was overwhelming evidence that the master of the Crown office who presided over the selection process worked hard to ensure that a small crew of trading special jurors ... would tilt jury sentiment in favour of the government'.[56] Such juries were 'struck': from the list of forty-eight freeholders, ostensibly selected at random by the Master of the Crown Office, who was assisted by the Under Sheriff, the attorneys for both parties would 'strike' twelve names each, leaving twenty-four prospective jurors.[57] But even the list itself could be packed. 'It seems more than likely', James C. Oldham writes, 'that the Under Sheriff or other impaneling officer maintained special lists for special juries, utilizing the list most appropriate for the type of case being tried'.[58] Such special juries worked. As we saw in the last chapter, the prosecution of Richard Francklin for *The Craftsman* in 1728 failed at least in part thanks to a recalcitrant Tory jury. A year after the legislation was passed, a special jury of Whigs was seemingly used to prosecute Francklin again—this time successfully.[59] During the latter half of the century Mansfield regularly used special juries, more than any judge before him. Most often he had them impanelled for cases touching on commerce, business, or bankruptcy.[60] But of the forty cases for libel recorded in his manuscripts, he impanelled a special jury in well over half.[61] By the end of the century, it was common practise in libel cases to use

---

[53] White to Nepean [?] (25 February 1794), HO 48/4, TNA.

[54] Douglas to Sheffield (17 August 1798), Sheffield MSS, Add. MSS 5440/322, Sussex Record Office.

[55] Samuel Johnson, *London*, in *The Works of Samuel Johnson*, vol. 6: Poems (1974), 2nd ed., edited by David Nichol Smith and Edward L. McAdam (New Haven: Yale University Press, 1958–2019), pp. 60–1, ll. 248–53.

[56] Harling, 'Law of Libel', p. 117.

[57] James C. Oldham, 'Origins of the Special Jury', *University of Chicago Law Review* 50, no. 1 (Winter 1983): p. 137.

[58] *Mansfield MSS*, vol. 1, p. 96.

[59] *An Act for the better Regulation of Juries*, 3 Geo. 2, ch. 25 (1730); *The Trial of Mr. Richard Francklin* (1731), rpt. 17 *State Trials* 625. See Hamburger, 'Seditious Libel', p. 760n312.

[60] *Mansfield MSS*, vol. 1, p. 98.   [61] *Mansfield MSS*, vol. 2, pp. 810–62.

such jurors, whose political leanings could be safely (and secretly) vetted in advance.[62]

The second prong of the government's strategy was even more effective: to lodge an ex officio information in King's Bench and thereby bypass the use of juries altogether. Such informations allowed the Crown to sidestep the usual procedure of defending a bill of indictment before a grand jury prior to trial. Often at the direction of the Secretary of State, these were lodged by the Attorney General, who would subpoena the accused (often a printer or bookseller), who would then have to answer the charges against him. Importantly, before 1820, there was no statutory requirement for the Attorney General to bring the accused to trial.[63] As a result, such prosecutions rarely went anywhere, though attendance in court remained necessary to avoid outlawry proceedings. In addition, even without actual trials and convictions, the nuisance and expense often proved enough to scare off printers and booksellers.[64] The accused was required to post sureties for good behaviour; if he lacked the funds for bail, which was not recoverable, then he might find himself stewing in gaol until trial. Those fees increased if the accused wanted a copy of the information outlining the offence, for which the Crown office charged a staggering £10.[65] Worst of all, even if acquitted, there was no way to recover costs, which could total upwards of £100 by the end of the century.[66] Ex officio informations simply proved a useful stopgap measure: a clever way to obviate bullheaded jurors while also financially incapacitating and thus silencing unruly booksellers and printers. This, contemporaries argued, was precisely their function.[67] Given the 'impossibility of getting Juries to convict', Lord Chancellor Hardwicke suggested to the prime minister, the duke of Newcastle, in 1756, 'it may be prudent to take up [libellers], though you don't intend to proceed to trial'.[68]

Little surprise then that the Crown turned increasingly to such informations. Between 1760 and 1790 some seventy-three ex officio informations were filed. Between 1790 and 1832, this figure more than doubled. One hundred and sixty-six were lodged at King's Bench, while only seventy-three traditional indictments by criminal information were filed.[69] Of these, some two hundred were initiated by

---

[62] Oldham, *English Common Law in the Age of Mansfield*, p. 217. See also documentary evidence that the Treasury Solicitor, Jonathan Sharpe, routinely packed juries: SP 36/131/87, TNA.

[63] Harling, 'Law of Libel', p. 113.

[64] Harris, *Politics and the Nation*, p. 75. On the harassment of stationers, see Black, *Press*, pp. 106–17.

[65] Harling, 'Law of Libel', p. 114.

[66] Douglas Hay, 'Controlling the English Prosecutor', *Osgoode Hall Law Journal* 21, no. 2 (October 1983): p. 168; Emsley, 'Prosecutions for Sedition', p. 168; and Black, *Press*, p. 111.

[67] For more on this 'most arbitrary Punishment' and 'very oppressive... manner of Proceeding' through ex officio warrants 'to break up the Press of a poor Printer', see [Hugh Hume, Earl of Marchmont], *A Serious Exhortation to the Electors of Great Britain* (London, 1740), p. 16.

[68] Hardwicke to Newcastle (29 August 1756), Add. MS 32867, f. 146, BL, qtd. Black, *Press*, p. 168.

[69] Harling, 'Law of Libel', p. 108.

Crown lawyers—a substantial increase over the roughly two hundred *total* prosecutions between 1702 and 1789.[70] As with all legal measures used to police the
press, such informations were employed tactically. This is clearest in the spikes: in
1770, fifteen were lodged; in 1775, twelve; in 1781, eleven; in 1792, nineteen; in
1808, twenty; and in 1810, seventeen.[71] During the 1760s, especially, ex officio
informations were used against Wilkite publishers.[72] And contemporaries noticed.
Charles James Fox felt the convictions of the dissenting minister Gilbert
Wakefield, the printers Joseph Johnson and Jeremiah Jordan, and the bookseller
John Cuthell by ex officio information for seditious libel were 'a death blow to the
liberty of the press'.[73] Ex officio informations were finally limited by statute in
1819.[74] But trials for seditious libel continued on unabated during the period of
reform, between 1817 and 1824, when some 167 seditious libel prosecutions were
undertaken.[75]

Court rulings from the first half of the eighteenth century and the prosecutorial
strategies of later decades ensured that satirists, printers, and booksellers faced a
selectively oppressive, systematic, and ad hoc regime of press regulation—to say
nothing of the aborted freedoms of the revolutionary and Romantic periods,
including the suspension of habeas corpus in 1794 and the treason trials so
expertly studied by John Barrell.[76] All of this should give us a sense, against our
progressive narratives of ever expanding press freedom—or even against our less
teleological accounts that nonetheless leave us with greater press freedom in the
nineteenth century than had existed in the seventeenth—that the Crown had in no
way in the eighteenth century abandoned the idea that the press should be
thoroughly if flexibly regulated. This was particularly true after mid-century and

[70] KB 33/24/2, TNA. See Michael Lobban, 'From Seditious Libel to Unlawful Conspiracy: Peterloo
and the Changing Face of Political Crime, c. 1770–1820', *Oxford Journal of Legal Studies* 10, no. 3
(1990): p. 309n11.

[71] 'Prosecutions for Libels by Information ex officio from 1760 to 1810', KB 33/24/2, TNA.

[72] John Brewer, 'The Wilkites and the Law, 1763–74', in *An Ungovernable People: The English and
their Law in the Seventeenth and Eighteenth Centuries*, edited by John Brewer and John Styles (London:
Hutchinson, 1980), pp. 161–2.

[73] Fox to Dennis O'Bryen (29 July 1798), Add. MSS 47566, f. 19, BL. See also F. K. Prochaska,
'English State Trials in the 1790s: A Case Study', *Journal of British Studies* 13, no. 1 (November 1973):
p. 71.

[74] 59 Geo. III, c. 12. See Siebert, *Freedom*, p. 386n66.

[75] Michael Scrivener (ed.), *Poetry and Reform: Periodical Verse from the English Democratic Press,
1792–1824* (Detroit: Wayne State University Press, 1992), p. 21. On the growth of seditious libel
prosecutions across the eighteenth century, see Wendell Bird, *Press and Speech Under Assault: The
Early Supreme Court Justices, the Sedition Act of 1798, and the Campaign against Dissent* (Oxford:
Oxford University Press, 2016), pp. 38–9; Lobban, 'From Seditious Libel to Unlawful Conspiracy',
pp. 307–9 and 'Treason, Sedition and the Radical Movements in the Age of the French Revolution',
Liverpool Law Review 22 (2000): pp. 205–34; Clive Emsley, 'Repression, "Terror" and the Rule of Law in
England During the Decade of the French Revolution', *The English Historical Review* 100, no. 397
(October 1985): pp. 801, 824; and Harling, 'The Law of Libel', p. 108.

[76] John Barrell, *Imagining the King's Death: Figurative Treason, Fantasies of Regicide, 1793–1796*
(Oxford: Oxford University Press, 2000); Paul Halliday, *Habeas Corpus: From England to Empire*
(Cambridge: Belknap Press, 2010); and Kenneth R. Johnston, *Unusual Suspects: Pitt's Reign of Alarm
and the Lost Generation of the 1790s* (Oxford: Oxford University Press, 2013), app. 1.

into the first decades of the nineteenth century, and especially so for sharply satirical works. Their printers, booksellers, and authors (when they could be squirrelled out) were routinely targeted, often during periods of heightened domestic anxiety. Press freedom, in fact, suddenly, stunningly, and repeatedly contracted at moments between 1760 and 1830.

Despite the Crown's best efforts to suppress such works, satire lived on, both in print and elsewhere. Over the next two sections, I focus on two forms of deverbalization. I begin with visual satire, which was manufactured on a massive scale after mid-century and could be just as vicious as any printed lampoon from the supposed Golden Age decades earlier. Nonetheless, there was not one successful prosecution for images alone during the latter half of the eighteenth century, despite the insidiousness and flexibility of this period's legal regime for regulating the press. Caricaturists and printsellers seem to have been given an almost free pass, and in what follows I review some of the visual and distributional strategies used to evade the authorities and to stymie prosecutions. Like printed and graphic satire, dramatic satire also lived on after mid-century, despite the passage of the Stage Licensing Act in 1737. In the final section of this chapter, I turn to this dramatic satire and pay particular attention to Samuel Foote. Like contemporary visual satirists, Foote increasingly employed non-textual forms of satire, especially mimicry and impersonation, which he coupled with suggestive staging and allusive costuming. In both visual and dramatic satire, the non-verbal came to serve an increasingly important function in the later eighteenth century, especially in works that lampooned prominent individuals.

6.2 The Deverbalization of Satire: Caricature and the Limits of Libel Law

In this section I offer a legal account of visual satire between roughly 1740 and 1830, offering a sense of how caricature operated during this period and why its emerging satiric conventions rendered earlier legal developments largely ineffective. I focus especially on caricature's visual language, its strategies for the production of meaning, and its resistance to prosecution. Many of the evasions that came to typify visual satire share some analogy with earlier printed works: a combination of semantic indeterminacy alongside shifty distribution practises. My larger goal is to show why one set of largely effective legal procedures made the publication of written satire perilous after mid-century and yet hardly affected visual works. In doing so, I explain how this diminution in print was offset by satire's migration to visual media.

This, however, is not only a story about the law. In part, caricature's rapid growth was an indirect consequence of the legal pressures written satire faced. But the growth of visual satire, perhaps above all, was aided by a constellation of non-legal developments: by the rise of caricature in the 1740s, an Italian art form characterized by comic and sometimes grotesque physiological and physiognomic distortions (from the Italian *caricare*: 'to charge' the features), that came in large measure to constitute the visual language of satire; by the emergence of eye-grabbing, richly hand-coloured prints in the 1760s; and by the eastward pan-metropolitan expansion of printsellers, whose shop-window displays expanded everyday viewership and promoted a specialized visual literacy even among the wholly illiterate. All of this suggests that visual satire's rapid rise after mid-century was in part only a fortuitous accident in media history: at the very moment when print satirists and their stationers faced the greatest legal pressure both from parliament and in the courts, a gripping new visual technology independently emerged that proved impervious to prosecution. It was only after the repeatedly failed and stymied prosecutions of visual materials that printsellers and carica-turists fully realized and capitalized on the resistance of visual satire to prosecution.

We might begin by noting just how aggressively and vindictively ad hominem visual satires could be.[77] Vic Gatrell has argued that visual satire actually 'became more scabrously personalized as the century wore on'.[78] This move toward increasingly personal attacks was part of a larger aesthetic shift. 'Caricature rapidly moved from the tradition of representing subjects emblematically', Michael Rosenthal has written, 'to portraying the individuals targeted. From the 1770s the squibs and satires became increasingly personal'.[79] Despite a broad critical prohibition against particular satire—one that applied to both printed and visual works, as we saw in chapter four—such prints evince an almost irrepressible urge to attack individuals, sending up everyone from familiar politicians to prominent aristocrats for almost any ungainly deed of political sleaze or everyday malfea-sance. For their part, satirists claimed that such visual lampoons served a true social function. The intense shift to personal satire after 1760 was a radical change in the supposed ethics of privacy and might be thought of as a response to the new and emerging perception that an individual should be measured by both his or her public identity and private moral failings.[80]

This intersection between public politics and private life was not lost on those living in London. Foreigners, for instance, were shocked by what they saw. The Spanish art historian Antonio Ponz could hardly believe the 'impunity of those who engrave and publish', noting disdainfully that 'the renowned English liberty is

---

[77] Diana Donald, *Age of Caricature: Satirical Prints in the Reign of George III* (New Haven: Yale University Press, 1996), p. viii.

[78] Gatrell, *City of Laughter*, p. 175.

[79] Michael Rosenthal, 'Public Reputation and Image Control in Late-Eighteenth-Century Britain', *Visual Culture in Britain* 7, no. 2 (Winter 2006): p. 69.

[80] Hellmuth, 'Liberty of the Press', p. 173; and Shearer West, 'The Darly Macaroni Prints and the Politics of "Private Man"', *Eighteenth-Century Life* 25, no. 2 (Spring 2001): p. 178.

most used ... to each day put ridiculing prints, which mock the Ministry'.[81] The German historian Johann Wilhelm von Archenholz also linked satire to English freedom, counting 'among the privileges of this country, the liberty to make satirical prints that ridicule the enemies of the moment'.[82] One visitor incredulously noted that Hannah Humphrey's print shop—'a manufactory ... working the press night and day, in throwing off libels against' the Crown—was just yards from the Royal Palace.[83] But what was one to do? As Horace Walpole observed, 'Ministers are, and ought to be lawful game; yet the law could not except them as proper to be abused'.[84] None of this was helped by the sense that visual satire was simply everywhere. Prints were produced on a massive scale and publicly displayed in shop windows across London and Westminster.[85] In Sheila O'Connell's estimate, by mid-century 'hundreds of thousands of prints were being sold every year'.[86] Between 1770 and 1830 alone, some 20,000 unique satiric prints were produced, roughly half of which were personal.

Despite visual satire's extensive distribution and endemic nastiness, the authorities had profound difficulty policing it. This is perhaps shocking given the government's eagerness to regulate written works and the availability of new courtroom procedures for prosecuting and litigating libel. Moreover, at least theoretically, images could be defamatory. Early on, Chief Justice Sir Edward Coke asserted that a libel 'may be ... *Picturis*'.[87] The legal writer William Hawkins also believed a libel could be by 'Signs or Pictures'.[88] Chief Baron of the Exchequer Sir John Comyns found pictures just as libellous as William Blackstone.[89] The problem, however, was how one was to demonstrate procedurally and to the satisfaction of jurors that an unflattering representation of some

---

[81] Qtd. In Reva Wolf, 'John Bull, Liberty, and Wit', in *The Efflorescence of Caricature, 1759–1838*, edited by Todd Porterfield (Burlington: Ashgate Publishing, 2011), pp. 55–7.

[82] Qtd. in Reva Wolf, *Goya and the Satirical Print in England and on the Continent, 1730–1850* (Boston: David R. Godine, 1991), p. 9.

[83] Qtd. Donald, *Age of Caricature*, p. 2.

[84] Horace Walpole, *Memoirs of the Reign of King George III*, edited by Derek Jarrett, vol. 4 (New Haven: Yale University Press, 2000), p. 183.

[85] Mark Bills, *The Art of Satire: London in Caricature* (London: Philip Wilson Publishers, 2006), pp. 222–3.

[86] Sheila O'Connell, 'The Print Trade in Hogarth's London', in *The London Book Trade: Topographies of Print in the Metropolis from the Sixteenth Century*, edited by Robin Meyers, Michael Harris, and Giles Mandelbrote (London: Oak Knoll Press & the British Library, 2003), p. 71.

[87] *Case de Libellis Famosis* (1605), 5 Coke 125 (K.B.), 77 Eng. Rep. 250. A recent overview of the early modern law of libel has uncovered only one case of pictorial defamation: *Taylor v. Mounds* (1618), STAC 8/284/23, TNA. See David Ibbetson, 'Edward Coke, Roman Law, and the Law of Libel', in *The Oxford Handbook of English Law and Literature, 1500–1700*, edited by Lorna Hutson (Oxford: Oxford University Press, 2017), pp. 498–501. Chief Justice Holt argued 'a libel may be either *per scripta* or *per signa*' though in that case the image of a pillory was also accompanied by words. See *Austin v. Culpeper* (1683), 2 Show. 313 (K.B.), 89 Eng. Rep. 960.

[88] William Hawkins, *A Treatise of the Pleas of the Crown*, vol. 1 (London, 1716), p. 193.

[89] All qtd. *Association Papers. Part I. Publications Printed by Special Order of the Society for Preserving Liberty and Property against Republicans and Levellers* (London, 1793), p. 15. See Blackstone, *Commentaries on the Laws of England*, Book IV: Of Public Wrongs, edited by Ruth Paley (Oxford: Oxford University Press, 2016), p. 99.

unnamed politician was legally defamatory. The legal procedures that the Crown and courts had developed focused above all on the ambiguous verbal elements of written defamation. This emphasis on libel's linguistic features meant that the laws addressing visual defamation remained embarrassingly underdeveloped. Early trials for visual materials soon exposed the law's inability to transliterate images. For all of the trouble *The Craftsman* faced, for instance, the Crown never initiated a prosecution against the periodical's inflammatory frontispieces until William Rayner had the poor sense to reprint them with explanatory poems. Even then, to go after the images the Crown was forced in Rayner's trial to focus on the publication's 'Verses'.[90] Simply put, no legal mechanism existed for converting defamatory images into prosecutable words.

The hermeneutic failure of libel law—its seemingly total inability to parse visual semantics—is key because it draws attention to the important aesthetic feature of visual satire that both caricaturists and printsellers came increasingly to capitalize on: its sparing use of words. Visual satires produced between 1760 and 1830 are not, of course, wordless. Eirwen Nicholson has argued that 'word/image relation-ships' are 'a defining and broadly common characteristic' of late eighteenth- and early nineteenth-century visual satires, and David Francis Taylor has amply demonstrated that graphic satire during this period is 'an intermedial cultural form'.[91] We would do well, moreover, to observe the extent to which visuality and especially intermediality were central to earlier eighteenth-century satires, perhaps most notably, for example, in the attacks on Pope during the fallout from the *Dunciad*.[92] Both Mark Hallett and Vincent Carretta have likewise studied the interaction between textual and visual satire, two forms in 'pictorial and textual dialogue'.[93] Finally, we need to attend to the inherent visuality of even printed satires as material objects during the first half of the century.[94] In particular, as I have argued elsewhere, satire during this period is not simply intermedial but perhaps even hypermedial; the visuality of textual satires extends not only to the cryptographic title pages and suggestive *mise-en-page* of this period, but also to the

---

[90] *The Tryal of William Rayner* (London, 1733), p. 15.

[91] Eirwen Nicholson, 'Soggy Prose and Verbiage', p. 33; and David Francis Taylor, *The Politics of Parody: A Literary History of Caricature, 1760–1830* (New Haven: Yale University Press, 2018), p. 10. On the text-image 'problematic' more generally, see W. J. T. Mitchell, *Picture Theory: Essays on Verbal and Visual Representation* (Chicago: University of Chicago Press, 1994), p. 7, in which he argues that 'all media are mixed media, and all representations are heterogeneous; there are no "purely" visual or verbal arts' (p. 9).

[92] See J. V. Guerinot, *Pamphlet Attacks on Alexander Pope, 1711–1744: A Descriptive Bibliography* (London: Methuen, 1969); and, for example, Herman Van Kruys' Frontispiece to *Pope Alexander's Supremacy and Infallibility Examin'd* (London, 1729).

[93] Mark Hallett, *The Spectacle of Difference: Graphic Satire in the Age of Hogarth* (New Haven: Yale University Press, 1999), pp. 2, 8–9; and Vincent Carretta, *The Snarling Muse: Verbal and Visual Political Satire from Pope to Churchill* (Philadelphia: University of Pennsylvania Press, 1983), pp. xiii–xx.

[94] Jerome J. McGann, *The Textual Condition* (Princeton: Princeton University Press, 1991), 77.

graphic qualities of writing and typography itself.[95] However, what needs to be kept in mind when discussing the verbality of later eighteenth-century caricatures is the *nature* of the words present in such satires. Deverbalization describes a purely prosecutorial or legalistic understanding of language in visual satire. From a legal (if not aesthetic) perspective, such verbal addenda served a largely *secondary* function, in adding a comic twist or pun or in stringing out an allusion; it was the image itself that often contained the satire's central defamatory imputation— and it was precisely this aspect that baffled the courts, which lacked a ready mechanism for delimiting imagistic meaning in linguistic and demonstrably libellous terms.

Paradoxically, the Crown's emphasis on prosecuting visual materials by focusing on their verbal elements only drew further attention to the shocking underdevelopment of legal procedures for handling images.[96] And satirists and booksellers noticed. Take the proposed prosecution of the figures behind the 'John of Gant' caricatures in 1749. The story went that, in spring or summer of that year, William Augustus, the duke of Cumberland and the third son of George II, had solicited a Savoyard girl after hearing her perform a version of the poem 'The Midsummer Wish' on a hurdy-gurdy. The girl rebuffed Cumberland's advances, as Horace Walpole giddily gossiped, and the affair ended there.[97] But later that summer, four prints turned up in allusion to the thwarted royal lover (Figure 6.1).[98] Many referred to the corpulent Cumberland as John of Gant, a joke about both his weight and his military failures in Ghent in 1745 and 1747 (the prints also carried more than a whiff of anti-Hanoverianism; Cumberland had for years been attacked as the butcher of Culloden in Jacobite verse).[99] Cumberland had earned the mocking Gant nickname in May of 1749, when *The Remembrancer* published a thinly veiled allegorical criticism of George II's preference for

---

[95] Andrew Benjamin Bricker, 'The Visual and the Verbal: The Intermediality of English Satire, *c.* 1695–1750', in *Changing Satire: Transformations and Continuities in Europe, 1600–1830*, edited by Cecilia Rosengren, Per Sivefors, and Rikard Wingård (Manchester: Manchester University Press, 2022), ch. 9. See also Mitchell, *Picture Theory*, on 'Writing, in its physical, graphic form, [as] an inseparable suturing of the visual and verbal' (p. 95); and Jesse Molesworth, 'Graphic Satire: Hogarth and Gillray', in *OHECS*, pp. 298–319, on 're-mediation' (p. 301) and the 'visual/verbal continuum' (p. 311) between satiric images and texts.

[96] Even before the rise of caricature in the mid-eighteenth century, the government had some inkling of the difficulties of interpreting images in the court. In Stephen College's trial for treason in 1681, the prosecution repeatedly presented and discussed a visual satire illustrating his anti-Charles II poem *The Raree Show* as further evidence of his treasonous intentions. Even then, however, the evidence for treason was in large measure derived from his public actions and the poem itself (*The Arraignment, Tryal and Condemnation of Stephen Colledge [sic] for High-Treason* [London, 1681], pp. 32 and 52–8). See M. D. George, *English Political Caricature to 1792: A Study of Opinion and Propaganda* (Oxford: Clarendon Press, 1959), pp. 56–7.

[97] Walpole to George Montagu (2 July 1749), *Correspondence*, vol. 9, p. 94.

[98] *The Cropper*, BM 3034; *John of Gant in Love*, BM 3037; *Solomons Glory*, BM 3030; and *The agreeable Contrast between the formidable John of Gant and Don Carlos of Southern Extraction*.

[99] Paul Kléber Monod, *Jacobitism and the English People, 1688–1788* (Cambridge: Cambridge University Press, 1989), pp. 60–1.

Figure 6.1 *John of Gant in Love, or Mars on his Knees* (1749). Courtesy of The Lewis Walpole Library, Yale University (749.07.15.01+ Impression 1)

Cumberland over his elder brother Frederick, Prince of Wales, which pretended only to describe the relationship between Edward III and his sons, John of Gaunt and the Prince of Wales. Later in September, shortly after the prints appeared, Lord Newcastle issued a warrant for their makers' arrest.[100] In short order, a group of printsellers were hauled in and interrogated.[101] But with almost comical redundancy, each told a similar story of managerial incompetence, claiming not to know where the prints came from or who was actually responsible for them.[102] Nonetheless, the Attorney General began to prepare a prosecution for those responsible, before quietly abandoning the affair altogether.

What needs to be kept in mind is the stunning verbal economy of these prints: none of them identified Cumberland by name and one even lacked the duke altogether. Yet through a complex set of literary, journalistic, and historical allusions, both viewers and the authorities were able to deduce the figures behind this bumbling love affair, an example of what Taylor has called the 'bewildering citational density' that typifies the most intelligent satirical prints from this period.[103] Moreover, the story of the thwarted royal lover and its fallout was the

---

[100] Herbert Atherton, *Political Prints in the Age of Hogarth: A Study of the Ideographic Representation of Politics* (Oxford: Clarendon Press, 1974), p. 77.

[101] *The Penny London Post, or The Morning Advertiser* (29 September–2 October 1749).

[102] SP 36/111 and KB 10/29/112, TNA.   [103] Taylor, *Politics of Parody*, p. 137.

media event of summer and autumn 1749: mockingly alluded to in print, satiric-ally represented in visual works, and archly covered in the London newspapers. The story simply illustrated a conclusion most had already arrived at: Cumberland was an obese, lusty, and incompetent boob.

For the emerging visual market, the fallout from the affair was perhaps even more interesting for what it had accidentally and obliquely revealed. Stymied prosecutions had the embarrassingly unintended consequence of pointing directly to the law's greatest interpretative failure. Even when those responsible for such works could be squirrelled out, there was no courtroom protocol for interpreting defamatory images. As a result, visual satire was given a largely free pass. The law was not the only element that encouraged the growth of caricature—both aesthetic and commercial developments prodded along the visual marketplace, as I have already noted—but it did unintentionally and indirectly help to encourage the visual marketplace by demonstrating the imperviousness of images to prosecu-tion. This, then, is how we might begin to explain the paradox of satiric produc-tion and its transition in media: the simultaneous diminishment of printed satire and yet the rapid and seemingly unabated growth of visual satire during the last half of the century.

In turn, visual satirists seemingly attacked whomever they wished. In 1812, for instance, the Solicitor General, with the exhaustion of a man who had to say the same thing over and over again, explained the situation to the Secretary of State: 'This is a most indecent and imprudent print but it would require so much of difficult explanation in stating it as a libel that it does not appear to us advisable to make it the subject of a criminal prosecution'.[104] Part of what made it so difficult to prosecute visual satire was its imagistic language—its techniques of identification and the way it produced satiric meaning. At the same time, visual satire's lingua franca, developed over decades, even centuries, made it easier for viewers to understand such prints while also allowing the prints themselves to pack an economical satiric punch. Hallett has argued that the visual language of satire was already in place by the 1730s, thanks to such early artists as William Hogarth.[105] By the 1760s, the recurring and developing visual aesthetics of personal satire—what Carretta has called its 'shared iconography'—had taken shape.[106] Some of the methods used were simply part of the common stock of images: allegorical appeals to history, scripture, and literature; recurring folk images, emblems, and pointed yet bizarre dream visions; personifications of abstractions like law, religion, and politics; and the reduction of nations and

---

[104] TS 11/580/1913, TNA. Qtd. Gatrell, *City of Laughter*, p. 503.
[105] Hallett, *Spectacle of Difference*, p. 131.
[106] Carretta, *Snarling Muse*, p. xix. See also Diana Donald, '"Calumny and Caricatura": Eighteenth-Century Political Prints and the Case of George Townshend', *Art History* 6, no. 1 (March 1983): pp. 44–66.

people down to animalistic types.[107] This also explains why words became increasingly rare in visual satire: imagistic language often made such verbalizations redundant. Such works were almost, as E. H. Gombrich has put it, 'illustrations of figures of speech', and yet they remained tantalizingly incommensurate with language, as Ronald Paulson has observed (and as prosecutors came to discover), 'as if the emblem were … beyond the capacity of the words attached to explain'.[108] Despite this, and despite the view generally held by art historians that later eighteenth-century caricature marks a definitive break with early modern emblematical traditions, there remains remarkable continuity in satire's visual language across this almost two-hundred-year period (Diana Donald, for one, has called this change 'more dialectical than evolutionary').[109] Even still, the language of visual satire had to be studied and learned. As the duke of Newcastle huffed, he couldn't make any sense of 'Prints, and Burlesques … if they are not decypher'd for Me'.[110] This in part explains why deverbalization posed such hermeneutic difficulties for the law—why it was seemingly impossible to reduce a pregnant visual satire down to a defamatory locution within the vacuum of the courtroom.

As a result, most images required interpretive work and even straightforward satires could fall victim to ambiguity. Take Thomas Rowlandson's *The Covent Garden Night Mare* (Figure 6.2), a perverse parody of Henry Fuseli's *The Nightmare* (Figure 6.3), which had been displayed to acclaim at the Royal Academy in London in 1782. Much of the humour of the print draws from the explicit juxtaposition between Fuseli's dreamer and Rowlandson's depiction of the Whig MP Charles James Fox: between the elegant, lithe body draped in a flowing, phantasmagoric nightgown and the oppressive embodiment of the denuded Fox, who seems to be less in the throes of a dream than some drunken hallucination. But what is the point to all of this? To some degree this print is most interesting for its seeming absence of a defined political agenda. The depiction of Fox is clearly unflattering. But how was one ever, within the stuffy confines of legal procedure, to reduce this parody's mocking depiction of Fox's nauseating physicality down to an explicitly libellous phrase? The muckraking nastiness of such satires—their obdurate love of exposure, their seeming indifference to their ramifications, even their absence of a clear social agenda or plan of reform—suggests that many prints were not undergirded by any deep-set or even superficial ethical mooring. Instead,

---

[107] See George, *English Political Caricature to 1792, passim.*

[108] E. H. Gombrich, *Meditations on a Hobby Horse and Other Essays on the Theory of Art* (London: Phaidon, 1963), p. 132; and Ronald Paulson, 'Pictorial Satire: From Emblem to Expression', in *A Companion to Satire: Ancient and Modern*, edited by Ruben Quintero (London: Blackwell, 2007), ch. 16.

[109] Donald, *Age of Caricature*, p. 44.

[110] Qtd. in John Brewer, *Party Ideology and Popular Politics at the Accession of George III* (Cambridge: Cambridge University Press, 1981), p. 227.

Figure 6.2 Henry Fuseli, *The Nightmare* (1781). Detroit Institute of Arts (55.5.A). Founders Society Purchase with funds from Mr. and Mrs. Bert L. Smokler and Mr. and Mrs. Lawrence A. Fleischmanf. Bridgeman Images

such satires could often be scandal-mongering entertainment, cruelty dressed in the clothes of oppositional reform.[111]

One of the questions we need to ask is how viewers managed, in the general absence of verbal clues, to identify satiric targets. Repetition was in large part aided by a visual shorthand for a familiar cast of public figures. Think of Sir Robert Walpole. So ingrained in the visual imagination of Londoners was the association between the prime minister and the fairground figure of Punch that one only needed to glimpse his hookish nose poking out from behind some dressing screen—covered in images silently attesting to ministerial corruption and would-be despotism—to make the connection.[112] The screen itself became visual shorthand for one of Walpole's sobriquets, this one earned for shielding his cronies: Screenmaster-General.[113]

---

[111] Mike Goode, 'The Public and the Limits of Persuasion in the Age of Caricature', in *The Efflorescence of Caricature, 1759–1838*, edited by Todd Porterfield (Burlington: Ashgate, 2011), p. 129.

[112] For a poem on Punch and screens, see the *London Evening-Post* (9–11 March 1742).

[113] Christine Gerrard, 'Poems on Politics', in *The Oxford Handbook of British Poetry, 1660–1800*, edited by Jack Lynch (Oxford: Oxford University Press, 20), p. 297; and *The Screen* (1742), BM 2539.

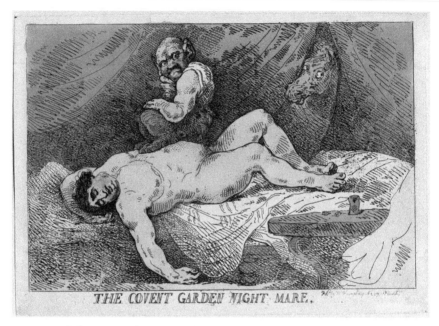

Figure 6.3 [Thomas Rowlandson], *The Covent Garden Night Mare* (1782). Courtesy of The Lewis Walpole Library, Yale University (784.04.20.01+)

Walpole, Punch, and his hookish nose were also part of a larger, more general representational reduction of men down to their physical traits.[114] Think of Fox's frown, eternal five o'clock shadow, and gelatinous belly, or Lord Stanhope's spindly legs—the kinds of physiological distillation and distortion that paradoxically produce what Amelia Rauser has called 'a more-like likeness'.[115] It hardly mattered, in fact, whether a print offered an accurate rendering of man so long as it followed closely the other prints at market. We might call this visual satire's closed system of representation. Amazingly, viewers knew what individuals looked like by their mere repetition—Burke, for instance, routinely shows up in Jesuit robes, a running joke about his creeping Catholicism. Even when a physiological mnemonic failed, a 'hieroglyph' or pun might coax the viewer along. Fox, for instance, was often literally depicted as a fox (though Newcastle, more circuitously, was a goose, the fox's Aesopian dupe).[116]

---

[114] Richard Godfrey, *English Caricature, 1620 to the Present: Caricaturists and Satirists, Their Art, Their Purpose and Influence* (London: Victoria & Albert Museum, 1984), p. 18.

[115] Amelia Rauser, *Caricature Unmasked: Irony, Authenticity, and Individualism in Eighteenth-Century English Prints* (Newark: University of Delaware Press, 2008), p. 15.

[116] *The Goose Lost* (1784), BM 6362.

The comprehensibility of such satires was also aided by topical context: political prints were often produced to coincide with the sitting of parliament.[117] Politics could be deduced from personalities, which in part explains why so many of these prints increasingly relied on the representation of individuals rather than emblematic abstractions (though it hardly explains why so many of those representations required such astonishing levels of personal animus). Nonetheless, this focus on Westminster politics meant that issues could sometimes be painfully obscure.[118] Some scholars have certainly overestimated the intelligibility of prints. But we might also say that identification hardly mattered. Part of caricature's rise lay simply in its blunt visual appeal. Unlike earlier allegorical or emblematic pieces— so perfectly hieroglyphic and in desperate need of unpacking, so lifelessly bland and as serious as the gravest puritan—caricature brought forth a simple explosion of laughter. Funniness itself even came to be viewed as an essential characteristic of prints more generally.[119] As one collection of Gillray's works put it in 1818, 'the humorous designs of his prolific pencil...contain so much of *graphic point*... they speak a language intelligible to the whole world' (an observation perhaps undermined by the half-dozen pages needed to explain each caricature).[120] Whether one fully understood the politics behind such works perhaps hardly mattered. Topical English prints actually sold widely outside of the British Isles: in Paris and Calais, in Berlin and Amsterdam.[121] This is not to downplay the semantic intricacy of visual satire from this period, but it is worth observing that caricature tended to operate at various levels of complexity. As Taylor has remarked on the intricacy of such prints, 'understanding is...a matter of degrees'.[122] At its most superficial, visual satire was grossly comic: antiquarians falling in the streets, ridiculous fashions, lecherous aristocrats, flatulent men, grimacing women.[123] But, at a deeper level, one might discern the backbiting indoor politics of Westminster or some whispered sexual romp at court. For many, however, the superficial level was perhaps enough.

In addition to technical innovations like the growth of caricature and systems of individual representation—techniques that both enabled lay identification while complicating prosecution—visual satirists had at their disposal a body of works, from beaux arts to belles-lettres, to draw on. For those on the wrong side of the Royal Academy's gates, which refused entry to engravers, the world of 'high' art

---

[117] Eirwen E. C. Nicholson, 'Consumers and Spectators: The Public of the Political Print in Eighteenth-Century England', *History* 81, no. 261 (January 1996): p. 14.

[118] Nicholson, 'Consumers and Spectators', p. 17.   [119] Donald, *Age of Caricature*, p. 32.

[120] 'Prospectus', in *The Caricatures of Gillray: With Historical and Political Illustrations*, 9 parts [?], pt. 1 (London, 1818), n.p.

[121] Donald, *Age of Caricature*, p. 20.   [122] Taylor, *Politics of Parody*, p. 134.

[123] For a pungent example of female flatulence, see C. D. Bengert's somewhat long-winded contribution, *Arse Musica; Or, The Lady's Back Report* (1722): *A Critical Edition with Apparatus* (Cold Lake: Haligonian Press, 1981).

was simply a visual rummage bin for satiric fodder.[124] Benjamin West's *Death of General Wolfe* (1770) (Figure 6.4), for instance, was burlesqued by John Boyne in a send-up of the ever-frowning Fox after his disastrous battle to pass the East India Bill in parliament (Figure 6.5).[125] Another satirist, perhaps Gillray, made pungent use of Friedrich Rehberg's *Drawings Faithfully Copied from Nature at Naples* (Figure 6.6), which depict Emma Hart, the youthful wife of the ancient Sir William Hamilton, the British Ambassador to the kingdom of Two Sicilies, and the later mistress of Captain Horatio Nelson. Rehberg's fine-limned sketches show Hart in her 'Attitudes', a series of supposedly classical poses she adopted for public performance while wearing ancient robes. Gillray's parody revised Rehberg's elegant classicizing image of Hart after she had taken on ungainly weight (Figure 6.7). Its dry title drove the message home, reducing Burkean aesthetics down to a puerile fat joke: *A New Edition Considerably Enlarged, of Attitudes Faithfully Copied from Nature and Humbly Dedicated to all Admirers of the Grand and Sublime*. Like those attacking the infamous Hart, so many of the visual satires

Figure 6.4 Benjamin West, *The Death of General Wolfe* (1770). ©National Trust Images/J. Whitaker (NT 851783)

---

[124] David Hunter, 'Copyright Protection for Engravings and Maps in Eighteenth-Century Britain', *Library* 6, no. 2 (1987): p. 144.

[125] H. V. Bowen, 'India: The Metropolitan Context', in *The Oxford History of the British Empire: The Eighteenth Century*, edited by P. J. Marshall (Oxford: Oxford University Press, 1998), p. 544.

Figure 6.5 [John Boyne], *General Blackbeard wounded at the Battle of Leadenhall* (5 January 1784). General Collection, Beinecke Rare Book & Manuscript Library, Yale University (11810304)

from this period are simply rotten with misogyny. They were part of 'a wider debate', Cindy McCreery has argued, 'what we might call the "satirical gaze", over women's role in English society'. According to McCreery, roughly 40 percent of the thousands of prints produced between 1760 and 1800 are satires on women.[126] Many of these works were generalized attacks on the supposed foibles of women. But many also found their starting point with the female *bon ton* living in London—particular women we can identify even today, thanks to the British Museum's extensive catalogues.[127]

In a similar way, visual satirists often turned to their literary predecessors, employing 'the narratives, characters, and themes of literary texts as a means of giving shape to the political present'.[128] Some even used an author's own works to skewer him. Frederick George Byron, for instance, sent up Burke in *Don Dismallo* (Figure 6.8), using a nickname that he had earned for his *Reflections on the Revolution in France* (1790). A satire on his defence of monarchy, the print alludes

---

[126] Cindy McCreery, *The Satirical Gaze: Prints of Women in Late Eighteenth-Century England* (Oxford: Clarendon Press, 2004), pp. 2, 6.

[127] Frederic George Stephens and Mary Dorothy George, *Catalogue of Prints and Drawings in the British Museum*, 11 vol. (London, 1870–1954).

[128] Taylor, *Politics of Parody*, p. 4.

Figure 6.6 Friedrich Rehberg, *Drawings Faithfully Copied from Nature at Naples* (1794) (London, 1797). Courtesy of The Lewis Walpole Library, Yale University (Quarto 75 R266 797)

to Burke's extravagant praise of Marie Antoinette. But the piece was also disgustingly personal, with Burke fawning over the French queen while his wife Jane (by this point almost sixty years of age) sobs in the background. 'Christ Jasus', Burke curses in his thick Irish brogue. 'What an ass have I been a number of Years; to have doated on an old woman—Heavens! What's her bacon and eggs to the delicious Dairy of this celestial Vision'.

Figure 6.7 [James Gillray?], *A New Edition Considerably Enlarged, of Attitudes Faithfully Copied from Nature and Humbly Dedicated to all Admirers of the Grand and Sublime* (1807). Courtesy of The Lewis Walpole Library, Yale University (Quarto 75 G41 807)

Figure 6.8 [Frederick George Byron], *Don Dismallo, after an Absence of Sixteen Years, Embracing his Beautiful Vision* (18 November 1790). © The Trustees of the British Museum (1868,0808.5973)

Such a slippery and allusive visual language was almost impossible to translate and corral to the satisfaction of jurors, but how these works were circulated only exacerbated the government's problems. Before 1750, most prints were anonymous.[129] We know many of the earliest practitioners—artists like Charles Mosley, George Bickham, Louis-Philippe Boitard, Anthony Walker, Joseph Groupy, Hubert-François Gravelot, and Paul Sandby—through reconstructions of specific satiric styles. Others went by pseudonyms. Gillray, for instance, often signed his crudest engravings with the perfectly generic 'J. Kent' or 'T. Adams'. At other times, printsellers relied on circumlocutory tricks to send the authorities on wild goose chases. Take *A Certain Dutchess Kissing Old Swelter-in-Grease the Butcher for his Vote* (1784), a vicious satire on Georgiana, duchess of Devonshire and her supposedly meddlesome efforts to solicit votes for Fox (Figure 6.9). The link between sex, politics, and light prostitution is clear enough, with Devonshire leaning down to kiss a grotesque little butcher, who greedily reciprocates. The print was ostensibly designed by 'R. Lyford', but this is clearly a pseudonym. Not a single other print by Lyford is known. The publisher, 'H. Macphail', is another red herring. The only telling detail from the piece is the address at which 'Macphail' was ostensibly resident: 68 High Holborn St, just north of Lincoln's Inn Fields. This was actually the former address of the printseller William Richardson, who had a shop on Holborn between 1778 and 1782. By 1784, when *A Certain Dutchess* was published, Richardson had relocated to Surrey Street, just south of the Strand. The outdated address was perhaps a clever printseller's ruse, a hint to knowledgeable customers intimating where more anti-Foxite prints could be found—not at Richardson's old shop, but his new one. In fact, Richardson seems to have repeatedly used the pseudonym 'H. Macphail' throughout the mid-1780s. A half-dozen prints published by 'Macphail' are still in existence, all of them attacking Fox, the Prince of Wales, and Devonshire.[130] In any case, printsellers knew what they could safely display in their windows for gawking passers-by. The *Times* suggested that printsellers were keeping their most radical wares below the counter.[131]

There was very little, legally speaking, that the government could officially do. Stern warnings remained an option. One was given to Gillray and the printseller Samuel William Fores for his travesty of religious art, *The Presentation, or, Wise Men's Offering* (1795), a satire on William Pitt and the Prince of Wales. The two were arrested for blasphemy, though the prosecution went nowhere.[132] At other times, though, officials felt their hands were tied. Fox, for instance, was infuriated with Gillray over *A Democrat, or Reason & Philosophy* (1793), in which a flatulent

---

[129] Godfrey, *English Caricature*, p. 13.
[130] See *The Political Beggar* (1784), BM 6500, possibly by Boyne, and *The Rival Canvessers* (1784), BM 6621.
[131] *Times* (19 December 1792).   [132] Donald, *Age of Caricature*, p. 166.

Figure 6.9 R. Lyford (pseud.), *A Certain Dutchess Kissing Old Swelter-in-Grease the Butcher for his Vote* (1784), for H. Macphail (pseud.). © The Trustees of the British Museum (1868,0808.5215)

Fox dances a bloody-handed jig in the guise of a *sans-culotte*, singing the popular revolutionary refrain 'Ça ira' ('It'll be fine') (Figure 6.10). Gillray should be 'trounced with a vengeance', a flustered Fox wrote, knowing full well, however, that a prosecution would only bring 'further ridicule and publicity'.[133]

Other measures proved just as useless. In 1787, trying to stem the tide, George III issued a proclamation against 'loose and licentious Prints, Books and Publications'.[134] Parliament followed suit, promulgating the Blasphemous and Seditious Libels Act (1819), which stipulated that those twice convicted of either offence could be punished by transportation. For all that, not even parliament proved far-sighted enough to see the value of a print registry. As we have already seen, the Act of Anne provided at least one tool for tying individual works to profit-minded booksellers. But neither the Engraving Copyright Act (1735) (8 Geo. II, c. 13), its successor, promulgated in 1767, nor the Prints Copyright Act of 1777 (17 Geo. III, c. 57) stipulated that prints be centrally registered. Those looking to protect their wares needed only to annotate each print with a date of publication and the proprietor, but even these were optional, if the copy owner was unwilling to fend off piracy.[135] Given the fact that the bar to entry was so low for registering copyright, there was no reason *not* to register a work, even if the registration was entirely fictional; to omit such information was simply to draw attention to the fact you were hiding something.

Nonetheless, despite the futility of their attempts, the authorities were unable to let visual satire be. Caricatures might have been impossible to prosecute when published in single sheets, but the Crown devised a workaround: by going after caricaturists and their printsellers by targeting written works. When visual satires appeared in newspapers and periodicals, they were sometimes accompanied by incriminating textual explanations.[136] As Gatrell notes, 'In view of the difficulties of prosecuting satirical *images*, it comes as no surprise that the most concerted legal attack of the 1810s, as in the 1790s, was directed against subversive *texts*'.[137] The printseller William Holland, for instance, long the radical scourge of the government for his Jacobin prints, was only finally tried in 1793 when a government informer discovered him selling one of Thomas Paine's anti-monarchical pamphlets. Even though these were widely available from other booksellers, Holland was fined, forced to give sureties for good behaviour, and imprisoned for a year in Newgate.[138] His trial was a cleverly instrumental use of what we would today call pretextual prosecution—like going after mobsters for tax evasion,

---

[133] Qtd. *Caricatures of Gillray*, pt. 2, p. 30.
[134] Rpt. *Gentleman's Magazine* 57, no. 1 (June 1787): p. 534.
[135] Hunter, 'Copyright Protection', pp. 136–45.
[136] Thomas Milton Kemnitz, 'The Cartoon As a Historical Source', *Journal of Interdisciplinary History* 4, no. 12 (Summer 1973): pp. 83–4.
[137] Gatrell, *City of Laughter*, p. 520.   [138] TS 11/175, TNA. See Gatrell, *City of Laughter*, p. 494.

Figure 6.10 [James Gillray], *A Democrat, or Reason & Philosophy* (1 March 1793). Courtesy of The Lewis Walpole Library, Yale University (793.03.01.01)

the Crown targeted texts to go after prints—but also a pungent if ultimately ineffective warning to other printsellers.

For the most part, though, prosecutions failed while also drumming up unwanted attention. What was the Crown to do? One option was simply to buy up entire impressions, no matter the cost, though this had the perverse effect of incentivizing the most scandalous prints.[139] Even better, in a page out of Robert Harley's book, one could produce counter-propaganda, written by 'political Prize fighters' and sold at a discount or given away.[140] Bribery proved the most useful tool. James Sayers, for example, received a sinecure from Pitt.[141] Many visual satirists simply illustrated for whoever put more money in their coffers. In the 1780s, during the battles between the pro-Pitt and pro-Fox factions, Rowlandson, Gillray, and Dent all 'habitually switched from one side to the other'.[142] Later, in the 1820s, George Cruikshank found himself supporting the radical measures of his colleague William Hone while simultaneously contributing to loyalist Tory satires.[143] As one writer in 1823 put it, Cruikshank was 'a free-handed, comical young fellow who will do anything he is paid for'.[144]

Hence George IV's efforts. As the Prince of Wales, he had been an extravagant womanizer and notorious drunkard. From the 1780s on, to the shock of many onlookers (even the sharp-tongued John Wilkes), his rakish, blubbery body was to be found on gruesome, almost anatomical public display in print shop windows.[145] Like those before him, the king hoped the courts might control the satirists, though with no success, asking whether the Attorney General thought 'the vendors of treason, and libellers…are to be prosecuted'.[146] Also like those before him, he paid satirists, such as Henry Wigstead and Rowlandson, to produce propaganda on his behalf.[147] He also attempted to buy up the most offensive

[139] John Wardroper, *Kings, Lords and Wicked Libellers: Satire and Protest, 1760–1837* (London: John Murray, 1973), p. 13.

[140] Downie, *Robert Harley and the Press*, pp. 2–5, 41–5, 106–16, 118–48, 162–70, 178–83, 191–5; Whitefoord MSS, Add. MSS. 36595 f. 201, BL; Brewer, *Party Ideology and Popular Politics*, p. 235, 228–39; and Donald, *Age of Caricature*, p. 147.

[141] Rosenthal, 'Public Reputation', p. 73.   [142] Donald, *Age of Caricature*, p. 26.

[143] Donald, *Age of Caricature*, p. 26.

[144] *Blackwood's Edinburgh Magazine* 14, no. 78 (1823): pp. 22–3.

[145] See, for instance, Letter LXVII (28 November 1788), *Letters, from the year 1774 to the year 1796, of John Wilkes, esq., addressed to his daughter, the late Miss Wilkes*, vol. 3 (London, 1804), p. 247; Sophie von la Roche, *Sophie in London, 1786: Being the Diary of Sophie v. la Roche*, trans. Clare Williams (London: J. Cape, 1933), p. 262; and Kenneth Baker, *George IV: A Life in Caricature* (London: Thames & Hudson, 2005).

[146] George IV to Lord Eldon (9 January 1821), rpt. Duke of Buckingham and Chandos, *Memoirs of the Court of George IV, 1820–1830*, vol. 1 (London, 1859), p. 107. See also the prints collected as evidence for a prospective prosecution, TS 11/115, TNA.

[147] Sir John Soane's Papers, VIII.c, f. 5, Soane Museum Archives. See Matthew Payne and James Payne, *Regarding Thomas Rowlandson, 1757–1827: His Life, Art and Acquaintance* (London: Hogarth, 2003).

Figure 6.11 'Suppressed' satire under George IV (note the manuscript annotation in the bottom right-hand corner). [Robert Cruikshank], *Royalty in a Rage or Family Quarrels* (1820), Prints and Photographs Division, Library of Congress (PC 3-1820 [A size])

prints—by the time of his death, the royal collection had swollen to some 2,750 caricatures—but found that this only encouraged printsellers to produce more prints in greater numbers.[148] In the end, George resorted to bribery on a massive scale. Between 1819 and 1822, the king paid out some £2,600 to individual printsellers and artists, including George and Robert Cruikshank, to suppress individual works (Figure 6.11).[149] As a result of these payouts, many of the largest printsellers and the most prominent caricaturists turned away from anti-monarchical satire.[150]

---

[148] GEO/MAIN/51382A, Royal Archives. See Kate Heard, 'The British Royal Family and Satirical Prints, 1760–1901', in *Collecting Prints and Drawings*, edited by Andrea M. Gáldy and Sylvia Heudecker (Cambridge: Cambridge Scholars Publishing, 2016), p. 146; and Kate Heard, *High Spirits: The Comic Art of Thomas Rowlandson* (London: Royal Collection Trust, 2013), p. 39.

[149] Wardroper, *Kings, Lords and Wicked Libellers*, p. 213. For George's bills and payments, see GEO/MAIN 51382, Royal Archives and HO73, TNA. For satires marked 'suppressed', see William Heath, *The Royal Milling Match* (1811), PC 1–11746 (B size), and John Lewis Marks, *The Cunning and Happy Family* (c.1822), PC 1–14404 (A size), both held in the Prints & Photographs Division of the Library of Congress. For help in sorting out George III's and IV's print-collecting activities, I would like to thank Martha Kennedy of the Library of Congress and Kate Heard, senior curator of prints and drawings, of the Royal Collection Trust at Windsor Castle.

[150] For more on George IV's response to visual satire, see Gatrell, *City of Laughter*, ch. 17; and Heard, 'The British Royal Family and Satirical Prints', pp. 142–7, and *High Spirits*, pp. 44–7.

Eventually, during the nineteenth and twentieth centuries, the law developed procedures for handling defamatory images—but such innovations came too late, after the visual market had again radically shifted in the 1830s.[151] Why it took so long to devise these procedures is, however, an oddity of legal history. In short, it seems that the courts, through their insistence on verbal evidence, drove libel law into a rut. By focusing so wholly on verbal reference, the law became 'path dependent', as legal historians put it: the development of defamation law effectively foreclosed the possibility that reference could also be understood in visual terms.[152] This procedural and doctrinal close-mindedness is even stranger when we consider how the courts, a century earlier, had come to handle irony in trials for libel. Verbal irony was a particular problem because it created textual evidence that seemed, on its face at least, to mean the opposite of what it said. In *R. v. Browne* the courts installed something similar to what today we call the obscenity test. As United States Supreme Court Justice Potter Stewart explained in *Jacobellis v. Ohio* in 1964, obscenity cannot be effectively defined, 'But I know it when I see it'. In a similar way, Chief Justice Holt held juries to a 'I know it when I see it' philosophy of ironic intention. Holt's ruling was undergirded by a clear sense that ironic meaning is produced by a community of readers rather than a simple and mechanistic set of verbal signals. In this sense, the courts came to hold a 'socio-centric' view of ironic interpretation: a belief that readers are ultimately responsible for ironic meaning and that the means of interpretation is a learned set of conventions produced by the institutions that have authorized them.[153]

Strangely, the courts failed to imagine a similar doctrine for visual materials. We might ask why jurors, when presented with a caricature, were unable to find it libellous or not, without demonstrating how precisely images signified. The alternative—that parliament pass a bill making caricatures defamatory—was simply a non-starter. As early as 1741, David Hume was calling liberty of the press 'a common right of mankind'.[154] By the latter half of the eighteenth century, any government attack on the press, no matter how reasonable, inevitably triggered a maelstrom of bad publicity and accusations of an ever-encroaching despotism.[155]

[151] Joseph Dean, *Ridicule, Hatred, or Contempt: A Book of Libel Cases* (New York: McMillan Co., 1954), ch. 11.

[152] Oona A. Hathaway, 'Path Dependence in the Law: The Course and Pattern of Legal Change in a Common Law System', *Iowa Law Review* 86, no. 2 (2001): pp. 601–65.

[153] Wayne Booth, 'A New Strategy for Establishing a Truly Democratic Criticism', *Daedalus* 112, no. 1 (Winter 1983): p. 197.

[154] David Hume, 'Essay of the Liberty of the Press', in *Essays, Moral and Political*, edited by Eugene F. Miller, rev. ed. (Indianapolis: Liberty Fund, 1987), p. 604, note d. Following the tumults of the Wilkites in the 1760s, Hume was considerably less sanguine about the pacifying effects of the press, however, and revised his essay extensively. See Hellmuth, 'Liberty of the Press', p. 180.

[155] For an early example, see *The Craftsman*, no. 4 (16 December 1726): 'If we descend to later Ages, we shall constantly observe, upon a strict Review of the Histories of all Nations, that *Liberty* in general has always flourished in the greatest Perfection, where the Liberty of *Writing* has been most encouraged; and when this Freedom declines by any Checks put upon the *Press*, that Tyranny and Servitude

Above all, though, there remained the problem of recalcitrant jurors, especially in trials for seditious libel and increasingly as the century wore on. As Thomas A. Green has remarked, 'Authorities drew the conclusion from years of jury resistance to the law of seditious libel that juries could not be trusted in such cases to return verdicts that accorded even loosely with the government's inter-pretation of facts'.[156]

That it took so long for the law to change was also in part the result of a massive shift in the visual marketplace. By the 1830s, the market for single-sheet political caricatures had simply dried up. When the radical satirists of the early nineteenth century abandoned satire, they did so to harness more profitable markets: chil-dren's literature, family magazines, literary periodicals, triple-decker Victorian novels, and underground pornography. As Wood notes:

> The single-sheet satiric etching had gone into decline and by 1830 it was dead and replaced by the benign lithographs of John Doyle (H.B.) and his followers . . . It was not just print technology but the satiric spirit of the age that had changed. Popular illustrated journalism flourished but became increasingly kindly in its attitudes towards the state. The savage and violent energies of the gutter press no longer poured into satire attacking the government and monarchy but were absorbed by the expanding horror market which focused on sensational murders and sex crimes.[157]

Donald has likewise argued that the Georgian satirical print entered a 'slow process of decline' in the 1820s and '30s, as printmakers moved to the 'genteel comic journal for family consumption'. It was all part of the 'stricter proprieties of the new age', which killed off the 'savage and envenomed character of the revolutionary period'.[158] The point is that the death of visual satire in the 1830s was largely a product of market forces, not legal ones; visual satirists only moved on to new media after the broadest base of consumers had finally soured on the chest thumping, finger pointing, and muckraking.

Through all of this, visual satirists were able to duck the authorities. Bribery offered the Crown one response, but it was the only effective mechanism in a legal culture that privileged words over images, where procedural rules for delimiting verbal ambiguity were impossible to co-opt for delimiting visual semantics. This itself was a stunning and unexpected twist of fate. Printed satire laboured under a series of rulings and a body of laws that made publishing extremely risky, and yet

---

increase in Proportion; for which Reason, those Persons who, in any Age, have been the Patrons of *Popular Liberty*, have always been the Champions of the Freedom of the *Press*; which was never restrained but in order to serve some bad Design, in wicked Reigns, or under corrupt Administrations'.

[156] Green, *Verdict*, p. 329.   [157] Wood, *Radical Satire and Print Culture*, p. 270.

[158] Donald, *Art of Caricature*, p. 184.

visual satire was simply not subject to the same laws and protocols and was consequently given a shockingly free pass.

6.3 The Deverbalization of Drama: Samuel Foote, Mimicry, and Impersonation after the Stage Licensing Act (1737)

In the late 1720s and throughout the 1730s, political and satiric drama also flourished, especially in London's minor theatres.[159] Though the government increasingly understood that direct prosecution could be troublingly counterproductive, Walpole himself remained eager to institute some form of theatrical control. His parliamentary efforts eventually resulted in the Stage Licensing Act of 1737, which reduced London to two patent theatres and mandated the pre-performance censorship of new plays.[160] In large measure, the Licensing Act was a response to the raucous dramatic satires staged, and sometimes suppressed, between 1728 and 1737. Nonetheless, few of the dramatic satires produced during this experimental period in London theatre could be described as direct (or even, perhaps, ideologically consistent if indirect) attacks on Walpole, his administration, or the Crown. They were, instead, much more vaguely oppositional satires.[161] Nevertheless, criticism, even obscure criticism, was undesirable, and we should little surprised to find that the first three plays banned under the Licensing Act— Henry Brooke's *Gustavus Vasa*, James Thomson's *Edward and Eleonora*, and William Patterson's *Arminius*—were all historical tragedies with political overtones that could be read in vaguely allegorical ways.[162]

The regulatory flexibility of the Licensing Act was also part and parcel of the Walpole administration's increasingly strategic approach to its critics in the 1730s. It certainly prosecuted satirists and stationers for libel when it could and proactively helped to develop courtroom procedures for delimiting verbal ambiguity. This, though, was only one strategy. When it came to the regulation of the stage, the Walpole administration took the long route, by seemingly drumming up the very controversy that would ensure that both the Commons and Lords would not, at that particular moment, oppose a bill for theatrical licensing. The institution of

---

[159] Robert D. Hume, *The Rakish Stage: Studies in English Drama, 1660–1800* (Carbondale: Southern Illinois University Press, 1983), pp. 270–311.

[160] Vincent J. Liesenfeld, *The Licensing Act of 1737* (Madison: University of Wisconsin Press, 1984), pp. 123–50; for the text of the Act, see pp. 191–3.

[161] See, for instance, William Eben Schultz, *Gay's Beggar's Opera: Its Content, History and Influence* (New Haven: Yale University Press, 1923), pp. 226–69; for critical disagreement across the twentieth century, see Hume, *Rakish Stage*, pp. 246–53.

[162] Matthew J. Kinservik, 'The Dialectics of Print and Performance after 1737', in *The Oxford Handbook of the Georgian Theatre, 1737–1832*, edited by Julia Swindells and David Francis Taylor (Oxford: Oxford University Press, 2014), p. 133.

dramatic censorship is thus in part worth reviewing because it reveals Walpole's canny ability to make legislative lemonade from satiric lemons.

Interestingly, the very thing that helped to ensure the bill's passage was an anti-ministerial and anti-Hanoverian allegorical satire: a two-part dream vision called the 'The Vision of the Golden Rump', which first appeared in March of 1737 in the journal *Common Sense*.[163] The vision describes the obeisance paid to the enormous posteriors of an idol with satyr-like legs (George II) controlled by the Chief Magician (Walpole). The High Priestess begins each ceremony by taking a 'Clyster-pipe' and injecting *aurum potabile*—the panacean drinkable gold of seventeenth-century alchemy—into the idol's 'F[un]d[amen]t'.[164] The idol is apparently 'very cholerick', however, and spontaneously 'lift[s] up his cloven Foot' to receive another dose, frequently with disastrous consequences: 'his Fury was sometimes so sudden and unexpected, that he imprinted visible Marks of it on all who stood near him' through these 'unnatural Sallies or Hurricanes'.

During the ceremony, the subjects prostrate themselves in front of the Rump, which in a flatulently 'hollow, hoarse Voice' demands their reverence. The Rump then receives its gifts, first from the Knights of the Golden Rump and then from the '*Castellans*', a group of twenty-two knights dressed in 'Party-coloured Robes'.[165] The Magician 'gently stroke[s]' the Rump with his wand, and 'the Idol swell[s] to an enormous size' equal to 'the Statue in *Grosvenor Square*, Horse and all'. The scene ends with the Knights and Castellans jostling for (and then complaining about) the monetary favours given out by the Rump, before the magician leaves to seduce 'some mortal Female' and the author receives a brief account of Jacobite-like 'Hereticks and Unbelievers' who worship 'the Rump of a *Buffalo*'. The entire dream vision ends in a puff of puffery: 'Here I was awakened by the bawling of an Hawker under my Window, who desired his Customers to open their Eyes, and purchase Two pennyworth of COMMON SENSE'.[166]

Though the authorities could have initiated a prosecution for seditious libel against *Common Sense*, Walpole saw that this same allegory might be leveraged in the service of even greater regulatory control. He seemingly bribed Henry Giffard, the hard-up theatre manager and co-owner of the Theatre in Goodman's Fields, to stage a now-lost dramatic version of the vision. Walpole then circulated extracts of the play to other MPs, read portions to the king, and recited lines from the script during parliamentary debate in May. His crafty manipulation of the entire event led to the almost wholly unopposed passage of the Stage Licensing Act (10 Geo. 2, c. 28), in late May and early June of 1737, which was not even a stand-alone bill

---

[163] Liesenfeld, *Licensing Act*, pp. 92, 129–37.

[164] Lawrence M. Principe, *The Secrets of Alchemy* (Chicago: University of Chicago Press, 2012), p. 113.

[165] *Common Sense: Or, The Englishman's Journal* no. 7 (19 March 1737).

[166] *Common Sense: Or, The Englishman's Journal* no. 8 (26 March 1737).

but merely an amendment to a 1714 act (12 Anne, c. 23) against itinerant players.[167]

The passage of the Licensing Act is in part interesting because it demonstrates the government's increasing tact in handling its opponents. But I am more interested, in this final section, in drawing attention to the process by which the Lords Chamberlain and the Examiners of Plays licensed plays and how such a system of regulation, like the interpretive doctrines for libel developed during this same period, promoted forms of dramatic deverbalization. In short, despite the precise *textual* aspects of licensing—the line-by-line censoring, erasure, or substitution of objectionable words or phrases—the onstage lampooning of prominent figures was still possible and in part permitted, for the licensers lacked a preliminary regulatory mechanism for censoring non-verbal gaps that only manifested themselves in performance.[168] As a result, playwrights, actors, and theatre managers—and especially Samuel Foote—exploited the process of licensing and managed to sneak some forms of non-verbal satire in through the backdoor of London theatres, even after the introduction of mandatory pre-performance censorship.

This is not to suggest that licensing was an utter failure or that more verbal forms of satire suddenly vanished from the post-licensing stage. Even after the passage of the Licensing Act, the Walpole administration seemingly permitted illegal, non-patent theatres to perform plays and other theatrical entertainments, so long as those same entertainments refrained from reflecting on him or parliament.[169] Moreover, Matthew J. Kinservik has shown that the goal of the Licensing Act was not the wholesale suppression of dramatic satire—something that would have led to public outcry and increased print sales of the most scurrilous and thus unstageable dramatic pieces. Instead, the goal was to discipline stage managers and playwrights: to show them what kinds of drama, and especially forms of satire, were permissible, thereby leading to stageable plays that neither gave offence, nor provoked the Crown, nor caused an uproar in the press.[170] In addition, according to David Thomas, the Licensing Act largely accomplished its objectives.[171]

---

[167] David Thomas (ed.), *Theatre in Europe: A Documentary History: Restoration and Georgian England, 1660–1788* (Cambridge: Cambridge University Press, 1989), pp. 211–14; and Julia Swindells, 'The Political Context of the 1737 Licensing Act', in *The Oxford Handbook of the Georgian Theatre, 1737–1832*, edited by Julia Swindells and David Francis Taylor (Oxford: Oxford University Press, 2014), p. 110.

[168] L. W. Conolly, *The Censorship of English Drama, 1737–1824* (San Marino: The Huntington Library, 1976), pp. 113–36.

[169] Matthew J. Kinservik, *Disciplining Satire: The Censorship of Satiric Comedy on the Eighteenth-Century London Stage* (Lewisburg: Bucknell University Press, 2002), pp. 102–4.

[170] Kinservik, *Disciplining Satire*, pp. 95–120.

[171] David Thomas, 'The 1737 Licensing Act and Its Impact', in *The Oxford Handbook of the Georgian Theatre, 1737–1832*, edited by Julia Swindells and David Francis Taylor (Oxford: Oxford University Press, 2014), pp. 91–106; and David Thomas, David Carlton, and Anne Etienne, *Theatre Censorship: From Walpole to Wilson* (Oxford: Oxford University Press, 2007), pp. 24–68.

Throughout the succeeding decades, concessions were made—the expansion of minor and provincial theatres, for instance, was increasingly permitted—but the administration's legislative aims were largely fulfilled by the Licensing Act and helped along by the avaricious management of the two patent theatres, which savoured their captive audiences and their shared metropolitan monopoly.[172]

Simply put, licensing worked not because the plays submitted for licensing witnessed radical excisions or were denied licenses. Licensing worked because politically incendiary and viciously satiric plays were never submitted at all. This resulted in part from the costs built into the process of staging a new work after 1737: managers were forced to submit and then wait on new plays; there was no certainty of a license; an illegal licensing fee had to be paid to the Examiner's office; actors had to learn new parts; and playscripts needed to be refined for performance. In any case, what was the point? Even if a new play were licensed, there was no guarantee of success, and dramatists routinely complained during this period that nothing novel could thrive on the increasingly conservative post-licensing stage. In 1759, for instance, Oliver Goldsmith lamented, in a doom-and-gloom essay on the mean state of the London stage, that the sycophantic modern playwright had to be equally skilled in 'the arts of courting the manager as well as the muse'.[173] (Perhaps. But Goldsmith's own success years later with *She Stoops to Conquer* [1773] might throw such Gibbonian griping into at least partial relief.) New plays, moreover, *did* appear on the post-licensing stage, even if there was a massive drop in overall new productions. Those new pieces, however, migrated away from the five-act main-piece and into those areas that made a night at an eighteenth-century London theatre a fully intermedial event: the epilogues, prologues, farces, afterpieces, dances, and entr'acte entertainments.[174] Theatre was a major draw in London and, between the two official theatres, there were enough attendees to go around. Moreover, a repertoire of free classics, independent of crotchety, fussy new playwrights and the tediously uncertain process of licensing, could fill the void.[175] Rivalry between the two patent theatres, in any case, hardly ensured better performances, as many argued at the time, but simply led to more crowd-pleasing pablum.[176]

Satire, nonetheless, found its way onto the stage during this later period, and not only in the 'sympathetic' satires most closely studied by Kinservik, with their

---

[172] See, for instance, Jane Moody, *Illegitimate Theatre in London, 1770–1840* (Cambridge: Cambridge University Press, 2007).
[173] Oliver Goldsmith, 'Of the Stage', in *The Collected Works of Oliver Goldsmith*, vol. 1: *An Enquiry into the Present State of Learning in Europe*, edited by Arthur Friedman (Oxford: Clarendon Press, 1966), p. 328.
[174] Kinservik, *Disciplining Satire*, pp. 99–101, 128–32.   [175] Hume, *Rakish Stage*, p. 311.
[176] Frederick Burwick, 'Georgian Theories of the Actor', in *The Oxford Handbook of the Georgian Theatre, 1737–1832*, edited by Julia Swindells and David Francis Taylor (Oxford: Oxford University Press, 2014), p. 180.

'reliance on the hortatory function of positive exemplary characters'.[177] Indeed, lashingly personal and even non-corrective satire regularly appeared on the post-licensing stage, though it tended to manifest itself in non-textual and highly ephemeral forms. Paradoxically, we have perhaps not paid enough attention to such performative workarounds in the age of licensing—how 'satirical meanings', in Ros Ballaster's words, 'accrued in performance'—thanks to the rich and yet strangely occlusive archives of theatrical regulation we possess today.[178] Theatre historians, early on, focused on the effects of censorship by studying a comprehensive collection of 2,500 play texts submitted to the Lord Chamberlain and later collected by John Larpent, the Examiner of Plays from 1778 to 1824.[179] The collection has been indispensable to theatre historians, but it is also a resource that has, in its very extensiveness and in its proximity to the mechanics of play writing, theatrical business, and censorship, obscured the most ephemeral and embodied aspects of London theatrical events by offering little insight into what actually happened on stage.

This performative quality, most importantly, lay beyond at least the initial reach and control of the licensers. Theatrical legislation, like earlier courtroom procedures that enabled the prosecution of satire, focused incessantly on the verbal or, more specifically, *textual* aspects of performance. It was through the non-verbal mechanics of performance that stage satirists were able to sidestep, at least temporarily and at least in this one regard, the initial process of regulation. Mimicry, for instance, was both widely practised among actors and incredibly popular on London stages: Tate Wilkinson, Charles Macklin, Kitty Clive, Charles Bannister, Ralph Sherwin, John Hill, and Charles Mathews, among so many other actors, were all gifted impersonators.[180] Even David Garrick was famed for it. In 1741, he played Bayes in a revival of *The Rehearsal* in a send-up of the excessively mannerist acting of his contemporaries, including Denis Delane, Sacheveral Hale, and Lacy Ryan.[181] Though celebrated in his own day for his portrayal of tragic Shakespearean heroes, Garrick spent most of his time on stage in comic and comedic roles, including in farces and afterpieces, and had a particular penchant for physical comedy and the portrayal of drunks.[182]

---

[177] Kinservik, *Disciplining Satire*, p. 46. See also Brian Corman, *Genre and Generic Change in English Comedy, 1660–1710* (Toronto: University of Toronto Press, 1993), p. 114.

[178] Ros Ballaster, 'Dramatic Satire', in *The Oxford Handbook of Eighteenth-Century Satire*, edited by Paddy Bullard (Oxford: Oxford University Press, 2019), p. 337.

[179] The Papers of John Larpent, 1737–1824, mssLA 1–2503, Hunt.L. See *The Censorship of British Theatre, 1737–1843*, edited by David O'Shaughnessy (Trinity College Dublin). https://tobeomitted.tcd.ie/index.html.

[180] Jim Davis, *Comic Acting and Portraiture in Late-Georgian and Regency England* (Cambridge: Cambridge University Press, 2015), p. 195.

[181] Kinservik, *Disciplining Satire*, p. 138.

[182] Misty G. Anderson, 'Genealogies of Comedy', in *The Oxford Handbook of the Georgian Theatre, 1737–1832*, edited by Julia Swindells and David Francis Taylor (Oxford: Oxford University Press, 2014), p. 356.

Most famous, even infamous, was Samuel Foote, the playwright, actor, and later manager and owner of the Little Theatre in the Haymarket. At the time, he was acclaimed for his 'chameleon-like capacity to inhabit the bodies of his satirical targets'.[183] Like the actors Edward Shuter and Henry Woodward, he often employed grimaces to comic effect—a physiognomic plasticity both marvelled at by spectators and condemned as excessive nonsense.[184] In *The Rosciad* (1761), his lacerating attack on actors and acting, Charles Churchill scoffingly observed:

> By turns transform'd into all kinds of shapes,
> Constant to none F[oo]TE laughs, cries, struts, and scrapes:
> Now in the center, now in van or rear,
> The Proteus shifts, Bawd, Parson, Auctioneer.
> His strokes of humour, and his bursts of sport
> Are all contain'd in this one word, Distort.
> Doth a man stutter, look a-squint, or halt?
> Mimics draw humour out of Nature's fault:
> With personal defects their mirth adorn,
> And hang misfortunes out to public scorn.[185]

We might disagree with Churchill's assessment of Foote's satiric ethics or his talents (though it is a commonplace of Foote scholarship to note that he was, at best, a mediocre actor). But Churchill's gloss nonetheless helps to explain the fascination with Foote's imitative powers—their physicality, their aurality, and, above all, their shockingly protean quality. Interestingly, it was precisely this form of sonic and embodied personal satire that transcended language and thus failed to appear in the play texts submitted for licensing, either for his plays and performances at the two patent theatres, Covent Garden and Drury Lane, or later, following his acquisition, in July of 1766, of a patent for the summer season, for his plays and performances at the Haymarket.[186]

What is most intriguing about Foote's mimicry is that it points directly to the insufficiency of the play text as a medium of dramatic policing.[187] As one critic wrote in 1765, Foote's plays 'could never be perfectly represented in black and white'; they required, instead, the 'strong colouring which Mr. Foote had given them in his personal representation'.[188] Jane Wessel has expanded on this idea, arguing that what Foote 'was offering was not a play that any theatre could

[183] Ballaster, 'Dramatic Satire', p. 347.

[184] Shearer West, *The Image of the Actor: Verbal and Visual Representation in the Age of Garrick and Kemble* (London: Printer Publishers, 1991), pp. 129–30.

[185] Charles Churchill, *The Rosciad*, in *The Poetical Works of Charles Churchill*, edited by Douglas Grant (Oxford: Clarendon Press, 1956), ll. 395–404.

[186] Phyllis T. Dircks, 'Foote, Samuel (bap. 1721, d. 1777)', *ODNB*.

[187] Ballaster, 'Dramatic Satire', p. 344.

[188] *Lloyd's Evening Post* 16, no. 1230 (27–9 May 1765): p. 508.

reproduce, but an experience in which he himself was the main feature . . . It was in theatres rather than in print that Foote was able to assert his singularity fully', she concludes, 'and he did so by creating "unfinished" texts that only he could complete in performance'.[189] Foote might not have modified his play texts for performance, but he did modify his *performance* of those play texts to create new overtones, characters, and especially satiric potshots.[190]

Mimicry and impersonation were thus a useful subterfuge in a single-minded regulatory culture that primarily policed words, but they were not evasions devised solely in response to licensing. Even before he began submitting play-scripts for licensing, when many of his performances were ambiguously illegal, Foote was using mimicry as a tool. In this regard, mimicry was not a newfound evasion but a refashioned 'affordance', as Caroline Levine might put it—a satirical-legal workaround that Foote had mined in the cultivation of not only his audiences but also his public persona.[191] Most importantly, though, it was a satiric tool that only became manifest, perhaps momentarily and always fleetingly, in the context of performance and through the instrument of the actor's body.[192] Unlike the French, the English did not observe the rules of either form or decorum in comic acting.[193] During this era, the comic actor's body, not the play text, was the locus of interest, and especially his or her improvisations and relations with the audience, physiognomic expressiveness, and use of theatrical byplay.[194] As Shearer West observes, London theatres witnessed 'a transition from a theatre of words at the beginning of the eighteenth century to a theatre of spectacle by the end': it was an increasingly *visual* and *aural* rather than exclusively verbal event.[195]

In addition, mimicry and impersonation were only one non-textual aspect of Georgian theatre, which had already developed over decades if not centuries prior to 1737 a rich non-verbal vocabulary. Theatregoers were prepared to understand dramatic evenings as semiotic events. This intermediality, this multisensory quality, was particularly the case for comedies, farces, and other comic entertainments. Pantomime, for instance, was wildly popular from the mid-1720s on, when

[189] Jane Wessel, 'Mimicry, Property, and the Reproduction of Celebrity in Eighteenth-Century England', *The Eighteenth Century* 60, no. 1 (Spring 2019): p. 73.

[190] Wessel, 'Mimicry', p. 71.

[191] Caroline Levine, *Forms: Whole, Rhythm, Hierarchy, Network* (Princeton: Princeton University Press, 2015), pp. 6–14.

[192] West, *Image of the Actor*, p. 123.

[193] Joseph R. Roach, *The Player's Passion: Studies in the Science of Acting* (Newark: University of Delaware Press, 1985), pp. 52–6.

[194] West, *Image of the Actor*, 123.

[195] Shearer West, 'Manufacturing Spectacle', in *The Oxford Handbook of the Georgian Theatre, 1737–1832*, edited by Julia Swindells and David Francis Taylor (Oxford: Oxford University Press, 2014), p. 287. On the importance of eighteenth-century theatre's auditory dimensions, see Peter Holland, 'Hearing the Dead: The Sound of David Garrick', in *Players, Playwrights, Playhouses: Investigating Performance, 1660–1800*, edited by Michael Cordner and Peter Holland (Basingstoke: Palgrave Macmillan, 2007), p. 249.

John Rich became famous for his illusionistic performances as Harlequin.[196] Dance, too, was increasingly everywhere in Georgian playhouses—from fully staged ballets and pantomimes to flourishes in operas and entr'actes *divertissements*. During this period, when dance lessons were routine and dance literacy was at an all-time high, dance itself increasingly became a non-verbal medium for visual storytelling with its own gestural grammar.[197] Already in the early eighteenth century, John Weaver had proposed the tripartition of dance: *la danse noble* (or *danse sérieuse* or *héroïque*); *la danse mixte* or *demi-sérieuse* or *demi-caractère*, for high comedy; and *la danse grotesque* (or *comique*).[198] Especially important was the emergence of the *ballet d'action*, which permitted dancers to produce cohesive narrative structures through movement alone—'an introduction, plot, and climax', as the French dancer Jean-Georges Noverre put it in 1760.[199] London theatre simply entailed a multisensory, and not merely verbal, experience— another aspect, perhaps, of what Peter de Bolla has called a growing mid-century 'culture of visuality', one that witnessed a critical shift in 'both how things were seen and what seeing meant to and for eighteenth-century viewers'.[200] All of this is to suggest that, by the time the Licensing Act went into effect, London theatres were already employing a range of non-verbal forms, all capable of communicating emotion, character, plot, and action, and that theatre attendees possessed the kind of literacy required to read the omnipresent theatrical language of the unspoken.

Among those non-verbal aspects most readily adaptable to satire were impersonation and mimicry. Both had a long history on stage, including, for instance, in Restoration plays seemingly built around satiric impersonation.[201] Moreover, a range of formal chironomic and chirological gestures, inherited from early modern guides to rhetoric and oratory and propagated throughout the eighteenth century in acting manuals, helped to produce and ingrain a form of emotive sign language.[202] But it was the mid-century evolution in acting styles—the emergence

---

[196] John O'Brien, *Harlequin Britain: Pantomime and Entertainment, 1690–1760* (Baltimore: Johns Hopkins University Press, 2004), pp. 3–4.

[197] Anne Bloomfield and Ruth Watts, 'Pedagogue of the Dance: The Dancing Master as Educator in the Long Eighteenth Century', *History of Education* 37, no. 4 (2008): pp. 605–18; Susan Leigh Foster, *Choreography and Narrative: Ballet's Staging of Story and Desire* (Bloomington: Indiana University Press, 1996); and Erin J. Smith, 'Dance and the Georgian Theatre', in *The Oxford Handbook of the Georgian Theatre, 1737–1832*, edited by Julia Swindells and David Francis Taylor (Oxford: Oxford University Press, 2014), p. 322.

[198] John Weaver, *An Essay Towards an History of Dancing* (London, 1712), pp. 157–72.

[199] Jean-Georges Noverre, *Lettres sur la danse, et sur les ballets* (Lyon, 1760), p. 32: 'son exposition, son nœud, & son dénouement'. See *Letters on Dancing and Ballets*, trans. Cyril W. Beaumont (Brooklyn: Dance Horizons, 1966), p. 19.

[200] Peter de Bolla, *Education of the Eye: Painting, Landscape, and Architecture in Eighteenth-Century Britain* (Stanford: Stanford University Press, 2003), p. 9.

[201] Robert D. Hume, *The Development of English Drama in the Late Seventeenth Century* (Oxford: Clarendon Press, 1976), pp. 90–1.

[202] Burwick, 'Georgian Theories of the Actor', pp. 182–3.

of so-called naturalistic forms of performance—that permitted those onstage to use their bodies as communicative media and encouraged the study of imitation among actors in the service of realistic and psychologically dynamic characterization.[203] Theatre in the eighteenth century, and perhaps even today, was simply an 'embodied medium'.[204]

None of this, though, showed up in play texts. Take, for instance, Foote's *The Orators*, first performed at the Haymarket in 1762, before he had acquired his patent, and then later in Dublin, which was not subject to the Licensing Act.[205] Less a play than a comic lecture, *The Orators* in part targets Thomas Sheridan. But the impersonation that most resounded was of George Faulkner, the one-legged Dublin printer, who appears as Peter Paragraph. The 'force of his mimickry', *The Theatrical Review* reported from Dublin, led to 'bursts of laughter', even among Foote's antagonists.[206] His imitation of Faulkner was part somatic, part phonetic: Foote 'hopp[ed] upon one leg' while telling lisping stories 'in a ridiculous manner'.[207] (Cruel, poetic justice, then, that Foote would have his own leg amputated a few years later following an idiotic aristocratic prank with an unbroken horse.) Faulkner eventually sued Foote for libel in Ireland, but it was just more fodder for his great satiric machine. Foote later published a 'Poetical Essay' about the run-in with Faulkner in the *Gentleman's Magazine*, a piece of self-puffery that helped him to cultivate the Aristophanic air of a satiric outlaw, as Kinservik has shown.[208] Again, what is worth emphasizing is the non-textual nature of his satire: 'the ridiculous gestures', his 'striking resemblance in the person', and the 'laughable... extravagance of the manners of Falkener [*sic*]', as *The Theatrical Review* put it.[209] Foote offered a similar account of the imitation in his poem:

[Foote] had, from the lumber, cull'd with curious care,
[Faulkner's] voice, his looks, his gesture, gait, and air,
His affectation, consequence, and mein,
And boldly launch'd him on the comic scene;
Loud peals of plaudits thro' the circle ran,
All felt the satire, for all knew the man.[210]

Both Foote's poem and *The Theatrical Review*'s account point to the shocking satiric power of mimicry. Comic representations produced the vicarious shame of

---

[203] Davis, *Comic Acting*, p. 10.   [204] O'Brien, *Harlequin Britain*, p. 83.

[205] For an account of the entire affair around *The Orators*, see Ian Kelly, *Mr Foote's Other Leg: Comedy, Tragedy and Murder in Georgian London* (London: Picador, 2012), pp. 161–6.

[206] *The Theatrical Review* (London, 1763), p. 126.

[207] William Cooke, *Memoirs of Samuel Foote, Esq.* vol. 1 (London, 1805), p. 122.

[208] Matthew J. Kinservik, 'The "English Aristophanes": Fielding, Foote, and Debates over Literary Satire', in *Brill's Companion to the Reception of Aristophanes*, edited by Philip Walsh (Leiden: Brill, 2016), pp. 109–28.

[209] *The Theatrical Review*, p. 126.   [210] *Gentleman's Magazine*, no. 33 (January 1763): p. 39.

witnessing one's own foibles and defects paraded out to peals of laughter by both strangers and acquaintances (and perhaps even friends, as Faulkner discovered). Even worse was the forced alterity: the uncanny shock of recognizing your alienated embodiment, perhaps without warning, on the stage in front of you. This was not only the power of satiric impersonation, but also the powerlessness it produced: the phantasmagoric, debilitating revelation of being under the mimetic control of another, like some living marionette. Hence Jane Moody's salient reminder that 'mimicry occupied a position on a knife edge between fame and defamation'.[211]   Foote's imitations met with occasional backlashes—from Churchill, of course, but also from Henry Fielding, who had his own run-ins with Foote in the late 1740s while running a satiric puppet theatre.[212] In his 'Court of Criticism', Fielding deemed 'Samuel Fut's' entire theatrical operation a 'Scandal-Shop' for personal defamation. For Fielding, his 'Mimickry', 'the meanest and vilest of all Arts', was little better than 'Buffoonry'.[213]

Legally, too, mimics were hardly given a free pass. The Lords Chamberlain and their Examiners and Deputy Examiners of Plays were eager to suppress satiric attacks on prominent public individuals—including the upper echelons of the London aristocracy and members of parliament—and often inspected play texts with an eye toward personal satire (in some instances they were even aided by those thought to be sent up).[214] This was easiest to do when aspects of a play alluded a little too clearly to some real-world individual and his or her sordid personal life. With Foote's A Trip to Calais (1775), later revised as The Capuchin (1776), nobody could miss the play's shots at Elizabeth Chudleigh, the notorious duchess of Kingston, whose trial for bigamy before the House of Lords filled the gossipy pages of London's pamphlets and periodicals.[215] She is sent up as Lady Kitty Crocodile, a name that pointed to her extravagant and even excessive mourning of her second husband. Kitty advises the play's heroine to marry two men—not only the man she loves, but also her father's choice of suitor—to help settle a familial row. Perhaps predictably, Francis Seymour Conway, marquis of Hertford, the Lord Chamberlain at the time, refused the play, the first and only work by Foote denied a license prior to performance.

[211] Jane Moody, 'Stolen Identities: Character, Mimicry and the Invention of Samuel Foote', in Theatre and Celebrity in Britain, 1660–2000, edited by Mary Luckhurst and Jane Moody (New York: Palgrave Macmillan, 2005), p. 68.

[212] Martin C. Battestin with Ruthe R. Battestin, Henry Fielding: A Life (London: Routledge, 1989), pp. 436–9. On Fielding's theatrical career, see Robert D. Hume, Henry Fielding and the London Theatre, 1728–1737 (Oxford: Clarendon Press, 1988); and Thomas Keymer, 'Fielding's Theatrical Career', in The Cambridge Companion to Henry Fielding, edited by Claude Rawson (Cambridge: Cambridge University Press, 2007), pp. 17–37.

[213] Henry Fielding, Jacobite's Journal, no. 22 (30 April 1748), in The Jacobite's Journal and Related Writings, edited by W. B. Coley (Oxford: Clarendon Press, 1974), pp. 262, 264–5.

[214] Conolly, Censorship of English Drama, 113ff.

[215] The Capuchin, msLA-413, Hunt.L; and Claire Gervat, Elizabeth: The Scandalous Life of the Duchess of Kingston (London: Century, 2003), pp. 136–54.

Even when the satire happened at the level of the play text, however, the censors often had difficulty catching every allusion or pregnant phrase. For instance, the antagonist of Foote's *The Nabob* (1772), Sir Matthew Mite (whose surname means 'cheesemonger'), a gauche East India merchant returned to England, was in part modelled after General Richard Smith, whose father owned a cheese shop.[216] Similar problems were presented by Foote's *The Minor* (1760), a send-up of Methodism and the preacher George Whitefield, who was depicted initially in the play's epilogue as Mr Squintum, an allusion to his deformed eye. Again and again in the play, characters speak of their 'new birth', a favourite Methodist idiom and one routinely mocked during this period.[217] Following a small storm of protest during the play's successful summer season at the Haymarket in 1760, a third, revised version of the play was submitted to the Chamberlain's Office for licensing for autumn, when it was slated to appear at Drury Lane. The Examiner of Plays, Edward Capell, axed not only allusions to 'new birth' but also the epilogue as a whole, featuring Foote's turn as Squintum, who was then rewritten into the play.[218] Even a vigilant examiner could only do so much to hear the full connotations of some obscure word or telling phrase before it was fully realized on the stage.

Much satire was not obvious until a play was put on, when impersonation could be combined with elaborate costumes and pointed staging. In *The Author* (1757), Foote openly mocked the odd and obese Sir Thomas Apreece, a Welshman known in London for his numerous physical and verbal idiosyncrasies, including his tendency to twitch and stare, his awkward gait, and his loud, rapid, and inarticulate speech.[219] At first, Capell and the Lord Chamberlain, Edward Cavendish, duke of Devonshire, missed the satire. The play was licensed in early 1757 and spent a successful year on stage at Drury Lane. Only later, after it was performed—and everyone, to Apreece's considerable dismay, roared with laughter at Foote's spot-on impersonation—did Devonshire suppress *The Author*, the first known incidence of a play having its license retroactively withdrawn.[220] Brief textual snippets simply tended to shore up physical impersonations on stage rather than supply them *in toto*.

All of this ought to point us not only to the limits of text-based licensing but also to the virtuosic body of the comic actor: the extent to which the miracle of simulation and of embodied imitation sometimes superseded and even overwhelmed the potential poignancy of the play itself. The performative aspects of

[216] *The Nabob*, msLA-335, Hunt.L. See W. K. Wimsatt, Jr, 'Foote and a Friend of Boswell's: A Note on *The Nabob*', *Modern Language Notes* 57, no. 5 (May 1942): pp. 326–8.

[217] Misty G. Anderson, *Imagining Methodism in Eighteenth-Century Britain: Enthusiasm, Belief, and the Borders of the Self* (Baltimore: Johns Hopkins University Press, 2012), p. 143.

[218] *The Minor*, msLA–177, Hunt.L. See Conolly, *Censorship of English Drama*, pp. 117–22; and Anderson, *Imagining Methodism*, pp. 141–50.

[219] *The Author*, msLA-129, Hunt.L.   [220] Conolly, *Censorship of English Drama*, pp. 114–17.

mimetic satire also opened it up to criticism. Mimicry promoted 'an actor's theatre', in Ballaster's words, something that was potentially little better than 'a politically-anodyne form of self-promotion, an empty trick of imitation'.[221] This is not to discount either the possible pointedness or political overtones of later eighteenth-century London drama. Daniel O'Quinn has amply demonstrated how 'the theatre distilled the social forces of imperial life in London and presented it on a nightly basis', just as Michael Ragussis has shown the extent to which Georgian theatres became spaces to showcase both 'domestic and colonial others' and therefore to define national identity.[222] David Francis Taylor has likewise shown the 'complex overlap of theatrical and parliamentary-political cultures' in the late eighteenth century, especially in Richard Brinsley Sheridan's 'politicization of the space of the playhouse', just as the dramatist Elizabeth Inchbald used 'the domestic', in Paula Backscheider's words, to provide 'a stark commentary on nationhood'.[223] The list could go on. In addition, any emphasis on new plays and their gradual reduction on the Georgian stage inevitably occludes how often repertory works could be topically refashioned.[224] Shakespeare, then as today, was repurposed in suggestively allegorical ways. Rumour—perhaps false—began to circulate in London in 1753 that the duke of Grafton, the Lord Chamberlain, had barred either patent house from performing *The Merchant of Venice* during the parliamentary debates around the so-called Jew Bill that later resulted in the Jewish Naturalization Act of 1753 (26 Geo. 2, c. 26) and which was repealed the following year.[225] The rumoured ban was likely bunk—a side product of anti-Jewish mockery in *The Craftsman*—but the incident itself signals the extent to which even 150-year-old plays about Venetian ghettos could be read in startlingly presentist terms.[226]

Nonetheless, any claim that the post-1737 stage was a hotbed of satiric or political radicalism, especially in comparison with visual satire during this period, should be taken with a grain of salt. As Dustin Griffin has pungently observed, the Licensing Act 'served to control the satirical tendencies of the London stage. Do

---

[221] Ballaster, 'Dramatic Satire', p. 347.

[222] Daniel O'Quinn, *Staging Governance: Theatrical Imperialism in London, 1770–1800* (Baltimore: Johns Hopkins University Press, 2005), p. 6; and Michael Ragussis, *Theatrical Nation: Jews and Other Outlandish Englishmen in Georgian Britain* (Philadelphia: University of Pennsylvania Press, 2010), p. 2.

[223] David Francis Taylor, *Theatres of Opposition: Empire, Revolution, and Richard Brinsley Sheridan* (Oxford: Oxford University Press, 2012), pp. 2–3; and Paula Backscheider, 'Retrieving Elizabeth Inchbald', in *The Oxford Handbook of the Georgian Theatre, 1737–1832*, edited by Julia Swindells and David Francis Taylor (Oxford: Oxford University Press, 2014), p. 616.

[224] O'Quinn, *Staging Governance*, p. 6.

[225] L. W. Conolly, '*The Merchant of Venice* and the Jew Bill of 1753', *Shakespeare Quarterly* 25, no. 1 (Winter 1974): pp. 125–7.

[226] *London Evening Post* (12–14 July 1753), which reprinted *The Craftsman* pieces. For an earlier example, see Katherine West Scheil, 'Early Georgian Politics and Shakespeare: The Black Act and Charles Johnsons' *Love in a Forest* (1723)', in *Shakespeare Survey*, vol. 51: Shakespeare in the Eighteenth Century, edited by Stanley Wells (Cambridge: Cambridge University Press, 1998), pp. 45–56.

such laws not constitute evidence that governments genuinely *believe* satire has the power to hurt? Hurt individuals, yes. Embarrass the government, perhaps. But seriously disturb the state—probably not'.[227] Instead, one might argue, we should focus on the targets of such satire. After the Licensing Act, 'Particular satire does not disappear from the stage but the particularity relates to figures in metropolitan society and culture rather than heads of state'.[228] These were, at least to some degree, safe targets. Foote's send-up of Whitefield in *The Minor*, for instance, was through Squintum, a character who initially only appeared in the play's epilogue. Squintum, moreover, was not even Whitefield per se, but in a much more complicated turn, the character Samuel Shift imitating Whitefield. Even then, in a seemingly endless recursion, Foote played Shift playing Squintum while also sending up and mimicking Tate Wilkinson, a protégé of Foote's and another gifted mimic who began his career by, of course, mimicking Foote (hence Churchill's redoubled snipe that Wilkinson was nothing more than 'a mere mere mimic's mimic').[229] Foote's mimicry in *The Minor* was thus a kind of two-for-one operation: a send-up of Methodism in the guise of some histrionic score-settling.

The question nonetheless remains of how precisely to make sense of Foote's mimicry. Kinservik has argued that his mimicry was not central but 'incidental' to his satire.[230] Moody has likewise argued that Foote's mimicry was merely 'artistic raw material for the creation of his own fame'.[231] Both of these statements are true: the mimicry in Foote's satiric plays is almost always a personal sideline that often falls outside of the central satiric agenda of a given play. Foote clearly understood that the *frisson* of comic impersonation was good for business—both for ticket sales and his pseudo-scandalous cult of celebrity. As Wessel notes, 'Audiences who went to see Foote's plays were often going specifically to see Foote'.[232] We might even raise a sceptical eyebrow about Foote's satire. Foote was no radical anti-ministerial, anti-Hanoverian incendiary. He was coddled by English elites and eventually given a royal patent to stage plays legally during the summer season. He maintained friendly relations with the Lords Chamberlain and Examiners of Play and, like so many of his theatrical peers, absorbed the lessons of licensing and how to produce largely unobjectionable plays.[233] And, for the most part, Foote knew whom to imitate: not prime ministers and monarchs but those who were nominally safe targets.

When viewed through the lens of lampoon, Foote's mimicry might be better understood not as the high-handed moral reform of a post-Augustan satirist or even the lashing exposure of a modern Aristophanes (as Foote branded himself),

---

[227] Griffin, *Satire*, p. 154.   [228] Ballaster, 'Dramatic Satire', p. 344.
[229] Churchill, *The Rosciad*, l. 414.   [230] Kinservik, *Disciplining Satire*, p. 155.
[231] Jane Moody, 'Stolen Identities', p. 65.   [232] Wessel, 'Mimicry', p. 71.
[233] Kinservik, *Disciplining Satire*, pp. 134–71.

but as personal attacks on identifiable personages, many of whom were targets without recourse. Sometimes, those personal attacks fed directly into a play's satiric topos. In *The Nabob*, for instance, the satirization of prominent nabobs was central to the play's central satiric thrust, onstage personifications who helped to explain the play's queasiness over newly enriched and empowered Britons returned from Asia.[234] At other times, though, Foote's mimicry was merely scattershot, personal, and thus secondary to the play's central satiric topos. Imitation, impersonation, and mimicry could all serve a satiric purpose, even if that purpose was not always in service of what we might think of as a central satiric argument.

Such forms of satiric imitation and mimicry were common on the eighteenth-century stage, both before and especially after 1737, even if the Licensing Act on the whole proved highly effective at limiting anti-ministerial and anti-monarchical satire. It proved less effective at policing personal satire on stage, thanks to the process of licensing with its primary focus on textual policing. Stage satirists, and especially Foote, realized increasingly the value of non-verbal satire for exploiting textual gaps. Mimicry simply became a performance technique that permitted one to evade the censors, at least initially, in a regulatory system more preoccupied with words than the mechanics of dramaturgy.

Studying the legal regimes in place to police satire, whether in print, in images, or onstage during this period, also has important implications for the literary-historical commonplace that satire simply vanishes at mid-century. That story of decline is in part true—printed satire is wildly diminished in quantity, quality, and cultural capital during the last half of the century—but it neglects a much more complicated history of satire across media. The overall satiric landscape between the middle of the eighteenth century and the 1830s paints a very different picture. In the first place, printed satire continued to be published after mid-century. But, even more importantly, non-verbal dramatic lampoons were common on the post-licensing stage and visual satires were produced on an absolutely massive scale during these decades. Both types, whether theatrical impersonations or cutting caricatures, could be just as nasty and personal as the poetic lampoons that appeared during the supposed Golden Age of Satire, and visual satires became a major medium for lashing commentary on political, ministerial, and monar-chical affairs. To miss this transition in media, this migration from verbal to visual and, to some degree, dramatic satire, is to make the same mistake the Crown itself made, but then only retrospectively realized: satire would live on, but in forms perhaps even more ambiguous than print—and, as a result, even harder to police.

---

[234] On Nabobs, see Derek Jarrett, *England in the Age of Hogarth* (New Haven: Yale University Press, 1992), p. 89; P. J. Marshall, *East Indian Fortunes: The British in Bengal in the Eighteenth Century* (Oxford: Clarendon Press, 1976), pp. 228–9; and Philip Lawson and Jim Phillips, '"Our Execrable Banditti": Perceptions of Nabobs in Mid-Eighteenth Century Britain', *Albion* 16, no. 3 (Autumn 1984): pp. 225–41.

By identifying the connections between written, visual, and dramatic satire across a variety of media—and by tracing those connections to the development of procedures for prosecuting defamation—*Libel and Lampoon* has offered an account of later seventeenth- and eighteenth-century satire that places the law at the centre of literary history. This story of development cuts across the cultural spheres that intersect throughout this 122-year period, across literature and the law, producing the verbally ambiguous works that came to define satire not only at the beginning of the eighteenth century but also, as I have argued, all the way up to today. At the heart of *Libel and Lampoon* has been a simple and yet wide-ranging thesis: without the law, there would have been no satire—or at least no satire of a very specific, verbally ambiguous kind, but a kind that has nonetheless provided satire with some rough rhetorical unity over the past 350 years.

Epilogue

A Shandean History of the Press

——What a journey!
Pray can you tell me,—that is, without anger, before I write my
chapter upon straight lines——by what mistake——who told them
so——or how it has come to pass, that your men of wit and genius
have all along confounded this line, with the line of GRAVITATION.
                          —Laurence Sterne, *Tristram Shandy*, vol. 6., p. 572.

What kinds of stories should we tell about the press during the eighteenth
century? Once upon a time, press freedom was merely one aspect of a larger
narrative about the growth of personal freedoms more generally during the spread
of liberal democracy.[1] Today, such stories of enlightenment and ineluctable
liberalization, told from a teleological present and framed by the flourishing liberal
democracies of the later nineteenth and early twentieth centuries, feel idealistic,
even quaint.[2] In 1931, Herbert Butterfield was one of the first to throw cold water
on such Whig interpretations of history, as he called them, which tended 'to
emphasise certain principles of progress in the past and to produce a story which
is the ratification if not the glorification of the present'.[3] Historians have sometimes fussed over Butterfield's brushstroke history of historiography, but his
general admonition still seems to hold true that any presentist, laudatory account
of the progressive past tends to reduce its overall complexity.[4]

 Moreover, over the last hundred years, stories about the growth of liberal democracy have begun to feel queasily inaccurate, no doubt thanks to the less democratic
regimes that filled the vacuum of power both before and after the Second
World War. As Debora Shuger has argued, a 'liberal-Whig historiography...
dominated the scholarship [on press freedom and censorship] into the 1980s',

---

[1] Arthur M. Schlesinger, *Prelude to Independence: The Newspaper War on Britain, 1764–1776* (New
York: Knopf, 1958); Robert R. Rea, *The English Press in Politics: 1769–1774* (Lincoln: University of
Nebraska Press, 1963); Siebert, *Freedom*, p. vi; and Hanson, *Government*.
[2] For an assessment of the 'evolutionary model', see Stephen Botein, Jack Censer, and Harriet Ritvo,
'The Periodical Press in Eighteenth-Century English and French Society: A Cross-Cultural Approach',
Comparative Studies in Society and History 23, no. 3 (July 1981): pp. 466–7.
[3] Herbert Butterfield, *The Whig Interpretation of History* (1932; New York: Norton, 1965), p. v.
[4] William Cronon, 'Two Cheers for the Whig Interpretation of History', *Perspectives on History* 50,
no. 6 (September 2012): pp. 5–6.

Libel and Lampoon: Satire in the Courts, 1670–1792. Andrew Benjamin Bricker, Oxford University Press.
© Andrew Benjamin Bricker 2022. DOI: 10.1093/oso/9780192846150.003.0008

and tended to depict early modern press regulation 'as a repressive instrument of political and ideological control, comparable "to censorship in Eastern Europe" under Communist rule'.[5] Stories about flourishing press freedoms were further undermined during the 1990s and the first two decades of the twenty-first century, as Eastern Bloc archives were opened up to researchers.[6]

A growing sense has likewise emerged, especially over the last few years, that freedom of the press—and freedom of speech more generally—does not mean equal freedoms for all.[7] Women, people of colour, the LGBTQIA+ community, the poor—none of these groups experiences the full complement of privileges supposedly entailed by unmitigated freedom of speech.[8] Even the First Amendment, once 'a defense of the powerless', Catharine A. MacKinnon has argued, has become 'a weapon of the powerful'.[9] Or, in Stanley Fish's Johnsonian quip: 'Nowadays the First Amendment is the First Refuge of Scoundrels'.[10]

The press today is, in any case, not entirely free. So-called 'libel tourism' remains commonplace in Europe and the United Kingdom and in its current and former Commonwealth countries, including Canada, Australia, New Zealand, and South Africa.[11] European countries likewise carefully police speech, through both defamation laws and hate-speech legislation.[12] Not even in the United States, where freedom of speech is part of 'civil religion', are the privileges of speech and the press wholly guaranteed.[13] You cannot utter 'true threats', you cannot incite imminent violence, and you cannot shout 'fire' in a crowded theatre, as any first-year law student will happily remind you.[14]

---

[5] Debora Shuger, *Censorship and Cultural Sensibility: The Regulation of Language in Tudor-Stuart England* (Philadelphia: University of Pennsylvania Press, 2011), pp. 1–2.

[6] Nicole Moore and Christina Spittel, 'South by East: World Literature's Cold War Compass', in *Australian Literature in the German Democratic Republic: Reading through the Iron Curtain*, edited by Nicole Moore and Christina Spittel (London: Anthem, 2016), pp. 1–32.

[7] 'The dark side of *Guardian* comments', *The Guardian* (12 April 2016): https://www.theguardian.com/technology/2016/apr/12/the-dark-side-of-guardian-comments.

[8] 'In Free Speech Debates, LGBTQ and People of Color at Risk', *WNYC News* (9 June 2017): https://www.wnyc.org/story/who-are-real-victims-crackdown-free-speech/.

[9] Catherine A. MacKinnon, 'The First Amendment: An Equality Reading', in *The Free Speech Century*, edited by Lee C. Bollinger and Geoffrey R. Stone (Oxford: Oxford University Press, 2019), p. 140.

[10] Stanley Fish, *There's No Such Thing as Free Speech . . . and it's a Good Thing, Too* (Oxford: Oxford University Press, 1994), p. 102.

[11] Richard Garnett and Megan Richardson, 'Libel Tourism or Just Redress?: Reconciling the (English) Right to Reputation With the (American) Right to Free Speech in Cross-Border Libel Cases', *Journal of Private International Law* 5, no. 3 (2009): 471–90.

[12] Uladzislau Belavusau, 'Fighting Hate Speech through EU Law', *Amsterdam Legal Forum* 4, no. 1 (2012): pp. 20–34; Kevin Boyle, 'Hate Speech—The United States Versus the Rest of the World?' *Maine Law Review* 53, no. 2 (2001): pp. 487–502; and Sarah H. Cleveland, 'Hate Speech at Home and Abroad', in *The Free Speech Century*, edited by Lee C. Bollinger and Geoffrey R. Stone (Oxford: Oxford University Press, 2019), pp. 210–31. For resistance, see Eric Heinze, *Hate Speech and Democratic Citizenship* (Oxford: Oxford University Press, 2006), pp. 4–7.

[13] Robert N. Bellah, *The Broken Covenant: American Civil Religion in Time of Trial* (1975), 2nd ed. (Chicago: University of Chicago Press, 1992).

[14] *Virginia v. Black* (2003), 538 U.S. 343; *Schenck v. United States* (1919), 249 U.S. 47. See also Lee C. Bollinger and Geoffrey R. Stone, 'Dialogue', in *The Free Speech Century*, pp. 1–2.

Though we have supposedly ceased to tell stories about the unmitigated growth of press freedom, scholars and journalists continue to point to the eighteenth century as the watershed moment when those carefully guarded liberties of speech and publication came most fully into being. Reiterating a classic genealogy of censorship, Nicole Moore has recently written that the eighteenth century witnessed 'seeming breakthroughs' in press freedom after the tenacious and sometimes persecutory regimes of ancient Rome, the Middle Ages, and the early modern period.[15] Even Robert Darnton, in his comparative history of censorship, concedes his own 'liberal sympathies' and 'a whiff of Whiggishness' in his willingness to trace an anti-censorship 'tradition that leads from the ancients through Milton and Locke to the First Amendment and the Universal Declaration of Human Rights'.[16]

To some degree, scholars like Moore and Darnton are entirely right to point to the eighteenth century as a critical fulcrum in the history of the press. Simply put, the expansion of press freedom over the course of the eighteenth century *was* remarkable. In 1695, England became the first and only European country with no prepublication system of government licensing; less than a century later, on 15 December 1791, when the government of the United States adopted the Bill of Rights, the first of its ten amendments to the Constitution sought to guarantee, among other freedoms, precisely those liberties of the press and speech. And, perhaps most amazingly, it was the government of the United States that actively chose to prohibit *itself* from abridging either the freedom of speech or the freedom of the press.[17] That these rights were among the first adopted by the US government is all the more remarkable considering how frequently the government of Great Britain prosecuted and harassed writers and publishers during this same era.[18]

Large-scale progressive stories about the radical liberalization of the press tend to simplify eighteenth-century debates around press freedom and the nature and philosophy of regulation itself. It is worth keeping in mind that the Press Licensing Act lapsed largely by accident in 1695.[19] As the House of Lords explained to the House of Commons, this was 'a Law which in no Wise answered the End for

---

[15] Nicole Moore, 'Censorship and Literature', in *Oxford Research Encyclopedia of Literature* (Oxford: Oxford University Press, 2016), p. 1.

[16] Robert Darnton, *Censors at Work: How States Shaped Literature* (New York: W. W. Norton & Co., 2014), pp. 17–19.

[17] Leonard Levy, *Emergence of a Free Press* (Oxford: Oxford University Press, 1985), ch. 7.

[18] Marcus Wood, *Radical Satire and Print Culture, 1790–1822* (Oxford: Clarendon Press, 1994), p. 3; Jon Mee, 'Treason, Seditious Libel, and Literature in the Romantic Period', in *Oxford Handbooks Online* (Oxford: Oxford University Press, 2016), pp. 1–23; and Michael T. Davis, Emma Macleod, and Gordon Pentland (eds.), *Political Trials in an Age of Revolutions: Britain and the North Atlantic, 1793–1848* (London: Palgrave Macmillan, 2018). See also Miles Ogborn, *The Freedom of Speech: Talk and Slavery in the Anglo-Caribbean World* (Chicago: University of Chicago Press, 2019).

[19] Raymond Astbury, 'The Renewal of the Licensing Act in 1693 and Its Lapse in 1695', *The Library*, 5th series 33, no. 4 (1978): pp. 296–322.

which it was made'.[20] The problem with the act was not licensing per se, the Lords concluded, but the partisan process by which those in power chose to censor their opponents. The House of Commons in turn believed that the lapse was only temporary, a mere hiatus like the one the government had witnessed in 1679 when the act had lapsed for six years, before being renewed for seven more. That the government at the beginning of the century had anything but happily abandoned press regulation is clearest in the repeated parliamentary attempts to re-enact licensing between 1695 and 1714.[21] That those bills failed, upending the omni-present structure of European press regulation, was a shock both to those in government and to Britain's neighbours on the Continent.

Moreover, the abolition of licensing in 1695 was hardly met with cheers. Instead, during the first decades of the eighteenth century 'demands for censor-ship to be reimposed were commonplace'.[22] Take George Lyttelton (later Baron Lyttelton). Just a dozen years after the publication of his own Montesquievian allegory of the Walpole administration, *Letters from a Persian in England* (1735)— 'a *Libel* on the present *Government*', as one commentator put it, stuffed with '*frothy Declamation*'[23]—even he was willing to argue that the authorities 'might, without any danger, exert with spirit and vigour the full power of legal govern-ment, check and even suppress the infamous licence of the press (unknown to all other ages and nations, and destructive of all civil society)'.[24] Calls for a new regime of moderate and yet increased press restraints were renewed throughout the first half of the century and gained a newfound rhetorical intensity during the 1760s and 1770s.[25]

Today, we might even be shocked to discover that many of those calling for press regulations were writers—writers who had themselves been targeted through licensing laws and libel prosecutions. Many authors adopted what we might think of as a Miltonic principle, one not unlike the House of Lords' own reasons for declining to renew the Press Licensing Act. In *Areopagitica* (1644), John Milton

---

[20] See 'Commons' reasons for not renewing the Licensing Act, 1695', in *The Eighteenth-Century Constitution, 1688–1815: Documents and Commentary*, edited by E. Neville Williams (Cambridge: Cambridge University Press, 1960), pp. 399–401.

[21] Hanson, *Government*, p. 260–3; John Feather, 'The Book Trade in Politics: The Making of the Copyright Act of 1710', *Publishing History* 8 (1980): pp. 21–2; Martin Dzelzainis, 'Managing the Later Stuart Press, 1662–1696', in *The Oxford Handbook of English Law and Literature, 1500–1700*, edited by Lorna Hutson (Oxford: Oxford University Press, 2017), p. 545; and Mark Goldie, 'Introduction', in *Censorship and the Press*, vol. 4: 1696–1720, edited by Mark Goldie and Geoff Kemp (London: Pickering & Chatto, 2009), p. xv.

[22] Bob Harris, 'Print Culture', in *A Companion to Eighteenth-Century Britain*, edited by H. T. Dickinson (Malden: Blackwell, 2002), p. 284.

[23] [George Lyttelton], *Letters from a Persian in England to his Friend at Ispahan* (London, 1735); and *The Persian strip'd of his Disguise* (London, 1735), pp. 3, 43.

[24] [George Lyttelton], *A Letter to the Tories* (London, 1747), p. 17.

[25] Eckhart Hellmuth, '"The palladium of all other English liberties": Reflections on the Liberty of the Press in England during the 1760s and 1770s', in *The Transformation of Political Culture: England and Germany in the Late Eighteenth Century*, edited by Eckhart Hellmuth (Oxford: Oxford University Press, 1990), ch. 19.

had argued that authors could be subject to post-publication censure, but that they should not be *prevented* from publishing their ideas (never mind that he himself became a licenser in 1649).[26] Eighteenth-century writers, for much of this era, took a similar tack, quibbling about the administration of the law while never denying the fundamental need for some form of press regulation. In 1704, just a year after he had been pilloried for *The Shortest Way with the Dissenters*, Daniel Defoe applauded the abolition of licensing—what he called 'A Padlock to the Press'.[27] At the same time, Defoe seemingly supported some form of regulation.[28] In so doing, he picked up on two long-standing arguments. The first posited that freedom of the press was an extension and guarantor of all personal liberties. As Cato, the corporate pseudonym of John Trenchard and Thomas Gordon, argued two decades later, in what became a rallying cry during the American Revolution, 'Freedom of speech is the great bulwark of liberty; they prosper and die together'.[29] To reinstate licensing 'To cure the ill Use of Liberty', Defoe reasoned, was 'like cutting off the Leg to cure the Gout in the Toe'.[30]

For many, prepublication censorship was simply an overblown response to a much more local problem. In this regard, rather than opposing press regulation, Defoe picked up on a second argument reiterated by Britons throughout the century. In the absence of licensing, a statutory libel law was needed, one that would clearly outline press offences while stating their attendant punishments, so that 'all Men will know when they Transgress'.[31] In short, Defoe and his fellow writers and booksellers wanted something like a bright-line rule: a set statutory principle that would define the offence of libel and its punishments in clear and comprehensive terms, thus militating against the seeming arbitrariness of post hoc libel prosecutions.[32] Laws are 'not made to draw Men into Crimes', he argued, 'but to prevent Crimes'.[33] Similar calls for statutory libel laws were made throughout the century, often founded on the principle that the best deterrent to crime was certainty in law and punishment.[34] In 1740, one author went so far as to draft a

[26] John Milton, *Areopagitica*, in *The Complete Prose Works of John Milton*, vol. 2: 1643–1648, edited by Ernest Sirluck (New Haven: Yale University Press, 1959), pp. 480–571. See Joad Raymond, 'Censorship in Law and Practice in Seventeenth–Century England: Milton's *Areopagitica*', in *The Oxford Handbook of English Law and Literature, 1500–1700*, edited by Lorna Hutson (Oxford: Oxford University Press, 2017), pp. 507–28.

[27] [Daniel Defoe], *An Essay on the Regulation of the Press* (London, 1704), p. 10.

[28] On the dubious process of attributing this pamphlet to Defoe, see Mark Vareschi, *Everywhere and Nowhere: Anonymity and Mediation in Eighteenth-Century England* (Minneapolis: University of Minnesota Press, 2018), pp. 114–15.

[29] *Cato's Letters: Or, Essays on Liberty, Civil and Religious, and other Important Subjects*, ed. Ronald Hamowy, vol. 1 (Indianapolis: Liberty Fund, 1995), p. 114.

[30] [Defoe], *Essay on the Regulation of the Press*, p. 8.

[31] [Defoe], *Essay on the Regulation of the Press*, p. 14.

[32] Leo Katz, *Why the Law Is So Perverse* (Chicago: University of Chicago Press, 2011), p. 145.

[33] [Defoe], *Essay on the Regulation of the Press*, p. 15.

[34] *The Thoughts of a Tory Author Concerning the Press* (London, 1712), p. 13. See Cesare Beccaria, *An Essay on Crimes and Punishments* (London, 1767), pp. 165–6; and [Sir Samuel Romilly], *Thoughts on a Late Pamphlet, Intituled, Thoughts on Executive Justice* (London, 1786), p. 38.

model bill against the 'licentious *Abuse* of the *Press*', leaving it to MPs to fill in the blanks as they saw fit: '———— *the Penalties hereafter to be mentioned*'.[35]

Such arguments should, of course, be taken with a grain of salt. In advocating for a statutory libel law, writers and stationers were also offering a disingenuous solution to a largely intractable problem—and precisely the sort of solution to which the government was wholly opposed. Any bright-line statutory law outlining what was libellous in positivistic terms would have hamstrung the government, preventing the authorities from regulating and censuring new and potentially even more pernicious forms of libel not spelled out clearly in the bill. Such a bill might have been wholly counterproductive, outlining for would-be incendiaries a clear set of negative guidelines to permissible forms of defamation and sedition. In the words of Cato: no law can be 'framed with so much contrivance, but artful men will slip out of it, and particularly in relation to libels'.[36] One of the reasons that the Crown turned increasingly to defamation at common law was precisely for its flexibility and, as it turned out, its malleability. As Philip Hamburger has written,

> The new role of the law of seditious libel as the government's chief means of prosecuting the printed press led to doctrinal modification of that law. The bench appears to have understood that the seventeenth century law . . . would have to be modified if it were to suit its eighteenth century function. Whereas it had been merely a subcategory of the law of libel or written defamation, it now became a separate law, with its own precedents.[37]

As part of an ill-defined umbrella of speech regulations, the broadness of defamation laws thus permitted the Crown and the bench ample discretion in defining what, at any given moment, it deemed libellous, whether that writing was defamatory and seditious or obscene and blasphemous.

For eighteenth-century thinkers, freedom of the press was intimately tied to the personal liberties of all Englishmen, but hardly did this mean that unregulated debate was a normative ideal. In 1740, one author scoffed that 'lewd Authors' who 'demand the *Liberty of the Press*' were little better than the '*Drunkard* [who] raves against a Law that deprives him of the *Liberty of the Gin-Shop*'.[38] For writers of a more patrician cast, unalloyed press freedom not only undermined the proper functioning of government, but also permitted the rabble to meddle in affairs beyond their understanding. In 1748, Henry Fielding, 'the most dominant professional playwright in London' in the 1730s who was put out of theatrical

---

[35] [Francis Squire], *A Faithful Report of a Genuine Debate Concerning the Liberty of the Press* (London, 1740), pp. 31–2.
[36] *Cato's Letters*, no. 101, p. 718.   [37] Hamburger, 'Seditious Libel', p. 725.
[38] [Squire], *A Faithful Report*, pp. 22–3.

business by the Stage Licensing Act of 1737, argued that the press was ill-suited to political debate.[39]

> The *Sanctum Sanctorum* of Government ... is a Place too sacred to be polluted by vulgar Eyes; nor are the Secrets there transacted the proper Subjects of News-Papers and Pamphlets. In a Free Country the People have the Right to complain of any Grievance which affects them, and this is the Privilege of the *Englishman*; but surely to canvas those high and nice Points, which move the finest Wheels of State, Matters merely belonging to the Royal Prerogative, and in no wise affecting the Body of the People, in Print, is in the highest Degree indecent, and a gross Abuse of the Liberty of the Press.[40]

During the *North Briton* controversies of the 1760s, Tobias Smollett, who had been successfully sued for libel and fined, before spending three months in King's Bench Prison in 1760, would return to a similar argument.[41] In his view, rather than creating greater personal liberties, an increasingly free press merely promoted a form of social devolution: not a levelling of society but a raising up of those who had no place rummaging around in the affairs of the nation. In part he feared the schadenfreude of 'the illiterate and illiberal dregs of the people, who ferment with every leaven, and are never better pleased, than when their spleen is gratified with some calumny, which tends to the disgrace of their superiors!'[42] Perhaps surprisingly, part of Smollett's fear was precisely the thing a free press was believed to guarantee. Rather than an expression of the liberty that was the birthright of every Englishman, freedom of the press turned the 'unthinking rabble'[43] into overweening mini-politicians, 'who proclaim themselves free-born *Englishmen*, and transported by a laudable spirit of patriotism, insist upon having a spoke in the wheel of government'.[44] Fielding agreed, pointing to the presumption of not only lower-class readers but also the 'Writers of these Libels ... [who] are not, nor cannot be Gentlemen; but must be sought after ... only among the lowest Dregs of the People'.[45]

Again, what is so remarkable about such eighteenth-century debates is that seemingly no one, at least in England and for much of the century, was in favour of a radically libertarian press—not even satirists. Christian Thorne has gone so

---

[39] Robert D. Hume, *Henry Fielding and the London Theatre, 1728–1737* (Oxford: Clarendon Press, 1988), p. xi; and Thomas Keymer, 'Fielding's Theatrical Career', in *The Cambridge Companion to Henry Fielding*, edited by Claude Rawson (Cambridge: Cambridge University Press, 2007), pp. 17–37.

[40] Henry Fielding, *Jacobite's Journal*, no. 26 (28 May 1748), in *The Jacobite's Journal and Related Writings*, edited by W. B. Coley (Oxford: Clarendon Press, 1974), p. 290.

[41] James G. Basker, *Tobias Smollett, Critic and Journalist* (Newark: University of Delaware Press, 1988), p. 149.

[42] *The Briton*, no. 20 (9 October 1762).   [43] *The Briton*, no. 6 (3 July 1762).

[44] Qtd. in Lance Bertelsen, *The Nonsense Club: Literature and Popular Culture, 1749–1764* (Oxford: Oxford University Press, 1986), p. 174.

[45] Fielding, *Jacobite's Journal*, no. 26 (28 May 1748), p. 290.

far as to argue that Jonathan Swift, Alexander Pope, and John Gay were united in 'their common loathing of discourse—not a particular discourse but discourse as such, the very procedure of public argument'.[46] Swift certainly believed in liberty of conscience and freedom of opinion. But he was also, in Ian Higgins' view, 'an advocate of censorship'.[47] Swift argued that certain publications, and especially those against established religion and in favour of republicanism, should 'be liable to the severest punishments the law can afflict'.[48]

As a result, discussions around the press tended to focus not on the desirability of a free press, but on the precise manner of its regulation. Those debates often centred on concerns over what we would today call 'due process': both on the necessity of rule of law, in opposition to the government's instrumental and pernicious repurposing of libel laws, especially during the first decades of the eighteenth century; and on the courts' troubling attempts to circumscribe the jury's purview.[49] As John Locke had argued in the seventeenth century, 'Absolute Arbitrary Power' is 'Governing without *settled standing Laws*'. Government power 'ought to be exercised by *established and promulgated Laws*', so that 'both the People may know their Duty, and be safe and secure within the limits of the Law, and the Rulers too kept within their due bounds'.[50] Following John Phillip Reid, we might borrow the Rawlsian argument that the rule of law was 'closely related to liberty' more generally for many seventeenth- and eighteenth-century Britons.[51] William Blackstone was explicit: 'the glory of the English law consists in clearly defining the times, the causes, and the extent, when, wherefore, and to what degree, the imprisonment of the subject may be lawful'.[52] Clear laws, not their absence, facilitated liberty and were essential to it.

[46] Christian Thorne, 'Thumbing Our Nose at the Public Sphere: Satire, the Market, and the Invention of Literature', *PMLA* 116, no. 3 (May 2001): p. 533. On the liberalization of public expression more generally during this era, see Trevor Ross, *Writing in Public: Literature and the Liberty of the Press in Eighteenth-Century Britain* (Baltimore: Johns Hopkins University Press, 2018).

[47] Ian Higgins, 'Censorship, Libel and Self-Censorship', in *Jonathan Swift and the Eighteenth-Century Book*, edited by Paddy Bullard and James McLaverty (Cambridge: Cambridge University Press, 2013), pp. 184–5.

[48] [Jonathan Swift], *Some Thoughts on Free-Thinking*, in *The Prose Writings of Jonathan Swift*, edited by Herbert Davis et al., vol. 4 (Oxford: Basil Blackwell, 1939–74), p. 49.

[49] Hamburger, 'Seditious Libel', pp. 661–765; and Green, *Verdict*, chs. 7 and 8.

[50] John Locke, *Two Treatises of Government*, edited by Ian Shapiro (New Haven: Yale University Press, 2004), 2.s.137.

[51] John Rawls, *Theory of Justice* (Cambridge: Harvard University Press, 1999), p. 207; and John Phillip Reid, *Rule of Law: The Jurisprudence of Liberty in the Seventeenth and Eighteenth Centuries* (DeKalb: Northern Illinois University Press, 2004), pp. 3–9.

[52] William Blackstone, *Commentaries on the Laws of England*, Book III: Of Private Wrongs, edited by Thomas P. Gallanis (Oxford: Oxford University Press, 2016), p. 90.

Hence this era's call for a statutory libel law, which harkened back to a debate started under Charles II and James II and continued under William III about the monarch's control over the judiciary.[53] The supposed obsequiousness of royally appointed judges who sat at the monarch's pleasure led to provisions in both the Bill of Rights (1689) and the Act of Settlement (1701), which sought in large measure to promulgate the rule of law by restricting royal prerogative.[54] Such attempts at securing judicial independence were only partially successful; judges might have been independent of the monarch after 1701, but hardly did that independence guarantee perfect rule of law.[55] As we saw in chapter three, Chief Justice Sir John Holt's modifications to the law of seditious libel at the turn of the seventeenth century were at times shocking given the growing consensus that the rule of law should be held above all else.[56] As I have argued throughout *Libel and Lampoon*, the appropriation and then radical modification of libel laws was in part a response to the verbal evasions that had come to typify satire during its Golden Age. Onlookers, moreover, noticed. *'Judges* and *Juries'*, one critic observed in 1740, had been forced 'to stretch the Laws' to convict 'these *Sophists in Calumny'*. But the courts had done so with good reason: 'so perfect are [these libellers] in all the Tricks and Wiles of Ambiguity, and Equivocation; in the Mysterious Art of raising Ideas by the Use of Words of a *contrary* Signification, of abusing and vilifying by affected *Encomiums*, of sneering Truth by Writing it in *Italicks*, of *assassinating* with a *Smile*, or *betraying* with a *Kiss'*.[57] In the absence of positive law, judges were forced to appropriate libel laws, turning them into a post-publication regulatory mechanism for an increasingly unruly press.

English writers, especially during the first half of the eighteenth century, simply believed in a very specific form of press freedom, one that combined a Lockean regard for rule of law with the principle that press freedom was merely the absence of prior restraint in the form of prepublication licensing or censorship. In Blackstone's famous formulation:

---

[53]   Alfred F. Havighurst, 'James II and the Twelve Men in Scarlet', *Law Quarterly Review* 69 (October 1953): pp. 522–46, 'The Judiciary and Politics in the Reign of Charles II (Part I, 1660–1676)', and 'The Judiciary and Politics in the Reign of Charles II (Part II, 1676–1685)', *Law Quarterly Review* 66 (January and April 1950): pp. 62–78 and 229–52.

[54]   Mark Kishlansky, *A Monarchy Transformed: Britain, 1603–1714* (London: Penguin, 1996), p. 290.

[55]   Wilfrid Prest, 'Judicial Corruption in Early Modern England', *Past & Present* 133 (November 1991): pp. 67–95; David Lemmings, 'The Independence of the Judiciary in Eighteenth-Century England', in *The Life of the Law*, edited by Peter Birks (London: The Hambledon Press, 1993), pp. 125–49; and Stewart Jay, 'Servants of Monarchs and Lords: The Advisory Role of Early English Judges', *American Journal of Legal History* 38, no. 3 (April 1994): pp. 117–96.

[56]   Harold J. Berman and Charles J. Reid, Jr., 'The Transformation of English Legal Science: From Hale to Blackstone', *Emory Law Journal* 45, no. 2 (Spring 1996): pp. 444–67; and Gerald J. Postema, 'Classical Common Law Jurisprudence (Part I)' and 'Classical Common Law Jurisprudence (Part II)', *Oxford University Commonwealth Law Journal* 2, no. 2 (Winter 2002): pp. 155–80 and 3, no. 1 (Summer 2003): pp. 1–28.

[57]   [Squire], *A Faithful Report*, pp. 17–18.

The liberty of the press is indeed essential to the nature of a free state: but this consists in laying no *previous* restraints upon publications, and not in freedom from censure for criminal matter when published. Every freeman has an undoubted right to lay what sentiments he pleases before the public: to forbid this, is to destroy the freedom of the press: but if he publishes what is improper, mischievous, or illegal, he must take the consequence of his own temerity.[58]

This freedom from prior restraint had been, even among advocates for a free press, a robust central tenet since at least the late seventeenth century, when Milton's *Areopagitica* was redeployed as a potent argument against prior restraint, though not against post-publication prosecution per se.

Across the entire eighteenth century in Britain, the explicit belief in a regulated press remained stunningly commonplace. Those debates began to shift in the 1770s, as more and more Britons questioned whether the doctrine of prior restraint was a sufficient guarantor of liberty. Such rumblings were especially pronounced after the Wilkes and Liberty campaigns of the 1760s, when calls for greater press freedom grew louder and louder as the government scrambled for new means to discourage its most vocal critics.[59] There simply existed a slippage, especially during the 1770s and 1780s, between English jurists like Blackstone and Lord Mansfield, who viewed the absence of 'prior restraint' as the lone condition for a free press, and an increasingly outspoken public and press that advocated for greater and greater freedoms.[60] As Wendell Bird has written, the Blackstonian 'definition and framework were not universally accepted in England or America in the 1770s and 1780s'.[61] But even this popular opposition to press regulation was short-lived in Britain, displaced in the long run, and especially during the French Revolution and the agitations of the 1790s, by the belief that regulation remained necessary to prevent anarchy.[62] The '*liberty of the press*' is 'essential to the nature of a free state', one writer remarked in 1795, but that liberty 'consists not in *freedom from censure* for any *criminal matter* that may be published, but in laying *no previous restraints* upon publication ... Thus the will of individuals is still left free; the *abuse* only of that *free-will* is the object of legal punishment'.[63]

The issue of prior restraint eventually became the cleft that opened up between Britons and their colonial brethren. Even when opposed to the Blackstonian

---

[58] William Blackstone, *Commentaries on the Laws of England*, Book IV: Of Public Wrongs, edited by Ruth Paley (Oxford: Oxford University Press, 2016), p. 100.

[59] John Brewer, *Party Ideology and Popular Politics at the Accession of George III* (Cambridge: Cambridge University Press, 1981), p. 220.

[60] Bird, 'Liberties of Press and Speech', pp. 3–4.

[61] Wendell Bird, *Press and Speech Under Assault: The Early Supreme Court Justices, the Sedition Act of 1798, and the Campaign against Dissent* (Oxford: Oxford University Press, 2016), p. 69.

[62] Kenneth R. Johnston, *Unusual Suspects: Pitt's Reign of Alarm and the Lost Generation of the 1790s* (Oxford: Oxford University Press, 2013), p. 5.

[63] *For all Ranks of People, Political Instructions* (London, 1795), pp. 18–19.

principle of 'prior restraint', Britons continued to argue that the press required some degree of regulation well into the nineteenth century. John Stuart Mill, for instance, waffled on unmitigated public debate throughout the 1830s.[64] Not until 1859 would he finally—and, for many Britons, radically—argue that press freedom should be absolute. Even if 'the law of England, on the subject of the press, is as servile to this day as it was in the time of the Tudors', Mill asserted, 'there ought to exist the fullest liberty of professing and discussing, as a matter of ethical conviction, any doctrine, however immoral it may be considered'.[65]

The ferment of the late 1760s in favour of press freedom became itself a referent for colonists who lived in increasing fear of a metropolitan conspiracy against those living in far-flung British dominions.[66] As Bernard Bailyn argued decades ago, 'Writings popular in the colonies insisted that the environment of eighteenth-century England was, to a dangerous degree, hostile to liberty'. By the 1760s, 'the belief was widespread in America that while liberty had been better preserved in England than elsewhere in the Old World, the immediate circumstances in [Britain] were far from conducive to the continued maintenance of liberty'.[67] In their distrust of British elites, colonists seemingly offered an early forerunner to the 'paranoid style' of American politics that Richard Hofstadter first identified in 1964, with its toxic mix of 'heated exaggeration, suspiciousness and conspiratorial fantasy'.[68] This sense that freedom had been irretrievably lost in the motherland is perhaps clearest in the motivations that undergirded the American Revolution. 'The primary goal of the American Revolution', Bailyn writes, 'was not the overthrow or even the alteration of the existing social order but the preservation of political liberty threatened by the apparent corruption of the constitution, and the establishment in principle of the existing conditions of liberty'.[69] That the government of the United States later sought to guarantee the allied rights of the press and speech, less than a century after the Press Licensing Act had lapsed, might be read as a direct response to the entire regime of press and speech regulation that British colonists had anxiously witnessed while living an ocean away from their king.

In Britain's American colonies, where many had come to view print, in Michael Warner's words, as 'the primary agent of world emancipation', a much more radical philosophy of press freedom was consistently espoused from at least the

[64] Alexander Brady, Introduction to *Essays on Politics and Society*, in *The Collected Works of John Stuart Mill*, edited by J. M. Robson et al., vol. 18 (Toronto: University of Toronto Press, 1963–91), p. lv.

[65] John Stuart Mill, *On Liberty*, in *Essays on Politics and Society*, edited by J. M. Robson, in *The Collected Works of John Stuart Mill*, p. 228, 228n.

[66] Bernard Bailyn, *The Ideological Origins of the American Revolution* (1967), enlarged edition (Cambridge: Belknap Press, 1992), pp. 122–30; and Hellmuth, 'Liberty of the Press', p. 472.

[67] Bailyn, *Ideological Origins*, p. 86.

[68] Richard Hofstadter, *The Paranoid Style in American Politics* (1964; New York: Alfred. A. Knopf, 1965), p. 3.

[69] Bailyn, *Ideological Origins*, p. 19.

mid-eighteenth century on.[70] For Britons, one was permitted to write or publish anything one wished, but that writing or speech could always be subject to later legal scrutiny. In the American colonies, and eventually the United States, both prior restraint *and* post-publication prosecution were opposed; the lone exception for early Americans was the personal defamation of private and public individuals. Both Jeffrey A. Smith and Wendell Bird have argued, contra Leonard Levy, that this libertarian tradition gained prominence in the British colonies following the failed 1735 prosecution of John Peter Zenger for libel in New York.[71] In Smith's words,

> Libertarians then, as now, believed the press should scrutinize government and express opinions freely, but thought the press had to accept some degree of responsibility in its treatment of the personal reputations of public officials... Libertarians routinely distinguished between the freedom to discuss public issues and the limited right to discuss public persons.[72]

This, to some degree, downplays the importance of the Federalists in government who continued to believe that the absence of prior restraint was the lone condition for a free press, especially during the final decades of the eighteenth century and even during the later 1790s, following the ratification of the First Amendment. Nonetheless, the reality remained that Americans in general, rather than their British counterparts, argued much more consistently that an unmitigated 'market-place of ideas'—the belief that 'truth naturally overcomes falsehood when they were allowed to compete'—was essential to a truly free press.[73]

The disparities between US and British law around press freedom endure even today—between a country with strong defamation laws and hate speech legislation and a country whose courts, first in civil cases and then in criminal cases in 1964, elected to protect even false statements, provided they are not made with 'actual malice'.[74] This faith in the marketplace of ideas—that 'the remedy to... falsehood and fallacies', as Justice Louis Brandeis of the US Supreme Court put it in 1927, 'is more speech, not enforced silence'—continues today.[75] As David

---

[70] Michael Warner, *The Letters of the Republic: Publication and the Public Sphere in Eighteenth-Century America* (Cambridge: Harvard University Press, 1990), p. 32.

[71] On the rejection among American legal historians of the 'new orthodoxy'—Leonard Levy's argument that neither Britons *nor* Americans conceived of press freedom in the 1790s as anything more than what Blackstone and Mansfield called an absence of 'prior restraint' (Levy, *Emergence of a Free Press*, p. vii)—see especially Wendell Bird, 'Liberties of Press and Speech: "Evidence Does Not Exist To Contradict the...Blackstonian Sense" in Late 18th Century England', *Oxford Journal of Legal Studies* 36, no. 1 (2016): pp. 1–5; and Jeffrey A. Smith, *Printers and Press Freedom: The Ideology of Early American Journalism* (Oxford: Oxford University Press, 1988), pp. 2–11.

[72] Smith, *Printers and Press Freedom*, pp. 10–11.

[73] Smith, *Printers and Press Freedom*, pp. 59, 31.

[74] *New York Times v. Sullivan* (1964), 376 U.S. 254; and *Garrison v. Louisiana* (1964), 379 U.S. 254.

[75] *Whitney v. California* (1927), 274 U.S. 377.

McCraw, deputy general counsel of *The New York Times*, has recently and, one might say, naïvely argued, the procession to truth is childishly simple: 'that journalists should tell stories straight, that readers can be trusted and that out of that process we as a country will get it right more often than not'.[76] This, shockingly, in an era when the Republican National Committee could hand out 'Fake News Awards' to *The New York Times*, *The Washington Post*, CNN, *Newsweek*, *Time*, and ABC News.[77]

We might instead look to William B. Warner, who has argued against the primacy of a libertarian 'marketplace of ideas' during the Revolutionary era and apply it to our own troubling historical moment. In Warner's account, the freedoms of speech and the press were viewed 'as a pragmatic mode of articulating resistance in a moment of political crisis; as a symptom of freedom as a spiritual possession of the people; and as a way boldly to perform or enact that freedom'. But, for 'both Whigs and Tories, a disinterested quest for truth took second place'.[78] Even the issue of truth early on opened up a fissure in Anglo-American law. In America, truth was first officially inscribed in law as a defence for libel in 1804.[79] In Britain, truth was permitted as a defence only in civil slander cases, but remained irrelevant in criminal proceedings until the passage of Lord Campbell's Libel Act in 1843.[80]

This is all to suggest that the comparative permissibility and toleration of press freedom in England during the eighteenth century has, to some degree, blinded us not only to its moments of oppressiveness but also to the extent to which everyday Britons supported some form of post-publication regulation. Generally speaking, religion, politics, and the monarch were topics not critically and openly discussed in the press in Europe in the eighteenth century.[81] Robert Darnton, for instance, has demonstrated how censorship, police investigations, and a monopolistic guild of booksellers in Old Regime France all protected official orthodoxies while forcing the most radical works underground, into the provinces, and across national borders for printing prior to covert importation.[82] That English writers experienced a *comparatively* free press—one, perhaps, in Robert Phiddian's pro-vocative account, that was even promoted by the rhetorical intemperance of satirists during this period—is to miss the extent to which the British government

---

[76] David McCraw, 'Think Like a Libel Lawyer', *New York Times* (9 March 2019).

[77] Yen Nee Lee, 'Trump and GOP attack CNN, New York Times and Washington Post in "fake news awards"', CNBC (17 January 2018): https://www.cnbc.com/2018/01/17/fake-news-awards-by-donald-trump-gop-cnn-new-york-times-washington-post.html.

[78] William B. Warner, *Protocols of Liberty: Communication Innovation and the American Revolution* (Chicago: University of Chicago Press, 2013), pp. 158–9.

[79] *The People of the State of New York v. Harry Croswell* (NY, 1804), 3 Johns. Cas. 337.

[80] 6 & 7 Vict. c96, sect. 6.

[81] Peter Gay, *The Enlightenment: An Interpretation*, vol. 2: The Science of Freedom (1966–69; New York: W.W. Norton & Co., 1977), pp. 70–9.

[82] Robert Darnton, *The Literary Underground of the Old Regime* (Cambridge: Harvard University Press, 1982).

remained eager to police speech and writing more generally.[83] The relative freedom of English writers was not a product of the government's support of a philosophical liberty as much as an acknowledgement of the limitations of its legal and regulatory tools.

In this regard, the legal history of satire provides a remarkable long-term case study in the story of eighteenth-century press regulation. As I have argued throughout *Libel and Lampoon*, the government actively pursued satirists and their stationers. Both judicial rulings and parliamentary legislation across the century make clear that the government was eager to regulate not only satiric speech but also the bibliographic forms in which such works circulated. Thomas Babington Macaulay was not simply Whiggish but wrong when he declared that 'English literature was emancipated, and emancipated forever, from the control of government' when the Press Licensing Act lapsed in 1695.[84] Almost all of this period's rulings, taxes on learning, and press-related statutes in some manner affected or targeted satiric practises and publishing; all, moreover, remained on the books and were used when convenient. As David Hume first remarked in 1741, 'The general laws against sedition and libelling are at present as strong as they possibly can be made'.[85] That we do not see hordes of new, significant rulings against satire after mid-century is to some degree testament to the fact that earlier regulatory measures had done their job. As Thomas Keymer has recently argued, the lapse of licensing was a watershed, not between a censored and a free press, but 'between one prevailing method of press control and another, perhaps more effective, method'.[86] The prosecution of printed satire had become easier, even if the authorities in many instances from the 1730s on elected to forgo formal prosecution in lieu of extralegal harassment, and even if those same laws, as I argued in my last chapter, proved nearly useless at policing deverbalized media after mid-century.[87]

Satirists and booksellers had, at least to some degree, and thanks to the machinery of constant coercion, internalized the dictates of censorship. In this regard, the swift and radical development of post-licensing regulatory mechanisms between 1695 and 1730 produced a kind of 'hortatory censorship': one that did not merely punish certain expressions, but implicitly prescribed, through punishment, the limits of permissibility for others.[88] Matthew J. Kinservik has argued, for instance, that the function of the 1737 Stage Licensing Act was not to

---

[83] Robert Phiddian, *Satire and the Public Emotions* (Cambridge: Cambridge University Press, 2019), pp. 32–5.
[84] Thomas Babington Macaulay, *The History of England from the Accession of James the Second*, vol. 7 (London: Longman, Green, 1860–62), p. 169.
[85] David Hume, 'Essay of the Liberty of the Press', in *Essays, Moral and Political*, ed. Eugene F. Miller, rev. ed. (Indianapolis: Liberty Fund, 1987), p. 605.
[86] Keymer, *Poetics*, p. 95.   [87] Black, *Press*, pp. 106–17.
[88] Michael Holquist, 'Corrupt Originals: The Paradox of Censorship', *PMLA* 109, no. 1 (January 1994): p. 16.

'eliminate satire, but to manage satires' by clarifying a 'censorial power' that would be both 'predictable and systematic'. The result, he claims, was an internalization of discipline among dramatists: the act 'achieve[d] its censorial goals by training playwrights ... to produce unobjectionable texts, not by punishing them for producing objectionable ones'.[89]

Satiric practises also helped to produce the very laws and procedures devised for delimiting verbal ambiguity and for increasing the liability of wayward stationers. But those same laws, while at times repressive, also encouraged the verbal, visual, and bibliographic evasions that came to typify satire during this period. This back and forth between the regulation of the press and the satiric evasions that proliferated under the Crown's watchful eye was thus not only dialectical and evolutionary but also generative and productive: of new literary forms, of new ways of publishing, and of new kinds of courtroom reading and regulation.[90] As Michel Foucault has argued, and as Judith Butler and Pierre Bourdieu have reiterated, repression itself can be a productive force.[91] For Foucault, the 'Censorship' of sexual terminology, the desire 'to subjugate it at the level of language', also paradoxically produced from the eighteenth century on 'a veritable discursive explosion' around sex itself.[92]

This same repressive energy exerted by the authorities on the press indirectly encouraged a similar proliferation. As I have attempted to show, satire and the law were two forces that shaped one another during this period. How the courts prosecuted satire was a response to how satire itself was practised; how satire was written and published, the forms it took, and the language it assumed was a response to the restraints of the law. That satire migrated to the deverbalized media of the later eighteenth century was in many ways the inevitable outcome of laws that sought to restrict verbal ambiguity itself. Satirists responded, and the non-verbal evasions of visual satire at times worked, temporarily stymying the courts and those looking to stop their most visible if silent critics. That satiric works often proved resistant to prosecution does not mean, however, that satire was given a free pass during the eighteenth century. The government eagerly prosecuted those they could and routinely harassed those they could not. Following the fates of satirists and their allies in the book trade during this period

---

[89] Matthew J. Kinservik, *Disciplining Satire: The Censorship of Satiric Comedy on the Eighteenth-Century London Stage* (Lewisburg: Bucknell University Press, 2002), pp. 10–11.

[90] Randy Robertson, *Censorship and Conflict in Seventeenth-Century England: The Subtle Art of Division* (University Park: Pennsylvania State University Press, 2010), pp. 19–21.

[91] Judith Butler, *Excitable Speech: A Politics of the Performative* (New York: Routledge, 1997), p. 139; and Pierre Bourdieu, *Language and Symbolic Power* (1982), edited by John B. Thompson, translated by Gino Raymond and Matthew Adamson (Cambridge: Harvard University Press, 1991), p. 37. For a critique of such 'constitutive' accounts of censorship, see Helen Freshwater, 'Towards a Redefinition of Censorship', in *Critical Studies (Vol. 22): Censorship & Cultural Regulation in the Modern Age*, edited by Beate Müller (Amsterdam: Ridopi, 2004), pp. 225–46.

[92] Michel Foucault, *The History of Sexuality: An Introduction* (1976), translated by Robert Hurley (1978; New York: Vintage, 1990), pp. 17–18.

provides an important reminder that the Crown continued to believe that the press should be strictly regulated, even after the Press Licensing Act finally and permanently lapsed and even if those attempts at regulation were sometimes both unsuccessful and counterproductive.

In addition, we need to attend to the cases against satirists and stationers that not only succeeded but also failed. Our current model of legal scholarship is a classic example of winner's history: legal and literary historians often point to trials that foundered or never got off the ground as evidence of ever-growing press freedom. This, however, is to misunderstand the function of much prosecution during this period. Imprisonment and fines were certainly welcomed by the Crown, but even failed prosecutions were systematic and had an important chilling effect on those in the book trade. As one commentator argued in 1740, convictions were fine, but it was better 'to weary...these *Hawkers of Iniquity*... with perpetual *Prosecutions*' and 'to punish them with the Charge of everlasting *Subpœnas, Appearances,* and *Defences*'.[93] Routine legal harassment financially hobbled stationers while effectively warning others in the trade.

This is all to say that satire is also a stand-in for a much larger, much less intuitive, and much more complicated history of the press. Rather than a crisp and uninterrupted arc to explain this messy story of press freedom, perhaps we should turn to Tristram Shandy and his comically convoluted narrative diagrams (Figure E.1). For all of our once Whiggish stories about press freedom during this period—that it inevitably grows and grows, part and parcel with our progression towards ever greater liberty—there can be little doubt that there were also sudden and stunning moments of contraction throughout the eighteenth century. We could easily point to some of those events and moments studied throughout *Libel and Lampoon*: the radical modification of libel laws under Chief Justice Holt, the routine prosecution of writers and stationers during the first two decades following the lapse of licensing, the systematic prosecutions of the Walpole administration during the 1720s and early 1730s, the Stage Licensing Act of 1737, the widespread use of ex officio informations and special juries, the Wilkes and Junius trials, the Gordon riots, the French Revolution, and the Napoleonic Wars, among many other controversies and instances. All of these are testament to the willingness of the government to use the courts to rein in the press when needed and especially during moments of heightened domestic anxiety. What we need, I would argue, is not a Whig History or even a piecemeal history but perhaps a Shandean history of the press. Such a history of the press, like Tristram's own meandering attempts to make sense of the forces that have shaped his life, would remain alive to the constant fluctuations in the practise of regulation, even if press freedoms did expand over the course of the century and in

---

[93] [Squire], *A Faithful Report*, p. 18.

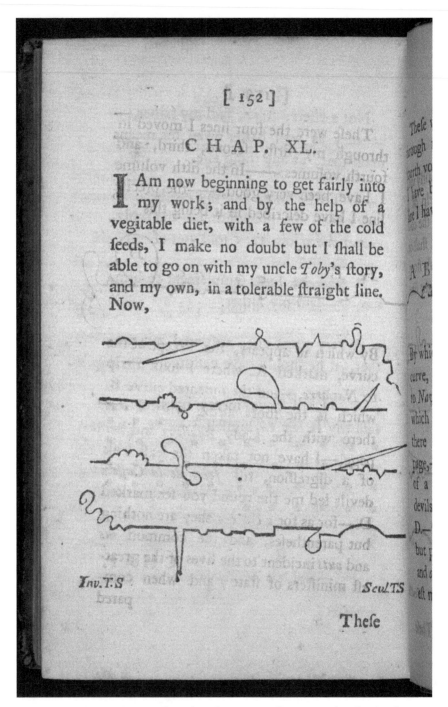

spite of the ad hoc policies of government after government and the staggeringly commonplace belief among Britons that freedom of the press was not—and should not be—absolute.

One benefit of a more circuitous or even Shandean model of press freedom is that it helps to temper and contextualize the role that the press played in the expansion of liberty more generally. A form of what we might call bibliophilic optimism has sometimes infected discussions of the press during the early modern period: the notion that printing, under all circumstances, will insolubly lead to the liberty of the subject. Some writers, like François Lambert in 1526 and John Foxe in 1563, framed the printing press as a 'divine' intervention in human affairs.[94] Others took a more quotidian approach, such as Samuel Hartlib, who declared in a utopian allegory in 1641, as the Long Parliament began dismantling the Stuart state apparatus, that 'the Art of Printing will so spread knowledge, that the common people, knowing their rights and liberties, will not be governed by way of oppression'.[95] Such optimism continued into the eighteenth century, when writers went so far as to argue that the Glorious Revolution, the Hanoverian Succession, and the Protestant Reformation, among so many other events, were all 'wholly owing to the press'.[96]

Scholars, in turn, have sometimes claimed too much noble-mindedness on behalf of a less than disinterested commercial industry. The American journalist Daniel Schorr, among others, has reminded us that 'the press is the only private industry afforded specific constitutional protection'—a supposed 'constitutional shelter in the public interest [that] primarily serv[es] substantial private interests'.[97] The arguments of eighteenth-century advocates for freedom of the press might raise similar eyebrows. Like the old-money families, Silicon Valley billionaires, and corporate entities that own today's media empires, eighteenth-century writers and stationers were, for the most part and increasingly, commercial entrepreneurs. Their interest in a free press was not wholly public-minded. A free press meant not only open debate and a well-informed electorate, but

---

[94] Jean-François Gilmont, 'Protestant Reformations and Reading', in *A History of Reading in the West*, edited by Guglielmo Cavallo and Roger Chartier, translated by Lydia G. Cochrane (Amherst: University of Massachusetts Press, 1999), pp. 213–37. Such rationalizations continued into the eighteenth century, when Matthew Tindal claimed that the 'Noble Art of Printing...was discovered...by Divine Providence...to free Men from under the Tyranny of the Clergy' ([Matthew Tindall], *Reasons Against Restraining the Press* [London, 1704], p. 7).

[95] [Samuel Hartlib], *A Description of the Famous Kingdome of Macaria* (London, 1641), pp. 6–7 or 13.

[96] Matthew Tindal, *A Letter to a Member of Parliament, shewing, that a Restraint on the Press is inconsistent with the Protestant Religion, and dangerous to the Liberties of the Nation* (London, 1698), p. 11; *England's Constitutional Test for the Year 1763* (London, 1763), p. 22; *The Extraordinary Case of William Bingley, Bookseller* (London, 1770), p. 33; and *Another Letter to Mr. Almon in Matter of Libel* (London, 1770), p. 6.

[97] Daniel Schorr, 'Foreword', in David A. Copeland, *The Idea of a Free Press: The Enlightenment and its Unruly Legacy* (Evanston: Northwestern University Press, 2006), p. ix.

also a flourishing business that faced fewer regulations, fewer variables, and, as a result, lower costs.[98] The brazen self-interest of stationers was not lost on contemporaries, and writers frequently pointed to 'the avarice and cupidity' of the 'monopolizing booksellers'.[99] Moreover, the press was hardly a lackey of the fourth estate, isolated from and in opposition to the powers to whom writers claimed to speak truth. As William St Clair, Adrian Johns, Jody Greene, and others scholars have amply demonstrated, the state and the press, especially through the Stationers' Company, maintained 'a close alliance' in which 'textual policing and self-censorship' were often delivered 'in exchange for economic privileges', including 'private intellectual property' and 'cartelisation within the [book] industry'.[100] The press might have been a guarantor of personal liberty, but it was also mediated by a commercial industry that was perfectly happy to dissemble its entrepreneurialism, issuing cries of 'press freedom' as a fig leaf in service of its own economic self-interest.

Like their early modern and Enlightenment-era forebears, scholars today have also been a bit too quick to celebrate the liberatory qualities of the press without due regard for either print's most pernicious aspects or publishers' rapacious self-interest. This form of optimism has in part extended from the radical impact of writing on 'mental and social structures', as such historians and theorists of orality and literacy as Walter J. Ong, Jack Goody, and Paula McDowell have shown.[101] But a specifically print rather than chirographic fetishism has also permeated academic discussions of the printing press. Perhaps most famously, Elizabeth L. Eisenstein argued that the shift 'from the copyist's desk to the printer's workshop ... revolutionized all forms of learning' by making texts available in numbers simply unthinkable in the era of manuscripts.[102] For Eisenstein, this 'unacknowledged revolution' in the form of publication created the conditions for the Renaissance, the Protestant Reformation, and the Scientific Revolution.

---

[98] James Raven, 'The Book as a Commodity', in *The Cambridge History of the Book in Britain*, vol. 5: 1695–1830, edited by Michael F. Suarez, S. J., and Michael L. Turner (Cambridge: Cambridge University Press, 2009), pp. 85–117; and Terry Belanger, 'Publishers and Writers in Eighteenth-Century England', in *Books and their Readers in Eighteenth-Century England*, edited by Isabel Rivers (New York: St. Martin's Press, 1982), pp. 5–23.

[99] *The Rambler's Magazine*, vol. 1 (London, 1822), pp. 395–6.

[100] William St Clair, *The Reading Nation in the Romantic Period* (Cambridge: Cambridge University Press, 2004), p. 438; Adrian Johns, *The Nature of the Book: Print and Knowledge in the Making* (Chicago: University of Chicago Press, 1998), pp. 37–8; Jody Greene, *The Trouble with Ownership: Literary Property and Authorial Liability in England, 1660–1730* (Philadelphia: University of Pennsylvania Press, 2005), pp. 4–6; and Joseph F. Lowenstein, 'Legal Proofs and Corrected Readings: Press-Agency and the New Bibliography', in *The Production of English Renaissance Culture*, edited by David Lee Miller, Sharon O'Dair, and Harold Weber (Ithaca: Cornell University Press, 1994), pp. 94–6.

[101] Walter J. Ong, *Orality and Literacy: The Technologizing of the Word* (1982; London: Routledge, 2010), p. 6; Jack Goody (ed.), *Literacy in Traditional Societies* (Cambridge: Cambridge University Press, 1968); and Paula McDowell, *The Invention of the Oral: Print Commerce and Fugitive Voices in Eighteenth-century Britain* (Chicago: University of Chicago Press, 2016).

[102] Elizabeth L. Eisenstein, *The Printing Press as an Agent of Change: Communications and Cultural Transformations in Early-Modern Europe*, vol. 1 (Cambridge: Cambridge University Press, 1979), p. 3.

Her claims have proven controversial among book historians and historians of reading.[103] Yet a tendency endures among scholars, even today, in Adrian Johns' words, to insist on the 'starkly revolutionary' quality of printing itself.[104]

Later historians, of especially American media and journalism, have exhibited a comparable enthusiasm, marvelling at the 'amazing evolution of the right of expression and, consequently, the liberty of the press' between the invention of moveable type and the American revolution.[105] A similar bibliophilic optimism has sometimes characterized studies of the eighteenth century.[106] This era was also, of course, the Enlightenment, the supposed period when Europeans attempted to emerge from their 'self-incurred' infancy and 'dared to know', in Immanuel Kant's famous words.[107] That coextensive daring and knowing was a product of liberty and publication for many, including Kant, who insisted 'in virtually all his political writings' that 'freedom of the press' was 'the instrument of enlightenment'.[108] According to David A. Copeland, the liberatory potential of the eighteenth-century press was 'the Enlightenment's gift' to Revolutionary-era Americans.[109] Even scholars sceptical of Kant's Horatian formulation ('*Sapere aude!*') have tended to put print more generally at the centre of early modernity. Clifford Siskin and William Warner, for instance, have provocatively argued that the Enlightenment itself was 'an event in the history of mediation', a moment (*c.*1730/40s–1780s) inside of a larger, longer story about how knowledge was created and organized through the various and variable tools of knowing—those mediations and interconnected remediations, like periodicals, encyclopedias, and review organs, in which 'print took center stage'.[110] Undeniably, the press was central to the distribution of Enlightenment ideals, not only through these 'cardinal' and 'proliferating mediations', as Siskin and Warner put it, but also

---

[103] Sabrina Alcorn Baron, Eric N. Lindquist, and Eleanor F. Shevlin, Introduction, in *Agent of Change: Print Culture Studies after Elizabeth L. Eisenstein*, edited by Baron et al. (Amherst: University of Massachusetts Press, 2007), pp. 1–12; and Marina Frasca-Spada and Nick Jardine (eds.), *Books and the Sciences in History* (Cambridge: Cambridge University Press, 2000).

[104] Adrian Johns, 'How to Acknowledge a Revolution', *American Historical Review* 107, no. 1 (February 2002): p. 107.

[105] David A. Copeland, *The Idea of a Free Press: The Enlightenment and its Unruly Legacy* (Evanston: Northwestern University Press, 2006), p. 215.

[106] For a particularly giddy account, in which 'battles of the pen' (p. 72) were a 'dynamo of change' (p. 79), see Roy Porter, *Enlightenment: Britain and the Creation of the Modern World* (London: Allen Lane, 2000), ch. 4.

[107] Immanuel Kant, 'An answer to the question: What is enlightenment? (1784)', in *The Cambridge Edition of the Works of Immanuel Kant: Practical Philosophy*, translated and edited by Mary J. Gregor (Cambridge: Cambridge University Press, 1996), pp. 17–22.

[108] Mary J. Gregor, Headnote, 'An answer to the question: What is enlightenment? (1784)', in *The Cambridge Edition of the Works of Immanuel Kant: Practical Philosophy*, p. 13.

[109] Copeland, *The Idea of a Free Press*, p. 226.

[110] Clifford Siskin and William Warner, 'This is Enlightenment: An Invitation in the Form of an Argument', in *This is Enlightenment*, edited by Clifford Siskin and William Warner (Chicago: University of Chicago Press, 2010), pp. 1–21, *passim*, esp. 5–7, 10.

frequently through dubious transnational reprintings or 'piracies', as Adrian Johns has shown.[111]

For scholars of both the early modern era and the Enlightenment, print has become a central actor in the stories we tell about these periods. At the same time, one might argue that the invention of the press, rather than liberating knowledge and thus the subject, actually intensified the government's desire to police written materials. With the possibility of mass, largely uniform, more efficient, and more economical printing, the authorities knew they were facing a much larger problem in need of sophisticated and at times repressive controls. Edoardo Tortarolo, for instance, has argued that the 'invention of the printing press with moveable type prompted a general awareness that systematic control of communication was becoming necessary and that governments had to devise agencies charged primarily with this task'.[112] The endurance of repressive press regimes across Europe—including England, through the rearguard action of libel prosecutions in the courts—is all the more remarkable for their prevalence during an intellectual movement, as Louis Dupré has argued, defined by its commitment to and belief in the emancipatory potential of public reason.[113] Even Kant was reprimanded by Frederick William II in 1793 for his *Religion within the Bounds of Bare Reason*. Little surprise, then, that he should argue in that same year that '*freedom of the pen* ... is the sole palladium of the people's rights'.[114]

A more cautious approach to the history of the press is not to downplay the liberatory potential of print or even the profound historical impact of the printing press. But it should remind us that freedom and censorship are two sides of the same coin: freedom of the press implies freedom *from* something; censorship became the something against which to define a negative liberty. The story of press freedom is not simply an adversarial tale between authoritarian government censors and noble-minded authors and booksellers. As I have tried to make clear in this final discussion, a third, often forgotten group typically gets pushed to the narrative wayside in such tales of legal combat: those who argued that the press should be free and yet still carefully regulated in some regard; those who worried that print was not a natural right and one that did not always ensure the liberty of the subject. Their reasoning shared something structurally in common with the arguments of both opponents to and advocates for press freedom: the

---

[111] Adrian Johns, *Piracy: The Intellectual Property Wars from Gutenberg to Gates* (Chicago: University of Chicago Press, 2009), chs. 1–4, *passim*, and 'The Piratical Enlightenment', in *This is Enlightenment*, p. 301.

[112] Edoardo Tortarolo, *The Invention of Free Press: Writers and Censorship in Eighteenth Century Europe* (Berlin: Springer, 2016), p. xiii.

[113] Louis Dupré, *The Enlightenment and the Intellectual Foundations of Modern Culture* (New Haven: Yale University Press, 2004), pp. 7–12.

[114] Kant, 'On the common saying: That may be correct in theory, but it is of no use in practice (1793)', in *The Cambridge Edition of the Works of Immanuel Kant: Practical Philosophy*, translated and edited by Mary J. Gregor (Cambridge: Cambridge University Press, 1996), p. 304.

press needed to be regulated precisely *because* of its troubling liberatory potential and capacity to spread misleading and ultimately uncorrectable information. As Jonathan Swift trenchantly observed in 1710,

> if a lie be believed only for an hour, it has done its work, and there is no farther occasion for it. Falsehood flies, and Truth comes limping after it; so that when men come to be undeceived, it is too late, the jest is over, and the tale has had its effect.[115]

Today, the worries of Swift and his fellow biblio-sceptics feel prescient.[116]

This twisting, Shandean history of press freedom is the larger narrative of *Libel and Lampoon* and the implicit story I have tried to tell of an ongoing, long-term back and forth between satirists, the authorities, and the courts. That story is about the ways in which legal concerns shaped the history of satire: how satire triggered legal responses; how those legal pressures changed the physical forms in which satiric works circulated, be they manuscript or print; and how an awareness of the difficulties of legal interpretation shaped both the heavily evasive language that came to typify the satire written during the final decades of the seventeenth century and across the eighteenth century and the deverbalized semantic indeterminacy of later-eighteenth-century caricature and drama.

This is also a story with provokingly Shandean forms of causation, of misunderstandings and misinterpretations. Legal concerns, even when misplaced, need to be at the centre of the stories we tell about this period and its literature. Ambiguous laws and rapidly changing courtroom procedures, routinely misinterpreted by writers and their stationers, also shaped satire's rhetorical qualities and its physical forms. Finally, as I have argued in closing, we might view this exchange as a synecdoche for the larger battle pitched between the press and its regulators throughout the eighteenth century. The story of satire in the courts is perhaps a salutary reminder that we should not think of press freedom in the eighteenth century as a mere rise or fall or even as a series of fragments; we should instead follow Tristram Shandy, so that we might tell this tale of press freedom in, at best, 'a tolerable straight line'.[117]

---

[115] [Jonathan Swift], *The Examiner*, no. 15 (2–9 November 1710).

[116] Soroush Vosoughi, Deb Roy, and Sinan Aral, 'The spread of true and false news online', *Science* 359, no. 6380 (9 March 2018): pp. 1146–51.

[117] Laurence Sterne, *The Life and Opinions of Tristram Shandy, Gentleman*, edited by Melvyn New and Joan New, vol. 3 (Gainesville: University Press of Florida, 1978), p. 570.

Bibliography

Cases

Anon. (1565). MS. Maynard 87, f. 34. *Sources*, pp. 637–8.

Anon. (1574). MS. LI. 3. 9, f. 402v, CUL.

Anon. (1575). MS. Maynard 77/313 (C.P.), Lincoln's Inn. *Sources*, p. 638.

Anon. (1579). MS. Misc. 488/48 (Q.B.), Lincoln's Inn.

Anon. (1580). MS Misc. 488/76 (Q.B.), Lincoln's Inn. *Sources*, pp. 638–9.

Austin v. Culpeper (1683), 2 Show. 313 (K.B.), 89 Eng. Rep. 960.

Baker v. Pierce (1704). 6 Mod. 24 (Q.B.). 87 Eng. Rep. 788.

Baldwin v. Elphinston (1775), 2 Black. W. 1038 (Ex.Ch.), 96 Eng. Rep. 610.

Trial of Sir Samuel Barnardiston (1684, K.B.). 9 *State Trials* 1349.

Barrow v. Lewellin (1615). Hobart 62 (S.C.). 80 Eng. Rep. 211.

Proceedings against Mr. Baxter (1685). 11 *State Trials* 502.

Bell v. Thatcher (1675). I Vent. 275 (K.B.). 86 Eng. Rep. 184.

Bourke v. Warren (1826). 2 Carr. & P. 307 (N.P.). 172 Eng. Rep. 138.

Brooke v. Wye (1602). Add. MS 25203, f. 471, BL.

Case de Libellis Famosis (1605). 5 Coke 125 (K.B.). 77 Eng. Rep. 250.

Case 114 (Anon.), 1 Comyns 263, 92 Eng. Rep. 106.

Carpenter's Case (1558). *Sources*, p. 637.

The Arraignment, Tryal and Condemnation of Stephen Colledge [sic] for High-Treason (London, 1681).

Cook v. Ward (1830). 6 Bing 409 (C.P.). 130 Eng. Rep. 1388.

Dickerson v. US (2000). 530 U.S. 428.

*Trial of Dover, Brewster and Brook*s (1663, K.B.). 6 *State Trials* 563, 10 *State Trials* 540.

Dr. Edwards v. Dr. Wooton (1607, K.B.). 12 Coke 35. 77 Eng. Rep. 1316.

Foster v. Browning (1624). Cro. Jac. 688 (C.P.). 79 Eng. Rep. 596.

The Trial of Mr. Richard Francklin (1731). 17 *State Trials* 666.

Garrison v. Louisiana (1964). 379 U.S. 254.

Gastrell v. Townsend (1591). Cro. Eliz. 239/8 (Q.B.). *Sources*, pp. 644.

Goodrick's Case (1612). Moore 821 (S.C.). 71 Eng. Rep. 927.

Hamond v. Kingsmill (1647), 22 Style 23 (K.B.). 82 Eng. Rep. 499.

Harrison v. Thornborough (1714). Gilb. Cas. 114, 10 Mod. 196 (Q.B.). 93 Eng. Rep. 277.

Hickes's Case (1618). Popham 139, Hobart 215 (K.B.). 79 Eng. Rep. 1240.

Holt v. Astrigg (1608). Cro. Jac. 184/4 (K.B.). *Sources*, pp. 643–4.

Jeames v. Rutlech (1599). 4 Co. Rep. 17 (Q.B.). *Sources*, pp. 642–3.

Jones v. Bird (1822), 5 B. & Ald. 845–846.

Kilvert v. Roe (1625). Bendl. 155 (K.B.). 73 Eng. Rep. 1022.

King v. Lake (1664), Hard. 364 and 388. 145 Eng. Rep. 499 and 511.

King v. Lake (1667). *Sources*, pp. 652–4.

King v. Lake (1668). *A Source Book of English Law*, edited by A. K. R. Kiralfy (London: Sweet & Maxwell Ltd, 1957), pp. 154–63.

King v. Lake (1670). Hard. 470–471 (Ex. Ch.). 145 Eng. Rep. 552–553, 146 Eng. Rep. 499.

King v. Lake (1671). 2 Vent. 28 (C.P.). 89 Eng. Rep. 12, 86 Eng. Rep. 289.

King v. Lake (1671). 1 Free. 14–15 (C.P.). 89 Eng. Rep. 12–13.

Knowlys v. Castleton (1754, K.B.). Harrowby MSS 12/14, Lincoln's Inn.

Lamb's Case (1610). 9 Coke 59 (S.C.). 77 Eng. Rep. 822.

Lewis v. Roberts (1661). Hard. 203. *Sources*, pp. 645.

Miles v. Bland (1609). 1 Rolle Abr. 67.

Morrison v. Cade (1607). Cro. Jac. 162. John March. *Actions for Slander.* 2nd ed. (London, 1674), p. 31.

New York Times v. Sullivan (1964). 376 U.S. 254.

Peard v. Jones (1635), Cro. Car. 382 (K.B.), 79 Eng. Rep. 934.

Earl of Pembroke v. Staniel (1672). 1 Free. 49 (K.B.). 89 Eng. Rep. 38.

The People of the State of New York v. Harry Croswell (NY, 1804). 3 Johns. Cas. 337.

Earl of Peterborough v. Sir John Mordant (1670). 1 Ventr. 60 (K.B.). 86 Eng. Rep. 42.

Earl of Peterborough v. Williams (1687). 2 Show. 505–506 (K.B.). 89 Eng. Rep. 1068.

Poe v. Mondford (1598). Cro. Eliz. 620 (Q.B.). 78 Eng. Rep. 861.*Prekington's Case* (1610). 1 Rolle Abr. 66.

R. v. Almon (1770, K.B.). *Mansfield MSS*, vol. 2, p. 833.

R. v. Baldwin (1770, K.B.). *Mansfield MSS.* vol. 2, p. 842.

R. v. Barnes (1749, K.B.). 10/29, TNA.

R. v. Bate (1782, K.B.). *Mansfield MSS*, vol. 2, p. 855.

R. v. Bear [*sic*] (1698). Holt 442 (K.B.). 90 Eng. Rep. 1132.

R. v. Bear [*sic*] (1699, K.B.). Hardwicke Papers, Add. MS 35981, BL.

R. v. Dr. Brown [*sic*] (1706, Q.B.). 88 Eng. Rep. 911.

R. v. Dr. Browne (1706, Q.B.). 90 Eng. Rep. 1134.

R. v. Burdett (1820). 3 B & Ald. 727–729, 750–2 (K.B.). 106 Eng. Rep. 827, 835.

R. v. Carr [or *Care*] (1680). 7 *State Trials* 1118.

R. v. Clerk [*sic*] (1728/9). 1 Barn. 305 (K.B.). 94 Eng. Rep. 207.

R. v. Cooper (1734). KB 1/4/2, TNA.

R. v. Drake (1706, Q.B.). Hardwicke Papers, Add. MS 35980, BL.

R. v. Harrop (1754). KB 1/11/6, TNA.

R. v. Hurt (1712). Williams Hawkins. *A Treatise of the Pleas of the Crown*, vol. 1 (London, 1716), p. 194.

R. v. Knell (1729). 1 Barn. 305–306 (K.B.). 94 Eng. Rep. 207–208.

R. v. Meres (1740). KB 10/25/1, TNA.

R. v. Miller (1781). KB 33/5/9, TNA.

R. v. Nutt (1728). 1 Barn. 306 (K.B.). 94 Eng. Rep. 208.

R. v. Paine (1696). 5 Mod. 163 (K.B.). 87 Eng. Rep. 584.

R. v. Tiffen (1768). D/DO/B24/5, Essex Record Office.

R. v. Tutchin (1704). Holt 424 (Q.B.). 90 Eng. Rep. 1133.

R. v. Woodfall (1774). KB 33/5/8, TNA.

The Tryal of William Rayner (London, 1733).

Roach v. Garvan (1742). 2 Atk. 469 (Ch.). 26 Eng. Rep. 683.

Roach v. Read (1742). 2 Atk. 469 (C.P.).

Schenck v. United States (1919). 249 U.S. 47.

Seven Bishops' Trial (1688, K.B.). 12 *State Trials* 401.

Smale v. Hammon (1610). 1 Bulst. 40 (K.B.). 80 Eng. Rep. 743.

Somers v. House (1693). Holt 39 (K.B.). 90 Eng. Rep. 919.

Stamp v. White (1621), Cro. Jac. 600 (K.B.), 79 Eng. Rep. 513.

Summers v. Summers (1664). 1 Lev. 138, 1 Keble 771, 788.

Taylor v. Mounds (1618), STAC 8/284/23, TNA.
Trial of John Tutchin (1704, Q.B.). 14 *State Trials* 1195.
Vaughan v. Menlove (1837), 3 Bing (N.C.) 468, 173 Eng. Rep. 232.
Virginia v. Black (2003). 538 U.S. 343.
Villers v. Monsley (1769). 2 Wils. 403 (K.B.).
Want's Case (1600). More 628 (S.C.). 72 Eng. Rep. 802.
Watson v. Vanderlash (1628). Hetley 71 (C.P.). 124 Eng. Rep. 351.
Whitney v. California (1927). 274 U.S. 377.

Manuscripts

Beinecke Rare Book and Manuscript Library, Yale University
GEN MSS 65
GEN MSS 313
GEN MSS 782
OSB MS 19
OSB MS 103, Boxes 1–4
OSB MS b54
OSB MS b105
OSB MS b216
OSB MS b327
OSB MS c103
OSB MS c111
OSB MS c162
OSB MS c171
OSB MS c252
OSB MS fb30
OSB MS fc137
OSB MS fb207
OSB MSS FILE 19698
Bodleian Library, Oxford University
Rawlinson MS D.72
British Library
Add. MS. 6880
Add. MS 16927
Add. MS 16922
Add. MS 16924
Add. MSS 27774–80
Add. MSS 30868–9
Add. MS 30877
Add. MS 32555
Add. MS 32867
Add. MS 33052
Add. MS 33230
Add. MSS 35980–1
Add. MS 36033
Add. MS 36128
Add. MS 36595

Add. MS 36663
Add. MS 38476
Add. MS 39200
Add. MS 41065
Add. MS 47566
Add. MS 61460
Egerton MS. 1951
['Libels on Pope'], General Reference Collection C.116.b.1–4
Cambridge University Library
Cholmondeley (Houghton) Papers MS
Harleian MS 6913/5
Lindsay SwJ 203
Harry Ransom Center, University of Texas at Austin
MS 1503
MS 1512
Houghton Library, Harvard University
MS Eng. 585
MS Eng. 598
MS Eng. 601.60
MS Eng. 602
MS Eng. 611
MS Eng. 623
MS Eng. 624
MS Eng. 636
MS Eng. 760
MS Eng. 760.1
MS Eng. 794
MS Eng. 827
MS Eng. 1038
MS Eng. 1063
MS Eng. 1065
MS Eng. 1123
MS Eng. 1131
MS Eng. 1137
The Huntington Library, San Marino, California
mssLA 93
mssLA 105
mssLA 129
mssLA 144
mssLA 149
mssLA 177
mssLA 192
mssLA 194
mssLA 200
mssLA 242
mssLA 274
mssLA 282
mssLA 310
mssLA 324

mssLA 335
mssLA 346
mssLA 355
mssLA 413
mssLA 467
mssLA 2470
The Lewis Walpole Library, Yale University
LWL Fol. 66 748 Sc43
LWL MSS Vol. 17
LWL MSS Vol. 71
LWL MSS Vol. 74
LWL MSS Vol. 98
LWL MSS Vol. 107
LWL MSS Vol. 108
LWL MSS Vol. 115
LWL MSS Vol. 120
LWL MSS Vol. 125
LWL MSS Vol. 126
LWL MSS Vol. 175
Lincoln's Inn Library, London, England
Harrowby MSS 12/14
Misc. MS 488/48
Misc. MS 488/76
MS. Maynard 77/313
Ryder Shorthand Document
The National Archives, England
C 11/2581/36
C 11/549/39
C 33/351
CP 35/6/1
KB 1/4/1–6
KB 1/5/1–3
KB 1/6/1–3
KB 1/10/2
KB 10/29
KB 1/11/3
KB 1/11/5–6
KB 1/12/1–3
KB 1/13/1–2
KB 15/25
KB 33/5/6
KB 33/5/5–9
KB 33/24/2
KB 101/1/5–9
SP 29/51/10
SP 36/8/74
SP 34/11/69
SP 34/37/11
SP 36/23

SP 36/23/134
SP 36/23/215
SP 36/26/120
SP 36/41/29
SP 36/46/4–7
SP 36/48
SP 36/48/14
SP 36/50–82
SP 36/65
SP 36/65/82–3
SP 36/70/67
SP 36/111
SP 36/131/87
SP 36/151/56–7
SP 36/151/75
SP 35/1/100
SP 43/66
SP 44/68/64
SP 44/78/65
SP 44/83
SP 44/114
SP 44/274
SP 44/352
SP 44/352/106
SP 63/396
TS 11/157
TS 11/175
TS 11/580/1913
TS 11/1076
TS 11/1078/5360
TS 11/10766
New York Public Library
MssCol 37
MssCol 4312
MssCol 6570
'Caricatures collected by Horace Walpole, 1769–91'. Miriam and Ira D. Wallach Division of
    Art, Prints and Photographs
Patricia D. Klingenstein Library, New-York Historical Society
John Almon, Correspondence and Papers [*c*.1760–1808]
Stationers' Company, London, England
Court Book F
Van Pelt Library, University of Pennsylvania
Ms. Coll. 167
Ms. Coll. 917
Misc. MSS (Jonathan Swift)
William Andrews Clark Memorial Library, University of California at Los Angeles
MS. STB Legal 2, f. 21
MS. 1951.021
MS. 1959.007

Royal Archives, Windsor Castle
Stuart Papers, 119/42
Stuart Papers, 120/85

Periodicals, Journals, and Newspapers

The Athenian Mercury (1690–1697). Burney Newspapers Collection, BL.
Blackwood's Edinburgh Magazine (1817–1905). Proquest British Periodicals.
The Briton (1762–1763). Burney Newspapers Collection, BL.
The Craftsman (1725–1750). Burney Newspapers Collection, BL.
The Critical Review (1756–1817). Proquest British Periodicals.
The Daily Journal (1721–1737). Burney Newspapers Collection, BL.
The Daily Post (1719–1746). Burney Newspapers Collection, BL.
The English Post (1700–1709). Burney Newspapers Collection, BL.
Fog's Weekly Journal (1728–1737). Burney Newspapers Collection, BL.
The Freeholder's Journal (1721–1723). Burney Newspapers Collection, BL.
The Gentleman's Magazine (1731–1833). Proquest British Periodicals.
The Grub-Street Journal (1730–1737). Proquest British Periodicals.
The Jacobite's Journal, edited by W. B. Coley (Oxford: Clarendon Press, 1974).
Lloyd's Evening Post (1757–1805). Burney Newspapers Collection, BL.
The London Evening-Post (1727–1799). Burney Newspapers Collection, BL.
The London Gazette (1666–1792). Burney Newspapers Collection, BL.
The London Journal (1719–1744). Burney Newspapers Collection, BL.
The London Packet: Or, New Evening Post (1771–1800). Burney Newspapers Collection, BL.
The London Post (1699–1705). Burney Newspapers Collection, BL.
Mist's Weekly Journal (1725–1728). Burney Newspapers Collection, BL.
The Monthly Review (1749–1844). Proquest British Periodicals.
The Monthly Chronicle (26 February 1729). Rpt. *Monthly Chronicle* ([London,] [1728–1732]).
The Morning Chronicle (1770–1800). Burney Newspapers Collection, BL.
The Morning Herald (1780–1800). Burney Newspapers Collection, BL.
The Morning Post (1773–1900). Burney Newspapers Collection, BL.
The North Briton (1762–1763). Burney Newspapers Collection, BL.
The Observator (1702–1707). Burney Newspapers Collection, BL.
The Parrot. 9 vol. (London, 1746). *Eighteenth-Century Collections Online*.
The Penny London Post, or The Morning Advertiser (*c.*1744–1751). Burney Newspapers Collection, BL.
The Public Advertiser (1752–1793). Burney Newspapers Collection, BL.
The Rambler's Magazine (1783–1791). Hathi Trust Digital Library.
The St. James's Journal (1722–1723). Burney Newspapers Collection, BL.
The Tatler. Edited by Donald F. Bond, 3 vol. (Oxford: Clarendon Press, 1987).
A Review of the State of the English Nation (1704–1713; New York: Columbia University Press, 1938).
The Spectator. Edited by Donald F. Bond, 5 vol. (Oxford: Clarendon Press, 1965).
The Times (1785–1800). Burney Newspapers Collection, BL.
The Weekly Journal, or, Saturday's Post (1716–1725). Burney Newspapers Collection, BL.
The World (1753–1756). Burney Newspapers Collection, BL.

Visual Materials

The Battle Royal between the Prig Major and Big Bess (1788). BM 7263.

The [boot] Interest in the [city] or a [bridge] in the [hole] (1760). BM Satires 3741.

Caricature Shop (1801). Lewis Walpole Library, Yale University, lwlpr10184.

A Certain Duchess Kissing Old Swelter-in-Grease the Butcher for his Vote (1784). BM 6533.

The Covent Garden Macaronies (1772). BM 5057.

Female Influence (1784). BM 6493.

Florizel granting Independency to Perdita (1783). BM 8318.

The Fly Catching Macaroni (1772). BM 4695.

And Herod and Pilate. . . (1783). BM 6194.

The Lilly Macaroni (1771). BM 4687.

The Old Goat and Young Kid (1798). BM 9304.

The Original Macaroni (1772). BM 5010.

The Rise of India Stock & Sinking fund of Oppression (1784). BM 6394.

The Screen (1742). BM 2539.

Signor Pi-z-i ravishing Mrs. Thr—e (1784 [?]). New York Public Library, 'Caricatures Collected by Horace Walpole, 1769–91', 1861472.

St. George & the Dragon & the Mademoiselle riposting (1789). BM 7557.

The Tiger Macaroni (1771). BM 4987.

'Twas Nobody saw The Lover's Leap & Let the Cat out of the Bag (1786). The Huntington Library, 6929.

The Vis. A. Vis Bisected. Or the Ladies Coop (1776). BM 5373.

A Windy Day: Scene outside the Shop of Bowles the Printseller (1790). Victoria & Albert Museum, D.43–1900.

Bickham, George. *A very Extraordinary Motion* (1744). BM 2613.

Boyne, John. *The Political Beggar* (1784). BM 6500.

Boyne, John. *General Blackbeard wounded at the Battle of Leadenhall* (1784). BM 6367.

Boyne, John. *Scrub and Archer* (1783). BM 6221.

Bretherton, James. *A Masquerade Scene Kensington Garden* (1772). BM 5083.

Burnet, Gilbert. *Burnet's History of My Own Time.* 2 vol., edited by Osmund Airy (Oxford: Clarendon Press, 1900).

Butler, Samuel. *Characters and Passages from Note-Books*, edited by A. R. Waller (Cambridge: Cambridge University Press, 1908).

Byron, Frederick George. *Don Dismallo, After an Absence of Sixteen Years, Embracing his Beautiful Vision* (1790). BM 7679.

Cruikshank, Isaac. *A Mansion House Treat: or Smoking Attitudes!* (1800). BM 9550.

Darly, Matthew. *A Macaroni Print Shop* (1772). BM 4701.

Dent, William. *A Right Hon. Democrat Dissected* (1793). BM 8291.

Dighton, Robert. *Old Q-uiz the old Goat of Picadilly* (1796). BM 8867.

Dighton, Robert. *A Real Scene in St. Paul's Church Yard on a Windy Day* (1782/4 [?]). BM 6352.

Elwood, J. (pseud.?). [A Crowd Outside a Print Shop.] (1790). British Museum, 1878,0511.654.

Kearsley, George. *The Feast of the Gods* (1780). BM 5692.

Gillray, James. *Very Slippy-Weather* (1808). BM 11100.

Gillray, James. *A New Edition Considerably Enlarged, of Attitudes Faithfully Copied for Nature and Humbly Dedicated to all Admirers of the Grand and Sublime* (1807). The Lewis Walpole Library, Yale University, Quarto 75 G41 807.

Gillray, James. *Dido, in Despair!* (1801). BM 9752.

Gillray, James. *A Cognoscenti contemplating the Beauties of the Antique* (1801). The British Museum, 1992,0516.14.

Gillray, James. *The Death of a Great Wolf* (1795). BM 8704.

Gillray, James. *Sandwich-Carrots! dainty Sandwich-Carrots* (1796). BM 8886.

Gillray, James. *The Presentation, or, Wise Men's Offering* (1795). BM 8779.

Gillray, James. *Smelling out a Rat; or The Atheistical-Revolutionist disturbed in his Midnight Calculations.* (1793). BM 7686.

Gillray, James. *A Democrat, or Reason & Philosophy* (1793). BM 8310.

Gillray, James. *A New Administration, or, The State Quacks Administring* (1783). BM 6201.

Gillray, James. *Paradise Regain'd* (1783). BM 6319.

Heath, William. *Good Humour* (1829). BM 15869.

Hogarth, William. *John Wilkes, Esq.* (1763). BM 4050.

Lyford, R. (pseud.). *The Rival Canvessers* (1784). BM 6621.

Newton, Richard. *Cries of London* (1797). BM [n/a].

Rehberg, Friedrich. *Drawings Faithfully Copied from Nature at Naples* (1794). The Lewis Walpole Library, Yale University, Quarto 75 R266 794.

Romney, George. Portrait of Emma Hart as Miranda (1785/6 [?]). Philadelphia Museum of Art, M1928-1-34.Rowlandson, Thomas. *Lady H******* Attitudes* (1791 [?]). BM 9571.

Rowlandson, Thomas. *The Poll* (1784). BM 6526.

Rowlandson, Thomas. *Box-Lobby Loungers* (1786). BM 8254.

Sandby, Paul. *A Poor Man Loaded with Mischief. Or John Bull and his Sister Peg* (1762). BM 3904.

Sayers, James. *Ld. St—e's Observations on Mr Pitt's Plan of Finance* (1786). BM 6960.

Smith, Benjamin. *Street Walkers* (1786). BM 7080.

Smith, J. R. *Spectators at a print shop in St Pauls Churchyard* (1774). BM 3758.

Smith, J. R. *Miss Macaroni and her Gallant at a Print-Shop* (1773). BM 5220.

Townshend, George. *Sawney discover'd, or, The Scotch Intruders* (1760). Lewis Walpole Library, Yale University, 761.00.00.03.2.

West, Benjamin. *Death of General Wolfe* (1770). The National Gallery of Canada, 8007.

Primary Sources

Another Letter to Mr. Almon in Matter of Libel (London, 1770).

Arse Musica; Or, The Lady's Back Report (London, 1722).

The Art of Poetry on a New Plan (London, 1762).

'Advice to Apollo' (1677). Rpt. *POAS*, vol. 1. pp. 392–4.

'An Answer to the Satire on the Court Ladies' (1680). Rpt. *CSR*, pp. 41–6.

The Art of Poetry (London, 1741).

'A Ballad to the Tune of Cheviot Chace, or Whenas King Henry Ruled this Land' (1682). Rpt. *CSR*, pp. 102–11.

Books printed for, and sold by John Clarke at the Bible under the Royal-Exchange Cornhill, London ([London?], [1734?]).

The Br—sh Embassadress's Speech to the French King (London, 1713). Rpt. *POAS*, vol. 7, pp. 590–6.

The Caricatures of Gillray: With Historical and Political Illustrations. 9 parts (London, 1818).

Characters of the Times; Or, An Impartial Account of... the several Nobelmen and Gentlemen, libell'd in a Preface to a late Miscellany (London, 1728).

Claudian's Rufinus (London, 1729).

A Collection of Pieces in Verse and Prose, which have been publish'd on Occasion of the Dunciad (London, 1732).

'Colin' (1679). Rpt. *CSR*, pp. 23–31.

A Compleat Collection Of all the Verses, Essays, Letters and Advertisements (London, 1728).

Counter-address to the Public (London, 1753).

The D—of A——e's Letter (London, 1740).

'A Dialogue between Vamp and his Patron'. In *A Letter to the Right Honourable The E— T—*. (London, 1766).

The Doctrine of Innuendo's Discuss'd, Or the Liberty of the Press Maintain'd (London, 1731).

England's Constitutional Test for the Year 1763 (London, 1763).

The English Theophrastus: Or, The Manners of the Age. 2nd ed. (London, 1706).

The Extraordinary Case of William Bingley, Bookseller (London, 1770).

For all Ranks of People, Political Instructions (London, 1795).

The Fox with his Fire-brand Unkennell'd and Insnared (London, 1703).

Gulliver Decypher'd (London, 1726).

Her Majesties Most Gracious Speech to Both Houses of Parliament, on Monday the Twenty Fifth Day of May 1702 (London, 1702).

'An Heroic Poem' (1681). Rpt. *CSR*, pp. 68–75.

The History and Proceedings of the House of Commons from the Restoration to the Present Times (London, 1742).

'A Hymn to the New Laureat, by a Native of Grub-Street'. In *The Windsor Medley* (London, 1731).

'Julian's Farewell to the Coquets' (1687). Rpt. *CSR*, pp. 138–40.

The Key to Atalantis. Part I ([London?: 1709?]).

The Key to Atalantis. Part II ([London?: 1709?]).

'The Ladies' March' (1681). Rpt. *CSR*, pp. 56–62.

The Law Corrupted; A Satire (London, 1706).

The Lawyer's Answer to the Country Parson's good Advice to My Lord Keeper (London, 1706). Rpt. *POAS*, vol. 7, pp. 160–4.

'The Litany of the Duke of Buckingham' (1680). Rpt. *POAS*, vol. 2, pp. 192–9.

'The Lovers' Session' (1687). Rpt. *CSR*, pp. 175–98.

The Martiniad. Pope Alexander's Supremacy and Infallibility examin'd (London, 1729).

'[On the Ladies of the Court]' (1663). Rpt. *CSR*, pp. 3–9.

The Persian strip'd of his Disguise (London, 1735).

Pope Alexander's Supremacy and Infallibility examin'd (London, 1729).

A Popp on Pope. Rpt. The Popiad (London, 1728).

The Present State of the Republick of Letters. 18 vol. (London, 1728–36).

The Protestant Jesuite Unmask'd (London, 1704).

Reasons for objecting to the renewal of the Licensing Act, London (1695). Rpt. *Primary Sources on Copyright (1450–1900),* edited by L. Bently & M. Kretschmer. www.copyrighthistory.org.

Reflections Upon a Late Scandalous and Malicious Pamphlet Entitul'd, The Shortest Way with the Dissenters (London, 1703).

Remarks, Critical and Political (London, 1726).

'Rochester's Farewell' (1680). Rpt. *POAS*, vol. 2, pp. 217–27.

The Safest-Way with the Dissenters (London, 1703).

'Satire' (1682). Rpt. *CSR*, pp. 81–5.

'Satire on Both Whigs and Tories' (1683). Rpt. *CSR*, pp. 121–30.

'Satire to Julian' (1682). Rpt. *CSR*, pp. 86–91.

A Sequel to the Dunciad: Being The famous British Sh—rs. A Satire (London, 1729).

A Session of the Poets (1676). Rpt. *POAS*, vol. 1, pp. 352–6.

The Session of the Poets (1668). Rpt. *POAS*, vol. 1, pp. 327–37.

The Shortest Way... With its Author's Brief Explanation Consider'd (London, 1703).

State Law: Or, The Doctrine of Libels. 2nd ed. ([London], [1730?]).

The Thoughts of a Tory Author Concerning the Press (London, 1712).

Tryal and Examination of Mr John Tutchin (London, 1704).

'Utile Dulce' (1681). Rpt. *CSR*, pp. 49–55.

Almon, John. *The Trial of John Almon, Bookseller* (London, 1770).

Almon, John. *Memoirs of a Late Eminent Bookseller* (London, 1790).

Almon, John. *Biographical, Literary, and Political Anecdotes of Several of the Most Eminent Persons of the Present Age* (London, 1797).

Arnauld, Antoine, and Pierre Nicole. *The Art of Speaking*, translated by Bernard Lamy (London, 1676).

Atkyns, J. T. *Reports of Cases Argued and Determined in the High Court of Chancery, in the Time of Lord Chancellor Hardwicke* (London, 1781).

Atterbury, Francis. *The Speech of Francis Late Lord Bishop of Rochester* (London, 1723).

Atterbury, Francis. *The Epistolary Correspondence, Visitation Charges, Speeches, and Miscellanies, of the Right Reverend Francis Atterbury, D.D.* 4 vol., edited by J. Nichol (London, 1783–87).

Bacon, Matthew. *A New Abridgment of the Law.* 5 vol. (London, 1736).

Beattie, James. 'An Essay on Laughter and Ludicrous Composition' (1764). In *Essays* (Edinburgh, 1776), pp. 321–486.

Beccaria, Cesare. *An Essay on Crimes and Punishments* (London, 1767).

Blackstone, William. *Commentaries on the Laws of England.* 4 vol., edited by Wilfrid Prest, et al. (Oxford: Oxford University Press, 2016).

Bohun, William. *Declarations and Pleadings in the Most Usual Actions* (London, 1733).

Boileau, Nicolas. *Le Lutrin* (1674). Rpt. *Oeuvres de Boileau Despréaux* (Paris, 1825), pp. 219–63.

Bolingbroke, Lord, Henry St John. *Contributions to the* Craftsman, edited by Simon Varey (Oxford: Oxford University Press, 1982).

Bramston, James. *Man of Taste* (London, 1733).

Browne, Joseph [?]. *The Country Parson's Honest Advice to The Judicious Lawyer, and Worthy Minister of State, My Lord Keeper* (London, 1706). Rpt. *POAS*, vol. 7, pp. 151–9.

Browne, Joseph. *A Letter To the Right Honourable Mr. Secretary Harley, by Dr. Browne* (London, 1706).

[Buller, Francis]. *An Introduction to the Law relative to Trials at Nisi Prius* (London, 1767).

Chambers, Ephraim. *Cyclopaedia: Or, An Universal Dictionary of Arts and Science*, 2 vol. (London, 1728).

Chardin, Sir John. *A New and Accurate Description of Persia*, 2 vol. (London, 1724).

Charles II. *A Proclamation for the Suppression of the Coffee-Houses* (London, 1675).

Charles II. *A Proclamation for the better Discovery of Seditious Libellers* (London, 1676).

Charles II. *An Additional Proclamation Concerning Coffee-Houses* (London, 1676).

Churchill, Charles. *The Poetical Works of Charles Churchill*, edited by Douglas Grant (Oxford: Clarendon Press, 1956).

Clitorides, Philogynes (pseud.). *Natural History of the Frutex Vulvaria, Or Flowering Shrub* (London, 1732).

Cock, Samuel (pseud.). *A Voyage to Lethe* (London, 1741).

Coke, Sir Edward. *Institutes of the Laws of England*, 4 vol. (London, 1628–44).

College, Stephen. 'The Raree Show' (1681). Rpt. *POAS*, vol. 2, pp. 425–31.

Cooke, William. *Memoirs of Samuel Foote, Esq.* (London, 1805).

Cowell, John. *The Interpreter: Or Booke, Containing the Signification of Words* (London, 1637).

Cowper, William. 'Table Talk'. In *Poems by William Cowper*, edited by John D. Baird and Charles Ryskamp, vol. 1: 1748–1782 (Oxford: Clarendon Press, 1980–95), pp. 241–61.

Curll, Edmund. *A Compleat Key to the Dunciad* (London, 1728).

Curll, Edmund. *The Curliad* (London, 1729).

D'Anvers, Knightley. *A General Abridgment of the Common Law*, 2 vol., 2nd ed. (London, 1722–25).

Defoe, Daniel. *A New Test of the Church of England's Loyalty* (London, 1702).

Defoe, Daniel. *A True Collection of the Writings of the Author of The True Born English- man* (London, 1703).

Defoe, Daniel. *An Essay on the Regulation of the Press* (London, 1704).

Defoe, Daniel. *Daniel Defoe: His Life and Recently Discovered Writings*, edited by William Lee, 3 vol. (London, 1869).

Defoe, Daniel. *The Letters of Daniel Defoe*, edited by George Harris Healey (Oxford: Clarendon Press, 1955).

Defoe, Daniel. *The True-Born Englishman* [1700] *and Other Writings*, edited by P. N. Furbank and W. R. Owens (New York: Penguin, 1997).

Defoe, Daniel. *A Brief Explanation of a Late Pamphlet, Entituled, The Shortest Way with the Dissenters* (1703). In *Political and Economic Writings of Daniel Defoe*, vol. 3: Dissent, edited by W. R. Owens (London: Pickering & Chatto, 2000), pp. 111–16.

Defoe, Daniel. *An Enquiry into the Occasional Conformity of Dissenters, in Cases of Preferment* (1697). In *Political and Economic Writings of Daniel Defoe*, vol. 3: Dissent, edited by W. R. Owens (London: Pickering & Chatto, 2000), pp. 37–56.

Defoe, Daniel. *The Shortest Way with the Dissenters: Or Proposals for the Establishment of the Church* (1702). In *Political and Economic Writings of Daniel Defoe*, vol. 3: Dissent, edited by W. R. Owens (London: Pickering & Chatto, 2000), pp. 95–110.

Dennis, John. *An Essay upon Publick Spirit* (London, 1711).

Dennis, John. *The Characters and Conduct of Sir John Edgar* (London, 1720).

Dennis, John. *Remarks Upon Several Passages In The Preliminaries to the Dunciad* (London, 1729).

Dryden, John. Prologue. In *The Tempest* (London, 1667).

Dryden, John. (trans.). *The Works of Virgil containing his Pastorals, Georgics and Aeneis* (London, 1697).

Dryden, John. *Discourse concerning the Original and Progress of Satire*. In *The Works of John Dryden*, vol. 4: Poems 1693–1696, edited by A. B. Chambers and William Frost (Berkeley and Los Angeles: University of California Press, 1974), pp. 3–90.

Dryden, John. *Absalom and Achitophel* (1681). In *The Poems of John Dryden*, vol. 1: 1649–1681, edited by Paul Hammond (New York: Longman, 1995), pp. 444–532.

Dryden, John. *Astraea Redux* (1660). In *The Poems of John Dryden*, vol. 1: 1649–1681, edited by Paul Hammond (New York: Longman, 1995), pp. 36–54.

Dryden, John. *Mac Fleckoe* (1676). In *The Poems of John Dryden*, vol. 1: 1649–1681, edited by Paul Hammond (New York: Longman, 1995), pp. 306–36.

Dryden, John. *To His Sacred Majesty: A Panegyric on his Coronation* (1661). In *The Poems of John Dryden*, vol. 1: 1649–1681, edited by Paul Hammond (New York: Longman, 1995), pp. 55–61.

Dryden, John. *To My Lord Chancellor* (1662). In *The Poems of John Dryden*, vol. 1: 1649–1681, edited by Paul Hammond (New York: Longman, 1995), pp. 62–9.

Dunton, John. *The Shortest Way with Whores and Rogues* (London, 1703).

Dunton, John. *The Hazard of a Death-Bed Repentance* (London, 1708).

Eaton, Daniel Isaac. *The Trial of Daniel Isaac Eaton, for Publishing a Supposed Libel* (London, 1793).

Fielding, Henry. *The Jacobite's Journal and Related Writings*, edited by W. B. Coley (Oxford: Clarendon Press, 1974).

Fielding, Henry. *The Author's Farce* (1734). In *Henry Fielding: Plays*, vol. 1: 1728–1731, edited by Thomas Lockwood (Oxford: Clarendon Press, 2004), pp. 221–358.

Fraunce, Abraham. *The Arcadian Rhetorike* (London, 1588).

Fulbecke, William. *A Direction or Preparatiue to the study of the Lawe* (London, 1600).

Garrick, David. *Private Correspondence of David Garrick*. 2 vol., edited by H. Colburn and R. Bentley (London, 1831).

Gay, John. *The Letters of John Gay*, edited by C. F. Burges (Oxford: Oxford University Press, 1966).

George, Prince of Wales. *The Correspondence of George, Prince of Wales, 1770–1812*. 4 vol, edited by A. Aspinall (London: Cassel, 1963–67).

Gildon, Charles. *A New Rehearsal, or Bays the Younger* (London, 1714).

Goldsmith, Oliver. *An Enquiry into the Present State of Polite Learning in Europe*. In *Collected Works of Oliver Goldsmith*, vol. 1, edited by Arthur Friedman (Oxford: Oxford University Press, 1966).

Gonson, Sir John. *A Charge to the Grand Jury* (London, 1729).

Gordon, Thomas. *The Art of Railing at Great Men* (London, 1723).

Gordon, Thomas. *The Humourist* (London, 1725).

Grose, Francis. *Rules for Drawing Caricaturas: With An Essay on Comic Painting* (London, 1788).

Haines, Henry. *Treachery, Baseness, and Cruelty Display'd to the Full; in the Hardships and Sufferings of Mr. Henry Haines, Late Printer of the Country Journal, or, Craftsman* (London, 1740).

Hale, Sir Matthew. *History of the Pleas of the Crown* (London, 1736).

Hall, Thomas. *Vindiciae literarum; The Schools Guarded* (London, 1655).

Hawkins, William. *A Treatise of the Pleas of the Crown* (1716), 2 vol., 2nd ed. (London, 1724).

Hearne, Thomas. *Remarks and Collections*. 11 vol., edited by C. E. Doble, et al. (Oxford: Clarendon Press, 1885–1921).

Hervey, John. *Memoirs of the Reign of George II from His Accession to the Death of Queen Caroline*. 3 vol. (London, 1855).

Hill, Aaron. *Progress of Wit* (London, 1730).

Historical Manuscripts Commission. *Manuscripts of the Duke of Portland*. 10 vol. (London, 1899).

History and Proceedings of the House of Commons, 3 vol. (London, 1741–42).

Hume, David. *Essays, Moral and Political*, edited by Eugene F. Miller, rev. ed. (Indianapolis: Liberty Fund, 1987).

Jacob, Giles. *A New Law-Dictionary* (London, 1729).

Johnson, Samuel. *Life of John Dryden*. In *The Yale Edition of the Works of Samuel Johnson*, edited by J. A. V. Chapple, vol. 21 (New Haven: Yale University Press, 1958–2019).

Johnson, Samuel. *Samuel Johnson's Dictionary: A Modern Selection*, edited by E. L. McAdam, Jr and George Milne (New York: Dover, 1964).

Johnson, Samuel. 'London' (1738). In *The Yale Edition of the Works of Samuel Johnson*, Vol. 6: Poems, edited by E. L. McAdam, Jr, with G. Milne (New Haven: Yale University Press, 1965).

Johnson, Samuel. 'The Vanity of Human Wishes' (1749). In *The Yale Edition of the Works of Samuel Johnson*, Vol. 6: Poems, edited by E. L. McAdam, Jr, with G. Milne (New Haven: Yale University Press, 1965).

Jones, William. *Treatise on the Law of Bailments* (London, 1781).

Junius (pseud.). *The Letters of Junius*, edited by John Cannon (Oxford: Oxford University Press, 1978).

Kant, Immanuel. 'An answer to the question: What is enlightenment? (1784)'. In *The Cambridge Edition of the Works of Immanuel Kant: Practical Philosophy*, translated and edited by Mary J. Gregor (Cambridge: Cambridge University Press, 1996), pp. 11–22.

Kant, Immanuel. 'On the common saying: That may be correct in theory, but it is of no use in practice (1793)'. In *The Cambridge Edition of the Works of Immanuel Kant: Practical Philosophy*, translated and edited by Mary J. Gregor (Cambridge: Cambridge University Press, 1996), pp. 273–310.

Krusinski, Judas Thaddeus. *The History of the Late Revolutions of Persia*, 2 vol. (London 1728).

L'Estrange, Roger. *A Word Concerning Libels and Libellers* (London, 1681).

Leslie, Charles. *The New Association, Part II* (London, 1703).

Littleton (or de Littleton), Sir Thomas. *Littleton's Tenures in English*, translated by Eugene Wambaugh (Littleton, CO: Rothman, 1985).

[Lyttelton, George]. *Letters from a Persian in England to his Friend at Ispahan* (London, 1735).

[Lyttelton, George]. *A Letter to the Tories* (London, 1747).

Locke, John. *An Essay Concerning Human Understanding*, edited by Peter H. Nidditch (Oxford: Clarendon Press, 1975).

Locke, John. *Two Treatises of Government*, edited by Ian Shapiro (New Haven: Yale University Press, 2004).

Longtool, Thomas (pseud.). *The New Epicurean* (London, 1740).

Lushington, E. H., ed. *An Account of the Persons Held to Bail to Answer in the Court of King's Bench for Libels, From 1 Anne to 57 Geo. 3* (London, 1818). KB 33/24/2, TNA.

Luttrell, Narcissus. *A Brief Historical Relation of State Affairs, from September 1678 to April 1714*. 6 vol. (Oxford: Oxford University Press, 1857).

Macky, John. *Memoirs of the Secret Services of John Macky* (London, 1733).

Manley, Delarivier. *The Adventures of Rivella* (1714). In *The Selected Works of Delarivier Manley*, edited by Rachel Carnell, vol. 4 (London: Pickering & Chatto, 2005).

Manley, Delarivier. *The New Atalantis (1709)*. In *The Selected Works of Delarivier Manley*, edited by Rachel Carnell and Ruth Herman, with W. R. Owens, vol. 3 (London: Routledge, 2005).

Marlborough, Sarah Churchill, duchess of. *An Account of the Conduct of the Dowager Duchess of Marlborough, from Her First Coming to Court to the Year 1710* (London, 1742).

Marlborough, Sarah Churchill, duchess of. *Private Correspondence of Sarah, Duchess of Marlborough* (London, 1838).

March, John. *Actions for Slander*, 2nd ed. (London, 1674).

[Marchmont, Hugh Hume, earl of], *A Serious Exhortation to the Electors of Great Britain* (London, 1740).

Marvell, Andrew. 'The Advice-to-a-Painter and Associated Poems'. In *The Poems of Andrew Marvell*, edited by Nigel Smith (New York: Pearson Longman, 2003), pp. 321–71.

Mason, William. *An Heroic Epistle to Sir William Chambers* (London, 1773).

Mason, William. *Poetical Works* (London, 1805).

Mill, John Stuart. *On Liberty*. In *Essays on Politics and Society*. In *The Collected Works of John Stuart Mill*, edited by J. M. Robson, et al., vol. 18 (Toronto: University of Toronto Press, 1963–91).

Miller, James. *The Coffee-House* (London, 1737).

Milton, John. *Areopagitica*. In *The Complete Prose Works of John Milton*, vol. 2: 1643–1648, edited by Ernest Sirluck (New Haven: Yale University Press, 1959), pp. 480–571.

Milton, John. *Paradise Lost*, edited by John Leonard (New York: Penguin, 2000).

Montesquieu, Charles de Secondat, baron de. *Persian Letters* (1721), 2 vol., trans. John Ozell (London, 1722).

Moxon, Joseph. *Mechanick Exercises on the Whole Art of Printing (1683-4)*, edited by Herbert Davis and Harry Carter, 2nd ed. (Oxford: Oxford University Press, 1962).

Mulgrave, John Sheffield, earl of. 'An Essay upon Satire' (1679). Rpt. *POAS*, vol. 1, pp. 403–13.

Nichols, Donald W. *Literary Anecdotes of the Eighteenth Century* (London, 1812–14).

Noverre, Jean-Georges. *Lettres sur la danse, et sur les ballets* (Lyon, 1760).

Oldham, John. *Satyrs upon the Jesuits* (1679). In *The Poems of John Oldham*, edited by Harold F. Brooks (Oxford: Clarendon Press, 1987), pp. 5–54.

Oldmixon, John. *Memoirs of... William Congreve* (London, 1730).

Peacham, Henry. *The Garden of Eloquence* (London, 1593).

Pheuquewell, Roger (pseud. for Thomas Stretzer). *A New Description of Merryland* (Bath [London], 1741).

Piguenit, C. D. *An Essay on the Art of News-Paper Defamation* (London, 1775).

Pilkington, Laetitia. *Memoirs of Laetitia Pilkington*, 2 vol., edited by A.C. Elias (Athens: University of Georgia Press, 1997).

Pope, Alexander. *A Full and True Account of a Horrid and Barbarous Revenge by Poison, on the Body of Mr. Edmund Curll, Bookseller* (London, 1716[?]).

Pope, Alexander. *The Works of Pope*, edited by Whitwell Elwin and William John Courthope. 10 vol. (London, 1871–86).

Pope, Alexander. *The Dunciad*. 2nd ed., edited by James Sutherland (New Haven: Yale University Press, 1953).

Pope, Alexander. *Epilogue to the Satires* (1738). In *Imitations of Horace: With An Epistle to Dr. Arbuthnot and The Epilogue to the Satires*, 2nd ed., edited by John Butt (New Haven: Yale University Press, 1953).

Pope, Alexander. *The Correspondence of Alexander Pope*. 5 vol., edited by George Sherburn (Oxford: Clarendon Press, 1956).

Pope, Alexander. 'Epilogue to the Satires: Dialogue II' (1738). In *The Poems of Alexander Pope*, edited by John Butt (New Haven: Yale University Press, 1963), pp. 694–703.

Pope, Alexander. 'First Satire of the Second Book of Horace Imitated' (1733). In *The Poems of Alexander Pope*, edited by John Butt (New Haven: Yale University Press, 1963), pp. 613–18.

Pope, Alexander. *Moral Essays: Epistle I. To Sir Richard Temple, Viscount Cobham* (1734). In *The Poems of Alexander Pope*, edited by John Butt (New Haven: Yale University Press, 1963), pp. 549–59.

Pope, Alexander. *Moral Essays: Epistle IV. To Richard Boyle, Earl of Burlington* (1731). In *The Poems of Alexander Pope*, edited by John Butt (New Haven: Yale University Press, 1963), pp. 586–95.

Pope, Alexander. 'Prologue, For the Benefit of Mr. Dennis' (1733). In *The Poems of Alexander Pope*, edited by John Butt (New Haven: Yale University Press, 1963), p. 819.

Pope, Alexander. *The Dunciad in Four Books*, edited by Valerie Rumbold (New York: Longman, 1999).

Pope, Alexander. *The Poems of Alexander Pope*, vol. 3: *The Dunciad (1728) & The Dunciad Variorum (1729)*, edited by Valerie Rumbold (New York: Longman, 2007).

Pope, Alexander, and Jonathan Swift. *The Art of Sinking in Poetry*, edited by Edna Lake Steeves (New York: King's Crown Press, 1952).

Prideaux, John. *Sacred Eloquence, Or the Act of Rhetorick* (London, 1659).

Prynne, William. *Histriomastix: The Player's Scourge or Actor's Tragedy* (London, 1633 [1632]).

Puttenham, George. *Arte of English Poesie* (London, 1589).

Quintilian. *The Orator's Education*, edited and translated by Donald A. Russell (Cambridge: Harvard University Press, 2002).

Ralph, James. *The Case of Authors by Profession or Trade, Stated* (London, 1758).

Ramsay, Allan. *An Essay on Ridicule* (London, 1753).

Rastell, John. *Les Termes de la Ley: Or, Certain Difficult and Obscure Words and Terms of the Common and Statute Laws of this Realm*, rpt. *An Exposition of Certaine Difficult and Obscure Words* (1579; London, 1721).

Rayner, John. *The Life of the Right Honourable Sir John Holt* (London, 1764).

Rayner, John. *A Digest of the Law Concerning Libels* (London, 1765).

Rochester, John Wilmot, earl of. *The Letters of John Wilmot, Earl of Rochester*, edited by Jeremy Treglown (Oxford: Basil Blackwell, 1980).

Rolle, Henry. *Un Abridgment des Plusieurs Cases et Resolutions del Common Ley* (London, 1668).

Romilly, Sir Samuel. *Thoughts on a Late Pamphlet, intituled, Thoughts on Executive Justice* (London, 1786).

Sacheverell, Henry. *The Political Union: A Discourse Shewing the Dependance of Government on Religion in General: And of the English Monarchy on the Church of England in Particular* (Oxford, 1702).

Salmon, Thomas. *Modern History: Or, The Present State of All Nations* (London, 1726).

Savage, Richard. *An Author to be Lett* (*London*, 1729).

Scroope, Sir Carr. 'In Defence of Satyr' (1677). Rpt. *POAS*, vol. 1, pp. 364–70.

Shadwell, Thomas. *The Virtuoso* (London, 1676).

Shaftesbury, Anthony Ashley Cooper, Lord. 'Sensus communis, an essay on the freedom of wit and humour in a letter to a friend'. In *Characteristics of Men, Manners, Opinions, Times*, edited by Lawrence E. Klein (Cambridge: Cambridge University Press, 1999), pp. 29–69.

Shakespeare, William. *Othello*. In *The Arden Edition of the Works of William Shakespeare*, edited by M. R. Ridley (Cambridge: Harvard University Press, 1958).

Sheffield, John, Earl of Mulgrave. *An Essay Upon Poetry* (London, 1682).

Sheppard, William. *Action upon the Case for Slander* (London, 1662).

Sherry, Richard. *A Treatise of the Figures of Grammer and Rhetorike* (London, 1555).

Smith, Adam. *Lectures on Jurisprudence*, edited by R. L. Meek, D. D. Raphael, P. G. Stein (Oxford: Clarendon Press, 1978).

Smith, John. *The Mysterie of Rhetorique Unvail'd* (London, 1657).

Smith, John. *The Printer's Grammar* (London, 1755).

Society for Preserving Liberty and Property against Republicans and Levellers. *Association Papers. Part I. Publications Printed by Special Order of the Society for Preserving Liberty and Property against Republicans and Levellers* (London, 1793).

Southey, Robert. *Essays, Moral and Political.* 2 vol. (London, 1832).

Spence, Joseph. *Observations, Anecdotes, and Characters of Books and Men*, edited by James M. Osborn (Oxford: Clarendon Press, 1966).

Spenser, Edmund. *The Faerie Queene*, edited by Carol V. Kaske (Indianapolis: Hackett, 2006–7).

Squire, Francis. *A Faithful Report of a Genuine Debate Concerning the Liberty of the Press* (London, 1740).

Sterne, Laurence. *The Life and Opinions of Tristram Shandy, Gentleman*, edited by Melvyn New and Joan New (Gainesville: University Press of Florida, 1978).

[Stretzer, Thomas.] *A New Description of Merryland* (Bath [London], 1741).

Suckling, John. *Fragmenta Aurea* (London, 1646).

Suckling, John. '[The Wits] (A Session of the Poets)'. In *The Works of Sir John Suckling: The Non-Dramatic Works*, edited by Thomas Clayton (Oxford: Clarendon Press, 1971), pp. 71–6.

Swift, Jonathan. 'Dean Smedley's Petition to the Duke of Grafton'. In *The Poetical Works of Jonathan Swift*, edited by John Mitford (London, 1833).

Swift, Jonathan. 'On the Irish Bishops' (1731). In *The Poetical Works of Jonathan Swift*, edited by John Mitford (London, 1833), pp. 158–60.

Swift, Jonathan. 'The Duke's Answer'. In *The Poetical Works of Jonathan Swift*, edited by John Mitford (London, 1833).

Swift, Jonathan. *Some Thoughts on Free-Thinking*. In *The Prose Writings of Jonathan Swift*, edited by Herbert Davis, et al., vol. 4 (Oxford: Basil Blackwell, 1939–74).

Swift, Jonathan. *Short character of his Ex. T.E. of W., LL of I__* (1710). In *The Prose Works of Jonathan Swift*, vol. 3: *The Examiner* and Other Pieces Written in 1710–11, edited by Herbert Davis (Oxford: Basil Blackwell, 1940), pp. 175–84.

Swift, Jonathan. *Journal to Stella*. 2 vol., edited by Harold Williams (Oxford: Clarendon Press, 1948).

Swift, Jonathan. *Proposal for the Universal Use of Irish Manufacture* (1720). In *The Prose Works of Jonathan Swift*, vol. 9: Irish Tracts, 1720–1723, and Sermons, edited by Louis Landa (Oxford: Basil Blackwell, 1948), pp. 13–22.

Swift, Jonathan. *Queries Wrote by Dr. J. Swift* (1732). In *The Prose Works of Jonathan Swift*, vol. 12: Irish Tracts, 1728–1733, edited by Herbert Davis (Oxford: Basil Blackwell, 1955), pp. 253–60.

Swift, Jonathan. *The Advantages Propos'd by Repealing the Sacramental Test, Impartially Considered* (1732). In *The Prose Works of Jonathan Swift*, vol. 12: Irish Tracts, 1728–1733, edited by Herbert Davis (Oxford: Basil Blackwell, 1955), pp. 239–52.

Swift, Jonathan. *The Presbyterians Plea of Merit* (1733). In *The Prose Works of Jonathan Swift*, vol. 12: Irish Tracts, 1728–1733, edited by Herbert Davis (Oxford: Basil Blackwell, 1955), pp. 261–80.

Swift, Jonathan. *An Epistle to a Lady* (1733). In *The Poems of Jonathan Swift*. 3 vol., 2nd ed, edited by Harold Williams (Oxford: Clarendon Press, 1958), pp. 628–38.

Swift, Jonathan. *On Poetry: A Rapsody* (1733). In *The Poems of Jonathan Swift*. 3 vol., 2nd ed, edited by Harold Williams (Oxford: Clarendon Press, 1958), pp. 639–59.

Swift, Jonathan. 'On the Words "Brother Protestants and Fellow Christians"' (1733). In *The Poems of Jonathan Swift*. 3 vol., 2nd ed, edited by Harold Williams (Oxford: Clarendon Press, 1958), pp. 809–13.

Swift, Jonathan. 'The Storm; or Minerva's Petition' (1722–23). In *The Poems of Jonathan Swift*. 3 vol., 2nd ed, edited by Harold Williams (Oxford: Clarendon Press, 1958), pp. 301–6.

Swift, Jonathan. *The Correspondence of Jonathan Swift*. 5 vol., edited by Harold Williams (Oxford: Clarendon Press, 1963–65).

Swift, Jonathan. *A Friend of Mr. St—le. The Importance of the Guardian Considered, in a Second Letter to the Bailiff of Stockbridge* (1713). In *English Political Writings, 1711–1714: The Conduct of the Allies and Other Works*, edited by Bertrand A. Goldgar and Ian Gadd (Cambridge: Cambridge University Press, 2008), pp. 217–40.

Swift, Jonathan. *The Conduct of the Allies* (1711). In *English Political Writings, 1711–1714: The Conduct of the Allies and Other Works*, edited by Bertrand A. Goldgar and Ian Gadd (Cambridge: Cambridge University Press, 2008), pp. 45–106.

Swift, Jonathan. *The Publick Spirit of the Whigs* (1713/4). In *English Political Writings, 1711–1714: The Conduct of the Allies and Other Works*, edited by Bertrand A. Goldgar and Ian Gadd (Cambridge: Cambridge University Press, 2008), pp. 241–84.

Swift, Jonathan. *A Tale of a Tub and Other Works*, edited by Marcus Walsh (Cambridge: Cambridge University Press, 2010).

Swift, Jonathan. *Journal to Stella: Letters to Esther Johnson and Rebecca Dingley, 1710–1713*, edited by Abigail Williams (Cambridge: Cambridge University Press, 2013).

Swift, Jonathan. *A Modest Proposal for Preventing the Children of Poor People from Being a Burthen to their Parents, or Country; and for Making Them Beneficial to the Publick*. In *Irish Political Writings after 1725: A Modest Proposal and Other Works*, edited by D. W. Hayton and Adam Rounce (Cambridge: Cambridge University Press, 2018), pp. 143–59.

Tindal, Matthew. *A Letter to a Member of Parliament, shewing, that a Restraint on the Press is inconsistent with the Protestant Religion, and dangerous to the Liberties of the Nation* (London, 1698).

Tindal, Matthew. *Reasons Against Restraining the Press* (London, 1704).

Touchit, Timothy (pseud.). *La Sourciè, Or The Mouse-trap* (London, 1794).

Trapp, Joseph. *Prælectiones Poeticæ* (1711–19), translated by William Bowyer and William Clarke as *Lectures on Poetry* (London, 1742).

Trenchard, John, and Thomas Gordon. *Cato's Letters: Or, Essays on Liberty, Civil and Religious, and Other Important Subjects*, edited by Ronald Hamowy (Indianapolis: Liberty Fund, 1995).

von la Roche, Roche. *Sophie in London, 1786: Being the Diary of Sophie v. la Roche*, translated by Clare Williams (London: J. Cape, 1933).

Walker, Obadiah. *Art of Oratory* (London, 1659).

Walpole, Horace. *Yale Edition of Horace Walpole's Correspondence*. 37 vol., edited by W. S. Lewis, et al. (New Haven: Yale University Press, 1937–83).

Walpole, Horace. *Memoirs of the Reign of King George III*, 4 vol., edited by Derek Jarrett (New Haven: Yale University Press, 2000).

Ward, Edward. *Apollo's Maggot in his Cups* (London, 1729).

Weaver, John. *An Essay Towards an History of Dancing* (London, 1712).

Welsted, Leonard, and James Moore Smythe. *One Epistle to Mr. A. Pope*, 2nd ed. (London, 1729).

Wilkes, John. *The Infamous Essay on Woman: Or John Wilkes Seated Between Vice and Virtue*, edited by Adrian Hamilton (London: Andre Deutsch, 1972).

Wood, Anthony. *The Life and Times of Anthony Wood, Antiquary, of Oxford, 1632–1695, described by Himself*. 5 vol., edited by Andrew Clark (Oxford: Clarendon Press, 1894).

Criticism and Scholarship

Alkon, Paul K. 'Defoe's Argument in *The Shortest Way with the Dissenters*'. *Modern Philology* 73, no. 4.2 (May 1976): pp. S12–23.

Amussen, Susan D., and Mark A. Kishlansky (eds.). *Political Culture and Cultural Politics in Early Modern England: Essays Presented to David Underdown* (Manchester: Manchester University Press, 1995).

Anderson, Misty G. *Imagining Methodism in Eighteenth-Century Britain: Enthusiasm, Belief, and the Borders of the Self* (Baltimore: Johns Hopkins University Press, 2012).

Anderson, Misty G. 'Genealogies of Comedy'. In *The Oxford Handbook of the Georgian Theatre, 1737–1832*, edited by Julia Swindells and David Francis Taylor (Oxford: Oxford University Press, 2014), pp. 347–67.

Astbury, Raymond. 'The Renewal of the Licensing Act in 1693 and its Lapse in 1695'. *The Library*, 5th series 33, no. 4 (1978): pp. 296–322.

Atherton, Herbert. *Political Prints in the Age of Hogarth: A Study of the Ideographic Representation of Politics* (Oxford: Clarendon Press, 1974).

Augustine, Matthew C. 'The Invention of Dryden as Satirist'. In *The Oxford Handbook of Eighteenth-Century Satire*, edited by Paddy Bullard (Oxford: Oxford University Press, 2019), pp. 161–76.

Backscheider, Paula R. 'No Defense: Defoe in 1703'. *PMLA* 103, no. 3 (May 1988): pp. 274–84.

Backscheider, Paula R. *Daniel Defoe: His Life* (Baltimore: Johns Hopkins University Press, 1989).

Backscheider, Paula R. 'Retrieving Elizabeth Inchbald'. In *The Oxford Handbook of the Georgian Theatre, 1737–1832*, edited by Julia Swindells and David Francis Taylor (Oxford: Oxford University Press, 2014), pp. 601–18.

Bailyn, Bernard. *The Ideological Origins of the American Revolution* (1967), enlarged edition (Cambridge: Belknap Press, 1992).

Baines, Paul. 'Crime and Punishment'. In *The Cambridge Companion to Alexander Pope*, edited by Pat Rogers (Cambridge: Cambridge University Press, 2007), pp. 150–60.

Baines, Paul, and Pat Rogers. *Edmund Curll, Bookseller* (Oxford: Oxford University Press, 2007).

Baker, John H. *An Introduction to English Legal History*, 4th ed. (Oxford: Oxford University Press, 1995).

Baker, J. H., and S. F. C. Milsom (eds.). *Sources of English Legal History: Private Law to 1750* (London: Butterworths, 1986).

Ballaster, Ros. *Seductive Forms: Women's Amatory Fiction from 1684 to 1740* (Oxford: Oxford University Press, 1992).

Ballaster, Ros. 'A Gender of Opposition: Eliza Haywood's Scandal Fiction'. In *The Passionate Fictions of Eliza Haywood: Essays on Her Life and Work*, edited by Kirsten T. Saxton and Rebecca P. Bocchicchio (Lexington: University Press of Kentucky, 2000), pp. 143–67.

Ballaster, Ros. *Fabulous Orients: Fictions of the East in England, 1662–1785* (Oxford: Oxford University Press, 2005).

Ballaster, Ros. 'Dramatic Satire'. In *The Oxford Handbook of Eighteenth-Century Satire*, edited by Paddy Bullard (Oxford: Oxford University Press, 2019), pp. 336–52.

Baltes, Sabine. '"The Grandson of that Ass Quin": Swift and Chief Justice Whitshed'. *Swift Studies* 23 (2008): pp. 126–46.

Bannet, Eve Tavor. '"Secret History": Or, Talebearing Inside and Outside the Secretoire'. *Huntington Library Quarterly* 68, no. 1-2 (March 2005): pp. 375-96.

Bannet, Eve Tavor. *Eighteenth-Century Manners of Reading: Print and Popular Instruction in the Anglophone Atlantic World* (Cambridge: Cambridge University Press, 2017).

Bannet, Eve Tavor. 'Secret History and Censorship'. In *The Secret History in Literature, 1660–1820*, edited by Rebecca Bullard and Rachel Carnell (Cambridge: Cambridge University Press, 2017), pp. 160-73.

Bardle, Stephen. *The Literary Underground in the 1660s: Andrew Marvell, George Wither, Ralph Wallis, and the World of Restoration Satire and Pamphleteering* (Oxford: Oxford University Press, 2013).

Barker, Hannah. *Newspapers and English Society, 1695–1855* (2000; London: Routledge, 2014).

Barker, Nicolas. 'Typography and the Meaning of Words: The Revolution in the Layout of Books in the Eighteenth Century'. In *Buch und Buchhandel in Europa im achtzehnten Jahrhundert*, edited by Giles Barber and Bernhard Fabian (Hamburg: Hauswedell, 1981), pp. 127-65.

Barnard, John, and D. F. McKenzie (eds.). *The Cambridge History of the Book in Britain*, vol. 4: 1557–1695 (Cambridge: Cambridge University Press, 2002).

Baron, Sabrina Alcorn, Eric N. Lindquist, and Eleanor F. Shevlin (eds.). *Agent of Change: Print Culture Studies after Elizabeth L. Eisenstein* (Amherst: University of Massachusetts Press, 2007).

Barrell, John. *Imagining the King's Death: Figurative Treason, Fantasies of Regicide* (Oxford: Oxford University Press, 2000).

Barrell, John. *The Spirit of Despotism: Invasions of Privacy in the 1790s* (Oxford: Oxford University Press, 2006).

Bartolomeo, Joseph F. 'Restoration and Eighteenth-century Satiric Fiction'. In *A Companion to Satire: Ancient and Modern*, edited by Ruben Quintero (Malden: Blackwell, 2007), pp. 257-75.

Basker, James G. *Tobias Smollett, Critic and Journalist* (Newark: University of Delaware Press, 1988).

Battestin, Martin C., with Ruthe R. Battestin. *Henry Fielding: A Life* (London: Routledge, 1989).

Beattie, J. M. *Crime and the Courts, 1660–1800* (Princeton: Princeton University Press, 1986).

Beattie, J. M. *Policing and Punishment in London, 1660–1750* (Oxford: Oxford University Press, 2001).

Belanger, Terry. 'Booksellers' Sale of Copyright: Aspects of the London Book Trade, 1718–1768' (PhD diss., Columbia University, 1970).

Belanger, Terry. 'Publishers and Writers in Eighteenth-Century England'. In *Books and their Readers in Eighteenth-Century England*, edited by Isabel Rivers (Leicester: Leicester University Press, 1982), pp. 5-25.

Belavusau, Uladzislau. 'Fighting Hate Speech through EU Law'. *Amsterdam Legal Forum* 4, no. 1 (2012): pp. 20-34.

Bellah, Robert N. *The Broken Covenant: American Civil Religion in Time of Trial*, 2nd ed. (Chicago: University of Chicago Press, 1992).

Bellany, Alastair, and Thomas Cogswell, *The Murder of King James I* (New Haven: Yale University Press, 2015).

Bender, John. *Imagining the Penitentiary: Fiction and the Architecture of Mind in Eighteenth-Century England* (Chicago: University of Chicago Press, 1987).

Bender, John. *The Ends of Enlightenment* (Stanford: Stanford University Press, 2012).

Bengert, C. D. (ed.). *Arse Musica; Or, The Lady's Back Report* (1722): *A Critical Edition with Apparatus* (Cold Lake: Haligonian Press, 1981).

Berman, Harold J. 'The Origins of Historical Jurisprudence: Coke, Selden, Hale'. *Yale Law Journal* 103, no. 7 (May 1993): pp. 1651–738.

Berman, Harold J., and Charles J. Reid, Jr. 'The Transformation of English Legal Science: From Hale to Blackstone'. *Emory Law Journal* 45, no. 2 (Spring 1996): pp. 444–67.

Bertelsen, Lance. *The Nonsense Club: Literature and Popular Culture, 1749–1764* (Oxford: Oxford University Press, 1986).

Bills, Mark. *The Art of Satire: London in Caricature* (London: Philip Wilson Publishers, 2006).

Beier, A. L., David Cannadine, and James M. Rosenheim (eds.). *The First Modern Society: Essays in English History in Honour of Lawrence Stone* (Cambridge: Cambridge University Press, 1989).

Birks, Peter (ed.). *The Life of the Law* (London: Hambledon Press, 1993).

Bird, Wendell. *Press and Speech Under Assault: The Early Supreme Court Justices, the Sedition Act of 1798, and the Campaign against Dissent* (Oxford: Oxford University Press, 2016).

Black, Jeremy. *The English Press in the Eighteenth Century* (London: Taylor & Francis, 1987).

Bloomfield, Anne, and Ruth Watts. 'Pedagogue of the Dance: The Dancing Master as Educator in the Long Eighteenth Century'. *History of Education* 37, no. 4 (2008): pp. 605–18.

Bodansky, Joel N. 'The Abolition of the Party-Witness Disqualification: An Historical Survey'. *Kentucky Law Journal* 70 (1981–82): pp. 91–130.

Bogel, Fredric V. *The Difference Satire Makes: Rhetoric and Reading from Jonson to Byron* (Ithaca: Cornell University Press, 2001).

Bollinger, Lee C., and Geoffrey R. Stone. 'Dialogue'. In *The Free Speech Century*, edited by Lee C. Bollinger and Geoffrey R. Stone (Oxford: Oxford University Press, 2019), pp. 1–10.

Bond, Richmond P., ed. *English Burlesque Poetry, 1700–1750* (Cambridge: Harvard University Press, 1932).

Booth, Wayne G. *A Rhetoric of Irony* (Chicago: University of Chicago Press, 1975).

Booth, Wayne G. 'A New Strategy for Establishing a Truly Democratic Criticism'. *Daedalus* 112, no. 1 (Winter 1983): pp. 193–214.

Botein, Stephen, Jack Censer, and Harriet Ritvo. 'The Periodical Press in Eighteenth-Century English and French Society: A Cross-Cultural Approach'. *Comparative Studies in Society and History* 23, no. 3 (July 1981): pp. 464–90.

Bourdieu, Pierre. *Language and Symbolic Power* (1982), edited by John B. Thompson, translated by Gino Raymond and Matthew Adamson (Cambridge: Harvard University Press, 1991).

Bowen, H. V. 'India: The Metropolitan Context'. In *The Oxford History of the British Empire: The Eighteenth Century*, edited by P. J. Marshall (Oxford: Oxford University Press, 1998), pp. 530–51.

Bowyer, John Wilson. *The Celebrated Mrs. Centlivre* (Durham: Duke University Press, 1952).

Boyle, Kevin. 'Hate Speech—The United States Versus the Rest of the World?' *Maine Law Review* 53, no. 2 (2001): pp. 487–502.

Brant, Irving. 'Seditious Libel: Myth and Reality'. *New York University Law Review* 39, no. 1 (January 1964): pp. 1–19.

Brewer, David A. 'Secret History and Allegory'. In *The Secret History in Literature, 1660–1820*, edited by Rebecca Bullard and Rachel Carnell (Cambridge: Cambridge University Press, 2017), pp. 60–73.

Brewer, John. *Party Ideology and Popular Politics at the Accession of George III* (Cambridge: Cambridge University Press, 1976).

Brewer, John. 'The Wilkites and the Law, 1763–74'. In *An Ungovernable People: The English and their Law in the Seventeenth and Eighteenth Centuries*, edited by John Brewer and John Styles (London: Hutchinson, 1980), pp. 128–71.

Bricker, Andrew Benjamin. 'Libel and Satire: The Problem with Naming'. *English Literary History* 81, no. 3 (Fall 2014): pp. 889–921.

Bricker, Andrew Benjamin. 'Who was "A. Moore"?: The Attribution of Eighteenth-Century Publications with False and Misleading Imprints'. *Papers of the Bibliographical Society of America* 110, no. 2 (June 2016): pp. 1–34.

Bricker, Andrew Benjamin. 'Fielding after Mandeville: Virtue, Self-Interest, and the Foundation of "Good Nature"'. *Eighteenth-Century Fiction* 30, no. 1 (Fall 2017): pp. 65–87.

Bricker, Andrew Benjamin. '"Laughing a Folly out of Countenance": Laughter and the Limits of Reform in Eighteenth-Century Satire'. In *The Power of Laughter and Satire in Early Modern Britain: Political and Religious Culture, 1500–1820*, edited by Mark Knights and Adam Morton (Woodbridge: Boydell Press, 2017), pp. 152–71.

Bricker, Andrew Benjamin. 'After the Golden Age: Caricature, Libel, and the Deverbalization of Satire'. *Eighteenth-Century Studies* 51, no. 3 (Spring 2018): pp. 305–36.

Bricker, Andrew Benjamin. 'Is Narrative Essential to the Law?: Precedent, Case Law and Judicial Emplotment', *Law, Culture and the Humanities* 15, no. 2 (June 2019): pp. 319–31.

Bricker, Andrew Benjamin. 'The Functions of Legal Literature and Case Reporting before and after *Stare Decisis*'. In *The Oxford Handbook of Law and Humanities*, edited by Simon Stern, Bernadette Meyler, and Maksymilian Del Mar (Oxford: Oxford University Press, 2020), pp. 617–36.

Bricker, Andrew Benjamin. 'The Visual and the Verbal: The Intermediality of English Satire, *c.* 1695–1750'. In *Changing Satire: Transformations and Continuities in Europe, 1600 – 1830*, edited by Cecilia Rosengren, Per Sivefors, and Rikard Wingård (Manchester: Manchester University Press, 2022), ch. 9.

Broich, Ulrich. *The Eighteenth-Century Mock-Heroic Poem* (1968). Trans. David Henry Wilson (Cambridge: Cambridge University Press, 1990).

Bronson, Bertrand H. *Printing as an Index of Taste in Eighteenth-Century England* (New York: New York Public Library, 1963).

Brooks, Cleanth. *The Well Wrought Urn: Studies in the Structure of Poetry* (New York: Harcourt Brace, 1947).

Brooks, Christopher, and Michael Lobban (eds.). *Communities and Courts in Britain, 1150–1900* (London: Hambledon Press, 1997).

Brooks, Christopher. 'Interpersonal Conflict and Social Tension: Civil Litigation in England, 1640–1830'. In *The First Modern Society: Essays in English History in Honour of Lawrence Stone*, edited by A. L. Beier, David Cannadine, and James M. Rosenheim (Cambridge: Cambridge University Press, 1989), pp. 357–400.

Brooks, Christopher. *Lawyers, Litigation, and English Society since 1450* (London: Hambledon Press, 1998).

Brooks, Harold F. 'English Verse Satire, 1640–1660: Prolegomena'. *The Seventeenth Century* 3, no. 1 (Spring 1988): pp. 17–46.

Bullard, Paddy (ed.). *The Oxford Handbook of Eighteenth-Century Satire* (Oxford: Oxford University Press, 2019).

Bullard, Paddy, and James McLaverty (eds.). *Jonathan Swift and the Eighteenth-Century Book* (Cambridge: Cambridge University Press, 2013).

Bullard, Rebecca. *The Politics of Disclosure, 1674–1725: Secret History Narratives* (London: Pickering & Chatto, 2009).

Bullard, Rebecca. 'Secret History, Politics, and the Early Novel'. In *The Oxford Handbook of the Eighteenth-Century Novel*, edited by J. A. Downie (Oxford: Oxford University Press, 2016), pp. 137–52.

Bullard, Rebecca. 'Introduction: Reconsidering Secret History'. In *The Secret History in Literature, 1660–1820*, edited by Rebecca Bullard and Rachel Carnell (Cambridge: Cambridge University Press, 2017), pp. 1–14.

Bülbring, Karl D. (ed.). *The Compleat English Gentleman by Daniel Defoe* (London: D. Nutt, 1890).

Burke, Peter. 'Publicizing the Private: The Rise of "Secret History"'. In *Changing Perceptions of the Public Sphere*, edited by Christian J. Emden and David Midgley (Oxford: Berghahn Books, 2012), ch. 3.

Burwick, Frederick. 'Georgian Theories of the Actor'. In *The Oxford Handbook of the Georgian Theatre, 1737–1832*, edited by Julia Swindells and David Francis Taylor (Oxford: Oxford University Press, 2014), pp. 177–91.

Butterfield, Herbert. *The Whig Interpretation of History* (1932; New York: Norton, 1965).

Butler, Judith. *Excitable Speech: A Politics of the Performative* (New York: Routledge, 1997).

Butler, Marilyn. *Romantics, Rebels, and Reactionaries: English Literature and its Background, 1760–1830* (Oxford: Oxford University Press, 1982).

Cannon, John (ed.). *The Letters of Junius* (Oxford: Oxford University Press, 1978).

Carnell, Rachel. *A Political Biography of Delarivier Manley* (London: Pickering & Chatto, 2008).

Carnell, Rachel. 'Slipping from Secret History to Novel'. *Eighteenth–Century Fiction* 28, no. 1 (Fall 2015): pp. 1–24.

Carretta, Vincent. *The Snarling Muse: Verbal and Visual Political Satire from Pope to Churchill* (Philadelphia: University of Pennsylvania Press, 1983).

Carter-Ruck, Peter F. *Libel and Slander* (Hamden: Archon, 1973).

Cash, Arthur. *John Wilkes: The Scandalous Father of Civil Liberty* (New Haven: Yale University Press, 2006).

Caudle, James J. 'Richard Francklin: A Controversial Publisher, Bookseller and Printer, 1718–1765'. In *The Cambridge History of the Book in Britain*, vol. 5: 1695–1830, edited by Michael F. Suarez, S. J., and Michael L. Turner (Cambridge: Cambridge University Press, 2009), pp. 383–96.

Champion, W. A. 'Recourse to Law and the Meaning of the Great Litigation Decline'. In *Communities and Courts in Britain, 1150–1900*, edited by Christopher Brooks and Michael Lobban (London: Hambledon Press, 1997), pp. 179–98.

Clayton, Tim. *The English Print, 1688–1802* (New Haven: Yale University Press, 1997).

Clegg, Cyndia Susan. *Press Censorship in Jacobean England* (Cambridge: Cambridge University Press, 1991).

Clegg, Cyndia Susan. *Press Censorship in Elizabethan England* (Cambridge: Cambridge University Press, 1997).

Clegg, Cyndia Susan. *Press Censorship in Caroline England* (Cambridge: Cambridge University Press, 2008).

Cleveland, Sarah H. 'Hate Speech at Home and Abroad'. In *The Free Speech Century*, edited by Lee C. Bollinger and Geoffrey R. Stone (Oxford: Oxford University Press, 2019), pp. 210–31.

Cobbett, William, and J. Wrights (eds.). *The Parliamentary History of England from the Earliest Times to the Year 1803*. 36 vol. (London, 1806–20).

Cobbett, William, et al. *Complete Collection of State Trials*. 21 vol. (London, 1809–26).

Cogswell, Thomas. 'Underground Verse and the Transformation of Early Stuart Political Culture'. In *Political Culture and Cultural Politics in Early Modern England: Essays Presented to David Underdown*, edited by Susan D Amussen and Mark A. Kishlansky (Manchester: Manchester University Press, 1995), pp. 277–300.

Cohen, Ralph. 'History and Genre'. *New Literary History* 17, no. 2 (Winter 1986): pp. 203–18.

Colley, Linda. *In Defiance of Oligarchy: The Tory Party 1714–60* (Cambridge: Cambridge University Press, 1982).

Colley, Linda. *Britons: Forging the Nation, 1707–1837*, rev. ed. (New Haven: Yale University Press, 2009).

Colomb, Gregory G. *Designs on Truth: The Poetics of the Augustan Mock-Epic* (University Park: Pennsylvania State University Press, 1992).

Conolly, L. W. *The Censorship of English Drama, 1737–1824* (San Marino: The Huntington Library, 1974).

Conolly, L. W. '*The Merchant of Venice* and the Jew Bill of 1753'. *Shakespeare Quarterly* 25, no. 1 (Winter 1974): pp. 125–7.

Conolly, L. W. 'Personal Satire on the English Eighteenth-Century Stage'. *Eighteenth-Century Studies* 9, no. 4 (Summer 1976): pp. 599–607.

Copeland, David A. *The Idea of a Free Press: The Enlightenment and its Unruly Legacy* (Evanston: Northwestern University Press, 2006).

Copeland, Rita, and Peter T. Struck, (eds.). *The Cambridge Companion to Allegory* (Cambridge: Cambridge University Press, 2010).

Cordasco, Francesco. 'John Miller—Associate with Woodfall in the Printing of the Junius Letters'. *N&Q* cxcv (July 1950): pp. 319–20.

Corman, Brian. *Genre and Generic Change in English Comedy, 1660–1710* (Toronto: University of Toronto Press, 1993).

Courtney, J. C. 'Absurdities of the Law of Slander and Libel'. *American Law Review* 36 (January–February 1902): pp. 552–64.

Cowan, Brian. *The State Trial of Doctor Henry Sacheverell* (Malden: Wiley-Blackwell, 2012).

Cowan, Brian. 'The History of Secret Histories'. *Huntington Library Quarterly* 81, no. 1 (Spring 2018): pp. 121–51.

Crist, Timothy. 'Government Control of the Press After the Expiration of the Printing Act in 1679'. *Publishing History* 5 (1979): pp. 49–77.

Cronon, William. 'Two Cheers for the Whig Interpretation of History'. *Perspectives on History* 50, no. 6 (September 2012): pp. 5–6.

Cross, Peter, ed. *The Moral World of the Law* (Cambridge: Cambridge University Press, 2000).

Cruickshanks, Eveline. 'Lord Cowper, Lord Orrery, the Duke of Wharton, and Jacobitism'. *Albion* 26, no. 1 (Spring 1994): pp. 27–40.

Crystal, David. *Making a Point: The Pernickety Story of English Punctuation* (London: Profile Books, 2015).

Culler, Jonathan. 'Lyric, History, and Genre'. *New Literary History* 40, no. 4 (Autumn 2009): pp. 879–99.

Damrosch, Leo. *Jonathan Swift: His Life and His World* (New Haven: Yale University Press, 2013).

'The dark side of *Guardian* comments'. *The Guardian* (12 April 2016): https://www. theguardian.com/technology/2016/apr/12/the-dark-side-of-guardian-comments.

Darnton, Robert. *The Literary Underground of the Old Regime* (Cambridge: Harvard University Press, 1982).

Darnton, Robert. *Censors at Work: How States Shaped Literature* (New York: W. W. Norton & Co., 2014).

Davis, Evan R. 'Pope's phantom Moore: Plagiarism and the Pseudonymous Imprint'. In *Producing the Eighteenth-Century Book: Writers and Publishers in England, 1650–1800*, edited by Laura Runge and Pat Rogers (Newark: University of Delaware Press, 2009), pp. 193–214.

Davis, Jim. *Comic Acting and Portraiture in Late-Georgian and Regency England* (Cambridge: Cambridge University Press, 2015).

Davis, Lennard. *Factual Fictions: The Origins of the English Novel* (Philadelphia: University of Pennsylvania Press, 1996).

Davis, Michael T., Emma Macleod, and Gordon Pentland (eds.). *Political Trials in an Age of Revolutions: Britain and the North Atlantic, 1793–1848* (London: Palgrave Macmillan, 2018).

Dawson, P. M. S. 'Poetry in an Age of Revolution'. In *The Cambridge Companion to British Romanticism*, edited by Stuart Curran (Cambridge: Cambridge University Press, 1993), ch. 3.

de Bolla, Peter. *Education of the Eye: Painting, Landscape, and Architecture in Eighteenth-Century Britain* (Stanford: Stanford University Press, 2003).

Dean, Joseph. *Ridicule, Hatred, or Contempt: A Book of Libel Cases* (New York: McMillan Co., 1954).

Deazley, Ronan. *On the Origin of the Right to Copy: Charting to the Movement of Copyright Law in Eighteenth-Century Britain (1695–1775)* (Portland: Hart, 2004).

Deazley, Ronan. *Rethinking Copyright: History, Theory, Language* (Northampton, MA: Edward Elgar, 2006).

Deazley, Ronan. 'Commentary on: *Pope v. Curl*, United Kingdom (1741)'. In *Primary Sources on Copyright (1450–1900)*, edited by Lionel Bently and Martin Kretschmer (2008). www.copyrighthistory.org.

Deutsch, Helen. *Resemblance & Disgrace: Alexander Pope and the Deformation of Culture* (Cambridge: Harvard University Press, 1996).

Devereaux, Simon. 'In Place of Death: Transportation, Penal Practices, and the English State, 1770–1830'. In *Qualities of Mercy: Justice, Punishment, and Discretion*, edited by Carolyn Strange (Vancouver: University of British Columbia Press, 1996), pp. 52–76.

De Man, Paul. *Allegories of Reading: Figural Language in Rousseau, Nietzsche, Rilke, and Proust* (New Haven: Yale University Press, 1979).

Dickie, Simon. *Cruelty and Laughter: Forgotten Comic Literature and the Unsentimental Eighteenth Century* (Chicago: University of Chicago Press, 2011).

Dickie, Simon. 'Deformity Poems and Other Nasties'. *Eighteenth-Century Life* 41, no. 1 (2017): pp. 197–230.

Donald, Diana. '"Calumny and Caricatura": Eighteenth-Century Political Prints and the Case of George Townshend'. *Art History* 6, no. 1 (March 1983): pp. 44–66.

Donald, Diana. *Age of Caricature: Satirical Prints in the Reign of George III* (New Haven: Yale University Press, 1996).

Doody, Margaret Anne. *The Daring Muse: Augustan Poetry Reconsidered* (Cambridge: Cambridge University Press, 1985).

Dowling, William. *The Epistolary Moment: The Poetics of the Eighteenth-Century Verse Epistle* (Princeton: Princeton University Press, 1991).

Downie, J. A. *Robert Harley and the Press: Propaganda and Public Opinion in the Age of Swift and Defoe* (Cambridge: Cambridge University Press, 1979).

Downie, J. A. 'Defoe's *Shortest Way with the Dissenters*: Irony, Intention and Reader-Response'. *Prose Studies* 9, no. 2 (September 1986): pp. 120–39.

Downie, J. A. 'Swift and the Oxford Ministry: New Evidence'. *Swift Studies* 1 (1986): pp. 2–8.

Downie, J. A. 'The Political Significance of *Gulliver's Travels*'. In *Swift and His Contexts*, edited by John Irwin Fischer, Hermann J. Real, and James Woolley (New York: AMS Press, 1989), ch. 1.

Duke, A. C., and C. A. Tamse (eds.). *Too Mighty to be Free: Censorship and the Press in Britain and the Netherlands* (Zutphen: De Walburg Press, 1987).

Dupré, Louis. *The Enlightenment and the Intellectual Foundations of Modern Culture* (New Haven: Yale University Press, 2004).

Dunan-Page, Anne, and Beth Lynch. *Roger L'Estrange and the Making of Restoration Culture* (Aldershot: Ashgate, 2008).

Dyer, Gary. *British Satire and the Politics of Style, 1789–1832* (Cambridge: Cambridge University Press, 1997).

Dyer, Gary. 'The Circulation of Satirical Poetry in the Regency'. *Keats-Shelley Journal* 61 (2012): pp. 66–74.

Dyer, Gary. 'Publishers and Lawyers'. *The Wordsworth Circle* 44, no. 2–3 (Spring–Summer 2013): pp. 121–6.

Dzelzainis, Martin. 'L'Estrange, Marvell and the *Directions to a Painter*: The Evidence of Bodleian Library, MS Gough London 14'. In *Roger L'Estrange and the Making of Restoration Culture*, edited by Anne Dunan-Page and Beth Lynch (Aldershot: Ashgate, 2008), pp. 53–66.

Dzelzainis, Martin. 'Managing the Later Stuart Press, 1662–1696'. In *The Oxford Handbook of English Law and Literature, 1500–1700*, edited by Lorna Hutson (Oxford: Oxford University Press, 2017), ch. 27.

Eisenstein, Elizabeth L. *The Printing Press as an Agent of Change: Communications and Cultural Transformations in Early-Modern Europe*, vol. 1 (Cambridge: Cambridge University Press, 1979).

Elias, A. C., et al. 'The Full Text of Swift's *On Poetry: A Rapsody* (1733)'. *Swift Studies* 9 (1994): pp. 17–32.

Elkin, P. K. *The Augustan Defense of Satire* (Oxford: Clarendon Press, 1973).

Elliott, Robert C. *The Power of Satire: Magic, Ritual, Art* (Princeton: Princeton University Press, 1960).

Emsley, Clive. 'An Aspect of Pitt's 'Terror': Prosecutions for Sedition during the 1790s'. *Social History* 6, no. 2 (May 1981): pp. 155–84.

Engell, James. 'Satiric Spirits of the Later Eighteenth Century: Johnson to Crabbe'. In *A Companion to Satire: Ancient and Modern*, edited by Ruben Quintero (Malden: Blackwell, 2007), pp. 233–56.

Fairer, David. *English Poetry of the Eighteenth Century* (London: Longman, 2003).

Feather, John. 'The Book Trade in Politics: The Making of the Copyright Act of 1710'. *Publishing History* 8 (1980): pp. 19–44.

Feather, John. 'The English Book Trade and the Law, 1695–1799', *Publishing History* 12 (1982): pp. 51–75.

Feather, John. *The Provincial Book Trade in Eighteenth-Century England* (Cambridge: Cambridge University Press, 1985).

Feather, John. *A History of British Publishing* (London: Croom Helm, 1988).

Feather, John. *Publishing, Piracy, and Politics: An Historical Study of Copyright in Britain* (London: Mansell, 1994).

Fischer, John Irwin. 'The Government's Response to Swift's "An Epistle to a Lady"'. *Philological Quarterly* 65, no. 1 (Winter 1986): pp. 39–59.

Fischer, John Irwin. 'The Legal Response to Swift's *The Public Spirit of the Whigs*'. In *Swift and his Contexts*, edited by John Irwin Fischer, et al. (New York: AMS Press, 1989), pp. 21–38.

Fish, Stanley. 'Short People Got No Reason to Live: Reading Irony'. *Daedalus* 112, no. 1 (Winter 1983): pp. 175–91.

Fish, Stanley. *There's No Such Thing as Free Speech... and it's a Good Thing, Too* (Oxford: Oxford University Press, 1994).

Flaningam, John. 'The Occasional Conformity Controversy: Ideology and Party Politics, 1697–1711'. *Journal of British Studies* 17 (1977): pp. 38–62.

Fletcher, Angus. *Allegory: The Theory of a Symbolic Mode* (Ithaca: Cornell University Press, 1964).

Foran, John. 'The Long Fall of the Safavid Dynasty: Moving beyond the Standard Views'. *International Journal of Middle East Studies* 24, no. 2 (May 1992): pp. 281–304.

Foster, Susan Leigh. *Choreography and Narrative: Ballet's Staging of Story and Desire* (Bloomington: Indiana University Press, 1996).

Foucault, Michel. *The History of Sexuality: An Introduction* (1976), translated by Robert Hurley (1978; New York: Vintage, 1990).

Fox, Adam. *Oral and Literate Culture in England, 1500–1700*. Oxford: Oxford University Press, 2000.

Foxon, David F. *Pope and the Early Eighteenth-Century Book Trade*, edited by James McLaverty (Oxford: Clarendon Press, 1991).

Fowler, Alastair. *Kinds of Literature: An Introduction to the Theory of Genres and Modes* (Cambridge: Harvard University Press, 1982).

Fowler, James. 'Moralizing Satire: Cross-Channel Perspectives'. In *The Oxford Handbook of Eighteenth-Century Satire*, edited by Paddy Bullard (Oxford: Oxford University Press, 2019), pp. 595–612.

Frasca-Spada, Marina, and Nick Jardine (eds.). *Books and the Sciences in History* (Cambridge: Cambridge University Press, 2000).

Fraser, Peter. *The Intelligence of the Secretaries of State and their Monopoly of Licensed News, 1660–1688* (Cambridge: Cambridge University Press, 1956).

'In Free Speech Debates, LGBTQ and People of Color at Risk'. *WNYC News* (9 June 2017): https://www.wnyc.org/story/who-are-real-victims-crackdown-free-speech/.

Freshwater, Helen. 'Towards a Redefinition of Censorship'. In *Critical Studies (Vol. 22): Censorship & Cultural Regulation in the Modern Age*, edited by Beate Müller (Amsterdam: Ridopi, 2004), pp. 225–46.

Frye, Northrop. *Anatomy of Criticism* (Princeton: Princeton University Press, 1957).

Gadd, Ian. 'Leaving the printer to his liberty: Swift and the London book trade, 1701–1714'. In *Jonathan Swift and the Eighteenth-Century Book*, edited by Paddy Bullard and James McLaverty (Cambridge: Cambridge University Press, 2013), pp. 51–64.

Gallagher, Catherine. *Nobody's Story: The Vanishing Acts of Women Writers in the Marketplace, 1670–1820* (Berkeley: University of California Press, 1995).

Gallagher, Noelle. *Historical Literatures: Writing about the Past in England, 1660–1740* (Manchester: Manchester University Press, 2018).

Garnett, Richard, and Megan Richardson. 'Libel Tourism or Just Redress?: Reconciling the (English) Right to Reputation With the (American) Right to Free Speech in Cross-Border Libel Cases'. *Journal of Private International Law* 5, no. 3 (2009): pp. 471–90.

Gatrell, Vic. *City of Laughter: Sex and Satire in Eighteenth-Century* (New York: Walker & Co., 2007).

Gay, Peter. *The Enlightenment: An Interpretation*, vol. 2: The Science of Freedom (1966–69; New York: W.W. Norton & Co., 1977).

George, M. Dorothy. *English Political Caricature to 1792: A Study of Opinion and Propaganda*. Oxford: Clarendon Press, 1959).

George, M. Dorothy. *Hogarth to Cruikshank: Social Change in Graphic Satire* (New York: Walker, 1967).

Gerrard, Christine. 'Poems on Politics'. In *The Oxford Handbook of British Poetry, 1660–1800*, edited by Jack Lynch (Oxford: Oxford University Press, 2016), pp. 286–302.

Gervat, Claire. *Elizabeth: The Scandalous Life of the Duchess of Kingston* (London: Century, 2003).

Gilmartin, Kevin. *Writing against Revolution: Literary Conservatism in Britain, 1790–1832* (Cambridge: Cambridge University Press, 2007).

Gilmont, Jean-François. 'Protestant Reformations and Reading'. In *A History of Reading in the West*, edited by Guglielmo Cavallo and Roger Chartier, translated by Lydia G. Cochrane (Amherst: University of Massachusetts Press, 1999), pp. 213–37.

Godfrey, Richard. *English Caricature, 1620 to the Present: Caricaturists and Satirists, Their Art, Their Purpose and Influence* (London: Victoria and Albert Museum, 1984).

Goldgar, Bertrand A. *Walpole and the Wits: The Relation of Politics to Literature, 1722–1742* (Lincoln: University of Nebraska Press, 1976).

Goldie, Mark, and Geoff Kemp (eds.). *Censorship and the Press*, vol. 4: 1696–1720 (London: Pickering & Chatto, 2009).

Gombrich, E. H. *Meditations on a Hobby Horse and Other Essays on the Theory of Art* (London: Phaidon, 1963).

Goode, Mike. 'The Public and the Limits of Persuasion in the Age of Caricature'. In *The Efflorescence of Caricature, 1759–1838*, edited by Todd Porterfield (Burlington: Ashgate, 2011), pp. 1–10.

Goody, Jack (ed.). *Literacy in Traditional Societies* (Cambridge: Cambridge University Press, 1968).

Gowing, Laura. *Domestic Dangers: Women, Words, and Sex in Early Modern London* (Oxford: Oxford University Press, 1996).

Gray, Douglas. 'Rough Music: Some Early Invectives and Flytings'. *Yearbook of English Studies* 14 (1984): pp. 21–43.

Green, Thomas A. *Verdict According to Conscience: Perspectives on the English Criminal Trial Jury, 1200–1800* (Chicago: University of Chicago Press, 1985).

Greene, Jody. *The Trouble with Ownership: Literary Property and Authorial Liability in England, 1660–1730* (Philadelphia: University of Pennsylvania Press, 2005).

Gregg, Edward. *Queen Anne* (New Haven: Yale University Press, 2001).

Griffin, Dustin. *Satire: A Critical Reintroduction* (Lexington: University Press of Kentucky, 1994).

Griffin, Dustin. *Swift and Pope: Satirists in Dialogue* (Cambridge: Cambridge University Press, 2010).

Griffin, Robert J. 'Anonymity and Authorship', *New Literary History* 30, no. 4 (Autumn 1999): pp. 877–95.

Griffith, R. H. 'The *Dunciad* of 1728'. *Modern Philology* 13, no. 1 (May 1915): pp. 1–18.

Guilhamet, Leon. *Satire and the Transformation of Genre* (Philadelphia: University of Pennsylvania Press, 1987).

Guerinot, J.V. *Pamphlet Attacks on Alexander Pope, 1711–1744: A Descriptive Bibliography* (London: Methuen, 1969).

Hallett, Mark. *The Spectacle of Difference: Graphic Satire in the Age of Hogarth* (New Haven: Yale University Press, 1999).

Halliday, Paul. *Dismembering the Body Politic: Partisan Politics in England's Towns, 1650–1730* (Cambridge: Cambridge University Press, 2003).

Halliday, Paul. *Habeas Corpus: From England to Empire* (Cambridge: Belknap Press, 2010).

Halsband, Robert. 'Pope's "Libel and Satire"'. *Eighteenth-Century Studies* 8, no. 4 (Summer 1975): pp. 473–4.

Hammond, Brean. 'Verse Satire'. In *A Companion to Eighteenth-Century Poetry*, edited by Christine Gerrard (Malden: Blackwell, 2006), ch. 27.

Hamburger, Philip. 'The Development of the Law of Seditious Libel and the Control of the Press', *Stanford Law Review* 37, no. 3 (February 1985): pp. 661–765.

Hamburger, Philip. 'Revolution and Judicial Review: Chief Justice John Holt's Opinion in *City of London v. Wood*'. *Columbia Law Review* 94, no. 7 (November 1994): pp. 2091–153.

Hanson, Laurence. *Government and the Press, 1695–1763* (Oxford: Clarendon Press, 1967).

Harling, Philip. 'The Law of Libel and the Limits of Repression, 1790–1832'. *The Historical Journal* 44, no. 1 (March 2001): pp. 107–34.

Harris, Michael. 'Figures Relating to the Printing and Distribution of the *Craftsman*, 1726 to 1730'. *Historical Research* 43, no. 108 (1970): pp. 233–42.

Harris, Michael. 'Newspaper Distribution during Queen Anne's Reign: Charles Delafaye and the Secretary of State's Office'. In *Studies in the Book Trade: In Honour of Graham Pollard*, edited by R. W. Hunt, I. G. Philip, and R. J. Roberts (Oxford: Oxford Bibliographical Society, 1975), pp. 139–51.

Harris, Michael. 'Print and Politics in the Age of Walpole'. In *Britain in the Age of Walpole*, edited by Jeremy Black (New York: St. Martin's Press, 1984), pp. 189–210.

Harris, Michael. *London Newspapers in the Age of Walpole: A Study of the Origins of the Modern English Press* (Rutherford: Fairleigh Dickinson University Press, 1987).

Harris, Michael. 'London newspapers'. In *The Cambridge History of the Book in Britain*, vol. 5: 1695–1830, edited by Michael F. Suarez, S. J., and Michael L. Turner (Cambridge: Cambridge University Press, 2009), pp. 413–33.

Harth, Phillip. 'The Problem of Political Allegory in *Gulliver's Travels*', *Modern Philology* 73, no. 4.2 (May 1976), pp. S40–7.

Hathaway, Oona A. 'Path Dependence in the Law: The Course and Pattern of Legal Change in a Common Law System'. *Iowa Law Review* 86, no. 2 (2001): pp. 601–65.

Havighurst, Alfred F. 'James II and the Twelve Men in Scarlet', *Law Quarterly Review* 69 (October 1953): pp. 522–46.

Havighurst, Alfred F. 'The Judiciary and Politics in the Reign of Charles II (Part II, 1676–1685)'. *Law Quarterly Review* 66 (April 1950): pp. 229–52.

Havighurst, Alfred F. 'The Judiciary and Politics in the Reign of Charles II (Part I, 1660–1676)'. *Law Quarterly Review* 66 (January 1950): pp. 62–78.

Harris, Bob. *Politics and the Rise of the Press, 1620–1800* (London: Routledge, 1996).

Harris, Bob. *Politics and the Nation: Britain in the Mid-Eighteenth Century* (Oxford: Oxford University Press, 2002).

Harris, Bob. 'Print Culture'. In *A Companion to Eighteenth-Century Britain*, edited by H. T. Dickinson (Malden: Blackwell, 2002), pp. 283–93.

Hay, Douglas. 'Controlling the English Prosecutor'. *Osgoode Hall Law Journal* 21, no. 2 (October 1983): pp. 165–286.

Hay, Douglas. 'Prosecution and Power: Malicious Prosecutions in the English Courts, 1750–1850'. In *Policing and Prosecution in Britain, 1750–1850*, edited by Douglas Hay and Francis Snyder (Oxford: Oxford University Press, 1989), pp. 343–93.

Hay, Douglas. 'Property, Authority and the Criminal Law'. In *Albion's Fatal Tree: Crime and Society in Eighteenth-Century England*, rev. ed., edited by Douglas Hay, et al. (London: Verso, 2011), pp. 49–65.

Hay, Douglas, Peter Linebaugh, and E. P. Thompson (eds.). *Albion's Fatal Tree: Crime and Society in Eighteenth-Century England*. 2nd ed. (London: Verso, 2011).

Hay, Douglas, and Francis Snyder (eds.) *Policing and Prosecution in Britain, 1750–1850* (Oxford: Oxford University Press, 1989).

Hay, Douglas, and Francis Snyder. 'Using the Criminal Law: Policing, Private Prosecution and the State'. In *Policing and Prosecution in Britain, 1750–1850*, edited by Douglas Hay and Francis Snyder (Oxford: Oxford University Press, 1989), pp. 3–52.

Heinze, Eric. *Hate Speech and Democratic Citizenship* (Oxford: Oxford University Press, 2006).

Heinzelman, Susan Sage. *Riding the Black Ram: Law, Literature, and Gender* (Stanford: Stanford University Press, 2010).

Heiserman, A. R. *Skelton and Satire* (Chicago: University of Chicago Press, 1961).

Hellmuth, Eckhart. '"The palladium of all other English liberties": Reflections on the Liberty of the Press in England during the 1760s and 1770s'. In *The Transformation of Political Culture: England and Germany in the Late Eighteenth Century*, edited by Eckhart Hellmuth (Oxford: Oxford University Press, 1990), pp. 467–501.

Hellmuth, Eckhart. 'Towards Hume—The Discourse on the Liberty of the Press in the Age of Walpole', *History of European Ideas* 44, no. 2 (2018): pp. 158–81.

Helmholz, Richard H., et al. *The Privilege Against Self-Incrimination* (Chicago: University of Chicago Press, 1997).

Helmholz, Richard H. 'Civil Trials and the Limits of Responsible Speech'. In *Juries, Libel, & Justice: The Role of the English Juries in Seventeenth- and Eighteenth-Century Trials for Libel and Slander* (Los Angeles: William Andrews Clark Memorial Library, University of California, Los Angeles, 1984), pp. 1–25.

Helmholz, Richard H. (ed.). *Select Cases on Defamation to 1600* (London: Selden Society, 1985).

Helmholz, Richard H. 'Continental Law and Common Law: Historical Strangers or Companions?' *Duke Law Journal* 1990, no. 6 (December 1990): pp. 1218–81.

Helmholz, Richard H. *The Oxford History of the Laws of England*, vol. 1: The Canon Law and Ecclesiastical Jurisdiction from 597 to the 1640s (Oxford: Oxford University Press, 2003).

Helmholz, Richard H. 'The *Mitior Sensus* Doctrine'. *Green Bag* 7 (Winter 2004): pp. 133–6.

Heard, Kate. *High Spirits: The Comic Art of Thomas Rowlandson* (London: Royal Collection Trust, 2013).

Heard, Kate. 'The British Royal Family and Satirical Prints, 1760–1901'. In *Collecting Prints and Drawings*, edited by Andrea M. Gáldy and Sylvia Heudecker (Cambridge: Cambridge Scholars Publishing, 2016), pp. 155–71.

Herman, Ruth. *The Business of a Woman: The Political Writings of Delarivier Manley* (Newark: University of Delaware Press, 2003).

Higgins, Ian. *Swift's Politics: A Study in Disaffection* (Cambridge: Cambridge University Press, 1994).

Higgins, Ian. 'Censorship, libel and self-censorship'. In *Jonathan Swift and the Eighteenth-Century Book*, edited by Paddy Bullard and James McLaverty (Cambridge: Cambridge University Press, 2013), pp. 179–98.

Highet, Gilbert. *The Anatomy of Satire* (Princeton: Princeton University Press, 1962).

Hile, Rachel E. *Spenserian Satire: A Tradition of Indirection* (Manchester: Manchester University Press, 2017).

Hinds, Peter. *'The Horrid Popish Plot': Roger L'Estrange and the Circulation of Political Discourse in Late Seventeenth-Century London* (Oxford: Oxford University Press, 2010).

Hodgson, Jessica. '*Private Eye* hails libel victory'. *The Guardian* (7 November 2001): https://www.theguardian.com/media/2001/nov/07/pressandpublishing1

Hofstadter, Richard. *The Paranoid Style in American Politics* (1964; New York: Alfred. A. Knopf, 1965).

Holmes, Geoffrey S. *British Politics in the Age of Anne*, rev. ed. (London: Hambledon Press, 1987).

Holmes, Geoffrey S. *The Making of a Great Power: Late Stuart and Early Georgian Britain, 1660–1722* (New York: Longman, 1993).

Holquist, Michael. 'Corrupt Originals: The Paradox of Censorship'. *PMLA* 109, no. 1 (January 1994): pp. 14–25.

Holdsworth, Sir William. *A History of English Law*. 2nd ed. 10 vol. (London: Methuen, 1937).

Holland, Peter. 'Hearing the Dead: The Sound of David Garrick'. In *Players, Playwrights, Playhouses: Investigating Performance, 1660–1800*, edited by Michael Cordner and Peter Holland (Basingstoke: Palgrave Macmillan, 2007), pp. 248–70.

Hone, Joseph. *Literature and Party Politics at the Accession of Queen Anne* (Oxford: Oxford University Press, 2017).

Hone, Joseph. 'Legal Constraints, Libellous Evasions'. In *The Oxford Handbook of Eighteenth-Century Satire*, edited by Paddy Bullard (Oxford: Oxford University Press, 2019), pp. 525–41.

Horsley, L. S. 'The Trial of John Tutchin, Author of the *Observator*', *Yearbook of English Studies* 3 (1973): pp. 124–40.

Horsley, L. S. 'Contemporary Reactions to Defoe's *Shortest Way with the Dissenters*'. *Studies in English Literature, 1500–1900* 16, no. 3 (Summer, 1976): pp. 407–20.

Hoxby, Blair. *Mammon's Music: Literature and Economics in the Age of Milton* (New Haven: Yale University Press, 2002).

Hume, Robert D. *The Development of English Drama in the Late Seventeenth Century* (Oxford: Clarendon Press, 1976).

Hume, Robert D. *The Rakish Stage: Studies in English Drama, 1660–1800* (Carbondale: Southern Illinois University Press, 1983).

Hume, Robert D. *Henry Fielding and the London Theatre, 1728–1737* (Oxford: Clarendon Press, 1988).

Hume, Robert D. '"Satire" in the Reign of Charles II'. *Modern Philology* 102, no. 3 (February 2005): pp. 332–71.

Hunt, Tamara L. 'Servants, Masters and Seditious Libel in Eighteenth-Century England', *Book History* 20 (2017): pp. 83–110.

Hunter, David. 'Copyright Protection for Engravings and Maps in Eighteenth-Century Britain'. *Library* 6, no. 2 (1987): pp. 136–45.

Hunter, J. Paul. 'Political, satirical, didactic and lyric poetry (I)'. In *The Cambridge History of English Literature, 1660–1800*, edited by John Richetti (Cambridge: Cambridge University Press, 2005), pp. 160–208.

Hutcheon, Linda. *A Theory of Parody: The Teachings of Twentieth-Century Art Forms* (London: Methuen, 1985).

Hutcheon, Linda. *Irony's Edge: The Theory and Politics of Irony* (London: Routledge, 1994).

Hyland, P. B. J. 'Liberty and Libel: Government and the Press during the Succession Crisis in Britain, 1712–1716'. *English Historical Review* 101 (October 1986): pp. 863–88.

Ibbetson, David. 'Edward Coke, Roman Law, and the Law of Libel'. In *The Oxford Handbook of English Law and Literature, 1500–1700*, edited by Lorna Hutson (Oxford: Oxford University Press, 2017), ch. 25.

Ingram, Martin. 'Ridings, Rough Music and Mocking Rhymes in Early Modern England'. In *Popular Culture in Seventeenth-Century England*, edited by Barry Reay (London: Routledge, 1985), pp. 166–97.

Ingram, Martin. 'Law, Litigants and the Construction of 'Honour': Slander Suits in Early Modern England'. In *The Moral World of the Law*, edited by Peter Cross (Cambridge: Cambridge University Press, 2000), pp. 134–60.

Iser, Wolfgang. *Prospecting: From Reader Response to Literary Anthropology* (Baltimore: Johns Hopkins University Press, 1993).

Jack, Ian. *Augustan Satire: Intention and Idiom in English Poetry, 1660–1750* (Oxford: Clarendon Press, 1952).

Jackson, H. J. *Marginalia: Readers Writing in Books* (New Haven: Yale University Press, 2001).

Jameson, Fredric. *The Political Unconscious: Narrative as a Socially Symbolic Act* (Ithaca: Cornell University Press, 1981).

Jarrett, Derek. *England in the Age of Hogarth* (New Haven: Yale University Press, 1992).

Jay, Stewart. 'Servants of Monarchs and Lords: The Advisory Role of Early English Judges'. *American Journal of Legal History* 38, no. 3 (April 1994): pp. 117–96.

Johns, Adrian. *The Nature of the Book: Print and Knowledge in the Making* (Chicago: University of Chicago Press, 1998).

Johns, Adrian. 'How to Acknowledge a Revolution'. *American Historical Review* 107, no. 1 (February 2002): pp. 106–25.

Johns, Adrian. *Piracy: The Intellectual Property Wars from Gutenberg to Gates* (Chicago: University of Chicago Press, 2009).

Johns, Adrian. 'The Piratical Enlightenment'. In *This is Enlightenment*, edited by Clifford Siskin and William Warner (Chicago: University of Chicago Press, 2010), pp. 301–20.

Johnston, Kenneth R. *Unusual Suspects: Pitt's Reign of Alarm and the Lost Generation of the 1790s* (Oxford: Oxford University Press, 2013).

Jones, Clyve. '"Too Wild to Succeed": The Occasional Conformity Bills and the Attempts by the House of Lords to Outlaw the Tack in the Reign of Anne'. *Parliamentary History* 30, no. 2 (2011): pp. 414–27.

Jones, Steven E. *Shelley's Satire: Violence, Exhortation, and Authority* (DeKalb: Northern Illinois University Press, 1994).

Jones, Steven E. *Satire and Romanticism* (London: Macmillan Press, 2000).

Jones, W. J. *Politics and the Bench: The Judges and the Origins of the English Civil War* (New York: Barnes & Noble, 1971).

Jones, William R. 'The Bishops' Ban of 1599 and the Ideology of English Satire'. *Literature Compass* 7, no. 5 (2010): pp. 332–46.

Jones, William R. *Satire in the Elizabethan Age: An Activistic Art* (New York: Routledge, 2018).

Kaplan, Lindsay M. *The Culture of Slander in Early Modern England* (Cambridge: Cambridge University Press, 1997).

Karian, Stephen. *Jonathan Swift in Print and Manuscript* (Cambridge: Cambridge University Press, 2010).

Karian, Stephen. 'Swift as a manuscript poet'. In *Jonathan Swift and the Eighteenth-Century Book*, edited by Paddy Bullard and James McLaverty (Cambridge: Cambridge University Press, 2013), pp. 31–50.

Katz, Leo. *Why the Law Is So Perverse* (Chicago: University of Chicago Press, 2011).

Keith, Jennifer. 'Pre-Romanticism and the Ends of Eighteenth-Century Poetry'. In *The Cambridge Companion to Eighteenth-Century Poetry*, edited by John Sitter (Cambridge: Cambridge University Press, 2001), pp. 271–90.

Kelly, Ian. *Mr Foote's Other Leg: Comedy, Tragedy and Murder in Georgian London* (London: Picador, 2012).

Kemnitz, Thomas Milton. 'The Cartoon as a Historical Source'. *Journal of Interdisciplinary History* 4, no. 12 (Summer 1973): pp. 81–93.

Kemp, Geoff (ed.). *Censorship and the Press*, vol. 3: 1660–1695 (London: Pickering & Chatto, 2009).

Kendrick, Laura. 'Medieval Satire'. In *A Companion to Satire*, edited by Ruben Quintero (Malden: Blackwell, 2007), pp. 52–69.

Kernan, Alan B. *The Cankered Muse: Satire of the English Renaissance* (New Haven: Yale University Press, 1959).

Kernan, Alan B. *The Plot of Satire* (New Haven: Yale University Press, 1965).

Keymer, Thomas. *Richardson's* Clarissa *and the Eighteenth-Century Reader* (Cambridge: Cambridge University Press, 1992).

Keymer, Thomas. *Sterne, the Moderns, and the Novel* (Oxford: Oxford University Press, 2002).

Keymer, Thomas. 'Fielding's Theatrical Career'. In *The Cambridge Companion to Henry Fielding*, edited by Claude Rawson (Cambridge: Cambridge University Press, 2007), pp. 17–37.

Keymer, Thomas. 'Defoe's Ears: *The Dunciad*, the Pillory, and Seditious Libel'. *The Eighteenth-Century Novel* 6–7 (2009): pp. 159–96.

Keymer, Thomas. *Poetics of the Pillory: English Literature and Seditious Libel, 1660–1820* (Oxford: Oxford University Press, 2019).

Keymer, Thomas, and Jon Mee (eds.). *The Cambridge Companion to English Literature, 1740–1830* (Cambridge: Cambridge University Press, 2004).

King, John N. 'Traditions of Complaint and Satire'. In *A New Companion to English Renaissance Literature and Culture*, 2 vol., edited by Michael Hattaway (Malden: Blackwell, 2010), pp. 326–40.

King, Peter. *Crime, Justice and Discretion in England, 1740–1820* (Oxford: Oxford University Press, 2000).

Kinservik, Matthew J. *Disciplining Satire: The Censorship of Satiric Comedy on the Eighteenth-Century London Stage* (Lewisburg: Bucknell University Press, 2002).

Kinservik, Matthew J. 'The Dialectics of Print and Performance after 1737'. In *The Oxford Handbook of the Georgian Theatre, 1737–1832*, edited by Julia Swindells and David Francis Taylor (Oxford: Oxford University Press, 2014), pp. 123–39.

Kinservik, Matthew J. 'The 'English Aristophanes': Fielding, Foote, and Debates over Literary Satire'. In *Brill's Companion to the Reception of Aristophanes*, edited by Philip Walsh (Leiden: Brill, 2016), pp. 109–28.

Kishlansky, Mark. 'Turning Frogs into Princes: Aesop's *Fables* and the Political Culture of Early Modern England'. In *Political Culture and Cultural Politics in Early Modern England: Essays Presented to David Underdown*, edited by Susan Dwyer Amussen and Mark A. Kishlansky (Manchester: Manchester University Press, 1995), pp. 338–60.

Kishlansky, Mark. *A Monarchy Transformed: Britain, 1603–1714* (London: Penguin, 1996).

Knights, Mark. *Representation and Misrepresentation in Later Stuart Britain: Partisanship and Political Culture* (Oxford: Oxford University Press, 2005).

Knox, Norman. *The Word Irony and its Context, 1500–1755* (Durham: Duke University Press, 1961).

Korshin, Paul (ed.). *Studies in Change and Revolution: Aspects of English Intellectual History 1640–1800* (Menston, Yorkshire: The Scolar Press, 1972).

Korshin, Paul. 'Types of Eighteenth-Century Literary Patronage'. *Eighteenth-Century Studies* 7, no. 4 (Summer 1974): pp. 453–73.

Kropf, C. R. 'Libel and Satire in the Eighteenth Century'. *Eighteenth-Century Studies* 8 (Winter 1974–75): pp. 153–68.

Lake, Peter. *Bad Queen Bess?: Libels, Secret Histories, and the Politics of Publicity in the Reign of Queen Elizabeth I* (Oxford: Oxford University Press, 2016).

Lamont, William. *Marginal Prynne, 1600–1669* (Toronto: University of Toronto Press, 1963).

Langbein, John H. 'The Historical Origins of the Privilege against Self-Incrimination at Common Law'. *Michigan Law Review* 92, no. 5 (March 1994): pp. 1047–85.

Langbein, John H. *The Origins of Adversary Criminal Trial* (Oxford: Oxford University Press, 2003).

Lassiter, John C. 'Defamation of Peers: The Rise and Decline of the Action for *Scandalum Magnatum*, 1497–1773'. *American Journal of Legal History* 22, no. 3 (July 1978): pp. 216–36.

Latham, Sean. *The Art of Scandal: Modernism, Libel Law, and the Roman à Clef* (Oxford: Oxford University Press, 2009).

Lawson, Philip, and Jim Phillips, '"Our Execrable Banditti": Perceptions of Nabobs in Mid-Eighteenth Century Britain'. *Albion* 16, no. 3 (Autumn 1984): pp. 225–41.

Le Goff, Jacques. *History and Memory*, translated by Steven Rendall and Elizabeth Claman (New York: Columbia University Press, 1992).

Lee, Yen Nee. 'Trump and GOP attack CNN, New York Times and Washington Post in "fake news awards"'. CNBC (17 January 2018): https://www.cnbc.com/2018/01/17/fake-news-awards-by-donald-trump-gop-cnn-new-york-times-washington-post.html

Lemmings, David. 'The Independence of the Judiciary in Eighteenth-Century England'. In *The Life of the Law*, edited by Peter Birks (London: Hambledon Press, 1993), pp. 125–49.

Lemmings, David. *Professors of the Law: Barristers and English Legal Culture in the Eighteenth Century* (Oxford: Oxford University Press, 2000).

Lemmings, David. *Law and Government in England during the Long Eighteenth Century: From Consent to Command* (New York: Palgrave Macmillan, 2011).

Liesenfeld, Vincent J. *The Licensing Act of 1737* (Madison: University of Wisconsin Press, 1984).

Levine, Caroline. *Forms: Whole, Rhythm, Hierarchy, Network* (Princeton: Princeton University Press, 2015).

Levy, Leonard. *Emergence of a Free Press* (Oxford: Oxford University Press, 1985).

Lobban, Michael. 'From Seditious Libel to Unlawful Conspiracy: Peterloo and the Changing Face of Political Crime, c1770–1820'. *Oxford Journal of Legal Studies* 10, no. 3 (1990): pp. 307–52.

Lobban, Michael. 'Treason, Sedition and the Radical Movements in the Age of the French Revolution'. *Liverpool Law Review* 22 (2000): pp. 205–34.

Lockwood, Thomas. *Post-Augustan Satire: Charles Churchill and Satirical Poetry, 1750–1800* (Seattle: University of Washington Press, 1979).

Loloi, Parvin. 'The Image of the Safavids in English and French Literature (1500–1800)'. In *Iran and the World in the Safavid Age*, edited by Willem Floor and Edmund Herzig (London: I. B. Taurus, 2012), pp. 347–55.

London, April. 'Secret History and Anecdote'. In *The Secret History in Literature, 1660–1820*, edited by Rebecca Bullard and Rachel Carnell (Cambridge University Press, 2017), pp. 174–87.

Lord, George DeF., et al. (eds.). *Augustan Satirical Verse, 1660–1714*. 7 vol. (New Haven: Yale University Press, 1963–75).

Love, Harold. 'Rochester and the Traditions of Satire'. In *Restoration Literature: Critical Approaches*, edited by Harold Love (London: Methuen, 1972), pp. 145–75.

Love, Harold. *Scribal Publication in Seventeenth-Century England* (Oxford: Clarendon Press, 1993).

Love, Harold. *English Clandestine Satire, 1660–1702* (Oxford: Oxford University Press, 2004).

Loveman, Kate. *Reading Fictions, 1660–1740: Deception in English Literary and Political Culture* (Burlington: Aldershot, 2008).

Loveman, Kate. 'Epigram and Spontaneous Wit'. In *The Oxford Handbook of Eighteenth-Century Satire*, edited by Paddy Bullard (Oxford: Oxford University Press, 2019), pp. 492–508.

Lowenstein, Joseph F. 'Legal Proofs and Corrected Readings: Press-Agency and the New Bibliography'. In *The Production of English Renaissance Culture*, edited by David Lee Miller, Sharon O'Dair, and Harold Weber (Ithaca: Cornell University Press, 1994), pp. 93–122.

Lund, Roger. 'The Ghosts of Epigram, False Wit, and the Augustan Mode'. *Eighteenth-Century Life* 27, no. 2 (Spring 2003): pp. 67–95.

Lund, Roger. 'Laughing at Cripples: Ridicule, Deformity and the Argument from Design'. *Eighteenth-Century Studies* 39, no. 1 (Fall 2005): pp. 91–114.

Lund, Roger. '"An Alembick of Innuendos": Satire, Libel, and *The Craftsman*'. *Philological Quarterly* 95, no. 2 (Spring 2016): pp. 243–68.

Macaulay, Thomas Babington. *The History of England from the Accession of James the Second*, vol. 7 (London: Longman, Green, 1860–62).

Macaulay, Thomas Babington. *The Complete Writings of Thomas Babington Macaulay* (Boston and New York: Houghton, Mifflin and Company, 1901).

Mack, Maynard. *The Last and Greatest Art: Some Unpublished Poetical Manuscripts of Alexander Pope* (Newark: University of Delaware Press, 1984).

Mack, Maynard. *Alexander Pope: A Life*. (New York: W. W. Norton & Company in association with Yale University Press, 1985).

Mack, Maynard. 'The Muse of Satire'. *Yale Review* 40 (1951): pp. 80–92.

MacKinnon, Catherine A. 'The First Amendment: An Equality Reading'. In *The Free Speech Century*, edited by Lee C. Bollinger and Geoffrey R. Stone (Oxford: Oxford University Press, 2019), pp. 140–61.

Malouf, David. 'Made in England'. *Quarterly Essay* 12 (2003): pp. 46–7.

Markiewicz, Henryk, and Uliana Gabara. 'Ut Pictura Poesis … A History of the Topos and the Problem'. *New Literary History* 18, no. 3 (Spring 1987): pp. 535–58.

Marsh, Joss. *Word Crimes: Blasphemy, Culture, and Literature in Nineteenth-Century England* (Chicago: University of Chicago Press, 1998).

Marshall, Alan. *Intelligence and Espionage in the Reign of Charles II, 1660–1685* (Cambridge: Cambridge University Press, 1994).

Marshall, Ashley. 'The Generic Context of Defoe's *The Shortest-Way with the Dissenters* and the Problem of Irony'. *Review of English Studies* 61, no. 249 (2010): pp. 234–58.

Marshall, Ashley. *The Practice of Satire in England, 1658–1770* (Baltimore: Johns Hopkins University Press, 2013).

Marshall, P. J. (ed.). *East Indian Fortunes: The British in Bengal in the Eighteenth Century* (Oxford: Clarendon Press, 1976).

Marshall, P. J. (ed.). *The Oxford History of the British Empire: The Eighteenth Century* (Oxford: Oxford University Press, 1998).

May, Steven M., and Alan Bryson. *Verse Libel in Renaissance England and Scotland* (Oxford: Oxford University Press, 2016).

McCabe, Richard A. 'Elizabethan Satire and the Bishops' Ban of 1599'. *Yearbook of English Studies* 11, no. 2 (1981): pp. 188–93.

McCalman, Iain. *Radical Underworld: Prophets, Revolutionaries and Pornographers in London, 1795–1840* (Cambridge: Cambridge University Press, 1988).

McCraw, David. 'Think Like a Libel Lawyer'. *New York Times*, 9 March 2019.

McCreery, Cindy. *The Satirical Gaze: Prints of Women in Late Eighteenth-Century England* (Oxford: Oxford University Press, 2004).

McDowell, Paula. *Women of Grub Street: Press, Politics, and Gender in the London Literary Marketplace, 1678–1730* (Oxford: Clarendon Press, 1998).

McDowell, Paula. *The Invention of the Oral: Print Commerce and Fugitive Voices in Eighteenth-century Britain* (Chicago: University of Chicago Press, 2016).

McGann, Jerome. *The Textual Condition* (Princeton: Princeton University Press, 1991).

McKendry, Andrew. 'Will the Public Please Step Forward?: Libel Law and Public Opinion in Byron's *The Vision of Judgment*'. *Studies in Romanticism* 54, no. 4 (2015): pp. 525–49.

McKenzie, D. F. 'The London Book Trade in the Later Seventeenth Century' (Sandars Lectures, 1976). MISC 217, SCSU.

McKenzie, D. F. *Making Meaning: 'Printers of the Mind' and Other Essays*, edited by Peter D. McDonald and Michael F. Suarez (Amherst: University of Massachusetts Press, 2002).

McKeon, Michael. 'What Were Poems on Affairs of State?' *1650–1850: Ideas, Aesthetics, and Inquiries in the Early Modern Era* 4 (1997): pp. 363–82.

McKeon, Michael. *The Secret History of Domesticity: Public, Private, and the Division of Knowledge* (Baltimore: Johns Hopkins University Press, 2005).

McLaverty, James. 'Lawton Gilliver: Pope's Bookseller'. *Studies in Bibliography* 32 (1979): pp. 101–24.

McLaverty, James. 'The Mode of Existence of Literary Works of Art: The Case of the *Dunciad Variorum*'. *Studies in Bibliography* 37 (1984): pp. 82–105.

McLaverty, James. 'Swift and the Art of the Political Publication: Hints and Title Pages, 1711–1714'. In *Politics and Literature in the Age of Swift: English and Irish Perspectives*, edited by Claude Rawson (Cambridge: Cambridge University Press, 2010), pp. 116–39.

McLaverty, James. 'Italics in Swift's Poems', *Swift Studies* 28 (2011): pp. 22–37.

McLynn, Frank. *Crime and Punishment in Eighteenth-Century England* (London: Routledge, 1989).

McRae, Andrew. *Literature, Satire and the Early Stuart State* (Cambridge: Cambridge University Press, 2004).

McTague, John. '*The New Atalantis* Arrests: A Reassessment'. *The Library* 15, no. 4 (December 2014): pp. 439–46.

Mee, Jon. 'Treason, Seditious Libel, and Literature in the Romantic Period'. In *Oxford Handbooks Online* (Oxford: Oxford University Press, 2016), pp. 1–23.

Meyers, Robin, Michael Harris, and Giles Mandelbrote (eds.). *The London Book Trade: Topographies of Print in the Metropolis from the Sixteenth Century* (London: Oak Knoll Press and the British Library, 2003).

Meyers, Robin, and Michael Harris (eds.) *Author/Publisher Relations During the Eighteenth and Nineteenth Centuries* (Oxford: Oxford Polytechnic Press, 1983).

Meyers, Robin, and Michael Harris (eds.). *Fakes and Frauds: Varieties of Deception in Print & Manuscript* (Detroit: St Paul's Bibliographies, 1989).

Mezey, Naomi. 'Law as Culture'. In *Cultural Analysis, Cultural Studies, and the Law: Moving beyond Legal Realism*, edited by Austin Sarat and Jonathan Simon (Durham: Duke University Press, 2003), pp. 37–72.

Miller, Alan D., and Ronen Perry. 'The Reasonable Person'. *New York University Law Review* 87, no. 2 (May 2012): pp. 323–92.

Millstone, Noah. 'Evil Counsel: *The Propositions to Bridle the Impertinency of Parliament* and the Critique of Caroline Government in the Late 1620s'. *Journal of British Studies* 50, no. 4 (October 2011): pp. 813–39.

Mitchell, Paul. *The Making of the Modern Law of Defamation* (Oxford: Hart, 2005).

Mitchell, W. J. T. *Picture Theory: Essays on Verbal and Visual Representation* (Chicago: University of Chicago Press, 1994).

Molesworth, Jesse. 'Graphic Satire: Hogarth and Gillray'. In *The Oxford Handbook of Eighteenth-Century Satire*, edited by Paddy Bullard (Oxford: Oxford University Press, 2019), pp. 298–319.

Monod, Paul Kléber. *Jacobitism and the English People, 1688–1788* (Cambridge: Cambridge University Press, 1989).

Moody, Jane. 'Stolen Identities: Character, Mimicry and the Invention of Samuel Foote'. In *Theatre and Celebrity in Britain, 1660–2000*, edited by Mary Luckhurst and Jane Moody (New York: Palgrave Macmillan, 2005), pp. 65–89.

Moody, Jane. *Illegitimate Theatre in London, 1770–1840* (Cambridge: Cambridge University Press, 2007).

Moore, Nicole, and Christina Spittel. 'South by East: World Literature's Cold War Compass'. In *Australian Literature in the German Democratic Republic: Reading through the Iron Curtain*, edited by Nicole Moore and Christina Spittel (London: Anthem, 2016), pp. 1–32.

Moore, Nicole. 'Censorship and Literature', *Oxford Research Encyclopedia of Literature* (Oxford: Oxford University Press, 2016).

Moran, Mayo. *Rethinking the Reasonable Person: An Egalitarian Reconstruction of the Objective Standard* (Oxford: Oxford University Press, 2003).

Morgan, Fidelis. *A Woman of No Character: An Autobiography of Mrs Manley* (Boston: Faber and Faber, 1986).

Mudge, Bradford K. *The Whore's Story: Women, Pornography, and the British Novel, 1684–1830* (Oxford: Oxford University Press, 2000).

Muecke, D. C. *The Compass of Irony* (London: Methuen, 1969).

Mueller, Andreas. 'Daniel Defoe, Master of Genres'. *Worcester Papers in English and Cultural Studies* 3 (2005): pp. 33–47.

Nathan, Edward P. 'The Bench and the Pulpit: Conflicting Elements in the Augustan Apology for Satire'. *English Literary History* 52, no. 2 (Summer 1985): pp. 375–96.

Nichols, Donald W. *Literary Anecdotes of the Eighteenth Century* (London, 1812–14).

Nicholson, Eirwen E. C. 'Consumers and Spectators: The Public of the Political Print in Eighteenth-Century England'. *History* 81, no. 261 (January 1996): pp. 5–21.

Nicholson, Eirwen. 'Soggy Prose and Verbiage: English Graphic Political Satire as a Visual/ Verbal Construct', *Word & Image: A Journal of Verbal/Visual Enquiry* 20, no. 1 (2004): pp. 28–40.

Nisbet, H. B., and Claude Rawson (eds.). *The Cambridge History of Literary Criticism: Vol. 4: The Eighteenth Century* (Cambridge: Cambridge University Press, 1997).

Nokes, David. 'Pope's Friends and Enemies: Fighting with Shadows'. In *The Cambridge Companion to Alexander Pope*, edited by Pat Rogers (Cambridge: Cambridge University Press, 2007), pp. 25–36.

Novak, Maximillian E. 'Defoe's *Shortest Way with the Dissenters*: Hoax, Parody, Paradox, Fiction, Irony, and Satire'. *Modern Language Quarterly* 27 (1966): pp. 402–17.

Novak, Maximillian E. *Daniel Defoe, Master of Fictions: His Life and Ideas* (Oxford: Oxford University Press, 2001).

Nussbaum, Felicity. *The Brink of All We Hate: English Satires on Women, 1660–1750* (Lexington: University Press of Kentucky, 1984).

O'Brien, John. *Harlequin Britain: Pantomime and Entertainment, 1690–1760* (Baltimore: Johns Hopkins University Press, 2004).

O'Brien, Karen. 'History and the Novel in Eighteenth-Century Britain'. *Huntington Library Quarterly* 68, no. 1–2 (March 2005): pp. 397–413.

O'Connell, Sheila. 'The Print Trade in Hogarth's London'. In *The London Book Trade: Topographies of Print in the Metropolis from the Sixteenth Century*, edited by Robin Meyers, Michael Harris and Giles Mandelbrote (London: Oak Knoll Press and the British Library, 2003), pp. 71–88.

O'Quinn, Daniel. *Staging Governance: Theatrical Imperialism in London, 1770–1800* (Baltimore: Johns Hopkins University Press, 2005).

O'Shaughnessy, David (ed.). *The Censorship of British Theatre, 1737–1843* (Trinity College Dublin): https://tobeomitted.tcd.ie/index.html.

Ogborn, Miles. *The Freedom of Speech: Talk and Slavery in the Anglo-Caribbean World* (Chicago: University of Chicago Press, 2019).

Oldham, James C. 'Origins of the Special Jury'. *University of Chicago Law Review* 50, no. 1 (Winter 1983): pp. 137–221.

Oldham, James C. *The Mansfield Manuscripts and the Growth of English Law in the Eighteenth Century*. 2 vol. (Chapel Hill: University of North Carolina Press, 1992).

Oldham, James C. 'Truth-Telling in the Eighteenth-Century English Courtroom'. *Law and History Review* 12, no. 1 (Spring 1994): pp. 95–121.

Oldham, James C. *English Common Law in the Age of Mansfield* (Chapel Hill: University of North Carolina Press, 2004).

Ong, Walter J. *Orality and Literacy: The Technologizing of the Word* (1982; London: Routledge, 2010).

Özdemir, Metin. 'Lampoon'. In *Encyclopedia of Humor Studies*, edited by Salvatore I. Attardo (Thousand Oaks: Sage, 2014), pp. 435–6.

Palmeri, Frank. *Satire, History, Novel: Narrative Forms, 1665–1815* (Newark: University of Delaware Press, 2003).

Parkes, M. B. *Pause and Effect: An Introduction to the History of Punctuation in the West* (Aldershot: Scolar Press, 1992).

Parks, Stephen. *John Dunton and the English Book Trade: A Study of his Career with a Checklist of his Publications* (New York: Garland, 1976).

Parsons, Nicola. 'Secrecy and Enlightenment: Delarivier Manley's *New Atalantis*'. In *Libertine Enlightenment: Sex, Liberty and Licence in the Eighteenth Century*, edited by Peter Cryle and Lisa O'Connell (London: Palgrave MacMillan, 2003), pp. 145–60.

Parsons, Nicola. *Reading Gossip in Early Eighteenth-Century England* (New York: Palgrave, 2009).

Patterson, Annabel. *Censorship and Interpretation: The Conditions of Writing and Reading in Early Modern England* (Madison: University of Wisconsin Press, 1984).

Patterson, Annabel. *Early Modern Liberalism* (Cambridge: Cambridge University Press, 1997).

Paulson, Ronald. *Satire and the Novel in Eighteenth-Century England* (New Haven: Yale University Press, 1967).

Paulson, Ronald. *Fictions of Satire* (Baltimore: Johns Hopkins University Press, 1967).

Paulson, Ronald. *Breaking and Remaking: Aesthetic Practice in England, 1700–1820* (New Brunswick: Rutgers University Press, 1989).

Paulson, Ronald. 'Pictorial Satire: From Emblem to Expression'. In *A Companion to Satire: Ancient and Modern*, edited by Ruben Quintero (London: Blackwell, 2007), pp. 293–324.

Paxson, James J. *Poetics of Personification* (Cambridge: Cambridge University Press, 1994).

Payne, Matthew, and James Payne, *Regarding Thomas Rowlandson, 1757–1827: His Life, Art and Acquaintance* (London: Hogarth, 2003).

Peakman, Julie. *Mighty Lewd Books: The Development of Pornography in Eighteenth-Century Britain* (New York: Palgrave Macmillan, 2003).

Peter, John. *Complaint and Satire in Early English Literature* (Oxford: Clarendon Press, 1956).

Peters, Julie Stone. 'Law, Literature, and the Vanishing Real: On the Future of an Interdisciplinary Illusion'. *PMLA* 120, no. 2 (March 2005): pp. 442–53.

Pettit, Alexander. *Illusory Consensus: Bolingbroke and the Polemical Response to Walpole, 1730–1737* (Newark: University of Delaware Press, 1997).

Pettit, Alexander, and Patrick Spedding (eds.). *Eighteenth-Century British Erotica*. 5 vol. (London: Pickering & Chatto, 2004).

Phiddian, Robert. 'Satire and the Limits of Literary Theories'. *Critical Quarterly* 55, no. 3 (October 2013): pp. 44–58.

Phiddian, Robert. *Satire and the Public Emotions* (Cambridge: Cambridge University Press, 2019).

Plomer, H. R., et al. *A Dictionary of the Printers and Booksellers who were at Work in England, Scotland and Ireland from 1668 to 1725* (Oxford: The Bibliographical Society, 1922).

Plomer, H. R., et al. *A Dictionary of the Printers and Booksellers who were at Work in England, Scotland and Ireland from 1726 to 1775* (Oxford: The Bibliographical Society, 1968).

Postema, Gerald J. 'Classical Common Law Jurisprudence (Part I)'. *Oxford University Commonwealth Law Journal* 2, no. 2 (Winter 2002): pp. 155–80.

Postema, Gerald J. 'Classical Common Law Jurisprudence (Part II)'. *Oxford University Commonwealth Law Journal* 3, no. 1 (Summer 2003): pp. 1–28.

Potter, Rachel. *Obscene Modernism: Literary Censorship and Experiment, 1900–1940* (Oxford: Oxford University Press, 2013).

Principe, Lawrence M. *The Secrets of Alchemy* (Chicago: University of Chicago Press, 2012).

Prochaska, F. K. 'English State Trials in the 1790s: A Case Study'. *Journal of British Studies* 13 (1973): pp. 63–82.

Plucknett, Theodore F. T. *A Concise History of the Common Law*. 5th ed. (Boston: Little, Brown and Co., 1956).

Pollard, Mary. *Dublin's Trade in Books, 1550–1800* (Oxford: Clarendon Press, 1989).

Pollard, Mary. 'Who's for Prison? Publishing Swift in Dublin'. *Swift Studies* 14 (1999): pp. 37–49.

Pollard, Mary (ed.). *A Dictionary of Members of the Dublin Book Trade 1550–1800* (London: Bibliographical Society, 2000).

Porter, Roy. *Enlightenment: Britain and the Creation of the Modern World* (London: Allen Lane, 2000).

Porterfield, Todd (ed.). *The Efflorescence of Caricature, 1759–1838* (Burlington: Ashgate, 2011).

Prest, Wilfrid. 'Judicial Corruption in Early Modern England'. *Past & Present* 133 (November 1991): pp. 67–95.

Prins, Yopie. 'What is Historical Poetics?' *Modern Language Quarterly* 77, no. 1 (2016): pp. 13–40.

Quilligan, Maureen. *The Language of Allegory: Defining the Genre* (Ithaca: Cornell University Press, 1979).

Quinlan, Maurice J. 'The Prosecution of Swift's *Public Spirit of the Whigs*'. *Texas Studies in Literature and Language* 9, no. 2 (1967): pp. 167–75.

Rabb, Melinda Alliker. *Satire and Secrecy in English Literature from 1650 to 1750* (New York: Palgrave Macmillan, 2007).

Ragussis, Michael. *Theatrical Nation: Jews and Other Outlandish Englishmen in Georgian Britain* (Philadelphia: University of Pennsylvania Press, 2010).

Rahn, B. J. 'A Ra-ree Show—a rare Cartoon: Revolutionary Propaganda in the Treason Trial of Stephen College'. In *Studies in Change and Revolution: Aspects of English Intellectual History 1640–1800*, edited by Paul J. Korshin (Menston, Yorkshire: The Scolar Press, 1972), pp. 77–98.

Rauser, Amelia. *Caricature Unmasked: Irony, Authenticity, and Individualism in Eighteenth-Century English Prints* (Newark: University of Delaware Press, 2008).

Raven, James. *The Business of Books: Booksellers and the English Book Trade, 1450–1850* (New Haven: Yale University Press, 2007).

Raven, James. 'The book as a commodity'. In *The Cambridge History of the Book in Britain*, vol. 5: 1695–1830, edited by Michael F. Suarez, S. J., and Michael L. Turner (Cambridge: Cambridge University Press, 2009), pp. 85–117.

Rawls, John. *Theory of Justice* (Cambridge: Harvard University Press, 1999).

Rawson, Claude. *Gulliver and the Gentle Reader: Studies in Swift and Our Time* (London: Routledge & Kegan Paul, 1973).

Rawson, Claude. *Satire and Sentiment, 1660–1830: Stress Points in the English Augustan Tradition*, rev. ed. (New Haven: Yale University Press, 2000).

Rawson, Claude (ed.). *The Cambridge Companion to Henry Fielding* (Cambridge: Cambridge University Press, 2007).

Rawson, Claude. 'Mock-heroic and English poetry'. In *The Cambridge Companion to the Epic*, edited by Catherine Bates (Cambridge: Cambridge University Press, 2010), pp. 167–92.

Raymond, Joad. 'The Newspaper, Public Opinion, and the Public Sphere in the Seventeenth Century'. *Prose Studies* 21, no. 2 (1998): pp. 109–36.

Raymond, Joad. 'Censorship in Law and Practice in Seventeenth-Century England: Milton's *Areopagitica*'. In *The Oxford Handbook of English Law and Literature, 1500–1700*, edited by Lorna Hutson (Oxford: Oxford University Press, 2017), ch. 26.

Rea, Robert R. 'Mason, Walpole, and That Rogue Almon'. *Huntington Library Quarterly* 23, no. 2 (February 1960): pp. 187–93.

Rea, Robert R. *The English Press in Politics: 1769–1774* (Lincoln: University of Nebraska Press, 1963).

Reid, John Phillip. *Rule of Law: The Jurisprudence of Liberty in the Seventeenth and Eighteenth Centuries* (DeKalb: Northern Illinois University Press, 2004).

Reynolds, Richard. 'Libels and Satires! Lawless Things Indeed!' *Eighteenth-Century Studies* 8, no. 4 (Summer 1975): pp. 475–7.

Richards, I. A. *Practical Criticism: A Study of Literary Judgment* (London: K. Paul, Trench, Trubner & Co., ltd., 1929).

Richetti, John (ed.) *The Cambridge History of English Literature, 1660–1800* (Cambridge: Cambridge University Press, 2005).

Riffaterre, Michael. *Semiotics of Poetry* (London: Methuen, 1980).

Rivers, Isabel (ed.). *Books and their Readers in Eighteenth-Century England* (Leicester: Leicester University Press, 1982).

Rivington, Charles A. *'Tyrant': The Story of John Barber, 1675–1741: Jacobite Lord Mayor of London and Printer and Friend to Dr. Swift* (York: William Sessions, 1989).

Roach, Joseph R. *The Player's Passion: Studies in the Science of Acting* (Newark: University of Delaware Press, 1985).

Robertson, Randy. *Censorship and Conflict in Seventeenth-Century England: The Subtle Art of Division* (University Park: Pennsylvania State University Press, 2010).

Robertson, Ritchie. *Mock-Epic Poetry from Pope to Heine* (Oxford: Oxford University Press, 2009).

Rogers, Deborah D. *Bookseller as Rogue: John Almon and the Politics of Eighteenth-Century Publishing* (New York: Peter Lang, 1986).

Rogers, Pat. *Grub Street: Studies in a Subculture* (London: Methuen & Co Ltd, 1972).

Rogers, Pat. *The Augustan Vision* (London: Methuen, 1974).

Rogers, Pat. 'Nathaniel Mist, Daniel Defoe, and the Perils of Publishing'. *The Library* 10, no. 3 (September 2009): pp. 298–313.

Rogers, Pat, and Paul Baines. 'The Prosecutions of Edmund Curll, 1725–28'. *The Library* 5, no. 2 (2004): pp. 176–94.

Rogers, Shef. 'Pope, Publishing, and Popular Interpretations of the *Dunciad Variorum*'. *Philological Quarterly* 74 (Summer 1995): pp. 279–95.

Roper, Alan. 'Who's Who in *Absalom and Achitophel*?', *Huntington Library Quarterly* 63, no. 1–2 (2000), pp. 93–138.

Rose, Carol M. 'Crystals and Mud in Property Law'. *Stanford Law Review* 40, no. 3 (February 1988): pp. 577–610.

Rose, Mark. *Authors and Owners: The Invention of Copyright* (Cambridge: Harvard University Press, 1993).

Rosenheim, Edward W. *Swift and the Satirist's Art* (Chicago: University of Chicago Press, 1963).

Rosenthal, Michael. 'Public Reputation and Image Control in Late-Eighteenth-Century Britain'. *Visual Culture in Britain* 7, no. 2 (Winter 2006): pp. 69–91.

Ross, Trevor. *Writing in Public: Literature and the Liberty of the Press in Eighteenth-Century Britain* (Baltimore: Johns Hopkins University Press, 2018).

Rothstein, Eric. *Restoration and Eighteenth-Century Poetry, 1660–1780* (Boston: Routledge & Kegan Paul, 1981).

Rounce, Adam. 'Swift's texts between Dublin and London'. In *Jonathan Swift and the Eighteenth-Century Book*, edited by Paddy Bullard and James McLaverty (Cambridge: Cambridge University Press, 2013), pp. 199–213.

Rubini, D. A. 'The Precarious Independence of the Judiciary, 1688–1701'. *The Law Quarterly Review* 83 (July 1967): pp. 343–5.

Runge, Laura, and Pat Rogers (eds.). *Producing the Eighteenth-Century Book: Writers and Publishers in England, 1650–1800* (Newark: University of Delaware Press, 2009).

Sambrook, James. 'Poetry, 1660–1740'. In *The Cambridge History of Literary Criticism*, vol. 4: The Eighteenth Century, edited by H. B. Nisbet and Claude Rawson (Cambridge: Cambridge University Press, 1997), pp. 73–116.

Santesso, Aaron. '*The New Atalantis* and Varronian Satire'. *Philological Quarterly* 79, no. 2 (Spring 2000): pp. 177–204.

Scheil, Katherine West. 'Early Georgian Politics and Shakespeare: The Black Act and Charles Johnsons' *Love in a Forest* (1723)'. In *Shakespeare Survey*, vol. 51, Shakespeare in the Eighteenth Century, edited by Stanley Wells (Cambridge: Cambridge University Press, 1998), pp. 45–56.

Schellenberg, Betty A. 'The Eighteenth Century: Print, Professionalization, and Defining the Author'. In *The Cambridge Handbook of Literary Authorship*, edited by Ingo Berensmeyer, Gert Buelens, and Marysa Demoor (Cambridge: Cambridge University Press, 2019), pp. 133–46.

Schlesinger, Arthur M. *Prelude to Independence: The Newspaper War on Britain, 1764–1776* (New York: Knopf, 1958).

Schorr, Daniel. 'Foreword'. In David A. Copeland, *The Idea of a Free Press: The Enlightenment and its Unruly Legacy* (Evanston: Northwestern University Press, 2006), pp. ix–xviii.

Schultz, William Eben. *Gay's Beggar's Opera: Its Content, History and Influence* (New Haven: Yale University Press, 1923).

Scrivener, Michael (ed.). *Poetry and Reform: Periodical Verse from the English Democratic Press, 1792–1824* (Detroit: Wayne State University Press, 1992).

Seidel, Michael. 'Satire, lampoon, libel, slander'. In *The Cambridge Companion to English Literature, 1650–1740*, edited by Steven Zwicker (Cambridge: Cambridge University Press, 1998), pp. 33–57.

Seitel, Peter. 'Theorizing Genres: Interpreting Works'. *New Literary History* 34, no. 2 (Spring 2003): pp. 275–97.

Sharpe, J. A. *Defamation and Sexual Slander in Early Modern England*. Borthwick Paper 58 (York: Borthwick Institute, University of York, 1980).

Shoemaker, Robert. 'Male Honour and the Decline of Public Violence in Eighteenth-Century London'. *Social History* 26, no. 2 (May 2001): pp. 190–208.

Shuger, Debora. *Censorship and Cultural Sensibility: The Regulation of Language in Tudor-Stuart England* (Philadelphia: University of Pennsylvania Press, 2006).

Siebert, Fredrick Seaton. *Freedom of the Press in England, 1476–1776: The Rise and Decline of Government Control* (Urbana: University of Illinois Press, 1965).

Simonds, Roger T. *Rational Individualism: The Perennial Philosophy of Legal Interpretation* (Amsterdam: Rodopi, 1995).

Simpson, Paul. *On the Discourse of Satire: Towards a Stylistic Model of Satirical Humour* (Amsterdam: John Benjamins, 2003).

Siskin, Clifford, and William Warner (eds.). *This is Enlightenment* (Chicago: University of Chicago Press, 2010).

Sitter, John. *The Cambridge Companion to Eighteenth-Century Poetry* (Cambridge: Cambridge University Press, 2001).

Sitter, John (ed.). *The Cambridge Introduction to Eighteenth-Century Poetry* (Cambridge: Cambridge University Press, 2011).

Smith, Erin J. 'Dance and the Georgian Theatre'. In *The Oxford Handbook of the Georgian Theatre, 1737–1832*, edited by Julia Swindells and David Francis Taylor (Oxford: Oxford University Press, 2014), pp. 321–32.

Smith, R. Jack. 'Shadwell's Impact Upon John Dryden'. *Review of English Studies* 20, no. 77 (January 1944): pp. 29–44.

Smith, Jeffrey A. *Printers and Press Freedom: The Ideology of Early American Journalism* (Oxford: Oxford University Press, 1988).

Smith, Nigel. *Literature and Revolution in England, 1640–1660* (New Haven: Yale University Press, 1994).

Snyder, Henry L. 'The Defeat of the Occasional Conformity Bill and the Tack: A Study in the Techniques of Parliamentary Management in the Reign of Queen Anne'. *Bulletin of the Institute of Historical Research* 41 (1968): pp. 173–86.

Starr, G. A. 'Defoe's Prose Style: 1. The Language of Interpretation'. *Modern Philology* 71, no. 3 (February 1974): pp. 277–94.

Stephens, Frederic George, George William Reid, and Dorothy M. George (eds.). *Catalogue of Prints and Drawings in the British Museum*. 11 vol. (London: British Museum, 1870–1954).

Stern, Simon. '*Tom Jones* and the Economies of Copyright'. *Eighteenth-Century Fiction* 9, no. 4 (1997): pp. 429–44.

Stern, Simon. 'Between Local Knowledge and National Politics: Debating Rationales for Jury Nullification after *Bushell's Case*'. *The Yale Law Journal* 111, no. 7 (May 2002): pp. 1815–59.

Stern, Simon. 'Copyright, Originality, and the Public Domain in Eighteenth-Century England'. In *Originality and Intellectual Property in the French and English Enlightenment*, edited by Reginald McGinnis (New York: Routledge, 2009), pp. 69–101.

Stern, Simon. 'From Author's Right to Property Right', *University of Toronto Law Journal* 62 (2012): pp. 29–91.

Stern, Simon. '*R v Jones* (1703)'. In *Landmark Cases in Criminal Law*, edited by Phil Handler, Henry Mares, and Ian Williams (Oxford: Hart, 2017), pp. 59–79.

Stern, Simon. 'Literary Analysis of Law: Reorienting the Connections Between Law and Literature'. *Critical Analysis of Law* 5, no. 2 (2018): pp. 1–8.

Stern, Tiffany. 'Nashe and Satire'. In *The Oxford History of the Novel in English: Vol. 1: Prose Fiction in English from the Origins of Print to 1750*, edited by Thomas Keymer (Oxford: Oxford University Press, 2017), pp. 180–95.

St Clair, William. *The Reading Nation in the Romantic Period* (Cambridge: Cambridge University Press, 2004).

Stone, Lawrence. *The Crisis of the Aristocracy* (Oxford: Oxford University Press, 1967).

Strachan, John. *British Satire, 1785–1840*. 5 vol. (London: Pickering & Chatto, 2002).

Strachan, John (ed.). *Advertising and Satirical Culture in the Romantic Period* (Cambridge: Cambridge University Press, 2007).

Suarez, Michael F., S. J., and Michael L. Turner (eds.). *The Cambridge History of the Book in Britain*, vol. 5: 1695–1830 (Cambridge: Cambridge University Press, 2009).

Suarez, Michael F., S. J. 'Towards a Bibliometric Analysis of the Surviving Record, 1701–1800'. In *The Cambridge History of the Book in Britain*, vol. 5: 1695–1830, edited by Michael F. Suarez, S. J., and Michael L. Turner (Cambridge: Cambridge University Press, 2009), pp. 39–65.

Sullivan, J. P., and A. J. Boyle (eds.). *Martial in English* (New York: Penguin, 1996).

Sutherland, James. 'The Dunciad of 1729'. *Modern Language Review* 31, no. 3 (July 1936): pp. 347–53.

Sutherland, James. *English Satire* (Cambridge: Cambridge University Press, 1958).

Sutherland, James. *The Restoration Newspaper and Its Development* (Cambridge: Cambridge University Press, 1986).

Swindells, Julia, and David Francis Taylor (eds.). *The Oxford Handbook of the Georgian Theatre, 1737–1832* (Oxford: Oxford University Press, 2014).

Swindells, Julia. 'The Political Context of the 1737 Licensing Act'. In *The Oxford Handbook of the Georgian Theatre, 1737–1832*, edited by Julia Swindells and David Francis Taylor (Oxford: Oxford University Press, 2014), pp. 107–22.

Symonds, Matthew Thomas. 'Grub Street Culture: The Newspapers of Nathaniel Mist, 1716–1737' (PhD diss., University College London, 2007).

Tambling, Jeremy. *Allegory* (New York: Routledge, 2010).

Targett, Simon. 'The premier scribbler himself': Sir Robert Walpole and the Management of Political Opinion', *Studies in Newspaper and Periodical History* 2, no. 1–2 (1994): pp. 19–33.

Tave, Stuart M. *The Amiable Humorist: A Study in the Comic and Theory and Criticism of the Eighteenth and Early Nineteenth Centuries* (Chicago: University of Chicago Press, 1960).

Taylor, Darrick N. 'L'Estrange His Life: Public and Persona in the Life and Career of Sir Roger L'Estrange' (PhD diss., University of Kansas, 2011).

Taylor, David Francis. *Theatres of Opposition: Empire, Revolution, and Richard Brinsley Sheridan* (Oxford: Oxford University Press, 2012).

Taylor, David Francis. *The Politics of Parody: A Literary History of Caricature, 1760–1830* (New Haven: Yale University Press, 2018).

Taylor, Stephen. '"Dr. Codex" and the Whig "Pope": Edmund Gibson, Bishop of Lincoln and London, 1716–1748'. In *Lords of Parliament: Studies, 1714–1914*, edited by R. W. Davis (Stanford: Stanford University Press, 1995), ch. 1.

Temple, Kathryn. 'Manley's 'Feigned Scene': The Fictions of Law at Westminster Hall'. *Eighteenth-Century Fiction* 22, no. 4 (2010): pp. 573–98.

Terry, Richard. 'Epic and Mock-Heroic'. In *A Companion to Eighteenth-Century Poetry*. Ed. Christine Gerrard (Malden: Blackwell, 2006), ch. 26.

Teskey, Gordon. *Allegory and Violence* (Ithaca: Cornell University Press, 1996).

Thorne, Christian. 'Thumbing Our Nose at the Public Sphere: Satire, the Market, and the Invention of Literature'. *PMLA* 116, no. 3 (May 2001): pp. 531–44.

Timperley, Charles Henry. *Encyclopedia of Literary and Typographical Anecdote* (London, 1842).

Thomas, David (ed.). *Theatre in Europe: A Documentary History: Restoration and Georgian England, 1660–1788* (Cambridge: Cambridge University Press, 1989).

Thomas, David, with David Carlton and Anne Etienne. *Theatre Censorship: From Walpole to Wilson* (Oxford: Oxford University Press, 2007).

Thomas, David. 'The 1737 Licensing Act and Its Impact'. In *The Oxford Handbook of the Georgian Theatre, 1737–1832*, edited by Julia Swindells and David Francis Taylor (Oxford: Oxford University Press, 2014), pp. 91–106.

Thomas, Gordon. *A Long Time Burning: The History of Literary Censorship in England* (London: Routledge and Kegan Paul, 1969).

Thomas, Keith. *The Ends of Life: Roads to Fulfilment in Early Modern England* (Oxford: Oxford University Press, 2009).

Tortarolo, Edoardo. *The Invention of Free Press: Writers and Censorship in Eighteenth Century Europe* (Berlin: Springer, 2016).

Treadwell, Michael. 'London Trade Publishers, 1675–1750'. *The Library*, Sixth series 4, no. 2 (June 1982): pp. 99–134.

Treadwell, Michael. 'Swift's Relations with the London Book Trade to 1714'. In *Author/Publisher Relations During the Eighteenth and Nineteenth Centuries*, edited by Robin Myers and Michael Harris (Oxford: Oxford Polytechnic Press, 1983), pp. 1–36.

Treadwell, Michael. 'On False and Misleading Imprints in the London Book Trade, 1660–1750'. In *Fakes and Frauds: Varieties of Deception in Print & Manuscript*, edited by Robin Meyers and Michael Harris (Detroit: St Paul's Bibliographies, 1989), pp. 29–46.

Urstad, Tone Sundt. *Sir Robert Walpole's Poets: The Use of Literature as Pro-Government Propaganda, 1721–1742* (Newark: University of Delaware Press, 1999).

Vandenberghe, Fauve. 'Caustic Burns and Moving Hearts: Satire and Affect in Eliza Haywood's *The Masqueraders*'. *Restoration: Studies in English Literary Culture, 1660–1700* 44, no. 1 (Spring 2020): pp. 39–66.

Vander Meulen, David L. 'The Printing of Pope's *Dunciad*, 1728'. *Studies in Bibliography* 35 (1982): pp. 271–85.

Vander Meulen, David L. *Pope's Dunciad of 1728: A History and Facsimile* (Charlottesville: University Press of Virginia, 1991).

Vareschi, Mark. *Everywhere and Nowhere: Anonymity and Mediation in Eighteenth-Century England* (Minneapolis: University of Minnesota Press, 2018).

Varey, Simon. 'Printers as Rivals: *The Craftsman*, 1739–40'. *The Library*, sixth series, 2, no. 2 (June 1980): pp. 220–2.

Varey, Simon. 'Growth of Capitalism and the Rise of the Press in the Age of Walpole'. In *Politics, Politeness and Patriotism: Papers Presented at the Folger Institute Seminar 'Politics and Politeness: British Political Thought in the Age of Walpole'*, edited by Gordon J. Schochet (Washington: Folger Institute, 1993), pp. 245–62.

Varey, Simon. 'The Craftsman'. *Prose Studies* 16, no. 1 (1993): pp. 58–77.

Vermeule, Blakey. 'Abstraction, Reference, and the Dualism of Pope's *Dunciad*'. *Modern Philology* 96, no. 1 (August 1998): pp. 16–41.

Vosoughi, Soroush, Deb Roy, and Sinan Aral. 'The spread of true and false news online'. *Science* 359, no. 6380 (9 March 2018): pp. 1146–51.

Wardroper, John. *Kings, Lords and Wicked Libellers: Satire and Protest, 1760–1837* (London: John Murray, 1973).

Warner, Michael. *The Letters of the Republic: Publication and the Public Sphere in Eighteenth-Century America* (Cambridge: Harvard University Press, 1990).

Warner, William B. *Protocols of Liberty: Communication Innovation and the American Revolution* (Chicago: University of Chicago Press, 2013).

Watt, Ian. *The Rise of the Novel: Studies in Defoe, Richardson, and Fielding* (Berkeley: University of California Press, 1957).

Weber, Harold M. *Paper Bullets: Print and Kingship under Charles II* (Lexington: University Press of Kentucky, 1996).

Weber, Harold M. 'The 'Garbage Heap' of Memory: At Play in Pope's Archives of Dullness'. *Eighteenth-Century Studies* 33, no. 1 (1999): pp. 1–19.

Weil, Rachel J. 'The Politics of Legitimacy: Women and the Warming-Pan Scandal'. In *The Revolution of 1688–89: Changing Perspectives*, edited by Lois G. Schwoerer (Cambridge: Cambridge University Press, 1992), ch. 4.

Weinbrot, Howard D. *The Formal Strain: Studies in Augustan Imitation and Satire* (Chicago: University of Chicago Press, 1969).

Weinbrot, Howard D. *Augustus Caesar in 'Augustan' England: The Decline of a Classical Norm* (Princeton: Princeton University Press, 1977).

Weinbrot, Howard D. *Alexander Pope and the Traditions of Formal Verse Satire* (Princeton: Princeton University Press, 1982).

Weinbrot, Howard D. 'Masked Men and Satire and Pope: Toward a Historical Basis for the Eighteenth-Century Persona', *Eighteenth-Century Studies* 16, no. 3 (Spring 1983): pp. 265–89.

Weinbrot, Howard D. *Eighteenth-Century Satire: Essays on Text and Context from Dryden to Peter Pindar* (Cambridge: Cambridge University Press, 1988).

Weinbrot, Howard D. *Britannia's Issue: The Rise of British Literature from Dryden to Ossian* (Cambridge: Cambridge University Press, 1995).

Weinbrot, Howard D. *Menippean Satire Reconsidered: From Antiquity to the Eighteenth Century* (Baltimore: Johns Hopkins University Press, 2005).

Weinbrot, Howard D. *Literature, Religion, and the Evolution of Culture, 1660-1780* (Baltimore: Johns Hopkins University Press, 2013).

Wessel, Jane. 'Performing 'A Ra-ree Show': Political Spectacle and the Treason Trial of Stephen College'. *Restoration* 38, no. 1 (Spring 2014): pp. 3–17.

Wessel, Jane. 'Mimicry, Property, and the Reproduction of Celebrity in Eighteenth-Century England'. *The Eighteenth Century* 60, no. 1 (Spring 2019): pp. 66–86.

West, Shearer. *The Image of the Actor: Verbal and Visual Representation in the Age of Garrick and Kemble* (London: Printer Publishers, 1991).

West, Shearer. 'Wilkes's Squint: Synecdochic Physiognomy and Political Identity in Eighteenth-Century Print Culture'. *Eighteenth-Century Studies* 33, no. 1 (1999): pp. 65–84.

West, Shearer. 'The Darly Macaroni Prints and the Politics of "Private Man"'. *Eighteenth-Century Life* 25, no. 2 (Spring 2001): pp. 170–82.

West, Shearer. 'Manufacturing Spectacle'. In *The Oxford Handbook of the Georgian Theatre, 1737-1832*, edited by Julia Swindells and David Francis Taylor (Oxford: Oxford University Press, 2014), pp. 286–303.

Wilkinson, Andrew M. 'The Decline of English Verse Satire in the Middle Years of the Eighteenth Century'. *Review of English Studies* 3, no. 11 (1952): pp. 222–33.

Williams, E. Neville (ed.). *The Eighteenth-Century Constitution, 1688-1815: Documents and Commentary* (Cambridge: Cambridge University Press, 1960).

Wimsatt, William K., Jr. 'Foote and a Friend of Boswell's: A Note on *The Nabob*'. *Modern Language Notes* 57, no. 5 (May 1942): pp. 326–8.

Wolf, Reva. 'John Bull, Liberty, and Wit'. In *The Efflorescence of Caricature, 1759-1838*, edited by Todd Porterfield (Burlington: Ashgate Publishing, 2011), pp. 49–60.

Wood, Marcus. *Radical Satire and Print Culture, 1790-1822* (Oxford: Oxford University Press, 1994).

Wood, Marcus. 'Radical Publishing'. In *The Cambridge History of the Book in Britain*, vol. 5: 1695–1830, edited by Michael F. Suarez, S. J., and Michael L. Turner (Cambridge: Cambridge University Press, 2009), pp. 834–48.

Woodmansee, Martha. *The Author, Art and the Market: Rereading the History of Aesthetics* (New York: Columbia University Press, 1994).

Woolley, David (ed.). *The Correspondence of Jonathan Swift, D.D.*, 5 vol. (Frankfurt am Main: Peter Lang, 1999-2014).

Woolley, James. 'Writing Libels on Germans: Swift's "Wicked Treasonable Libel"'. In *Swift: The Enigmatic Dean, Festschrift for Hermann Josef Real*, edited by Rudolf Freiburg, et al. (Tübingen: Stauffenburg Verlag, 1998), pp. 303–16.

Worden, Blair. 'Literature and Political Censorship in Early Modern England'. In *Too Mighty to be Free: Censorship and the Press in Britain and the Netherlands*, edited by A. C. Duke and C. A. Tamse (Zutphen: De Walburg Press, 1987), pp. 45–62.

Zachs, William. *The First John Murray and the Late Eighteenth-Century Book Trade: With a Checklist of his Publications* (Oxford: The British Academy, Oxford University Press, 1998).

Zwicker, Steven N. *The Arts of Disguise: Politics and Language in Dryden's Poetry* (Princeton: Princeton University Press, 1984).

Zwicker, Steven N. *Lines of Authority: Politics and English Literary Culture, 1649–1689* (Ithaca: Cornell University Press, 1993).

Zwicker, Steven N. 'Dryden and the Invention of Irony'. In *Swift's Travels: Eighteenth-Century Satire and its Legacy*, edited by Nicholas Hudson and Aaron Santesso (Cambridge: Cambridge University Press, 2008), ch. 5.

Index

'A. Moore' (false imprint) 79, 84
Act of Anne (1709/10) 66–74, 200–1, 227
Act of Settlement (1701) 125–6, 202, 256
Addison, Joseph 135
Advice to a Painter poems 50–1
Afshar, Nader Shah 186
allegory 5–8, 12, 14, 21–4, 35, 56, 87, 167,
     169–71
  as basis for libel prosecution 14–15, 163–81
  as defence 172n.57
  etymology of 163n.10
  innuendoes in 169–70
  personification in 164–6
  publication of 'satiric keys' for 168
Almon, John 64–5, 69–70, 72–3, 203–4, 265–6
  libel prosecutions of 64–5
ambiguity
  as the common denominator of satire 24–5
  functional 3
  verbal 4–5, 22
American Revolution 201–2, 251–2, 258, 267–8
Anne, Queen 30–1, 95–6, 132–3, 165, 172–3
Antoinette, Marie 221–2
Apreece, Thomas 243
Arbuthnot, John 154–5
Aris, Samuel 70–2
Armine, Susan 38
Astley, Thomas 83
Atterbury, Francis 185, 243

Backscheider, Paula 123, 243–4
Bailyn, Bernard 258
Baines, Paul 62–3, 156–7
Baldwin, Henry 203
Ballaster, Ros 236–9, 243–5
  on interpretation of allegory 167
ballet 240
Bannister, Charles 237
Barber, John 68, 71–2, 80–1, 171
Barber, Mary 71–2
Bath, William Pulteney, earl of 61, 175
Battle of the Frogs and Mice 51
Beaufort, Henry Somerset, first duke of 165
Beaufort, Henry Somerset, second duke of 165
Belasyse, Henry 38
Bengert, C. D. 219n.123

'bibliophilic optimism' 265–8
Bickham, George 225
Bill of Rights (1689) 256
Bill of Rights (1789) 250
Bird, Wendell 257–9
Bishops' Ban 26–7, 26n.2
Blackstone, William 31–2, 125–6, 133–4,
     211, 255–7, 259
Blasphemous and Seditious Libels Act
     (1819) 227
Bogel, Fredric V. 22, 52–3, 106, 166
  on parody 106
  on satire 52
Boileau, Nicolas 46, 51
  Le Lutrin 46, 51
Boitard, Louis-Philippe 225
Bolingbroke, Henry St John, first viscount of
     60–1, 133, 175, 177–8, 191–2
Booth, Judith 112
Booth, Wayne 20, 119
  on 'doctrinal adhesions' in the perception of
     irony 106
  on verbal irony 104–5
Bourdieu, Pierre 262
Bowyer, William 67–8
Boyle, Charles, fourth earl of 185
Boyle, Richard, third earl of 82–3, 139–40,
     142
Boyne, John 220
Brandeis, Louis 259
Brewer, David A. 166, 177
Brome, Richard 146
Brooke, Henry 233
  Gustavus Vasa 233
Broome, William 146–8
Browne, Joseph 113, 115–21
  The Country Parson's Honest Advice 12–13,
     94, 111–18, 123–4
  *Letter To the Right Honourable Mr. Secretary
     Harley, by Dr. Browne, A* 115–17
Buckingham, George Villiers, second
     duke of 36
  Rehearsal, The 154
Bullard, Rebecca 176
Bunyan, John
  Pilgrim's Progress, The 167

Burke, Edmund 70, 218
    Reflections on the Revolution in France 221–2
Burke, Jane Mary (née Nugent) 222
Burlington, Allen Bathurst, first earl of 82–3
Busenello, Giovanni Francesco 50
Bute, John Stuart, third earl of 145
Butler, Judith 262
Butler, Samuel 2–3
    on libel 2–3
Butterfield, Herbert
    on historiography 248
Byron, Frederick George
    Don Dismallo 221–2, 224

Calvering, Mary 112
Capell, Edward 243
caricature
    as libel 15, 209–33
    rise of 209–10
Carlile, Richard 202–3
Carnell, Rachel 172
Carretta, Vincent 212, 215
Caryll, John 82
Cato's Letters 252
Chappelle's Show (television show) 24
Charles II, King 2–3, 36, 166, 176
Chaucer, Geoffrey 39
Chetwood, William Rufus 140
Churchill, Charles 24, 242, 245
    Rosciad, The 238, 245
Clarke, John 83, 161–2, 182, 188, 190–1
Cleland, William 153–4
Clive, Kitty 237
Cobbett, William 203
Coffeehouse Proclamations (1675, 1676) 41–2
coffeehouses 42, 61, 73, 107
Cogswell, Thomas 41
Cohen, Ralph 20
Coke, Edward 109–10, 150, 205, 211
Colepeper, Thomas 169
College, Stephen 2–3, 60–1, 213n.96
    Ra-Ree Show, The 2–3, 60–1, 213–14
    treason prosecution of 2–3, 3n.14
'common intendment' 11, 29–35, 56–7, 119–20
    defined 10–11
Comyns, John 211
Copeland, David A. 267
Copeland, Rita 164
Corporation Act 95
Cowan, Brian 175
Cowley, Abraham 40
Cowper, William, first earl of 111–12
Craftsman, The 12, 14–15, 60–1, 63–5, 71–2, 78,
    139–40, 173–83

libel prosecutions of 173–81
Crofts, Catherine 38
Cruikshank, (Isaac) Robert 229–30
Cruikshank, George 229–30
Cruikshanks 12
Culex (The Gnat) 51
Culler, Jonathan 20
Culling, Elizabeth 112
Curll, Edmund 63, 68, 75–8, 80, 140–2, 146–8,
    152
Curry, Michael 68
Cuthell, John 208
Clegg, Cyndia Susan 19

dance 239–40
Darnton, Robert 250
    on press regulation in Old Regime France 260
David Garrick 88–9, 237
Davis, Lennard 178
de Bolla, Peter 240
de Man, Paul 181
defamation 7n.28
    ecclesiastical origins 10n.41
    images as 211–12, 213n.96
defamatory imputations 32n.20, 37
Defoe, Daniel 4–5, 12–14, 93–100, 102–7, 120–5,
    182–3, 251–3
    on misinterpretation of satiric works 4–5
    prosecution for libel 121–6
    Essay on the Regulation of the Press, An 251–3
    Shortest Way with the Dissenters, The 96–101
    Works: *An Enquiry into the Occasional
        Conformity of Dissenters* 95–6
Delafaye, Charles 62, 192
Delane, Denis 237
Denham, John 40
Dennis, John 7, 54–6, 141, 150–1, 153–4,
    157
    on Dryden 53–4
Deutsch, Helen 16, 149
Devonshire, Edward Cavendish, duke of 243
Devonshire, Georgina Cavendish, duchess
    of 225
Devonshire, William Cavendish, first earl and
    fourth duke of 13, 112
Dodd, Ann 151
Dodsley, Robert 87
Don Dismallo (Byron) 221–2
Donald, Diana 210, 215, 232
Donne, John 39
d'Orléans, Philippe 186
Douglas, Sylvester 206
Downie, J. A. 99, 121
    on allegory 164

Dryden, John 1, 28
  approach to satire 54–7
  disagreement with Shadwell on
      dramaturgy 43–4
  on satire 47
  on satire and lampoon 23
  socio-literary agenda 54–5
  use of irony 51–2
  Works: *Absalom and Achitophel* 51, 53–4, 56,
      165–7
  Astraea Redux 51
  *Discourse Concerning the Original and
      Progress of Satire* 43, 47, 55–6
  Mac Flecknoe 6–8, 28–9, 43–57
    double entendre in 143
    as epic poem 49–50, 53–4
    literary forms in 47–8
    as mock-heroic poem 51
    as model for verbal evasion 43–57
    publication and distribution of 49
    and 'self-irony' 52–3
    use of irony in as verbal evasion 28–9
  To My Lord Chancellor 51
Dundas, Lawrence 145–6
Dunton, John 62–3
  avoidance of libel prosecutions 75
Dupré, Louis 268
Dyer, Gary 203

Edwin, Humphrey 95
Eisenstein, Elizabeth L. 266–7
Elliott, Robert C. 151–2
Engraving Copyright Act (1735) 227
Enlightenment, The 267–8
'erotic topography' 75–8, 75n.103
evasion:
  bibliographic 7, 74–92
  in printselling 225
  in manuscript circulation 26–7
  by editing 87–8
  by gutting of names 127–34, 138–48
  by use of false imprints 78–84
  by use of rebus 145–6
  rhetorical 3
  satiric 6–7
  verbal 3, 28, 74–84
  by use of double entendres 75–8
  by verbal irony. *See* irony, verbal
ex officio informations 207–8

Faulkner, George 241
Fazakerley, Nicholas 87, 139–40
Felton, Betty 38
Fenton, Elijah 146

Fielding, Henry 60, 79, 101, 242, 253–4
Fish, Stanley 249
  on verbal irony 118–19
Flecknoe, Richard 44, 46
Fleming, Thomas 131
Fletcher, Angus 173
flytings 40
Foote, Samuel 16, 145–6
  and mimicry 238–46
  Works: *Author, The* 243
  Capuchin, The 242–3
  Minor, The 243–5
  Nabob, The 243, 245–6
  Orators, The 241–2
  Trip to Calais, A 242
Fores, Samuel William 225–7
Foucault, Michel 262
Fowler, Alastair 21
Fox, Charles James 207–8, 216–17, 219–21,
      225–7
Foxe, John 265
  Acts and Monuments, The 39
Fox's Libel Act (1792) 9, 198, 205–6
Francis, Philip 70
Francklin, Richard 71–2, 78, 139–40, 175,
      191–2, 206–7
  avoidance of libel prosecution 60–1, 63–4,
      205–6
  libel prosecutions 63–4
Frederick William II 268
freedom of the press 6, 12, 18–19, 20n.68, 24–5,
      199–202, 205–6, 208–9, 212–13, 267–8
  history of 248–69
  U.S. and British compared 259–61
French Revolution 257, 263–5
Frye, Northrop 21
  on 'sophisticated irony' 104
Fuseli, Henry
  Nightmare, The 216–17

Gallagher, Catherine 74–5, 143, 167, 171
Garrick, David 88–9, 237
Gatrell, Vic 227–9, 231
  on visual satire 210
Gay, John 175, 255
'generality of readers' standard 10–11, 35,
      119–20, 182, 190–1, 200
George I, King 91, 183
George II, King 14–15, 70–1, 89–90, 183–4,
      186–9, 193, 213–14, 234
George III, King 70, 88, 227
George IV, King 229–31
Gibson, Edmund 184
Giffard, Henry 193, 234

Gildon, Charles 154
  New Rehearsal, A 154
Gilliver, Lawton 71–2, 82–3
Gillray, James 12, 219, 225
  Works: *Certain Dutchess Kissing Old Swelter-
    in-Grease the Butcher for his Vote,
    A* 225
  Democrat, or Reason & Philosophy, A 225–7
  *Presentation, or, Wise Men's Offering,
    The* 225–7
Godolphin, Sidney, first earl 112
Goldsmith, Oliver
  She Stoops to Conquer 236
Goody, Jack 266
Gordon, Lord George 70
Gordon, Thomas 101–2, 105–6, 145–6, 178,
    251–2
  on ambiguity 143
  on verbal irony 101
Gordon Riots 263
Gravelot, Hubert-François 225
Gray, Samuel 61, 204
Green, Thomas A.
  on juries 232
Greene, Jody 66–7, 266
Grenville, Richard 68
Griffin, Dustin 16
  on the effects of the Stage Licensing Act
    244–5
Groupy, Joseph 225
Guilhamet, Leon 16
gutted names (emvowelling or
    emvowellment) 122–3, 127–30, 132–7,
    143–8, 151, 158–9

Haines, Henry 64
Hale, Matthew 9–10, 31–3, 43
Hallett, Mark 212, 215
Hamburger, Philip 9–10, 29–30, 63, 107–10,
    179–80, 253
  on libel laws 9–10, 179–80, 253
Hanson, Laurence 68
Hardwicke, Philip Yorke, first earl of 8,
    187–92, 207
Harley, Robert 80–1, 115, 122–3, 125, 133,
    165, 172
Harling, Philip 204, 206
Harris, Henry 48
Hart, Emma 220–1
Hartlib, Samuel 265
Haversham, John Thompson, first
    baron 112
Hawkins, William 133, 188–9, 211
Hay, Douglas 65, 204

Haywood, Eliza 22, 140, 158, 167
Heinzelman, Susan Sage 170n.53
Hellfire Club 185
Hertford, Francis Seymour Conway, marquis
    of 242
Higgins, Ian 255
Hildebrand, Jacob
  Silent Flute, The 84
Hill, John 237
Hobart, Henry 38
Hofstadter, Richard 258
Hogarth, William 215
Holland, William 227–9
Holt, John 10–14, 94–111, 114–20, 123–6,
    150–1, 160–1, 190–1, 199–200
Hone, Joseph 17, 99, 99n.26
Hone, William 203
Horace 40, 52, 73, 267
How, John 87–8
Howard, Thomas 39
Howe, John Grobham 41
Huggonson, John 89
Hume, David 15, 193, 231, 261
  on libel laws 15
Humphrey, Hannah 211
Hunt, John 203
Hunt, Leigh 203
Hunter, J. Paul 40
Hurt, William
  libel prosecution of 132–3
Husayn, Sultan 186
Hutcheon, Linda 98, 106

imprints, false and misleading 78–81
In Living Color (television show) 24
Inchbald, Elizabeth 244
Ingram, Martin
  on slander lawsuits 139
innuendo, legal 130, 132, 169–70, 178–81
interpretation
  legal protocols of 3–12, 30–2, 113–14, 134–7,
    168–71, 173, 199–200
  among readers 4–5, 11n.47, 74–84, 97–8,
    114–15, 138, 141–3, 148–9, 151–2, 159,
    162–8, 214–17
  reasonable and 'objective' standards of 7–11,
    199–200
  codification of 10n.43
irony 7–8, 160
  verbal 4–8, 11–14, 20–5, 51–2, 93–107
  'extrinsic' 93–4, 103–5
  history and development of 99–103
  italics as signifier of 101–3
  shared prejudices as basis for 103–5

Iser, Wolfgang 143
  on textual indeterminacy 164

Jack, Ian 16
Jacobites and Jacobitism 14–15, 64–5, 104–5,
        161–2, 165, 173, 182–5, 187,
        213–14, 234
James II, King 30–1, 39, 62–3, 165–6,
        183–4, 256
Jameson, Fredric 21
Jermyn, Henry 38
'John of Gant' caricatures 213–15
Johns, Adrian 265–8
Johnson, Samuel 23, 87, 181, 206
  definition of satire 23
  London 87
Johnson, Joseph 207–8
Johnston, William 87
Jonson, Ben 44, 46, 148
Jordan, Jeremiah 207–8
judicial independence 6, 20–1, 30–1, 58–9,
        125–6, 202, 256
judicial tenure 13–14
Junius 12, 64–5, 72–3, 88–9, 203, 263–5
juries and jurors 3–4, 6, 8–11, 9n.38, 13, 27,
        32–3, 35, 56–7, 94, 116, 118–20, 130–2,
        161–2, 169–70, 190–1, 198–200, 205–7,
        231–2, 256
judicial directions to 34–5, 199–200
jury nullification 9, 9n.37, 205n.51
Juvenal 26, 40, 52, 55

Kaplan, Lindsay M. 19
Karian, Stephen 90
Kay, John 145
Kernan, Alvin B. 16
Keymer, Thomas 16–17, 57, 99n.29, 112–13,
        123, 140, 261
Kids in the Hall (television show) 24
King v. Lake (1671) 9–10, 31–5
Kingston, Elizabeth Chudleigh, duchess of 242
Kinservik, Matthew J. 235–7, 241, 245
  on the effects of the Stage Licensing Act
        (1737) 261–2
Knox, Norman 100
  on verbal irony 100
Knox, William 69
Kropf, C. R.
  on libel and satire 16–17
Kynaston, Thomas 204

Lacy, John 48
Lambert, François 265
lampoon 23, 28, 32, 36–43, 53–6, 245–6

Langland, William 39
Larpent, John 237
Latham, Sean 17
legal punishments 2–4, 252–5
'legal-defence fallacy' 129, 158–9
Leslie, Charles 96
L'Estrange, Roger 2, 30, 42, 62
Leveson, Richard 38
Levine, Caroline 6–7, 24, 239
Levy, Leonard 259
Libel
  defamatory imputations 193–4
  distinguished from slander 24, 31–2
  legal elements of 7–9, 130
  legal elements of, *mitior sensus* doctrine. See
        mitior sensus doctrine
  legal elements of, 'reasonable man'
        standard 34–5
  requirement of knowledge of contents as
        element of 62
  seditious 107–21
  seditious, and irony 125
  seditious, legal elements of 108–10
  seditious, prosecutions for 203, 205–8
libel laws
  development in latter half of the eighteenth
        century 199
  enforcement against publishers and
        booksellers 60–6
  enforcement in latter half of the eighteenth
        century 201–9
Lloyd, Charles 69
Lloyd, Evan 202
Locke, John 250, 255
Lord Campbell's Libel Act (1843) 260
Louis XIV, King 132, 176, 186
Loveman, Kate 97–8
Lowenstein, Joseph F. 61–2
Lund, Roger 17, 21–2, 181
'luxury obscenity' 37n.45
Lyons, Solomon 205
Lyttelton, George, first baron
  Letters from a Persian in England 251

Macaulay, Thomas Babington 261
MacKinnon, Catharine A. 249
Macklin, Charles 142, 237
Manley, Delarivier
  Works: *Adventures of Rivella, The* 170–3
        New Atalantis, The 14, 161–3, 165, 169–71,
        176–7
  libel prosecution of 162–73
Mansfield, William Murray, first earl of 202,
        205–7, 257, 259

manuscript circulation 26–8, 30, 32, 36–44, 49
Margaretta, Anne 38
Marlborough, Sarah Churchill, duchess of
    165–6, 172–3
Marshall, Ashley 16, 20–2, 54n.115, 99n.29
Marston, John 39
Martial 41, 52
Marvell, Andrew 50–1
Mason, Dorothy 38
Mason, Richard 38
Mason, William 69
Mathews, Charles 237
Matthews, John 68, 186–7
Mawson, Robert 182
McCraw, David 259–60
McCreery, Cindy 221
McDowell, Paula 22, 87, 266
McGann, Jerome 74
McKeon, Michael 11n.47, 49
McLaverty, James 102
Meres, John 79
Mezey, Naomi 117, 137
    on law and culture 18
Mill, John Stuart 258
Miller, James 142
Miller, John 203
Milton, John 49–50, 250–2
    Works: *Areopagitica* 251–2, 257
        Paradise Lost 45
Mist, Nathaniel 64–5
Mist's Weekly Journal 182–3
    libel prosecution for 'The Persian Letter'
        14–15, 161–2, 182–94
Mitchell, W. J. T. 212n.91
mitior sensus doctrine 32–3, 130–2, 180, 200
Modena, Mary of 38, 184
Mohun, Charles, fourth baron 112
Montesquieu, Charles de Secondat, baron de
    Persian Letters 186
Moody, Jane 242
Moore, Nicole 250
Moore, William 58
Morning Advertiser, The 69–70, 72–4, 88, 203
Morphew, John 80–2, 170–1
Mosley, Charles 225
Motte, Andrew 87–8
Motte, Benjamin, Jr. 70–2, 81–2, 87–8
Moxon, Joseph 101–2, 187–8
Mudge, Bradford K. 162–3
Muecke, D. C. 20, 104–5
Murray, John 75

Napoleonic Wars 263
Nashe, Thomas 39
Nathan, Edward P. 143
Nelson, Horatio 219–21

Neville, Samuel 79
Newcastle, Thomas Pelham-Holles, duke of 8,
    187, 207, 213–16, 218
Novak, Maximillian 123
Noverre, Jean-Georges 240
Nussbaum, Felicity 16
Nutt, Richard 58, 79

occasional conformity 94–7, 105, 111, 121–4
Ogle, Lady Elizabeth Percy, countess of 38–9
O'Connell, Sheila 211
Oldham, James C. 107–8, 202, 206
Oldham, John 40
O'Neill O'Beirne, Maria Theresa 185
Ong, Walter J. 266
O'Quinn, Daniel 244
Orrery, John Boyle, fifth earl of 89–90
Orrery, Roger Boyle, second earl 38, 185
Oxford, Edward Harley, second earl of 145–6

Paine, Thomas 227
Paleotti, Adellinda 132
pantomime 239–40
Parker, Thomas 7, 127–8, 131–3, 200
parody 23–4, 50, 106
Parsons, Nicola 168, 172
'path dependence' in law 231
Patterson, Annabel 176
    on functional ambiguity 3
Patterson, William
    Arminius 233
Paulson, Ronald 16
Persius 40–1, 52, 73
Peterloo Massacre 202
Peters, Julie Stone 17–18
Pettit, Alexander 192
Phiddian, Robert 20, 114, 261
Pilkington, Matthew 67–8
Pindar, Peter 24
Pitt, James 177–80
Ponz, Antonio 210–11
Pope, Alexander
    evasion of libel prosecutions 82–3, 87
        Works: *Dunciad* 14, 126–9, 139–43, 146–8,
            153–8
        Dunciad Variorum 62–3, 82–3, 152–8
Press Licensing Act (1662) 29–30, 250–1
Prynne, William 2
Punch (magazine) 24

Queen Caroline affair 202
Quilligan, Maureen 178
Quintilian 103

R. v. Dr. Browne (1706) 110–21
Rabb, Melinda Alliker 22

Ragussis, Michael 244
Ralegh, Walter 167
Ramsay, Allan 105
  on verbal irony 105
Rauser, Amelia 218
Rawls, John 255
Rawson, Claude 16, 173–4
  on allegory 173–4
Raymond, Robert 10–11, 15, 182, 189–90
Rayner, William 212
Read, Thomas 75n.102
reciprocity between law and literature 5–6, 16–20, 24–5
Rehberg, Friedrich
  Drawings Faithfully Copied from Nature at Naples 220–1
Reid, John Phillip 255
reputation 149–52
Restoration 'censorship' 2n.6
Restoration, Stuart (1660) 1–3, 11, 26–7, 39–43, 54–5, 100, 129
retributive violence for words 1n.1
Rich, John 239–40
Richardson, Samuel
  Clarissa 185
Richardson, William 225
Riffaterre, Michael 164
Robinson, George 203
Rochester, John Wilmot, second earl of 40
Rogers, Pat 16, 63, 156–7
Roper, Alan
  on allegory in Absalom and Achitophel 166
Rose, Carol M. 18
Rosenheim, Edward W. 21
Rosenthal, Michael
  on caricature 210
Ross, Trevor 9, 66, 205, 255n.46
Rowlandson, Thomas 12, 229–30
  The Covent Garden Night Mare 213–14, 216–17
Royal Academy of Arts 219–20
Ryan, Lacy 237
Rye House Plot 39

Sacheverell, Henry 95–6
Sackville, Mary 38
Safavid Dynasty 185–6
Sandby, Paul 225
Sandwich, John Montagu, fourth earl of 70
Satire
  defined 20–4
  deverbalization, by caricature 15, 209–33
  deverbalization, by mimicry and impersonation 233–47
  and epigrams 40–1, 51
  and female authors 22

'indirect' counter-tradition 26n.3
manuscript 7, 36–7, 42–3
medieval and early modern 26
market-square tradition 40n.58
neoclassical 54n.115
Restoration 2–3, 16–18
and women 16, 22, 44
Saturday Night Live (television show) 24
Savage, Richard 141
Say, Charles 203
Sayer, Charles 87
Sayers, James 229
Scandalum Magnatum 30, 107, 135
Schorr, Daniel 265–6
Scriblerus, Martin 156
Scroggs, William 42, 60–1
'secret history' 22, 175–7
Sedley, Katherine 38
Seidel, Michael 23, 54–5
Seitel, Peter 21
sensibility and sentimentality 15, 195
'sessions' poems 47–8
Shakespeare, William 44, 244
  Merchant of Venice, The 244
Sharpe, Jonathan 58
Sheridan, Richard Brinsley 244
Sheridan, Thomas 241
Sherwin, Ralph 237
Shrewsbury, Charles Talbot, first baron 132, 188
Shuger, Debora 19
  on historiography 248–9
Shuter, Edward 238
Siskin, Clifford 267–8
Skelton, John 39
skimmington 40
slander, distinguished from libel 31
slippage 18, 117, 137, 257
Smart, Christopher 69–70
Smith, Adam 150–1
  on libel 138–9
Smith, Jeffrey A. 259
Smith, John
  Printer's Grammar 101–2, 188
Smith, Nigel 54–5
Smollett, Tobias 254
South Sea Bubble 183
Southey, Robert 203
'special juries' 63–4, 198–9, 206–7
Spence, Thomas 202–3
Spenser, Edmund
  Faerie Queene, The 167
Squire, Francis
  Faithful Report of a Genuine Debate Concerning the Liberty of the Press, A 4–5

St Clair, William 266
Stage Licensing Act (1737) 16, 233–6
Stagg, John 83
Stanhope, James, first earl 184
Stern, Simon 18
Sterne, Laurence
    Tristram Shandy 248, 263–5, 269
Stevenson, John Hall 69
Struck, Peter T. 164–5
Stuart, James Francis Edward 183
Suckling, John 48
Sunderland, Charles Spencer, third earl of
    170–1, 173
Sutherland, James 16
Swift, Jonathan 132, 135–6
    avoidance of libel prosecution 12, 67–8, 70–2,
        81–3, 87–91
    Works: *Conduct of the Allies, The* 80–1
    Gulliver's Travels 81–2, 87–8, 164
        as allegory 164
    Epistle to a Lady, An 70–1
    Importance of the Guardian Considered,
        The 80–1, 135–6
    Modest Proposal, A 13, 103, 160–1
    On Poetry: A Rapsody 89–91
    'On the Irish Bishops' 91
    'On the Words "Brother Protestants and
        Fellow Christians"' 91
    Publick Spirit of the Whigs, The 80–1
    Short character of his Ex. T.E. of W., LL of I__ 81
    'The Storm; or Minerva's Petition' 91
    Tale of a Tub, A 135–6, 164
    'A Wicked Treasonable Libel' 91

Tassoni, Alessandro 51
    Secchia Rapita (The Stolen Bucket) 51
Tave, Stuart M. 195
Taylor, David Francis 212, 214, 219, 244
Temple, Kathryn 168, 171
text-image 'problematic' 212n.91
That Mitchell and Webb Look (television show) 24
Thomson, James
    Edward and Eleonora 233
Thorne, Christian 254–5
Thynne, Thomas 39
Tooke, Benjamin Jr. 68
John Horne 70
Tortarolo, Edoardo 268
Townshend, Charles 69
Townshend, George 61, 215
Treadwell, Michael 80
Trenchard, John 4, 252
Tudor, Mary 38
Turner, Sharon 87

Tutchin, John 99, 110, 125, 169
Twyn, John 2

underground printing 26–7, 29–30, 42–3, 232,
    260–1

Vareschi, Mark 114n.100, 252n.28
Virgil 50
    Aeneid 45
Vision of the Golden Rump, The 193, 234
von Archenholz, Johann Wilhelm 211
Vox Dei, Vox Populi 186–7
'vulgar intendment' 11

Wake, William 184
Wakefield, Gilbert 208
Walker, Anthony 225
Waller, Edmund 50–1
    Instructions to a Painter 50
    Last Instructions to a Painter 51
Walpole, Horace 69–70, 210–11, 213–14
Walpole, Robert 14–15, 63–4, 70–2, 79, 82–3,
    139–40, 145–6, 161–2, 173–6, 183, 185–7,
    191–3, 217, 233–5, 263–5
'warming-pan' myth 183–4
Warner, Michael 258–9
Warner, William B. 260, 267–8
    on freedom of speech 260
Watt, Ian 99n.29
Weaver, John 240
Weber, Harold 60–1
Weinbrot, Howard D. 16, 97n.15, 100n.30
Wessel, Jane 3, 61, 238–9, 245
West, Benjamin
    Death of General Wolfe 219–21
West, Shearer 239
Wharton, Philip James, duke of 184–7
White, Joseph 205–6
Whitefield, George 146, 243–5
Wilkes, John 68–70, 72, 87, 229–30, 263–5
    North Briton 69, 87, 201–2, 254
Wilkinson, Tate 237
Willes, John 71
William III, King 96–7, 165–6, 256
Williams, Susannah 37
Wood, Marcus 196, 203, 232
Woodfall, Henry Sampson 72–3, 88–9
    avoidance of libel prosecutions 73
    libel prosecutions 65, 70
    and *Public Advertiser* 70, 72–4, 88, 203
Woodward, Henry 238
Wooler, Thomas 203

Zwicker, Steven N. 6, 28, 51–2